东莞统计年鉴

DONGGUAN STATISTICAL YEARBOOK

2010

(总第20期 NO.20)

东莞市统计局
国家统计局东莞调查队编
Compiled by
Dongguan Municipal Bureau of Statistics
Dongguan Survey Office of National Bureau of Statistics

中国统计出版社
China Statistics Press

（京）新登字 041 号

图书在版编目（CIP）数据
东莞统计年鉴. 2010 / 东莞市统计局，国家统计局东莞调查队编.
—北京：中国统计出版社，2010. 9
ISBN 978 - 7 - 5037 - 6084 - 6

Ⅰ. ①东…
Ⅱ. ①东… ②国…
Ⅲ. ①统计资料 - 东莞市 - 2010 - 年鉴
Ⅳ. ①C832. 653 - 54

中国版本图书馆 CIP 数据核字（2010）第 181436 号

东莞统计年鉴 - 2010

作　　者/ 东莞市统计局　国家统计局东莞调查队
责任编辑/ 佘竞雄
责任校对/ 李妙荷　李琳达
封面设计/ 张永艳　钟锦漩
出版发行/ 中国统计出版社
通信地址/ 北京市丰台区西三环南路甲 6 号　中国统计出版社
邮　　编/ 100073
电　　话/（010）63376907
E - mail / yearbook@ gj. stats. cn
印　　刷/ 东莞市本色印刷有限公司
经　　销/ 新华书店
开　　本/ 880 × 1230 毫米 1/16
字　　数/135 万字
印　　张/ 36. 5 印张
印　　数/1500 册
版　　别/ 2010 年 9 月第 1 版
版　　次/ 2010 年 9 月第 1 次印刷
书　　号/ ISBN 978 - 7 - 5037 - 6084 - 6/C · 2427
定　　价/ 350. 00 元

《东莞统计年鉴－2010》
编委会和编辑出版人员

编 者 说 明

一、《东莞统计年鉴－2010》（以下简称年鉴）是一部反映东莞国民经济和社会发展情况的资料性年刊，本书收录了东莞 2009 年大量的统计数据和历史主要年份的一些主要统计数据，旨在全面系统地反映东莞在经济和社会方面的发展变化，为社会各界和海内外人士了解和研究东莞提供翔实的资料。

二、全书分四部分。第一部分，概述；第二部分，统计资料，具体分为综合、人口与劳动力、农业、工业、固定资产投资与建筑业、运输邮电、国内贸易、物价、外经旅游、财政与金融、人民生活、社会事业、能源、镇街主要指标、村（居）委会主要指标、建国以来国民经济和社会发展主要指标和东莞与全国、全省、珠江三角洲主要经济指标等 17 部分；第三部分，基本单位情况；第四部分，政策法规。

三、本年鉴资料大部分来自政府统计部门和调查队的各种定期统计报表和抽样调查资料，部分来自中央省属单位和市属各主管部门。

四、使用本年鉴时，请注意指标的统计口径，计量单位及计算价格。本年鉴指标计算所采用的价格除注明外均为当年价格。

五、年鉴统计表中的符号说明：" #" 表示其中主要项；" 空格" 表示该项统计指标数据不详或无该项数据；" ＊" 表示本表下有注解。

六、本年鉴在编辑出版过程中，得到市直有关部门和镇街的大力支持，在此表示衷心感谢。限于编辑水平，本书难免有疏漏之处，敬请批评指正。

目　　录
CONTENTS

第一部分　概　述
Part One　Outline

第二部分　统计资料
Part Two　Statistics

一、综　合
General Survey

二、人口与劳动力
Population and Labor Force

三、农业
Agriculture

四、工业
Industry

五、固定资产投资与建筑业
Investment in Fixed Assets and Construction

六、运输邮电
Transport, Postal and Telecommunication Services

七、国内贸易
Domestic Trade

八、价格指数
Price Indices

九、对外经济贸易与旅游
Foreign Economy，Trade and Tourism

十、财政、金融与保险
Government Finance, Banking and Insurance

十一、人民生活
People's Live Conditions

十二、社会事业
Social Undertakings

十三、能源
Energy

十四、镇街主要指标
Main Indicatory of Towns

十五、村（居）委会主要指标
Main Indicatory of Villagers'（Neighborhood）Committees

十六、建国以来国民经济和社会发展主要指标
Main Indicators on National Economy and Social Development from the Founding of the PRC

十七、东莞与全国、全省及三角洲城市主要指标比较
Comparison of Main Indicators between Dongguan and China, Guangdong Province, the Cities of the Pearl River Delta

第三部分　基本单位情况

Part Three　Basic Units

第四部分　政策法规

Part Four　Policies and Legislation

东莞市生产总值(亿元)

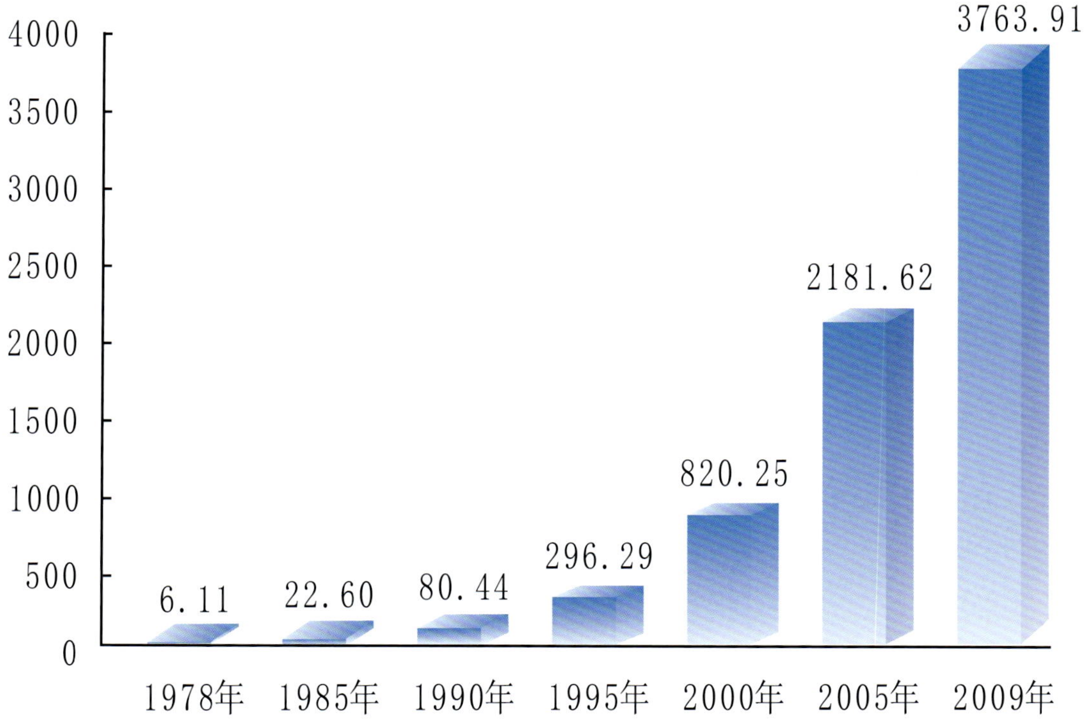

东莞市生产总值构成(%)

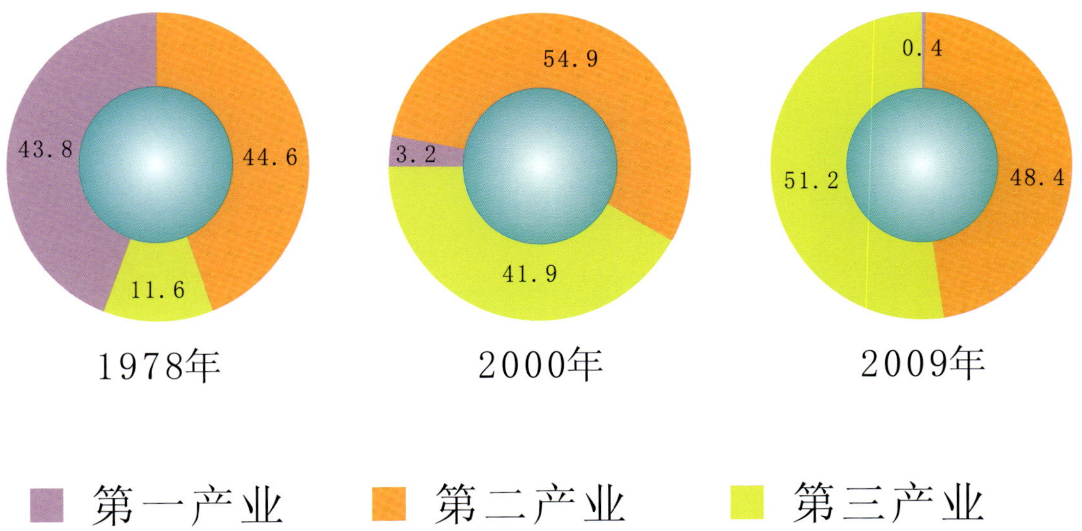

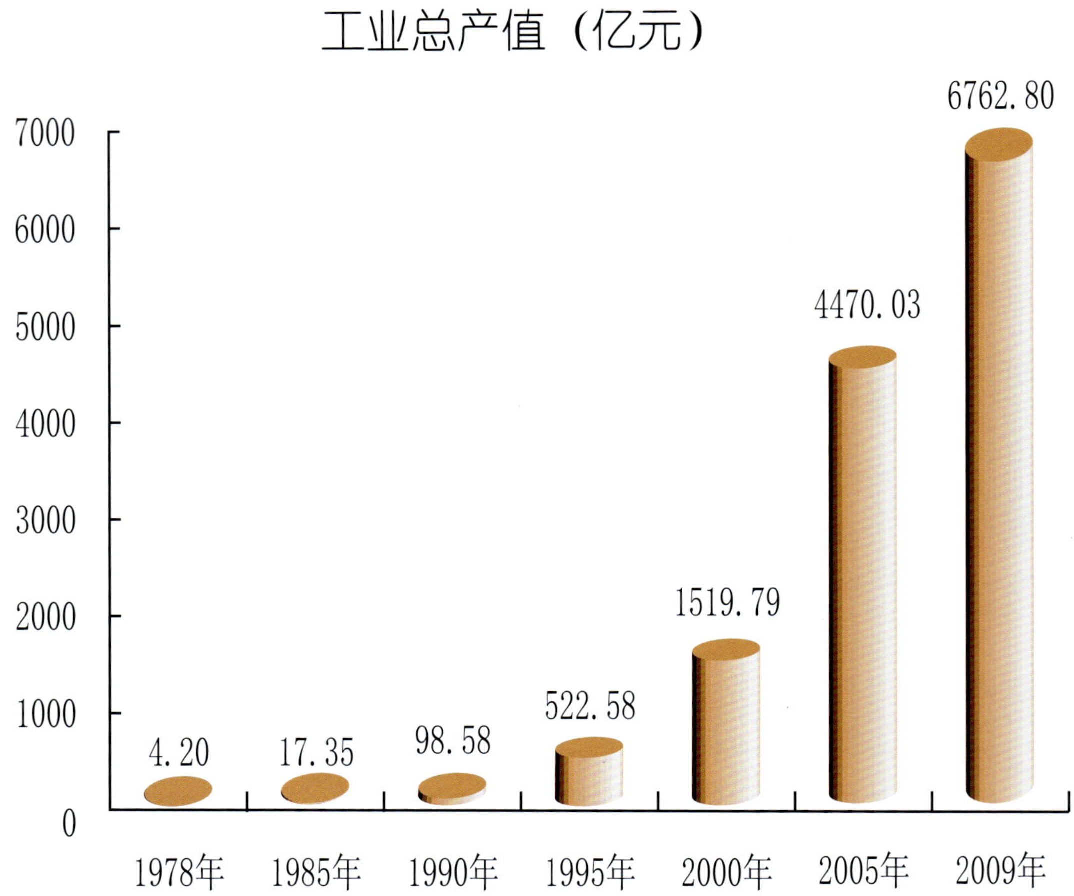
工业总产值（亿元）
7000
6000
5000
4000
3000
2000
1000
0
4.20
17.35
98.58
522.58
1519.79
4470.03
6762.80
1978年
1985年
1990年
1995年
2000年
2005年
2009年

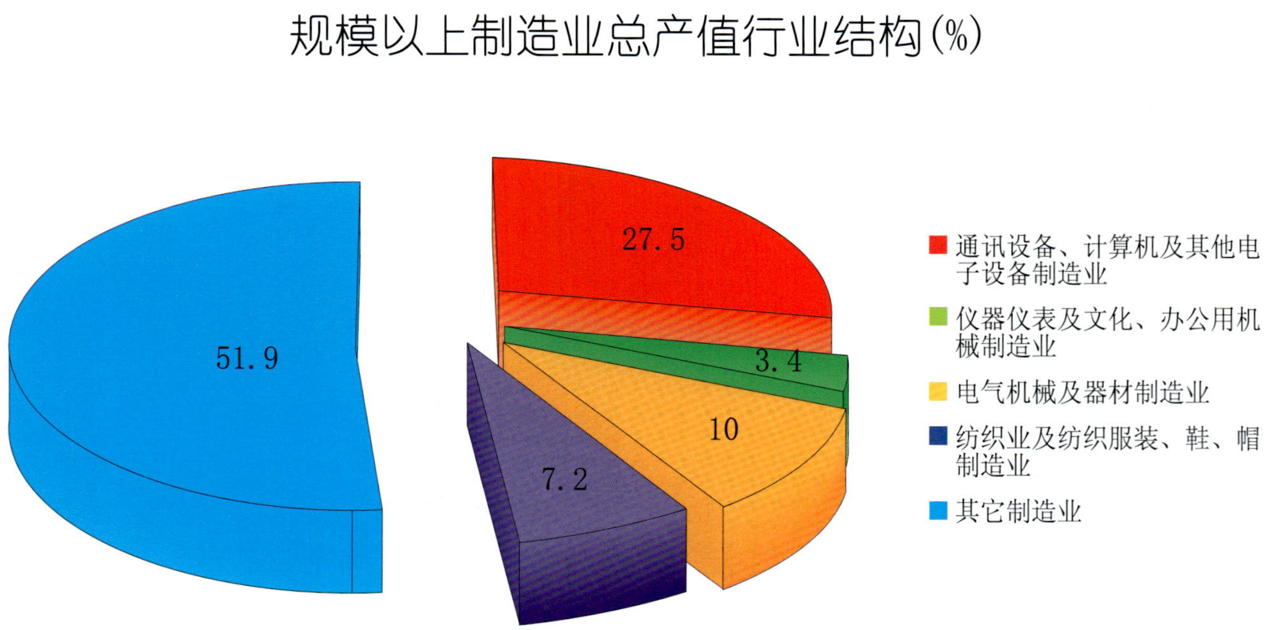
规模以上制造业总产值行业结构(%)
51.9
27.5
3.4
10
7.2
通讯设备、计算机及其他电子设备制造业
仪器仪表及文化、办公用机械制造业
电气机械及器材制造业
纺织业及纺织服装、鞋、帽制造业
其它制造业

进口总额、出口总额（亿美元）

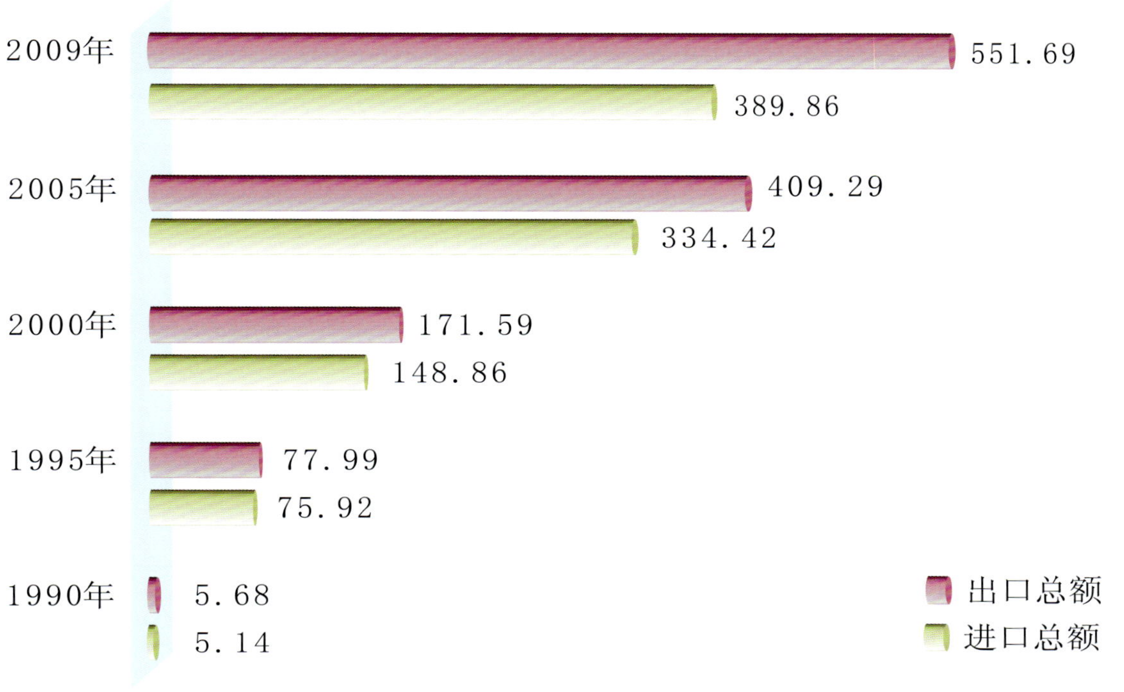

当年实际利用外资（新口径）（亿美元）

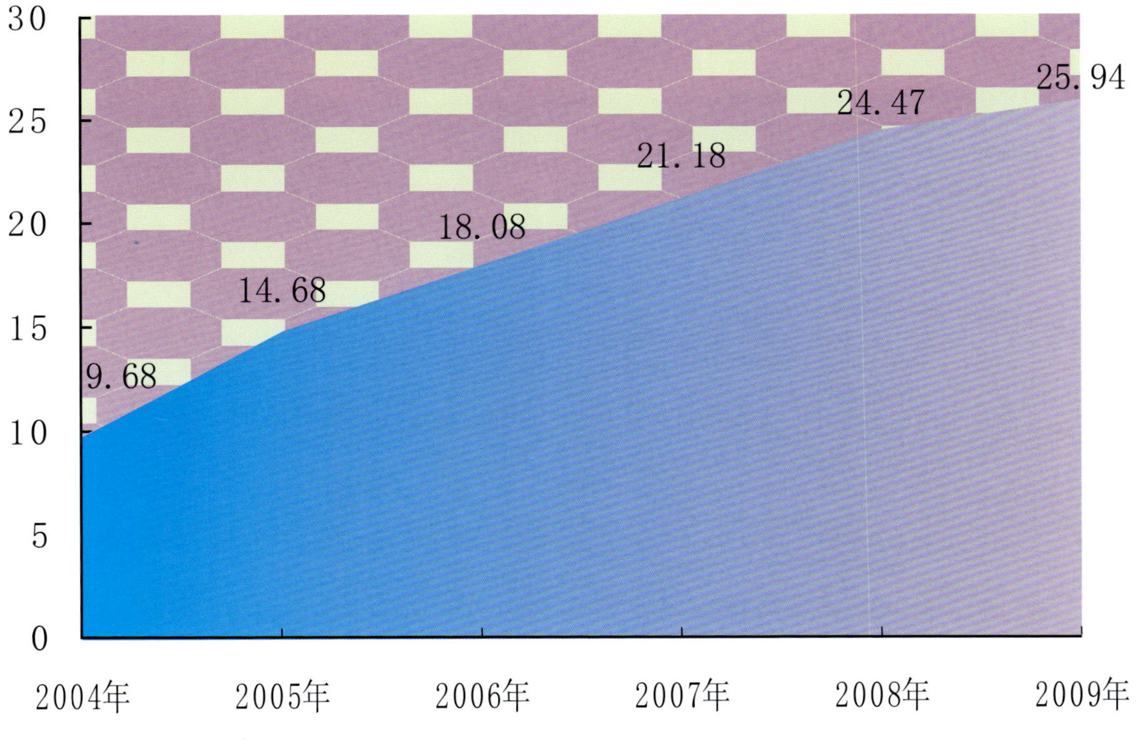

来源于东莞的财政收入(不含关税)(亿元)

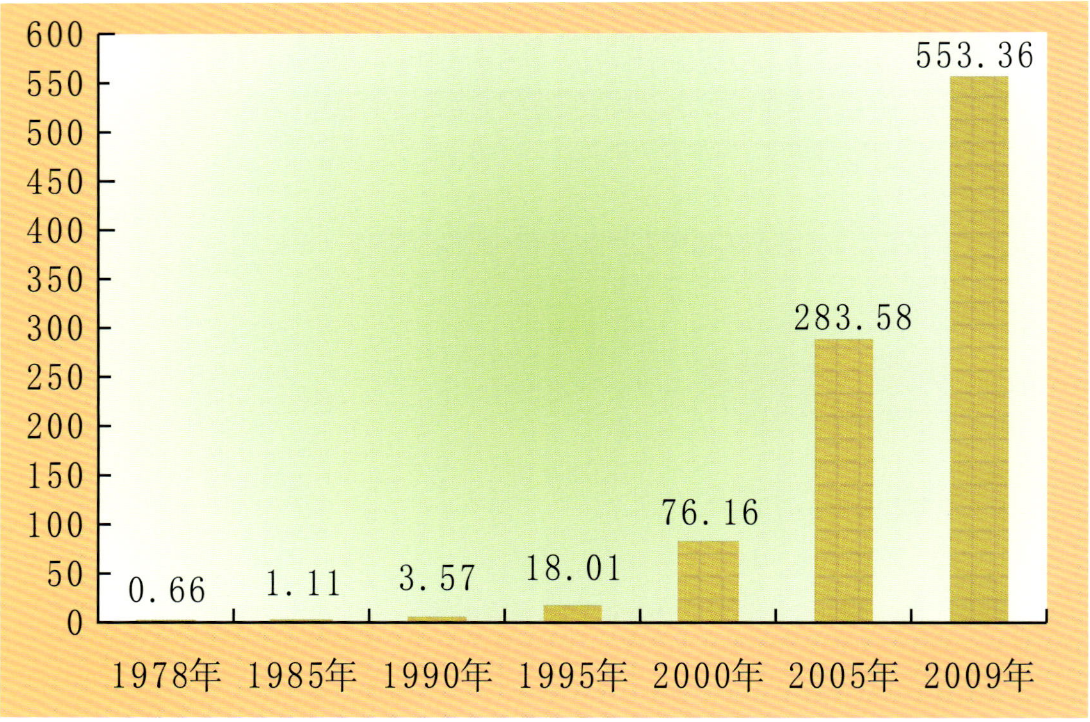

各项人民币存贷款余额(亿元)

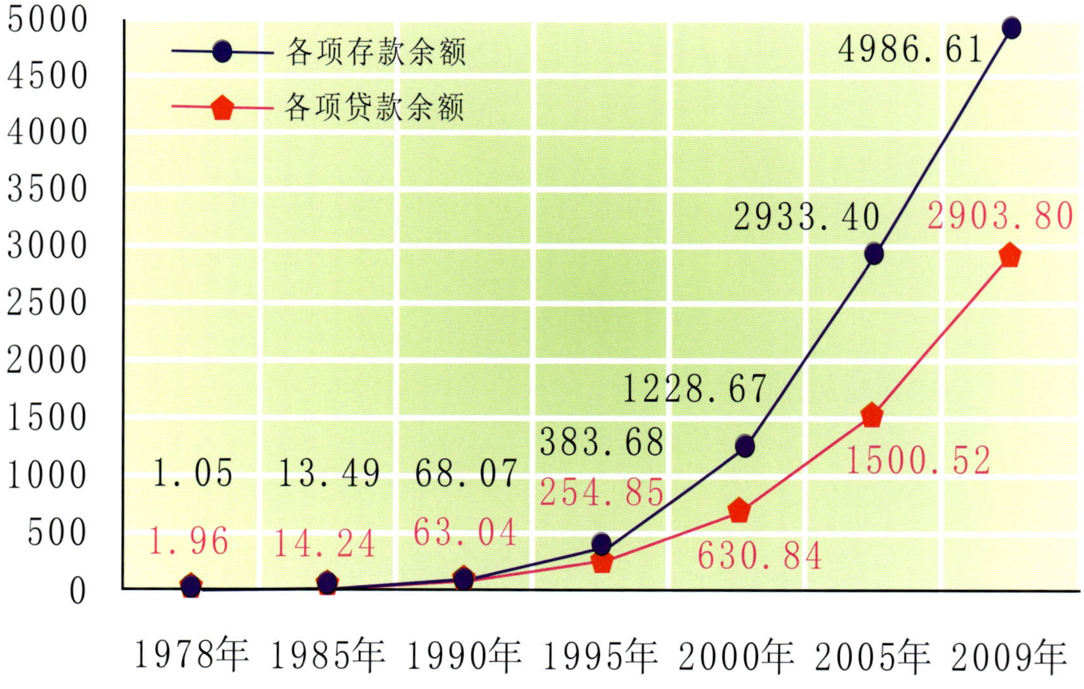

居民消费价格总指数（以上年为100）
120
115
110
105
100
95
90
85
106.5
96.6
113.9
106.8
101.5
99.9
97.9
101.5
96.6
98.1
100.7
103.0
102.4
101.2
103.1
105.5
96.9
1985年
1990年
1995年
1996年
1997年
1998年
1999年
2000年
2001年
2002年
2003年
2004年
2005年
2006年
2007年
2008年
2009年

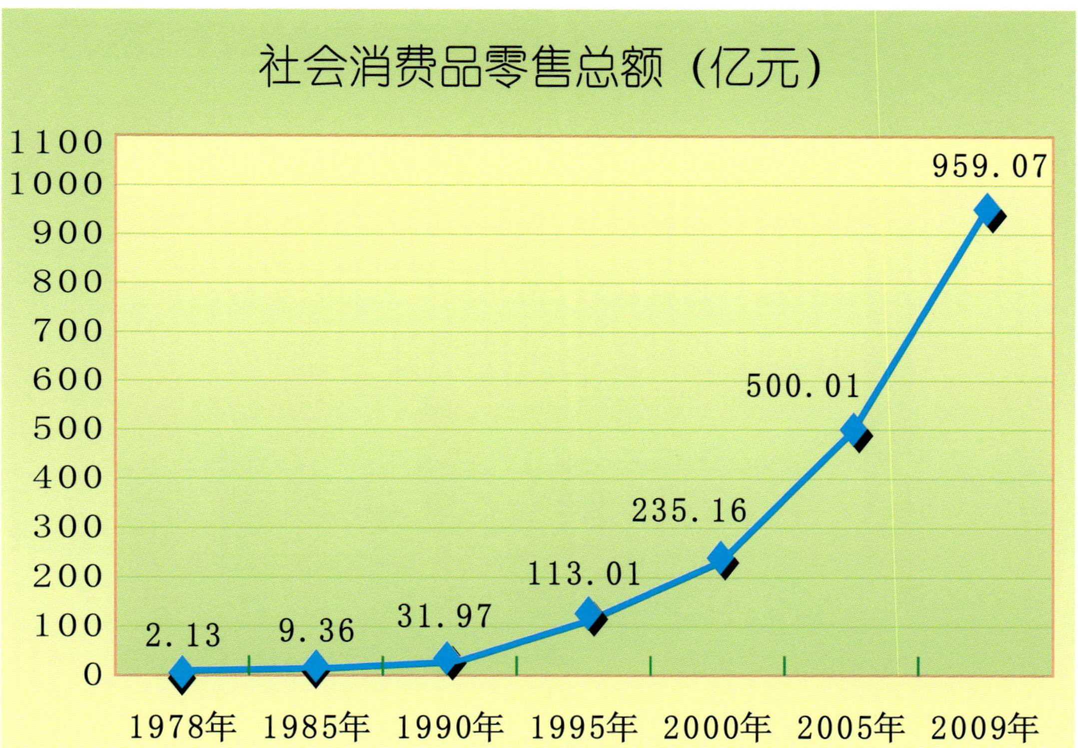
社会消费品零售总额（亿元）
1100
1000
900
800
700
600
500
400
300
200
100
0
2.13
9.36
31.97
113.01
235.16
500.01
959.07
1978年
1985年
1990年
1995年
2000年
2005年
2009年

城乡居民人民币储蓄存款余额(亿元)

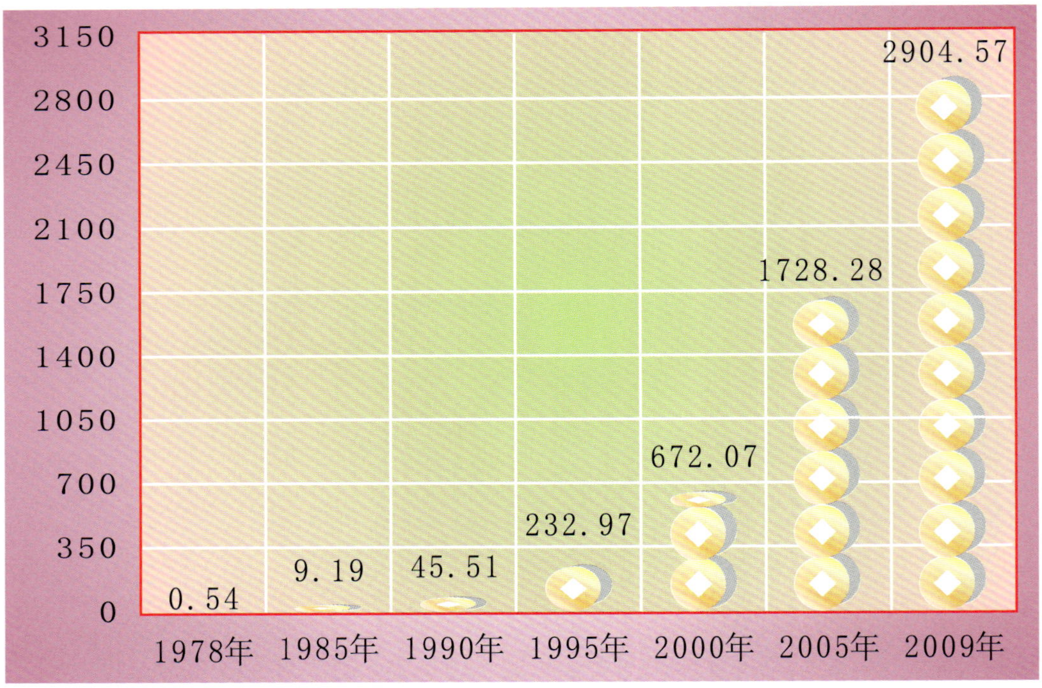

城乡居民收入(元)

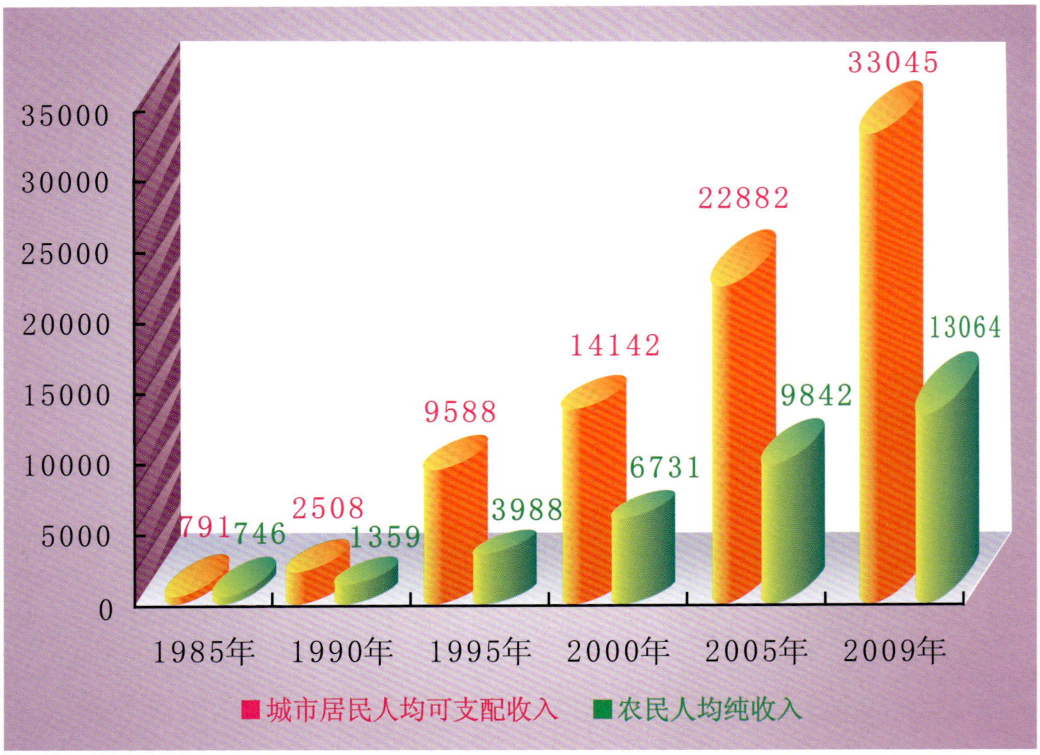

全社会固定资产投资总额(亿元)

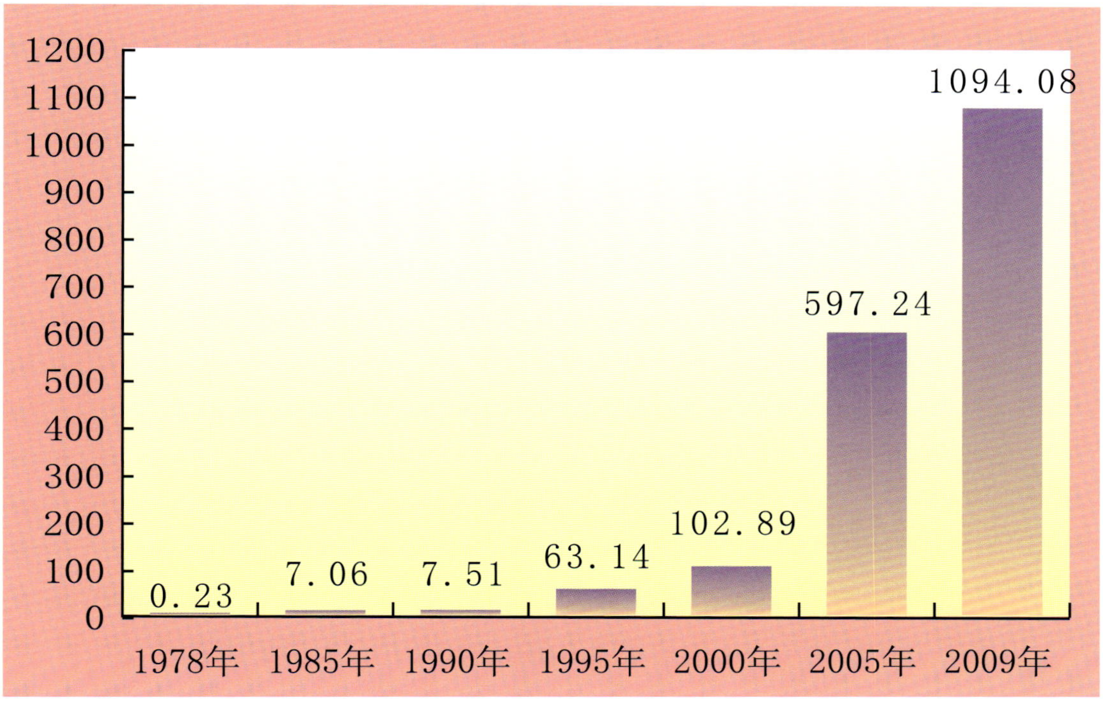

总供电量和总售电量(亿千瓦时)

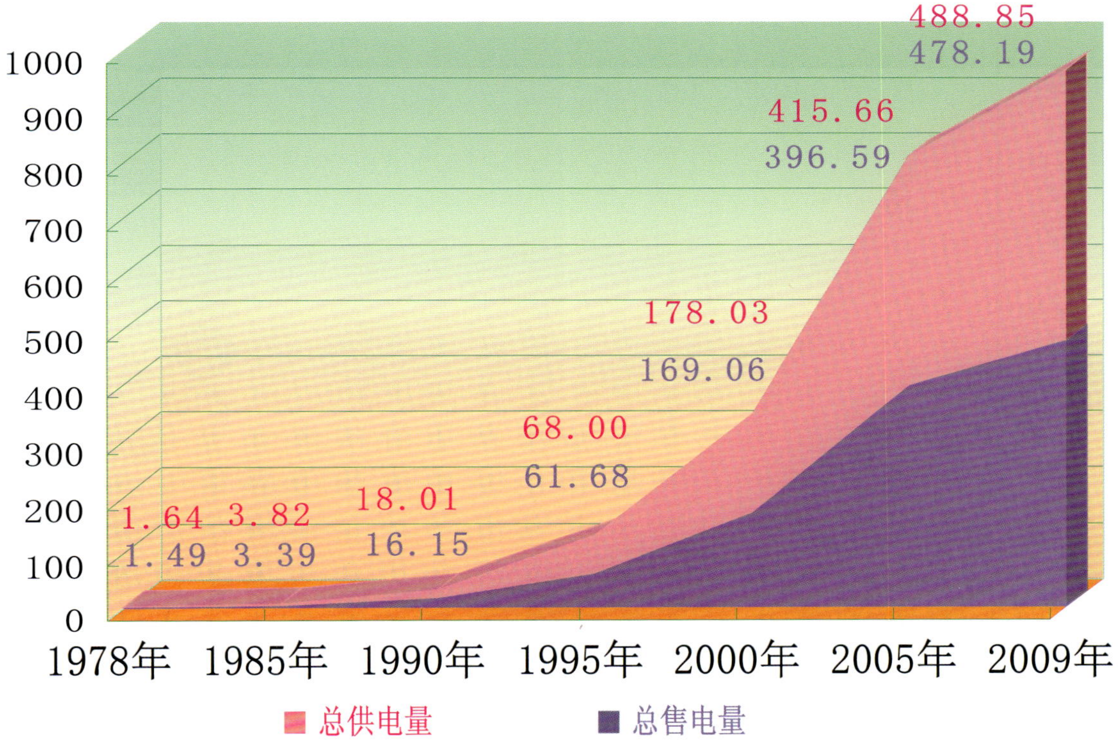

公路密度（公里/百平方公里）

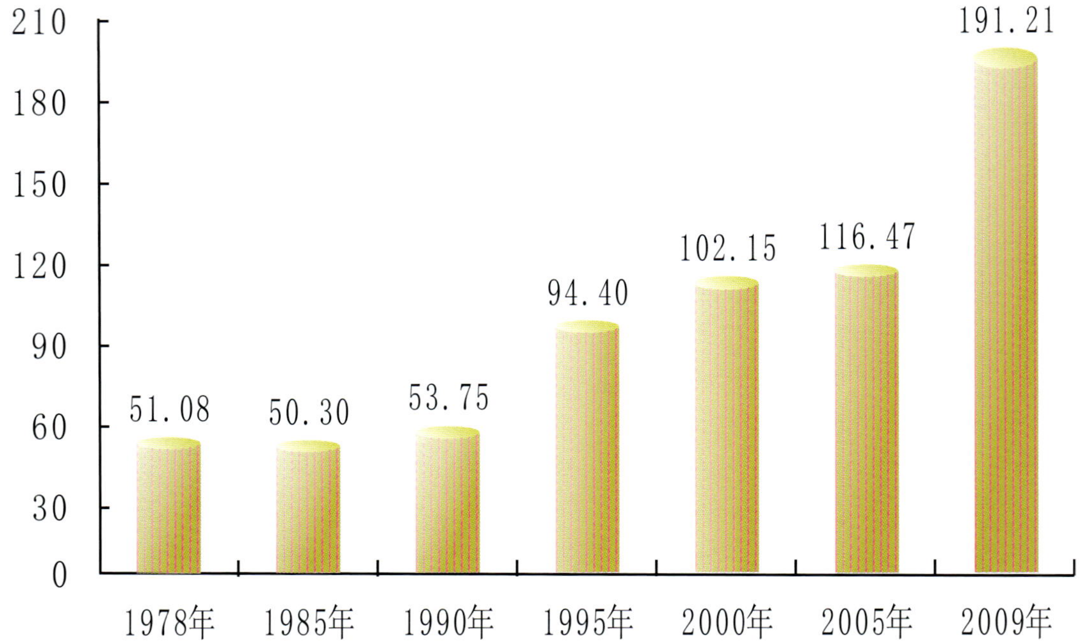

注：公路密度2000年起含高速公路，2006年起含专用公路和村道。

本地电话用户、移动电话用户（万户）

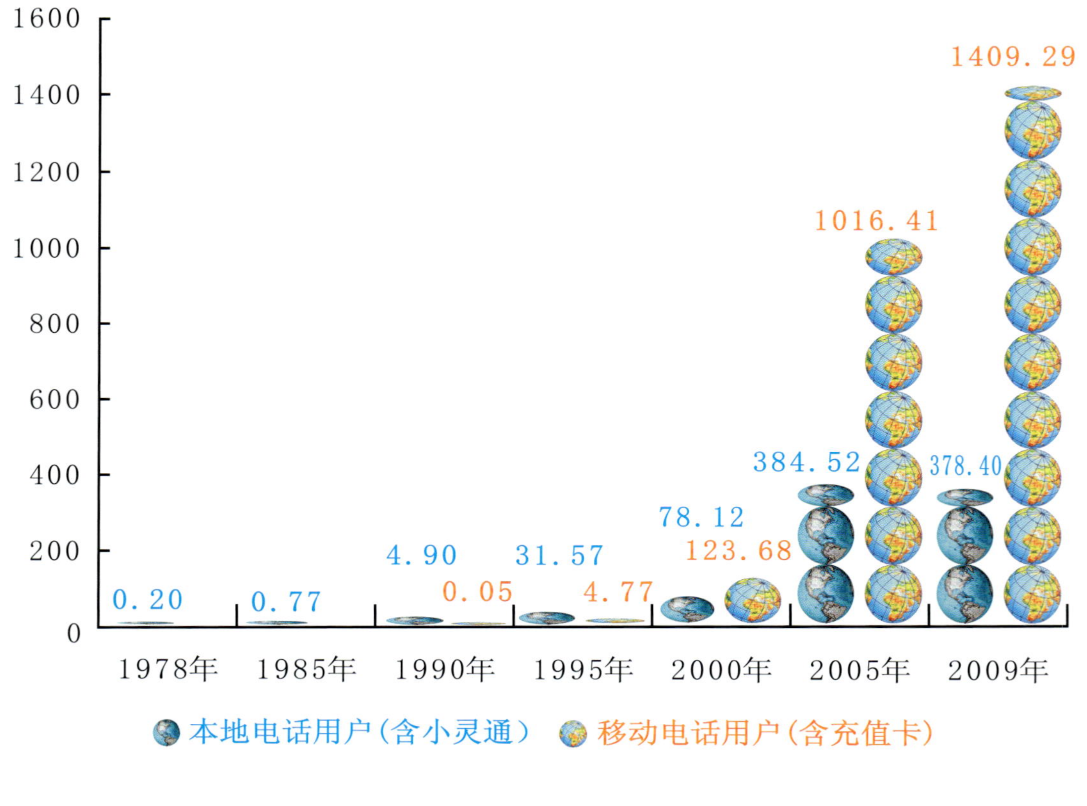

第一部分　概　述

Part One　Outline

2009 年东莞市国民经济和社会发展统计公报

2009 年，东莞面对国际金融危机带来的严重冲击，全市人民在市委、市政府的坚强领导下，以科学发展观为指导，认真贯彻执行国家和省的各项宏观调控政策与措施，化危为机，砥砺奋进，加快推进经济社会双转型，全力以赴保增长，有效遏制了经济下滑的势头，国民经济形势总体回升向好，社会事业不断进步，在逆境中实现了新的发展。

一、经济发展

经济总量

初步核算，2009 年东莞市生产总值（GDP）3763.26 亿元，按可比价格计算，比上年增长 5.3%。其中第一产业增加值 14.99 亿元，增长 5.1%；第二产业增加值 1771.77 亿元，下降 3.7%；第三产业增加值 1976.50 亿元，增长 15.1%。三大产业比例为 0.4∶47.1∶52.5。在第三产业中，批发和零售业增长 17.5%，住宿和餐饮业增长 8.8%，金融业增长 25.5%，房地产业增长 23.4%，其他服务业增长 13.5%。人均生产总值达 56591 元，增长 10.0%。

图一 1978—2009 年地区生产总值及增长速度

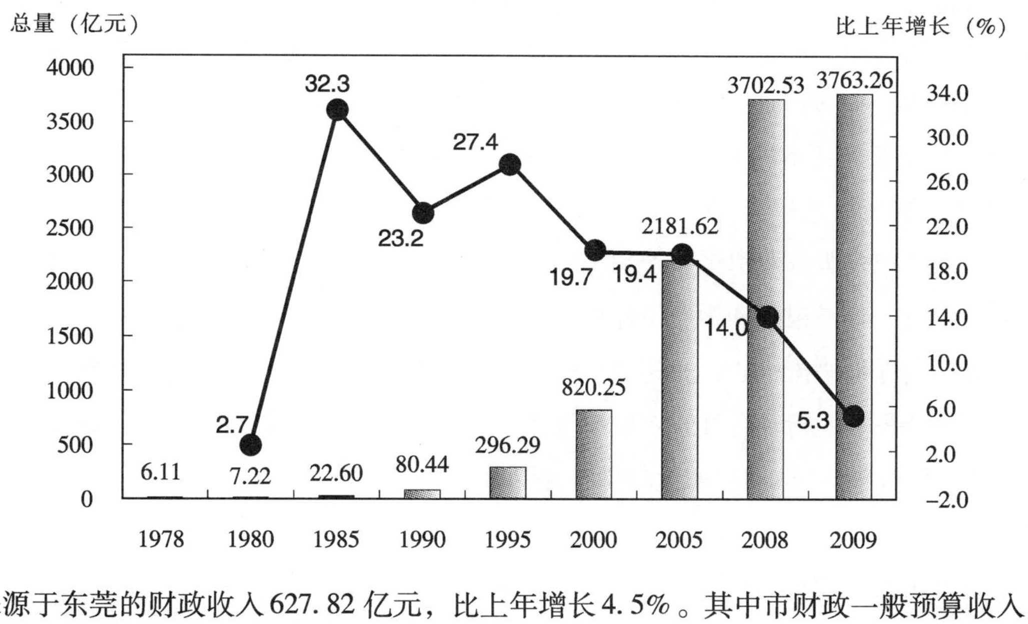

全年来源于东莞的财政收入 627.82 亿元，比上年增长 4.5%。其中市财政一般预算收入 231.16 亿元，增长 10.5%。在市财政一般预算收入中，增值税 53.44 亿元，下降 3.3%；营业税 44.69 亿元，增长 5.8%；企业所得税 17.68 亿元，下降 4.2%；个人所得税 8.73 亿元，下降 0.7%；城市维护建设税 9.21 亿元，增长 9.6%；房产税 7.58 亿元，增长 15.6%；契税 15.75 亿元，增长 38.8%。全年全市工商税收总额 547.51 亿元，比上年增长 2.1%。其中国税 338.47 亿元，下降 0.2%；地税 209.04 亿元，增长 6.1%。全年地方一般财政支出 225.94 亿元，比上年增长 3.5%。其中，一般公共服务支出 19.30 亿元，公共安全支出 30.93 亿元，教育支出 12.97 亿元，科学技术支出 11.68 亿元，文化体育与传媒

支出2.50亿元，社会保障和就业支出15.09亿元，医疗卫生支出3.09亿元，环境保护支出5.41亿元，城乡社区事务支出3.88亿元，农林水事务支出7.89亿元，交通运输支出7.25亿元。

所有制结构

初步核算，在全市生产总值中，公有制经济增加值1002.14亿元，比上年增长12.0%，占26.6%；民营经济增加值1326.28亿元，增长10.2%，占35.2%；外资经济增加值1434.84亿元，下降2.6%，占38.1%。

在全市规模以上工业总产值中，国有控股工业总产值545.29亿元，比上年下降0.5%；集体工业总产值97.29亿元，增长1.9%；外商投资工业总产值1900.54亿元，下降11.1%；港澳台投资工业总产值2564.50亿元，下降8.0%。私营经济工业总产值529.97亿元，增长2.8%。

在固定资产投资中，国有经济投资177.58亿元，比上年增长73.7%，占固定资产投资总额的比重为16.2%；集体经济投资195.71亿元，增长1.9%，占17.9%；民营经济投资423.59亿元，增长15.1%，占38.7%；外商及港澳台投资203.50亿元，下降24.9%，占18.6%。

在限额以上批发零售贸易业零售额中，内资企业实现零售额364.38亿元，比上年增长11.0%，占总零售额的比重为88.8%。其中，国有企业占2.0%，集体企业占4.4%，股份制企业占45.6%，私营企业占36.8%；外资企业实现零售额45.90亿元，增长30.4%，占11.2%。

在出口总额中，国有企业出口额111.24亿美元，比上年下降30.1%；三资企业出口额334.56亿美元，下降12.0%；集体企业出口额9.39亿美元，下降12.6%。

转型升级

东莞市积极搭建服务平台，完善就地不停产转型的操作办法，帮助339家来料加工企业成功转为三资或民营企业。用好加工贸易转型升级专项资金，激励企业加强技术研发和品牌经营，全市新设立外资企业研发机构84家；拥有自主品牌的加工贸易企业900家，增长15%。完善科技东莞配套政策，积极培育“两自”企业，新增国家高新技术企业90家、省民营科技企业89家；新增省级以上名牌名标25个；全市工业更新改造投资154亿元，增长1.5倍。支持科技企业融资，设立5000万元科技贷款风险准备金。加强现代服务业引进，推动金融、物流、会展等生产性服务业加快发展。东莞农信社改制为农村商业银行，新增银行和融资担保机构8家、上市公司1家，引进中外运等一批大型物流仓储项目。启动虎门港保税物流中心，一期项目投入8亿元，已通过验收。强化责任落实，加强重点耗能企业监管，开展全民节能行动，推进企业清洁生产，加强土地执法监察。二氧化硫和化学需氧量排放分别下降9.2%和6.8%，达到省总量减排年度要求。

固定资产投资

全年全社会固定资产投资1094.08亿元，比上年增长13.0%。

在固定资产投资总额中，基本建设投资464.07亿元，比上年增长18.0%；更新改造投资212.88亿元，增长150.8%；房地产开发投资277.66亿元，增长2.3%。从产业投向看，投资集中在二、三产业。第二产业投资395.43亿元，其中制造业投资335.71亿元；第三产业投资698.04亿元。

全年完成投资5000万元以上的项目292个，完成投资409.83亿元。其中，工业类项目126个，完成投资152.09亿元。完成投资1亿元以上项目93个，完成投资267.91亿元。其中，工业类项目33个，完成投资86.21亿元。

价格

全年居民消费价格总水平比上年下降3.1%。其中居住类价格下降8.7%，娱乐教育文化用品及服务类价格下降4.7%，衣着类价格下降2.8%，食品类价格下降1.9%，医疗保健和个人用品类价格下降1.8%，烟酒及用品类价格上涨1.4%，交通和通信类价格下降1.3%，家庭设备用品及维修服务类价格上涨0.2%。商品零售价格下降4.7%。工业品出厂价格下降3.2%。

图二　1978–2009年全社会固定资产投资总额及其增长速度

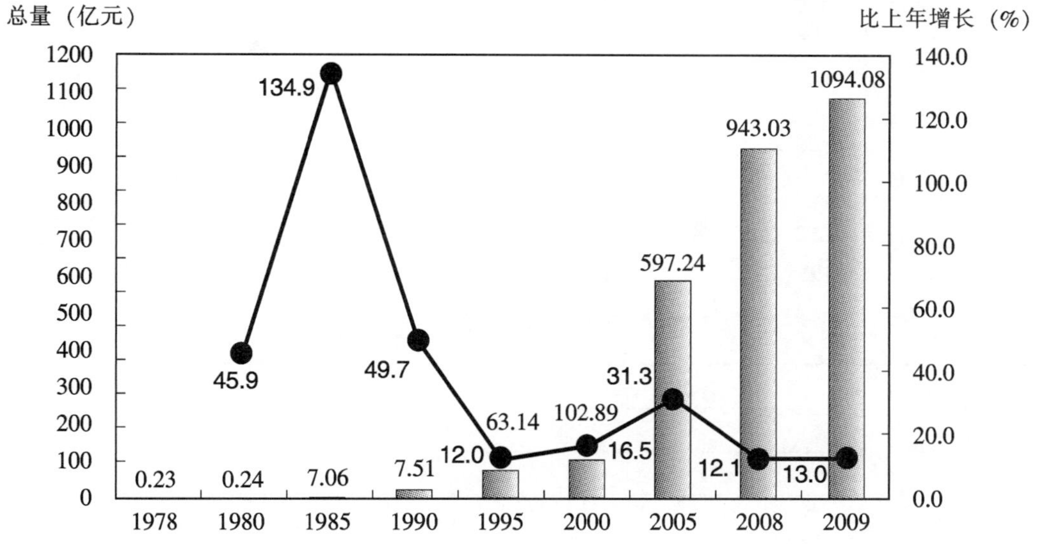

表一：2009年分行业固定资产投资额情况

单位：万元

行　业	投资额	增长%
总计	10940753	13.0
农、林、牧、渔业	6009	-15.7
制造业	3357103	-9.1
电力、燃气及水的生产和供应业	595645	110.0
建筑业	1574	-90.8
交通运输、仓储和邮政业	1267998	157.0
信息传输、计算机服务和软件业	207335	-15.9
批发和零售业	163146	-22.1
住宿与饮食业	225418	163.1
金融业	11242	56.3
房地产业	3533940	7.8
租赁和商务服务业	152034	17.6
科研、技术服务和地质勘察业	49643	-25.4
水利、环境和公共设施管理业	771160	18.2
居民服务和其他服务业	19928	219.4
教育	140411	-12.1
卫生、社会保障和社会福利业	212290	72.6
文化、体育和娱乐业	74655	65.3
公共管理和社会组织	151222	-3.3

图三　1978–2009 年居民消费价格涨跌幅度

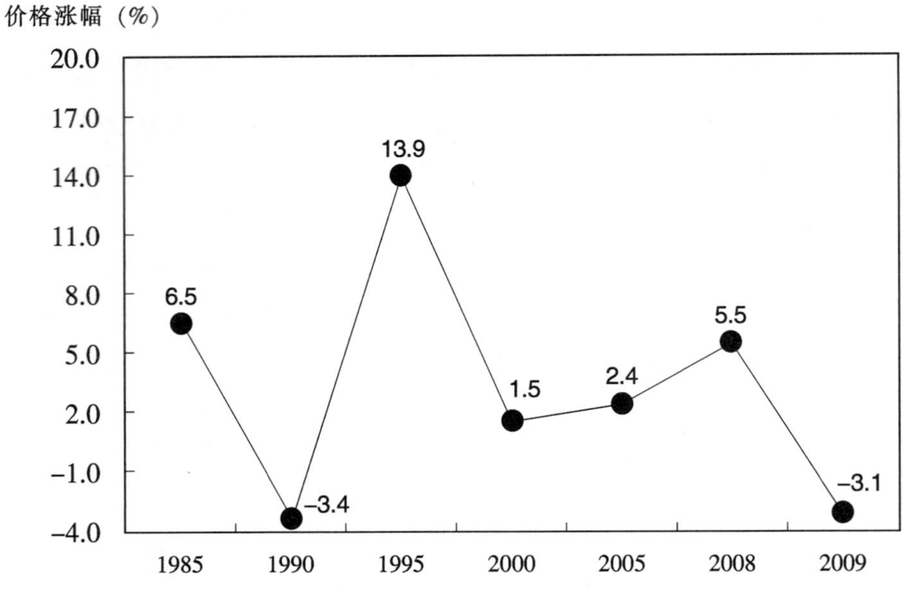

表二：2009 年价格变动情况

类　　别	价格指数（%）	比上年升降幅度（%）
居民消费价格指数	96.9	-3.1
食　品	98.1	-1.9
其中：粮食	104.2	4.2
肉禽及其制品	94.2	-5.8
油脂	83.1	-16.9
蛋	97.4	-2.6
鲜菜	95.7	-4.3
水产品	101.0	1.0
烟酒及用品	101.4	1.4
衣着	97.2	-2.8
家庭设备用品及服务	100.2	0.2
医疗保健及个人用品	98.2	-1.8
交通和通信	98.7	-1.3
娱乐教育文化用品及服务	95.3	-4.7
居住	91.3	-8.7
商品零售价格指数	95.3	-4.7
工业品出厂价格指数	96.8	-3.2

农业

全年全市完成农业总产值 25.31 亿元，按可比价计算，比上年增长 3.3%。其中种植业产值 13.20 亿元，增长 3.2%，占 52.2%；林业产值 0.21 亿元，下降 37.5%，占 0.8%；牧业产值 5.00 亿元，增长 6.8%，占 19.8%；渔业产值 6.06 亿元，增长 3.3%，占 23.9%。全年粮食种植面积 4.16 万亩，粮食产量 1.19 万吨；水产品产量 7.33 万吨，增长 1.4%；蔬菜产量 40.03 万吨，增长 2.3%；生猪出栏数 28.08 万头，增长 8.4%；家禽出栏数 752.20 万只，增长 2.7%。

新增省级农业龙头企业 2 家、市级农业龙头企业 2 家、新增农民专业合作组织 3 家。年末全市共有 20 家农业龙头企业和 25 家农民专业合作组织，其中省级以上龙头企业 6 家、国家级 2 家。年末全市共有广东省名牌产品（农业类）26 个、无公害农产品 47 个、绿色食品 38 个、有机食品 10 个。

工业

全年全市实现工业增加值 1690.22 亿元，比上年下降 4.0%，占 GDP 的比重为 44.9%。全市完成工业总产值 6762.8 亿元，下降 3.3%。其中规模以上工业总产值 5935.2 亿元，下降 6.3%。在规模以上工业中，重工业产值 3290.6 亿元，下降 7.7%，所占比重为 55.4%；轻工业产值 2644.6 亿元，下降 4.6%，占 44.6%。大中型企业完成工业总产值 4127.1 亿元，占规模以上工业总产值的 69.5%。规模以上工业实现利润总额 155.55 亿元，比上年增长 12.6%；资产负债率为 60.5%；工业经济综合效益指数为 113.77，比上年上升 1.78 个点。

全年规模以上八大支柱产业总产值 3728.72 亿元，比上年下降 7.2%。其中通信设备、计算机及其他电子设备制造业产值 1590.84 亿元，下降 8.4%。规模以上电子信息制造业产值 2402.67 亿元，下降 9.4%；实现利润总额 41.95 亿元，下降 17.1%。

表三：2009 年规模以上工业主要产品产量

产品名称	计量单位	产 量	比上年增长%
发电量	亿千瓦时	337.11	-5.3
化学纤维	吨	11528.12	-36.1
纱	吨	11780.10	-72.0
服装	万件	117600.52	-8.4
皮革鞋靴	万双	36296.75	-16.3
人造板	万立方米	16.94	74.8
家具	万件	5745.75	-36.4
机制纸及纸板	万吨	866.67	21.8
塑料制品	万吨	272.90	-13.7
平板玻璃	万重量箱	3058.71	81.6
金属切削机床	台	2976	-61.7
泵（液体泵）	万台	937.63	-28.2
交流电动机	万千瓦	155.30	-5.1
变压器	万千伏安	412.79	-23.6
电话单机	万台	2948.81	-29.0
移动通信手持机（手机）	万台	1203.47	33.0
微型电子计算机	万台	16.80	
打印机	万台	54.24	-45.7
激光视盘机	万台	2892.25	-31.2
集成电路	万块	26.40	-89.5
电子元件	亿只	6892.10	-7.2
印制电路板	万平方米	2077.23	13.8
彩色电视机	万台	514.48	4.3
组合音响	万台	2667.76	-27.8
自动化仪表及系统	万台（套）	75.86	10.3
电工仪器仪表	万台	321.19	-22.8
光学仪器	万台	1.91	-63.6

建筑业

全年全市建筑业增加值 81.55 亿元，比上年增长 4.7%。

建筑企业完成施工产值 96.42 亿元，比上年下降 11.4%；施工面积 728.79 万平方米，下降 24.4%；竣工面积 344.05 万平方米，下降 39.2%。建筑企业按施工产值计算的全员劳动生产率人均达 17.8 万元，比上年增长 1.8%。

交通运输、仓储和邮政业

全年全市交通运输、仓储和邮政业增加值 73.16 亿元，比上年下降 12.8%。

年末全市境内公路通车里程（含乡村道路）4713.33 公里，公路密度 191.21 公里/百平方公里。其中等级公路 4598.13 公里，密度 186.54 公里/百平方公里；高速公路 207 公里，密度 8.40 公里/百平方公里。年末全市机动车保有量 126.91 万辆，比上年增长 3.6%。其中汽车保有量 79.56 万辆，增长 13.4%。公路货物运输 6944 万吨，公路货物周转量 45.29 亿吨公里；水路货物运输 1789 万吨，水路货物周转量 56.36 亿吨公里。全年公路运输完成旅客客运量 7.33 亿人，旅客周转量 105.13 亿人公里；水路运输 33 万人，旅客周转量 2145 万人公里。全年港口旅客吞吐量 34.48 万人，港口货物吞吐量 3530.08 万吨。

全年完成邮电业务收入 156.31 亿元，比上年下降 9.3%。其中电信业务收入 149.16 亿元，下降 9.6%；移动业务收入 101.29 亿元，下降 4.9%；邮政业务收入 7.15 亿元，下降 3.0%。全年发送信函 4276 万件，下降 35.42%；特快专递 557 万件，增长 16.3%；全年邮政汇款汇出金额 222.24 亿元，下降 6.9%。

国内贸易

全年全市批发和零售业增加值 367.45 亿元，比上年增长 17.5%；住宿和餐饮业增加值 153.24 亿元，增长 8.8%。

全年全市社会消费品零售总额 956.25 亿元，比上年增长 14.1%，扣除物价因素，实际增长 19.7%。分行业看，批发零售贸易业零售额 831.96 亿元，增长 14.7%；住宿餐饮业零售额 124.23 亿元，增长 10.1%。

在限额以上贸易业中，食品、饮料、烟酒类零售额增长 16.8%；服装鞋帽、针、纺织品类增长 31.8%；日用品类增长 26.3%；汽车类增长 53.7%。

全年批发零售贸易业实现商品销售总额 1571.92 亿元，比上年增长 9.5%。

图四 1978–2009 年社会消费品零售总额及其增长速度

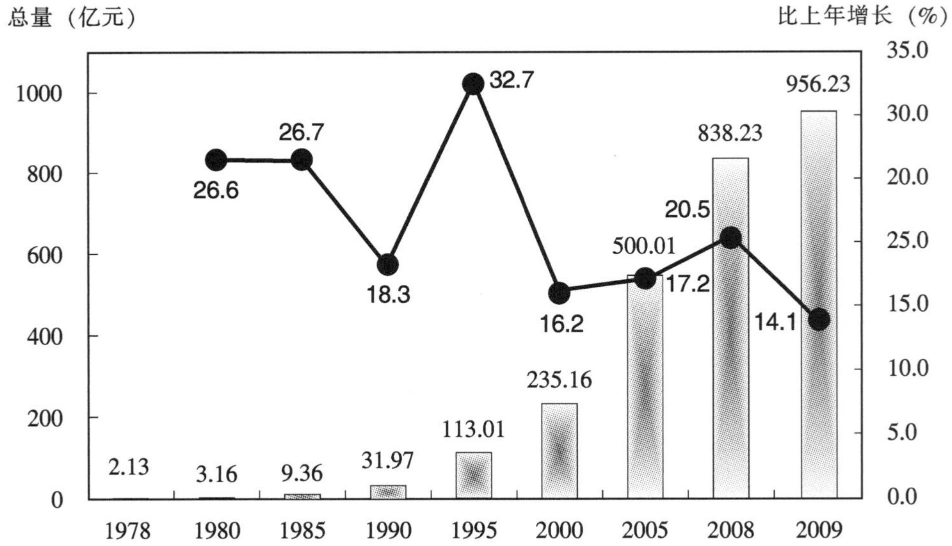

金融业

全年全市金融业增加值166.42亿元，比上年增长25.5%。

全年新增各类金融机构3家。年末全市有各类金融机构75家，其中银行类机构23家，保险类机构37家，证券期货类机构15家。

年末全市金融机构各项人民币存款余额4986.61亿元，比年初增长14.6%。其中企业存款余额1419.94亿元，增长20.0%；财政性存款余额52.45亿元，增长5.9%。各项人民币贷款余额2903.80亿元，比年初增长22.2%。其中工业贷款余额237.12亿元，增长8.2%；商业贷款余额261.75亿元，增长49.2%；个人消费贷款余额714.56亿元，增长25.2%。在个人消费贷款余额中，个人住房按揭贷款余额606.70亿元，增长22.7%；个人汽车消费贷款余额24.06亿元，增长22.2%。全年金融机构现金收入8449.47亿元，现金支出8486.22亿元，收支相抵现金净投放36.75亿元。全市金融机构不良贷款率比年初下降0.62个百分点。年末各类银行机构人民币资产总额5863.15亿元，比上年增长15.2%。

年末全市各类证券公司共有开户数77.60万户，比上年增加42.92万户。全年股票总成交额11677.38亿元，比上年增长251.7%。年末保证金余额162.60亿元，比上年增长113.5%。

年末全市有各类保险公司37家，保险中介机构31家，比上年增加7家。保险从业人员2.8万人。全年保费收入115.08亿元，比上年增长27.4%。其中财产险保费收入35.36亿元，增长11.2%；人寿险保费收入79.72亿元，增长36.3%。全年保险赔款与给付金额27亿元，其中财产险赔款19亿元，综合赔付率为14.25%。人身险赔款与给付8亿元，赔付率为11.24%。

房地产业

全年全市房地产业增加值333.37亿元，比上年增长23.4%。

全年完成房地产开发投资277.66亿元，比上年增长2.3%。商品房施工面积2223.4万平方米，增长11.3%；竣工面积188.83万平方米，下降60.5%；销售面积604.11万平方米，增长18.1%，其中商品住宅销售面积585.68万平方米，增长25.2%。全年商品房销售额353.17亿元，增长22.4%，其中商品住宅销售额336.86亿元，增长36.9%。

民营经济

年末全市民营单位登记注册户数47.80万户，比上年增长0.3%。其中私营企业增长较快，达到7.42万户，增长17.4%；个体工商户40.33万户，下降2.3%。全年规模以上民营工业完成总产值782.36亿元，增长6.9%；民营经济完成固定资产投资423.59亿元，增长15.1%；民营经济消费品零售额798.80亿元，增长14.6%；民营经济缴税总额197.98亿元，下降1.2%。

区域经济

年末全市32个镇街本级总资产934.31亿元，净资产626.47亿元，分别比上年增长19.1%和16.5%；32个镇街税收总额419.16亿元，增长0.4%。年末全市村组两级集体总资产1149.87亿元，增长3.6%；净资产888.77亿元，增长4.3%；全年镇街本级可支配收入197.54亿元，下降5.3%。当年可支配财政收入超10亿元的镇街有4个，GDP超100亿元的镇街有12个。可支配收入（扣除土地物业转让纯收入）超亿元的村有19个，超千万的村有405个，比上年增加20个，超5千万的村有59个。

2009年11个欠发达镇工商税收总额69.35亿元，比上年增长4.6%；可支配财政收入43.15亿元，增长4.2%。90个欠发达村总资产66.43亿元、净资产41.86亿元，分别增长7.4%和8.5%；经营纯收入1.79亿元，增长1.3%。

松山湖项目引进和投产步伐加快，工业总产值和税收分别增长43%和40%；虎门港成功开辟首条国际班轮航线，获批深水泊位项目共21个，其中6个正式投产运营；东莞生态园完成土地征收83.4%，启动重点工程30项；长安新区用海申报、规划环评、港区总体规划等通过专家审查。

二、对外开放

对外贸易

全年全市进出口总额941.55亿美元，比上年下降17.0%。其中进口总额389.86亿美元，下降18.4%；出口总额551.69亿美元，下降16.0%。

按贸易方式分，一般贸易出口57.17亿美元，增长17.3%；加工贸易出口487.82亿美元，下降19.0%；其他出口6.69亿美元，增长27.4%。

按出口的国家和地区分，对亚洲出口273.35亿美元，下降9.9%；对欧洲出口96.30亿美元，下降26.6%；对北美洲出口157.70亿美元，下降17.3%；对拉丁美洲出口13.24亿美元，下降23.2%；对大洋洲出口8.13亿美元，下降17.9%。

全年机电产品出口387.52亿美元，下降18.2%，占出口总额的比重为70.2%。高新技术产品出口159.39亿美元，下降19.8%，占28.9%。

表四：2009年主要商品出口情况

单位：万美元

商品名称	金额	增长%
自动数据处理设备及其部件	422632	-35.9
服装及衣着附件	281072	-12.0
自动数据处理设备的零件	266800	-16.6
鞋类	245746	-9.3
家具及其零件	242631	-12.7
静止式变流器	231368	-13.5
游戏机	182400	-26.5
有线电话机（包括无绳电话机）	148365	-3.5
纺织纱线、织物及制品	136791	-6.9
数字式相机	127126	-14.0
电视、收音机及无线电讯设备的零附件	125923	-22.4
玩具	122820	-16.5
旅行用品及箱包	114392	4.6
电线和电缆	108069	-23.0
电视机（包括整套散件）	101880	27.6
通断保护电路装置及零件	103723	-16.1
塑料制品	90919	-15.4
录、放像机	84151	-30.3
手持或车载无线电话机	79983	87.0

吸收外资

按新口径统计，全年全市新签外商直接投资项目 579 宗，合同外资金额 16.16 亿美元（含增资和减资），比上年下降 37.5%。实际利用外资 25.94 亿美元，增长 6.0%。其中电子及通信设备制造业实际利用外资 6.32 亿美元，增长 26.2%；专用设备制造业实际利用外资 1.33 亿美元，增长 16.4%。全市新签投资总额超 1000 万美元项目 27 宗，增加 4 宗；新增世界 500 强企业投资项目 3 宗，世界 500 强企业增资 2 宗；新签第三产业项目合同外资 23398 万美元，占全市的 14.5%，比 2008 年提高 2.7 个百分点。外商进入商贸领域加快。全市新签批发和零售业项目有 86 宗，合同吸收外资 12403 万美元，增长 53.7%，占第三产业吸收外资的 53.0%。

全市外资企业共设立研发机构 84 家，比上年增长 15.5 倍。成功设立 2 家外商投资地区总部，实现外资引进地区总部新突破。全市新增外商投资的服务外包企业有 9 家，增加 8 家，占我市历年吸收服务外包项目的 75%。

表五：2009 年分行业利用外资及其增长速度

单位：万美元

行业名称	合同外资金额	比上年增长%	实际利用外资	比上年增长%
总计	149577	-37.5	243219	6.0
农、林、牧、渔业	13	0.0	35	-59.3
制造业	136926	-39.7	235137	4.5
其中：纺织业	5457	-23.3	8071	-41.9
纺织服装、鞋、帽制造业	3474	-66.4	11563	6.9
家具制造业	3287	-48.5	6383	-4.2
普通机械制造业	2994	-60.5	7105	8.0
专用设备制造业	6230	-58.5	13276	16.4
电气机械及器材制造业	12554	-57.1	17075	-24.6
电子及通信设备制造业	36972	-32.7	63247	26.2
金属制品业	8955	13.4	8328	-1.3
塑料制品业	11422	1.7	11544	-4.3
文教体育用品制造业	4545	-33.4	11054	71.5
造纸及纸制品业	2183	-82.3	24198	21.9
其他制造业	38853	-33.0	53293	0.0
信息、计算机服务和软件业	235	-55.2	571	114.7
批发和零售业	12403	53.7	7476	264.9

旅游

年末全市有星级酒店 95 家。其中五星级酒店 19 家，四星级酒店 26 家，三星级酒店 35 家，二星级酒店 14 家，一星级酒店 1 家。全市有旅行社 51 家，其中国际旅行社 9 家，国内旅行社 38 家，其他 4 家。全年接待国际及港澳台旅游入境人数 286 万人次，比上年增长 6.6%。其中入境外国人 104.23 万人次，增长 1.3%；港、澳、台同胞 181.76 万人次，增长 10.0%。国际旅游外汇收入 5.17 亿美元，增长 13.5%。全年接待国内旅游人数 1751 万人次，增长 9.2%。国内旅游总收入 151.49 亿元，增长 17.7%。

全年东莞组团外出旅游人数 127.1 万人，比上年增长 17.3%。其中，国内旅游人数 114.45 万人，增长 17.1%；出境旅游人数 12.65 万人，增长 20.0%。

三、城市建设

城市绿化

年末全市建成区土地面积 780.15 平方公里，公共设施用地面积 59.57 平方公里。全市林业用地面积 92.1 万亩，全市森林覆盖率为 36.5%，林地绿化率为 99.01%；城市建成区绿地率为 40.98%，绿化覆盖率为 44.27%，人均公共绿地面积 15.21 平方米；全市已建成公园广场 777 个，面积 5919 公顷。

公用事业

年末全市有公交线路 91 条，公交运营车辆 1407 辆，运营出租小汽车 6811 辆。全年市内公共汽车旅客客运量 2.25 亿人次。

全市自来水日供水能力达到 700 万立方米，全年自来水供水总量 16.08 亿立方米。年末供水管道总长度 12667.99 公里。全年全社会用电量 495.57 亿千瓦时，下降 3.6%，其中工业用电 376.10 亿千瓦时，下降 4.3%；照明用电 101.15 亿千瓦时，增长 8.1%。年末全市液化石油气家庭用户 87.32 万户，天然气家庭用户 11.15 万户。全年液化石油气供应量 35.19 万吨，天然气供气量 2.93 亿立方米。

信息化

2009 年信息化综合指数为 73.2（按常住人口计算）。年末全市普通固定电话 206.56 万户，比上年增加 11.16 万户；移动电话用户 1409.29 万户，减少 45.01 万户，其中充值卡用户 1271.15 万户，减少 91.76 万户。全年长途电话通话时长 174.32 亿分钟，其中对国际及港澳台电话通话时长 2.47 亿分钟。年末互联网用户 118.02 万户，比上年增加 21.65 万户；宽带接入用户 114.22 万户，增加 22.6 万户。

四、社会事业

科技

全年新增 90 家国家高新技术企业和 89 家广东省民营科技企业，总数分别达到 246 家和 562 家；全年承担省级以上科技计划项目 224 项，获得了 1.37 亿元经费资助。其中，获国家中小企业技术创新基金立项 30 个和 1395 万元资助经费，分别比上年增长 150% 和 140%；预计全市高新技术产业产值 2316 亿元。

全年专利申请量 19106 件、授权量 12918 件，分别比上年增长 32.6% 和 59.6%。其中发明专利申请量 1593 件，授权量 254 件；实用新型申请量 6557 件，授权量 4370 件；外观设计申请量 10956 件，授权量 8294 件。

教育

全市共有幼儿园 680 所，比上年增加 63 所，其中公立集体办园 174 所，民办园 506 所。共有省、市一级幼儿园 99 所。3—6 周岁在园（班）幼儿共 17.62 万人，入园（班）率达 95.1%，比上年提高

0.08 个百分点。绝大部分镇街基本普及三年学前教育，实行六周岁入小学。

全市共有小学 337 所，比上年减少 15 所；在校学生 51.12 万人；适龄儿童入学率达 100%，本市户籍毕业生升学率达 100%。全市有初中 144 所，初中在校学生 18.27 万人，户籍适龄少年入学率为 100%，辍学率为 0.22%，毕业生升学率为 97%。

全市高中阶段学校有 71 所（含民办学校 3 所），在校学生 11.64 万人，其中普通高中（含完中）42 所，在校学生 6.68 万人，中职学校 29 所（含技工学校 4 所），在校学生 4.97 万人。本市户籍初中毕业生 3.68 万人，升入各类高中阶段学校就读的学生 3.57 万人，其中普通高中 2.25 万人，中职学校 1.32 万人。本市户籍初中毕业生升学率达 97.0%，比上年提高 0.4 个百分点。普通高中在校学生与中等职业技术教育在校学生的比例约为 6:4。

全市有成人高等教育机构 5 所、镇街成人文化技术学校 32 所、民办成人非学历教育机构 268 个，各类成人教育年培训量达 49 万多人次。

全市有普通高等院校 5 所。其中本科院校 2 所，专科院校 3 所。在校学生 3.40 万人。全年普通高等院校共招收本科、专科学生 1.29 万人，毕业生 7292 人。

本年全市参加高考总人数 24707 人，其中普通类 21286 人，高职类 3421 人。在普通类考生中，上重点线 2229 人，比上年增加 387 人；上本科线 8384 人，增加 1349 人。

文化

东莞举办首届中国国际影视动漫版权保护和贸易博览会，达成动漫版权成交意向 120 项，成交总金额 82 亿元。年末全市有群众艺术馆 1 个，文化站 33 个，公共图书馆 504 个，博物馆 31 个，文化广场 697 个，艺术表演场所 63 个，电影放映单位 40 个，网吧 1056 间，公共文化设施建筑面积 923 万平方米。全市有公共广播节目 66 套，公共电视节目 32 套。广播、电视综合覆盖率均达到 100%。有线电视“村村通”工程继续推进，全市覆盖率达 100%。全年共出版报纸 8462.2 万份，各类杂志 168.18 万册，图书 4.6 万册，《东莞日报》发行量 4745 万份，电影放映 1.05 万场次，观众 298 万人次。

卫生

年末全市有医疗机构总数 2106 个，其中门诊、诊所、卫生站、医务室、社区卫生服务机构等基层医疗机构 2033 个，卫生技术人员 35766 人，医院病床 18080 张。全市建成并投入使用的社区卫生服务中心 348 个，覆盖了全市 300 多个村（社区）。全年诊疗总人数上升 8.0%。

体育

全年东莞运动员共获得 122 枚金牌、104 枚银牌、128 枚铜牌。其中夺得国际赛金牌 8 枚；夺得全国赛金牌 20 枚；夺得广东省赛金牌 94 枚、银牌 92 枚、铜牌 113 枚。

全年举办市级综合和单项比赛 18 次，参加人数 5.08 万人次；举办镇街级单项比赛 1178 次，参加人数 68.10 万人次。全市有体育彩票发行网点 644 个，销售总额 5.2 亿元，体彩公益金 1.32 亿元。

社会福利与救助

年末全市有收养类福利事业单位 39 个，其中社会福利院 2 个，儿童福利院 1 个，敬老院 33 个，敬老院供养老人 1464 人。社会福利事业单位 36 个，收养人数 2570 人，安排“四残”人员就业人数 247 人，全年社会救济人数 4.04 万人。城市居民最低生活保障支出 7022 万元，社会救济福利费用 2.37 亿元，自然灾害救济费用 234.8 万元，慈善基金结余 2.05 亿元。全市纳入“五保户”对象有 1364 人，“五保户”费用支出 998.8 万元。32 个镇街全部建立了社会保障网络，纳入街道级最低生活保障范围的有1606户3770人，纳入镇级最低生活保障范围的有13106户33549人。

社会稳定

全年市财政安排公共安全支出30.93亿元，比上年增长15.6%。推进科技强警，建设视频监控联网平台，全市在用各类视频监控点12.8万个。新建平安社区200个。全市接报违法犯罪宗数下降4.3%，刑事案件破案宗数增长50.1%。新建镇街综治信访维稳中心22个，村（社区）、企业综治工作站（室）317个。全市受理群众信访总量下降39.4%，群体性事件下降44%。完善企业倒闭风险预警机制，严厉打击欠薪逃匿行为，为9.3万名工人追回工资1.2亿元。

安全生产

全年全市共发生各类生产事故5074宗，比上年下降6.4%；死亡582人，受伤5565人，分别下降8.1%和7.2%；直接经济损失796.13万元，下降40.6%。其中，道路交通事故5037宗，下降6.3%；造成死亡545人，受伤5560人，分别下降7.6%和7.1%。亿元地区生产总值生产安全事故死亡率为0.15，道路交通万车死亡率为4.29。

资源和环境保护

全年雨日天数167天，全年日照时数1967.8小时，平均气温22.8摄氏度，相对湿度70%。全年降水量1881.6毫米，全年全市水资源总量22.13亿立方米。

年末全市有森林公园17个，林地面积92.1万亩，生态公益林37.45万亩，林木积蓄量241.41万立方米，林木总生长量15.56万立方米。全年完成水源涵养林改造1335.33公顷，种植乡土阔叶树苗木152万株，完成幼林抚育2896.6公顷，营造防火林带65公里，抚育374.34公里。

全年空气污染指数平均值为57，比上年降低5个百分点，空气质量优良天数占99.2%，比上年提高4.12个百分点，灰霾天数比上年减少61天。全市34项污水处理厂建成32项，投入运营19项，累计完成投资24.4亿元；全市35项配套截污管网已基本建成20项，建成管线长度681.92公里，占总长度的78.93%，累计完成投资30.8亿元；全市有28家企业通过省、市清洁生产验收；有40家企业被评为首批市级环境友好企业，有30家第二批市级环境友好企业通过验收。

五、人民生活

人口

年末全市户籍人口178.73万人。全年出生人口1.86万人，出生率为10.67‰；死亡人口7587人，死亡率为4.36‰；人口自然增长率为6.31‰。年末全市常住人口635万人。人口城镇化率为86.39%，城镇常住人口548.58万人。

就业

全年接收大中专毕业生1.45万人。全年人才市场求职登记人数155.12万人，比上年下降21.3%；成功应聘人数42.91万人，下降50%。年末城镇实有登记失业人数7674人，全年失业人员安置就业人数11923人，城镇登记失业率为1.61%。

居民收入

初步统计，2009年全市职工年平均工资14416元，比上年增长6.6%。其中，城镇在岗职工年平均工资42585元，增长7.8%。城市居民人均可支配收入33045元，农村居民人均纯收入13064元，分别比上年增长9.1%和6.0%。城镇最高10%收入组人均可支配收入71031元，城镇最低10%收入组人均可支配收入13642元。

图五　1978-2009年城市居民人均可支配收入及其增长速度

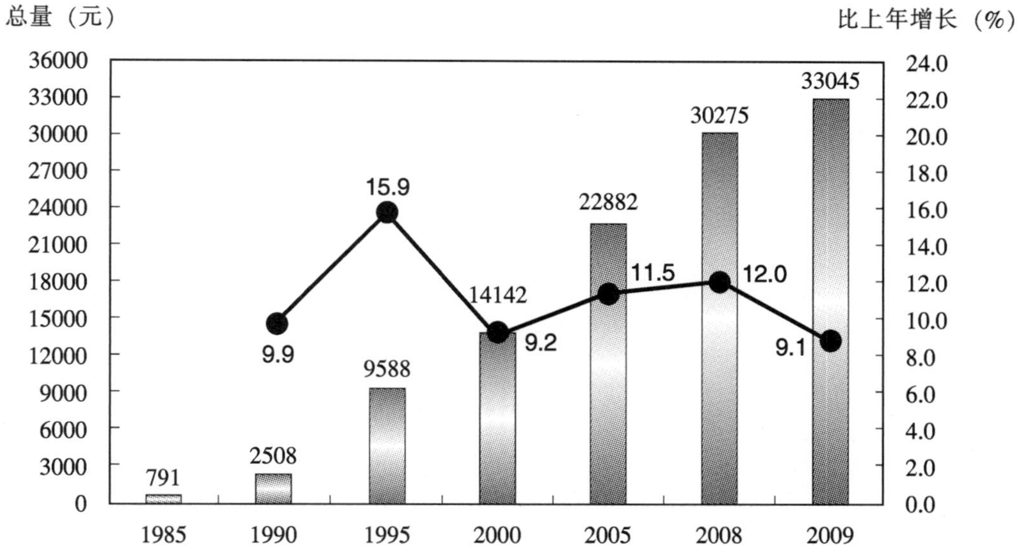

图六　1978-2009年农民人均纯收入及其增长速度

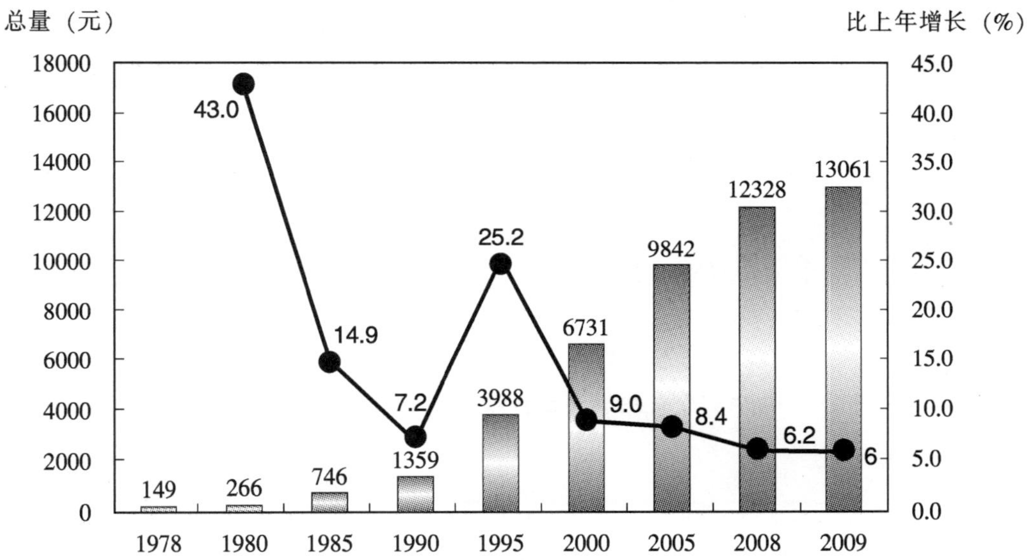

居民消费

全年城市居民人均消费性支出24270元，比上年增长4.6%。其中食品消费支出7972元，增长2.5%；衣着消费支出1492元，增长10.6%；居住消费支出2232元，下降13.7%；家庭设备用品及服务支出1616元，增长5.0%；医疗保健支出1401元，增长5.2%；交通和通信支出5456元，增长22.3%；教育文化娱乐服务支出3326元，下降4.0%；其他商品和服务支出777元，增长11.0%。城市居民家庭恩格尔系数为32.8%。在农民生活消费现金支出中，食品消费支出占35.0%，衣着消费支出占6.0%，居住消费支出占14.0%，家庭设备用品及服务支出占4.4%，医疗保健支出占5.3%，交通通讯支出占16.6%，文教娱乐用品及服务支出占11.5%，其他商品和服务消费支出占7.0%。

表六：2009 年居民收支情况

指　　标	收入或支出额（元）	比上年增长（%）
城市居民人均可支配收入	33045	9.1
# 工资性收入	23723	13.7
财产性收入	4209	19.4
转移性收入	3094	1.6
城市居民人均消费性支出	24270	4.6
食品	7972	2.5
衣着	1492	10.6
居住	2232	-13.7
家庭设备用品及服务	1616	5.0
医疗保健	1401	5.2
交通和通信	5456	22.3
教育文化娱乐服务	3326	-4.0
其他商品和服务	777	11.0

年末平均每百户城市居民家庭耐用消费品拥有量：家用空调 233 台，组合音响 69 套，移动电话 261 部，家用电脑 112 台，淋浴热水器 128 台，家用汽车 63 辆。年末城市居民人均住房建筑面积 53.75 平方米。平均每百户农村居民家庭耐用消费品拥有量：彩电 160 台，摩托车 83 辆，洗衣机 103 台，淋浴热水器 129 台，移动电话 257 部，影碟机 74 台，家用空调 210 台，家用电脑 109 台，家用汽车 53 辆。

居民储蓄

年末全市城乡居民人民币储蓄存款余额 2904.57 亿元，当年新增 266.59 亿元。其中，定期储蓄存款余额 1265.57 亿元，新增 161.65 亿元；活期储蓄存款余额 1639.00 亿元，新增 104.94 亿元。

图七　1978–2009 年城乡居民储蓄存款余额及其增长速度

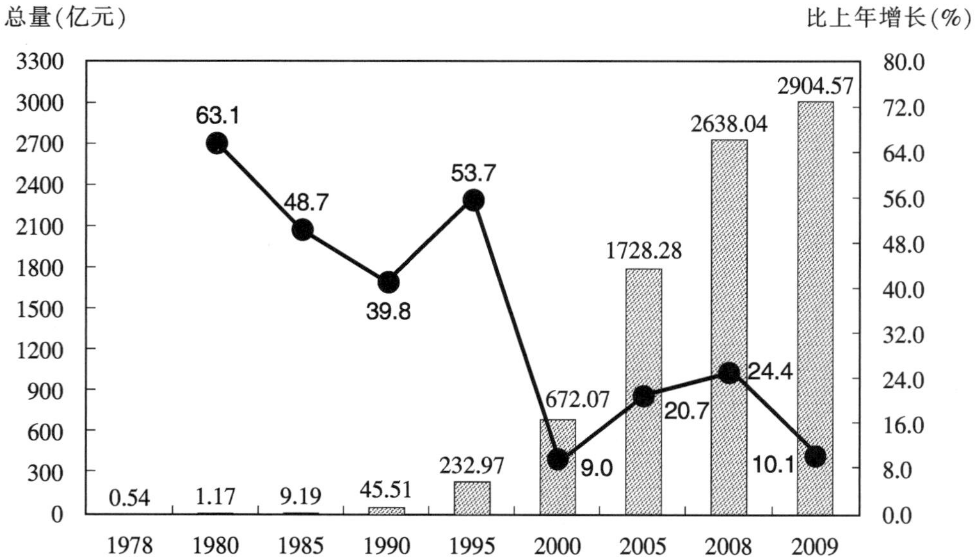

社会保障

年末全市参加职工基本养老保险315.81万人，基本医疗保险536.57万人，失业保险259.15万人，工伤保险438.87万人，地方养老保险310.87万人。全年社会保险基金总收入120.13亿元，保险基金总支出64.53亿元，年末保险基金累计余额310.24亿元。全市农（居）民基本养老保险人数45.83万人。全年累计征缴各项保险（不含机关养老保险）基金109.27亿元，比上年增长12.0%。

国民经济和社会发展中存在的主要困难和问题是：经济回升基础尚不牢固，企业经营仍有困难；产业转型升级和结构调整仍待加强，自主创新能力和抗御风险能力有待进一步提高；社会不稳定因素依然较多，安全消防隐患需进一步整治等。

注：1. 本公报数为初步统计数，最后统计数据以《东莞统计年鉴－2010》为准。

2. 地区生产总值、各行业增加值、工业总产值绝对数按当年价格计算，增长速度按可比价格计算。

3. 全市职工年平均工资的调查范围为东莞市辖区内除农户以外各类经济实体，具体包括：①辖区内中央、省、市属各类企业、事业、机关单位；②各镇街办企业；③村及村以下办企业；④私营企业和个体工商户。

城镇在岗职工年平均工资的调查范围包括：①东莞市辖区内中央、省、市属全部独立核算的企业、事业、机关单位；②莞城、石龙、虎门3个镇街范围内镇街属单位（不包括莞城、石龙、虎门3个镇街以下及其它镇街的单位、全市的私营单位和个体工商户）。

以上两个指标的调查范围不同，调查结果不同，请勿误用。

4. 阅读本公报时，请注意统计指标的时间、口径和计算方法等。

Dongguan Statistical Communiquéon National Economic and Social Development 2009

Facing with the serious impact of international finance crisis, the people of Dongguan city implemented the national and provincial macro-control policies conscientiously and turned crises into opportunities, accelerated the transformation of economic and social, ensured the growth of economy, with the guidance of scientific concept of development and the strong leadership of the municipal government. By the Efforts of the people in the city, the economic downturn was contained, economic recovered, social undertakings got continued progress, and Dongguan achieved a new development adversity.

Economical development

I Economic aggregate

According to preliminary accounting, Dongguan realized a GDP of RMB 376. 33 billion in 2009, up by 5. 3% over the previous year calculating at comparable price. In specific terms, primary industry contributed RMB 1. 50 billion to the overall growth, up by 5. 1% ; secondary industry contributed RMB 177. 18 billion, down by 3. 7% ; and tertiary industry contributed RMB 197. 65 billion, showing an increase of 15. 1%. The added value of primary, secondary and tertiary industries respectively accounted for 0. 4% , 47. 1% and 52. 5% of the GDP of Dongguan for the year 2009. In the tertiary industry, the growth of value added of the wholesales and retail trade was 17. 5% over the previous year, of the housing and catering services 8. 8% , of the finance 25. 5% , of the real estate 23. 4% , of the others 13. 5%. Per Capita GDP was RMB 56591, up by 10. 0%.

Figure 1: Gross Domestic Product and Its Growth,1978–2009

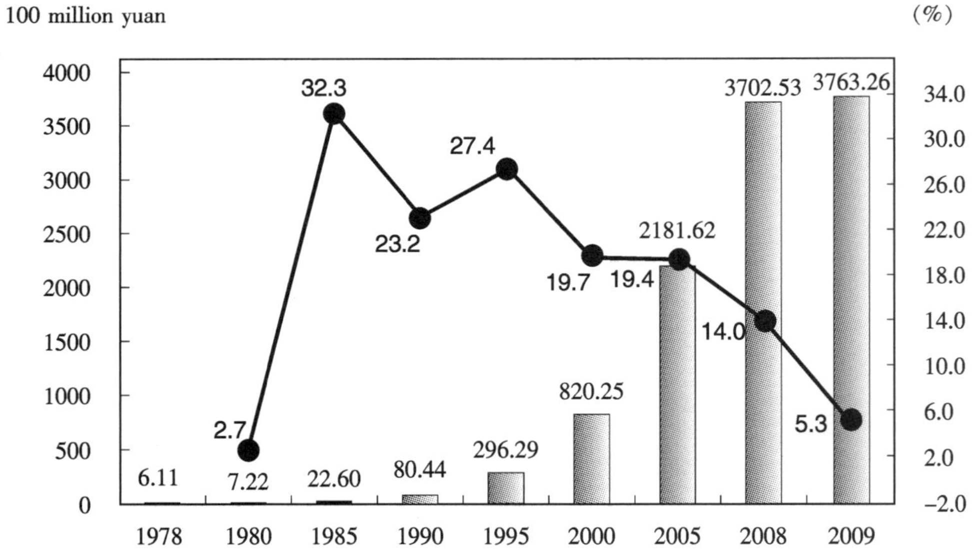

Fiscal revenue rooted in Dongguan was RMB 62. 78 billion for the year, up by 4. 5% , in which, the General budgeted revenue was RMB 23. 12 billion, up by 10. 5%. Among the General budgeted revenue, for the value-added tax revenue was RMB 5. 34 billion, down by 3. 3% ; for the business tax revenue was RMB 4. 47 billion, up by 5. 8% ; for the enterprise income tax revenue was RMB 1. 77 billion, down by 4. 2% ; for the individual income tax revenue was RMB 0. 87 billion, down by 0. 7% ; for the city maintenance and construction tax revenue was RMB 0. 92 billion, up by 9. 6% ; for the house property tax revenue was RMB 0. 76 billion, up by 15. 6% ; for the deed tax revenue was RMB 1. 58 billion, up by 38. 8%. Industrial and commercial tax revenue for the year was RMB 54. 75 billion, up by 2. 1% , in which the national tax revenue was RMB 33. 85 billion, down by 0. 2% , and the local tax revenue was RMB 20. 90 billion, up by 6. 1%. General budget expenditures amounted to RMB 22. 59 billion, increasing by 3. 5% , in which the general public services expenditures totaled RMB 1. 93 billion; the expenditure for public security amounted to RMB 3. 09 billion; for education was RMB 1. 30 billion; for science and technology was RMB 1. 17 billion; for culture, sports and media expenditures totaled RMB 0. 25 billion; for safety net and employment effort was RMB 1. 51 billion; for medical and health care services was RMB 0. 31 billion; for environmental protection was RMB 0. 54 billion; for urban and rural community affairs was RMB 0. 39 billion; for agriculture, forestry and water conservancy was RMB 0. 79 billion; for transportation was RMB 0. 73 billion.

Ⅱ Structure of ownership

According to preliminary accounting, the added value of the public ownership economy was RMB 100. 21 billion, up by 12. 0% ; the private ownership economy was RMB 132. 63 billion, up by 10. 2% ; foreign investment economy was RMB 143. 5 billion, down by 2. 6%. The added value of public ownership economy, private ownership economy and foreign investment economy respectively accounted for 26. 6% , 35. 2% and 38. 1% in the GDP of Dongguan for the year 2009.

The output value of state-owned enterprises in which of industrial enterprises above designated size in Dongguan was RMB 54. 53 billion, down by 0. 5% ; collective-owned industrial enterprises was RMB 9. 73 billion, increasing 1. 9% over previous year; industrial enterprises with foreign funds was RMB 190. 05 billion, down by 11. 1% ; HK/Macao/Taiwan-invested industrial enterprises realized RMB 256. 45 billion, down by 8. 0% ; private industrial enterprises increased 2. 8% to RMB 53. 00 billion.

With regard to the sources of the investment in fixed assets, investment from state-owned economy increased 73. 7% to RMB 17. 76 billion, accounting for 16. 2% ; investment from collective-owned economy increased 1. 9% to RMB 19. 57 billion, accounting for 17. 9% ; investment from private economy increased 15. 1% to RMB 42. 36 billion, accounting for 38. 7% ; funds from foreign and HK/Macao/Taiwan was RMB 20. 35 billion, down by 24. 9% , accounting for 18. 6%.

The total retail sales of domestic enterprises of wholesale and retail enterprises above designated size increased 11. 0% to RMB 36. 44 billion, accounting for 88. 8% . Of the total, state-owned enterprises, collective enterprises, share-holding enterprises and private enterprises accounted for 2. 0% , 4. 4% , 45. 6% and 36. 8% respectively; The total retail sales of foreign enterprises realized RMB 4. 59 billion, increased 30. 4% over the previous year, accounting for 11. 2% of the total.

In specific terms, the value of export by state-owned enterprises was US $ 11. 12 billion, down by 30. 1% ; the foreign enterprise was US $ 33. 46 billion, down by 12. 0% ; the collective enterprise was US $ 0. 94 billion, down by 12. 6%.

Ⅲ Economy Structure Transformation and Upgrading

Dongguan actively built a service platform, for improving the operation of local non-stop production in transition, to help 339 P. S. M. enterprises (processing with supplied materials enterprises) turn into

Foreign-funded enterprises or private enterprises successfully. Encouraging enterprises to strengthen technology research and brand management by using of special funds for upgrading, 84 foreign R & D institutions was newly established; 900 processing trade enterprises have established their own brand, up by 15%. Improved the related policies to support science and technology, actively cultivate the enterprises which have their own brand and technology. 90 newly national High-New Technology enterprises added, totaled 89 provincial technology private enterprises, and 25 newly famous brands added. The investment of technical innovation was RMB 15.4 billion, up by 150%. Dongguan established loan loss provision totaled RMB 50 million to support technical enterprises for Capital raising. Strengthening the introduction of modern services, improving financial、logistics, exhibition and other production services to development. Dongguan Rural Credit Cooperatives Reform for Rural Commercial Banks, and 8 newly bank or financing guarantees organizations and 1 newly quoted company added, and introduction Sinotrans Logistics warehousing and other large items. Enable the Humen Port Bonded Logistics Center, the first phase invested RMB 800 million and has been approved. Strengthening the responsibility to implement, especially the supervision of key energy-consuming enterprises, carrying out the civil energy conservation, promote clean production, strengthen supervision of land utilization Emissions of sulfur dioxide and chemical oxygen demand dropped 9.2% and 6.8% respectively, reached the provincial annual emission reduction requirements.

Ⅳ Investment in Fixed Assets

The total investment in fixed assets reached RMB 109.40 billion in 2009, an increase of 13.0% over the previous year. Specifically, the investment in capital construction increased 18.0% to RMB 46.41 billion; the investment in renovation and reconstruction increased 150.8% to RMB 21.29 billion and the investment in real estate development increased 2.3% to RMB 27.77 billion. With regard to industry, the investment was concentrated toward the secondary and tertiary industries. Investment in secondary industry was RMB 39.54 billion, including manufacturing industry investment of RMB 33.57 billion; Investment in tertiary industry was RMB 69.80 billion.

A total of RMB 40.98 billion of investment was completed on 292 projects above RMB 50 million, in specific terms, completed investment RMB 15.21 billion on 126 industrial projects. A total of RMB 26.79 billion of investment was completed on 93 projects above 100 million, completed investment RMB 8.62 billion on 33 industrial projects.

Figure 2: Investment in Fixed Assets and Its Growth, 1978–2009

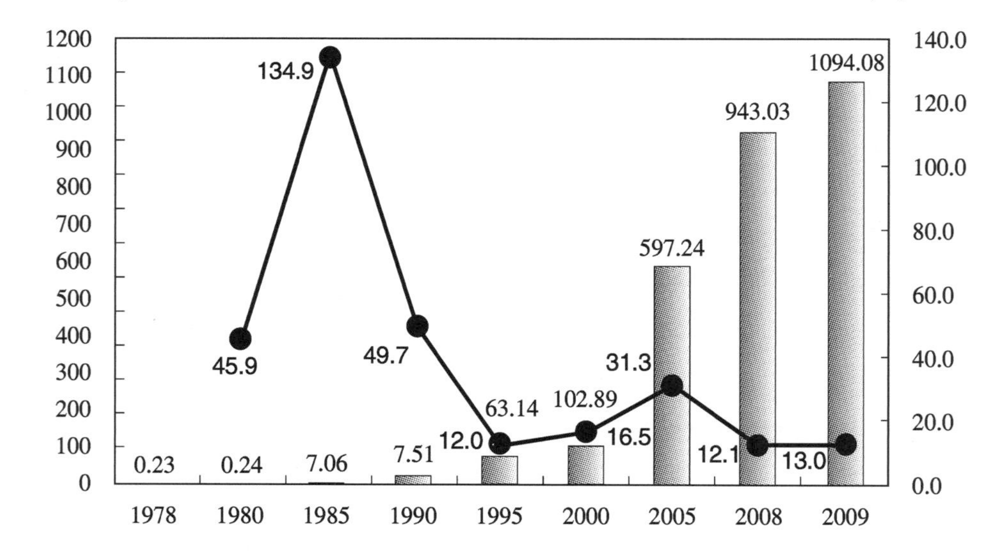

Table 1: Investment in Fixed Assets by sector in 2009

Sector	Investment	% over the previous year
Total	10940753	13. 0
Farming, Forestry, Animal Husbandry and Fishery	6009	-15. 7
Manufacture	3357103	-9. 1
Production and Supply of Electric Power, Gas and Water	595645	110. 0
Construction	1574	-90. 8
Transport, Storage and Postal Services	1267998	157. 0
Information Transmission, Computer Services and Software	207335	-15. 9
Wholesale and Retail Trade	163146	-22. 1
Hotel and Catering Services	225418	163. 1
Finance	11242	56. 3
Real Estate	3533940	7. 8
Leasing and Business Services	152034	17. 6
Scientific Research, Technical Services and Geological Prospecting	49643	-25. 4
Water Conservancy, Environment and Public Facilities Management	771160	18. 2
Resident Services and Other Services	19928	219. 4
Education	140411	-12. 1
Health Care, Social Security and social Welfare	212290	72. 6
Culture, Sports and Recreation	74655	65. 3
Public Administration and Social Organizations	151222	-3. 3

V Prices

2009 CPI (consumer price index) down by 3. 1% in Dongguan, among which residence down by 8. 7%; recreational, education and culture articles down by 4. 7%; clothing down by 2. 8%; food prices down by 1. 9%; healthy care and personal articles down by 1. 8%; tobacco, liquor and articles up by 1. 4%; transportation and communication down by 1. 3%; household facilities, articles and services up by 0. 2%; retail price down by 4. 7% and PPI (producer price index) down by 3. 2% over the pervious year in Dongguan.

Figure 3: Change in Consumer Prices, 1978–2009

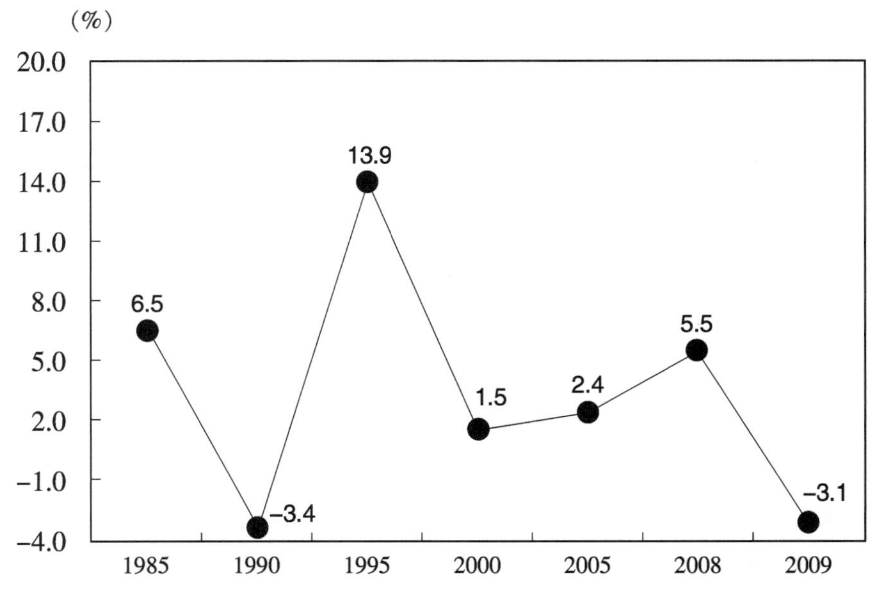

Table 2: Change in Prices in 2009

Item	Price Index (%)	Increase over 2008 (%)
Consumer Price Index	96.9	-3.1
Food	98.1	-1.9
of which: Grain	104.2	4.2
Meal, Poultry and Processed Products	94.2	-5.8
Oil or Fat	83.1	-16.9
Eggs	97.4	-2.6
Fresh	95.7	-4.3
Aquatic Products	101.0	1.0
Tobacco, Liquor and Articles	101.4	1.4
Clothing	97.2	-2.8
Household Facilities, Articles and Services	100.2	0.2
Health Care and Personal Articles	98.2	-1.8
Transportation and Communication	98.7	-1.3
Recreation, Education and Culture Articles	95.3	-4.7
Residence	91.3	-8.7
Retail Price Index	95.3	-4.7
Producer Price Index	96.8	-3.2

Ⅵ Agriculture

In 2009, the gross output value of agriculture forestry animal husbandry and fishery was RMB 2.53 billion, up by 3.3% calculating at comparable price. Specifically, the output value of agriculture was RMB 1.32 billion, with an increase of 3.2%, account for 52.2%; the output value of forestry was RMB 21 million, down by 37.5%, account for 0.8%; the output value of animal husbandry RMB 500 million, up by 6.8%, account for 19.8%; the output of fishery increased 3.3% to RMB 606 million, account for 23.9%. In 2009 the sown area of grain was 27.73 million m^2. The total output of grain was 11.9 thousand tons; the total output of aquatic products was 73.3 thousand tons, up by 1.4%; the total output of vegetables was 400.3 thousand tons, up by 2.3%. The number of slaughtered fattened hogs was 280.8 thousand heads, up by 8.4%; and that of poultry was 7.5 million, up by 2.7%.

In 2009, there were 2 newly approved leading agricultural enterprises at the municipality level, 2 at the provincial level, 3 newly farmer's specialized cooperation units. At the end of this year, there were 20 leading agricultural enterprises and 25 farmer's specialized cooperation units, specifically, 6 provincial level and 2 state level leading enterprises on agricultural industrialization respectively. By the year end, Dongguan boasted 26 province-level famous brand names in agriculture, 47 pesticide-free farming products, 38 eco-friendly foods and 10 organic foods.

Ⅶ Industry

In 2009, the total value added of the industry sector was RMB 169.02 billion, down by 4.0% and represented 44.9% of the city's GDP. The gross industrial output value was RMB 676.28 billion, down by 3.3%, among which, the industrial enterprises above the designated size was RMB 593.52 billion, down by 6.3%. Specifically, heavy industry realized an output value of RMB 329.06 billion, down by 7.7%, accounting for 55. 4% of the output value of industry above the designated size; that of light industry was RMB 264. 46 billion, down by 4. 6% , accounting for 44. 6%. The output value of large and medium sized enterprises was RMB 412. 71 billion, accounting for 69. 5% of the output value of the industrial enterprises above the designed size. The industrial enterprises above the designed size realized total profit RMB 15. 56 billion, up by 12. 6% over the previous year, the assets liability ratio was 60. 5% ; and the comprehensive index of economic efficiency levels was 113. 77, up by 1. 78 index points.

In 2009, the total output value of 8 pillar industry was RMB 372. 87 billion, down by 7. 2% , among them, the output value of communication equipment, computer and other electronic equipment manufacturing was RMB 159. 08 billion, down by 8. 4%. The output value of electronic information and manufacturing enterprises above designated size was RMB 240. 27 billion, down by 9. 4% , showing a total profit of RMB 4. 20 billion, which represents a decrease of 17. 1% over the previous year.

Table 3: Output of Major Industrial Products of industrial Enterprises above the Designated Size and the Growth Rates in 2009

Industry	Unit	Qty	Increase over 2008 (%)
Electricity	100 million kilowatt-hours	337. 11	-5. 3
Chemical Fibers	tons	11528. 12	-36. 1
Yarn	tons	11780. 10	-72. 0
Garment	10000 Pcs	117600. 52	-8. 4
Leather Shoes	10000 pairs	36296. 75	-16. 3
Artificial slabs	10000 stere	16. 94	74. 8
Furniture	10000 Pcs	5745. 75	-36. 4
Machine-made Paper & Paperboard	10000 tons	866. 67	21. 8
Plastic products	10000 tons	272. 90	-13. 7
Plain Glass	10000 Weight case	3058. 71	81. 6
Metal-cutting Machine Tools	units	2976	-61. 7
Pump (liquid pump)	10000 units	937. 63	-28. 2
Alternating Current motivation	10000 kilowatt	155. 30	-5. 1
Transformer	KVA	412. 79	-23. 6
Telephone sets	10000 sets	2948. 81	-29. 0
Mobile Telephone	10000 sets	1203. 47	33. 0
Micro-Computers	10000 sets	16. 80	
Printer	10000 sets	54. 24	-45. 7
Laser disk player	10000 sets	2892. 25	-31. 2
Integrated circuits	10000 sets	26. 40	-89. 5
Electronic components	100 million Pcs	6892. 10	-7. 2
Print circuit board	100 million Pcs	2077. 23	13. 8
Color TV	10000 sets	514. 48	4. 3
Hi-Fi Stereo Component Players	10000 sets	2667. 76	-27. 8
Automatization meter and system	10000 sets	75. 86	10. 3
Electricians Instruments and Meters	10000 sets	321. 19	-22. 8
Optical instruments	10000 sets	1. 91	-63. 6

Ⅷ Construction

The value added of construction was RMB 8. 16 billion, up by 4. 7% over the previous year.

The output value of buildings completed of construction enterprises in Dongguan was RMB 9. 64 billion, down by 11. 4% ; the floor space of buildings under construction was 7. 29 million m^2, down by 24. 4% ; the floor space of buildings completed was 3. 44 million m^2, down by 39. 2%. Calculated at the output value of buildings completed, the overall labor productivity was RMB 178, 000 per person, up by 1. 8% over the previous year.

Ⅸ Transportation, storage, post and telecommunications

The value added of the transportation, storage, post and telecommunications sector reached RMB 7. 32 billion in 2009, down by 12. 8%.

At the end of 2009, the total length of highways in Dongguan (including the highway in the rural area) was 4713. 3 kilometers; the highway density was 191. 2 kilometers per 100 sq. km.. Among them the length of expressway and class I to IV highways was 4598. 1 km, the density was 186. 5km per 100 sq. km. ; the length of expressways in the whole city reached 207 kilometers, and the density reached 8. 4 km per 100 sq. km.. The possession of motor vehicles reached 1. 27 million units, up by 3. 6% , among which the possession of civil motor vehicles was 795. 6 thousand units, up by 13. 4%. The freight traffic of highways was 69. 44 million tons, and the freight ton-kilometers of highways were 4. 53 billion ton-kilometers; the freight traffic of waterways was 17. 89 million tons, and the freight ton-kilometers of waterways were 5. 64 billion ton-kilometers. The passenger traffic of highways was 733 million by the end of 2009, the passenger-kilometers of highways were 10. 51 billion passenger-km; the passenger traffic of waterways was 330 thousand persons by the end of 2009, the passenger-kilometers of waterways was 21. 45 million passenger-km. The volume of freight handled in Dongguan's coastal ports was 35. 3 million tons and passenger traffic was 344. 8 thousand persons.

The total business volume of postal and telecommunication services was RMB 15. 63 billion in the year, down by 9. 3%. Specifically, the business volume of telecommunications was RMB 14. 92 billion, down by 9. 6% ; the business volume of mobile telephone services was RMB 10. 13 billion, down by 4. 9% ; the business volume of post was RMB 715 million, down by 3. 0%. In 2009, 42. 76 million letters were posted, down by 35. 42% ; 5. 57 million EMS were posted, up by 16. 3% ; the amount of postal remittance was RMB 22. 22 billion, down by 6. 9%.

Ⅹ Domestic trade

The total value-added of wholesale & retail sales was RMB 36. 75 billion by the end of 2009, up by 17. 5% over the previous year; that of the lodging and catering industry was RMB 15. 32 billion, up by 8. 8%.

The total retail sales of consumer goods reached RMB 95. 63 billion, up by 14. 1% over the previous year (up by 19. 7% in real terms) . Specifically, the retail value of wholesale and retail trades reached RMB 83. 20 billion, up by 14. 7% , the lodging and catering industry reached RMB 12. 42 billion, up by 10. 1%.

With regard to enterprises above designated size of wholesale and retail trades, the sales value of food、beverages、tobacco and liquor, clothing、shoes、hats and textiles, daily necessities, automobiles increased 16. 8% , 31. 8% , 26. 3% and 53. 7% over the previous year.

The total sales value of wholesales and retail trades increased 9. 5% over the previous year, reaching RMB

157. 19 billion.

Figure 4: The Retail Sales of Consumer Goods and Its Growth, 1978–2009

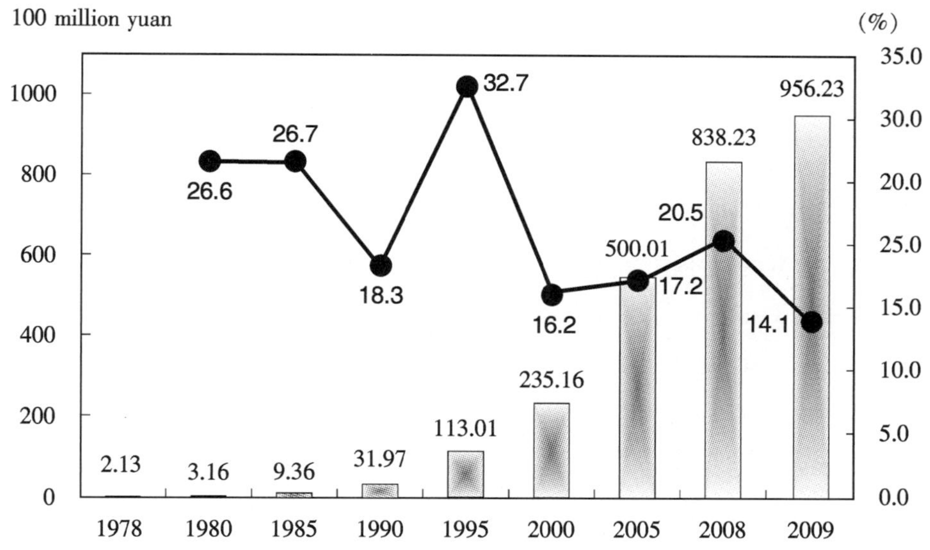

XI **Finance**

By the end of 2009, the value added of finance was RMB 16. 64 billion, up by 25. 5% over the previous year.

In 2009, Dongguan had 75 financial institutions, including 3 newly added. Specifically, there were 23 banking institutions, 37 insurance companies, 15 securities and futures institutes.

The year-end balance of RMB savings in domestic financial institutions totaled 498. 66 billion, up by 14. 6% , in which Deposits by Enterprises totaled RMB 141. 99 billion, an increase of 20% over the previous year; Fiscal Deposits amounted to RMB 5. 25 billion, up by 5. 9%. The year-end balance of RMB loans in domestic financial institutions totaled RMB 290. 38 billion, up by 22. 2%. With respect to the amount of the loans, loans to Industrial Sector totaled RMB 23. 71 billion, up by 8. 2% over the previous year; loans to Commercial Sector totaled RMB 26. 18 billion, up by 49. 2% ; loans to personal individual consumption loans reached RMB 71. 46 billion, up by 25. 2% , Specifically the balance of personal housing loans reached RMB 60. 67 billion, up by 22. 7% ; personal auto loans totaled RMB 2. 41 billion, up by 22. 2%. The cash income of financial institutions totaled RMB 844. 95 billion, cash expenditure totaled RMB 848. 62 billion, withdrawal of currency from circulation in balance totaled RMB 3. 68 billion. The NPLs of Dongguan financial institutions reduced 0. 62 index over the previous year. The assets of all kinds of banks totaled RMB 586. 32 billion, up by 15. 2%.

The total investors of all kinds of securities institutes was 776. 0 thousand accounts by the end of 2009, increased about 429. 2 thousand accounts over the previous year. The total turnover of stock trading increased 251. 7% to RMB 1167. 74 billion. The guarantee fund balance totaled RMB 16. 26 billion, up by 113. 5%.

The total number of Insurance Institutes reached 37, the Insurance Intermediary Institutes increasing by 7 amounted to 31, 28 thousand persons engaged. Insurance Institutes earned premiums was RMB 11. 51 billion, up by 27. 4% over the previous year, in which property insurance premiums was RMB 3. 54 billion, up by 11. 2% , and life insurance premiums was RMB 7. 97 billion, up by 36. 3%. The claim and payment reached

RMB 2. 7 billion, including property insurance indemnity of RMB 1. 9 billion, and life insurance indemnity of RMB 0. 8 billion, the loss ratio reached 14. 25% , 11. 24% respectively.

Ⅻ Real estate

The value-added of real estate was RMB 33. 34 billion, up by 23. 4% over the previous year.

The total investment in real estate reached RMB 27. 77 billion in 2009, an increase of 2. 3% over the previous year. The total floor space under construction of commercialized buildings was 22. 23 million m^2, up by 11. 3%; the total floor space completed reached to 1. 89 million m^2, down by 60. 5%; the floor space of commercialized buildings sold amounted to 6. 04 million m^2, up by 18. 1%, in which the floor space of residential buildings sold this year was 5. 86 million m^2, up by 25. 2%. The total sales value of commercialized buildings was RMB 35. 32 billion, up by 22. 4% , specifically the sales value of residential buildings was RMB 33. 69 billion, up by 36. 9%.

XIII Private Economy

The number of private units registered was 478 thousand, up by 0. 3% over the previous year; in which, private enterprises was 74. 2 thousand units, up by 17. 4% over the pervious year; self-employed individuals was 403. 3 thousand, down by 2. 3% over the previous year. The gross output value of the private enterprises above designated size was RMB 78. 24 billion, up by 6. 9% ; the total investment in fixed asset of the private economy reached RMB 42. 36 billion, up by 15. 1% ; the total retail sales of consumer goods of private economy was RMB 79. 88 billion, up by 14. 6% over the previous year; the total tax payable was RMB 19. 80 billion, down by 1. 2%.

XIV Regional Economy

The total assets of the 32 towns in Dongguan was recorded at RMB 93. 43 billion, the net assets was RMB 62. 65 billion, up by 19. 1% and 16. 5% respectively over the previous year. The total tax was RMB 41. 92 billion, up by 0. 4%. The total collective assets of suburban & village groups was RMB 114. 99 billion, up by 3. 6% ; the net assets was RMB 88. 88 billion, up by 4. 3% ; the net disposable income was RMB 19. 75 billion, down by 5. 3%. The number of towns whose disposable fiscal revenue over RMB 1 billion was 4 towns, and the GDP over RMB 10 billion was 12 towns. The number of villages whose disposable income (excluding the net income of land & tenement transferred) over RMB 100 million was 19 villages, over RMB 10 million was 405 villages, 20 new added, over RMB 50 million was 59 villages.

The total industrial and commercial tax revenue of the 11 developing towns was RMB 6. 94 billion, up by 4. 6% over the previous year. The total disposable fiscal revenue was RMB 4. 32 billion, up by 4. 2%. The total assets of 90 developing villages was RMB 6. 64 billion and the net assets was RMB 4. 19 billion, up by 7. 4% and 8. 5% respectively over previous year, and the net total revenue was RMB 179 million, up by 1. 3%.

The process of projects introducing and operation of Song Shan Lake was speeding up, the gross industrial output value and tax revenue up by 43% and 40% respectively. The Human Harbor established the first international regular shipping liner, and the approved deepwater berths reached 21 (6 have been put into production); collecting land accomplish ratio reached 83. 4% of the Dongguan Ecologically Friendly Park, 30 major projects were launched; Preliminary programming work of Changan oceanfront new area construction was approved.

Reform and opening up

Ⅰ Foreign trade

The total value of imports and exports in 2009 reached US $94.16 billion, down by 17.0% over the previous year, of which the total value of imports reached US $38.99 billion, down by 18.4%; the total value of exports reached US $55.17 billion, down by 16.0%.

Divided by mode of trade, the export value of general trade reached US $5.72 billion, an increase of 17.3%; The export value of processing trade reached US $48.78 billion, down by 19.0%; other trades for export reached US $0.67 billion, representing an increase of 27.4%.

Divided by countries and regions of export, the exports to Asia reached US $27.34 billion, down by 9.9%; the exports to EU reached US $9.63 billion, down by 26.6%; the exports to North America reached US $15.77 billion, down by 17.3%; the exports to Latin America reached US $1.32 billion, down by 23.2%; the exports to Oceania reached US $0.81 billion, down by 17.9%.

The total export volume of electromechanical products reached US $38.75 billion, down by 18.2%, accounting for 70.2% of the total exports. The export of hi-tech products reached US $15.94 billion, down by 19.8%, accounting for 28.9% of total export value of the entire city.

Table 4: Main Export Commodities in Value and the Growth Rates in 2009

Unit: 10000 US dollars

Commodities	Value	Increase over 2008 (%)
Automatic Data Processing Machines and Components	422632	-35.9
Clothes and Clothing Accessories	281072	-12.0
Parts of Automatic Data Processing Machines	266800	-16.6
Shoes	245746	-9.3
Furniture and Components	242631	-12.7
Static Converters	231368	-13.5
Game Machines	182400	-26.5
Cable Telephone (Including Cordless Telephone)	148365	-3.5
Spinning Yarn, Fabric and Products	136791	-6.9
Digital Cameras	127126	-14.0
Parts of Television, Radio and Wireless Telecommunication Equipment	125923	-22.4
Toys	122820	-16.5
Traveling Articles and Cases (value)	114392	4.6
Insulated Wire or Cable	108069	-23.0
TV Sets (including a complete set of spare parts)	101880	27.6
Electric Apparatus for Switching or Protecting Electrical Circuits	103723	-16.1
Plastic Articles	90919	-15.4
Video Recorder and Video Player	84151	-30.3
Handle Mobiles and Car Telephones	79983	87.0

Ⅱ Foreign investment absorbance

According to new statistical standard, the number of recently signed projects of direct foreign investment was 579, the amount of contracted foreign capital (including capital increase and capital reduction) reached US $1.62 billion, down by 37.5% over the previous year. The amount of foreign capital actually utilized reached US $2.59 billion, up by 6.0%; in which, the amount of foreign capital actually utilized by manufacture of electronic equipment and communication equipment reached US $0.63 billion, up by 26.2%; the amount of foreign capital actually utilized by manufacture of special purpose machinery reached US $0.13 billion, up by 16.4%. The number of recently signed projects whose investments were over US $10 million was 27, representing an increase of 4 over the previous year; the number of capital increasing projects from World Top 500 Enterprises was 3, and the number of increase investment from World Top 500 Enterprises was 2. The recently signed projects of tertiary industry reached US $23.40 million, accounting for 14.5% of entire city, representing an increase of 2.7%. The step of foreign traders entering business domain was getting faster. The number of recently signed projects of wholesale and retail trade was 86, the amount of contracted foreign capital reached US $124.03 million, up by 53.7%, accounting for 53.0% of total contracted foreign capital of tertiary industry.

Foreign-funded enterprises of whole city had established 84 research and development organizations, up by 15.5 times over the previous year. Two Foreign funded regional headquarters were established, making new breakthroughs on bringing in foreign funded regional headquarter. The number of outsourcing enterprises of new increase foreign investment was 9, risen by 8 over last year, accounting for 75% of introducing service outsourcing projects in the city.

Table 5: Total value of Foreign Capital Actually Utilized and the Growth Rates by sector in 2009

Unit: 10000 US dollar

Sector	contracted foreign capital	Increase over 2008 (%)	Foreign Capital Actually Utilized Value	Increase over 2008 (%)
Total	149577	-37.5	243219	6.0
Agriculture, Forestry, Animal Husbandry and Fishing	13	0.0	35	-59.3
Manufacturing	136926	-39.7	235137	4.5
Of Which: Textile Industry	5457	-23.3	8071	-41.9
Manufacture of Textiles, garments, shoes and hats	3474	-66.4	11563	6.9
Manufacture of furniture	3287	-48.5	6383	-4.2
Manufacture of General Machinery	2994	-60.5	7105	8.0
Manufacture of Special Purpose Machinery	6230	-58.5	13276	16.4
Manufacture of Electric Machinery and Equipment	12554	-57.1	17075	-24.6
Manufacture of Electronic Equipment and Communication Equipment	36972	-32.7	63247	26.2
Manufacture of Metal Products	8955	13.4	8328	-1.3
Manufacture of Plastics Products	11422	1.7	11544	-4.3
Manufacture of stationery and sporting Products	4545	-33.4	11054	71.5
Manufacture of papermaking and Paper Products	2183	-82.3	24198	21.9
Manufacture of others	38853	-33.0	53293	0.0
Information Transmission, Computer Services and Software	235	-55.2	571	114.7
Wholesale and Retail Trade	12403	53.7	7476	264.9

Ⅲ Tourism

At the end of 2009, there were 95 star-rated hotels in the city, including 19 five-star hotels, 26 four-star hotels, 35 three-star hotels, 14 two-star hotel and 1 one-star hotels. There were 51 travel agencies, including 9 international travel agencies, 38 domestic travel agencies and 4 other travel agencies. The number of tourists from foreign economic zones, including Hong Kong, Macao and Taiwan, was 2. 86 million, up by 6. 6% over the previous year; among them, the number of foreign tourists was 1. 04 million, up by 1. 3% over the previous year; the number of tourists from Hong Kong, Macao and Taiwan was 1. 82 million, up by 10. 0%. The foreign exchange income from international tourism increased 13. 5% to US $0. 52 billion. The number of domestic tourists was 17. 51 million, up by 9. 2% over the previous year; and the total income from domestic tourism increased 17. 7% to RMB 15. 15 billion.

The number of people of Dong Guan out on tours was 1. 27 million in 2009, up by 17. 3% ; of which, the number of domestic tourists was 1. 45 million, up by 17. 1% ; the number of outgoing visitors was 126. 5 thousand, up by 20. 0%.

Urban construction

Ⅰ Urban greening

At the end of 2009, the total developed areas reached 780. 15km^2. In Dongguan, the land used for public facilities reached 59. 57km^2. The area of afforested land in DongGuan was 61. 4 thousand hectares; forest cover rate reached 36. 5% , the green cover rate in afforested land reached 99. 01% . The green covered area of completed area reached 40. 98% in the city, the green covered area was 44. 27% of completed areas. Per capita public green areas were 15. 21m^2. The number of park plaza was 777 and the total area was 5919 hectares.

Ⅱ Public Utilities

There were 91 bus lines, 1407 public transit vehicles and 6811 taxis in operation at year-end of 2009. Passenger' s traffic reached 225 million by public transportation for the year.

The daily water supply capacity was 7 million cubic meters and the total annual volume of water supply totaled 1. 61 billion cubic meters in Dongguan. At the end of 2009, the total length of water supply pipelines reached 12. 67 thousand kilometers. Electricity consumption overall the society was 49. 56 billion Kwh, down by 3. 6%. Of which, industrial electricity was 37. 61 billion Kwh, down by 4. 3% and lighting electricity was 10. 12 billion Kwh, up by 8. 1%. At the end of 2009, the total of households using liquefied petroleum gas numbered 873. 2 thousand, and the households using natural gas was 111. 5 thousand. The total LPG supply was 351. 9 thousand tons, and the supply of natural gas was 293 million cubic meters.

Ⅲ Infomationization

In 2009, the general informationization index was 73. 2 in Dongguan (according to resident population). The number of fixed telephone subscribers at year-end was 2. 07 million, increasing by 111. 6 thousand. The number of mobile phone subscribers reached 14. 09 million, decreasing by 450. 1 thousand, of which by recharge card were 12. 71 million, decreasing by 917. 6 thousand. The length of long-distance calls totaled

17.43 billion minutes in 2009, of which those connected to overseas nations and to Hong Kong, Macao and Taiwan were 247 million minutes. At the end of 2009, there were 1.18 million internet subscribers, up by 216.5 thousand, and broad band subscribers reached 1.14 million, an increase of 226 thousand.

Social Undertaking

Ⅰ Science and Technology

90 new national hi-tech enterprises and 89 new provincial private hi-tech enterprises were approved in 2009; totally reach 246 national and 562 provincial hi-tech enterprises in Dongguan. 224 projects counting up to RMB 137 million were subsidized by the national and provincial government. Of the total, 30 projects counting up to RMB 13.95 million were subsidized by the National Innovation Fund for Small Technology-Based Firms, increasing by 150% and 140% respectively. Dongguan's gross output value of high-tech industry was RMB 231.6 billion in 2009.

The number of patents application accepted and granted reached 19106 and 12918, up by 32.6% and 59.6% over the previous year respectively. Of the total, 1593 patent applications for inventions were accepted, and 254 were granted; 6557 patent applications for utility model were accepted, and 4370 were granted; 10956 patent applications for design were accepted, and 8294 were granted.

Ⅱ Education

There were 680 kindergartens in Dongguan, 63 more than the previous year, of which 174 were founded by education departments and collectives and 506 were founded by private institutions. 99 kindergartens were certified as Provincial or Municipal 1st Class kindergarten. There were 17.62 thousand three-six year old children enrolled, and the enrollment rate of kindergarten reached 95.1%, up by 0.08%. Three-year pre-school education and six years old children admission to primary school were enforced in most towns.

There were 337 primary schools in Dongguan, 15 fewer than the previous year; there were totally 511.2 thousand students enrolled in primary school; school-age children enrollment ratio had reached 100%, and the promotion rate from primary schools to junior secondary schools for Dongguan residents was 100%. There were 144 junior secondary schools, with 182.7 thousand enrolled students. For Dongguan's registered residents, the net enrollment ratio of junior secondary schools, drop-out rate and graduation rate were 100%, 0.22% and 97% respectively.

There were 71 senior secondary schools (including 3 private schools) with 116.4 thousand students enrolled in Dongguan. Of this total, there were 42 senior secondary schools (including six-grade secondary schools) with 66.8 thousand students and 29 secondary vocational schools (including 4 technical schools) with 49.7 thousand students. The junior secondary school graduates of Dongguan residents were 36.8 thousand students, and 35.7 thousand of them entered various types of senior secondary schools. Those graduates who entered into senior secondary schools and enrolled into vocational secondary schools were 22.5 thousand and 13.2 thousand respectively. The promotion rate from junior secondary schools to senior secondary school for Dongguan residents was 97%, up by 0.4%. The proportion of students in senior secondary schools compared with secondary vocational schools was 6:4.

There were 5 adult institutions of higher education, 32 township cultural and technical schools for adults, and 268 private non-degree adult education institutions. More than 490 thousand people participated in various types of training in adult education.

There were 5 institutions of regular higher education. Among which, 2 were universities with full undergraduate courses and 3 were collages with specialized courses. There were 34 thousand total enrollments. In institutions of higher education, there were totally 12.9 thousand students new enrolled and 7292 students graduated in 2009.

24707 people participated in college entrance examination in 2009. Of which 21286 were regular category, 3421 were senior occupational category. In the regular category candidates, 2229 people have passed the priority score line, 387 people more than previous year; 8384 people have passed the line for the undergraduates, an increase of 1349 people.

Ⅲ Culture

In 2009, the First China International Animation Copyright Fair was held in Dongguan. 120 projects for animation copyright were signed, with total contract funds RMB 8.2 billion. By the end of 2009, there were 1 mass art center, 33 cultural stations, 504 public libraries, 31 museums, 697 cultural squares, 63 arts performance places, 40 movie screening units and 1056 internet cafes. Public cultural facilities construction area reached 9.23 million square meters. Dongguan had 66 public radio programs and 32 public television programs. Radio and television coverage of population had reached 100%. CATV for " Every Village" project is continuing. Coverage of households has reached 100%. In 2009, 84.62 million copies of newspapers, 1.68 million copies of magazines and 46 thousand copies of books were published. Dongguan Daily reports a circulation of 47.45 million copies. There were 10.5 thousand film screenings and 2.98 million viewers in 2009.

Ⅳ Health and Medicine

By the end of 2009, Dongguan had 2106 heath care institutions, including 2033 grass-roots health care institutions such as outpatient departments, clinics, health stations, infirmaries and community health service centers, with 35766 medical technical personnel and 18080 hospital beds. In Dongguan, 348 community health service institutions were built and put into service, covering more than 300 villages (communities) throughout the city. The patients who received treatment throughout the year were increased by 8.0%.

Ⅴ Sports

Dongguan athletes won 122 gold, 104 silver and 128 bronze medals in 2009, including 8 gold medals in international tournaments and 20 gold medals in national tournaments. In provincial tournaments, athletes won 94 gold, 92 silver and 113 bronze medals.

Dongguan held 18 municipal integrated and individual sport games, in which 50.8 thousand people participated. There were 681 thousand participants who took part in 1178 township individual sport games. Dongguan had 644 sports lottery networks, total sale was RMB 520 million and public welfare fund of sports lottery was RMB 132 million.

Ⅵ Social Welfare and Relief

By the end of 2009, there were 39 residential institutions in Dongguan, including 2 social welfare homes, 1 children's welfare home and 33 gerocomiums where 1464 old people were supported. There were 36 social welfare institutions with 2570 people adopted and 247 "Four Types of Handicapped" people to obtain employment. 40. 4 thousand people received social assistance in 2009. The expenditure of urban minimum living allowance was RMB 70. 22 million. Expenditure of social relief was RMB 237 million. Expenditure of social relief for natural disaster was RMB2. 35 million. Source of charitable funds was RMB 205 million. 1364 persons were brought into the "Five-Guaranteed" project, and which cost RMB 9. 99 million. All 32 towns in Dongguan had established social security network. 1606 households counting up to 3770 persons were brought into street minimum living allowance project and 13106 households counting up to 33549 persons were brought into township receiving minimum living allowance project.

Ⅶ Social Stability

In 2009, Dongguan had arranged fiscal expenditure of RMB 3. 09 billion for public security, up by 15. 6%. Strengthening police force by technology, video surveillance network platform had been built in the city. There were 128 thousand locations of video surveillance in use in the city. 200 Safe Communities had been built. The number of reported crimes dropped by 4. 3%, number of detected criminal cases increased by 50. 1%. 22 township comprehensive govern, petition and stability maintenance centers and 317 village (community) or enterprise comprehensive govern workstation (room) had been built. A decline of 39. 4% was shown in total acceptance of mass petitions, and the number of mass incidents decreased by 44%. Improving the warning mechanism of business failure risk, and cracking down escape from owing wages, RMB 120 million wages were recovered for 93 thousand workers.

Ⅷ Safe Production

In 2009, 5074 cases of accidents occurred in Dongguan, down by 6. 4%; 582 people died and 5565 people were injured, which decreased by 8. 1% and 7. 2% respectively; direct economic loss was RMB 7. 96 million, down by 40. 6%. Of this total, the number of road traffic accidents was 5037, a decline of 6. 3%, which resulted in 545 deaths and 5560 injured, a decrease of 7. 6% and 7. 1% respectively. Production-related accident mortality rate per 100 million GDP was 0. 15, and road traffic mortality rate per 10 thousand vehicles was 4. 29.

Ⅸ Resource and environmental protection

Throughout the year, rainy days numbered 167 days; sunshine hours were 1967. 8 hours; average temperature was 22. 8 degrees Celsius; relative humidity was 70%. Precipitation of the year was 1881. 6 millimeters. Total water consumption of Dongguan was 2. 21 billion cubic meters.

By the end of 2009, 17 forest parks with 61. 4 thousand hectares of woodland area and 25 thousand hectares of ecological public forest, which contained 2. 41 million cubic meters of tree storage and 155. 6 thousand cubic meters of total tree growth. All year around, 1335. 33 hectares of reconstruction of conservation forest had completed. 1. 52 million broad-leaved trees had been planted. 2896. 6 hectares of young forest were successfully bred. 65 kilometers of fire prevention forest had been built and 374. 43 kilometers had been bred.

Annual average air pollution index was 57, down by 5%, good air quality days accounted for 99. 2%, increased by 4. 12%, and 61 haze days less than last year. 32 out of 34 sewage treatment plants had been built, 19 of them in operation, and total investment was RMB 2. 44 billion; 20 of 35 sewage interception pipeline network projects had completed, of which the length of 681. 92 kilometers pipeline was built, accounting for 78. 93% of total length, and the cumulative completed investment was RMB 3. 08 billion; 28 companies had passed provincial and municipal cleaner production inspection; There were 40 companies that received the first batch of municipal environment-friendly enterprises, and 30 companies in the second batch of environment-friendly enterprises had passed inspection.

People's living conditions

Ⅰ Population

By the end of 2009, Dongguan's registered population reached 1.79 million. The annual births in 2009 were 18.6 thousand, the birth rate was 10.67 per thousand, and the annual deaths in 2009 were 7587 persons, the death rate was 4.36 per thousand. The natural growth rate was 6.31 per thousand. By the end of the year the total number of resident population reached 6.35 million. Urban households' percentage was 86.39%, and the urban resident population reached 5.49 million.

Ⅱ Employment

In 2009, Dongguan accepted 14.5 thousand college graduates. And the total registered job-seeks in the talent market was 1.55 million persons, down by 21.3%; 429.1 thousand persons were employed, down by 50% over the previous year. By the end of 2009, the actual number of registered unemployed persons was 7674, the annual number of unemployed job placement was 11.92 thousand, and the registered unemployment rate in urban area was 1.61%.

Ⅲ Income

In 2009, the average annual salary was an estimated RMB14416, up by 6.6% over the previous year. Specifically, the average annual wage of the urban fully employed staff and workers was RMB 42585, up by 7.8%. The per capital annual disposable income of urban households increased by 9.1% over the previous year to RMB 33045, and the per capita annual disposable income of rural households increased by 6.0% over the previous year to RMB 13064. The per capital annual disposable income of the urban 10% highest income households was RMB 71031, and the per capital annual disposable income of the urban 10% lowest income households was RMB 13642.

Figure 5: Per capita disposable income of urban households and its growth, 1978–2009

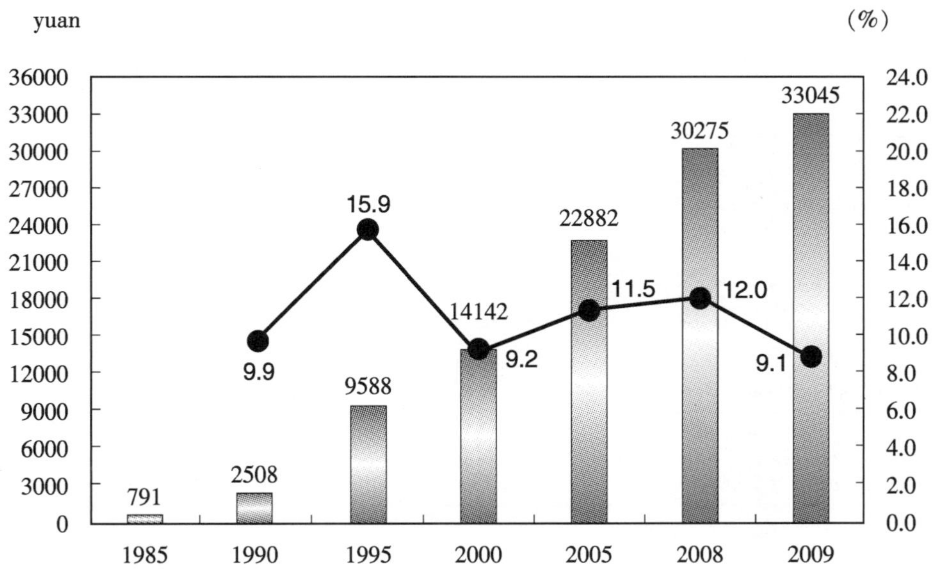

Ⅳ Consumer expenditure

The annual per capital consumption expenditure of urban residents was RMB 24270, up by 4.6%. Specifically, the expenditure on food was RMB 7972, up by 2.5%; the expenditure on clothing was RMB 1492, up by 10.6%; the expenditure on residence was RMB 2232, down by 13.7 %; the expenditure on household facilities, articles and services was RMB 1616, up by 5.0%; the expenditure on health care and medical services was RMB 1401, up by 5.2%; the expenditure on transport and communications was RMB 5456, up by 22.3%; the expenditure on education, cultural and recreation services was RMB 3326, down by 4.0%; and the expenditure on miscellaneous goods and services was RMB 777, up by 11.0%. The Engel's Coefficient of urban households was 32.8%. In consumption expenditure of rural households, 35.0% was spent on food; 6.0% on clothing; 14.0% on living; 4.4% on household facilities, articles and services; 5.3% on health care and medical services; 16.6% on transport and communications; 11.5% on education, cultural and recreation services; 7.0% on miscellaneous goods and services.

Figure 6: per capita disposable income of rural households and its growth, 1978–2009

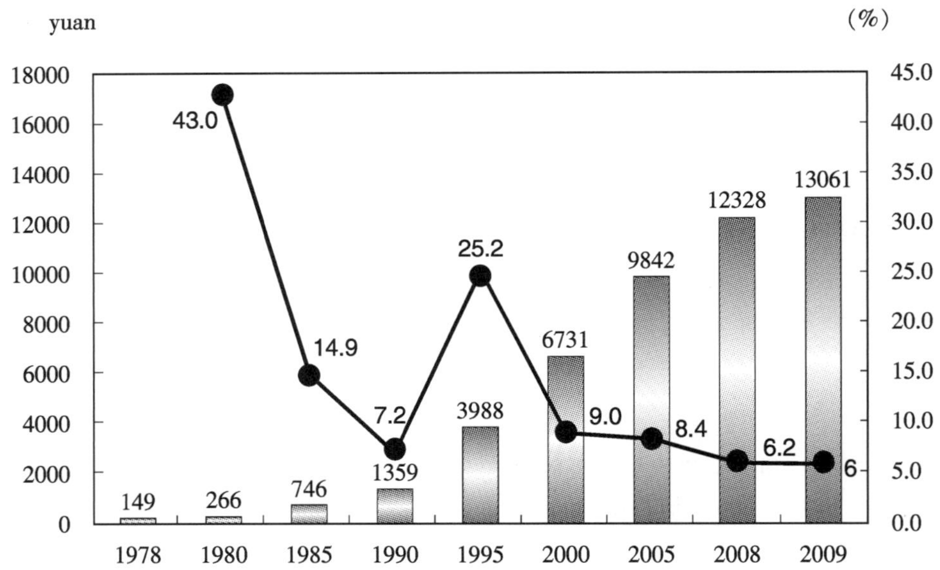

Table 6: Income and expenditure of urban households 2009

Item	Income or expenditure (yuan)	Increase over 2007 (%)
Per Capita Disposable Income of Urban Residents	33045	9.1
Income from Wages and Salaries	23723	13.7
Income from Properties	4209	19.4
Income from Transfer	3094	1.6
Per Capita Consumption Expenditure of Urban Residents	24270	4.6
Food	7972	2.5
Clothing	1492	10.6
Residence	2232	-13.7
Household Facilities, Articles and Services	1616	5.0
Health Care and Medical Services	1401	5.2
Transport and Telecommunication	5456	22.3
Educational, Cultural Recreation Services	3326	-4.0
Miscellaneous Goods and Services	777	11.0

The ownership of major durable consumer goods per 100 urban households at the year-end were: 233 air conditioners, 69 Hi-Fi stereo component system, 261 mobile phones, 112 computers, 128 water heaters, 63 cars. The per capita housing floor space of urban households was 53.75 square meters. The same index concerning rural households were: 160 color TV, 83 motorcycles, 103 washing machines, 129 water heaters, 257 mobile phones, 74 disc players, 210 air conditioner, 109 computers, 53 cars.

Ⅴ household savings

At the end of 2009, the balance of savings deposit of urban and rural households was RMB 2 90. 46 billion, an increase of RMB 26. 66 billion. Of this total, the time deposits were RMB 126. 56 billion, an increase of RMB 16. 17 billion; the demand deposits were RMB 163. 90 billion, an increase of RMB 10. 49 billion.

Ⅵ Social Security

At year-end, the number of employee joining basic pension insurance was 3. 16 million, that of who joining basic medical care system was 5. 37 million persons, 2. 59 million persons joined unemployment insurance; 4. 39 million persons injury joined maternity insurance, and 3. 11 million persons joined local basic pension insurance. The annual total revenue of social insurance fund was RMB12. 01 billion, the total expense at year-end of the insurance fund was RMB 6. 45 billion, and the end of the accumulated balance of the insurance fund was RMB 31. 02 billion. By the end of 2009, a total of 0. 46 million rural resident households participated in basic pension program. A total collection of the insurance fund (excluding department pension program) was RMB 10. 93 billion in 2009, up by 12. 0%.

The main difficulties and problems in national economic and social development were: the basis for economic recovery was not strong, different difficulties in business operations still remained; industrial transformation & upgrading and structural adjustment still to strengthen, the capacity for independent innovation to cope with risks needed to be improved; too many unstable factors still existed security and fire safety required further remediation.

政府工作报告

Government Work Report

——2010年1月20日在东莞市第十四届人民代表大会第五次会议上

东莞市人民政府市长　李毓全

各位代表：

现在，我代表市人民政府向大会作政府工作报告，请予审议，并请政协各位委员和其他列席人员提出意见。

2009年工作回顾

过去一年，是新世纪以来东莞经济社会发展最为困难的一年，也是我们砥砺奋进、经受严峻考验的一年。面对罕见国际金融危机带来的严重冲击，我们在上级和市委的坚强领导下，以科学发展观为指导，以实施《珠江三角洲地区改革发展规划纲要》为动力，认真落实“三促进一保持”的工作要求，加快推进经济社会双转型，着力保增长、扩内需、调结构、强管理、惠民生，在逆境中实现了新的发展。预计全市生产总值3760亿元，按可比价计算比上年增长5.3%，人均生产总值56500元，增长10%。来源于东莞的财政收入628亿元，增长4.5%，其中市财政一般预算收入231亿元，增长10.5%。城市居民人均可支配收入33045元，农村居民人均纯收入13061元，分别增长9.1%和6%。金融机构本外币各项存款余额5095亿元，比年初增长14.3%。三大产业比例由上年底的0.3∶52.8∶46.9调整为0.3∶47.8∶51.9。东莞先后获得全国文明城市、全国社会治安综合治理优秀市、全国民族团结进步模范集体等荣誉。创建国家环保模范城市顺利通过国家技术评估。

——这一年，我们千方百计保增长，实现了逆势回升。把保增长作为首要任务，全面实施并不断完善应对危机的一揽子计划，成功遏制了经济下滑势头，推动了稳步回升。*着力帮扶企业共渡难关。*实施“六个10亿元”帮扶计划，深入走访企业，帮助解决实际困难，稳定企业扎根发展。积极开展跨境贸易人民币结算试点和知识产权质押融资试点工作，出台已建房屋补办产权办法，以贴息和担保方式帮助企业融资，推动金融机构为1430家企业累计发放贷款548亿元；推广“两仓合一”保税物流模式，降低企业物流成本，建成保税仓和出口监管仓34个，东莞保税物流中心投入运营。有效增强了社会信心，企业经营逐步好转。全市外资企业关停外迁宗数减少24%。*着力扩大投资刺激消费。*实施五年7300亿元的投资计划，加大政府投资力度，积极引导社会投资。完成市镇两级土地规划修编，出台新的征地拆迁补偿标准；加大重点项目统筹推进力度，实行领导挂钩督导和审批绿色通道制度，对财政投资项目实行并联审批，500万元以下项目招投标权限下放镇街。开展“欢乐消费年”系列活动，实施家电下乡等八大商贸促进工程，推进国民旅游休闲计划，刺激居民消费。全社会固定资产投资1094亿元，增长13%；社会消费品零售总额956亿元，扣除物价因素影响实际增长19.7%，成为拉动经济增长的重要动力。*着力鼓励出口拓展内销。*出台16项出口优惠措施，协同海关提高口岸通关效率，建立出口300强企业外贸快速通道，全市出口551.7亿美元，降幅比年初收窄16.1个百分点。积极引导和帮助企业开拓国内市场，举办大中型展会48场，组织莞货促销活动24场，资助企业参加国内外大型展会50场，推动企业与销售商家、电子商务平台对接。全市规模以上工业产品内销产值2710亿元，占工业销售总产值的46%，比上年提高4.6个百分点。

——这一年，我们坚定不移调结构，加快了转型步伐。总结试点经验，出台"1+26"政策文件，加大结构调整力度，有效推动了三大产业结构、内外源型经济结构、企业投资结构、经营模式、加工贸易企业形态优化，以及人均经济指标、自主创新能力、节能减排水平提升。*以加工贸易转型优化存量。*积极搭建服务平台，完善就地不停产转型的操作办法，帮助339家来料加工企业成功转为三资或民营企业。用好加工贸易转型升级专项资金，激励企业加强技术研发和品牌经营，全市新设立外资企业研发机构84家；拥有自主品牌的加工贸易企业900家，增长15%。加工贸易合同电子审批实现全覆盖。*以加强园区招商提升增量。*依托市镇工业园区，调整引资目录，实行招商奖励，精心组织赴欧日韩、港台、广州、杭州等地招商推介。全市实际吸收外资26亿美元、内资122亿元，分别增长6%和42.4%。松山湖项目引进和投产步伐加快，工业产值、税收分别增长43%和40%；虎门港成功开辟首条国际班轮航线，获批深水泊位项目共21个，其中6个正式投产运营；东莞生态园完成土地征收83.4%，启动重点工程30项；长安新区用海申报、规划环评、港区总体规划等通过专家审查。*以推进自主创新提高质量。*完善科技东莞配套政策，积极培育"两自"企业，新增国家高新技术企业90家、省民营科技企业89家；新增省级以上名牌名标25个；专利授权量增长59.6%，总量跃居全省第二位；参与制定修订各类标准32项。加强创新平台建设，深化产学研合作，加快技术更新改造，建成省级以上各类研发和检测中心36个，新增省级产业集群升级示范区2个，承接省级以上科技项目313个，获批省部院市产学研合作项目99个，全市工业更新改造投资154亿元，增长1.5倍。支持科技企业融资，设立5000万元科技贷款风险准备金。整合出台扶持民营经济22条措施，落实排忧解难协调制度，民营企业注册资金增长13.4%；内源型经济占生产总值的62.5%，比重提高4.5个百分点。*以发展第三产业强化支撑。*加强现代服务业引进，推动金融、物流、会展等生产性服务业加快发展。东莞农信社改制为农村商业银行，新增银行和融资担保机构8家、上市公司1家，引进中外运等一批大型物流仓储项目，成功承办首届中国动漫博览会和广东外博会，电博会、虎门服装、厚街家具、大朗毛织、长安五金模具等品牌展会的影响力稳步扩大。出台鼓励总部经济发展的政策和实施细则，启动首批总部企业认定工作。第三产业增加值占生产总值的比重提高5个百分点。*以落实节能减排严格约束。*强化责任落实，加强重点耗能企业监管，开展全民节能行动，推进企业清洁生产，加强土地执法监察，严守耕地保护红线。全市单位生产总值耗地、耗电分别下降3.1%和4.2%。二氧化硫和化学需氧量排放分别下降9.2%和6.8%，达到省总量减排年度要求。

——这一年，我们加大力度扶镇村，夯实了基层基础。把镇村作为全市发展和稳定的基础，市财政共支出40.9亿元，大力支持镇村建设和发展。*加大经济扶持管理力度。*完善财政激励政策，欠发达镇超收分成由30%提高到40%，继续实施贷款贴息等帮扶政策，市财政共贴息2.2亿元，帮助欠发达镇村累计获得贷款49亿元，对285个村（社区）补助公共管理经费2.35亿元。加强镇村收支和资产监管，出台农村干部违反集体资产管理行为责任追究办法，开展重大事项审查和村级绩效审计，强化农村集体土地款、借贷款与经济合同管理，严格控制集体开支和福利分红。32个镇街可支配收入221.5亿元，增长15.9%；村组两级净资产890.2亿元，增长3.5%。*加大基础设施建设力度。*"三院一中心”等28项市属重点工程竣工，市轨道交通R2线起点站、东莞大道延长线、东莞篮球中心等38项动工。环城路全线贯通，莞深高速三期、虎岗高速顺利通车，建成镇村联网路14条、大型输变电工程17项、水利防灾减灾工程123宗。整合村级水厂16家，改造老化水管547公里，新增LNG管网163公里，整治市区内涝点11个。加大城乡环境整治力度。调整优化生态控制线和饮用水源保护区，实施生态补偿，促进生态保护。加快环保基础设施建设，累计建成污水处理工程32项、截污主干管网工程18项，医疗废物处理中心投入营运。扎实推进运河综合整治，运河水质明显改善。加强环境执法监察和污染企业监管，积极治理养殖业污染、水库污染、油气污染和机动车尾气排放。出台“三旧”改造办法和实施细则，深入推进“五整治”，加强城管综合执法，狠抓城市“六乱”治理，进一步提升了市容环境水平。加大现代农业发展力度。加快农业产业园建设，已批10个中6个完成了主要基础设施建设，2个被认定为省级园区。推动农业产业化、规模化、标准化经营，新增省、市级农业龙头企业各2家。启动集体林权制度改革试点工作。

——这一年，我们多管齐下强管理，维护了安全稳定。把综治维稳作为第一责任，着力加强社会管理，妥善化解矛盾纠纷，保障了安定局面。强化社会治安综合治理。加强巡逻防控，整治重点区域，保持严打高压态势，突出打击“两抢一盗”、拐卖儿童等犯罪行为，开展禁毒禁赌扫黄专项行动。推进科技强警，建设视频监控联网平台，扩大视频监控覆盖面，全市在用各类视频监控点12.8万个。新建平安社区200个。全市接报违法犯罪宗数下降4.3%，刑事案件破案宗数增长60.4%。强化安全隐患整治。加快安全生产应急救援指挥平台建设，划定了21个应急避险场所，全市所有村（社区）都成立了安全办。深入开展消防隐患、危险化学品、食品药品和建筑安全等专项整治行动。加强农产品检疫检测，建成食品安全样板市场38个。强化交通安全管理，禁止摩托车在环城路以内行驶，大力查处酒后驾驶等违章行为。全市发生各类事故起数、死亡人数分别下降6.4%和7.3%。强化矛盾纠纷调解。新建镇街综治信访维稳中心22个，村（社区）、企业综治工作站（室）317个。扎实开展“基层大接访”和“信访积案化解年”活动，全市受理群众信访总量下降39.4%，群体性事件下降44%。完善企业倒闭风险预警机制，严厉打击欠薪逃匿行为，为9.3万名工人追回工资1.2亿元。

——这一年，我们高度重视惠民生，增进了社会和谐。把改善民生作为政府工作的出发点和落脚点，全面发展社会事业，基本完成向市民承诺的十件实事，市财政用于民生事业支出102.8亿元。办好教育实事。以积分制方式新接受1.39万名新莞人子女入读公办学校。取消义务教育公办学校非本市户籍借读生书杂费，免收金额2.3亿元。切实解决中小学代课教师待遇问题。出台扶持民办教育发展政策。推进高中阶段学校布局调整，实施中小学校舍安全工程，新建学生宿舍10座，增加床位近万个。落实“六优先”政策，促进各级各类教育优质均衡发展，每万户籍人口升大学人数排名全省第一。繁荣文体事业。实施“提升城市文明十大行动”和“文化惠民工程”，新建图书馆和博物馆12个、农家书屋和妇女书屋142个，免费开放了一批文化馆所。开展庆祝建国六十周年活动，举办省音乐舞蹈花会和东莞音乐剧节，启动历史人文创作工程，莞城“文化周末”活动荣获文化部创新奖，12个文艺精品获得全国全省重大奖项。大力发展群众体育和竞技体育，成功承办举办第四届全国妇女健身活动展示大赛、市第七届运动会等大型赛事20余次，莞籍运动员在第十二届全运会上取得7项冠军，获得省第二届体育大会团体总分第四名。完善社会保障体系。统筹农居民与职工养老保险制度，两次提高医保待遇，将大中院校学生纳入基本医保范围。增加生育医疗待遇，整合医疗和生育保险。完善低保制度，提高“五保户”供养标准，开展居家养老服务试点。为23800多名户籍困难残疾人提供生活专项补助和服务。加快社会工作发展，扶持社工机构建设。解决2658户困难家庭的住房问题，建成经济适用房1454套，完善住房公积金管理，制定改善新莞人居住条件指导意见。全面发展卫生、劳动就业、计划生育等事业。完善社区卫生服务体系建设，积极防控甲型H1N1流感，开展职业卫生和生活饮用水专项整治。帮助户籍大中专毕业生和零就业家庭就业，完成户籍劳动力资助培训和新莞人技能提升培训6.7万人次。城镇登记失业率1.7%。建立37个新型社区，解决人才落户难问题。大力发展公共交通，投放城市小巴，设立学生临时专线，新增公交运力302辆、线路48条。提升人口计生服务管理水平，人口自然增长率6.31‰。完成第二次全国经济普查。国防人防、科普法普、外事侨务、工青妇幼、民族宗教、统计审计、气象测报、档案方志、打私等工作扎实推进。

——这一年，我们改进作风抓落实，提高了政府效能。把加强政府自身建设摆在突出位置，以更务实高效的作风抓好工作落实。推动相关改革。实施政府机构改革，市政府部门从37个整合为32个。以石龙、塘厦为试点推进扩权强镇，下放管理权限248项。完成第三轮行政审批制度改革，取消审批事项85项。恢复驻京联络处，密切与中央机构和企业的联系。弘扬务实作风。加强督查督办，推广现场办公、联合会审等工作方式，帮助基层和企业解决实际问题。出台法治政府建设意见和重大行政决策程序规定，推进政务公开，进一步规范政府行为。落实廉政责任，开展机关作风暗访和行业纠风行动，加强电子纪检监察系统应用，职能部门审批业务提前办结率达98.8%。全年办理人大代表和政协委员的建议提案489件。厉行勤俭节约。加强财政资金绩效评价和审计，提高资金使用效益。严格控制楼堂馆所等非生产性项目投资，严格控制一般性行政经费支出，市直机关行政经费缩减5.3亿元，由财政出资或政府主办的晚会、展览、庆典、论坛活动经费减少47.5%。

——这一年，我们落实《纲要》谋合作，促进了区域协调。深入实施珠三角规划纲要，积极加强区域合作，努力开创区域协调发展新局面。扎实推进深莞惠一体化。建立三市联席会议制度、政府工作协调机制、专责小组协调推进机制，召开党政主要领导联席会议3次，签署框架协议文件13份，确定并积极推动近期合作的25项重点事项。扎实推进莞港台合作。加强与港台地区在帮扶企业、招商推介、内外贸易等方面的合作，成立莞港生产力促进中心，促成台湾10大产业服务机构在莞设点，创办松山湖台湾高科技园。扎实推进双转移战略。制定产业转移规划和实施方案。市财政投入1亿元加快建设莞韶、莞惠产业转移工业园。接收我省东西北地区近50万劳动力就业。扎实推进对口援建扶贫。按照三年任务两年完成的要求，加快汶川映秀镇灾后对口援建，总投资近10亿元的33项“交钥匙”工程和25项资金补助项目已完成总工程量的50%。全市捐助台湾同胞抗灾重建1.4亿元，援助广西河池、西藏林芝等对口帮扶地区财物5742万元。

各位代表！

回顾一年来同舟共济的拼搏之路，我们深感成绩凝聚汗水，团结就是力量。我市在极其困难的形势下保持了经济社会的平稳发展，离不开上级和市委的正确领导，离不开各级各部门的精诚协作，离不开市人大、市政协、各民主党派及社会各界的监督支持，离不开广大投资者的信赖、坚守和勤奋经营，离不开全体市民和驻莞部队的共同努力，离不开港澳台同胞、海外侨胞以及国际友人的关心帮助。在此，我们表示衷心的感谢！

回顾一年来逆势前行的突围之路，我们深感信心异常可贵，坚持就是胜利。困难是常有的，也是暂时的，战胜困难的过程，就是推动改革发展大步向前的过程。东莞能够成就今天的城市地位，靠的就是敢为人先，务实奋进，靠的就是不畏险阻，艰苦奋斗，靠的就是坚定信念，永不言败。

回顾一年来化危为机的进取之路，我们深感科学发展制胜，转型才有出路。实践证明，只有坚定不移地落实科学发展观，坚定不移地推进经济社会双转型，才能有效转变发展方式，提高核心竞争能力和抗御风险能力，才能推动东莞经济社会不断取得新的发展。

回顾一年来攻坚克难的奋斗之路，我们深感问题不容忽视，忧患才能兴市。当前东莞仍存在不少问题和隐忧：经济回升基础尚不牢固。主要指标增长与年度目标有一定差距，外贸出口尚未完全恢复，合同利用外资降幅较大，企业经营还有不少困难。转变发展方式任重道远。引进培育大项目等工作亟需加力，自主创新能力和抗御风险能力有待进一步提高，污染整治的成效仍未充分显现。社会管理工作仍然繁重。社会不稳定因素依然较多，治安形势仍未实现根本好转，群体性事件、安全和消防事故时有发生。我们必须高度清醒，以强烈的责任感和紧迫感，积极寻求破解之策。

2010年工作安排

今年是实施“十一五”规划的最后一年，做好全年各项工作，对夺取应对国际金融危机全面胜利、加快经济社会转型步伐、为“十二五”规划奠定良好基础具有十分重要的意义。我们要清醒地看到，新一年的形势仍然复杂严峻，国际金融危机对东莞的影响尚未完全消除，后危机时代还会有一段比较艰难的时期，必须切实增强危机意识和风险意识，决不能有丝毫的懈怠。同时，我们也要满怀信心地看到，当前综合发展环境正在不断好转：从外部环境看，世界经济逐步显现出复苏迹象，外部需求有所回升，我市外贸出口压力将得到一定程度的缓解；不少跨国公司正在酝酿产业的重新布局，有利于我市开展招商引资。从国内环境看，中央和地方一系列刺激经济政策日益见效，中央继续实施积极的财政政策和适度宽松的货币政策，珠三角规划纲要深入实施，有利于我市开拓国内市场，深化区域合作。从我市实际看，经过一段调整适应期，经济企稳向好的势头明显，全市上下应对危机的信心和能力不断强化，推动转型发展的积极性和主动性进一步增强。只要我们审时度势，坚定信心，趋利避害，奋发有为，就一定能够实现新的更大的发展。

综合考虑各方面因素，**全市经济社会发展的目标是**：生产总值增长8%；市财政一般预算收入增长6%；固定资产投资和社会消费品零售总额增长14%；外贸出口增长5%；城市居民人均可支配收入和农民人均纯收入增长7%；单位生产总值能耗下降4.4%；城镇登记失业率、人口自然增长率分别控制在2.5%和7‰以内。

政府工作的总体要求是：**以科学发展观为指导，全面贯彻党的十七届四中全会、中央经济工作会议、胡锦涛总书记视察广东重要讲话、省委十届六次全会和市委十二届六次全会精神，深入实施珠三角规划纲要，落实“五个更加注重”和“三促进一保持”要求，突出以转变经济发展方式为核心，继续稳增长，加力调结构，积极优环境，锐意抓改革，更加重民生，全面促和谐，坚定不移地推动全市经济社会在平稳发展的基础上加快转型，全面完成“十一五”规划各项目标任务，努力建设以信息产业为特色的现代制造业名城、适宜创新创业安居乐业的生态城市、珠三角新兴物流城市，当好推动科学发展、促进社会和谐的排头兵。**

具体抓好以下八个方面的工作：

一、坚持多策并举，巩固经济回升基础

珍惜来之不易的回暖局面，把扩大内需作为战略基点，继续实施刺激经济增长的一系列政策措施，不断巩固和增强回升向好的势头。

完善落实扶企政策。加强政策宣讲辅导，完善管理办法和操作指引，切实发挥好科技东莞、创业东莞、转型升级、支持融资等多个专项资金的作用。融资贴息、社保金缓交等政策延期一年，扩大政策普惠面，加快补办土地使用证和房屋产权证，帮助企业盘活资产。积极推进跨境贸易人民币结算试点工作。加强劳务协作，完善用工平台，帮助企业解决招工难题。

加快投资项目建设。全面加快重点基础设施和优质产业项目建设，将政府投资5000万元、社会投资2亿元以上的项目列为重点项目，给予纳入审批绿色通道、减收城市基础设施配套费等支持。结合产业导向和引资目录，制定优质产业项目认定标准，做到用地指标优先安排、审批事项优先办理。完善和落实领导挂钩督导等制度，定期协调解决实际问题，加大投资拉动力度。

积极开拓内外市场。落实激励政策，帮助企业抢抓订单、稳定出口，积极开拓东盟等新兴海外市场，优化外贸出口结构。加力资助企业拓展内销，推广内销“集中申报”模式，加快保税物流和口岸大通关建设，积极举办形式多样的莞货展销活动，认真筹办省第二届外博会，资助企业参加各类大型展会，组建东莞工厂直销中心，推动生产企业与大型商家、电子商务平台对接。积极举办各类商贸促销活动，加大家电和汽车下乡、以旧换新等政策的宣传力度，发展和完善消费信贷，有效刺激和扩大居民消费。

二、加快结构调整，构建现代产业体系

坚定不移地把产业结构调整作为核心任务和工作主线，加大典型示范和推进力度，有效转变经济发展方式。

加快打造三大经济带。着力打造以松山湖为龙头的园区经济带。完善松山湖各项功能配套，推进台湾高科技园和IT研发园建设，加速集聚高端产业和人才；同步加强东莞生态园的基建与招商工作，完成主要路网设施建设，力争在项目引进上有所突破；推进长安新区规划报批，基本完成收地任务，尽快转入实质性建设阶段。着力打造以虎门港为依托的物流经济带，积极寻求战略合作，加速码头泊位建设运营，研究出台港口物流优惠政策，提升港口集散能力，推动早日繁荣；加强西大坦物流园和立沙岛石化园的招商，积极引进精细化工和装备制造等产业。着力打造以主城区为核心的商贸经济带，推进中央商务区、商贸区和休闲区的规划建设，强化主城区的辐射带动功能。

加快推进加工贸易和传统产业转型升级。完善专项资金使用办法，优化一站式服务，重点跟进资金技术密集型来料加工企业，推动其不停产转三资或民营企业，在拓展内销、技术改造、设立研发机构和地区总部等方面取得实效。加强与港台专业机构合作，帮助企业提升技术和管理水平。以信息化和高新技术改造提升传统产业，推动五金模具、服装、毛织、家具等产业集群优化升级。

加快引进培育优质项目和龙头企业。加强已有产业分析和投资动向研究，落实重大及关键项目引资奖励措施。加大城市营销力度，充分利用现有企业资源，对重点企业开展登门招商，对日韩台等地区实行驻点招商，积极引进国内外大型企业和行业龙头企业，引进新兴战略性产业、先进制造业及其配套缺失项目。着力扶优扶强，落实24项倾斜措施，突出扶持市选定的521家重点工业企业。力争用3年时间形成一批年主营业务收入超十亿、百亿元的大企业。

加快发展现代服务产业。从今年起连续5年，市财政每年安排3000万元，采用竞争性招标方式资助信息服务业项目。出台建设珠三角新兴物流城市的实施意见，认定十大连锁企业、十大物流项目、十大专业市场和十大展会，从政策和资金上重点扶持。加强对同类型专业市场及展会的规划整合。大力发展工业设计、金融、旅游、中介等产业，稳步发展总部经济。把文化产业作为支柱产业来扶持，制订发展规划和配套政策。认真筹办第二届动漫博览会，引进培育文化创意产业基地，推动现代传媒、演艺娱乐、印刷等文化产业集群发展。

加快落实节能降耗减排。强化污染企业监管，严把产业项目准入关，加快7个环保专业基地建设。务实发展低碳经济，落实重点耗能企业节能计划，扶持发展节能服务机构，鼓励企业开展清洁生产。推广清洁能源、节能建筑、绿色照明，实施LED路灯应用示范工程，深化机动车尾气和加油站油气污染治理。严格落实责任，确保完成“十一五”节能减排任务。

三、强化自主创新，提高核心竞争能力

把自主创新作为引领东莞未来发展的核心推动力，深入实施“科技东莞”工程，积极培育“两自”企业，大力发展民营经济，不断提升自主发展能力。

推动企业研发和品牌经营。落实专项扶持资金，鼓励企业加大技改投入，设立研发机构，承接参与国家和省市重大科技专项，争取新建一批省级以上工程技术中心，推动一批企业成为省级工业设计示范基地。做好首届市政府质量奖评审工作，鼓励企业参与各级各类标准的制定和修订。深入实施名牌带动战略，支持企业争创名牌名标，加强知识产权和品牌保护。

推动科技平台建设和管理。推进国家设计中心试点工作，推动散裂中子源项目动工，加快中山大学研究院、国家消费品重点实验室等公共平台建设，新建鞋业、模具等行业技术平台，组建太阳能、智能玩具等省部产学研创新联盟，引导镇街以“民办公助”方式建设科技企业孵化平台。加强分类指导和管理，促进现有科技平台提高运营水平和效益。办好科技合作周等活动，推动高等院校与企业的产学研合作，积极谋求关键领域和关键技术突破，加快科研成果转化应用。完善和落实人才政策，争取在科技创新团队和领军人才的引进培育方面有所突破。

推动民营经济做大做强。进一步放宽市场准入，落实扶持民营经济发展22条措施，突出帮扶省百强民营企业和市50强民营企业。实行核发筹建执照等办法，推动规模较大的民营企业加快落户。制定相关激励政策，引导民间资本更多地进入先进制造业领域。对民营企业的大额技改投资贷款给予贴息，对技术开发和转让的相关税费给予减免，完善扶持民营企业的政府采购政策。充分发挥商会行会作用，加强对民营企业家的培训，鼓励企业实行强强联合、并购重组，实现规模化发展。

推动科技金融更紧密结合。全面落实金融业发展规划，加快市金融商务区和松山湖金融改革创新服务区建设，积极组建外商和台商信用担保公司，推动设立村镇银行，稳步发展融资、租赁机构。做好后备企业改制上市培育工作，力争新增上市企业2—3家。积极开展省首批科技金融试点市工作，制定市联动科技贷款风险准备金使用办法，推动知识产权质押融资，发挥创业投资和风险投资作用，引导更多资金投向科技创新领域。

四、着力帮扶镇村，以强镇促进强市

镇村是东莞的发展之基、特色所在、惠民所依，强镇才能强市。必须坚持不懈地扶持镇村，筑牢全市发展基础。

加强政策资金扶持，加大转移支付力度。全年市财政安排49.4亿元扶持镇村发展。落实好财政超收分成、公共管理支出补助、生态补偿、结对帮扶等政策措施。继续按一定比例分担联网公路、水利工程等基础建设费用，村际联网路补贴政策期限延长一年。对镇村集体已建项目补办手续给予费用优惠。突出帮扶欠发达镇村加快发展，继续实施扶贫贷款贴息政策，适当放宽贷款使用范围。引导欠发达村用好市免息借款，不断增强造血功能。

加强土地统筹开发，转变镇村发展模式。强化镇级统筹发展的主导作用，鼓励各镇街以租赁、入股、征收等多种形式，加强对土地的统筹利用，实行统一规划、统一建设、统一招商，不断完善镇村“统筹开发、利益共享”的发展模式。探索建立相关激励机制，对镇街涉及土地统筹的贷款给予贴息，重大项目的税收给予所在村一定比例的返还。

加强集体资产监管，力促增收节支减债。制定村组年度收支计划，合理控制资产负债率。积极扶持集体增收项目。逐步减轻村组社会管理负担。严格落实重大事项审查、土地款管理、合同管理等制度，加强农村集体经济审计和责任追究。规范农村干部薪酬管理。继续严控一般性支出，严控贱卖集体资产，严控超支福利分红。

坚持生态高效方向，扶持现代农业发展。按照“强化规划、突出产业、标准适度”的原则，逐步把全市符合条件的农业用地纳入园区范围。推进标准化基本农田建设，承接优质高产的农业项目。积极培育农业产业化组织，推动专业合作社发展，推广现代农业机械和技术，探索土地流转和规模经营的有效方式，推动农业产业园建设速度加快、效益提高。

五、统筹规划建设，提升城乡环境水平

坚持组团发展方向和环境取胜战略，不断强化城市功能，改善城乡环境，建设生态宜居城市。

加速推进城市基础设施建设。配合推进穗莞深、穗莞惠城际轨道交通工程，全面启动市轨道交通R2线建设，推进石龙火车新站工程。加快完善“一环六纵六横三连”的高快速路网，建成虎岗高速虎门港支线一期、广深高速石鼓连接线，推进广深沿江高速、从莞高速、博深高速、深圳外环高速东莞段以及东莞大道延长线、环莞快速路二期、松山湖大道至常平连接线、高埗连接市区梨川大桥等建设。加快中麻公路、石大公路、省道S120石排至桥头段、S256南城至虎门段、S357谢岗段、S358长安至虎门段等改造工程。加快水、电、气网建设，完成东江与水库联网一期工程，建成水利防灾减灾工程126宗，改造供水管网1300公里；建成110千伏及以上输变电工程15项；新建天然气管网131公里。加快打造“无线城市”，推进电信网、广电网、互联网三网融合。

加速推进城市功能配套建设。加快大市区建设，抓紧完成广电中心、篮球中心、市中医院新院、市民艺术中心、工人文化宫、市廉租房和经济适用房等项目建设，增强城市功能和辐射带动作用。加快各镇中心区建设，按照中小城市的标准完善公共设施，着力打造若干个各具特色的标志性片区。加快成熟社区建设，制定量化标准，完善公交、商业、休闲等功能配套，力争年内每个镇打造出2—3个成熟社区，市区四个街道成熟社区覆盖率达到40%。

加速推进旧城旧村旧厂改造。把“三旧”改造作为优化城市布局、改善城乡面貌、促进经济发展的重要抓手强力推进。设立市财政连续五年、每年10亿元的专项资金，落实减免市属税费、简化供地方式、优先用地指标、加快项目审批、返还出让收益等优惠政策。抓好分类典型示范，通过开发商业区和商住楼、改建现代化工业厂房、联建农民公寓、保护历史村落、建设主题公园等多种模式推进改造。各镇街年内完成改造专项规划，至少启动一个成片改造和若干个单宗改造项目。

加速推进城乡环境综合整治。落实生态绿线规划，严格保护农田山林绿地。按照“一年基本建成、两年全部到位、三年成熟完善”的要求，扎实推进珠三角绿道网建设。加快黄旗山城市公园的建设改造，完善市植物园和银瓶山、大岭山、大屏嶂森林公园的设施配套。鼓励各镇村因地制宜建设乡村公园。坚持广泛植树、见缝插绿，按照新区不低于30%、旧城改造区不低于25%的面积标准配套绿地。加大运河综合整治力度，推进内河涌和水库污染治理。全面建成34项污水处理厂及配套管网，加强运营管理。新建4座垃圾处理厂。加大城管综合执法力度，深入整治城市“六乱”。争取成功创建国家环保模范城市。

六、加强社会管理，切实维护安全稳定

稳定压倒一切，必须毫不放松强化公共安全管理和矛盾排查调解，切实维护安定有序的社会局面。

坚持不懈推动社会治安持续明显好转。保持高压态势，继续严打各类恶性犯罪和多发性犯罪，突出打击入室抢盗、公交扒窃、拐卖儿童等。深入开展打黑除恶禁毒扫黄等专项行动，大力整治治安重点区域和行业。实行有奖举报，严格责任追究，坚决清除“老虎机”和地下“六合彩”赌博行为。加大路面巡逻力度，加快视频监控网络建设，加强出租屋管理，推动社区群防群治，力争全市80%的社区（村）成为平安社区。推进公安信息化、执法规范化和队伍正规化建设。

坚持不懈狠抓安全生产排查整治。夯实基层基础，创新监管机制，突出抓好危险化学品、特种设备、“三小”场所、人员密集场所、建筑安全等专项整治，对存在重大隐患、未能限时整改到位的场所，坚决实施关停，严防重特大事故发生。加强食品药品和农产品安全监管，创建62个食品安全样板市场，确保百姓用药安全、饮食放心。强化宣教培训，营造全社会关爱生命、关注安全的良好氛围。

坚持不懈做好信访调解和应急管理。深入推进镇、村和企业综治信访维稳机构建设，强化矛盾纠纷排查化解，推行领导接访包案和干部下访制度。加强劳动监察执法，提高劳动仲裁处理效率，进一步健全欠薪逃匿防范机制。加快打造市综合应急平台，强化信息研判、指挥调度、辅助决策等功能，推进应急避险中心和镇街值班室建设，完善应急预案管理体系，不断提高应对和处置突发事件的能力。

坚持不懈推进新型和谐社区建设。以社区为基本单元，完善警务区建设，落实辖区治安队、安全生产监管人员等工作职责，加强城乡社区网格化、全覆盖的管理。指导各居住小区成立业主委员会，推进物业管理进社区。年内规范完善215个城市社区的服务设施和机构队伍，逐步建立政府向社会组织购买公共服务机制，积极健全社区服务体系。深入创建省“六好”平安和谐社区，力争80%以上的城市社区达标；积极创建全国和谐社区示范单位。

七、办好民生实事，全面发展社会事业

坚持以人为本、惠民先行，大力发展社会民生事业，继续办好“十件实事”，不断改善群众生活，共享发展成果。

促进充分就业、全面保障。加强就业服务，设立实名制劳动力资源库，推广“村民车间”模式，帮助户籍劳动力特别是“零就业”家庭和大学毕业生就业。实施全民技能提升储备计划，不断提高劳动力就业素质。全面深化社会养老保险体系建设，市镇村三级分期投入43.4亿元，其中今年14.5亿元，逐步提高59万名原农居民参保人员的保障水平。加快组建市社会福利中心，新建4间敬老院，向全市80岁以上老人发放政府津贴，争取一、二档镇街居家养老服务覆盖面达到20%。对低保对象实施分类保障和基本医疗救助，对特殊困难对象增发保障金。积极推进社会工作，力争专职社工达到500名。逐步提高困难残疾人补助标准，加强残疾人服务体系建设。推进住房公积金事业发展和廉租房、经济适用房建设，解决2404户困难家庭住房问题。深入开展关爱新莞人系列活动。

促进教育质量更高、医疗卫生服务更优。坚持教育优先战略，推进各级各类教育优质均衡发展。加快高中阶段学校布局调整，新建扩建16所高中学校。推进技师学院、高技能公共实训中心和理工学校、卫校新校区等建设，加快打造职教城。探索公办中职学校学生逐步实现学费全免。支持办好东莞理工学院城市学院新校和中山大学新华学院，推进与香港理工大学联合办学，加强民办教育的扶持、引导和监管。推进市镇医院和重点特色医疗专科建设，继续完善社区卫生服务体系，实施基本药物制度，加强甲型H1N1流感防控，为群众提供优质安全、价廉便利的医疗保健服务。

促进交通更顺畅、出行更便利。完善镇村（社区）交通分流系统，加强交通疏导和执法管理，深入推进“治摩”工作，改造3条主干公路12个交通堵塞点，整治事故多发和市镇中心区拥堵路段，努力做到安全顺畅有序。设立道路交通事故社会救助基金。大力发展公共交通，加大运力投放，优化线路设置。更新出租车1200辆，完善公交枢纽站、首末站、候车亭、出租车停靠点和交通标识、自行车道等设施，增建人行天桥和地下通道，使群众出行更加便利。

促进文化、体育等社会事业全面发展。着力巩固全国文明城市创建成果，鼓励发展志愿服务，引导市民践行道德规范，形成良好文明风尚。完善公共文化服务体系，推进社区文化和企业文化建设，鼓励文艺精品创作，加强社会科学研究，传承文化遗产，弘扬东莞特色文化，积极创建全国历史文化名城。落实《全民健身条例》，增加健身场所和完善设施，广泛开展群众体育运动，积极承办第十六届亚运会举重赛事。科学编制“十二五”规划，开展第六次全国人口普查，加强人口计生服务管理，继续做好国防人防、双拥共建、科普法普、外事侨务、工青妇幼、民族宗教、统计审计、档案方志、打私、气象等工作。

八、继续深化改革，激发体制机制活力

坚持先行先试，锐意创新，大力推进管理体制机制改革，不断提升政府行政效能和公共事业活力。

深化行政管理体制改革。全面推进政府机构改革后续工作，加快制定实施部门“三定”方案，理顺职责关系，完善运行机制，切实强化统筹管理职能。建立机构编制实名管理制度。深化户籍制度改革，落实居住证制度，进一步放宽入户门槛。推进事业单位人事制度改革。开展第四轮行政审批事项清理，完善推广集中审批、并联审批、网上审批。抓好石龙、塘厦扩权强镇试点，在总结经验基础上全面铺开。在镇街尝试设立政府法制机构，提高镇一级依法行政水平。探索推进黄江、厚街村级体制改革试点工作。

深化公共事业改革。推进市政管理改革，制定精细化管理的标准和考核办法，探索实行市区数字化城管，全面推广市政设施和环卫绿化“市场化＋监理制”模式。推进水务一体化管理改革，提高供水质量。坚持公益方向，推进医疗卫生体制改革，开展公立医院改革试点。深化民政改革发展，履行部省协议，全面推进8大方面60项试点工作。深化经营性文化事业单位改革，支持民办公益性文化机构发展。完成林权改革试点。

深化区域合作发展。深入推进深莞惠一体化发展，做好规划编制衔接，积极推动道路连接、跨界公交、收费站年票互认等工作，加强治安、治污、劳动保障、市场监管等方面的对接。深化与港台地区的经贸合作。落实产业和劳动力双转移战略，积极推进莞韶、莞惠产业转移园开发建设。加快映秀镇对口援建，确保5月12日前基本完成整体援建任务。继续帮扶河池等地区，推进与云浮、韶关两市“规划到户、责任到人”扶贫开发。

深化机关作风建设。深入实施改进机关作风六项制度，切实提高行政效率和服务质量。弘扬艰苦奋斗，厉行勤俭节约，继续严控一般性行政经费支出，强化财政资金绩效评价，提高资金使用效率。扎实推进依法行政和廉政建设，落实重大行政决策程序和政务公开制度，主动接受市人大、市政协及社会各界监督。加大督查督办力度，以时不我待的强烈责任、以奋发有为的精神状态，以令行禁止的纪律观念，以脚踏实地的工作作风，不折不扣落实各项工作部署，努力建设“为民、务实、清廉”的服务型政府。

各位代表！过去一年，我们众志成城、风雨同舟，经受了国际金融危机的考验，取得了极其不易的成绩。新的一年，让我们再接再厉，团结奋进，扎实做好各项工作，为推进经济社会双转型、建设富强和谐新东莞而努力奋斗！

名词注解：

三促进一保持：这是广东省委提出的经济工作的重要要求，即促进提高自主创新能力、促进传统产业转型升级、促进建设现代产业体系，保持经济平稳较快增长。

两仓合一保税物流：两仓即监管仓和进口保税仓。两仓合一保税物流主要功能是让来料加工贸易产品通过国内结转型监管仓实现内销，替代以往的“香港一日游”内销，节约企业运输成本，提高运作效率。

八大商贸促进工程：即家电下乡工程、万村千乡市场工程、社区商业双进工程、餐饮业分等定级工程、汽车销售服务升级工程、农贸市场升级改造工程、放心肉放心酒工程、重点商贸项目工程。

“1+26”政策文件：2008年4月东莞正式启动产业结构调整和转型升级试点工作，研究推进14个课题27项配套政策文件出台。其中“1”是指《关于推进产业结构调整促进产业转型升级的意见》，“26”是指《东莞市推进加工贸易转型升级工作方案》、《东莞市转型升级实施“三旧改造”土地管理暂行办法》等26项具体配套政策文件。

三院一中心：即市人民医院新院、市第三人民医院、市妇幼保健院新院、市疾病预防控制中心。这是2009年建成的大型医疗卫生机构。加上仍在建设的市中医院新院又称为“四院一中心”。

“六优先”政策：这是我市坚持教育优先战略的原则要求，即教育发展优先规划，教育投入优先安排，教育用地优先保障，教育人才优先引进，教师待遇优先落实，教育问题优先解决。

提升城市文明十大行动：即社会治安综合治理深化行动、思想道德素质提升行动、市容环境美化行动、交通秩序整合行动、城市亲和力强化行动、和谐社区家庭创建行动、志愿服务拓展行动、社会诚信建设行动、行政效能优化行动、全民学习行动。

五个更加注重：这是中央经济工作会议提出关于2010年全国经济工作的总体要求，即：更加注重提高经济增长质量和效益，更加注重推动经济发展方式转变和经济结构调整，更加注重推进改革开放和自主创新、增强经济增长活力和动力，更加注重改善民生、保持社会和谐稳定，更加注重统筹国内国际两个大局。

“一环六纵六横三连”高快速路网：一环是指环城路；六纵是指沿江高速、广深高速、国道107、增莞深高速、从莞高速、博深高速；六横中的第一横为北环快速，第二横为西部干道、东部快速，第三横为番莞高速跨江大桥、番莞高速东延，第四横为虎门大桥、虎岗高速虎门港支线一期、虎岗高速，第五横为龙林高速及延长线，第六横为深圳外环；三连是指虎岗高速虎门港支线二期、龙大高速、清平高速。

2010年市政府十件实事

一、创建一批平安社区。新建150个平安社区（村），将全市80%以上的社区（村）建成平安社区（村）。

二、提高养老和医疗保险待遇。投入14.52亿元，确保社会养老保险制度改革顺利实施，社会基本医疗保险年度最高支付限额由10万元提高到15万元。

三、建设一批学校。投入16.8亿元，新建扩建16所中学，年内建成6所。

四、改善困难家庭住房。投入4000万元，解决2400户城乡低收入困难家庭的住房问题。

五、改造农村老化水管。投入9000万元，完成全市83个欠发达村共1250公里的老化水管改造。

六、促进城乡就业。完成城乡劳动力资助性技能培训1.25万人次，实现东莞生源普通高校毕业生就业率90%

以上。

七、建成一批样板市场。创建62个食品安全样板市场，全市食品安全样板市场达到100个。

八、整治市区内涝。投入1.9亿元，完成南城街道雀巢片区、莞城街道市桥河系统、东城街道下桥河系统内涝整治工程。

九、推进运河整治。投入4亿元，完成塘板水闸扩建、樟村水闸扩建和合浦市陂—梅塘水汇入口段堤防建设及扩河工程，建成运河峡口至新基段堤路及景观整治工程。

十、改善交通出行条件。投放公交运力100辆，优化市区、跨镇和镇内公汽三级网络，提升公交服务水平；建成9.2公里运河路自行车专用道示范工程。

全球金融危机下东莞工业类中小企业的发展困境与突围之路

The Development Dilemma and Breakthrough Road of Industrial SMEs in Dongguan in the Global financial crisis

改革开放30年来，东莞经济一直保持较快速增长，形成了以制造业为主，外向依存度较高的经济发展模式，工业企业成为推动东莞经济高速前进的强劲引擎，而在东莞工业企业中，中小企业则是主体力量。2008年，东莞22697家工业企业中，有22650家是中小企业；在规模以上工业中，中小企业的数量所占比重达到99.1%，可以说东莞工业类中小企业的发展直接决定了东莞工业，乃至东莞经济的发展。从2008年第4季度开始，当席卷全球的金融危机爆发后，东莞的工业企业遭受了较大的冲击，订单减少、产值下降、效益下滑、部分企业外迁、倒闭等现象接踵而来。受其影响，东莞经济也出现了较大程度的下滑。2009年一季度东莞的GDP出现了负增长，上半年仅增长0.6%，其中工业的下滑是主导原因。在此背景下，本文着重分析全球金融危机前后，东莞工业类中小企业的发展情况，结合产业转型与升级，探求危机下中小企业摆脱困境的途径，以促进东莞经济的可持续发展。

一、东莞工业类中小企业的发展现状

东莞工业类中小企业是东莞经济增长的主要推动力量，是工业生产的主力军，是社会就业的重要渠道，是民间投资的重要载体，是技术创新的活跃因素和重要主体，在国际合作与贸易中发挥着越来越重要的作用。但是东莞经济外资型、加工型和资源主导型特色显著，中小企业自身发展存在很多的不足和局限。一是行业处于产业链低端，产品附加值不高。大部分中小企业从事贴牌生产为主，技术含量不高，主要依靠土地、劳动力等生产要素价格优势换取低微加工利润；二是产业布局散乱。少数产业和镇街形成了产业集群规模，大部分镇街产业种类多规模少；三是外资型企业多，企业根植性差。对外依存度较高，经济自主性差、产业根植性弱，抗外部风险的能力不高；四是企业缺乏自主创新能力，大多数企业没有创立品牌和创新研发的意识。因此，中小企业寻求新的发展路径成为当务之急。

（一）数量与分布

东莞市工业类中小企业发达，数量众多，至2008年，全市工业类中小企业22650家，其中规模以上工业类中小企业4940家，占规模以上工业企业总数的99.1%。

从轻重工业看，轻工业企业数量较多，为2731家，重工业企业2209家；但产值上，重工业占较大比重，2008年工业类中小企业轻重工业产值比重为45.4∶54.6。

从企业大小看，小型企业数量较多，有3818家，中型企业有1122家。

从行业分布看，东莞工业类中小企业门类齐全，覆盖了30多个制造行业。其中，所占比重较大的有纺织业（6.1%）、纺织服装、鞋、帽制造业（5.2%）、家具制造业（3.5%）、造纸及纸制品业（5.6%）、文教体育用品制造业（4.1%）、化学原料及化学制品制造业（3.2%）、塑料制品业（10.4%）、金属制品业（7.1%）、通用设备制造业（2.8%）、专用设备制造业（4.5%）、电气机械及器材制造业（11.1%）、电气机械及器材制造业和仪器仪表及文化（14.6%）和仪器仪表及文化、办公用机械制造业（2.1%）。

2008 年东莞工业类中小企业行业分布

行业名称	企业单位数（个）	企业个数所占比重（%）	产值比重（%）
总计	4940	100	100
非金属矿采选业	3	0.1	0.01
农副食品加工业	28	0.6	3.71
食品制造业	46	0.9	1.22
饮料制造业	11	0.2	2.12
纺织业	302	6.1	2.79
纺织服装、鞋、帽制造业	259	5.2	3.79
皮革、毛皮、羽毛（绒）及其制品业	274	5.5	3.10
木材加工及木、竹、藤、棕、草制品业	42	0.9	0.25
家具制造业	172	3.5	2.43
造纸及纸制品业	277	5.6	5.32
印刷业和记录媒介的复制	97	2.0	1.36
文教体育用品制造业	201	4.1	3.03
石油加工、炼焦及核燃料加工业	5	0.1	0.21
化学原料及化学制品制造业	160	3.2	2.54
医药制造业	10	0.2	0.14
化学纤维制造业	18	0.4	0.30
橡胶制品业	78	1.6	0.73
塑料制品业	514	10.4	5.07
非金属矿物制品业	105	2.1	1.70
黑色金属冶炼及压延加工业	26	0.5	0.86
有色金属冶炼及压延加工业	48	1.0	1.08
金属制品业	353	7.1	4.27
通用设备制造业	138	2.8	1.76
专用设备制造业	221	4.5	2.53
交通运输设备制造业	40	0.8	1.06
电气机械及器材制造业	548	11.1	11.98
通信设备、计算机及其他电子设备制造业	721	14.6	23.38
仪器仪表及文化、办公用机械制造业	104	2.1	2.29
工艺品及其他制造业	90	1.8	1.53
电力、热力的生产和供应业	12	0.2	8.88
水的生产和供应业	37	0.7	0.55

（二）产值与规模

2008 年工业类中小企业实现工业总产值 6016.24 亿元，占全市工业企业总产值的 83.3%。其中规模以上工业类中小企业实现工业总产值5361.75亿元，占全市规模以上工业企业总产值的84.1%；实现销售收入5087.65亿元，占全市规模以上工业企业销售收入的83.9%；利税总额193.32亿元，占市全市规模以上工业企业利税总额的89.3%。工业类中小企业是吸纳就业的主要力量，2008年，东莞工业类中小企业全年平均从业人员221.47万个，占全市规模以上工业企业从业人员总数的90.4%。根据1%人口抽样调查得到的劳动力比重推算，规模以上工业类中小企业吸纳了东莞35.7%的劳动力。

（三）主要优势行业

电子信息和电气机械两大行业规模较大，2008年这两个行业的企业数量分别为721和548家，占工业类中小企业总数的14.6%和11.1%。产值分别为1253.42亿元和642.15亿元，占总量的23.4%和12.0%。电子信息产业以电脑零部件及周边设备、电子元器件为主，配套率高达95%，部分产品在全球市场占有10%至40%的份额；电气机械以输配电及控制设备、电线电缆、电池为主要产品，这两大产业加工配套环节用工较多，每百元实现利税约为1.26元。

纺织服装、家具、塑料制品三个行业是东莞的传统优势产业，企业数量也较多，2008年三个行业企业数量分别为561家、172家和514家。这三个行业劳动密集特征明显，2008年人均产值分别为13.19万元、17.0万元和18.91万元，与全市平均水平（24.21万元）有较大差距。纺织服装业生产规模较大，产业链较为完善，在虎门、大朗两镇形成了两大产业集群，技术改造投入力度明显加大，品牌建设也取得良好成效，全市纺织服装产业百元产值实现利税约为3.11元。家具、玩具产业的专业化程度较高，但从事贴牌加工为主，较少掌握核心技术、品牌，生产环节用工多。

食品饮料、造纸行业呈现出良好规模发展优势，对地方经济拉动效应大。这两种产业集聚度高，大型企业、知名企业数量多。行业技术水平较佳，运用先进大型自动化生产设备，用工少、盈利能力强，对地方税收贡献大。以食品饮料产业为例，2008年东莞食品饮料业中小企业数量仅57家，产值为179.25亿元，平均企业产值规模为3.14亿元，是全市平均水平的2.9倍，从业人员人均产值85.4万元，是全市平均水平的3.5倍，百元产值实现利税约为12.33元，是全市平均水平的3.4倍。

（四）企业研发状况

在企业研发能力方面，东莞市中小企业普遍研发能力比较弱，存在研发人员数量较少、层次较低的问题。从行业来看，工业类中小企业研发人员主要集中于纺织服装、鞋帽制造业、家具制造业、造纸及纸制品业、金属制品业、电气机械及器材制造业、通信设备、计算机及其他电子设备制造业、工艺品及其他制造业这些行业。而其中又以金属制品业和电气机械及器材制造业最为突出，二者研发人员共占到了总研发人数的1/2。

研发投入不足，处于低水平。工业类中小企业按行业划分，食品制造业企业的研发投入最为突出，其研发投入占销售收入的比重大约为4%左右，远远高于其他行业水平。大多数行业的研发投入比例大概维持在1%到3%之间。

二、全球金融危机下东莞工业类中小企业的发展困境与原因分析

（一）金融危机影响下工业类中小企业的发展困境

困境之一：生产规模萎缩，产值下降

金融危机爆发以来，东莞外资型中小企业首先受到冲击，订单减少以及难以收到货款等问题的出现，促使企业难以继续生产，生产规模迅速萎缩。2007年，东莞工业类中小企业产值为4903.10亿元，到2008年底金融危机出现，产值为5163.75亿元，虽然仍有增长，但同往年相比增速已经大幅下

滑。而到了2009年上半年，产值仅有1966.15亿元，按现价计算，与上年同期相比下降20.5%。32个工业行业大类中，大部分出现了不同程度的下降，仅有7个行业保持增长。占主导地位的优势产业通信设备、计算机及其他电子设备制造业和电气机械及器材制造业的下降幅度也在30%以上。平均企业产值规模缩减严重。2009年上半年工业类中小企业的平均产值为3424万元，与上年同期相比缩减近1/3。影响较大且缩减较为严重的行业有通信设备、计算机及其他电子设备制造业，电气机械及器材制造业，金属制品业等，缩减幅度均超过35%以上。

困境之二：产品出口压力增大

金融危机带来的国际市场萎缩给东莞的出口造成巨大压力，2009年开始，东莞出口开始负增长，中小企业的出口形势更加困难。2009年上半年，东莞工业类中小企业出口产品交货值为933.85亿元，同比下降28.6%。以往的主要出口行业电子信息类行业降幅达到39%，值得关注的是装备制造业却出现了增长，特别是交通运输设备制造业增长达到80%。

困境之三：企业亏损加剧，亏损面扩大

2007年，东莞工业类中小企业中亏损企业1223家，亏损面为24.8%；2008年底亏损企业增加至1850家，亏损面扩大为37.4%，到2009年上半年亏损企业达到2978家，亏损面扩大到51.9%，超过半数的中小企业出现了亏损。亏损额也大幅上升，2009年上半年，中小企业亏损额为56.52亿元，同比增长56.1%。

困境之四：关停的企业中小居多，新增企业不足

2009年上半年全市关闭、停产或搬迁的规模以上工业企业共206家，大部分属于中小企业。其中，17.5%属于通信设备、计算机及其他电子设备制造业，10.2%属于电气机械及器材制造业，9.7%属于塑料制品业，55.8%属于港、澳、台商投资企业，17.0%属于外商投资企业，共减少54.09亿元工业产值，拉低全市规模以上工业产值增速2个百分点。

（二）工业类中小企业陷入困境的原因分析

其实，近年来东莞工业类中小企业发展已经出现了一定程度上的阻碍，东莞的中小企业不仅经受着中国大多数中小企业遇到的“融资难”、企业竞争力弱、创新不足、受近年来原材料成本上涨、出口政策调整、人民币汇率升值、劳动法实施等因素的影响而造成的经营困难等问题，还必须面对东莞工业的外向型和加工贸易等特点所造成的自主调控能力低，产品附加值低、产品销售渠道单一、开拓市场能力不强等“先天不足”的现实。金融危机的到来，无疑成为上述矛盾加速激化的催化剂。加之东莞目前正在加快实施产业转型升级，多种因素的叠加，造成了目前东莞工业类中小企业发展的困境。深刻剖析主要有以下几个方面的原因：

1. 结构性方面。东莞的工业类中小企业大多属于加工贸易企业。该类企业主要以贴牌加工为主，生产方式是以销定产，产品主要用于出口。这类模式导致企业的生存与发展的自我调控能力低，被动地接受外部市场调节，而企业开拓国内市场的能力又比较欠缺。当金融危机使国际的市场需求明显放缓，打破了企业原有的产品市场结构，迫使企业必须积极开拓国内市场，然而，珠三角企业眼光长期向外，经营方式单一，大部分企业只有承接订单加工的能力，缺少开拓市场，打造企业产品品牌的经验；有的企业甚至长期专门为少数几家外资企业做贴牌加工，既不熟悉国际市场，又不熟悉国内市场。在金融危机深度冲击下，外资企业订单减少或中断，这类中小企业就只能减产、停产甚至倒闭。

2. 产业链方面。东莞企业被动接受国际产业分工，生产两头在外，导致所处产业被挤压于国际产

业链低端，产业发展中存在着许多结构性缺陷，如产业结构层次低，产业空间布局不协调，技术来源及市场结构对外依赖程度高等，产业结构战略性调整的压力较大。由于企业处于价值链低端，尽管经过长期经营，一些企业抵御风险的能力仍然很低，面对金融风暴更加无所适从。

3. *经营模式方面*。改革开放30年来，东莞许多企业处于快速发展时期，企业规模迅速扩张，业务量急剧增长，掩盖了管理效率低和运作成本高的问题。但随着市场竞争的加剧，尤其是金融危机带来的外部环境的突然变化，迫使企业向管理要效益，推动精细化管理。高成本运作成为企业生存的最大枷锁。许多企业出现了成本不断上升，利润下降，经营困难的局面。

4. *品牌方面*。中小企业创品牌的动力和能力不足。名牌企业不强、品牌数量和质量与经济发展不相适应的情况依然存在。品牌的产业分布不合理，品牌的产业知名度不大，传统优势产业名牌少，影响了产业优势。企业创建品牌的意识不强，缺少运作品牌的动力和能力，许多中小企业满足于贴牌加工，许多企业甚至无牌加工。

5. *体制方面*。东莞的村级是与企业联系最紧密的单位，通常集“村民自治、经济发展、公共管理和服务”于一体。由于村级承担着大量的行政管理事务，提供着大量的地方性公共服务，担负着较为庞大的公共支出。在现行利益分配格局下，市镇两级倾向淘汰落后的中小企业，调整中小企业的结构来提升整体实力；村级则更倾向于留住能带来厂租、带来人气的低端的劳动密集型企业，在一定程度上阻碍了中小企业整体的发展。

三、金融危机下工业类中小企业的突围之路

金融危机虽然给东莞的中小企业生存发展带来了冲击，但从倒闭的中小企业来看，多数都不符合政府产业调整倡导的方向，早晚都要为市场所淘汰，全球金融危机只是加速了这一进程。目前，东莞正在进行产业转型与升级，又适逢珠三角《规划纲要》的实施，中小企业如果能坚持自主创新、积极转型、创立品牌，金融危机未尝不是机遇。

（一）逆境突围的有利条件

1. *基础雄厚，产业配套已具规模*。经过30多年的发展，东莞市已跻身为颇具规模的国际性加工制造业基地，形成了以电子信息及光电、机械及汽车配套、高档服装及织物、家具及建材、五金塑胶等支柱行业为主的现代化工业体系，行业间和上下游产品之间的产业配套体系完善，结构合理，效率卓越，具有较强的国际竞争力。同时还形成了以制造业为主，以电子资讯产业为支柱的外向型经济结构，成为国际性的制造业基地和中国重要出口基地，世界上大多数工业产品都可以在东莞市找到与其相配套的行业和产品，鞋业、服装、玩具、家具等产品也大量远销欧、美等国际市场，“东莞制造”誉满全球。以电子信息产业为例，东莞全市注册登记的电脑资讯工业企业有3000多家，电脑整机零部件配套率达95%，目前东莞市的电脑资讯产品在世界市场占有份额超过10%的有十几种。

2. *政府相继出台的相关政策帮扶中小企业的发展*。为贯彻落实中央关于扩大内需、促进经济平稳较快增长特别是扶持中小企业发展的各项政策措施，加大对中小企业的扶持力度，帮助中小企业渡过难关，保持经济社会又好又快发展，东莞出台了一系列政策切实缓解中小企业融资难问题，支持中小企业实行产业转型和结构优化升级，加强和改善对中小企业的服务以及加强组织领导，如提出了经济社会“双转型”的发展战略，推出了《东莞市产业结构调整和转型升级试点工作方案》，促进和鼓励企业转型升级，出台了“五个10亿”帮扶政策，实施1400亿元投资计划等，利用好这些政策将有助于中小企业走出困境。

3. *珠三角《规划纲要》的实施给中小企业发展带来新的机遇。*珠三角《规划纲要》的出台，是国家针对珠三角30年的发展的实际情况，考虑到珠三角原来的模式在新发展环境下已经不可持续，分享全球化产业链低端收益的方式已经走不通的事实，从战略全局和长远发展出发，着眼于提升我国综合国力和国际竞争力，着眼于珠三角地区增创科学发展新优势作出的重大战略决策。突如其来的金融危机，加剧了珠三角转型升级的阵痛，让珠三角劳动密集型产业的深层次矛盾暴露无遗，传统的生产经营模式难以为继，而《规划纲要》的实施则加大了珠三角深化改革、转型升级的力度，《纲要》中一些先行先试的项目，如建设物流信息交换中心、产业转移示范园、加工贸易转型升级试点，打造先进制造业和现代服务业基地等战略布署，都给东莞中小企业带来新的发展机遇。

4. *金融危机会锻炼了中小企业抵御风险的能力，促进产业集群的发展。*在严峻的环境下，一些中小企业难以获得发展机会，为了生存，可以通过兼并和利用中小企业聚集形成的企业集群所产生的规模效应，增强竞争力、谋求生存与发展。中小企业的集群化，有利于降低集群内企业间的交易费用，降低生产成本和管理成本，提高企业的技术创新能力。企业集群能够保持中小企业灵活多变、反应敏捷的特点，并形成群体规模，使中小企业在获得竞争优势的过程中提高自身的核心竞争力。

（二）成功个案带来的启示

在金融危机下，东莞一些企业立足自身实际，早做准备，积极转变，克服重重困难，通过抓技改、重研发、做品牌等一系列科学途径，仍然保持了较快的发展速度，2009年上半年，东莞规模以上工业企业产值增长的企业数量占28.9%，增长型企业产值占规模以上工业产值的30.3%。增长超过100%的企业有277家，总产值173.9亿元，占规模以上工业总产值的7.0%；增长超过50%以上的企业有527家，总产值299.4亿元，占12.0%，其中一些企业的做法值得总结与推广。

1. 技术改造，突破劳动力密集瓶颈

东莞市颖祺实业有限公司是一家毛织企业，主要生产针织服装，是一家典型的劳动密集型企业。自2001年起，颖祺便对部分劳动密集型的生产工序实施有序梯度转移，陆续将织片、缝盘等劳动密集型前整工序转移到内陆城市，为东莞总部腾出了更大发展空间。2007年3月开始，颖祺开始陆续从日本和德国引进国际先进电脑编织机，目前该公司已累计引进500台电脑编织机，耗资2000多万。据该企业生产主管介绍，一台电脑编织机可以减少企业8人用工量，1名熟练工又可以同时进行8台电脑编织机的操作，先进设备的大范围应用，大大提升了生产效率，降低了单位制造成本。目前，颖祺仅织造这一道工序便节省了85%的用工量。经过一系列技术改造，颖祺公司今年将实现1200万件的生产规模，利润空间明显增加，市场占有率也获得大幅提升。颖祺已准备加大技术改造和自动化设备引进的步伐，按照计划，企业将建成拥有超过1000台国际先进设备的生产流水线，并投入4亿元致力于中长期的技术改造。通过这一系列的技术改造，该企业提高了产值，降低了成本，减少了用工，2009年上半年，该企业工业总产值2.86亿元，同比增长54.7%；资产总额增加近1倍；利润403.7万元，同比增长13.6倍；从业人员则下降20%左右。

2. 注重研发，激发企业自主创新潜力

东莞瑞柯电机有限公司是一家生产气体压缩机和微电机的企业，创建之初，曾经面临过技术、资金、市场等诸多难题，企业一度为生存犯愁，到处找米下锅。历经许多弯路与坎坷之后，瑞柯公司决策层毅然认定自主创新这条发展主轴，在产品开发上树立“人无我有，人有我精”的指导思想，推进产品结构优化，取得显著成效，使企业逐渐进入良性发展轨道。瑞柯首先对企业传统主打产品汽车应急充胎机进行了全方位创新，大胆采用新材料，运用新结构，在国内首次自行研发出高精度电子压力表、液压组合机装配线、连续寿命自动化测试台等一系列新产品，并在此基础上前后推出了新款便携式轮胎充气机30余款，新款数字式胎压机5项，国内外市场份额不断增加。与此同时，凭借在国际市场树立的良好声誉，2007年瑞柯与英国某公司联合开发了家庭用电显示感应器，使企业从单一的机电产品制造转变为机电产品和电子信息产品的双向发展。此后，瑞柯又乘势与东莞电子科技大学电子信息研究院进行技术合作，共同开发出“双向无线电能监控器”的核心部件——射频IC芯片组，形成了自主知识产权的拳头产品，为企业发展带来了新的生机。2009年上半年，该企业工业总产值4691.2万元，同比增长61.5%；其中新产品产值2663.8万元，同比增长50.5%；利润总额293.8万元，同比增长56.9%；从业人员下降25%。

四、结论与相关建议

综上，金融危机确实使东莞工业类中小企业的发展进入困境，但面对危机只要积极转变，深入贯彻实施“双转型”战略，企业的逆境突围依然可期。结合我市实际，特提出以下建议：

1. *千方百计减轻企业负担*。当前大多企业出现经营困难，千方百计为企业减轻“包袱”，使企业轻装上阵，是充分激发企业新活力的重要途径。要认真清理行政事业性收费，规范各项规费的收取；设立加工贸易保证金台帐担保专项资金，支持有关中介机构对符合我市产业发展导向、需缴纳保证金的进料加工企业提供保函担保；对符合我市发展规划的企业，加快其土地、厂房确权办理手续，盘活企业的沉淀资金。

2. *加大对企业的扶持力度*。近年来，我市已经针对加工贸易企业在科技攻关、技术改造和品牌建设等方面制定了一系列政策措施，并取得初步成效，面对金融危机影响，应进一步加大扶持力度，使加工贸易企业真正扎根发展，走出困境。要促进加工贸易生产与研发的有机结合，强化企业与高校院所的专题对接，在科技发展专项资金中设立专门的加工贸易研发奖励资金，梳理有待突破的重大技术问题。要鼓励企业优化出口结构，要帮助企业积极适应货币政策，引导各金融机构优先对产业结构调整试点企业项目给予信贷支持和提供优质金融服务，为具有高成长性的加工贸易企业拓宽融资渠道。

3. *健全支持服务体系*。各级政府部门必须牢固树立主动服务意识，进一步优化工作流程。在促进中小企业社会服务体系的相关政策建设上要加大力度，以整体搞活中小企业经济为主线，内抓服务规范、外创服务品牌，大力推进技术创新、技术改造、贷款担保、综合服务和人才培训，营造适合中小企业生存发展的环境，建设一个充满生机与活力的服务体系，促进中小企业健康发展。要密切关注国家加工贸易政策调整和宏观经济形势变化，健全企业联系制度，及时了解企业生产经营状况。加快建设加工贸易转型信息服务平台，整合政府职能部门和社会组织的最新信息资源，提供职能部门最新的业务操作指引和涉及加工贸易企业升级转型的行业信息、培训信息等，为全市加工贸易企业升级转型提供更全面、权威的信息服务。

4. *推进自主创新，提升核心竞争力*。要加快推进企业自主技术创新工作，重点扶持优势企业进行技术创新，努力构建以市场为导向、企业为主体的技术创新体系。要实现财政扶持的政策引导作用，要提高扶持资金使用效率，走重点扶持路线。促成企业与科研院所、大专院校的合作，着力培育技术源和项目源。扶持具有行业优势的企业、企业技术中心进行自有知识产权的产品和技术开发，形成产业竞争优势；支持专利（专有）技术产业化的转化和应用。实施名牌带动战略，提升中小企业核心竞争力。

5. 推进村级行政改革。积极推进村级体制改革试点工作，理顺市、镇、村之间的事权划分，稳步剥离村级行政管理职能，建立事权与财权相统一、适应城市型生产方式的管理体制。加快建立和完善惠及村级的利益分配格局，继续加大市镇两级财政对基层的投入，通过专项补助或镇（街）政府剥离等形式，逐步降低村级对治安、环卫、市政建设和公共管理等投入的负担，减轻支出压力，增强村级承受产业结构调整的能力。同时，探索重大基础设施投融资领域适当向集体经济组织放开，增加集体经济收入途径。对村级盘活土地资源、引进符合市产业导向项目，给予村级财政奖励，进一步提高村级推进产业结构调整积极性。

初探开放条件下的珠三角地区产业结构调整与升级

The Primarily Exploration of the Industrial Restructuring and Upgrading of the Pearl River Delta in Opening Conditions

在解释金融危机以及由此带来的经济周期如何产生时，大多数人都在金融体系和信用制度内寻找原因。而且，既然危机通常是从某一个特定国家开始爆发，继而通过金融链条或者产业链条波及到其他国家乃至全球经济，因此对于绝大多数经济体，尤其是在开放条件下以出口导向为主的劳动密集型珠三角经济体，都可以宣称危机来自外部的冲击。但是，无论是从经济史还是从本次危机的实质来看，危机所施加的影响，在不同国家、地区、产业和企业都不尽相同。所以我们应该说，即便危机来自于外部的冲击，但受危机冲击的大小总是与一个国家、地区的经济发展模式、与特定产业所处的地位和环境，以及与企业选择的技术结构和经营方式有关。就这一点来说，我们需要跳出货币和信用结构的框架，从实体经济和产业结构方面考察在危机中求发展机遇的方法。

一、产业结构特点

中国并没有发生金融危机，但是中国，特别是珠三角经济体，面对国际性金融危机遭受的出口冲击，显示出的结构问题、引起的经济下滑和就业冲击却非常明显。全球金融危机冲击对中国实体经济的影响因地区、产业和企业的不同特点而表现出不同的影响方式，换句话说，经济周期是内生与经济发展的，冲击只是“最后一根稻草”，这一轮的经济冲击带给中国的启示，特别是冲击明显的珠三角经济体，不仅是国际市场的低迷和国际投资的下滑造成经济增长的回落，更深层次的是经济体内部的产业结构和分配体制的积重难返。经济体对国际贸易、国际投资的极度依赖，对经济体内分配体制的置若罔闻，造成了经济增长的主动权旁落，而在其发展过程过度依赖某些产业或大型企业，生产要素的行政性定价，企业或者产业，甚至经济体的创新活动被寻租取代，导致冲击的影响被放大，经济恢复的方式不合理，恢复时间被拉长。

在中国保持长达30年的高速经济增长过程中，具有突出的地区特点，就珠三角而言，其利用本地发展外向型经济的便利，以及中西部近乎无限的劳动力供给，在国际市场上取得了竞争优势，推动了“沿海先发、中西联动”的国内发展模式，但同时其结构问题也十分突出：首先，形成并维系的单纯依靠资本和劳动投入推动型的增长方式，技术进步、产业结构升级和生产率提高对经济增长的贡献相对小，容易对企业主和地区经济形成“惯性”、造成“惰性”，而这种经济增长模式的需求拉动因素突出表现为出口和投资需求，出口投资造成了珠三角的经济增长引擎两头在外，自身能把握的刺激方案效果不突出；其次，国家的沿海地区先发的战略，造成沿海地区形成了一种路径依赖的后果，通过实施沿海率先发展的地区发展战略，形成既有的区域发展格局，在一定程度上缩小甚至扭曲了产业结构调整的空间，并且是地区产业结构的选择与形成，并不与比较优势相一致，尤其是中央政府与地方政府的行政性产业结构规划，对区域经济发展介入过深，对生产要素资源的使用政策化，在财政上对某些成规模的产业或者企业产生依赖性，以致政策被产业和企业的既得利益所俘获，一系列补贴、优惠、垄断地位乃至其他保护和制度租金源源不断流向产业和企业，扭曲的生产要素价格迟迟得不到矫正，企业无法正确判断生产要素相对稀缺性的变化，以致地方政府期待的创新活动被寻租所代替，经济增长方式将积重难返。

作为一个经济体来说，主动改变其固有或“熟悉”的经济增长模式都是十分困难的，而且从上面的分析也知道，两头在外的经济增长引擎，内生的扩张财政政策与宽松的货币政策带来的刺激效果不会十分突出，而且有可能引起通货膨胀、资产泡沫以及国际贸易失衡带来的贸易冲突，就目前我国的刺激政策对珠三角经济体而言，复苏的迹象虽有所显现，但是却表现出无就业复苏、短期库存调整式复苏的端倪，这一点我们可以从近期重新出现在东莞的“招工难”现象以及反映珠三角来料加工模式的进出口数据中可以看出。但从长远来看，只要引导应对危机的策略得当，转危为机是完全有可能的。因为在经济衰退时期，企业为了在市场上站住脚跟，必须作出努力以提高竞争力，同时产业结构调整也比往常来得更加激烈（蔡昉等，2009）。产业结构会表现得更加资本密集化，产业流动会向具有更高比较优势的地区转移。任何一种经济增长模式的转变都是一次创造性毁灭的过程（熊彼特，1990），虽然对成熟的经济体而言，这将是一次漫长而又痛苦的过程，但对其今后的可持续增长却是十分必需和必要的，而增长模式的改变也即意味着产业结构和分配体制的转变，这将是一个长期而又连续的过程。

1. 珠三角产业结构升级的特征

在熊彼特看来，经济发展是由企业创造新消费品、新生产方法或运输方法、新市场，以及新产业组织的形式等一系列创新活动所推动的。（熊彼特，2007）通过创新首先形成一批与老企业并驾齐驱的新企业，后者进而以竞争的方式试图消灭老企业，并造成诸多发展条件的改变，需要特殊的并且常常表现为经济周期的适应过程，从而构成所谓的“创造性毁灭”。（熊彼特，1990）而从表面上来看，我国，特别是以外向型代表的珠三角经济体，其产业升级过程遵循雁阵模型的预期，不论是从早期的国际分工还是如今的产业国际布局而言都可以证明这一点，但如果我们从一个复杂的雁阵理论，结合熊彼特创造性毁灭理论，应用到其区域发展特征中，则可以得出如下图示的产业升级过程。

图 1　跨越式的产业升级模式

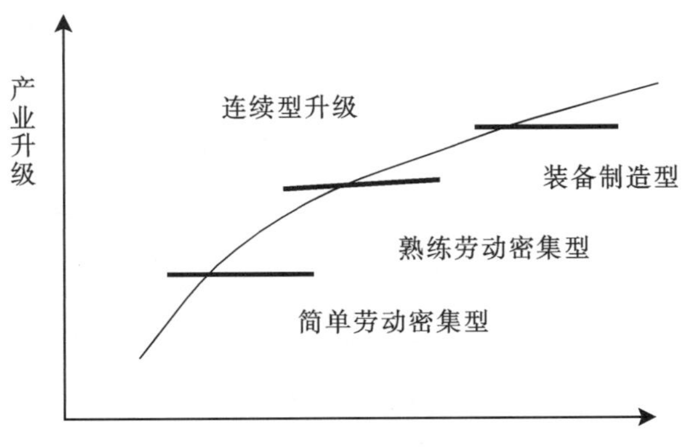

图 1 所示不仅代表着全国产业升级的模式，同样也是珠三角内部产业转移的一个缩影。按照前述熊彼特的理论逻辑，经济增长方式的转变应该是一个“创造性毁灭”的过程，然而对已经显示出优越性、带来可观发展利益的产业模式转型，企业、产业和地方政府都缺乏足够的动力主动进行创造性毁灭，或者说没有能力承受这种毁灭，使得这种转变迟迟不能进行，但是产业转型是一个不可逆转的发展进程，由于地域和地方政府的利益分割性，产业转型升级呈现出蛙跳式的发展模式，也即只能通过

跨跃式技术构成升级模式，由另一个地域承担升级后的产业结构，以替代早期发展地区在产业攀升上的困境，经济体内部出现产业结构高低共存的局面。深圳的产业发展历程也较为清晰地反映了这一现象，改革开放初期，深圳引领开始了工业化进程，90年代末深圳利用其先发和地域优势直接从以轻工业为主的“初期”阶段，跨越了以重化工业化为主的“中期”阶段，直接进入到以深加工和高新技术产业为主的“中后期”阶段，并进而加速向后工业化的“后期”阶段迈进，这种跨越虽然带来了经济的超常发展，但同时也造成了产业结构的早熟与先天发育不良，主要表现为产业结构单一，重型化不足，制造业基础薄弱，第三产业发展空间狭小，就目前看来，电子及通信设备制造业在整个深圳产业结构中发挥着举足轻重的作用，从表面上看好像深圳的产业定位十分明确，支柱产业突出，有利于发挥该产业的区域优势，但却几乎对其他产业部门没有起到任何带动作用，对产业结构的调整从来也没有毁灭过，充其量也就是从简单劳动密集型向熟练劳动密集型的转变。而整个珠三角经济体内部，以东莞、中山等为代表的简单劳动密集型、以深圳等为代表的熟练劳动密集型和以广佛经济联合体为代表的汽车装备制造业共存，同时华南沿海与中部等地区的产业转移也是表现了这种蛙跳式的产业升级过程。

这样的区域经济增长和产业结构变化特征，固然是一些体制因素特别是政府不恰当干预地方经济增长的结果，但是也说明蛙跳式区域增长本身反映了一个变种的产业升级和增长方式转变。说它是一种产业升级和增长方式转变，是因为这种区域跨越式发展，的确伴随着技术进步和生产率提高；说它是一个变种，是因为这种转变虽然在某种程度上与比较优势动态变化相关，但却不必然准确反映区域的资源禀赋结构特征。换句话说，由于劳动力的大规模迁移，以及产业结构调整过程中的潮涌现象（林毅夫，2007），导致这里观察到的产业结构跨跃式升级特点和格局显得比较独特，现实性比较优势似乎与资源禀赋结构存在一定程度上脱离。

2. 珠三角经济体产业结构的特点

前面我们已经对珠三角经济体的产业升级特征进行了分析，这里选取最具代表性的广佛经济联合体、深圳和东莞作比较分析，以求在城市产业结构发展历程中，找到结构变迁的特点和主角，以产业变迁主体及变迁驱动力为分析角度，对经济体内部各城市产业结构变化特点和发展路径做探讨。

广州　改革开放前，广州是一个以商贸为主的城市，建成区（城市建成区指具有一系列城市功能的区域实际面积及其占总面积比重）只有9212平方公里左右。工业生产多是一些日用轻工业，从三次产业比例来看，则以工业为主，其1978年地区生产总值的产值占比从大到小排列是：第二产业（58.59%）、第三产业（29.74%）、第一产业（11.67%），工业生产中轻工业占63.24%，重工业占36.76%，产业结构水平均较低，改革开放以后，广州产业结构的调整按照“稳定提高第一产业，调整优化第二产业，大力发展第三产业”的思路进行，“八五”、“九五”计划的实施是广州产业结构调整的第一个关键时期，以电子通讯设备、交通运输设备、家用电器、摩托车、电气机械和新型食品饮料为主导的产业群逐渐清晰，明确了高新技术制造业的龙头地位，同时将汽车工业、电子通信工业、石油化工工业等三大支柱产业并明确列入八个龙头制造业，培育了一批具有较强国内外市场竞争优势的名牌产品和企业集团，从“十五”计划开始，后续的“十一五”计划都以强调结构调整、优化升级为广州今后产业发展的方向，提出建设软件产业基地、计算机及外围设备制造基地，大力发展高新技术产业，加大对传统产业改造的力度，通过结构调整，继续扶持壮大一批、重组发展一批、放开搞活一批、关闭破产一批，尽快形成具有特色优势和较强市场竞争力的若干产业（行业）板块全面提高工业化水平，到如今，广州已经形成了以汽车、石化、电子信息制造及生物医药制造为主导的主导产业群，传统产业作为产业板块的有益补充，新兴服务业作为经济新的增长极的新的产业布局。

图 2　1952–2005 年广州产业结构变化(%)

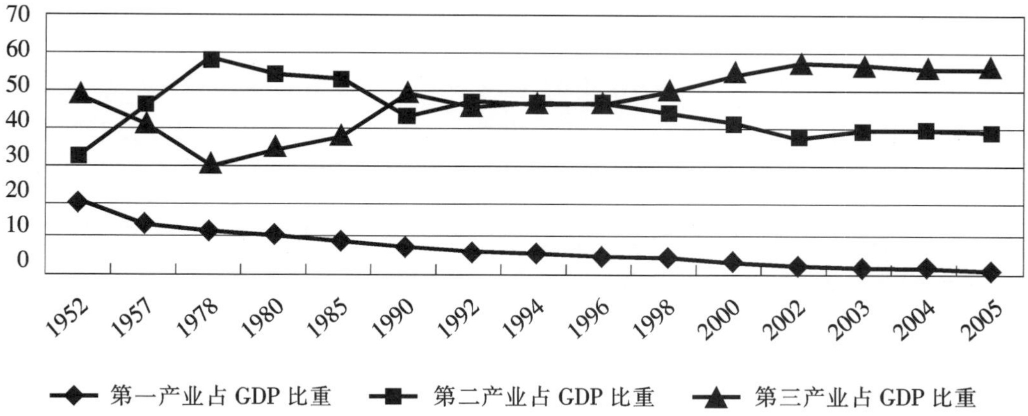

从图 2 可以看出，第一产业产值在 GDP 中所占比重呈下降趋势，第二产业产值在 GDP 中所占的比重呈现上升后下降的趋势，第三产业产值在 GDP 中的比重则呈现下降后上升的趋势，尤其是在改革开放后呈现出快速上升的发展势头。

深圳　改革开放之初深圳还是一个边陲小镇，利用改革开放的政策优势和毗邻香港的地缘优势，借助香港制造业大规模北移的产业转移契机，深圳大力引进发展“三来一补”出口加工工业，1979 年深圳 GDP 的三次产业结构比例为 37∶20.5∶42.5，随着“三来一补”企业的不断发展，由工业比重增加带来服务业的增长，到 1990 年三次产业结构变化为 4.1∶44.8∶51.1，这与深圳作为单一的出口加工区的定位是相吻合的。由于“三来一补”多为劳动密集型的低层次产业，20 世纪 90 年代初深圳对“三来一补”产业进行转型提高，“八五”期间深圳开始重视产业规划、调整产业比重，提出建立“以高新技术产业为先导，以先进工业为基础”的工业体系，到“八五”末期的 1995 年深圳的三次产业结构调整为 1.5∶50.1∶48.4，其中工业比重占 40%。“九五”期间，更进一步明确把“深圳建成高新技术产业生产基地”，“加快发展先进和高新技术产业，加大技术改造力度”，此后经济持续增长，产业结构高级化加快，2000 年产业结构发展为 0.7∶49.7∶49.6，其中工业比重达 44%，产业结构从 1979 年的一、二、三型发展为 1990 年的三、二、一型，呈现第一产业比重大幅下降，第二、三产业比重上升的局面，从 1991 年到 2002 年呈现第一产业比重继续下降，第二、三产业比重波动式发展，相对较为均衡，两种结构型三、二、一与二、三、一交替出现，从 2003 年起，第二产业的比重开始超过第三产业，此后除 2006 年外均出现第二产业比重逐年上升，第三产业比重逐年下降趋势，产业结构呈现二、三、一型，说明深圳的高新技术产业已进入了持续增长期，高新技术制造业在产业结构中所占比重不断上升。第三产业中的金融、房地产及批发零售等行业飞速发展，带来了产业结构发展的进程加快，而工业已经成为深圳国民经济的重要支柱，撑起了深圳经济的“半壁江山”，工业总产值的构成中，轻重工业比从 1980 年 83.81∶16.19，1990 年为 74.6∶25.4，1996 年为 49.37∶50.63，2003 年为 31.41∶68.59，2006 年为 24.15∶75.85，整体呈现轻工业比重不断下降，重工业比重逐年上升之态势，深圳的工业发展进程中，1980 – 1986 年以劳动密集型的来料加工产业为主，1987 – 1995 年以发展资本密集型的外向型出口加工工业为主；1996年至今深圳的高新技术产业崛起，由高新技术产业的发展创立了一批重要的工业主导产品，高新技术产业成为深圳经济增长最快的部门，且1996年深圳轻重工业的比重已相当接近，并在2006年重工业的比重已占压倒性优势，然而深圳的重工业以电子及通讯设备制造业为主，而通信设备、计算机及其他电子设备制造业占工业总产值的比重达59.79%，电子信息产业一业独大，产业结构过于单一。重工业内部的结构也偏轻，重型机械工业制造业的有色、黑色金属冶压、金属制品业，化学工业的化学原料及制品、石化、化纤、橡胶、塑料等占比重分别为0.24%、0.12%、2.27%、1.39%、0.05%、0.04%、0.37%、2.23%，重化工业比重偏轻，按照钱纳里的工业阶段分级论，随着工业化程度的提高，产业结构由轻型化为主到重型化为主，再到高新技术产业为主的新兴工业阶段，但深圳的产业结构由于其特定的历史原因和经济全球化带来的国际产业结构转移与重建而呈现出跨越式的发展，即未经过重型化阶段而直接进入新兴工业阶段，呈现明显的轻型化结构。在重工业完成生产力布局及实现产能之前深圳缺乏重化工业支撑这一结构特征在短期内仍将存在。深圳的工业化直接从以轻工业为主的“初期”阶段，跨越了以重化工业化为主的“中期”阶段，直接进入到以深加工和高新技术产业为主的“中后期”阶段，并进而加速向后工业化的“后期”阶段迈进。这种跨越虽然带来了经济的超常发展，但同时也造成了产业结构的早熟与先天发育不良，主要表现为产业结构单一，重型化不足，制造业基础薄弱，第三产业发展空间狭小等，并且这些弱点开始影响深圳经济的发展，深圳工业主体的制造业呈现竞争力下降的趋势，结构性缺陷开始暴露。目前，电子及通信设备制造业在整个深圳产业结构中发挥着举足轻重的作用，从表面上看好像深圳的产业定位十分明确，支柱产业突出，有利于发挥该产业的区域优势。但是在深圳，却几乎对其他产业部门没有起到任何带动作用，其中很大的原因是由于深圳的特殊城市功能。深圳作为我国对外开放的窗口，本身就是在一个没有任何产业的基础上建立起来的，它的原材料及生产配件主要来自国外，在深圳装配制造完成后又大多销往国外，可以说深圳只是起到了一个装配车间的作用，所以对当地区域的前向和后向连锁效应很小。

佛山　改革开放近30年来，佛山的经济社会发生了翻天覆地的变化，以产值或增加值的比重和各产业的从业人数的比重从增加值的比重变化来考察其产业结构的历史演变，如图3示，第一、二、三产业增加值占生产总值的比重由1978年的31∶51∶18转变为2006年的2.6∶62.9∶34.5。较明显的是，近30年来佛山三大产业中处于领先地位的是第二产业，第二产业增加值比重始终占半壁江山，第二产业尤其是工业成为拉动佛山经济快速发展的最直接、最关键的因素。同时，第一产业在三大产业中的比例以较快速度大幅收缩，其变化在20世纪90年代中后期以前更为明显，2006年第一产业比重还不到1978年的10%，其自身产值在世纪之交略有波动增长，反映出农业开始要走向现代化的特点；产业结构由“二一三”型转为“二三一”型结构状态，第三产业自身产值的增长一直呈现出平稳上升趋势。从三次产业顺次发展的趋势和规律及佛山三大产业增长速度的变化来看，在21世纪初，佛山市产业结构略呈现出由第二产业主导转向第三产业主导阶段的趋势，但在2002年以后又出现工业化反弹现象。

从劳动者就业人数比重变化来看，如图4所示，在1994年－2006年期间，佛山市社会从业人员年末人数在三大产业的分布一直保持“二三一”的结构形态，其中第二产业的社会从业人员年末人数在2002年以后飞速增长，这点与上述的以增加值的变化考察的结果相同，尤其是劳动者就业人数变化更为明显，增长幅度高达近1倍。

图 3　1978–2006 年佛山市三次产业增加值比重变动图

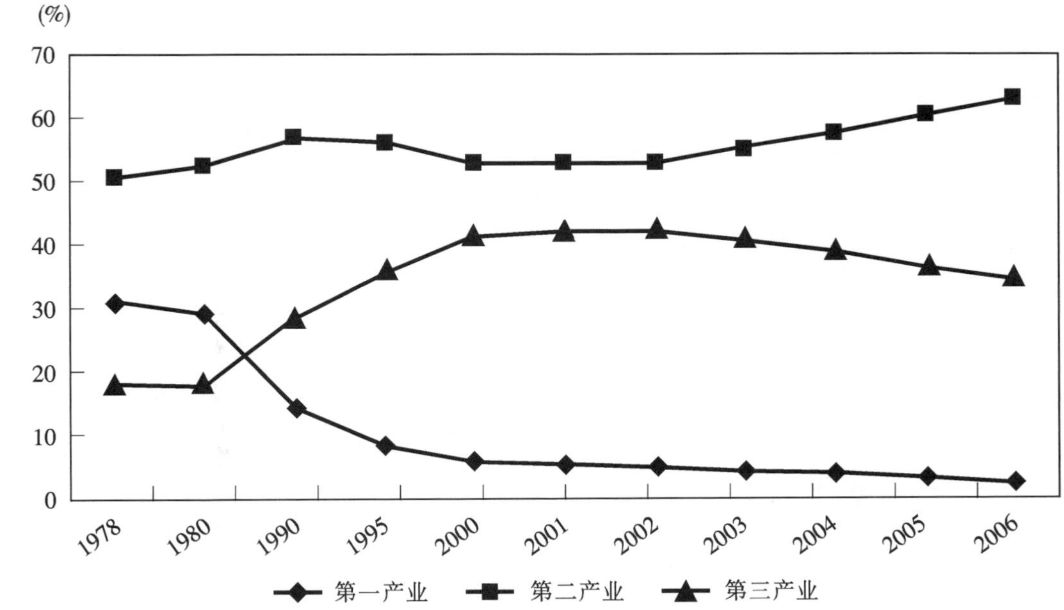

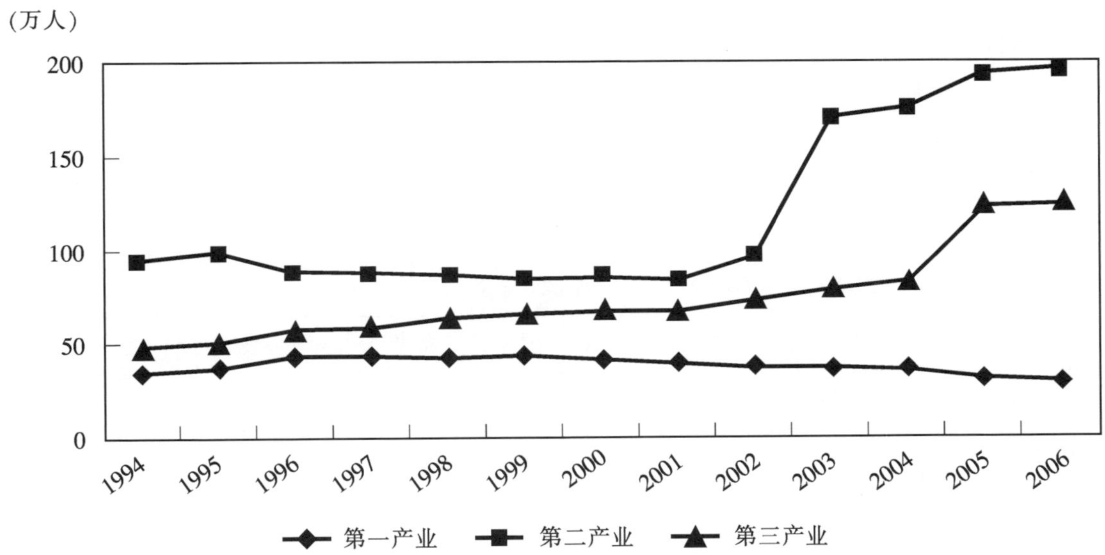

从佛山产业结构演变的阶段性特征来看，其演变过程可以分为 3 个阶段：1978 年 – 20 世纪 90 年代初，工业化初期发展阶段。由图 3 可以看出，90 年代之前，第二产业一枝独秀，而紧随其后的是第一产业，第三产业比第一产业落后 10 个百分点左右，形成“二一三”结构。这个时期，在计划经济主导下，满足基本生活需要的第一产业和消耗大、劳动力密集、附加值较低的传统工业占了较大比重。第三产业整体水平偏低，仅包括一般流通业如商业、运输业、饮食业以及其他为生活服务的产业；20 世纪 90 年代初至 21 世纪初，工业化中期发展阶段。此阶段的服务业获得快速增长，超越农业成为国民经济增长的第二推动力，形成“二三一”结构，直到 1999 年，第二产业和第三产业的增长率分别是 9% 和 11.6%，第三产业增长率超过第二产业，并且占据全市 GDP 的 40.3%，第三产业除了集中于流通部门之外，与产业升级相关的高层次服务部门也有较快发展；21 世纪以后为工业化的成熟阶段，即工业化中后期阶段，第二产业通过进一步扩大份额，巩固其在三次产业中的地位，并且形成以纺织、陶瓷、塑料、电子、食品包装、电器照明为代表的支柱产业，尤其是 2002 年的行政区划调整更加促进第二产业的持续高速增长，第三产业的生产总值每年递增，增长的比例保持在15%左右，在继续发展为生产部门服务的产业的基础上，信息服务、中介咨询部门逐步成为新亮点，现代物流业更是成为代表本地优势服务业的“龙头”。通过对佛山产业结构的历史演变及阶段特征的分析，可以看出佛山三大产业各自的发展趋势总体上有如下特点，一是第一产业的增加值和劳动力人数比重均出现持续下跌；二是第二产业增加值和劳动力人数在三大产业中的比重一直处于领先地位，第二产业中处于优势的行业仍为纺织、陶瓷、塑料、电器照明等传统劳动力密集型行业；三是佛山第三产业也呈现出以劳动密集型服务业为主的结构特色，到目前为止，佛山第三产业仍集中于运输、邮电、贸易及餐饮等流通部门，与产业结构升级密切相关的生产性服务业所占比重较低，劳动者和企业家素质有待提高。

东莞　改革开放以来，东莞市通过优先发展基础产业、基础设施建设，重点发展制造业，积极调整制造业内部结构，大力发展第三产业等一系列政策和措施，产业结构发生了积极而深刻的变革，并向优化和升级的方向发展。二、三产业占有绝对优势：三大产业增加值在宏观经济总量中的比例关系，由2000年的3.2∶54.9∶41.9调整为2007年的0.4∶56.8∶42.8，二、三产业增加值占GDP的99.6%。见下表1。

表1　三大产业增加值构成

年　份	GDP（亿元）	第一产业（亿元）	构成（%）	第二产业（亿元）	构成（%）	第三产业（亿元）	构成（%）	人均GDP（元/人）
2000	820.25	25.91	3.2	450.71	54.9	343.64	41.9	13679
2001	991.89	26.10	2.6	540.51	54.5	425.28	42.9	15268
2002	1186.94	24.88	2.1	648.81	54.7	513.25	43.2	18131
2003	1452.52	22.82	1.6	798.20	55.0	631.51	43.5	22174
2004	1806.03	22.71	1.3	1016.04	56.3	767.28	42.5	27554
2005	2182.62	19.62	0.9	1236.25	56.7	925.76	42.4	33263
2006	2626.51	11.76	0.5	1527.28	58.1	1087.47	41.4	39468
2007	3151.01	12.28	0.4	1790.68	56.8	1348.04	42.8	46014

注：人均GDP按常住人口计算。

从年度间的连续变化上来看，三大产业增加值在GDP中所占比重的变动规律互不相同，呈现出的特点也不一样。第一产业比重呈逐步下降趋势，农业产业规模调减，行业结构不断调整，加大了农作物结构的调整力度，大幅度减少甘蔗、花生、蔬菜和稻谷等农作物面积，增加花卉、优质水果等的种植面积，较好地发挥了现有农业园地的效益，逐步向“三高”农业、商品农业、休闲农业方向发展；第二产业比重呈上升趋势，支柱产业凸显，适度重工业开始显现，如表2示，工业行业分类齐全，电子通信设备、电气机械及器材、纺织服装、塑料、鞋业、家具等行业形成东莞工业的领头羊；第三产业相对稳定，其中流通部门和为生产和生活服务的部门发展较快，为提高科学文化水平和居民素质服务的部门和为社会公共需要服务的部门所占比重较小，从行业看，2006年与2004年相比，房地产业上升5.3个百分点，教育业上升0.3个百分点，金融保险业上升0.1个百分点。批发零售贸易业下降3.7个百分点，居民服务业下降0.1个百分点，第三产业的劳动密集型特征还是比较突出。三大产业结构的上述变化，反映了以下几个特点：第一，东莞市三大产业结构变化基本符合世界范围的产业结构演变规律，即第一产业比重下降，而第二产业、第三产业比重上升。第二，工业化进程在经历“优先发展消费品工业—加强基础产业—加快重化工业发展”等一系列变化中有所加快，第二产业特别是工业的增长成为经济快速增长的主要动力之一。

表2　主要年份东莞轻重工业比重

单位:%

年　份	全　市	轻工业	重工业
1978	100.0	75.0	25.0
1980	100.0	73.7	26.3
1985	100.0	74.6	25.4
1990	100.0	61.2	38.8
1995	100.0	63.2	36.8
2000	100.0	52.7	47.3
2004	100.0	45.4	54.6
2006	100.0	42.8	57.2
2007	100.0	42.7	57.3

注：本表按当年价工业总产值计算。

现阶段下，东莞市产业结构还存在以下几个方面的问题与不足，这些矛盾与问题随着经济发展日益突出。一是，经济结构过分依赖外源经济，结构性矛盾突出，东莞过去20多年的发展，形成了以外源带动为主、以劳务出口为主、以外延扩张为主的发展模式，结构上突出体现为工业布局分散零乱，投资分散、资源浪费、环境污染、经济效益低下等问题，企业尤其是民营企业大多从事加工制造环节，掌握和拥有核心技术、自主知识产权的不多，工艺、装备制造、信息化水平不高，企业品牌实力不强，产业协作水平需要提高，在整个产业链条中，突出存在着制造加工中间环节强、研发和物流两头弱的结构性问题；二是，第二产业大而不强，从下面两个对比表中可以看出（如表3所示），突出表现为企业规模较小，产出效益不高，2006年东莞市大中型工业企业有951家，全省排第二位，但企业规模偏小，平均每家产值只有3.70亿元，比全省平均水平的5.78亿元低2.08亿元，在2007年4987家规模以上工业企业中，低于全市平均劳动生产率的企业有3659家，占73.4%；低于全市平均增加值率的企业有2100家，占42.1%。与其他市比较，东莞工业效益明显低于全省平均水平，从工业综合效益指数看，2006年东莞为130.85，比全省的169.7低38.85个点；三是产品结构不合理，产品开发滞后，长期以来工业产品以出口加工贸易为主，技术设备要求不高，部分企业和生产环节仍维持传统的手工作业方式，劳动生产率低，产品的质量、档次、品种与国际先进水平有较大差距，新产品的开发能力薄弱，产品的更新换代过分依赖国际市场，特别体现在R&D投资上，2007年东莞市高新技术产品研究开发经费只有28.98亿元，占产品销售收入的比例为1.7%，远低于国际上高新技术产业企业研究开发经费占销售额5%以上的水平；三是第三产业比重偏低，发展层次较低，发展水平滞后，还是以劳动密集型特征出现。

表3　2006年规模以上大中型工业主要指标对比

名　称	企业数（个）	工业总产值（亿元）		资产总额（亿元）	
		总量	平均	总量	平均
全　省	5334	30828.93	5.78	23498.32	4.41
东莞市	951	3521.93	3.70	3015.36	3.17
广州市	672	5222.01	7.77	5383.52	8.01
深圳市	1210	9595.60	7.93	6141.63	5.08
佛山市	654	3609.44	5.52	2357.43	2.53

从上述对四市的产业结构发展历程及特征对比来看，珠三角经济体的产业结构特征表现出以下几个特点：一是产业结构变化外资唱主角，产业同构现象比较明显，且产业内企业分工不明确，各自为阵。珠三角经济体作为我国对外经济发展的窗口，无论在外资的引用规模、引用范围和政策扶持上都处于全国前列。按照第二次国际分工的路线图可以看出，珠三角承接的基本上以第二产业、劳动密集型、出口替代型和产品生命周期末端产业为主，FDI挤占了珠三角产业第一次变革期间的国内投资，在产业发展沿革过程中，FDI主导了产业转型，国内投资的流向以产业发展配套为主，特别突出的是，东莞、深圳两市，在改革开放前没有任何产业基础上引进产业布局，引进外资自主程度偏弱和产业同构现象突出，例如2007年东莞全市工业总产值6667.9亿元，其中港澳台及外资经济工业产值4614.9亿元，占全市69%，1978年比重更高，且从上面对四市的产业演变历程可以看出，两市的主导产业比较类似，主要产品雷同，产业同构现象比较突出。而广州、佛山的轻工业发展历史比较悠久，商贸有特色，其外资的利用自主程度相较深圳、东莞较高，而佛山在引进外资过程中，自身民营经济发展较快，形成了自身的轻工业体系，且积极与广州的重工业基地配套发展，自主性和目的性也较为突出，产业间和产业内的同构现象不突出，产业配套发展和产业链条式发展前景较好，广州外向且以三来一补起步，佛山内向，民营经济、镇街经济特色突出，两个城市在轻工业产业布局有基础，产业发展有家底，特别是以南海模式、顺德模式发展起来的佛山民营经济，在全国家电、陶瓷、铝材制造等行业有先发和历史优势，这样，在外资引进和产业联合布局中过程中就可以根据自己的先发优势和已有的产业链基础进行自主调节，充分调动自身联合体内的产业发展优势；二是主导产业不主导，产业升级跨越式发展。这个特征主要体现在东莞的产业发展上，同时其他市由于现代化产业基础不厚，产业间和产业内的前后联系不紧，也存在产业升级过程中。以东莞为例，在经历了改革开放初期的来料加工产业“群雄争霸”后，东莞主导产业看似逐渐清晰，但其产业间和产业内联系不紧密，各企业只对自己的制造成本利润率负责，对产业的竞争力和利润率贡献率偏低，主导产业不主导，产业升级过程因缺乏产业发展基础，升级没有实现“创造性毁灭”，只能将产业转移而不能升级；三是产业链松散，上下游的设计下单、原料供应、物流营销掌握在国外，企业没有定价权，只能被动接受成本上升。就目前情况而言，珠三角经济体内的产业自主创新升级难度较大，所需时间较长，而低端制造业也并非只有自主创新一条出路，可以通过整合产业链提升整体产业竞争力，可以参照西班牙ZARA、瑞典的H&M甚至国内晋江企业的成功，都是由纯制造转型成为产业链高效整合的传统劳动力密集产业，将原料批发、仓储、运输、订单处理、制造、产品设计整合，控制产品定价权、定性权。而在松散的产业

链影响下，各企业成为散兵游勇，企业群一盘散沙，各企业为寻求生存权，不仅要接受上游原料上涨的压力，而且受下游销售、批发商的定价压力，只有尽量压缩生产成本和产品利润率才能勉强维持生存，更谈不上分出微薄的利润去进行自主创新；四是输入式的产业发展，三次产业模式以简单劳动密集型为主。这种劳动密集型不仅体现在第二产业上，在第三产业和所谓的高新技术密集企业同样或多或少存在。以四个市第三产业的布局来看，批发零售业、物流业等行业都是以低成本劳动为主，金融等新兴服务业还处于低水平的借贷上，金融创新能力不强。而在所谓的高新技术行业里面，比如通信设备制造、成套装备制造等等，劳动密集型模式的印记还是很深。珠三角经济体内呈现出跨越式发展与基础性发展共存、出口替代型与进口替代型模式共存、发展加工贸易型与产业配套型发展方向共存的局面。这就使得对于不同的经济联合体或地区的产业升级转型模式需要区别对待。一下对各地区全要素生产率和内生经济增长路径进行经验分析，探讨各类型产业模式的发展方向。

二、全要素生产率及内生经济增长路径：经验分析

1. 数据说明

考虑到现有统计数据的可获性和完整性，本文使用的样本数据为广州和东莞两地 1995 – 2007 年的数据，并作对比分析。样本数据集包括两地的生产总值（GDP）、全社会固定投资总额（K）、劳动力人数（L）以及科技变量（RDS1①）。数据来源自历年统计年鉴。

2. 全要素生产率的测算

全要素生产率适用于观察一个国家（地区或产业）增长绩效的重要指标，可分为效率增长贡献率和技术增长贡献率，这里以深圳、广州、东莞作为对比决策单元，通过对三地全要素生产率变化的测算，确定效率变化抑或是技术变化给三地的生产率增长带来的影响。具体如下表 2②：

表 4　广州、深圳东莞三市 Malmquist 指数均值

FIRMS	EFFCH	TECHCH	TFPCH
广州	1.002	1.111	1.113
深圳	1.004	1.124	1.125
东莞	1.000	1.053	1.053

基于上表数据而言，2000 年以后，各市的 Malmquist 指数均大于 1，说明普遍存在生产率的提高，且从全要素生产率的分解看出，效率变化不明显，三地全要素生产率提高的主要来源是技术变化，且东莞的技术变化对全要素生产率的影响远小于广州和深圳两市。如果结合下表来看，数据结果就非常有意思了，珠三角经济体的华南沿海地区与华东沿海地区的 TFP 增长率与西部地区接近，验证了产业结构演变的特点和与比较优势及资源禀赋脱离的产业升级模式，说明虽然在出口拉动需求下，沿海地区特别是珠三角经济体获得了较快的产出增长，但 TFP 增长速度较慢，意味着沿海地区通过创新和产业升级转变经济增长的效果不明显，产业升级与比较优势的动态变化脱离，通过科技或创新拉动的产业升级困难重重。

---

①科技发展变量用｜R&D｜*｜专门技术从业人员｜^{T} 表示

②从以公布的数据角度来看，有些市的数据的完整性以及连贯性都存在不足，时序数据的选取只能在一定程度上反映三市的情况，特别是从业人员数据对 TCH 的影响较大

表 5　2000 - 2007 年全要素生产率增长率和贡献率

	产出（总产值）	资本	劳动	中间投入	TFP
平均增长率（%）					
华南沿海	22.51	14.07	12.87	18.81	4.6
华东沿海	23.84	18.17	11.59	20.17	4.38
华北沿海	24.28	14.77	5.26	20.95	5.6
东北地区	19.74	8.08	-0.05	15.82	5.46
中部地区	22.98	12.32	2	19.86	6.17
西部地区	21.38	10.34	1.05	18.76	4.13
平均贡献率（%）					
华南沿海	100	1.88	5.21	72.47	20.45
华东沿海	100	1.75	2.96	76.91	18.37
华北沿海	100	2.01	1.84	73.09	23.06
东北地区	100	0.74	-0.02	71.63	27.65
中部地区	100	2.09	0.87	70.2	26.84
西部地区	100	0.58	0.3	79.82	19.3

3. 模型构建

对珠三角经济体内各外向型产业而言，转变经济增长方式，确立产业升级转型的工作方向对可持续发展是非常重要的。从上述全要素生产率的分析来看，华南沿海的 TFP 虽然保持正向增长，但其落在了中部地区和东北地区后列，且与西部相差无几，结合表 4 来看的话，技术对产业升级的贡献率相当低，还是以劳动投入为主。在此部分中，通过建立向量自回归模型（VAR model）对 GDP 进行回归分析，并通过 Granger 检验和脉冲响应图反映各变量与解释变量的关系，从而找出在经济快速增长时期路径的缺陷，明确技术变量作为新增长阶段源动力的重要地位。将 GDP、全社会固定投资总额（K）、劳动力人数（L）以及科技实力（RDS）变量建立模型如下：

$$GDP_{it} = \alpha_{it} + \beta_{it} X_{it} + \varepsilon_{it} \quad (1)$$

$$Y_t = A_1 Y_{t-1} + A_2 Y_{t-2} + \cdots A_P Y_{t-P} + \varepsilon_t \quad (2)$$

其中，在（3）中，X_{it}代表（K、L、RDS）T 的列矩阵，即各变量对 GDP 的贡献率，α_{it}为模型常数项，ε_{it}为随机扰动项；（4）式中，Y_t 是上述四个内生变量的向量组合，即，Y_t =（*GDP*，*K*，*L*，*RDS*），ε_t为随机扰动项，A_i 为参数矩阵，*P* 的选取依照 AIC 和 SC 准则。考虑到时序数列可能存在的异方差性，对两式各变量取自然对数，即

$$\ln GDP_{it} = \alpha_{it} + \beta_{it} lnX_{it} + \varepsilon_{it} \quad (3)$$

$$\ln Y_t = A'_1 lnY_{t-1} + A'_2 lnY_{t-2} + \cdots A'_P lnY_{t-P} + \varepsilon_t \quad (4)$$

为更好反映在内生经济增长路径中各要素的贡献率，以及各要素基于发达地区的差异度，对（4）式的分析结果与广州市进行对比；并通过（5）式的 VAR 模型的脉冲响应及 Granger 结果检验各要素的逻辑关系。

4. 实证结果

由（4）式的模型分析出发，得出 GDP 分别与 K、L、RDS 之间的双变量模型的结果，初步估算各

内生变量对 GDP 的影响度，结果如下表：

表 6 对应（4）式的回归结果

变量	东莞市 各变量系数			广州市 各变量系数		
	model 1	model 2	model 3	model 1	model 2	model 3
lnK	0.76 (12.81)			1.48 (22.36)		
lnL		1.66 (11.85)			3.67 (18.68)	
lnRDS			0.39 (8.10)			0.77 (21.44)
adj R^2	0.93	0.92	0.84	0.98	0.97	0.97
std	0.06	0.14	0.05	0.07	0.20	0.04

注：（1）各内生变量系数值下括号内数值为 t 检验值；

（2）adj R^2 代表修正后的 R^2 值，std 为标准差

从表 6 可以看出，广州与东莞两市的科技实力影响程度相较于 K、L 来看还是比较小的，L 的影响程度最高，K 次之，说明两市的生产要素密集度还是以劳动力密集为主；东莞市各变量的弹性系数均小于广州市相应值，说明东莞市的生产要素集约化程度不及广州市；从东莞市的回归分析结果可以看出，科技变量对 GDP 的贡献度最小，劳动密集型的发展模式还是较为突出，资本投入次之，结合图 1 来看，若东莞经济发展模式不改变，必将落入“中等收入发展陷阱”，即发展模式的不可持续性必将凸显。

进一步地，我们通过（5）式的具体分析结果，对各自变量对 GDP 的长期协整关系进行评价和分析。首先使用 EG 两步法对各变量进行协整分析，由协整定义可知，如果 N 个时间序列存在协整关系，则非均衡误差必然是 I（0）的，反之，则是 I（1）的。由此对变量用 OLS 建立回归模型，对其残差项进行单位根检验，通过分析残差项的特征来判断是否存在协整关系。建立 OLS 回归模型如下：

$$LnGDP = \alpha_0 + \alpha_1 LnK + \alpha_2 LnL + \alpha_3 LnRDS + \varepsilon \quad (5)$$

通过回归检验，其主要的统计指标比较理想，直接对残差进行 ADF 检验得出，其在 10% 水平下可以拒绝单位根假设，基本可以确定各变量之间存在协整关系，选择滞后一期变量建立误差修正模型如下（括号为各系数的 t 检验值）：

$$LnGDP = 0.62\ (3.12) + 1.03\ (21.01)\ LnGDP(-1) + 0.08\ (1.18)\ LnK - 0.12\ (-0.93)\ LnK(-1) - 0.01\ (-0.18)\ LnL - 0.09\ (-1.60)\ LnL(-1) + 0.03\ (1.26)\ LnRDS - 0.002\ (-0.11)\ LnRDS(-1) \quad (6)$$

从（6）式可以看出，误差修正模型的检验结果还是较为理想的，各相关变量的检验值较为显著，可以初步了解 GDP 的长期影响机制。GDP 的长期影响机制除受到前期量影响较为显著以外，受当期的固定投资和科技实力变量影响也为正，但滞后一期的固定投资显现出了较大的反向影响，说明固定投资对 GDP 正向的作用是递减的，劳动力对 GDP 的影响长期为负，说明在 GDP 的长期影响机制中，劳动力数量的提高并不能使得 GDP 增长，反而会出现负向影响。

为更进一步反映各变量间的协整和长期关系，在这里使用 VAR 模型对各变量进行检验。J－J 检验

后可以看出在5%水平下存在一个协整关系，VAR结果如下表：

表7　各变量VAR检验各系数计统计特征值

VAR	Ln（GDP）	Ln（K）	Ln（L）	Ln（RDS）
Ln（GDP（-1））	1.02 （0.03） （30.30）	0.14 （0.23） （0.59）	0.75 （0.30） （2.44）	-0.46 （0.63） （-0.74）
Ln（K（-1））	0.07 （0.03） （2.07）	1.07 （0.22） （4.85）	-0.42 （0.29） （-1.45）	3.37 （0.59） （5.71）
Ln（L（-1））	-0.09 （0.05） （-1.82）	0.31 （0.33） （0.95）	0.30 （0.43） （0.70）	-0.74 （0.88） （-0.84）
Ln（RDS（-1））	-0.03 （0.01） （-2.00）	-0.14 （0.09） （-1.58）	0.07 （0.12） （0.58）	-0.40 （0.24） （-1.63）
C	0.41 （0.09） （4.38）	-2.11 （0.66） （-3.22）	0.88 （0.86） （1.02）	-1.07 （1.76） （-0.61）

VAR结果与EG两步法结论基本保持一致，根据建立的VAR模型，我们可以描绘出变量间的脉冲响应关系图，示图如下：

图5　各变量对其他变量的脉冲响应图

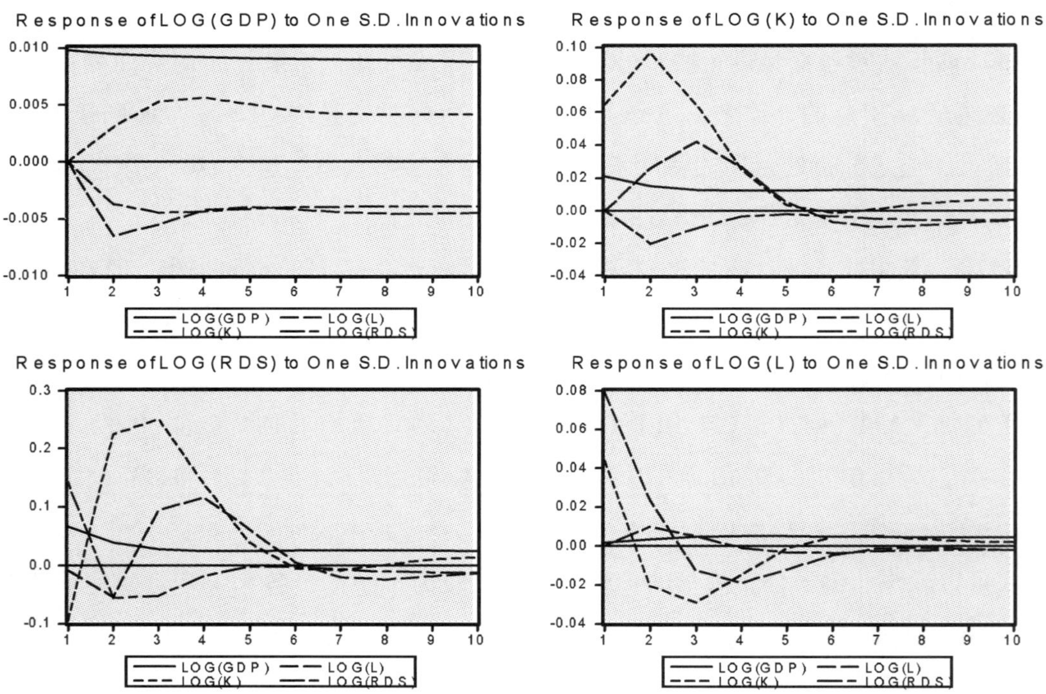

从图5可以看出，GDP除对自身前期量的脉冲响应明显以外，受固定投资标准差新息的脉冲也比较明显，且为正向；劳动力显著为负；科技变量由于历史欠账，响应过程不明显，但可看出其响应趋势为正。更进一步地，为从数据间逻辑关系验证GDP与科技变量的关系，将两者进行Granger检验，

结果如下：

表 8　Granger 检验结果及显著特征

Null Hypothesis:	Obs	F - Statistic	Probability
LOG（RDS）does not Granger Cause LOG（GDP）	11	0. 81724	0. 48542
LOG（GDP）does not Granger Cause LOG（RDS）		2. 08473	0. 20538

从上表的结果可以看出，GDP 与科技变量互为因果关系，即 GDP 的增加是科技实力提高的原因，且科技变量的提高也是 GDP 增长的原因。结合表 1、表 3、（8）式的结果，科技变量显然对东莞的经济增长有正向的促进作用，但近期效果不是很明显。

三、结论与建议

*避免出现产业空洞化。*类型资本决定产业模式。资本的背后是整条产业链的性质，珠三角在外向型经济发展了 30 年的基础上，产业链已经逐步确定下来，要想一朝一夕实现产业转型升级，一是难度大，二是容易造成产业空洞化，很多现实的例子给了我们启示：美国 70 年代后期贸易赤字的迅猛上升，汽车、钢铁制造业竞争力不断下降，是美国政府对美国产业基础发展认识存在偏差，将主要精力放在第三产业的发展上，使得日本制造业企业在美国本土市场超越了其本身的市场覆盖率；香港在 90 年代初大力发展金融服务业、贸易、旅游以及房地产业，制造业占 GDP 比重从 1984 年的 24. 8% 下降到 1994 年的 9. 2%，出现了产业空洞化，90 年代末期金融危机的影响超过其对台湾及其他周边东南亚制造业为主导的国家或地区，如今在全球竞争力排名中，香港已从 1998 年的第 2 逐渐降至 2001 —2002 年度的第 17，台湾却从第 6 升至第 3；如果我们再回顾一下 1992 年后在海南、北海、淡水等地出现的那波投资热，就会更清楚地看到脱离制造业而超前、孤立发展第三产业的后果，当时全国各地企业对上述热点地区趋之若鹜，大量资金集中投向房地产、贸易、金融、旅游等服务业，但当地相对滞后的第一、第二产业却未能提供与之相匹配的有效需求，结果不可避免地造成房地产过热和经济泡沫，留下的只是无数的闲置地皮、空置楼、烂尾楼、被死死套牢的资金加上惨痛的教训。珠三角作为输入型产业结构的在亚洲新兴经济体的代表，其产业结构调整更具典型性。通过产业结构调整提升区域的产业国际竞争力，实现经济的可持续发展。产业结构调整不仅是针对国民产业三次产业间的调整升级，也包括对产业内部的优化调整实现产品带动产业竞争力的提升，拔苗助长。

*创新并不全指技术创新，要抓住行业本质。*行业本质决定企业发展。现实发展阶段，珠三角劳动密集型产业、企业都存在科技创新能力不强，品牌树立能力不强的局面，企业运行的利润率一直在低水平徘徊，摒弃现有的产业基础和企业销售渠道，凌驾于目前的现实发展高科技，发展局面会比较尴尬。其实就劳动密集型产品而言，抓住了行业本质后的利润率并不比高科技产品低，高科技产品高度吻合产品生命周期理论，其研发成本和后续开发成本相当高，对于目前珠三角的家底而言，发展前景不乐观，而劳动密集型产品，在抓住行业本质后，可以在产业链整合和产品价值上赋予它新的价值增长点，譬如说服装产业，其价值取向不仅仅是奢侈品，换种角度来看，以产业链整合为手段创造的利润率并不比奢侈品低，尤其是在金融危机爆发的现时，西班牙的 ZARA、瑞典的 H&M，虽说他们的服装设计师不是世界顶尖的、制造成本不是最低的，但他们抓住了服装行业在现时的本质，通过将设计、批发、仓储、运输、订单处理、制造环节整合起来，实现“快速、少量、多款”的规模经济效应，根本不需要靠廉价劳动力来降低成本或是请顶尖设计师设计最时尚经典的服装款式，金融危机深入影响的 2009 年，其第一季度净销售额为 23. 38 亿欧元，同比增长 5%，相较于其他服装品牌甚至顶

尖品牌而言这都是一个销售奇迹。

*用实用好《纲要》规划，打造紧密的块状经济带。*一是要做好规划，解决经济体的产业同构问题，扎实推进产业链的整合，在《纲要》出台后，经济体内各城市都在根据自身发展需要联合周边城市，规划联合体的产业发展方向，但在笔者看来，只要做好产业规划，切实解决产业同构问题，打破地域限制、行政限制和利益分配体制，利用现有的产业基础和产业链，就能将经济体呈现出各有特色、有品牌、有竞争力的联合体；二是发扬广东人拓荒精神，敢于先行一步，充分利用国家在广东试点人民币结算业务的机会，将人民币结算推广使用，有效降低国际市场的汇率分险，毕竟珠三角还是东亚及东南亚最大的制造基地，在人民币结算的条件下逐步开放人民币自由兑换等其他金融服务；三是泛珠三角和粤港澳台经济联合体综合考虑，有转移有升级，逐步有序承接高新技术产业、转移淘汰落后产能，利用港澳台的熟练劳动密集型产业和中央政府给予其优惠的政策实现从简单劳动密集型产业扎实升级到熟练和技术含量较高的产业。

*分配制度的改革。*经济发展的代表是产业发展，产业发展是有一定的规律性的，产业结构与经济发展相互促进，相互影响（库兹涅茨，1955），产业结构是一个经济系统内在规律的外化，产业结构优化形成强力优势，促进经济的快速发展。美国经济学家钱纳里将工业化过程划分为初期、中期、中后期和后期四个阶段。一国工业化道路一般从早期的轻工业过渡到中期工业，然后过渡到以重化工业为主的中后期工业，经过深加工工业阶段，为新兴工业阶段所取代，进入后工业化阶段。在工业化的进程中，每一阶段都有其不可替代和不可逾越性。随着工业化程度的提高，产业结构由轻型化的轻工业为主到重型化的重工业为主，再到高新技术产业为主的新兴工业阶段。但珠三角输入性的产业发展模式，已经出现了跨越式发展，产业升级的基础薄弱，实现升级转型的关键就更强调在了科技实力的厚积薄发。从上面的经验分析可以看出，GDP 与 RDS 互为因果，但贡献率远落后于资本和劳动要素，要提升产品的竞争力、产业的集中度和优势，科技和人才的投入必须补足在跨越式发展中留下的空缺，资金容易解决，但资金能否形成创新需要人才的积累，这就需要珠三角各区域政府要对现有的分配制度进行深度改革，历年来本土劳动力与外来劳动力形成的巨型价格剪刀差已经迫使更多的人才流向报酬和福利更高的长三角地区，人才特别是熟练人才的流失给珠三角的技术外溢效应带来了很大的负面影响，对其内部的产业升级转型也带来了不小的阻碍。

风雨六十年　拼搏铸辉煌

——新中国成立60年来东莞经济社会发展成就

The Achievements in Economic and Social Development in Dongguan Since the People's Republic of China has been founded for 60 years

1949年中华人民共和国成立以来，共和国走过了60年的辉煌历程，在毛泽东思想、邓小平理论、“三个代表”重要思想和科学发展观的指引下，在历届领导班子的带领下，以“敢为天下先”著称的东莞人，海纳百川，厚德务实，坚持以经济建设为中心，解放思想，抢抓机遇，不断深化改革，扩大开放，团结奋进，顽强拼搏，创造了一个又一个奇迹。60年来，东莞综合经济实力显著增强，社会事业全面进步，人民生活水平不断提高，城市面貌发生了翻天覆地的巨大变化，东莞的发展成为我国改革开放精彩而生动的缩影。

一、经济总量实现大跨越，创造了经济增长奇迹

中华人民共和国成立以来，特别是党的十一届三中全会以来，东莞经济持续快速发展、经济实力快速提高，向着全面建设小康社会迈出了坚实的步伐。1949年东莞县按不变价计算的工农业总产值只有0.83亿元，1950年东莞财政收入0.11亿元。到1978年生产总值6.11亿元，人均生产总值533元，财政收入0.66亿元。在改革开放的历史新时期，经济总量迅猛扩张。1988年东莞市生产总值实现比1980年翻两番，提前12年完成生产总值比80年翻两番的任务。2000年全市生产总值比1980年翻五番。2001年以后，经济快速发展，2002年全市生产总值突破1000亿元大关，2005年又跨上2000亿元台阶，2007年再次突破3000亿元，2008年达到3702.5亿元，按可比价计算比1978年增长了136.9倍，年均增长17.8%。1949年东莞户籍人口68.24万人，1978年发展到111.23万人，2008年全市户籍人口174.87万人，常住人口694.98万人。人均生产总值53285元，比1978年增长28.4倍，年均增长11.9%。

图一　1978–2008年地区生产总值

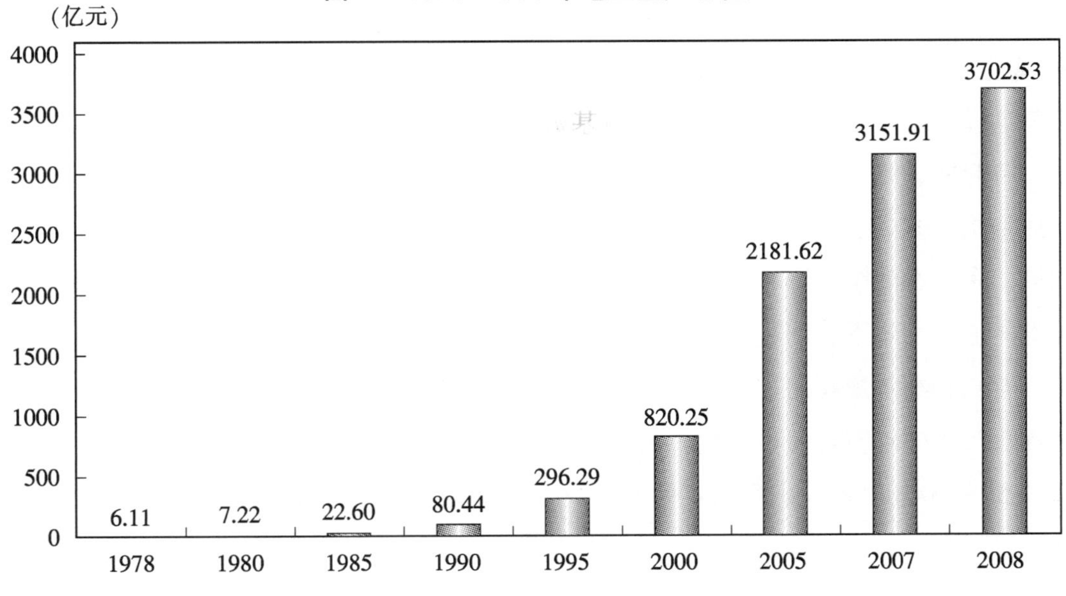

图二　1990-2008 年东莞市常住人口

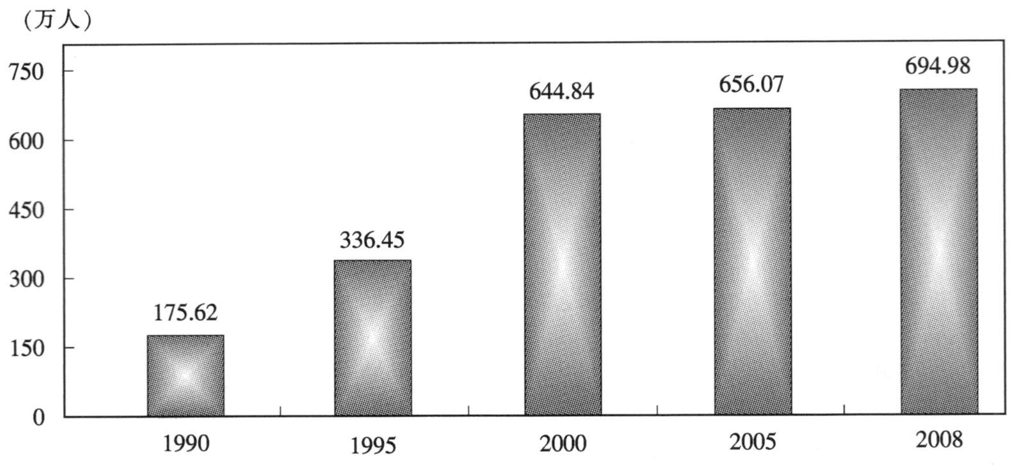

图三　1949-2008 年东莞市户籍人口

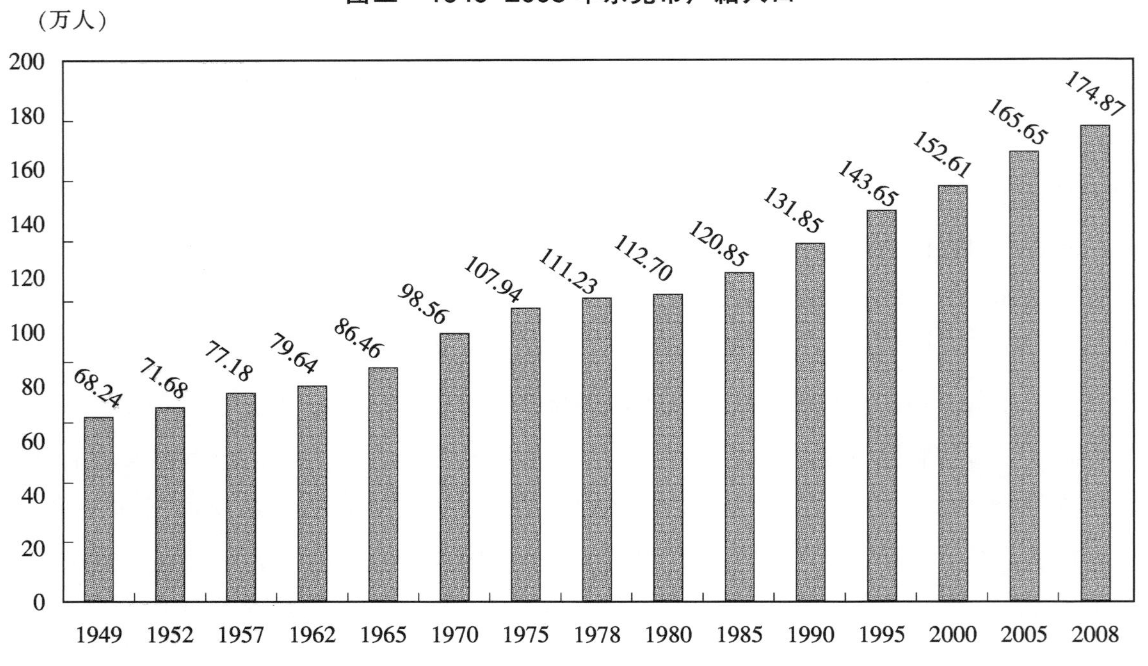

随着经济的高速发展和经济总量的不断壮大，东莞地方财力明显增强。2008 年来源于东莞的财政收入601.06 亿元，与1950 年相比，增长5463 倍，与1978 年相比，增长910 倍；东莞地方财政一般预算收入209.22 亿元，比1978 年增长316 倍，年均增长21.2%。

对于东莞这样一个经济发展起点低、人口基数不断庞大的城市，在60 年之内能够取得这样的进步，是一个了不起的成绩。

二、产业结构化蛹成蝶，实现了二、三产业飞跃发展

解放初期，东莞经济结构不尽合理，主要以农业为主，所有制结构单一，分配绝对平均主义，城镇化水平很低，地区发展不协调。农林牧渔业总产值0.54 万元，占工农业总产值的比重达到65.1%，伴随着经济的增长和经济规模的扩大，1978 年这一比重下降到50.2%。经过改革开放后30 年的发展，经济结构在逐步改善中趋向合理和优化，三次产业增加值在经济总量中的比例关系由1978 年的44.6:43.8:11.6 调整为2008 年的0.3:52.8:46.9，第一产业比重大幅下降，二、三产业比重快速上升，由55.4%上升到99.7%。

图四 1952-2008 年市财政一般预算收入

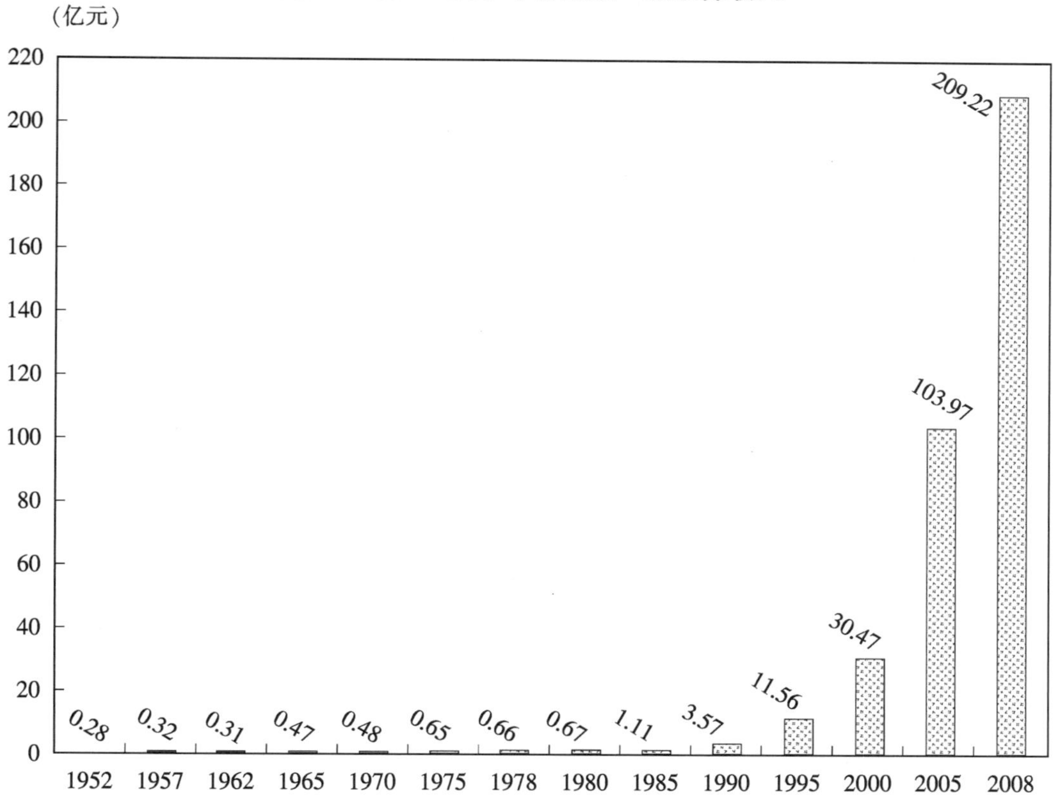

东莞市生产总值构成(%)

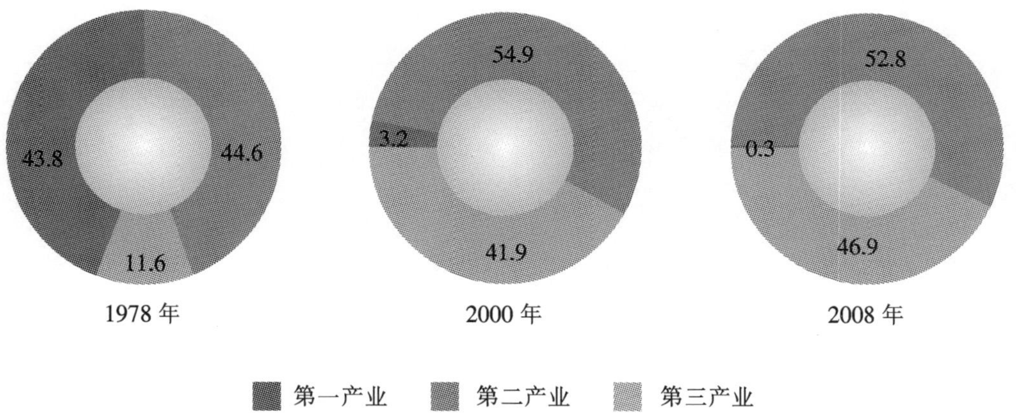

改革开放以来，家庭联产承包责任制率先在农村推广，农业生产力得到了极大解放，农业科技不断进步，东莞农业已由过去形式单一的传统农业向“三高”农业、商品农业、休闲农业方向发展，良种良法得到普及和推广，农业内部结构发生了深刻变革，种养比例由 1978 年的 70:30 调整为 2008 年的 50.9:44.4（不含林业和农林牧渔服务业）。

工业不断升级与腾飞。以引进“三来一补”企业为突破口，外资型工业迅速崛起，产业集中度明显提高，经济结构实现了由传统农业向现代工业的转变。

第三产业快速发展。2008 年第三产业增加值已经达到 1736.06 亿元。从第三产业内部结构看，流通部门和为生产和生活服务的部门发展较快，为提高科学文化水平和居民素质服务的部门及为社会公共需要服务的部门所占比重较小。不仅如此，伴随着第三产业的发展，一些新兴产业也如雨后春笋，在改革开放30年中萌芽并迅速发展起来，初步形成了以批发零售业、住宿餐饮业、房地产业、租赁服务业、信息传输、计算机服务和软件业为主体，其他服务业并存的第三产业体系。

所有制结构从单一向多元化发展。1978年民营经济占极少部分，外资经济还是空白，形成了国有集体经济一统天下的局面。改革开放以来，外资工业和民营工业迅速发展，到2008年国有集体企业约占全部工业的1%，绝大部分为外资和民营企业，在2008年生产总值中，外资经济占42.0%，公有经济占25.5%，民营经济占32.5%。

三、工业化进程突破性发展，铸就了现代制造业名城

建国初期，东莞工业基础薄弱，基本上以农副产品加工和采掘业为主，工业整体水平很低。经过60年发展，东莞工业已具有了相当的基础和规模，工业门类较齐全，形成了以电子信息产业为支柱，以出口为主的比较完整的工业经济结构体系，成为IT产业的大市。1952年东莞工业企业有3522家，其中个体工业3363家，国营工业仅有14家，工业总产值4031万元，发展到1978年，东莞工业企业有1290家，工业总产值4.20亿元，到2008年全市工业企业有2.27万家，全市工业总产值7222.38亿元，按可比价计算比1978年增长1092倍，年均增长26.3%。规模以上工业总产值6372.28亿元，其中国有工业总产值359.71亿元，外资型工业总产值4973.97亿元，民营工业总产值909.95亿元。工业经济效益稳步提高。2008年全市规模以上工业实现利润123.45亿元，比1978年的0.26亿元增长474倍，年平均增长22.8%。主要产品产量发展迅速，许多产品从无到有，且增长较快，东莞制造业享誉海内外。东莞的开拓之路，更是创下了一个工业发展史上的神话——仅仅30年，就完成了西方发达国家用了100多年、亚洲“四小龙”用了40多年的工业化进程。

图五　1949–2008年工业总产值

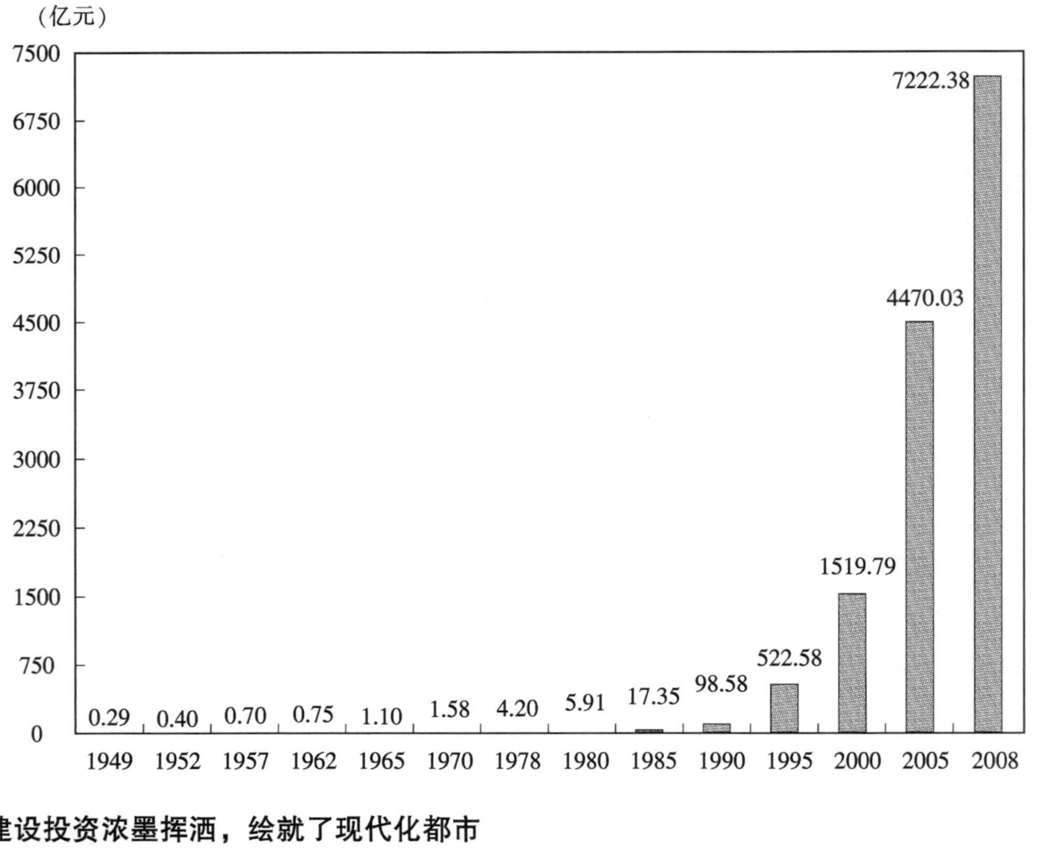

四、建设投资浓墨挥洒，绘就了现代化都市

东莞抓住改革开放的机遇，加大招商引资力度，加快基础设施建设，固定资产投资规模不断扩大，基础设施建设突飞猛进，现代化城市格局基本建成，城市魅力显现。2008 年全社会固定资产投资 944. 3 亿元，1978 -2008 年累计完成固定资产投资总额 4920 亿元，年均增长 31. 9%。城市承载能力逐步提高，道路、供水、供气等公益设施日臻完善，城市整体功能不断增强。到 2008 年，全市境内公路通车里程（含乡村道路）4000. 9 公里，比 1978 年增长 2. 2 倍，公路密度 162. 3 公里/百平方公里。2008 年公路货物周转量 30. 33 亿吨公里，旅客周转量 137. 58 亿人公里；水路货物周转量 7. 11 亿吨公里，旅客周转量 0. 29 亿人公里，港口货物吞吐量 3208 万吨。全市自来水日供水能力 650 万立方米，自来水供水总量 17. 36 亿立方米，液化石油气家庭用户 87. 66 万户，天然气家庭用户 8. 23 万户。2008 年全市程控电话用户（不含小灵通）254. 13 万户，移动电话用户 1454. 29 万户，互联网用户 96. 37 万户。城市对外交通更加便捷，高速公路、铁路纵横交错，与深、穗建成 1 小时交通圈。2008 年全市规模以上工业固定资产原值 2848. 43 亿元，镇（街）、村（社区）、组三级净资产累积达到 1402. 54 亿元。

图六　1978–2008 年全社会固定资产投资总额

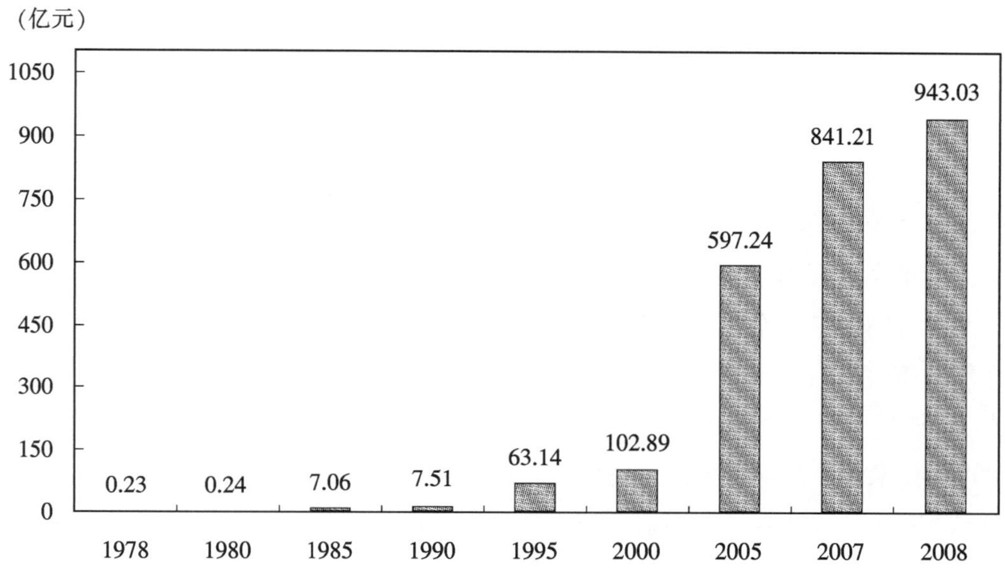

五、解放思想对外开放，开辟了对外经济新天地

60 年来，东莞经济发展经历了由封闭走向开放的历程。1949 -1978 年间，由于当时的国际环境与国内计划经济体制等多方面因素，对外贸易处于半封闭状态，发展速度缓慢。党的十一届三中全会以后，东莞乘改革开放的东风，充分利用地缘优势和政策优势，积极承接港澳地区制造业转移，大力发展“三来一补”贸易并开始注重引进外资，对外贸易得到长足的发展，形成了全方位、多层次、多形式的对外开放格局，取得了丰硕的成果。

改革开放 30 年，东莞对外贸易蓬勃发展，成为促进东莞经济快速发展的重要支柱，外贸出口在较高平台保持平稳快速发展，保证了这一时期东莞经济成为改革开放以来少有的快速增长期。1978 年东莞出口总额不到 0. 4 亿美元，1991 年突破 10 亿美元，1997 年突破 100 亿美元，2008 年达到了 655. 37 亿美元。2001 年我国正式加入世界贸易组织，东莞对外贸易迈上新台阶。东莞进出口总额 2002 年比 2001 年增加近百亿美元，2007 年突破千亿美元，到 2008 年，东莞进出口总额达 1132. 99 亿美元，比 2000 年翻了近两番；出口总额 655. 37 亿美元，是 2000 年的 3. 8 倍；进口总额 477. 62 亿美元，是 2000 年的 3. 2 倍。2008 年东莞进出口总额占全国的比重为 4. 42%，占全省的比重为 16. 58%，其中出口占全国的比重为4.59%，占全省的比重为16.22%。改革开放30年，中国跻身国际贸易主要大国，广东跻身对外贸易大省，东莞功不可没。

图七　1952–2008年出口总额

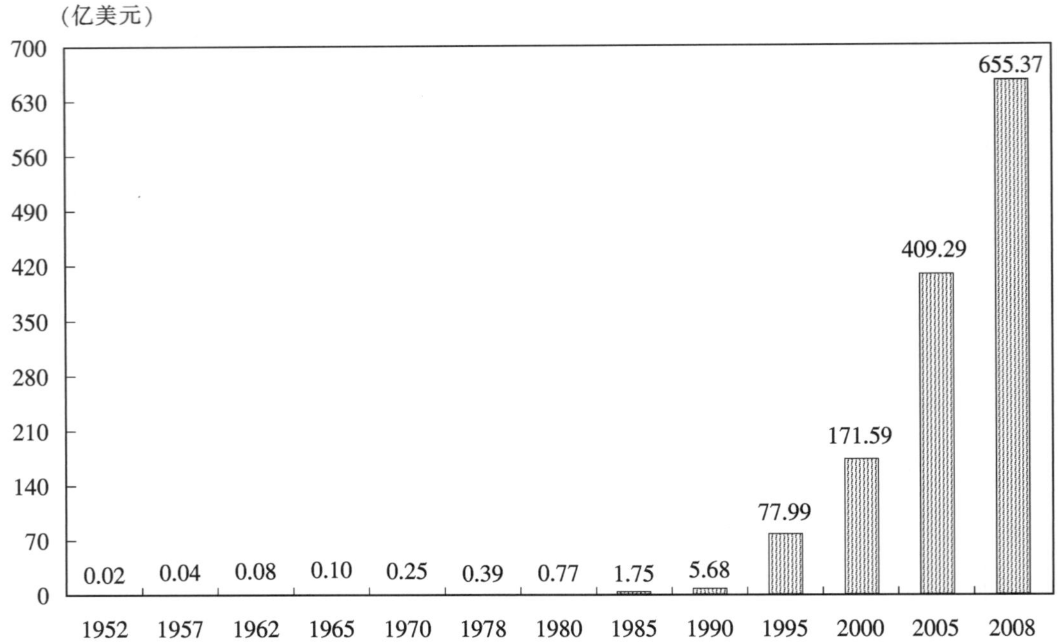

建国之初到1978年，东莞利用外资渠道单一，规模很小。改革开放以来，利用外资在近乎空白的基础上迅速发展。随着1978年全国第一家来料加工厂——太平手袋厂落户东莞，就此拉开了东莞利用外资的序幕。1979–2008年，全市累计实际利用外资（不含对外借款）423.58亿美元，平均每年14亿美元。1979年共签订来料加工项目140宗，实际利用外资（不含对外借款，下同）173万美元，发展到1990年的2.43亿美元，到1999年的14.57亿美元，再到2008年的32.26亿美元。随着东莞经济实力的增强和管理技术水平的提高，以“借船出海”、“筑巢引凤”为特点的对外经济合作逐步转型升级。东莞的外资来源已由改革开放初期单一的港资转变为呈多元化发展的态势。针对加工贸易占全市贸易主导地位的实际，东莞对外开放在致力于量扩张的同时，也着重引进技术含量高的项目，投资规模不断扩大，从劳动密集型向资本密集型和技术密集型转移，不少设备和产品已达到世界先进水平，在国内外市场有较强的竞争力。世界级的大财团、大公司、跨国公司纷纷落户东莞，全世界排名前100位的企业已有13家在东莞投资办厂，如杜邦、雀巢、赫司特、汤母逊、菲利浦、太古集团、诺基亚、京瓷、美能达、索尼、新日铁、住友、通用电气等国际性大公司都在这里投资办厂或进行技术合作。

六、居民收入大幅提高，实现了百姓生活由“量”变到“质”变

60年来，城乡居民生活伴随着国民经济迅速发展发生了深刻的变化，尤其是改革开放以来，经济的持续快速增长，为人民生活水平的迅速提高创造了物质条件，人们的衣、食、住、行等方面发生了根本性的变化。

收入水平快速提高。1952年城乡居民储蓄存款余额28.7万元。1978年城乡居民储蓄存款余额0.54亿元，农民人均纯收入只有149元。2008年城市居民人均可支配收入30275元，比1978年增长94倍，年均增长16.4%；农民人均纯收入12328元，比1978年增长81.7倍，年均增长15.9%；城乡居民储蓄存款余额2638.04亿元，比1952年增长91.9万倍，比1978年增长4884倍，年均增长32.7%。

图八　1979-2008 年实际利用外资情况

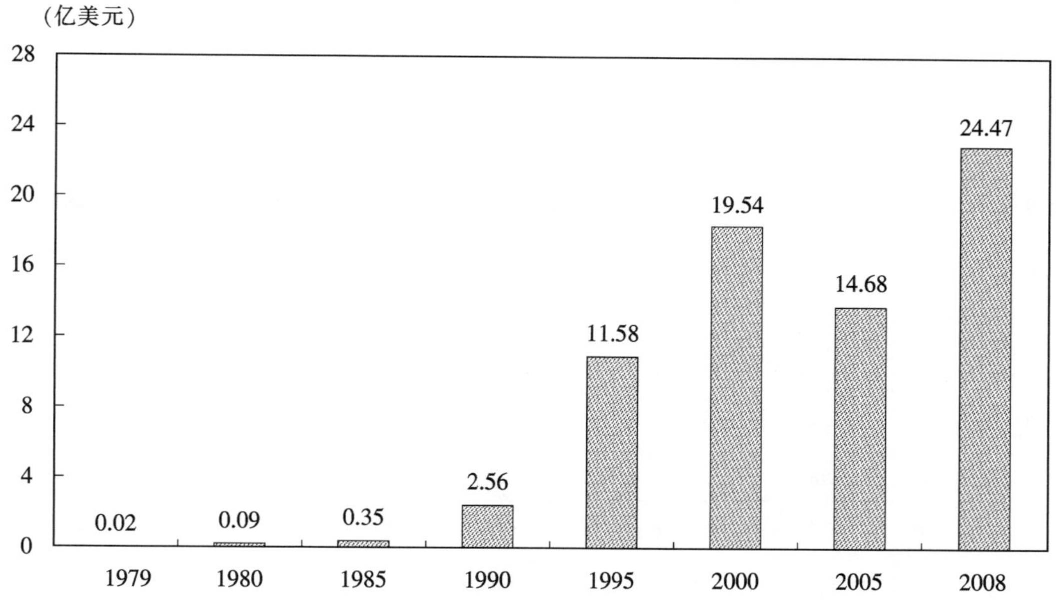

图九　1978-2008 年城乡居民储蓄存款余额

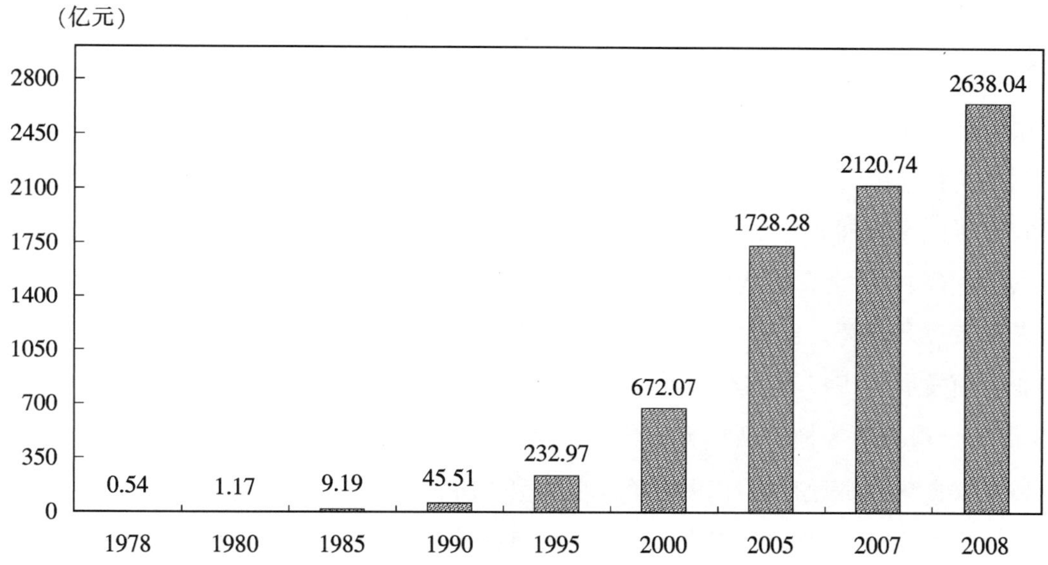

图十　1985-2008 年城市居民人均可支配收入

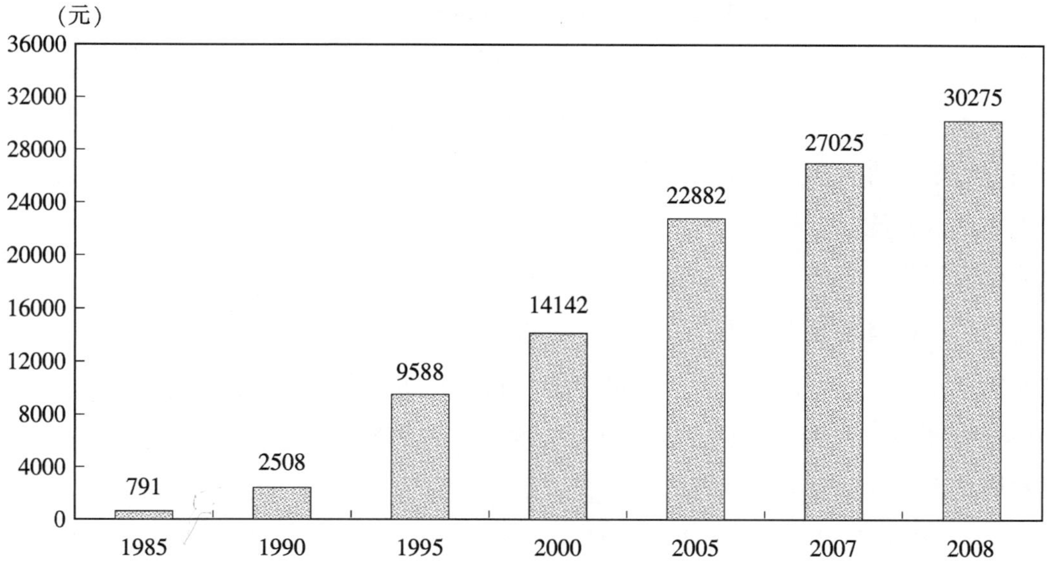

图十一　1978-2008年农民人均纯收入

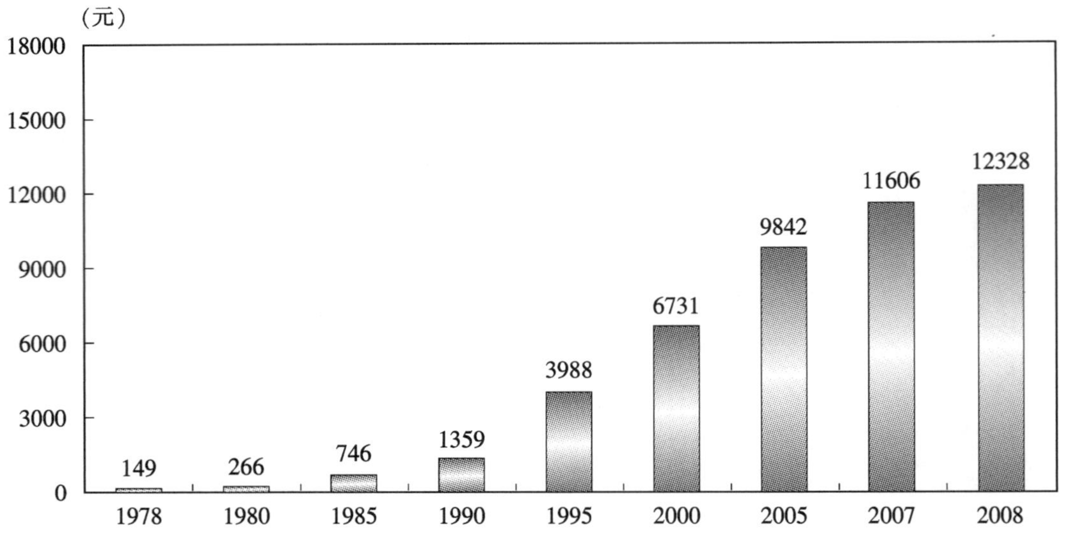

生活方式发生根本性变化。城市居民人均住房使用面积由1985年的10.98平方米增加到2008年的40.25平方米，耐用消费品越来越高档。城市居民人均消费性支出由1985年的689元增加到2008年的23208元，年均增长16.5%；老百姓的生活从解决温饱到全面小康，高档消费品从改革开放前的手表、自行车、缝纫机"老三大件"，逐渐演变到九十年代的电视机、电冰箱、洗衣机"新三大件"，到今天的家用电脑、组合音响、移动电话、家用汽车等现代高档消费品。2008年每百户城市居民家庭拥有家用空调200台，组合音响59套，移动电话248部，家用电脑100台，彩电180台，家用汽车47辆。每百户农村居民家庭拥有彩电183台，洗衣机107台，淋浴热水器142台，移动电话261部，影碟机95台，家用空调234台，家用电脑97台。

七、振兴科技提升教育，实现了科教事业的大发展

教育事业全面发展。1949年东莞有小学481所，中学8所，师范1所，在校学生共5.5万人。经过60年的建设，全市教育规模不断扩大，各项教育事业协调发展，文盲率大幅下降，义务教育普及率不断提高，高等教育规模迅速扩张。1978年有小学794所，中学39所，师范一所，在校学生共23.77万人，专任教师9316人。1988年升格地级市以后，教育加快发展，当年教育投入1.15亿元，1989年普及九年义务教育，1995年在全省率先普及高中阶段教育。建立了幼儿教育、基础教育、职业教育、成人教育、高等教育等各阶段教育比较完整的国民教育体系。2008年全市有幼儿园617所，小学352所，适龄儿童入学率达100%，本市户籍毕业生升学率达100%。初中139所，初中在校学生18.45万人，户籍适龄少年入学率为99.15%，毕业率为99.78%。全市有高中阶段学校67所，在校学生10.94万人；普通高等院校4所，在校学生2.87万人。教育布局得到优化，教学条件得到较大改善，普及高中阶段教育工作深入实施。

科技事业硕果累累。中华人民共和国成立初期，东莞科技事业基本上是空白。经过60年特别是改革开放以来的努力，科技教育事业飞速发展，自主创新能力持续增强，科技成果举世瞩目，一些技术领域取得世界先进水平。改革开放以后，积极实施"科教兴市"战略，科技事业迅速发展，创新能力不断提高。1988年出现第一家民科企业，1994年出现第一家高新技术企业，此后，民营科技和高新技术企业不断发展壮大，一批著名企业如广东彩管、东莞伟易达、五星太阳能、中成化工等不断涌现出来。2008年东莞获批国家高新技术企业153家，新增省民营科技企业55家，总数已经达到470家。

2008 年建成公共技术创新平台 6 个。新增省级企业工程中心和技术中心 11 个，总数达 34 个。新认定省专业镇和专业镇技术创新平台各 2 个，总数分别达到 11 个和 10 个。新增企业博士后科研工作站 4 家。2008 年获国家和省资助项目 110 个。全市高新技术产业工业总产值 2403 亿元，占全市工业总产值的 33.4%。2008 年专利申请量 14406 件、授权量 8093 件，分别比 1990 年增长 422.7 倍和 268.8 倍。

八、繁荣卫生、文化、体育事业，奏响了民生和谐乐章

卫生事业长足发展。老有所养，病有所医是人民最关心、最直接、最现实的利益问题，也是政府孜孜以求的目标。1949 年东莞仅有卫生医疗机构 5 个，病床数 219 张，卫生技术人员 156 人，东莞城乡缺医少药，医疗设施落后。1978 年有卫生医疗机构 82 个，病床 2257 张，卫生技术人员 2636 人。改革开放后，东莞开始进行较大规模的卫生基础设施建设，医疗机构、先进设备、技术人员逐年增加，2008 年全市有医疗机构 2106 个，比 1978 年增长 24.7 倍；卫生技术人员 33113 人，增长 11.6 倍；病床数 16778 张，增长 6.4 倍。全市建成并投入使用的社区卫生服务机构 318 个，其中社区卫生服务中心 33 个，社区卫生服务站 285 个，覆盖了全市 300 多个村（社区）。先后消灭了天花、鼠疫、丝虫病、麻风病，控制了脊髓灰质炎、白喉、百日咳、乙脑、麻疹等传染病，人民群众的健康水平大幅提高。

文化事业蓬勃发展。解放初期，东莞文化体系不健全，文化生活单调，全市文化设施数量很少而且简陋，1949 年全县仅有电影院 3 座，其他文化设施均为空白。发展到 1978 年，陆续增加了文化馆、图书馆、广播站等设施，但仍然很难满足人民群众的文化需求。党的十一届三中全会以来，东莞重视文化建设，先后共投入 15 亿元建设文化设施，大剧院、展览馆、图书馆、群众艺术馆、岭南画院等文化设施相继落成。投入 40 多亿元建成镇村文化中心 80 个，图书馆（室）367 个、文化广场 360 个、电影院和影剧院 49 间，市、镇、村三级文化设施网络初步形成。定期举办以高雅艺术和知识普及为特色的“文化周末”、“文化高地直播车”、“东莞学习论坛”、“读书节”、“图书流动服务车”，各镇村举办了特色鲜明的广场文化活动。2008 年全市有群众艺术馆 1 个，文化站 33 个，公共图书馆 387 个，博物馆 23 个，文化广场 653 个，艺术表演场所 62 个，电影放映单位 40 个，网吧 1056 间，公共文化设施建筑面积 626 万平方米。全市有公共广播节目 66 套，公共电视节目 37 套。广播、电视综合覆盖率均达到 100%。2008 年出版报纸 6647.3 万份，各类杂志 158.32 万册，图书 5.6 万册，《东莞日报》发行量 4380 万份，电影放映 1.29 万场次，观众 320.56 万人次。

体育事业成绩斐然。1956 年，东莞籍举重运动员陈镜开成为新中国第一个打破世界纪录的运动员。伴随着经济和社会的发展，东莞体育事业也呈现蓬勃发展的局面，体育设施不断完善，竞技体育成果丰硕。改革开放前东莞仅有游泳、篮球、足球运动等几十个体育设施，目前东莞拥有网球、射击、保龄球、高尔夫球场、各类健身房、举重馆、乒乓球馆、羽毛球馆等几千个各类大型完善的体育设施。1994 年创办全国首个篮球俱乐部，承办了多次上规模的世界比赛，竞技比赛取得好成绩，2008 年东莞运动员共获得 68 枚金牌、71 枚银牌、55 枚铜牌。其中夺得国际赛金牌 3 枚；夺得亚洲赛金牌 1 枚；夺得全国赛金牌 16 枚；夺得广东省赛金牌 49 枚、银牌 71 枚、铜牌 55 枚。近年来，东莞坚持发展群众体育，醒狮、龙舟、万人长跑等成为东莞每年的品牌活动，各镇街、各学校、各单位举行的运动会也逐年增多。2008 年举办市级综合和单项比赛 11 次，参加人数 3000 人次；举办全民健身活动 33 次，参加人数 2.60 万人次。全市有体育彩票发行网点 430 个，销售总额 3.47 亿元，体彩公益金 2702 万元。

回顾 60 年来的东莞经济社会发展取得的巨大成就，归纳起来，有如下几条主要经验：

1. 始终坚持对外开放不动摇是东莞经济社会实现跨越发展的重要保证

纵观东莞 60 年的发展历程，经济社会的辉煌成就主要是改革开放以后取得的。1978 年东莞地区生产总值（GDP）只有6.11亿元，改革开放后，经济迅猛发展，2002年GDP超过一千亿元，2005年超过两千亿元，2007年超过三千亿元。改革开放后东莞GDP年均增长19.2%，东莞的发展成果得益于改革开放。全国第一家“三来一补”企业——太平手袋厂落户东莞，拉开了东莞对外开放的序幕，改革开放从根本上改变了我市封闭落后的和沉闷僵化的状况，打破了束缚人们的思想桎梏，调动了人民群众的积极性，大大解放了生产力，有力地推动了经济社会的大发展，使经济社会充满蓬勃生机和活力，只有长期坚持改革开放不动摇，才是经济发展和社会进步的永恒动力，才是富民强市的正确道路。东莞人民具有海纳百川、厚德务实的优良传统和智慧，只要改革开放不动摇，东莞经济社会发展将不断实现新跨越。

2. 始终勇立时代潮头是东莞经济社会实现跨越发展的重要推动力

新中国成立60年来，特别是改革开放30年以来，东莞始终坚持解放思想，开拓创新，始终走在时代的前列，东莞改革开放30年的发展史可以说是我国改革开放的一段浓缩史，东莞在全国首先开展商品流通和价格的市场化改革，在所有制的改革上先行一步。一方面，努力探索公有制有效的实现形式。按照现代企业制度，对公有制企业进行规范化的公司制改革，提高公有资本的控制力和竞争力，并建立制度严密的国有资产监督和营运体系，防止资产流失，实现资产增值。另一方面，大力鼓励和支持非公有制经济发展。东莞在利用外资方面多次在全国首开先河。全国首创的东莞县来料加工装配办公室成立，一个窗口办公、一条龙服务的服务型政府为东莞经济装上了发展的“加速器”。正是东莞人这种勇于探索、敢为人先的精神推动了东莞经济社会的跨越发展。

3. 始终坚持以科学发展观为指导是确保东莞经济社会又好又快发展的根本途径

东莞60年来的发展，特别是改革开放30年来的经验告诉我们，只有坚持以科学发展观为指导，按照统筹城乡发展，统筹区域发展、统筹经济社会发展、统筹人与自然和谐发展的要求，都能确保东莞经济社会又好又快地发展。党的十六大以来，东莞市委、市政府认真贯彻落实党的创新理论，坚持以科学发展观为指导，全面推进经济、政治、文化建设，努力构建和谐社会，使经济社会发展不断迈上新台阶。近年来，东莞不断调整优化产业结构，转变经济发展方式，着力构建现代产业体系，我市产业结构日趋优化，第三产业成为拉动全市经济增长的主要动力。东莞不断推进区域协调发展，坚持产业合理布局与人力资源优化配置相结合，扎实推进“双转型”和“双转移”工作。市委、市政府坚持以人为本，重视民生建设，建设社会主义和谐社会。在国际经济危机的背景下，东莞认真贯彻落实全省“三促进一保持”的中心任务，把保增长、调结构、促发展作为重中之重来抓，出台了扩大内需、刺激经济的措施，落实“五个10亿”帮扶企业渡过难关，确保经济平稳增长。实践证明，只有坚持以科学发展观为指导，经济社会才能经得起复杂形势和困难的考验，保持又好又快向前发展。

60年风雨历程铸就辉煌成就，东莞由农业大县发展成为一座实力强盛、环境优美、文化繁荣、社会和谐的现代化都市，城市功能和城市面貌发生了翻天覆地变化。如今，顶着“中国经济综合实力百强城市”、“中国最具经济活力城市”、“中国最佳魅力城市”、“中国优秀旅游城市”、“国家卫生城市”、“国家篮球城市”、“国际花园城市”、“全国绿化模范城市”和“全国文明城市”等多个光环的东莞，正大步迈向“经济社会双转型”的新道路。我们相信，在未来，面对新形势、新任务、新机遇、新挑战，东莞人民也会满怀信心，在东莞市委、市政府的正确领导下，以科学发展观统领经济社会发展全局，推进经济社会双转型，建设富强和谐新东莞，团结拼搏，扎实苦干，东莞的明天将会更加辉煌。

新莞人的工作与生活状况有待改善

Working and living conditions of New Dongguan Citizens need to be improved

为全面了解和掌握新莞人在东莞的居住、教育、就业等有关情况，以及金融危机对新莞人的工作和生活等方面的影响，及时为市委、市政府及有关部门进行科学决策提供依据。国家统计局广东调查总队与东莞市统计局于2009年7月联合开展了第二次的“新莞人”基本情况调查。

一、抽样原则和调查的内容与方式

本次调查采用随机抽样原则，在全市抽取33个镇（街），65个村（居）委，131个调查小区，回收有效调查问卷2013份。调查内容包括居住情况、子女及成人教育情况、收入、社会保障和其他情况等。调查方式采取调查员直接入户，根据调查对象的意见进行填报。

二、调查对象

在调查对象中，男性较多，占调查总人数的64.1%；中青年占的比例较高，其中年龄以21—30岁为主，占42.8%；31—40岁，占37.2%；来自省外的新莞人最多，占75.0%；受教育程度主要是初中、中高（含中专），占79.6%；在东莞工作居住的时间以5年以上至10年的为主，占25.0%；职业主要是雇员，占70.0%。调查对象的基本情况具体如表1所示：

表1　调查对象的基本情况（%）

性别		年龄				
男	女	16-20岁	21-30岁	31-40岁	41-50岁	50岁以上
64.1	35.9	6.4	42.8	37.2	11.4	2.2
户籍		受教育程度				
省内	省外	小学及以下	初中	高中（包括中专）	大专	本科及以上
25	75	8.5	46.4	33.2	9.2	2.7
在东莞居住的时间						
半年以上-1年	1年以上-3年	3年以上-5年	5年以上-10年	10年以上-15年	15年以上-20年	20年以上
11.0	23.6	20.5	25.0	15.1	4.5	0.4
职业						
雇员	雇主	自由职业者	家务劳动者	其他	没有职业	
70.0	11.6	12.0	1.2	2.9	2.3	

三、居住情况

1. 大部分新莞人以租赁私人房和单位提供的免费住房为主，住房面积较小，部分新莞人对目前居住条件不太满意

新莞人由于受经济条件的限制，无经济能力购买房子，唯一以低价位的租赁私人房和普通楼房为主。居住在普通楼房的占59.4%，居住在单元房的占23.6%。住房面积大多数（78.2%）在60平方米以下，其中30平方米及以下占53.1%，31-60平方米的占25.1%。住房的产权类型主要是租赁私人房，占62.5%；其次是工作单位提供的免费住房，占30.3%；只有1.2%住在廉租房。新莞人总体

上对目前居住条件实际可以接受，其中对居住条件表示满意的有32.7%，表示一般的为54.1%。

新莞人主要居住在低价位的租赁房，每月需付房租集中在100－300元（占57.5%）和300－600元（占17.6%）。对于房租的价格，过半（52.2%）的被访者认为合适，46.6%认为高。新莞人租房的最主要原因是为了生活便利（占28.8%）和能够与家人或朋友住在一起（占28.5%），其次是离工作地点近（22.8%）。

2. 希望租住政府提供的廉租房的比例有所上升，低文化群体对租住廉租房反映不够积极

东莞政府计划对低收入群体提供廉租房。对于政府提供的廉租房，54.4%的受访者表示会租住，租住的比例不太高，但仍比去年上升5.4个百分点。一般来讲，文化程度越低的群体经济状况越差，理应更积极地租住廉租房，但是，据调查，小学及以下文化的群体只有40.4%希望租住政府提供的廉租房，初中文化的比例为50.6%，高中（包括中专）文化的比例为58.7%，大专的比例为66.7%，本科及以上的比例为70.4%。调查显示，文化程度越低的群体表示会租住政府提供廉租房的比例却越低，这与文化程度越低的群体对社会的接触面少，对政府的廉租房政策相关信息不太了解。因此，如果政府要针对低收入群体提供廉租房，还应向低收入、低文化群体大力宣传相关的政策。

从收入来看，不同收入的群体希望租住政府提供的廉租房的比例并无明显差异。

3. 新莞人对廉租房面积的期望不高，但希望廉租房租金便宜些

由于大多数新莞人的收入水平都不高，他们对廉租房面积的期望也不太高。据调查，被访者最希望政府提供廉租房的面积在31－60平方米的占39.1%；希望廉租房面积在61－80平方米的占25.5%，希望廉租房面积在30平方米及以下的占14.5%，81－100平方米的占12.9%，100平方米以上的只占8.9%。

从廉租房的租金来看，占多数（66.1%）的被访者希望政府提供的廉租房租金在5元及以下/平方米，希望廉租房租金在5－10元/平方米的占25.3%，希望廉租房租金在11—15元/平方米与希望租金在16元/平方米以上的比例为4.3%。

4. 新莞人购房意愿上升，高文化和高收入群体购房意愿相对强烈，但期望的房价较低

在东莞拥有自己的住房是许多长期在东莞工作的新莞人的梦想。调查显示，有28.9%的受访者打算今后在东莞购房，比去年高7.3个百分点，但仍有绝大多数人不打算购房。从文化程度来看，文化程度越高的群体打算购房的比例越高，显示出高文化程度群体的经济状况较好，对未来的信心较足。（详见图1所示）

图1　不同文化群体打算购房的比例

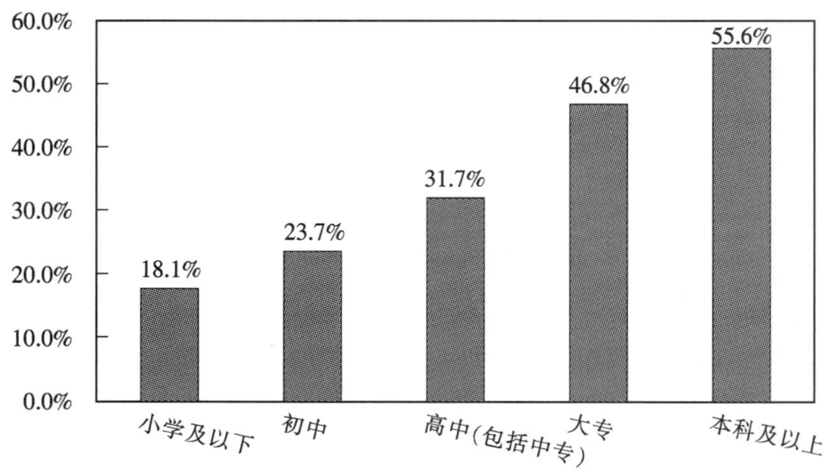

收入越高的群体购房欲望也越高，个人月收入在1000元及以下组的新莞人表示今后将购买住房的比例为22.9%，月收入在1001－3000元组中有购买意向者的比例为27.1%，而3000元以上组的受访者有购买意向的比例为50.2%。

受访者打算购房的面积则主要集中在60－120平方米，其中61－80平方米占16.9%，81－100平方米占37.7%，101—120平方米占24.3%。对于可接受的房价，受访者期望房价较低，89.6%的受访者表示在每平方米3500元以下，其中2500元及以下的占63.3%，2501—3500元的占26.3%。

5. 购买住房的主要原因是为了在东莞发展，但房价高严重制约了新莞人购房

长期租房存在着诸多的不便，部分有能力的新莞人计划购买住房。打算今后在东莞购房的被访者中，有75.9%购买住房的原因是为了在东莞发展；其次是为了工作方便（50.8%）；第三是为了子女教育（49.2%）；第四是为了提高家人生活质量（47.3%）；为了投资（21.3%）和其他（0.5%）的比例很小。

但房价高企严重制约了新莞人的购房意愿。调查显示，不打算在东莞购房的被访者中，有70.1%不打算购房的原因是东莞房价太高，负担不起；其次是因为今后不一定在东莞发展（42.0%）；第三是因为目前工作不稳定（31.8%）；目前已经购买了住房（6.6%）和自己或家人不适应东莞的生活环境（7.3%）的比例很小。

四、子女及成人教育情况

1. 教育费用高，负担沉重成为新莞人子女教育中存在的最主要问题

由于教育费用高，招生制度不公平，没时间照顾子女等原因，大多数的新莞人家庭都没有子女在东莞接受教育，只有22.8%的新莞人家庭有子女在东莞接受教育。子女在东莞接受教育的新莞人家庭中，有43.3%需要交赞助费或借读费。58.9%的被访者表示子女在东莞教育支出的负担过重，41.1%表示可以承受或不算负担。对于目前新莞人子女教育中存在的主要问题，这些家庭中有62.8%认为主要是“教育费用高，负担沉重”，其次是“新莞人子女难以享受国家义务教育”（55.4%），以及“目前的招生制度不公平”（42.4%），其他情况详见图2所示。

图2　新莞人子女教育中存在的主要问题

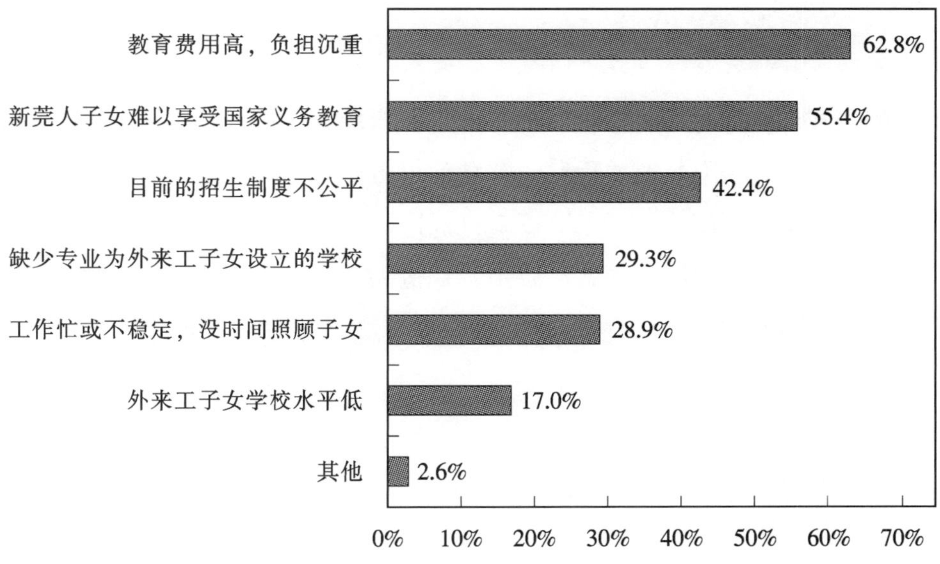

2. 新莞人子女在东莞就读的学校最需要改进教师素质

由于公办学校的门槛较高，在东莞接受教育的新莞人子女中，有68%就读民办学校，32%就读公办学校。这些学校的教师素质、办学水平、管理规范程度和教学设施都参差不平。据调查，有63.5%的被访者反映新莞人子女在东莞就读的学校最需要改进教师素质，其次需要改进管理规范（52.4%）和办学水平（50.4%），详见图3所示。

图3　新莞人子女在东莞就读的学校有待改进的方面

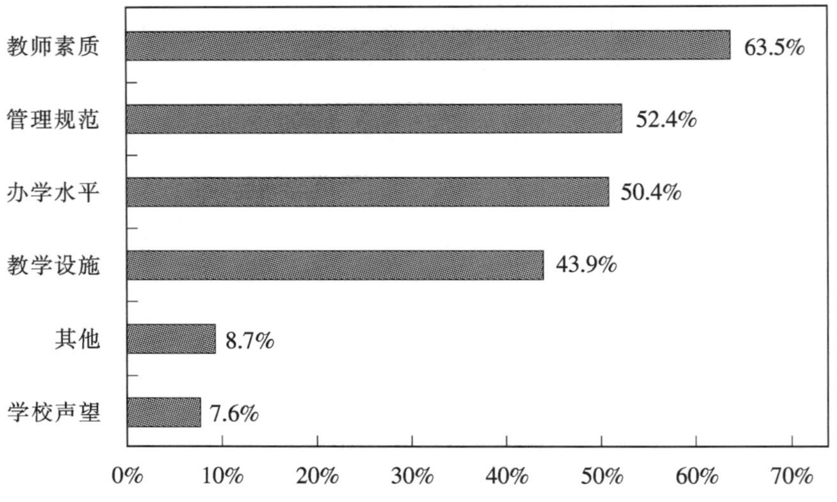

3. 成人教育对改善工作环境或收入有较大帮助，但新莞人在东莞接受过成人教育的比例很低

成人教育对改善工作环境或收入是非常重要的，特别是对于文化程度较低的群体。在这个问题上，新莞人似乎有些忽视。据调查，有13.2%的新莞人家中的成员在东莞接受过成人教育，比去年增加4.6个百分点，但比例仍然很低。在东莞接受的成人教育中，有65.7%属于专业技术资格或职称类培训，14.7%属于学历类培训（函授、电大等），31.3%属于劳动技能培训，其他占4.2%。接受成人教育学习的费用，全部由单位支付的占38.1%，单位支付部分的占11.3%，完全由个人支付的占50.6%。大多数（84.9%）的被访者表示家庭成员接受成人教育后对改善工作环境或提高收入有帮助。

五、就业、社会保障和归属认同感情况

1. 新莞人在东莞的工作机会多，工作不够稳定，失业后会继续在东莞寻找工作机会

东莞的社会经济比较繁荣，就业机会多，是外地人寻找工作的理想之地。但是，由于大多数新莞人从事的是劳动密集型的工作，技术含量较低，劳动的可替代性强，新莞人工作的稳定性相对较低。据调查，96%的新莞人在东莞有工作，但只有43%的新莞人工作稳定，过半（57%）的被访者在东莞工作不够稳定。在被访的失业者中，过半（57.0%）的被访者表示会继续在东莞寻找工作机会，20.3%的被访者会回老家发展，20.3%的被访者去珠三角其它城市发展。可以看出，由于东莞的就业机会较多，东莞还是新莞人寻找就业机会的首选。

2. 国际金融危机对新莞人的影响主要体现在经济收入方面

国际金融危机对在东莞工作的新莞人的影响较大，主要影响表现在对经济收入的影响，占60.7%；影响工作稳定性，占10.5%。另外，有21.5%的被访者表示无影响，详见图4所示。

图 4　国际金融危机对在东莞工作的新莞人的影响

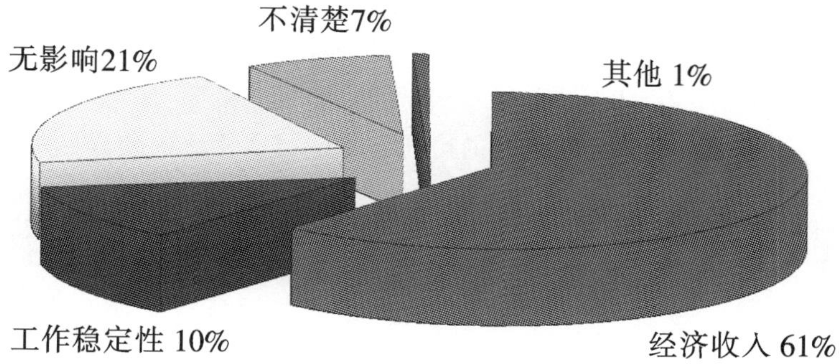

3. 新莞人享受社会保障的比例不高，与本地同事的最主要差别在于社保福利方面

由于我国的社会保障体制还不够完善，加上人们的法律意识和自我保护意识不强，只有部分（62.7%）在东莞工作的新莞人与用人单位或雇主签订了劳动合同，其中，签订固定期限合同的占48.8%，签订不固定期限（长期）合同的占13.9%。参加社会保险的比例不高，只有51.1%的新莞人享有医疗保险，49.1%享有工伤保险，43.2%享有养老保险，其他情况详见图5所示。

图 5　享有各种保险项目的比例

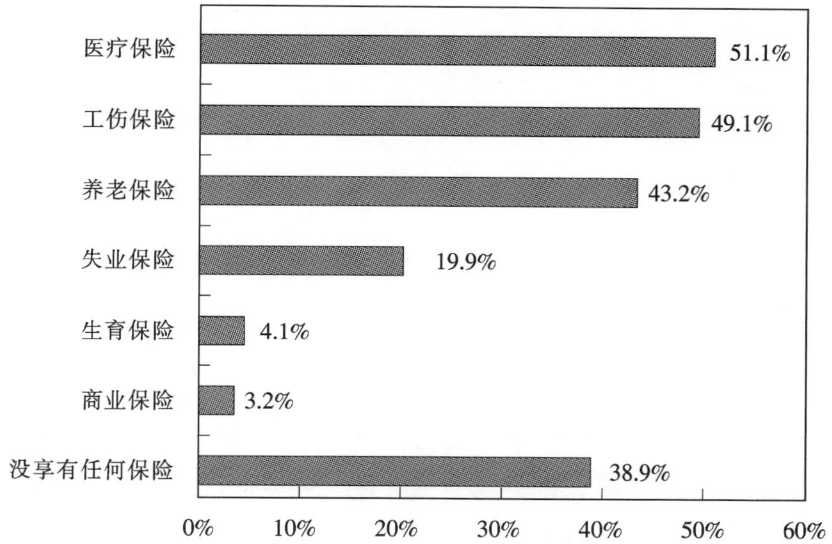

新莞人与本地同事的待遇也有差别。据调查，有53%的被访者认为在单位的待遇与本地同事相比有差异，47%认为无差异。与本地同事相比的主要差别在于福利社保方面，有24.2%的被访者认为如此。在其他方面的差异不大，详见图6所示。

4. 新莞人对东莞的归属认同感相对较模糊，但觉得本地人对待自己的态度较好，赚钱后首选继续在东莞发展

对于是否有归属认同感这个问题，较多新莞人的看法比较模糊，他们对归属认同感不太确定，处于比较尴尬的状态。调查显示，相对较多（44.9%）的新莞人对于是否有归属认同感说不清，42.8%的新莞人对东莞有归属认同感，只有12.3%没有归属认同感，新莞人对东莞的归属认同感说不清的比例最高，明确表示没有的比例其实也很低。对比刚来的时候，有69.4%的被访者觉得目前本地人对待新莞人的态度一直比较好或比以前好，只有2.0%的被访者认为比以前差。可以看出，虽然新莞人对东莞有归属认同感的比例不算高，但由于东莞的经济发达，就业机会相对较多，本地人对待新莞人的

态度较好等各种原因，新莞人在东莞赚钱后的首选仍然是继续在东莞发展。调查显示，有46.2%的新莞人表示赚钱后打算继续在东莞发展，远远高于其他选择；回原籍发展是第二选择，比例为22.2%；去北京、长三角地区以及其他地方发展的比例非常小；另有两成多的新莞人对于发展去向还没确定。

图6　新莞人在单位的待遇与本地同事相比的差异

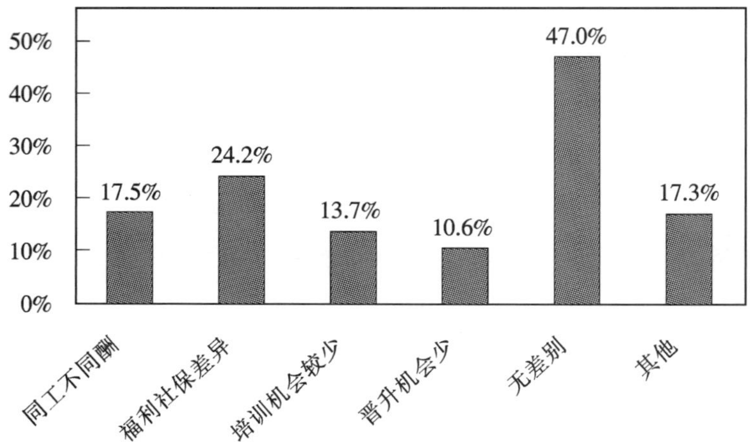

5. 新莞人最需要在社会保障方面得到政府的政策支持

大多数的新莞人都是相对弱势的群体，他们大多在东莞没有住房，收入不高，户籍不在东莞，社会保障、子女教育还存在较多问题，得到的待遇也不够公平等，因此，他们需要得到政府的政策支持。据调查，新莞人最需要得到政府政策支持的是社会保障（养老、住房、医疗、工伤保险等），占74.3%，然后是公平待遇（66.5%）和子女教育（50.6%），详见图7所示。

图7　新莞人最需要得到政府政策支持的方面

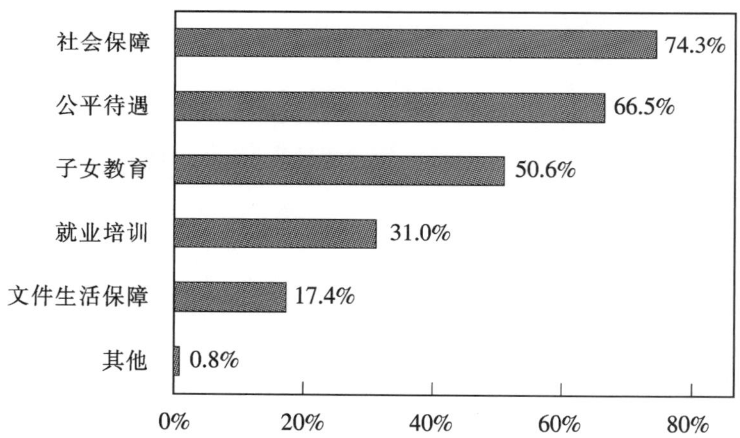

六、收入支出和生活消费情况

1. 新莞人的收入和支出均偏低，寄（带）回家乡的钱很少

接受调查的新莞人中只有一成是雇主，其余的都是雇员、自由职业和家务劳动者或没有职业者，他们的个人月均收入主要集中在1001－2000元（占48.8%）和1000元以下（21.5%）。家庭月均收入主要集中在1001－2000元（占38.4%）和2001－3000元（23.9%），详见表2所示。按上限公式计算的个人月均收入的中位数只有1531元，只有2008年东莞市城镇在岗职工的月平均工资（3293元）的46.5%。家庭月均收入的中位数为2061.2元，可以看出，新莞人的个人和家庭月均收入均

偏低。

表 2　2009 年上半年新莞人的月均收入分组比例

单位:%

项目	1000以下元	1001 - 2000 元	2001 - 3000 元	3001 - 4000 元	4001 - 5000 元	5001 - 10000 元	10001元以上	无收入	合计
个人	21.5	48.8	15.7	5.7	3.1	1.8	0.7	2.6	100
家庭	9.9	38.4	23.9	11.8	6.6	6.3	2.4	0.5	100

由于新莞人的收入较低，新莞人大多很节俭，尽量把消费支出降到最低，以期多剩余些钱，因为大部分（73%）的新莞人还需要寄（带）钱回家乡。调查显示，新莞人的家庭月均支出集中在 501 - 1000 元（占 32.4%）和 1001 - 2000（33.6%）元，详见表 3 所示。按上限公式计算的家庭月均支出的中位数为 1106.5 元。一年寄回（带回）家乡的钱的中位数为 3677.6 元，可以看出，新莞人一年能够寄回（带回）家乡的钱并不多。

表 3　2009 年上半年的月均支出的分组比例

单位:%

项目	500 元以下	501 - 1000 元	1001 - 2000 元	2001 - 3000 元	3001 - 4000 元	4001 - 10000 元	10001元以上	合计
家庭	14.0	32.4	33.6	10.5	5.5	3.1	0.7	100

2. 新莞人消费水平偏低，食品消费占首位，低价位的耐用消费品偏多

大多新莞人的经济状况都比较拮据，他们的收入主要是应付最基本的日常生活，主要用在吃饭、住房等基本消费，对其他消费不敢有太多的奢望。按照被访者消费的多少顺序选出家庭平时消费最多的项目，以第一回答的比例高低来排序，可以得出，家庭平时消费最多的是食品，有 70.5% 的被访者认为食品是平时消费最多的项目，远远高于其他；第二位是住房费用（8.6%），第三位是教育费用（4.8%），详见表 4 所示。

表 4　家庭平时消费最多的项目

项　目	第一回答的比例（%）
食品	70.5
住房费用	8.6
教育费用	4.8
家庭设备用品及服务	4.7
衣着	4.3
交通与通讯	2.8
医疗保健	2.3
娱乐休闲费用	1.9

新莞人家庭拥有的耐用消费品也多是低价位的，最多的是电视机，有 93.0% 的被访者拥有，第二是电脑（44.2%），第三是电冰箱（39.4%），拥有钢琴、汽车等高档消费品的比例很小。值得关注的是，拥有电脑的比例排在了第二位，说明现在的新莞人比较重视学习知识和关心现代信息，这是一个

可喜的现象。

图 8　新莞人家庭拥有的耐用消费品

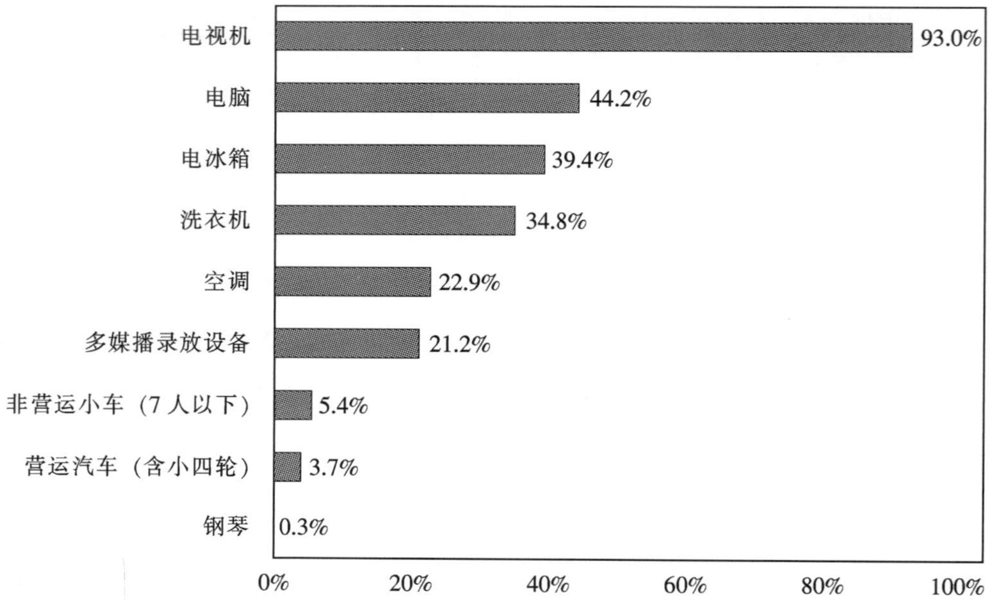

七、对政府的期望和建议

本次调查得到新莞人的大力支持和密切配合，他们对政府提出了许多期望和建议，归纳如下：

1. 创造良好的治安环境。社会治安问题是这次调查反映最多的问题，许多新莞人都希望有关部门能够创造良好的治安环境，严厉打击犯罪分子。

2. 解决公平待遇问题。公平待遇问题是新莞人反映第二多的问题。新莞人非常希望能够获得公平待遇，与本地市民享有平等的福利待遇和社会保障。同时，还希望政府出台避免户籍歧视的措施，取消或放松入户限制，取消或降低某些费用（例如暂住证办证费等）。

3. 关心新莞人子女教育和成人教育问题。新莞人子女教育和成人教育问题在新莞人反映的问题中居于第三。新莞人希望政府多关心新莞人子女教育问题，使新莞人子女能享受义务教育，并改善民办学校及外来工子女学校的教学质量。同时，还希望政府能够为新莞人提供免费的技能培训，以及为新莞人提供更多的就业机会。

4. 提供文化生活保障。新莞人大多远离家乡、文化生活单调，因此，希望政府提供更多免费的文化娱乐设施，丰富新莞人的业余文化生活。

5. 改善住房条件。新莞人大多收入较低、居住条件不太好，希望政府向新莞人提供更多的廉租房，降低新莞人的生活成本。同时，希望政府建设经济适用房并给予新莞人一定的购房优惠政策。

6. 加强公共管理。希望政府改善空气污染和水污染情况，保护公共环境；改善公共交通系统，方便市民出行；加强食品安全监督管理；提高行政部门的办事效率。

7. 加大对企业的扶持力度。经济危机对企业造成了一定的影响，希望政府加大对企业的扶持力度，减少经济危机的不利影响，提高经济活力。另外，还希望有关部门加强劳动合同管理，协调企业与雇员之间的劳资关系。

第二部分　统计资料

Part Two　Statistics

一、综　合

General Survey

1-1 东莞行政区划（2009年）

Divisions of Administrative Areas in Dongguan (2009)

镇街	村（居）委会		
	个数		名称
合计	村委会	383	
	社区居委会	215	
莞城	社区居委会	9	东正 市桥 罗沙 北隅 西隅 博厦 细村 兴塘 创业
石龙	村委会	7	西湖 忠维 林屋 蒲溪 新维 王屋洲 黄家山
	社区居委会	3	中山东 中山西 兴龙
虎门	社区居委会	30	虎门寨 东方 则徐 大宁 树田 白沙 沙角 怀德 博涌 镇口 村头 新联 九门寨 居岐 金洲 南面 北栅 小捷滘 北面 陈村 东风 武山沙 黄村 南栅 龙眼 宴岗 赤岗 路东 新湾 民泰
东城	社区居委会	23	岗贝 花园新村 东泰 温塘 桑园 周屋 余屋 鳌峙塘 峡口 柏洲边 上桥 下桥 樟村 梨川 堑头 主山 石井 同沙 光明 牛山 立新 火炼树 星城
万江	社区居委会	28	万江墟 万江 石美 莫屋 拔蛟窝 黄粘洲 蚬涌 谷涌 小享 滘联 上甲 新村 新谷涌 共联 水蛇涌 大莲塘 牌楼基 严屋 大汾 流涌尾 金泰 曲海 坝头 胜利 官桥滘 简沙洲 新和 新城
南城	社区居委会	17	宏远 胜和 元美 亨美 三元里 篁村 新基 周溪 袁屋边 白马 石鼓 蛤地 西平 雅园 水濂 新城 鸿福
中堂	村委会	15	潢涌 三涌 湛翠 凤冲 袁家涌 吴家涌 鹤田 中堂 一村 东向 蕉利 槎滘 下芦 马沥 四乡
	社区居委会	5	中心 斗朗 红锋 东泊 江南
望牛墩	村委会	21	李屋 望东 扶涌 赤滘 五涌 下漕 上合 聚龙江 望联 洲湾 洲涡 杜屋 寮厦 芙蓉沙 官桥涌 横沥 福安 石排 官洲 朱平沙 锦涡
	社区居委会	1	望牛墩
麻涌	村委会	13	麻一 麻三 麻四 大步 东太 新基 川槎 鸥涌 华阳 南洲 大盛 漳澎 黎滘
	社区居委会	2	麻涌 麻二
石碣	村委会	14	石碣 唐洪 黄泗围 西南 单屋 梁家村 沙腰 刘屋 水南 四甲 鹤田厦 涌口 横滘 桔洲
	社区居委会	1	城中
高埗	村委会	18	冼沙 卢溪 宝莲 塘厦 草墩 护安围 保安围 三联 横滘头 低涌 朱磡 新联 欧邓 芦村 高埗 凌屋 上江城 下江城
	社区居委会	1	新创
道滘	村委会	13	南城 南丫 闸口 大鱼沙 小河 永庆 北永 昌平 厚德 九曲 大罗沙 大岭丫 蔡白
	社区居委会	1	兴隆
洪梅	村委会	9	洪屋涡 新庄 梅沙 氹涌 黎洲角 夏汇 尧均 乌沙 金鳌沙
	社区居委会	1	洪梅
沙田	村委会	16	中围 和安 大流 泥洲 杨公洲 福禄沙 阇西 民田 先锋 西大坦 穗丰年 大泥 齐沙 稔洲 义沙 西太隆
	社区居委会	2	横流 滨港
厚街	村委会	22	厚街 珊美 宝屯 三屯 陈屋 赤岭 河田 寮厦 汀山 环冈 大迳 新围 桥头 南五 新塘 涌口 双岗 溪头 沙塘 宝塘 下汴 白濠
	社区居委会	1	竹溪
长安	社区居委会	13	涌头 沙头 霄边 上沙 咸西 厦岗 锦厦 厦边 上角 乌沙 新民 长盛 新安

1-1 续表

(2009年)

镇街	村(居)委会		
	个数		名称
寮步	村委会	20	西溪 凫山 石龙坑 石步 良边 富竹山 塘唇 向西 霞边 上屯 下岭贝 竹园 上底 药勒 刘屋巷 浮竹山 陈家埔 井巷 小坑 长坑
	社区居委会	10	寮步 塘边 横坑 岭厦 新旧围 缪边 牛杨 泉塘 坑口 良平
大岭山	村委会	21	太公岭 大塘朗 下高田 连平 鸡翅岭 马蹄岗 金桔 大沙 百花洞 大塘 水朗 杨屋 矮岭冚 颜屋 大片美 梅林 元岭 大岭 新塘 旧飞鹅 大环
	社区居委会	3	大岭山 农场 领居
大朗	村委会	16	高英 洋乌 洋坑塘 松柏朗 黎贝岭 松木山 犀牛陂 水平 宝陂 石厦 杨涌 沙步 新马莲 佛子凹 蔡边 水口
	社区居委会	12	大朗 佛新 巷头 巷尾 大井头 屏山 竹山 求富路 长塘 黄草朗 圣堂 长富
黄江	村委会	11	社贝 鸡啼岗 袁屋围 合路 北岸 田心 龙见田 大冚 长龙 星光 旧村
	社区居委会	3	新市 田美 三新
樟木头	社区居委会	9	圩镇 樟罗 百果洞 樟洋 石新 柏地 官仓 裕丰 金河
清溪	村委会	20	浮岗 上元 清厦 铁松 铁场 谢坑 青皇 大埔 长山头 三中 九乡 三星 渔樑围 厦坭 大利 土桥 重河 松岗 罗马 荔横
	社区居委会	1	清溪
塘厦	社区居委会	22	塘厦 三局 林村 石潭埔 四村 振兴围 大坪 莆心湖 平山 诸佛岭 桥陇 龙背岭 石鼓 田心 横塘 蛟乙塘 凤凰岗 莲湖 沙湖 石马 清湖头 塘新
凤岗	村委会	11	雁田 官井头 油甘埔 凤德岭 塘沥 黄洞 竹塘 竹尾田 三联 五联 天堂围
	社区居委会	1	凤岗
谢岗	村委会	11	黎村 窑山 南面 大龙 大厚 赵林 稔子园 五星 曹乐 谢岗 谢山
	社区居委会	1	泰园
常平	村委会	31	岗梓 塘角 苏坑 袁山贝 金美 还珠沥 朗贝 桥沥 卢屋 九江水 朗洲 陈屋贝 司马 霞坑 漱旧 漱新 黄泥塘 元江元 横江厦 沙湖口 白石岗 松柏塘 上坑 木棆 下墟 板石 田尾 白花沥 桥梓 麦元 土塘
	社区居委会	2	常平 新民
桥头	村委会	11	田头角 李屋 朗厦 岗头 屋厦 禾坑 邓屋 邵岗头 东江 山和 石水口
	社区居委会	6	桥头 田新 莲城 大洲 迳联 岭头
横沥	村委会	16	石涌 隔坑 半仙山 田头 田坑 横沥 村头 长巷 田饶步 六甲 村尾 水边 新四 山厦 月塘 张坑
	社区居委会	1	恒泉
东坑	村委会	14	东坑 坑美 角社 塔岗 黄麻岭 初坑 凤大 黄屋 寮边头 长安塘 新门楼 井美 彭屋 丁屋
	社区居委会	1	草塘
企石	村委会	19	铁岗 深巷 湖美 博夏 上洞 江边 旧围 清湖 东平 上截 下截 东山 莫屋 杨屋 新南 南坑 铁炉坑 企石 霞朗
	社区居委会	1	宝石
石排	村委会	18	石排 下沙 福隆 庙边王 沙角 黄家壆 赤坎 向西 水贝 田寮 横山 埔心 谷吓 塘尾 李家坊 田边 中坑 燕窝
	社区居委会	1	太和
茶山	村委会	16	上元 茶山 下朗 横江 增埗 卢边 寒溪水 南社 塘角 博头 冲美 粟边 孙屋 超朗 京山 刘黄
	社区居委会	2	茶山圩 茶溪
松山湖	社区居委会	1	松山湖

1-2 历年东莞行政区划

Divisions of Administrative Areas in Dongguan over Years

单位：个

年 份	镇 街	村(居)委会	村委会	居委会
1978	33	526	496	30
1979	33	531	501	30
1980	33	545	515	30
1981	34	554	524	30
1982	34	561	531	30
1983	34	561	531	30
1984	34	542	512	30
1985	33	546	516	30
1986	33	560	530	30
1987	34	580	537	43
1988	33	582	542	40
1989	33	583	544	39
1990	33	583	543	40
1991	33	586	546	40
1992	33	590	549	41
1993	33	590	549	41
1994	33	592	551	41
1995	33	592	551	41
1996	33	593	552	41
1997	33	594	551	43
1998	32	594	551	43
1999	32	593	546	47
2000	32	675	546	129
2001	32	678	546	132
2002	32	678	546	132
2003	32	616	487	129
2004	32	596	440	156
2005	32	596	404	192
2006	32	596	394	202
2007	32	591	386	205
2008	32	591	383	208
2009	32	598	383	215

1-3 主要年份户数、人口与自然资源

Number of Households, Population and Natural Resources in Main Years

项目	单位	1978年	1985年	1990年	1995年	2000年	2005年	2008年	2009年
一、户数									
年末户籍总户数	万户	24.82	28.95	32.73	36.43	41.40	46.50	50.64	52.12
#非农业户	万户	4.37	6.97	8.91	10.06	11.44	18.90	22.42	24.05
二、人口与劳动力									
年末常住人口	万人			175.62	336.45	644.84	656.07	694.98	635.00
年末户籍人口	万人	111.23	120.85	131.85	143.65	152.61	165.65	174.87	178.73
#非农业人口	万人	18.49	25.49	30.87	35.38	39.61	65.84	76.80	81.46
年末户籍从业人员数	万人	54.97	67.35	75.10	82.40	88.62	101.30	109.67	112.18
#企事业机关	万人	8.20	12.30	13.16	18.40	16.80	19.14	13.68	15.07
人口密度(常住人口)	人/平方公里			712	1365	2616	2662	2819	2576
人口密度(户籍人口)	人/平方公里	451	490	535	583	619	672	709	725
三、土地									
土地面积	平方公里	2465	2465	2465	2465	2465	2465	2465	2465
年末耕地面积	万亩	118.39	96.67	88.26	70.86	66.33	50.29	47.93	51.66
人均耕地面积	亩	1.06	0.80	0.67	0.49	0.43	0.30	0.27	0.29
城镇建成区面积	平方公里				82.48	147.68	620.31	706.54	780.15
#城区建成区面积	平方公里					28.13	108.10	82.50	87.29
四、气候									
年降水量	毫米	1748.3	1678.0	1602.9	1664.8	2019.3	1837.6	2710.9	1881.6
年平均气温	摄氏度	21.9	21.8	22.8	22.4	23.2	22.7	22.2	22.8
极端最高气温	摄氏度	35.7	35.8	37.8	36.2	37.0	37.4	36.8	36.3
极端最低气温	摄氏度	2.7	4.2	4.3	6.7	5.6	1.8	4.8	5.3
年日照时数	小时	1958.8	1671.7	1910.2	1935.7	2059.5	1736.3	1879.3	1967.8
五、森林									
有林地面积	万亩		78.34	83.48	91.48	92.16	89.23	88.60	90.05
林木蓄积量	万立方米		155.97	167.18	123.02	136.11	175.38	227.90	241.41
森林覆盖率	%		28.6	31.4	29.7	30.6	33.1	36.2	36.5
六、水资源									
大陆海岸线总长度	公里	61.4	61.4	61.4	61.4	115.9	92.1	97.2	97.2
海水养殖可养面积	万亩	5.0	5.0	5.0	5.5	2.6	16.9	2.5	2.0
淡水养殖可养面积	万亩	30.0	30.0	30.0	28.0	14.3	30.7	15.0	10.0

注：1. 人均耕地面积按户籍人口计算。
2. 大陆海岸线从2000年起以咸水为界定。

1-4 历年土地与自然资源

Land and Natural Resources over Years

年份	土地面积(平方公里)	气候				
		年降水量(毫米)	年平均气温(摄氏度)	极端最高气温(摄氏度)	极端最低气温(摄氏度)	年日照时数(小时)
1978	2465	1748.3	21.9	35.7	2.7	1958.8
1979	2465	2007.1	21.9	36.5	2.9	1991.4
1980	2465	1434.7	22.3	37.7	3.3	2157.1
1981	2465	2394.9	22.1	35.6	3.2	1792.2
1982	2465	1454.1	22.1	37.5	3.8	1754.1
1983	2465	1947.1	21.8	35.8	3.3	1909.7
1984	2465	1444.5	21.5	35.9	3.1	1749.2
1985	2465	1678.0	21.8	35.8	4.2	1671.7
1986	2465	1665.2	22.2	35.9	3.0	2098.1
1987	2465	1908.8	22.9	37.0	4.3	1816.6
1988	2465	1735.0	22.0	37.0	7.0	1836.5
1989	2465	1567.2	22.5	37.6	5.2	1926.0
1990	2465	1602.9	22.8	37.8	4.3	1910.2
1991	2465	1219.6	23.0	36.6	1.2	1968.8
1992	2465	1827.1	22.3	37.0	4.5	1854.5
1993	2465	2393.6	22.5	35.6	3.0	1965.7
1994	2465	1809.1	23.0	38.2	5.4	1828.6
1995	2465	1664.8	22.4	36.2	6.7	1935.7
1996	2465	1547.4	22.7	37.1	3.4	2036.0
1997	2465	2074.0	22.8	36.3	6.1	1558.1
1998	2465	1844.5	23.6	36.5	5.6	1699.0
1999	2465	1614.5	23.3	37.8	3.1	2015.8
2000	2465	2019.3	23.2	37.0	5.6	2059.5
2001	2465	2042.6	23.3	36.6	6.6	1978.2
2002	2465	1557.4	23.6	36.7	4.5	2046.9
2003	2465	1416.7	23.0	36.1	3.8	2268.7
2004	2465	1705.8	22.8	38.0	3.5	2192.9
2005	2465	1837.6	22.7	37.4	1.8	1736.3
2006	2465	2412.0	22.7	36.8	4.7	1616.4
2007	2465	1806.9	22.9	35.9	6.7	1876.7
2008	2465	2710.9	22.2	36.8	4.8	1879.3
2009	2465	1881.6	22.8	36.3	5.3	1967.8

1-4 续表

年份	森林			水资源		
	森林面积(万亩)	林木蓄积量(万立方米)	森林覆盖率(%)	大陆海岸线总长度(公里)	海水养殖可养面积(万亩)	淡水养殖可养面积(万亩)
1978				61.4	5.0	30.0
1979	44.4	110.3	14.7	61.4	5.0	30.0
1980				61.4	5.0	30.0
1981				61.4	5.0	30.0
1982				61.4	5.0	30.0
1983				61.4	5.0	30.0
1984	76.6	160.5	21.9	61.4	5.0	30.0
1985	78.3	156.0	28.6	61.4	5.0	30.0
1986	82.4	157.8	30.0	61.4	5.0	30.0
1987	83.9	183.9	34.5	61.4	5.0	30.0
1988	84.3	169.1	34.7	61.4	5.0	30.0
1989	80.9	164.8	31.1	61.4	5.0	30.0
1990	83.5	167.2	31.4	61.4	5.0	30.0
1991	85.0	169.2	31.6	61.4	5.0	29.0
1992	86.3	169.8	31.3	61.4	5.5	29.0
1993	87.3	168.9	31.9	61.4	5.5	28.0
1994	86.1	116.8	28.3	61.4	5.5	28.0
1995	91.5	123.0	29.7	61.4	5.5	28.0
1996	91.9	115.7	29.9	61.4	5.5	28.5
1997	93.5	121.1	29.9	61.4	5.7	28.7
1998	93.4	126.0	30.1	61.4	5.7	28.7
1999	92.2	120.4	30.1	115.9	4.8	28.7
2000	92.2	136.1	30.6	115.9	2.6	14.3
2001	93.3	146.0	31.2	116.0	2.8	12.9
2002	93.8	155.0	31.7	115.9	4.1	11.7
2003	93.3	165.1	32.2	92.1	4.2	10.4
2004	93.3	165.1	32.2	92.1	4.0	10.0
2005	89.2	175.4	33.1	92.1	16.9	30.7
2006	88.9	194.4	35.1	92.1	16.6	30.5
2007	89.1	215.1	35.5	92.1	16.9	30.7
2008	88.6	227.9	36.2	97.2	2.5	15.0
2009	90.1	241.4	36.5	97.2	2.0	10.0

1-5 主要年份国民经济主要指标

Main Indicators of National Economy in Main Years

项　　目	单位	1978年	1985年	1990年	1995年	2000年	2005年	2008年	2009年
一、经济总量指标									
地区生产总值	亿元	6.11	22.60	80.44	296.29	820.25	2183.20	3703.60	3763.91
第一产业	亿元	2.72	6.15	13.28	21.43	25.91	20.55	14.83	14.79
第二产业	亿元	2.68	11.66	40.53	166.97	450.71	1227.86	1901.61	1823.08
#工业	亿元			39.18	154.19	430.45	1173.23	1819.22	1741.53
第三产业	亿元	0.71	4.80	26.63	107.89	343.64	934.78	1787.17	1926.04
工农业总产值(当年价)	亿元	8.44	26.47	122.23	565.27	1574.42	4514.22	7337.82	6788.11
二、农村经济									
农业总产值(当年价)	亿元	4.24	9.12	23.64	42.69	54.64	42.05	25.53	25.31
农村集体经营总收入	亿元			7.18	41.23	77.50	120.57	141.05	136.10
年末耕地面积	万亩			88.26	70.86	66.33	50.29	47.93	51.66
三、工　业									
工业总产值(当年价)	亿元	4.20	17.35	98.58	522.58	1519.79	4470.03	7312.29	6762.80
轻工业	亿元	3.15	12.95	60.33	330.05	801.22	1966.16	3279.34	3013.34
重工业	亿元	1.05	4.40	38.25	192.53	718.57	2503.87	4032.95	3749.46
规模以上工业企业财务指标									
主营业务收入	亿元	2.69	9.23	47.27	275.84	988.91	3912.15	6536.08	6007.76
年末固定资产原值	亿元	0.78	1.68	14.29	60.14	728.85	1856.09	2734.92	3079.92
年末固定资产净值	亿元	0.51	1.20	11.95	46.26	470.19	1105.26	1658.31	1724.00
年末流动资产余额	亿元	0.26	0.58	1.74	21.28	529.82	1873.28	2949.29	3165.25
资产总额	亿元		1.73	13.51	52.98	1122.60	3345.33	5114.42	5286.18
负债总额	亿元					563.04	1858.09	2939.23	3043.46
资产负债率	%					50.2	55.5	57.5	57.6
利税总额	亿元					84.10	183.10	268.43	403.47
综合效益指数	%					114.0	119.9	116.6	127.2
四、能源消费									
地区能源消费总量(等价值)	万吨标准煤						1885.78	2589.66	2603.52
地区能源消费总量(当量值)	万吨标准煤						1800.14	2280.31	2311.86
电力消耗	亿千瓦时						419.83	514.16	495.58
单位GDP能耗(等价值，2005年可比价)	吨标准煤/万元						0.864	0.738	0.705
单位GDP能耗(当量值，2005年可比价)	吨标准煤/万元						0.825	0.650	0.626
单位GDP电耗(2005可比价)	千瓦小时/万元						1923.00	1465.25	1341.26
规模以上工业综合能源消费量(当量值)	万吨标准煤						1203.77	1452.85	1367.94
规模以上工业增加值能耗(当量值,2005年可比价)	吨标准煤/万元						1.14	0.82	0.82

注：1.2005年以前地区生产总值采用全国第一次经济普查资料修订的数据；2005-2008年采用第二次经济普查资料修订的数据；2004年以前使用旧行业分类，2004年起使用新行业分类，下同。

2.规模以上工业企业1997年及以前年份为独立核算工业企业口径，1998-2005年为全部国有工业及年销售收入500万元以上非国有工业企业口径，2006年起为年主营业务收入500万元及以上工业企业口径，下同。

3.2005年以前工业相关数据采用第一次经济普查资料修订的数据，2008年采用第二次经济普查资料修订的数据，下同。

1-5 续表 1

项　　目	单 位	1978年	1985年	1990年	1995年	2000年	2005年	2008年	2009年
五、运输邮电									
公路通车里程	公里	1259	1240	1325	2327	2518	2871	4001	4713
#高速公路	公里					89	154	159	207
旅客周转量	亿人公里	0.94	9.52	32.22	44.62	100.19	118.53	224.85	105.35
水　运	亿人公里	0.43	0.43	0.15	0.19	0.14	0.33	0.24	0.21
公　路	亿人公里	0.51	9.10	32.07	44.43	100.05	118.20	224.61	105.13
货物周转量	亿吨公里	1.51	17.16	18.47	26.46	40.47	42.48	174.75	101.65
水　运	亿吨公里	1.42	5.86	11.25	13.66	15.86	15.23	128.47	56.36
公　路	亿吨公里	0.09	11.30	7.22	12.80	24.60	27.25	46.28	45.29
港口货物吞吐量	万吨	293	276	233	201	746	2280	3208	3530
邮政业务收入	亿元							7.37	7.15
电信业务收入	亿元							165.01	149.16
局用交换机容量	万门		1.14	6.98	52.29	103.13	286.25	340.71	347.15
年末移动电话交换机总容量	万户				4.80	154.20	1059.10	1602.10	1621.60
本地电话用户	万户	0.20	0.77	4.90	31.58	78.12	384.52	439.41	378.40
移动电话用户(含充值卡)	万户			0.05	4.77	123.68	1016.41	1454.29	1409.29
#充值卡	万户					42.71	839.58	1362.91	1271.15
互联网用户	万户				0.05	13.78	52.90	96.37	118.02
六、供用电									
总供电量	亿千瓦时	1.64	3.82	18.01	68.00	178.03	415.66	507.35	488.85
#网供	亿千瓦时	1.64	3.39	11.18	38.48	134.91	342.26	442.31	431.89
总售电量	亿千瓦时	1.49	3.39	16.15	61.68	169.06	396.59	487.32	478.19
#工业用电	亿千瓦时	1.08	2.21	11.93	48.79	134.58	330.31	392.81	376.10
七、固定资产投资									
全社会固定资产投资总额	亿元	0.23	7.06	7.51	63.14	102.89	597.24	944.34	1094.08
#基本建设	亿元	0.17	1.41	2.51	28.43	28.07	262.14	377.45	
更新改造	亿元	0.01	0.29	1.91	2.92	11.23	62.04	81.56	
房地产开发	亿元				8.52	11.25	144.43	271.42	277..66
房地产开发当年房屋施工面积	万平方米						1160.20	1998.00	2333.90
房地产开发当年房屋竣工面积	万平方米						132.90	478.00	310.22
商品房销售面积	万平方米						321.90	511.59	600.27
商品房销售额	亿元						119.40	288.60	353.00
国有单位新增固定资产	亿元	0.17	0.56	2.77	6.76	15.68	2.45	8.67	23.47
国有单位固定资产交付使用率	%	93.3	33.0	54.7	63.2	79.3	3.6	13.0	14.1
八、国内商业									
社会商业商品销售总额	亿元	7.49	23.16	43.41	155.69	279.19	824.82	1444.66	1581.91
社会消费品零售总额	亿元	2.13	9.36	31.97	113.01	235.16	506.29	881.15	959.07

注：1.2006年起公路通车里程含专用公路和村道，与往年数据不可比，下同。
2.全社会固定资产投资总额1995年不含沙角C厂投资；2005年基本建设,更新改造及其他投资中包含农村集投资额，因此该部分数据与往年数据不可比。
3.2009年客货运输量中，公路和水路运输量统计改用新调查方法，2008年数据已做同口径调整，与往年不比，下同。
4.2005年以前国内商业相关数据采用第一次经济普查资料修订的数据，2005-2008年采用第二次经济普查料修订的数据，下同。

1-5 续表 2

项　　目	单 位	1978年	1985年	1990年	1995年	2000年	2005年	2008年	2009年
九、物价指数(以上年价格为100)									
商品零售物价总指数	%	100.4	106.9	94.9	109.7	100.1	103.0	107.9	95.3
居民消费价格总指数	%		106.5	96.6	113.9	101.5	102.4	105.5	96.9
消费品价格指数	%		106.9	94.9	109.7	100.1	103.0	107.3	97.1
服务项目价格指数	%		103.3	111.0	128.9	112.8	100.4	100.1	96.3
十、外经、外贸、旅游									
进出口总额(海关口径)	亿美元			10.82	153.91	320.45	743.72	1132.99	941.55
进口总额	亿美元			5.14	75.92	148.86	334.42	477.62	389.86
出口总额	亿美元			5.68	77.99	171.59	409.29	655.37	551.69
#一般贸易	亿美元				2.32	2.09	17.55	48.72	57.17
来料加工装配	亿美元				43.46	83.43	161.17	242.84	182.32
进料加工	亿美元				32.02	85.84	230.43	358.56	305.50
其他	亿美元				0.19	0.22	0.14	5.26	6.70
新签利用外资协议	宗		625	1267	3077	1276	992	588	601
协议规定外商投资额(旧口径)	亿美元		0.68	3.02	33.09	18.36	47.52	39.37	20.30
协议规定外商投资额(新口径)	亿美元						29.80	25.87	16.16
实际利用外资(旧口径，含对外借款)	亿美元		0.35	2.56	11.58	19.54	42.48	47.09	42.12
实际利用外资(新口径)	亿美元						14.67	24.47	25.94
全年接待旅游人数	万人次			125	89	291	1156	1872	2037
#国际及港澳台旅游者	万人次			27	27	106	169	268	286
旅游外汇收入	万美元					7617	28189	45614	51756
十一、财政、金融									
来源于东莞的财政收入(不含关税)	亿元	0.66	1.11	3.57	18.01	76.16	283.58	537.68	553.36
市财政一般预算收入	亿元				11.56	30.47	103.97	209.22	231.16
市财政一般预算支出	亿元	0.18	0.50	2.28	12.42	33.61	117.04	218.26	232.62
金融机构各项人民币存款余额	亿元	1.05	13.49	68.07	383.68	1228.67	2933.40	4354.53	4986.61
金融机构各项人民币贷款余额	亿元	1.96	14.24	63.04	254.85	630.84	1500.52	2380.36	2903.80
现金总支出	亿元	2.21	17.32	125.88	897.43	3718.78	7178.50	9071.05	8486.22
现金总收入	亿元	2.08	14.03	120.97	858.45	3594.58	7375.25	9134.38	8449.47
十二、人民生活									
全市职工平均工资	元							13523	14416
城镇在岗职工平均工资	元	474	1456	3552	9682	14051	28253	39516	42585
城市居民人均可支配收入	元		791	2508	9588	14142	22882	30275	33045
城市居民人均消费性支出	元		689	2038	9220	12529	21768	23208	24270
农民人均纯收入	元	149	746	1359	3988	6731	9842	12328	13064
城乡居民人民币储蓄存款余额	亿元	0.54	9.19	45.51	232.97	672.07	1728.28	2638.04	2904.57

注：1. 现金总支出与现金总收入1997年及以前年份是银行口径，1998年起为金融机构口径。
2. 城镇在岗职工工资总额和人均工资2000年前是城镇职工工资，2000年起是城镇在岗职工工资，不含乡镇及以下办企业职工，下同。
3. 接待过夜旅客数、国际旅客数和旅游外汇收入2002年起是旅游局口径，与往年数不可比。

1-6 主要年份国民经济和社会发展主要比例与效益指标

Main Indicators of Proportions and Efficiency in National Economic and Social Development in Main Years

项　目	单 位	1990年	1995年	2000年	2005年	2008年	2009年
一、户籍人口							
出生率	‰	17.07	17.59	12.11	10.62	10.77	10.67
死亡率	‰	4.76	4.84	4.59	4.60	4.54	4.36
自然增长率	‰	12.31	12.75	7.52	6.02	6.23	6.31
人口性别比(男/女)	%	97.10	100.40	102.43	103.05	103.37	103.21
二、就　业(按户籍人口计算)							
就业者负担人口	人	1.8	1.7	1.7	1.6	1.6	1.6
各产业劳动力比例							
第一产业	%	36.2	23.7	19.6	8.6	5.5	5.1
第二产业	%	40.6	46.1	46.8	45.6	37.4	41.2
第三产业	%	23.2	30.2	33.6	45.9	57.1	53.7
三、地区生产总值中三次产业比重							
第一产业	%	16.5	7.2	3.2	0.9	0.4	0.4
第二产业	%	50.4	56.4	54.9	56.2	51.3	48.4
工　业	%	48.7	52.0	52.5	53.7	49.1	46.3
建筑业	%	1.7	4.3	2.5	2.5	2.2	2.2
第三产业	%	33.1	36.4	41.9	42.8	48.3	51.2
四、全社会劳动生产率	元/人	**10794**	**36261**	**92978**	**218685**	**342418**	**339314**
(按户籍从业人员、增加值计算)							
第一产业	元/人	4853	10934	13841	21794	24362	25243
第二产业	元/人	13581	44828	113318	267365	442168	417944
第三产业	元/人	15380	43395	115595	210172	302559	313439
五、工农业总产值中农、轻、重比例							
农　业	%	19.3	7.6	3.5	0.9	0.4	0.4
轻工业	%	49.4	58.4	50.9	43.6	43.6	44.4
重工业	%	31.3	34.1	45.6	55.5	56.0	55.2
六、农　业							
农业总产值中“五业”比例							
种植业	%	54.9	45.7	39.6	27.0	54.2	55.4
林　业	%	1.8	2.1	0.7	0.4	1.4	0.9
牧　业	%	19.2	30.0	41.4	57.7	20.8	19.7
副　业	%	11.1	6.2	3.5			
渔　业	%	13.3	16.1	14.9	14.9	23.6	24.0

注：2002年起农业中副业并入种植业。

1-6 续表 1

项　　目	单 位	1990年	1995年	2000年	2005年	2008年	2009年
七、工　业							
工业总产值中轻、重工业比例							
轻工业	%	61.2	63.2	52.7	44.0	43.8	44.6
重工业	%	38.8	36.8	47.3	56.0	56.2	55.4
规模以上工业企业效益							
固定资产利税率	%	8.5	10.7	11.5	9.9	7.6	23.4
资金利税率	%	6.3	7.7	7.5	5.5	4.5	7.6
产值利税率	%	5.4	10.0	9.2	4.6	3.4	6.6
八、建筑业							
技术装备率	万元/人		0.37	0.43	0.68	0.9	1.37
产值利税率	%		3.9	5.4	7.5	6.9	10.0
劳动生产率(按施工产值计算)	元/人	18636	42766	60849	108136	174827	184034
九、固定资产投资							
全社会固定资产投资相当于地区生产总值比例(投资率)	%	9.3	17.0	12.5	27.4	25.5	29.1
全社会房屋建筑面积竣工率	%	45.2	34.1	60.7	22.5	33.0	19.9
基本建设固定资产交付使用率	%	47.1	101.8	84.9	24.7	30.0	
基本建设项目建成投产率	%	47.5	26.5	70.9		9.9	
基本建设投资中三大产业比例							
第一产业	%	0.2		0.1		0.1	
第二产业	%	80.7	74.5	39.2	53.4	42.9	
第三产业	%	19.2	25.5	60.8	46.6	56.9	
十、财　政							
来源于东莞的财政收入(不含关税)相当于地区生产总值比例	%	4.4	6.1	9.3	13.0	14.5	14.7
市财政一般预算支出相当于地区生产总值比例	%	2.8	4.2	4.1	5.4	5.9	6.2
十一、外经外贸							
利用外资结构							
外商直接投资	%	41.2	63.6	66.0	75.2	75.8	88.2
外商其他投资	%	58.8	36.4	34.0	24.8	24.2	11.8
实际利用外资额相当于协议规定外商投资额比例(旧口径)	%	80.6	31.9	89.7	78.9	81.9	144.9
进出口总额比例							
进口总额	%	47.5	49.3	46.5	45.0	42.2	41.4
出口总额	%	52.5	50.7	53.6	55.0	57.8	58.6
#一般贸易	%		3.0	1.2	4.3	7.4	10.4
来料加工装配	%		55.7	48.6	39.4	37.1	33.0
进料加工	%		41.1	50.0	56.3	54.7	55.4
其他	%		0.2	0.2		0.8	1.2

1-6 续表 2

项目	单位	1990年	1995年	2000年	2005年	2008年	2009年
十二、交通、邮电通信业							
货运量中各种运输方式比例							
公路	%	58.2	55.7	63.3	71.7	86.4	79.5
水运	%	41.8	44.3	36.7	28.3	13.6	20.5
十三、金融							
各项人民币存款相当于生产总值比例	%	84.6	129.5	149.8	134.5	117.6	132.5
各项人民币贷款相当于生产总值比例	%	78.4	86.0	76.9	68.8	64.3	77.1
金融机构现金支出相当于收入的比例	%	104.1	104.5	103.5	97.3	99.3	100.4
各项人民币存款余额中主要存款比例							
#企业存款	%	17.1	23.3	35.7	29.2	27.2	28.5
财政性存款	%	1.2	2.2	0.3	0.9	1.1	1.1
储蓄存款	%	66.9	60.7	54.7	58.9	60.6	58.2
农业存款	%	7.4	6.2	5.9	4.1	3.7	4.2
各项人民币贷款余额中主要贷款比例							
#短期贷款	%	90.5	64.6	84.2	48.9	42.6	43.4
#农业贷款	%	10.8	3.2	3.4	0.3	0.04	0.05
中长期贷款	%	2.1	10.8	7.4	46.7	50.6	50.0
十四、科技、教育、文化、卫生							
科教文卫事业费占财政支出比例	%	28.7	24.5	25.8	17.8	30.1	31.5
学龄儿童入学率	%	99.9	100.0	100.0	100.0	100.0	100.0
小学毕业生升学率	%	95.4	99.2	99.8	99.9	100.0	100.0
初中毕业生升学率	%	44.1	85.4	90.3	94.1	96.6	97.0
普通高中毕业生升学率	%	31.2	64.9	70.5	96.5	91.0	87.5
学校教师负担学生数							
普通高等学校	人		13.7	20.1	15.4	16.9	18.0
中等职业技术学校	人	20.6	21.8	19.0	18.2	20.5	20.0
普通中学	人	20.7	21.1	22.4	19.8	19.1	18.3
小学	人	24.0	24.2	34.3	27.5	24.9	24.2
每万人有电影放映单位	个	0.87	1.53	1.27	0.43	0.23	0.22
每万人《东莞日报》发行量	万份	1.36	6.93	10.40	16.79	25.05	26.55
每万人医生数	人	13.21	16.13	21.81	42.13	67.87	72.09
每万人医院病床数	张	29.67	40.68	46.67	71.35	95.95	101.16
十五、人民生活							
城市居民消费结构							
食品类	%	63.5	39.5	32.3	27.7	33.5	32.8
衣着类	%	4.7	6.6	3.9	5.9	5.8	6.1
其他	%	31.8	53.9	63.8	66.4	60.7	61.1

注：本表中人均指标按户籍人口计算。

1-7 国民经济主要指标分月变化情况（2009年，累计绝对数）

Changes of Main Indicators of National Economy by Month (2009, Accumulative Figures in Value Terms)

项　　目	单位	1 月	1-2 月	1-3 月	1-4 月	1-5 月	1-6 月
规模以上工业总产值	亿元		749.61	1175.42	1600.33	2027.29	2496.89
#国有经济	亿元		50.91	73.22	102.45	129.36	160.70
外资型经济	亿元		568.04	890.26	1215.59	1543.12	1903.65
#民营企业	亿元		115.84	146.90	195.13	249.98	306.93
#八大支柱产业	亿元		463.69	712.41	973.94	1246.44	1536.13
规模以上工业增加值	亿元		167.42	263.13	361.24	456.15	562.22
规模以上工业销售产值	亿元		747.98	1173.47	1596.94	2023.16	2469.10
规模以上工业出口产品产值	亿元		414.44	633.83	863.31	1094.35	1338.97
规模以上工业产品产销率	%		99.8	99.8	99.8	99.8	98.9
规模以上工业企业产品销售收入	亿元		717.68	1171.95	1595.29	2012.30	2446.90
规模以上工业企业利税总额	亿元		23.40	35.85	44.24	52.67	70.05
全社会固定资产投资总额	亿元		58.09	137.66	223.26	310.05	398.18
#基本建设	亿元		23.52	57.95	111.33	161.31	203.46
更新改造	亿元		11.10	26.14	34.38	41.95	54.02
房地产开发	亿元		14.29	41.00	58.32	83.36	103.89
来源于东莞的财政收入	亿元	56.44	111.56	157.42	216.60	267.56	318.76
市财政一般预算收入	亿元	22.04	40.59	57.45	77.58	95.15	113.82
市财政一般预算支出	亿元	26.03	36.72	53.99	73.27	86.23	105.65
金融机构各项人民币存款余额	亿元	4297.54	4374.12	4561.35	4508.60	4563.59	4709.42
#城乡居民储蓄存款余额	亿元	2677.00	2714.62	2762.11	2762.21	2772.26	2805.31
金融机构各项人民币贷款余额	亿元	2405.87	2450.15	2566.95	2531.74	2569.25	2670.07
货币总投放(现金支出)	亿元	808.91	1341.07	1983.31	2654.27	3264.71	3958.60
货币总回笼(现金收入)	亿元	719.14	1293.24	1957.68	2612.20	3237.59	3942.44
进出口总额(海关口径)	亿美元	55.59	109.38	178.72	251.84	325.36	403.53
#出口总额	亿美元	36.82	67.23	108.47	150.14	193.54	237.54
新签项目宗数	宗	36	70	115	156	180	216
合同规定外商投资额	亿美元	1.22	2.73	3.65	4.62	4.96	5.59
实际利用外资(不含对外借款)	亿美元	2.25	3.95	6.55	8.46	10.88	13.29
社会消费品零售总额	亿元		155.65	229.43	305.31	382.68	462.60
居民消费价格总指数	%	100.2	97.8	97.5	97.3	97.2	97.0
#服务项目价格指数	%	98.1	96.1	96.1	96.1	96.3	96.5
总供电量	亿千瓦时	24.45	53.17	89.53	126.17	166.46	211.32
总售电量	亿千瓦时	38.96	67.31	100.22	138.43	173.49	212.82
邮电业务收入	亿元	12.95	26.21	39.10	51.91	64.95	77.87
城市居民人均可支配收入	元/人			11278			18231
城市居民人均消费性支出	元/人			6277			12071

注：1. 物价指数与上年同期相比；各项指标1-12月累计不等于年报数。
　　2. 城市居民收支调查改为季报。

1-7 续表

(2009年，累计绝对数)

项　　目	单位	1-7 月	1-8 月	1-9 月	1-10 月	1-11 月	1-12 月
规模以上工业总产值	亿元	2951.15	3457.44	4055.01	4622.78	5244.97	5935.15
#国有经济	亿元	192.31	228.61	270.72	306.26	340.93	377.57
外资型经济	亿元	2243.15	2625.12	3072.19	3508.57	3952.05	4465.03
#民营企业	亿元	370.11	427.42	500.55	567.98	679.12	782.36
#八大支柱产业	亿元	1817.74	2132.60	2509.82	2874.67	3285.40	3728.72
规模以上工业增加值	亿元	665.16	778.87	912.54	1038.86	1174.60	1325.95
规模以上工业销售产值	亿元	2938.91	3446.16	4023.66	4589.22	5205.66	5890.71
规模以上工业出口产品产值	亿元	1586.82	1868.51	2186.12	2500.48	2813.54	3180.78
规模以上工业产品产销率	%	99.6	99.7	99.2	99.3	99.3	99.3
规模以上工业企业产品销售收入	亿元	2935.97	3424.34	3970.57	4544.18	5077.47	5651.32
规模以上工业企业利税总额	亿元	92.47	121.22	150.37	184.17	218.20	248.15
全社会固定资产投资总额	亿元	469.72	560.13	685.77	753.21	836.78	1094.08
#基本建设	亿元	234.57	265.81	304.47	323.46	361.32	464.07
更新改造	亿元	75.28	98.32	134.16	166.29	184.78	212.88
房地产开发	亿元	114.81	138.02	174.37	185.03	204.69	277.66
来源于东莞的财政收入	亿元	372.90	416.71	471.98	530.79	578.74	627.82
市财政一般预算收入	亿元	132.48	148.90	168.16	187.99	207.68	231.16
市财政一般预算支出	亿元	127.36	146.34	162.98	178.19	196.00	225.94
金融机构各项人民币存款余额	亿元	4656.31	4692.14	4773.20	4804.23	4894.35	4986.61
#城乡居民储蓄存款余额	亿元	2788.47	2772.70	2837.72	2834.00	2851.82	2904.57
金融机构各项人民币贷款余额	亿元	2713.23	2796.38	2822.11	2853.02	2870.01	2903.80
货币总投放(现金支出)	亿元	4705.49	5435.67	6253.78	6915.62	7646.15	8486.22
货币总回笼(现金收入)	亿元	4687.23	5423.48	6204.00	6885.33	7628.09	8449.47
进出口总额(海关口径)	亿美元	490.46	576.13	672.10	759.48	848.62	941.55
#出口总额	亿美元	287.39	337.04	393.06	445.20	498.17	551.69
新签项目宗数	宗	277	330	390	450	532	579
合同规定外商投资额	亿美元	7.28	9.22	11.02	12.35	14.31	16.16
实际利用外资(不含对外借款)	亿美元	15.64	18.76	21.86	23.28	24.56	25.94
社会消费品零售总额	亿元	542.98	623.72	704.91	788.24	872.40	956.25
居民消费价格总指数	%	96.7	96.6	96.5	96.5	96.7	96.9
#服务项目价格指数	%	96.4	96.0	96.0	96.0	96.0	96.3
总供电量	亿千瓦时	261.97	313.74	364.45	407.98	448.65	488.85
总售电量	亿千瓦时	256.81	305.47	356.15	401.11	439.49	478.19
邮电业务收入	亿元	91.11	104.57	117.62	130.97	143.43	156.31
城市居民人均可支配收入	元/人			25772			33045
城市居民人均消费性支出	元/人			18166			24270

1-8 国民经济主要指标分月变化情况（2009年，比上年同期增长）

Changes of Main Indicators of National Economy by Month (2009, Compare with Same Period of Preceding Year)

项　　目	单位	1 月	1-2 月	1-3 月	1-4 月	1-5 月	1-6 月
规模以上工业总产值	%		-23.5	-17.2	-17.1	-16.6	-15.0
#国有经济	%		-6.4	-3.2	-3.2	-4.0	-3.6
外资型经济	%		-26.8	-20.1	-19.9	-19.1	-17.2
#民营企业	%		-8.0	-8.4	-8.5	-9.4	-9.1
#八大支柱产业	%		-25.5	-19.1	-18.7	-17.8	-16.3
规模以上工业增加值	%		-22.3	-16.6	-16.6	-16.4	-14.8
规模以上工业销售产值	%		-29.6	-23.1	-22.5	-22.6	-21.4
规模以上工业出口产品产值	%		-29.6	-28.0	-27.9	-27.5	-26.4
规模以上工业产品产销率	%		-0.2	-0.2	0.7	0.2	-0.5
规模以上工业企业产品销售收入	%		-31.5	-23.8	-23.1	-22.7	-22.0
规模以上工业企业利税总额	%		-58.4	-50.5	-48.8	-50.8	-42.9
全社会固定资产投资总额	%		18.0	13.6	10.1	10.1	8.2
#基本建设	%		19.0	4.3	24.3	27.8	35.2
更新改造	%		158.0	155.2	79.1	86.3	68.3
房地产开发	%		20.2	29.6	4.6	2.5	-8.6
来源于东莞的财政收入	%	-20.7	-3.9	-0.4	0.1	1.8	-0.3
市财政一般预算收入	%	3.1	7.8	8.8	9.1	8.3	5.4
市财政一般预算支出	%	54.0	37.0	33.1	35.8	25.8	16.4
金融机构各项人民币存款余额	%	-1.3	0.5	4.8	3.6	4.9	8.2
#城乡居民储蓄存款余额	%	1.5	2.9	4.7	4.7	5.1	6.3
金融机构各项人民币贷款余额	%	1.1	2.9	7.8	6.6	8.1	12.4
货币总投放(现金支出)	%	-25.5	-19.5	-18.0	-17.4	-17.3	-14.7
货币总回笼(现金收入)	%	-26.0	-18.5	-17.5	-17.3	-17.4	-14.8
进出口总额(海关口径)	%	-42.8	-34.1	-32.0	-30.4	-29.6	-27.8
#出口总额	%	-32.1	-27.2	-25.9	-25.5	-24.9	-24.2
新签项目宗数	%	-66.4	-50.7	-38.5	-31.6	-33.1	-29.9
合同规定外商投资额	%	-58.1	-57.6	-53.5	-52.5	-56.2	-54.1
实际利用外资(不含对外借款)	%	-17.9	-9.5	1.8	5.1	8.0	7.7
社会消费品零售总额	%		11.1	10.2	10.3	10.5	11.1
居民消费价格总指数	%	0.2	-2.2	-2.5	-2.7	-2.8	-3.0
#服务项目价格指数	%	-1.9	-3.9	-3.9	-3.9	-3.7	-3.5
总供电量	%	-34.7	-16.8	-13.5	-13.1	-12.9	-10.7
总售电量	%	-5.8	-13.1	-4.6	-4.5	-6.3	-7.2
邮电业务收入	%	-10.7	-6.3	-9.7	-9.5	-10.4	-9.7
城市居民人均可支配收入	%			10.5			9.9
城市居民人均消费性支出	%			2.9			3.8

1-8 续表

(2009年，比上年同期增长)

项　　目	单位	1-7 月	1-8 月	1-9 月	1-10 月	1-11 月	1-12 月
规模以上工业总产值	%	-14.1	-12.7	-11.3	-10.3	-8.4	-6.3
#国有经济	%	-4.1	-4.6	-3.9	-2.6	-2.5	-0.3
外资型经济	%	-16.2	-14.9	-13.7	-12.6	-11.2	-9.4
#民营企业	%	-7.3	-6.1	-4.0	-2.9	3.5	6.9
#八大支柱产业	%	-15.4	-14.0	-12.6	-11.6	-9.3	-7.2
规模以上工业增加值	%	-13.7	-12.3	-11.0	-10.0	-8.3	-6.4
规模以上工业销售产值	%	-19.8	-18.5	-17.4	-16.0	-13.6	-11.0
规模以上工业出口产品产值	%	-25.1	-23.8	-22.9	-21.7	-20.1	-18.0
规模以上工业产品产销率	%	0.2	-0.1	-0.6	-0.4	-0.5	-0.5
规模以上工业企业产品销售收入	%	-19.9	-19.4	-17.8	-16.3	-14.8	-12.2
规模以上工业企业利税总额	%	-33.9	-27.6	-18.9	-11.1	-4.5	3.4
全社会固定资产投资总额	%	9.1	13.8	14.5	13.4	10.4	13.0
#基本建设	%	35.4	37.7	34.1	22.8	18.3	18.0
更新改造	%	103.9	122.4	147.4	179.6	159.8	150.8
房地产开发	%	-9.8	-6.0	-0.4	-2.1	-2.6	2.3
来源于东莞的财政收入	%	-0.04	-1.9	1.6	2.0	2.5	4.5
市财政一般预算收入	%	5.7	3.6	5.9	6.4	8.0	10.5
市财政一般预算支出	%	14.0	13.3	8.5	7.0	5.4	3.5
金融机构各项人民币存款余额	%	7.0	7.9	9.7	10.4	12.5	14.6
#城乡居民储蓄存款余额	%	5.7	5.1	7.6	7.4	8.1	10.1
金融机构各项人民币贷款余额	%	14.2	17.7	18.8	20.1	20.8	22.2
货币总投放(现金支出)	%	-13.2	-11.6	-9.8	-9.5	-8.1	-6.8
货币总回笼(现金收入)	%	-13.6	-12.0	-10.6	-10.5	-9.1	-7.8
进出口总额(海关口径)	%	-26.4	-25.3	-23.8	-22.4	-20.1	-17.0
#出口总额	%	-23.1	-22.5	-21.3	-20.4	-18.5	-16.0
新签项目宗数	%	-21.8	-15.2	-6.0	1.4	8.1	4.7
合同规定外商投资额	%	-48.7	-47.6	-43.8	-41.2	-39.3	-37.5
实际利用外资(不含对外借款)	%	5.4	3.8	4.0	5.7	5.8	6.0
社会消费品零售总额	%	12.0	12.4	12.9	13.4	13.9	14.1
居民消费价格总指数	%	-3.3	-3.4	-3.5	-3.5	-3.3	-3.1
#服务项目价格指数	%	-3.6	-4.0	-4.0	-4.0	-4.0	-3.7
总供电量	%	-9.1	-7.7	-6.2	-5.8	-4.6	-3.7
总售电量	%	-6.9	-6.0	-5.0	-3.8	-4.7	-1.9
邮电业务收入	%	-10.0	-9.4	-9.8	-9.5	-9.6	-9.3
城市居民人均可支配收入	%			9.4			9.1
城市居民人均消费性支出	%			3.6			4.6

1-9 历年地区生产总值

Gross Domestic Product over Years

年 份	地区生产总值 (万元)				人均生产总值 (元)
		第一产业	第二产业	第三产业	
1978	61122	27235	26781	7106	553
1979	66233	26460	29244	10528	593
1980	72199	26323	33290	12586	643
1981	91131	32772	42980	15379	802
1982	114322	37257	58137	18927	991
1983	130340	39847	68962	21531	1115
1984	159632	45671	78091	35869	1350
1985	226033	61475	116584	47973	1885
1986	300167	81416	135735	83016	2462
1987	392859	98236	177249	117373	3170
1988	554583	118888	282771	152924	4408
1989	609202	126568	279724	202910	4768
1990	804401	132787	405290	266325	6173
1991	959073	134523	503220	321330	5095
1992	1108922	144115	592701	372106	5038
1993	1570491	143953	873114	553424	5850
1994	2170341	174796	1194928	800616	6357
1995	2962892	214306	1669723	1078863	7421
1996	3617502	248645	1994826	1374031	8444
1997	4485981	256388	2432816	1796777	9747
1998	5579964	259437	3056779	2263749	11265
1999	6672386	257863	3670519	2744004	12494
2000	8202530	259087	4507072	3436372	13679
2001	9918905	260968	5405092	4252845	15268
2002	11869374	248791	6488109	5132474	18131
2003	14525186	228165	7981954	6315068	22174
2004	18060258	227087	10160382	7672789	27554
2005	21831961	205546	12278624	9347791	33287
2006	26279791	120089	15065985	11093717	39490
2007	31600489	118991	17546573	13934924	46146
2008	37036004	148251	19016068	17871685	53301
2009	37639142	147877	18230836	19260428	56601

注：1.本表绝对值按当年价计算，指数按可比价计算,下同。
2.人均生产总值1990年以前按户籍人口计算，1991年起按常住人口计算，与以前年份不可比。

1-10 历年地区生产总值指数（上年＝100）

Indices of Gross Domestic Product over Years(preceding year=100)

年 份	地区生产总值指数	第一产业	第二产业	第三产业	人均生产总值指数	人均GDP指数与GDP指数之比
1979	99.5	86.5	107.0	146.4	98.6	0.991
1980	102.7	90.3	117.3	113.9	102.0	0.993
1981	116.6	115.0	122.1	110.8	115.4	0.989
1982	116.9	105.3	131.0	117.6	115.1	0.985
1983	110.4	104.8	115.7	111.3	108.9	0.987
1984	114.2	109.0	107.0	140.9	112.9	0.988
1985	132.3	118.9	144.5	132.7	130.5	0.986
1986	126.1	111.9	110.3	174.7	124.0	0.983
1987	122.5	111.6	127.7	126.0	120.5	0.984
1988	115.7	90.6	143.7	103.0	114.0	0.985
1989	107.1	99.8	106.2	113.7	105.5	0.985
1990	123.2	104.4	127.6	128.0	120.8	0.980
1991	117.5	103.1	121.5	118.6	108.8	0.926
1992	108.3	100.0	112.6	105.1	92.6	0.855
1993	127.9	79.4	139.2	129.0	104.8	0.820
1994	122.5	107.2	124.7	122.3	96.3	0.786
1995	127.4	110.5	135.1	116.8	108.9	0.855
1996	117.5	109.4	115.5	123.5	109.5	0.932
1997	119.6	104.5	119.8	121.8	111.3	0.931
1998	121.8	100.9	122.1	124.5	113.1	0.929
1999	119.7	102.3	120.6	120.3	111.0	0.928
2000	119.7	99.8	120.7	120.0	106.6	0.891
2001	119.9	103.0	121.6	118.9	110.7	0.923
2002	120.5	97.6	122.6	119.1	119.6	0.992
2003	120.5	90.2	122.3	119.7	120.4	0.999
2004	121.0	90.0	125.6	115.8	120.9	0.999
2005	119.5	102.3	120.0	119.3	119.4	0.999
2006	119.2	58.9	121.9	117.1	117.5	0.986
2007	118.3	89.9	114.8	123.3	114.9	0.972
2008	114.0	110.6	106.1	124.0	112.4	0.986
2009	105.3	102.3	99.7	111.4	110.0	1.045

1-11 历年地区生产总值产业构成

Composition of Gross Domestic Product over Years

单位：%

年 份	地区生产总值	第一产业	第二产业	第三产业
1978	100.0	44.6	43.8	11.6
1979	100.0	40.0	44.2	15.9
1980	100.0	36.5	46.1	17.4
1981	100.0	36.0	47.2	16.9
1982	100.0	32.6	50.9	16.6
1983	100.0	30.6	52.9	16.5
1984	100.0	28.6	48.9	22.5
1985	100.0	27.2	51.6	21.2
1986	100.0	27.1	45.2	27.7
1987	100.0	25.0	45.1	29.9
1988	100.0	21.4	51.0	27.6
1989	100.0	20.8	45.9	33.3
1990	100.0	16.5	50.4	33.1
1991	100.0	14.0	52.5	33.5
1992	100.0	13.0	53.5	33.6
1993	100.0	9.2	55.6	35.2
1994	100.0	8.1	55.1	36.9
1995	100.0	7.2	56.4	36.4
1996	100.0	6.9	55.1	38.0
1997	100.0	5.7	54.2	40.1
1998	100.0	4.7	54.8	40.6
1999	100.0	3.9	55.0	41.1
2000	100.0	3.2	55.0	41.9
2001	100.0	2.6	54.5	42.9
2002	100.0	2.1	54.7	43.2
2003	100.0	1.6	55.0	43.5
2004	100.0	1.3	56.3	42.5
2005	100.0	0.9	56.2	42.8
2006	100.0	0.5	57.3	42.2
2007	100.0	0.4	55.5	44.1
2008	100.0	0.4	51.3	48.3
2009	100.0	0.4	48.4	51.2

1-12 各行业增加值项目（2009年）

Composition of Value-added by Industry (2009)

单位:万元

项　　目	增加值	劳动者报酬	生产税净额	固定资产折旧	营业盈余
地区生产总值	**37639142**	**15365173**	**3850333**	**6996340**	**11427296**
第一产业	147877	56168		91709	
第二产业	18230836	8523791	1571970	2424987	5710088
工业	17415347	8161742	1443635	2365041	5444929
建筑业	815489	362049	128335	59946	265159
第三产业	19260428	6785214	2278363	4479644	5717208
交通运输、仓储和邮政业	799116	317337	57270	242587	181922
交通运输和仓储业	763692	301864	55772	238227	167829
邮政业	35425	15474	1497	4361	14093
信息传输、计算机服务和软件业	1717874	278065	91614	296640	1051554
批发和零售业	3605753	1765762	1276383	166066	397542
住宿和餐饮业	1473255	1205964	72578	203620	-8908
金融业	1540408	466963	236621	36565	800259
#银行业	1190514	388659	108080	31996	661778
房地产业	2830855	136899	343694	2002367	347895
房地产开发经营	639589	53552	293178	20498	272361
物业管理	177680	61532	11861	88054	16233
房地产中介服务	20218	9305	2704	2759	5450
其他房地产活动	148042	12511	35951	45729	53851
居民自有住房服务	1845327			1845327	
租赁和商务服务业	3862084	326328	125919	660126	2749712
科学研究、技术服务和地质勘查业	233198	60613	11958	100194	60434
水利、环境和公共设施管理业	87245	40726	3337	25479	17703
居民服务和其他服务业	878067	715666	27763	81214	53424
教育	574101	472712	2887	91953	6548
卫生、社会保障和社会福利业	365263	254681	6136	53274	51173
文化、体育和娱乐业	173472	84842	21326	59350	7953
#娱乐业	114585	54037	18453	47105	-5011
公共管理和社会组织	1119738	658655	876	460207	

1-13 主要年份支出法地区生产总值

Gross Domestic Product by Expenditure Approach in Main Years

项　　目	1995年	1998年	2000年	2004年	2005年	2008年	2009年
支出法地区生产总值(万元)	2962892	5579964	8202530	18060258	21831961	37036004	37639142
最终消费	1502524	2803708	4342481	9263952	11201390	19295758	19883133
资本形成总额	1210079	1969877	2369818	5562324	7148513	11548959	11972192
货物和服务净出口	250290	806380	1490232	3233982	3482058	6191287	5783817
资本形成率(投资率)(%)	40.8	35.3	28.9	30.8	32.7	31.2	31.8
最终消费率(消费率)(%)	50.7	50.2	52.9	51.3	51.3	52.1	52.8

1-14 主要年份资本形成总额及构成

Gross Capital Formation and Its Composition in Main Years

项　　目		1995年	1998年	2000年	2004年	2005年	2008年	2009年
资本形成总额(万元)		1210079	1969877	2369818	5562324	7148513	11548959	11972192
固定资产形成总额		884671	1535531	1775228	4614797	6115306	9624345	10122708
存货增加		325407	434345	594590	947527	1033207	1924614	1849484
比重(资本形成总额=100)	固定资产形成总额	73.1	78.0	74.9	83.0	85.5	83.3	84.6
	存货增加	26.9	22.0	25.1	17.0	14.5	16.7	15.4

1-15 主要年份最终消费支出及构成

Final Consumption Expenditure and Its Composition in Main Years

项　　目		1995年	1998年	2000年	2004年	2005年	2008年	2009年
最终消费(万元)		1502524	2803708	4342481	9263952	11201390	19295758	19883133
居民消费		1262972	2484308	3752814	8029368	9798031	16962490	17320612
政府消费		239552	319400	589666	1234584	1403359	2333268	2562521
比重(最终消费=100)	居民消费	84.1	88.6	86.4	86.7	87.5	87.9	87.1
	政府消费	15.9	11.4	13.6	13.3	12.5	12.1	12.9

1-16　季度地区生产总值（2005-2009年）

Quarter of Gross Domestic product (2005-2009)

项　　目		地区生产总值	
		累计数（亿元）	同比增长（%）
2005年	1季度	478.98	18.0
	1-2季度	1023.17	18.7
	1-3季度	1602.39	19.4
	1-4季度	2183.20	19.5
2006年	1季度	562.96	18.3
	1-2季度	1223.08	18.7
	1-3季度	1930.18	19.2
	1-4季度	2627.98	19.2
2007年	1季度	665.26	17.4
	1-2季度	1456.48	17.5
	1-3季度	2300.44	17.5
	1-4季度	3160.05	18.3
2008年	1季度	805.97	16.2
	1-2季度	1740.97	16.0
	1-3季度	2737.00	15.1
	1-4季度	3703.60	14.0
2009年	1季度	768.94	-2.3
	1-2季度	1692.81	0.6
	1-3季度	2705.78	3.1
	1-4季度	3763.91	5.3

1-17　季度民营经济增加值发展速度（2005-2009年）

Quarter of Growth Rates of Private Economy value-added (2005-2009)

项　　目		民营经济增加值发展速度(%)	项　　目		民营经济增加值发展速度(%)
2005年	1季度	118.3	2007年	1-3季度	118.9
	1-2季度	119.5		1-4季度	119.3
	1-3季度	120.3	2008年	1季度	118.9
	1-4季度	120.2		1-2季度	117.9
2006年	1季度	119.1		1-3季度	117.3
	1-2季度	119.5		1-4季度	115.6
	1-3季度	119.8	2009年	1季度	104.6
	1-4季度	120.6		1-2季度	106.1
2007年	1季度	121.0		1-3季度	108.6
	1-2季度	118.6		1-4季度	110.2

1-18 历年工农业总产值

Gross Output Value of Industry and Agriculture over Years

单位：万元

年份	工农业总产值	农业	工业		
				轻工业	重工业
1978	84440	42394	42046	31539	10507
1979	90361	41527	48834	36230	12604
1980	101003	41943	59060	43495	15565
1981	118999	50388	68611	51570	17041
1982	138419	55881	82538	60681	21857
1983	151262	56439	94823	69320	25503
1984	184417	70180	114237	81802	32435
1985	264739	91244	173495	129464	44031
1986	362336	122988	239348	174251	65097
1987	515273	148414	366859	265157	101702
1988	820929	203685	617244	394088	223156
1989	995695	221079	774616	491260	283356
1990	1222259	236412	985847	603329	382518
1991	1526152	242587	1283565	797899	485666
1992	2138039	271293	1866746	1232505	634241
1993	2961230	284539	2676691	1765600	911091
1994	4238731	347451	3891280	2480380	1410900
1995	5652727	426901	5225826	3319385	1906441
1996	7259021	497161	6761860	4337001	2424859
1997	8500548	514373	7986175	5273909	2712266
1998	10413801	536047	9877754	5812367	4065387
1999	12956449	537442	12419007	6662589	5756418
2000	15744241	546383	15197858	8012197	7185661
2001	19027514	559280	18468234	9800160	8668074
2002	23510827	546383	22964444	11345286	11619158
2003	29238097	490206	28747891	14412890	14335001
2004	37278037	441912	36836125	15965813	20870312
2005	45120842	420496	44700346	19661630	25038716
2006	55509635	212632	55297003	24676434	30620569
2007	66878337	199782	66678555	28440950	38237605
2008	73378209	255307	73122902	32793386	40329516
2009	67881114	253077	67628037	30133426	37494611

1-19 主要年份全市企业和个体工商户登记注册年末实有数量

Number of Enterprises and Self-employed Individuals registered at Year-end in Main Years

单位：户

项　　目	2001年	2002年	2003年	2004年	2005年	2006年	2007年	2008年	2009年
工商登记户数合计	**163743**	**215631**	**248433**	**280483**	**353266**	**403403**	**476125**	**504978**	**505502**
内资企业	18055	16080	15427	15916	13898	12953	13401	13074	12493
#国有	3119	2989	2869	2521	1977	1554	1404	1313	1141
集体	12142	10066	8984	8786	6478	4989	4487	3385	2899
有限责任公司	2573	2841	1382	1606	1606	1468	1493	7017	7886
外商投资企业	4815	5842	6411	7387	7675	7695	7973	9437	9748
#合资	1412	1398	1228	1199	1013	822	718	860	1206
合作	751	739	629	593	482	379	307	218	197
独资	2649	3702	4551	5592	6177	6492	6946	6956	7678
"三来一补"企业	11310	11557	10515	10388	9552	8206	7417	6552	5748
私营企业	9260	12529	16820	23225	29017	38282	48955	63241	74229
个体工商户	120303	169623	199260	223567	293124	336267	398379	412674	403284

注：本表数据来源于市工商局。

1-20 个体工商户情况（2009年）

Statistics on Self-employed Individuals (2009)

项　　目	户数（户）	从业人员（人）	资金数额（万元）	其中城镇		
				户数（户）	从业人员（人）	资金数额（万元）
合　计	**403284**	**1030413**	**891715**	**207301**	**504259**	**434761**
农、林、牧、渔业	207	791	4874	88	315	1712
工　业	53314	278440	320406	20152	97827	117411
建筑业	1108	2977	5050	603	1528	1928
交通运输、仓储和邮政业	1528	4214	5915	530	1762	1663
信息传输、计算机服务和软件业	3776	5618	3282	1835	2659	1459
批发和零售业	267679	542687	369324	144034	290248	204311
住宿和餐饮业	36774	105720	95699	18951	60298	56734
房地产业	182	356	573	121	233	316
租赁和商务服务业	2303	5523	6858	1555	3652	4382
居民服务和其他服务业	35541	81120	70074	18937	44020	38818
卫生、社会保障和社会福利业	32	88	153	28	79	141
文化、体育和娱乐业	526	2041	8046	283	1183	5029
其他行业	314	838	1461	184	455	857

注：本表数据来源于市工商局。

1-21 私营工商企业基本情况（2009年）

Basic Conditions of Private Industrial and Commercial Enterprises (2009)

项　　目	户数(户)	投资者人数(人)	雇工人数(人)	注册资本(万元)	其中：1. 独资企业 户数(户)	投资者人数(人)	雇工人数(人)	注册资本(万元)
合　计	**74229**	**135149**	**475942**	**9356447**	**7633**	**7569**	**82173**	**278847**
农、林、牧、渔业	721	1081	11724	69213	443	407	9349	33167
工　业	23187	43689	183427	2465845	3863	3876	51543	123094
建筑业	3537	6735	22046	655654	44	44	249	390
交通运输、仓储和邮政业	1422	2629	7831	236123	27	25	114	307
信息传输、计算机服务和软件业	1882	3387	12520	227069	527	527	5029	52019
批发和零售业	27074	46942	141995	2142863	1510	1513	5618	13847
住宿和餐饮业	1021	1665	12721	194686	328	323	4288	33754
房地产业	2669	5432	14029	763477	10	12	43	55
租赁和商务服务业	6570	12924	35549	1236406	233	236	853	2479
居民服务和其他服务业	3213	4815	17151	174666	531	480	3957	13422
卫生、社会保障和社会福利业	24	47	311	48663				
文化、体育和娱乐业	467	834	3315	64853	82	87	961	5626
其他行业	2442	4969	13324	1076929	35	39	169	689

1-21 续表

项　　目	2. 合伙企业 户数(户)	投资者人数(人)	雇工人数(人)	注册资本(万元)	3. 有限责任公司 户数(户)	投资者人数(人)	雇工人数(人)	注册资本(万元)
合　计					**65544**	**124965**	**385124**	**8825117**
农、林、牧、渔业					155	342	809	23160
工　业					18950	38806	128059	2254742
建筑业					3484	6686	21751	655234
交通运输、仓储和邮政业					1387	2592	7676	235211
信息传输、计算机服务和软件业					1207	2508	6605	160770
批发和零售业					25408	45026	135892	2103569
住宿和餐饮业					647	1230	7582	149542
房地产业					2645	5406	13932	746446
租赁和商务服务业					6272	12506	34417	1208294
居民服务和其他服务业					2617	4203	12864	158781
卫生、社会保障和社会福利业					24	47	311	48663
文化、体育和娱乐业					373	723	2283	58489
其他行业					2375	4890	12943	1022216

注：本表数据来源于市工商局。

1-22 历年总供用电

Gross Electricity Supply over Years

单位：万千瓦时

年份	总供电量	#网供	总用电量	#工业用电	#农村工业用电	照明用电
1978	16375	16376	14909	10828		1741
1979	19271	19271	17325	12474		2338
1980	21659	21569	19663	13407		3372
1981	22247	22247	19902	14194		4650
1982	26871	26351	23502	14618		6272
1983	31527	31527	27461	17496		8052
1984	32617	28566	28403	18019		9484
1985	38183	33907	33907	22139		9934
1986	39305	35100	35099	25567		10204
1987	64258	45129	57083	38076		16657
1988	94842	66295	84738	60226		22347
1989	120861	76762	108387	80050	60116	26139
1990	180142	111800	161479	119322	70459	39677
1991	240471	139841	216657	157062	99767	56504
1992	320003	180902	288688	210373	144391	25578
1993	436231	242205	393962	287400	205687	103583
1994	585763	393312	530232	416128	297479	110357
1995	680030	384764	616788	487873	386413	125135
1996	800300	506062	727093	569317	423898	153093
1997	949296	612907	866456	702811	519325	180583
1998	1094816	724758	1009086	781811	597601	221750
1999	1327788	973427	1234183	965945	756713	261629
2000	1780290	1349134	1690557	1345766	1104301	337044
2001	2077248	1649458	1965858	1567083	1400915	584700
2002	2585474	2219054	2471342	2070709	1877278	392879
2003	3216468	2846679	2835389	2401970	2071712	424869
2004	3728441	3196454	3502821	2966131	2539962	527332
2005	4156629	3422603	3965892	3303140	2873734	652514
2006	4644506	3676492	4455157	3686266	3234929	759384
2007	5078933	4167125	4825614	3956118	3483474	859851
2008	5073489	4423085	4873204	3928108	3424868	935510
2009	4888467	4318868	4781895	3761046	3292716	1011494

1-23 企业景气指数（2009年）

Business Climate Index (2009)

项　　目	一季度	二季度	三季度	四季度
企业景气指数	**98.83**	**114.33**	**131.17**	**133.40**
按行业门类分				
工业	98.59	115.14	130.87	135.06
建筑业	90.00	96.58	107.11	103.27
交通运输、仓储和邮政业	111.57	76.46	91.57	78.23
批发和零售业	95.24	146.12	156.13	159.31
房地产业	104.60	97.27	132.28	152.28
社会服务业	100.00	110.28	124.72	116.96
信息传输、计算机服务和软件	109.70	131.43	149.85	113.33
住宿和餐饮业	73.19	85.20	101.33	108.72
按企业登记注册类型分				
国有企业	156.47	180.17	181.47	196.64
集体企业	117.13	127.66	132.92	139.02
股份合作企业				
有限责任公司	112.57	120.57	132.39	125.80
股份有限公司	54.40	116.48	143.93	141.48
私营企业	106.72	104.55	154.15	152.61
外商及港、澳、台投资企业	89.35	103.32	118.11	122.08
按企业规模分				
大型	115.15	137.13	153.42	153.70
中型	94.38	97.75	111.36	112.64
小型	86.54	115.38	125.00	121.15
按观察指标分				
生产总量	67.69	107.46	132.06	124.61
盈利(亏损)变化	66.80	110.10	126.18	108.40
流动资金	102.99	114.62	127.71	131.10
货款拖欠	96.36	100.95	112.67	97.47
劳动力需求	67.04	97.37	125.31	122.16
固定资产投资	67.09	100.76	110.58	113.83
产品订货	65.34	90.16	110.49	109.60
企业融资	103.70	101.92	108.33	119.17

1-24 企业家信心指数（2009年）

Entrepreneurs' Confidence Index (2009)

项　　目	一季度	二季度	三季度	四季度
企业家信心指数	**85.12**	**96.52**	**122.30**	**128.02**
按行业门类分				
工业	83.87	91.87	121.44	128.51
建筑业	90.77	90.68	99.92	103.27
交通运输、仓储和邮政业	78.23	63.13	91.57	91.57
批发和零售业	99.46	139.55	144.23	164.78
房地产业	72.32	95.24	113.18	126.51
社会服务业	89.47	94.47	127.23	122.51
信息传输、计算机服务和软件	109.87	129.87	138.27	111.92
住宿和餐饮业	52.40	53.72	92.06	92.76
按企业登记注册类型分				
国有企业	181.66	180.36	181.66	184.32
集体企业	89.47	117.13	122.40	133.76
股份合作企业				
有限责任公司	97.43	113.13	125.75	123.85
股份有限公司	60.28	102.96	141.50	138.16
私营企业	91.80	98.53	107.99	131.82
外商及港、澳、台投资企业	69.33	74.41	106.88	113.53
按企业规模分				
大型	96.02	111.15	141.16	137.91
中型	78.65	83.15	111.36	118.39
小型	92.31	105.77	109.62	123.08

1-25 各行业企业景气指数（2009年）

Business Climate Index by Sector (2009)

指　　标	一季度	二季度	三季度	四季度
总指数	**98.83**	**114.33**	**131.17**	**133.40**
工业				
企业综合生产经营	98.59	115.14	130.87	135.06
生产成本	101.57	93.48	75.43	70.79
生产总量	64.40	123.77	147.49	136.72
产品订货	61.22	100.42	117.66	108.19
＃国外订货	53.77	92.65	115.40	101.46
产品销售量	46.44	133.78	153.22	113.49
产品销售价格	66.53	92.32	97.42	99.23
产成品库存	102.83	121.82	122.95	122.78
税后利润	63.80	126.60	144.69	112.60
流动资金	109.85	117.42	128.79	133.40
企业融资	110.10	102.86	111.35	126.69
货款拖欠	90.16	94.10	118.12	93.64
劳动力需求	64.11	101.72	139.38	133.64
固定资产投资	58.80	100.60	118.10	121.13
科技创新	90.88	112.47	106.33	101.59
主要原材料及能源购进价格	101.99	93.12	60.10	75.38
主要原材料及能源供应	142.41	153.96	152.88	150.55
建筑业				
企业综合生产经营	90.00	96.58	107.11	103.27
工程合同	118.04	44.63	125.59	122.97
＃国(境)外合同	66.42	98.98	74.24	92.31
建筑工程量	107.24	91.54	81.33	138.36
新开工工程量	53.42	51.30	132.82	122.97
技术设备能力	157.19	165.40	152.87	157.12
工程进度	111.27	113.33	114.15	116.95
工程结算收入	113.91	84.88	74.24	130.66
建筑材料购进价格	151.01	71.87	75.19	68.33
工程结算成本	80.02	117.01	133.63	76.15
税后利润	100.33	118.21	74.29	77.06
流动资金	128.06	124.18	164.22	156.99
企业融资	117.00	103.25	114.20	109.26
工程款拖欠	90.52	112.11	130.76	93.88
劳动力需求	67.00	84.88	119.29	106.79
固定资产投资	51.39	111.88	107.98	93.88
交通运输、仓储及邮政业				
企业综合生产经营	111.57	76.46	91.57	78.23
业务预订	64.90	56.46	111.57	80.00
业务量	71.57	56.46	111.57	66.67
业务收费价格	80.00	80.00	93.33	100.00

1-25 续表 1

指　　标	一季度	二季度	三季度	四季度
营业成本	93.33	68.43	58.23	13.33
税后利润	86.67	56.46	73.33	61.77
流动资金	98.23	91.57	78.23	98.23
企业融资	84.90	91.57	106.67	104.90
货款拖欠	113.33	93.33	84.90	81.77
劳动力需求	86.67	93.33	78.23	95.10
固定资产投资	83.54	89.80	81.77	95.10
批发和零售贸易业				
企业综合生产经营	95.24	146.12	156.13	159.31
商品购进	72.05	120.31	132.23	135.23
商品购进价格	122.73	83.95	85.99	67.04
商品销售	70.78	112.38	105.39	105.35
#出口	73.16	98.05	98.12	103.33
商品销售价格	67.20	97.98	93.74	131.45
商品库存	116.37	125.01	139.69	145.78
经营费用	100.40	110.20	85.48	90.94
竞争能力	129.53	154.46	152.37	150.64
税后利润	80.46	127.18	115.26	125.56
流动资金	102.37	131.77	143.32	150.72
企业融资	112.87	127.83	136.77	136.77
货款拖欠	98.80	100.46	87.49	114.94
劳动力需求	63.70	93.00	116.13	126.06
固定资产投资	99.51	117.31	98.93	96.67
房地产业				
企业综合生产经营	104.60	97.27	132.28	152.28
土地开发面积	77.78	92.44	111.41	138.05
完成投资	65.46	89.35	125.22	136.14
新开工面积	50.10	68.84	105.76	130.88
房屋竣工面积	66.67	63.07	121.67	134.50
商品房预售面积	82.92	71.61	83.93	125.34
商品房销售面积	78.83	73.14	88.69	119.57
商品房销售价格	72.32	95.02	115.91	121.01
空置商品房面积	134.85	141.16	117.94	128.69
税后利润	87.56	79.80	87.68	126.78
流动资金	65.61	92.78	121.63	138.90
企业融资	72.28	86.62	86.62	95.20
货款拖欠	139.61	132.28	134.15	123.93
劳动力需求	30.65	55.21	74.85	110.33
固定资产投资	68.19	100.00	108.69	125.23
社会服务业				
企业综合生产经营	100.00	110.28	124.72	116.96
服务预订	73.91	60.00	95.00	90.00

1-25 续表 2

指　　标	一 季 度	二 季 度	三 季 度	四 季 度
竞争能力	140.00	132.23	134.72	152.77
旅游客源	113.03	50.00	166.67	66.67
收费服务价格	68.91	74.44	95.00	70.00
业务量	88.91	65.00	110.00	85.00
营业成本	81.09	80.56	50.00	80.00
税后利润	59.19	60.00	100.00	80.00
流动资金	94.72	112.23	121.96	109.44
企业融资	91.96	91.96	91.96	101.96
货款拖欠	85.81	110.28	87.23	96.96
劳动力需求	103.91	110.00	120.00	85.00
固定资产投资	71.96	91.96	86.96	86.96
信息传输、计算机服务和软件业				
企业综合生产经营	109.70	131.43	149.85	113.33
产品销售	51.77	65.11	121.75	76.98
产品订货	38.44	51.77	85.11	86.84
竞争能力	158.10	136.37	176.52	154.94
销售价格	91.60	71.60	71.60	70.15
营业收入	51.60	71.60	106.52	70.30
营业成本	84.77	44.77	73.01	79.71
税后利润	63.04	89.70	116.37	75.23
流动资金	117.93	111.27	124.60	113.16
企业融资	103.14	103.14	114.74	103.02
货款拖欠	123.21	96.54	134.96	71.77
劳动力需求	93.33	115.06	101.73	108.40
固定资产投资	103.31	96.64	96.64	113.16
住宿和餐饮业				
企业综合生产经营	73.19	85.20	101.33	108.72
业务预订	11.60	87.24	60.01	139.10
业务量	8.88	86.72	57.60	144.36
竞争能力	112.12	85.57	105.81	119.44
客房出租	0.00	0.00	0.00	33.33
收费服务价格	49.99	71.32	62.40	89.47
营业收入	1.60	78.79	68.06	128.57
营业成本	161.78	96.59	70.92	82.19
税后利润	11.60	73.52	85.49	135.61
流动资金	74.43	88.24	91.65	107.93
企业融资	92.83	105.22	91.65	96.60
货款拖欠	90.08	101.81	77.20	83.30
劳动力需求	42.63	86.66	92.39	118.36
固定资产投资	89.03	98.45	137.56	123.66

1-26 企业宏观经济景气状况

Macro Economic Climate Situations of Enterprises

指 标	2003年	2004年	2005年	2006年	2007年	2008年	2009年
一季度							
乐观	49.22	49.12	39.84	45.56	53.43	44.86	21.32
一般	41.90	42.49	54.26	46.28	37.89	46.78	42.48
不乐观	8.88	8.39	5.9	8.16	8.68	8.36	36.20
企业家信心指数	140.35	140.73	133.95	137.41	144.75	136.51	85.12
二季度							
乐观	44.42	49.19	40.67	45.15	53.04	41.18	24.00
一般	41.20	40.65	50.71	44.22	36.51	49.61	48.52
不乐观	14.38	10.16	8.63	10.63	10.46	9.21	27.48
企业家信心指数	130.04	139.03	132.04	134.53	142.57	131.96	96.52
三季度							
乐观	49.18	49.10	41.32	46.79	52.47	32.49	32.43
一般	48.49	40.85	49.22	46.46	38.28	55.07	57.44
不乐观	5.33	10.05	9.46	6.75	9.26	12.45	10.13
企业家信心指数	140.85	139.05	131.86	140.03	143.21	120.04	122.30
四季度							
乐观	49.03	49.05	43.59	49.91	54.11	19.81	36.40
一般	49.13	43.51	45.86	41.94	39.96	48.46	55.22
不乐观	6.83	11.45	10.54	8.15	5.93	31.72	8.38
企业家信心指数	140.20	133.60	133.05	141.76	148.18	88.10	128.02

1-27 企业综合生产经营状况

Comprehensive Production and Management Situations of Enterprises

指 标	2003年	2004年	2005年	2006年	2007年	2008年	2009年
一季度							
良好	46.13	41.55	42.26	42.90	49.06	43.76	23.01
一般	46.55	52.59	48.27	48.00	39.90	44.41	52.81
不佳	7.32	5.86	9.47	9.10	11.04	11.83	24.18
企业景气指数	138.81	135.69	132.79	133.80	138.02	131.94	98.83
二季度							
良好	38.17	45.61	43.39	43.95	48.04	37.58	27.65
一般	4.00	47.64	47.96	47.61	45.36	52.34	59.03
不佳	18.84	6.75	8.65	8.44	6.60	10.08	13.31
企业景气指数	119.33	138.85	134.75	135.51	141.44	127.50	114.33
三季度							
良好	46.67	46.38	38.46	47.09	52.18	34.90	39.20
一般	52.40	45.74	54.57	47.67	42.84	52.53	52.78
不佳	3.93	7.89	6.97	5.24	4.97	12.58	8.02
企业景气指数	139.73	138.48	131.49	141.85	147.21	122.32	131.17
四季度							
良好	46.34	44.44	39.85	45.90	51.67	24.31	41.72
一般	49.52	46.18	51.39	49.38	39.42	51.89	49.96
不佳	4.14	9.38	8.76	4.72	8.91	23.81	8.32
企业景气指数	142.20	135.06	131.09	141.19	142.76	100.50	133.40

1-28 历年国民经济主要指标人均水平

The Per Capita Level of Main National Economic Indicators over Years

年 份	人均生产总值(元)	人均地方财政收入(元)	人均出口总额(美元)	人均消费品零售额(元)	人均固定资产投资额(元)	人均用电量(千瓦时)	年末人均储蓄存款余额(元)
1978	553	60	36	192	21	135	49
1979	593	59	48	224	15	155	64
1980	643	60	69	281	21	175	104
1981	802	60	81	354	33	175	178
1982	991	70	94	417	157	204	238
1983	1115	73	102	447	157	235	328
1984	1350	72	110	625	254	240	520
1985	1885	93	146	781	589	283	761
1986	2462	132	191	1004	945	288	1068
1987	3170	163	216	1214	1145	461	1519
1988	4408	215	253	1959	1315	674	1965
1989	4768	250	273	2116	392	848	2529
1990	6173	274	436	2454	576	1239	2592
1991	5095	236	879	1943	732	1154	3074
1992	5038	263	1217	2073	883	1350	3580
1993	5850	385	1318	2615	1345	1617	4131
1994	6357	277	1548	3070	5074	1911	5130
1995	7421	366	2468	3577	1998	1952	6924
1996	8444	268	2553	3489	1879	2021	8300
1997	9747	278	2774	3564	1608	2114	9758
1998	11265	324	2799	3753	1650	2162	10740
1999	12494	344	2851	3806	1662	2322	10890
2000	13679	503	2834	3884	1700	2792	10422
2001	15268	693	2923	4244	1932	3026	12212
2002	18131	845	3626	4907	2926	3775	15297
2003	22174	1030	4275	5645	4876	4329	18788
2004	27554	1261	5369	6506	6940	5344	21836
2005	33287	1585	6240	7624	9106	6047	26343
2006	39490	1938	7119	8784	10601	6695	29833
2007	46146	2723	8796	10162	12284	7047	30527
2008	53301	3011	9432	12064	13572	7013	37966
2009	56601	3476	8296	14422	16453	7191	45741

注：人均指标1991年以前按户籍人口计算，1991年起时点数按常住人口计算，时期数按平均常住人口计算。

主要统计指标解释

地区生产总值 指按国土原则计算的一个国家（或地区）物质生产部门和非物质生产部门在一定时期内所生产和提供最终使用的产品和劳务的货币表现。它不包括中间消耗的产品和劳务的价值。这些最终产品和劳务，不论是本国居民投资、本国居民生产的，还是外国居民投资、外国居民生产的，只要是在这个国家的领土范围之内，就全部计入这个国家（或地区）的地区生产总值。

地区生产总值从生产角度来说，是国民经济各部门的增加值之和；从分配角度来说，是这些部门劳动者收入、税金、利润、固定资产折旧等项目之和；从使用角度来说，是最终使用于消费、投资以及净出口的产品和劳务的价值总和。所以地区生产总值有三种计算方法，即生产法、分配法、使用法。国外净要素收入与生产总值之和，即为国民生产总值。

增加值 增加值是指常住单位生产过程创造的新增价值和固定资产的转移价值。它可以按生产法计算，也可以按收入法计算，按生产法计算，它等于总产出减去中间投入；按收入法计算，它等于劳动者报酬、生产税净额、固定资产折旧和营业盈余之和。

劳动者报酬 指劳动者为常住单位提供劳务而获得的各种报酬，它反映劳动者参与增加值创造而获得的原始收入。具体包括从各种来源开支的货币工资和实物工资，即单位以工资、福利、社会保险等形式，从成本、费用和利润中为劳动者支付的各种开支，以及个体和其他劳动者通过参加社会生产活动所获得的各种劳动报酬。

生产税净额 指生产税与补贴之差，它反映政府从本期创造的增加值中所得的原始收入份额。生产税是指政府对生产单位的生产经营活动所征收的各种税、附加和规费，具体包括销售（营业）税金及附加、增值税、管理费开支的税、应交纳的养路费、排污费和水电附加等，以及烟酒专卖上缴政府的专项收入。补贴与生产税相反，是政府对生产单位的单方面收入转移，因此视为负税处理，包括政策亏损补贴、粮食系统价格补贴、外贸企业出口退税收入等。

固定资产折旧 指一定时期内为弥补固定资产损耗而应提取的补偿价值，它反映了全部固定资产在本期生产中的资产转移价值。各类企业的固定资产折旧是指从成本费用中提取的折旧费。对不计提折旧的单位，如政府机关、事业单位、学校医院、部队和居民住房则应进行虚拟折旧。

营业盈余 指常住单位创造的增加值扣除固定资产折旧价值、支付劳动者报酬和上缴政府生产税净额后的余额，它反映企业参与增加值创造而应得到的原始收入份额。该指标相当于企业的营业利润，但要扣除利税后项目中支付的工资、福利及公益金等。

三次产业 根据社会生产活动历史发展的顺序对产业结构的划分，产品直接取自自然界的部门称为第一产业，初级产品进行再加工的部门称为第二产业，为生产和消费提供各种服务的部门称为第三产业。它是世界上通用的产业结构分类，但各国的划分不尽一致。我国的三次产业划分是：

第一产业：农业（包括种植业、林业、牧业、副业和渔业）

第二产业：工业（包括采掘工业、制造业、自来水、电力、蒸汽、热水、煤气）和建筑业。

第三产业：除第一、第二产业以外的其他各业。由于第三产业包括的行业多、范围广，根据我国的实际情况，第三产业可分为两部分；一是流通部门，二是服务部门。

景气指数 亦称景气度，是对企业景气调查中的定性指标通过定量方法加工汇总，综合反映某一特定调查群体或某一社会经济现象所处的状态或发展趋势的一种指标，景气指数介于 0—200 之间，100 为景气指数的临界值；当景气指数大于 100 时，表明经济状况趋于上升或改善，处于景气状态；当景气指数小于

100 时，表明经济状况趋于下降或恶化，处于不景气状态。

企业景气指数 亦称企业综合生产经营景气指数，是根据企业家对本企业综合生产经营情况的判断与预期（通常为对“良好”、“一般”、“不佳”的选择）而编制的指数，用以综合反映企业的生产经营状况。

企业家信心指数 亦称宏观经济景气指数，. 是根据企业家对企业对外部市场经济环境与宏观政策的认识、看法、判断与预期（通常为对“乐观”、“一般”、“不乐观”的选择）而编制的指数，用以综合反映企业家对宏观经济环境的感受与信心。

发展速度 用以反映社会经济发展程度的相对指标，根据两个时期发展水平的对比而得。由于比较的标准时期不同，发展速度可分为定基发展速度和环比发展速度两种。

增长速度 发展速度 - 1 （或 100%）就是增长速度。即增长速度=发展速度 - 1（或 100%）。

平均每年增长速度 我国计算平均增长速度有两种方法，一种是习惯上经常使用的“水平法”，又称几何平均法，是以间隔最后一年的水平同基期水平对比来计算平均每年增长（或下降）的速度；另一种是“累计法”又称代数平均法或方程法，是以间隔年内各年水平的总和同基期水平对比来计算平均每年增长（或下降）的速度。具体计算方法，可参照中国财经出版社出版的《平均增长速度查对表》。

在一般正常情况下，两种方法计算的平均每年增长速度比较接近，但在经济发展不平衡出现大起大落时，两种方法计算的结果差别较大。

本《年鉴》内所列的平均每年增长速度都是用水平法计算的。从某年到某年平均增长速度的年份，均不包基期年在内。如 1981-2006 年平均每年增长速度，是以 1980 年为基期，2006 年为报告期，年份从 1981 年算起，共 26 年。

二、人口与劳动力

Population and Labor Force

2-1 历年总人口数与人口密度

Total Population and Population Density over Years

单位：万人

年 份	户籍人口	按性别分		按农业、非农业分		外来暂住人口	常住人口	人口密度（人/平方公里）
		男	女	农业人口	非农业人口			
1949	68.24	32.87	35.37	56.29	11.95			
1952	71.68	34.53	37.15	58.69	12.99			
1957	77.48	37.50	39.98	62.52	14.96			
1962	79.64	38.07	41.57	64.42	15.22			
1965	86.46	41.83	44.63	70.28	16.18			
1970	98.56	47.91	50.65	81.26	17.30			
1975	107.94	52.70	55.24	90.37	17.57			
1978	111.23	54.34	56.89	92.74	18.29			451
1979	112.04	54.45	57.59	92.86	19.18			455
1980	112.70	54.43	58.27	92.87	19.83			457
1981	114.46	55.36	59.10	94.08	20.38			464
1982	116.19	56.28	59.91	95.32	20.87			471
1983	117.59	57.05	60.54	96.36	21.23			477
1984	118.95	57.80	61.15	96.47	22.48			483
1985	120.85	58.84	62.01	95.36	25.49			490
1986	123.01	59.95	63.06	96.53	26.48	15.62		499
1987	124.86	61.02	63.84	97.20	27.66	25.29		507
1988	126.76	62.09	64.67	97.96	28.80	36.89		514
1989	128.76	63.27	65.49	98.82	29.94	47.19		522
1990	131.85	64.96	66.89	100.99	30.86	65.59	175.62	712
1991	133.65	66.10	67.55	101.79	31.86	80.58	200.01	811
1992	136.06	67.55	68.51	103.35	32.71	114.48	227.78	924
1993	138.92	69.20	69.72	105.18	33.74	121.70	259.41	1052
1994	141.40	70.64	70.76	106.85	34.55	139.09	295.43	1198
1995	143.65	71.97	71.68	108.27	35.38	142.18	336.45	1365
1996	145.25	72.92	72.33	109.11	36.14	143.32	383.17	1554
1997	147.12	74.04	73.08	110.15	36.97	144.68	436.38	1770
1998	148.77	74.99	73.78	110.93	37.84	199.11	496.97	2016
1999	150.82	76.18	74.64	112.09	38.73	244.81	565.98	2296
2000	152.61	77.22	75.39	113.00	39.61	254.72	644.84	2616
2001	153.89	77.94	75.95	113.52	40.37	457.82	654.43	2655
2002	156.19	79.14	77.05	115.17	41.02	433.65	654.84	2657
2003	158.96	80.65	78.31	102.09	56.87	440.45	655.25	2658
2004	161.97	82.25	79.72	100.49	61.48	486.95	655.66	2660
2005	165.65	84.07	81.58	99.81	65.84	584.98	656.07	2662
2006	168.31	85.43	82.88	97.89	70.42	586.76	674.88	2738
2007	171.26	87.00	84.26	97.59	73.67	557.80	694.72	2818
2008	174.86	88.88	85.98	98.06	76.80	552.50	694.98	2819
2009	178.73	90.78	87.95	97.27	81.46	429.96	635.00	2576

注：人口密度1990年以前户籍人口计算，1990年起按常住人口计算。

2-2 主要年份户籍人口与劳动力指标

Main Indicators of Household Registration Population and Labor Force in Main Years

指　　标	单 位	1985年	1990年	1995年	2000年	2005年	2008年	2009年
年末户籍人口	人	1208515	1318526	1436525	1526090	1656541	1748658	1787283
#农业人口	人	953582	1009857	1082703	1130002	998159	980693	972706
人口性别比(女性人口=100)	%	94.9	97.1	100.4	102.4	103.1	103.4	103.2
人口密度	人/平方公里	490	535	583	619	672	709	725
人口出生率	‰	15.4	17.1	17.6	12.1	10.6	10.8	10.7
人口死亡率	‰	4.5	4.8	4.8	4.6	4.6	4.5	4.4
人口自然增长率	‰	10.8	12.3	12.8	7.5	6.0	6.2	6.3
人口净迁移率	‰	3.0	1.9	1.9	2.2	16.4	15.8	16.2
户籍从业人员总数	人	673494	750980	824014	886169	983628	1096704	1121839
按类型分								
企事业机关从业人员	人	122951	131631	184047	168013	178495	136771	150747
国有单位	人	56534	63469	75308	79738	86665	104512	99804
企业	人			32080	32964	22225	19202	15033
事业和机关	人			43228	46774	64440	85310	84771
城镇集体单位	人	63383	58749	65145	51088	45654	15482	20893
其他所有制单位	人	3034	9413	43594	37187	46176	16777	30050
#外商经济单位	人				11208	9725	4548	6711
港澳台经济单位	人				17482	25479	3213	12608
城镇私营个体劳动者人数	人	5809	20438	45122	83457	178793	359598	351366
农村乡镇劳动者人数	人	544734	598911	594845	634699	626340	600335	619726
按产业分								
第一产业劳动者人数	人	285857	271513	194895	173829	101936	60150	57012
第二产业劳动者人数	人	233231	305190	380101	414273	457039	410124	462281
第三产业劳动者人数	人	154406	174277	249018	298067	424653	626430	602545
离、退休及退职人员	人		24930	29568	34768	41323		
#国有单位	人		12255	18623	19915	12163		
城镇新登记的失业人员人数	人			6536	6524	7080	7936	7674
城镇失业人员安置就业人数	人				5683	6088	7515	11923

2-3 历年户籍人口自然变动情况

Natural Changes of Household Registration Population over Years

年 份	出 生		死 亡		自然增长	
	人 数 (人)	出生率 (‰)	人 数 (人)	死亡率 (‰)	人 数 (人)	自然增长率(‰)
1978	20728	18.73	5451	4.92	15277	13.81
1979	26931	24.13	5755	5.13	21176	19.00
1980	27428	24.41	5747	5.10	21681	19.31
1981	24828	21.86	6016	5.29	18812	16.57
1982	21991	19.07	5681	4.93	16310	14.14
1983	19573	16.74	6100	5.21	13473	11.53
1984	18380	15.54	5841	4.94	12539	10.60
1985	18432	15.37	5439	4.54	12993	10.83
1986	20049	16.44	5955	4.88	14094	11.56
1987	19962	16.11	5502	4.44	14459	11.67
1988	21077	16.75	5863	4.66	15214	12.09
1989	23457	17.06	5966	4.67	17491	12.39
1990	22238	17.07	6208	4.76	16030	12.31
1991	23771	17.91	6070	4.57	17701	13.34
1992	26040	19.31	6485	4.81	19555	14.50
1993	25270	18.38	6833	4.97	18437	13.41
1994	24152	17.88	6319	4.51	17833	13.37
1995	25312	17.59	6898	4.84	18414	12.75
1996	24635	17.05	7333	5.08	17302	11.97
1997	24106	16.50	6448	4.41	17658	12.09
1998	22563	15.31	6553	4.45	16010	10.86
1999	21673	14.55	6460	4.34	15213	10.22
2000	18260	12.11	6923	4.59	11337	7.52
2001	17083	11.16	6344	4.14	10739	7.01
2002	16029	10.35	6873	4.44	9156	5.91
2003	16204	10.34	7346	4.69	8858	5.65
2004	17312	10.86	7814	4.90	9498	5.96
2005	17301	10.62	7497	4.60	9804	6.02
2006	16819	10.14	7103	4.28	9716	5.86
2007	17482	10.39	7418	4.41	10064	5.98
2008	18382	10.77	7752	4.54	10630	6.23
2009	18584	10.67	7587	4.36	10997	6.31

2-4 历年户籍人口迁移变动情况

Changes of Household Registration Population Migration over Years

年份	迁入		迁出		总迁移		净迁移	
	人数（人）	迁入率（‰）	人数（人）	迁出率（‰）	人数（人）	总迁移率（‰）	人数（人）	净迁移率（‰）
1978	10148	9.2	13179	11.9	23327	21.1	-3031	-2.7
1980	13345	11.9	28624	25.5	41969	37.4	-15279	-13.6
1985	19205	16.0	15636	13.0	34841	29.1	3569	3.0
1990	13485	10.4	11061	8.5	24546	18.8	2424	1.9
1991	12628	9.5	12531	9.4	25159	19.0	97	0.1
1992	14622	10.8	11168	8.3	25790	19.1	3454	2.5
1993	10801	7.9	4886	3.6	15687	11.4	5915	4.3
1994	10127	7.2	6406	4.6	16533	11.8	3721	2.7
1995	10312	7.2	7675	5.4	17987	12.6	2637	1.9
1996	9273	6.4	11508	8.0	20781	14.4	-2235	-1.6
1997	10284	7.0	9469	6.5	19753	13.5	815	0.6
1998	12400	8.4	11253	7.6	23653	16.0	1147	0.8
1999	15049	10.0	11497	7.6	26546	17.6	3552	2.4
2000	15618	10.2	12314	8.1	27932	18.3	3304	2.2
2001	15968	10.4	11099	7.2	27067	17.6	4869	3.2
2002	20214	12.9	8033	5.1	28247	18.1	12181	7.8
2003	27143	17.1	7173	4.5	34316	21.6	19970	12.6
2004	29621	18.3	7618	4.7	37239	23.0	22003	13.6
2005	43026	26.0	15798	9.5	58824	35.5	27228	16.4
2006	30710	18.2	11442	6.8	42152	25.0	19268	11.4
2007	26940	15.7	4847	2.8	31787	18.6	22093	12.9
2008	33595	19.2	5974	3.4	39569	22.6	27621	15.8
2009	36387	20.4	7381	4.1	43768	24.5	29006	16.2

2-5 主要年份新莞人和劳动力

Migrant Population and Migrant Labor Force in Main Years

单位：人

项　　目	1995年	1996年	1997年	1998年	1999年	2000年	2001年	2002年
一、新莞人总计	**1421754**	**1433157**	**1446830**	**1991122**	**2448134**	**2547221**	**4578163**	**4336453**
(一) 按性别分								
男	581304	606524	554193	850266	1084492	1155277	2138218	1973316
女	840450	826633	892637	1140856	1363642	1391944	2439945	2363137
(二) 按来自地区分								
省内	371816	305821	298510	402267	504722	485889	731931	722894
省外	1023510	1106749	1130981	1569963	1921206	2041959	3826830	3593034
#湖南省	253574	232329	243384	330241	391491	377257	718295	685311
四川省	223727	223315	227077	294149	387730	319039	622166	555569
广西自治区	149478	137933	140483	183734	236936	240923	442904	394088
湖北省	84727	90528	89140	143662	173787	196697	359872	389735
江西省	67562	79730	83272	118685	149000	157323	294740	294086
港澳台	23729	18094	16048	17557	20664	17547	17975	18856
国外	2699	2493	1291	1335	1542	1826	1427	1669
二、新莞人劳动力总计	**1265368**	**1276626**	**1307279**	**1831939**	**2161487**	**2448415**	**4496771**	**4260142**
按行业分								
工业	1084860	1084330	1114235	1577922	1609539	2043270	3681099	3573355
农业	54714	64732	57214	68143	113324	88195	174936	127584
商业	52965	61092	67242	100041	282938	187015	283277	300642
服务业	72829	66472	68588	85833	155686	129935	357459	258561

注：本表根据市公安局统计数据整理。

2-5 续表

单位：人

项　　目	2003年	2004年	2005年	2006年	2007年	2008年	2009年
一、新莞人总计	**4404467**	**4869462**	**5849785**	**5867555**	**5577988**	**5525022**	**4299615**
(一) 按性别分							
男	2198324	2347115	2746833	2775718	2666292	2657712	2093055
女	2206143	2522347	3102952	3091837	2911696	2867310	2206560
(二) 按来自地区分							
省内	665549	747804	1036417	1012637	986062	1012341	889160
省外	3720408	4096599	4747692	4807064	4551507	4468505	3367565
#湖南省	663487	812976	844053	875904	816688	828779	604891
四川省	591145	581272	642170	617644	553907	533496	441758
广西自治区	432738	483329	574634	556961	497438	488226	396425
湖北省	443603	490063	514760	531987	521529	517519	391650
江西省	339518	329715	376526	367094	355798	353738	269133
港澳台	16986	21700	59798	44653	36321	37329	35630
国外	1524	3359	5878	3201	4098	6847	7260
二、新莞人劳动力总计	**4327312**	**4733903**	**5534248**	**5669798**	**5389490**	**5303008**	**4134581**
按行业分							
工业	3753904	4078400	4676454	4820388	4480800	4227211	3361306
农业	85109	98272	107933	124942	102519	97597	74982
商业	278632	315021	420810	412180	460114	560345	430183
服务业	209667	242210	329051	312288	346057	417855	268110

2-6 历年新莞人与劳动力

Migrant Population and Migrant Labor Force over Years

单位：人

年 份	新莞人总 计	按性别分		按省内省外分		新莞人劳动力	工 业	商 业	服务业	农 业
		男 性	女 性	本 省	外 省					
1986	156222					104091	87154	2509	4579	9849
1987	252895					180285	154842	4181	8152	13110
1988	368913					292499	260237	5797	9554	16911
1989	481850					405287	365840	7763	11791	19893
1990	655902			333180	322722	572044	518971	10793	16704	25576
1991	805790			360379	445411	701982	633400	17945	24799	25838
1992	1144753	440500	704253	494278	650475	1071048	874149	88087	46488	62324
1993	1217010	529096	687914	370770	846240	1126813	933147	88524	64965	40177
1994	1390884	547435	843449	380790	1010094	1241814	1069478	39869	80321	52146
1995	1421754	581304	840450	371816	1023510	1265368	1084860	52965	72829	54714
1996	1433157	606524	826633	305821	1106749	1276626	1084330	61092	66472	64732
1997	1446830	554193	892637	298510	1130981	1307279	1114235	67242	68588	57214
1998	1991122	850266	1140856	402267	1569963	1831939	1577922	100041	85833	68143
1999	2448134	1084492	1363642	504722	1921206	2161487	1609539	282938	155686	113324
2000	2547221	1155277	1391944	485889	2041959	2448415	2043270	187015	129935	88195
2001	4578163	2138218	2439945	731931	3826830	4496771	3681099	283277	357459	174936
2002	4336453	1973316	2363137	722894	3593034	4260142	3573355	300642	258561	127584
2003	4404467	2198324	2206143	665549	3720408	4327312	3753904	278632	209667	85109
2004	4869462	2347115	2522347	747804	4096599	4733903	4078400	315021	242210	98272
2005	5849785	2746833	3102952	1036417	4747692	5534248	4676454	420810	329051	107933
2006	5867555	2775718	3091837	1012637	4807064	5669798	4820388	412180	312288	124942
2007	5577988	2666292	2911696	986062	4551507	5389490	4480800	460114	346057	102519
2008	5525022	2657712	2867310	1012341	4468505	5303008	4227211	560345	417855	97597
2009	4299615	2093055	2206560	889160	3367565	4134581	3361306	430183	268110	74982

2-7 历年社会劳动者人数

Number of Social Laborers over Years

单位：万人

年份	合计	企事业机关从业人员	国有单位	城镇集体	其他	城镇私营个体从业人员人数	农村户籍社会劳动者人数
1957	37.57	4.65	3.90	0.75			32.92
1962	36.78	3.94	2.93	1.01			32.84
1965	40.56	4.61	3.17	1.44			35.95
1970	49.97	5.39	3.29	2.10			44.58
1975	51.44	6.32	3.80	2.52			45.12
1978	54.97	8.20	4.84	3.36			46.78
1979	56.51	9.68	5.17	4.51		0.02	46.81
1980	57.86	9.86	4.94	4.92		0.14	47.86
1981	59.42	10.66	5.19	5.47		0.32	48.43
1982	61.76	11.41	6.14	5.27		0.11	50.24
1983	63.25	11.59	6.12	5.48		0.43	51.22
1984	65.51	11.76	5.40	6.37		1.07	52.68
1985	67.35	12.30	5.65	6.34	0.30	0.58	54.47
1986	69.68	13.27	6.17	6.77	0.34	0.70	55.70
1987	71.63	13.67	6.20	6.85	0.61	0.85	57.11
1988	71.99	12.71	6.15	5.70	0.86	1.04	58.24
1989	73.95	13.10	6.17	6.37	0.56	1.85	58.99
1990	75.10	13.16	6.35	5.87	0.94	2.04	59.89
1991	76.99	14.59	6.54	6.42	1.63	2.26	60.15
1992	77.55	15.47	6.81	6.68	1.98	2.85	59.23
1993	79.36	17.66	6.92	7.37	3.37	3.41	58.30
1994	81.02	17.78	7.36	6.83	3.59	3.00	60.24
1995	82.40	18.40	7.53	6.51	4.36	4.51	59.48
1996	83.52	18.05	7.66	6.37	4.03	5.77	59.70
1997	84.78	16.73	7.38	5.90	3.45	6.51	61.54
1998	85.98	16.45	7.57	5.36	3.51	5.14	64.39
1999	87.82	16.66	7.74	5.32	3.61	8.67	62.49
2000	88.62	16.80	7.97	5.11	3.72	8.35	63.47
2001	90.80	16.98	8.02	4.82	4.14	8.78	65.03
2002	92.93	17.23	7.93	5.36	3.94	11.44	64.27
2003	95.64	16.88	8.50	4.36	4.02	14.52	64.24
2004	98.36	17.85	8.67	4.57	4.62	17.88	62.63
2005	101.30	19.14	9.91	4.48	4.75	21.18	60.99
2006	103.76	20.23	10.61	4.38	5.24	23.18	60.35
2007	106.65	21.44	11.65	4.02	5.77	25.58	59.63
2008	109.67	13.68	10.45	1.55	1.68	35.96	60.03
2009	112.18	15.08	9.98	2.09	3.01	35.14	61.97

注：1. 本表不含新莞人劳动力，下同。
2. 2008年起采用新口径，与往年数不可比。

2-8 主要年份分行业年末户籍从业人员数

Number of Employed Resident Persons at Year-end by Sector in Main Years

单位：人

项　　目	1985年	1990年	1995年	2000年	2005年	2008年	2009年
合　　计	**673494**	**750980**	**824014**	**886169**	**1013029**	**1096704**	**1121839**
第一产业	**285857**	**271513**	**194895**	**173829**	**86694**	**60150**	**57012**
第二产业	**233231**	**305190**	**380101**	**414273**	**461451**	**410124**	**462281**
工　业	195846	266867	348107	382674	435208	379780	432464
采矿业			121	75	707	235	61
制造业			341954	377632	426649	373024	425852
电力、燃气及水的生产和供应业			6032	4967	7852	6521	6551
建筑业	37385	38323	31994	31599	26243	30345	29817
第三产业	**154406**	**174277**	**249018**	**298067**	**464884**	**626430**	**602546**
#金融业	2942	5635	12900	20380	18446	17057	15636
房地产业			2377	3774	777	3848	3122
公共管理和社会组织	5854	7887	9407	14829	27987	35059	36872

2-9 主要年份城镇职工年末人数

Number of Staff and Workers in Urban Areas at Year-end in Main Years

单位：人

项　　目	1985年	1990年	1995年	2000年	2005年	2008年	2009年
合　　计	**122951**	**131631**	**178724**	**164080**	**188579**	**207234**	**225990**
第一产业	**2432**	**2053**	**620**	**476**	**483**	**459**	**477**
第二产业	**64525**	**72993**	**110885**	**76153**	**80596**	**77982**	**94365**
工　业	60571	68508	105782	68354	79359	76563	92943
采矿业			130	62	59	50	50
制造业			99194	62790	71569	69381	85496
电力、燃气及水的生产和供应业			6458	5502	7731	7132	7397
建筑业			5103	7799	1237	1419	1422
第三产业	**55994**	**56585**	**67219**	**87451**	**107500**	**128793**	**131148**
#金融业	2270	4291	9487	13945	16584	18176	18290
房地产业	1551	2529	73	387	427	395	472
公共管理和社会组织	5854	7887	9711	15733	28542	38479	39017

注：2000年起为城镇在岗职工人数。

2-10 历年分行业户籍从业人员与城镇职工人数

Number of Employed Resident Persons & Staff and Workers in Urban Areas by Sector over Years

单位：人

年份	年末户籍从业人员	第一产业	第二产业	#工业	第三产业	年末城镇职工人数合计	第一产业	第二产业	#工业	第三产业
1978	549728	393460	92601	85380	63667	81971	2875	41179	38729	37917
1979	565106	376489	130211	127797	58406	96807	3051	44905	42251	48851
1980	578587	370959	142273	139636	65355	98587	2637	47374	44737	48576
1981	594207	370122	139996	137728	84089	106626	2897	52638	50370	51091
1982	617578	362320	162932	145325	92326	114119	2133	56391	52418	55595
1983	632486	307693	204435	178546	120358	115926	1978	58139	53246	55809
1984	655121	250339	240330	204914	164452	117627	1933	59129	54916	56565
1985	673494	285857	233231	195846	154406	122951	2432	64525	60571	55994
1986	696758	279337	264289	218257	153132	132744	2252	73922	65674	56570
1987	716287	272343	281926	238059	162018	136666	2359	76393	69985	57914
1988	719942	273059	286785	246743	160098	127098	2702	69385	64631	55011
1989	739474	275774	291640	254727	172060	131039	2397	73042	68738	55600
1990	750980	271513	305190	266867	174277	131631	2053	72993	68508	56585
1991	769895	263385	323235	285691	183275	145873	2083	84992	79389	58798
1992	775498	238442	337736	300848	199320	154712	2043	89713	82611	62956
1993	793618	212881	357969	313281	222769	176578	1933	107296	92212	67349
1994	810180	197120	364846	324883	248213	160872	621	95378	83322	64873
1995	824014	194895	380101	348107	249018	178724	620	110885	105782	67219
1996	835174	199715	377401	343021	258058	174964	497	98061	91228	76406
1997	847812	203616	378073	338911	266123	164987	616	82513	76619	81858
1998	859797	202926	381278	344588	275594	164047	779	80510	70499	82758
1999	878242	200559	381198	346341	296485	163917	583	76905	68860	86429
2000	886169	173829	414273	382674	298067	164080	476	76153	68354	87451
2001	907962	159116	436684	407142	312162	164226	444	76181	69260	87601
2002	929321	132403	439266	402030	357652	164209	431	75384	68348	88394
2003	956442	114911	449963	424507	391568	165978	522	73357	72118	92099
2004	983628	101936	457039	427880	424653	175415	565	78003	76786	96847
2005	1013029	86694	461451	435208	464884	188579	483	80596	79359	107500
2006	1037587	67300	468080	440192	502207	199878	483	84618	83328	114777
2007	1066498	61555	450004	421588	554940	205640	487	81448	79949	123705
2008	1096704	60150	410124	379780	626430	207234	459	77982	76563	128793
2009	1121839	57012	462281	432464	602546	225990	477	94365	92943	131148

注：2000年起城镇职工为城镇在岗职工口径。

2-11 主要年份国有单位分行业年末职工人数

Number of Staff and Workers in State-owned Units at Year-end by Sector in Main Years

单位：人

指　　标	1985年	1990年	1995年	2000年	2005年	2008年	2009年
合　　计	**56534**	**63469**	**71165**	**78216**	**94902**	**112956**	**116088**
按企业、事业、机关单位分							
企业	40201	43538	38022	31988	20401	19673	19873
事业	11362	13072	23147	31506	46382	55967	57846
机关	4971	6859	9996	14722	28119	37316	38369
按国民经济行业分							
第一产业	2264	1956	712	476	483	459	477
第二产业	22373	22877	17363	11658	4442	4670	4687
工　业	20919	19390	14610	10119	3471	3448	3465
采矿业	423	72	130	62	59	50	50
制造业	19625	16912	12908	6611	1217	974	940
电力、燃气及水的生产和供应业	871	2406	1572	3446	2195	2424	2475
建筑业	1454	3487	2753	1539	971	1222	1222
第三产业	31897	38571	53090	66082	89977	107827	110924
交通运输、仓储及邮政业					3381	2172	2263
信息传输、计算机服务和软件业					2243	2174	2281
批发和零售业					1582	1364	1377
住宿和餐饮业							
金融业	943	2215	5634	7343	9401	9245	9293
房地产业	138	149	44	98	244	245	310
租赁和商务服务业					676	1426	1438
科学研究、技术服务和地质勘查业					1496	1735	1854
水利、环境和公共设施管理业					484	516	516
居民服务和其他服务业					95	104	108
教育					23301	25425	25778
卫生、社会保障和社会福利业					17134	23644	24904
文化、体育和娱乐业					1398	1729	1785
公共管理和社会组织	4971	6859	9563	15372	28542	38048	39017
国际组织							

注：2000年起为城镇在岗职工人数，下同。

2-12 主要年份城镇集体单位分行业年末职工人数

Number of Staff and Workers in Urban Collective-owned Units at Year-end by Sector in Main Years

单位：人

指　　标	1985年	1990年	1995年	2000年	2005年	2008年	2009年
合　计	**63383**	**58749**	**64923**	**50592**	**44251**	**38870**	**35159**
按企业、事业、机关单位分							
企业	58258	54671	63194	49257	43200	37569	34269
事业	4062	3050	1581	974	1051	994	890
机关	1063	1028	148	361		307	
按国民经济行业分							
第一产业	168	97	33				
第二产业	39858	41795	52334	34958	32778	26161	23586
工　业	37358	40979	49984	28698	32527	25975	23397
采矿业		433					
制造业		40458	48600	27268	30772	24803	21931
电力、燃气及水的生产和供应业		88	1384	1430	1755	1172	1466
建筑业	2500	998	2350	6260	251	186	189
第三产业	23357	16857	12556	15634	11473	12709	11573
交通运输、仓储及邮政业					3446	3413	3845
信息传输、计算机服务和软件业					45	40	40
批发和零售业					2078	3107	1897
住宿和餐饮业					307	272	272
金融业	1327	2076	3844	3437	4184	4321	4349
房地产业			29	289	183	150	162
租赁和商务服务业					843	689	703
科学研究、技术服务和地质勘查业					16	56	56
水利、环境和公共设施管理业					237	111	117
居民服务和其他服务业							
教育							
卫生、社会保障和社会福利业					92	64	66
文化、体育和娱乐业					42	55	66
公共管理和社会组织	1063	1028	148	361		431	
国际组织							

2-13 主要年份其他所有制单位分行业年末职工人数

Number of Staff and Workers in Other Ownership Units at Year-end by Sector in Main Years

单位：人

指　　标	1985年	1990年	1995年	2000年	2005年	2008年	2009年
合　　计	**3034**	**9413**	**42636**	**35272**	**49426**	**55408**	**74743**
按企业、事业、机关单位分							
企业	2312	9413	42597	35272	49426	55408	74743
事业	722		39				
机关							
按国民经济行业分							
第一产业							
第二产业	2294	8321	41188	29537	43376	47151	66092
工　业	2294	8321	41188	29537	43361	47140	66081
采矿业		48					
制造业		8273	37686	28911	39580	43604	62625
电力、燃气及水的生产和供应业			3502	626	3781	3536	3456
建筑业					15	11	11
第三产业					6050	8257	8651
#交通运输、仓储及邮政业					412	603	682
信息传输、计算机服务和软件业					240	218	220
批发和零售业					1530	2155	2523
住宿和餐饮业					678	503	450
金融业			9	3165	2999	4610	4648
房地产业	722						
租赁和商务服务业					191	168	128
卫生、社会保障和社会福利业							

2-14 主要年份工业、建筑业企业年末城镇职工人数

Number of Urban Staff and Workers in Industrial and Construction Enterprises at Year-end in Main Years

单位：人

指　　标	1985年	1990年	1995年	2000年	2005年	2008年	2009年
一、工业总计	**105782**	**91228**	**82474**	**68354**	**79359**	**76563**	**92943**
(一) 按经济类型分							
国有经济单位	14610	15121	14477	10119	3471	3448	3465
城镇集体经济单位	49984	38822	32620	28698	32527	25975	23397
其他各种经济单位	41188	37285	35377	29537	43361	47140	66081
(二) 按工业行业分(大类)							
非金属矿采选业	130	43	66	62	59	50	50
木材及竹材采运业							
食品加工业	4664	4419	3978	2884	249	351	397
食品制造业	1842	542	583	368	159	143	138
饮料制造业	3944	2976	2814	584	570	720	1400
烟草加工业							
纺 织 业	2722	1561	1547	1990	1928	1495	1499
服装及其他纤维制品制造业	11769	13199	6749	4162	5068	5625	6687
皮革、毛皮、羽绒及其制品	3692	2756	1688	106	209	207	5692
木材加工及竹、藤、棕、草制品业	1190	1056	910	362	45		
家具制造业	433	192	154	29	5246	6518	4888
造纸及纸制品业	1697	1540	938	1079	1241	970	928
印刷业、记录媒介的复制	2065	1493	1734	773	1074	1064	1015
文教、体育用品制造业	7192	1463	1173	9	254	249	1003
石油加工及炼焦业							
化学原料及化学制品制造业	1921	1325	1284	869	662	391	1053
医药制造业	1115	915	689	2719	1890	1675	1846
化学纤维制造业	25	25					
橡胶制品业		9	520	148			
塑料制品业	3783	3855	3235	1418	1739	1907	3265
非金属矿物制品业	4909	3882	3159	1939	3556	3878	671
黑色金属冶炼及压延加工业							
有色金属冶炼及压延加工业	59	205	205	86	74	80	83
金属制品业	2862	1767	1664	2226	768	695	476
普通机械制造业	2097	2825	2666	1308	890	1118	1048
专用设备制造业	1819	942	1968	560	240	230	509
交通运输设备制造业	1729	972	827	375	329	965	2681
电气机械及器材制造业	14755	10017	11197	16028	13638	10478	10857
电子及通信设备制造业	14129	12589	14310	14121	17812	17103	20958
仪器、仪表及文化办公机械制造业	4884	6617	8107	7262	13759	12753	17635
其他制造业				1385	130	745	745
电力、蒸汽、热水生产和供应业	6068	4993	5199	4579	6487	5795	5731
自来水、煤气生产和供应业	390	415	590	923	1244	1337	1666
二、建筑业总计	**5103**	**6833**		**7799**	**1237**	**1419**	**1422**
国有经济单位	2753	1462	1362	1539	971	1222	1222
城镇集体经济单位	2350	4771	4532	6260	251	186	189
其他各种经济单位		600			15	11	11

2-15 主要年份城镇职工变动情况

Changes of Staff and Workers in Urban Areas in Main Years

单位：人

项目	1995年	1996年	1997年	1998年	2000年	2005年	2008年	2009年
当年增加人数	**25995**	**12155**	**10658**	**14326**	**17604**	**35604**	**36138**	**37712**
从农村招收	13318	4883	4007	6551	7208	17746	16220	16737
从城镇招收	3025	2059	2269	2241	2391	4109	4100	3930
录用退伍军人	299	183	144	240	306	412	227	229
录用大、中专、技工学校毕业生	3082	1894	2527	3230	4852	7409	8530	8778
调入	1806	1021	912	1135	947	1156	1349	1425
其他	4465	2115	799	929	1900	4772	5712	6613
当年减少人数	**19109**	**14039**	**11565**	**16349**	**12881**	**29785**	**36614**	**39481**
离、退休、退职	2784	2230	3040	2682	2764	8532	12629	15121
开除、除名、辞退	6561	2887	2170	2483	2565	3491	1245	1618
终止解除合同	4695	4989	4136	7544	3989	12587	15961	17396
离开单位仍保留劳资关系	1131			1127	634	74	88	36
调出	30	932	726	555	524	610	996	1190
其他	3908	3001	1493	1958	2405	4491	5695	4120

2-16 单位从业人员变动情况（2008-2009年）

Changes of Employed Persons in Units (2008-2009)

单位：人

项目	2008年				2009年			
	总计	国有单位	城镇集体单位	其他单位	总计	国有单位	城镇集体单位	其他单位
当年增加人数	**36138**	**8640**	**11189**	**16309**	**37712**	**7431**	**8725**	**21556**
从农村招收	16220	697	7313	8210	16737	556	5398	10783
从城镇招收	4100	926	950	2224	3930	781	639	2510
录用退伍军人	227	132	34	61	229	128	31	70
录用大、中专、技工学校毕业生	8530	3779	919	3832	8778	3246	884	4648
调入	1349	1206	73	70	1425	1139	19	267
#由外省、自治区直辖市调入	323	305	2	16	340	320	1	19
其他	5712	1900	1900	1912	6613	1581	1754	3278
当年减少人数	**36614**	**5418**	**13164**	**18032**	**39481**	**3805**	**10156**	**25520**
离、退休、退职	12629	666	3374	8589	15121	710	2802	11609
开除、除名、辞退	1245	381	293	571	1618	441	675	502
终止解除合同	15961	2265	7341	6355	17396	1335	4559	11502
调出	996	928	43	25	1190	864	33	293
#调往外省、自治区直辖市	26	25		1	29	27		2
其他	5597	1091	2027	2479	4036	391	2041	1604

2-17 按经济类型分行业城镇职工人数及构成（2009年）

Number and Composition of Staff and Workers in Urban Areas by Registration Status and Sector (2009)

项　　目	合　计	国有经济单位	城镇集体经济单位	其他经济单位
合　计(人)	**225990**	**116088**	**35159**	**74743**
第一产业	477	477		
第二产业	94365	4687	23586	66092
工　业	92943	3465	23397	66081
采矿业	50	50		
制造业	85496	940	21931	62625
电力、燃气及水的生产和供应业	7397	2475	1466	3456
建筑业	1422	1222	189	11
第三产业	131148	110924	11573	8651
交通运输、仓储及邮政业	6790	2263	3845	682
信息传输、计算机服务和软件业	2541	2281	40	220
批发和零售业	5797	1377	1897	2523
住宿和餐饮业	722		272	450
金融业	18290	9293	4349	4648
房地产业	472	310	162	
租赁和商务服务业	2269	1438	703	128
科学研究、技术服务和地质勘查业	1910	1854	56	
水利、环境和公共设施管理业	633	516	117	
居民服务和其他服务业	108	108		
教育	25778	25778		
卫生、社会保障和社会福利业	24970	24904	66	
文化、体育和娱乐业	1851	1785	66	
公共管理和社会组织	39017	39017		
国际组织				
占全部职工人数的比重(%)	**100.00**	**51.37**	**15.56**	**33.07**
第一产业	0.21	0.21		
第二产业	41.76	2.07	10.44	29.25
工　业	41.13	1.53	10.35	29.24
采矿业	0.02	0.02		
制造业	37.83	0.42	9.70	27.71
电力、燃气及水的生产和供应业	3.27	1.10	0.65	1.53
建筑业	0.63	0.54	0.08	0.00
第三产业	58.03	49.08	5.12	3.83
交通运输、仓储及邮政业	3.00	1.00	1.70	0.30
信息传输、计算机服务和软件业	1.12	1.01	0.02	0.10
批发和零售业	2.57	0.61	0.84	1.12
住宿和餐饮业	0.32		0.12	0.20
金融业	8.09	4.11	1.92	2.06
房地产业	0.21	0.14	0.07	
租赁和商务服务业	1.00	0.64	0.31	0.06
科学研究、技术服务和地质勘查业	0.85	0.82	0.02	
水利、环境和公共设施管理业	0.28	0.23	0.05	
居民服务和其他服务业	0.05	0.05		
教育	11.41	11.41		
卫生、社会保障和社会福利业	11.05	11.02	0.03	
文化、体育和娱乐业	0.82	0.79	0.03	
公共管理和社会组织	17.26	17.26		
国际组织				

2-18 主要年份城乡私营企业和城乡个体劳动者分行业年末从业人数

Number of Employed Persons in Private Enterprises and Self-employed Individuals in Urban and Rural Areas at Year-end by Sector in Main Years

单位：人

项　　目	1985年	1990年	1995年	2000年	2005年	2008年	2009年
合　　计	**18813**	**64875**	**171136**	**356748**	**1120116**	**1475741**	**1506355**
第一产业(农、林、牧、渔业)			**83**	**395**	**43784**	**16220**	**12515**
第二产业	**575**	**19924**	**54174**	**122907**	**362041**	**465549**	**486890**
工　业	575	19548	51968	119342	344854	442602	461867
采矿业			1230	81	5884	2151	77
制造业			50738	119261	338737	440131	461393
电力、煤气及水的生产和供应业					233	320	397
建筑业		376	2206	3565	17187	22947	25023
第三产业	**18238**	**44951**	**116879**	**233446**	**714291**	**993972**	**1006950**
交通运输、仓储及邮政业					12031	11298	12045
信息传输、计算机服务和软件业					17493	19497	18138
批发和零售业					484087	676767	684682
住宿和餐饮业					83895	121581	118441
房地产业					9190	13298	14385
租赁和商务服务业					21529	36862	41072
居民服务和其他服务业					75334	97316	98271
卫生、社会保障和社会福利业					122	386	399
文化、体育和娱乐业					2818	5019	5356
其他行业					7792	11948	14161

注：本表根据工商登记注册资料整理。

主要统计指标解释

人口数 指一定时点、一定地区范围内的有生命的个人的总和。年度统计的年末人口数是指每年12月31日24时的人口数。

外来暂住人口 指户口登记地在外县、市而目前在本市暂住的人口。

性别比 反映两性人口之间比例的指标。指在总人口中或在各年龄人口中，男性人数与女性人数之比。通常用每100个女性人口相应有多少男性人口表示。

出生率（又称粗出生率） 指在一定时期内（通常为一年）平均每千人所出生的人数的比率，一般用千分率表示。

死亡率（又称粗死亡率） 指在一定时期内（通常为一年）一定地区的死亡人数与同期平均人数（或期中人数）之比，一般用千分率表示。

人口自然增长率 指在一定时期内（通常为一年）人口自然增加数（出生人数减死亡人数）与该时期内平均人口数（或期中人数）之比，一般用千分率表示。

总迁移率 是反映人口迁移变动总规模的相对指标，是某地区一定时期内（通常为一年）迁入人数及迁出人数之和与同时期平均人口数之比，一般用千分率表示。

净迁移率 是反映人口迁移变动的相对指标之一，是某地区一定时期内（通常为一年）迁入与迁出相抵销后的余额与同时期平均人口数之比，一般用千分率表示。

计划生育率 是指一定时期内（通常为一年）计划内出生人数与总出生人数之间的比率，一般用百分率表示。

节育率 指一定时期内（通常为一年）已落实节育措施的已婚育龄妇女人数与同期已婚育龄妇女人数之间的比率，一般用百分率表示。

从业人员 指在劳动年龄内，有劳动能力，参加社会劳动取得劳动报酬或经营收入的人口。

职工 在单位工作，以工资为生活费主要来源的从业人员。

城镇集体经济单位职工 指在城镇集体经济单位及其管理部门工作，并由其支付工资的各类人员。

其他经济单位职工 指在联营经济、股份制经济、外商投资经济、港、澳、台投资经济单位工作，并由其支付工资的各类人员。

三、农　业

Agriculture

3-1 主要年份农业指标

Main Indicators of Agriculture in Main Years

指　　标	单　位	1978年	1980年	1985年	1990年	1995年	2000年	2001年
镇(街)户籍总户数	户	248167	256572	289512	327344	364273	414007	421177
镇(街)户籍总人口数	人	1112299	1126973	1208515	1318526	1436525	1526090	1538919
镇(街)农村劳动力	人	467757	478599	544734	598911	639985	727328	743662
第一产业	人	390585	368322	283425	269460	202138	189349	174786
第二产业	人	51422	94576	167116	228114	283050	362666	383363
第三产业	人	25750	15701	94193	101337	154797	175313	185513
年末耕地面积	亩	1183926	1177400	966725	882602	708595	663304	643648
农业机械总动力	千瓦	248760	354250	667750	1003980	795120	586063	515689
水利建设总投资	万元	413	927	886	5428	16900	35550	33416
化肥施用量(实物量)	吨	113296	100776	150083	235836	124263	103570	99146
农药施用量	吨	4276	3382	2951	3453	1924	1836	1819
农村用电量	万千瓦时	5667	7355	14365	82545	406327	1312931	1475778
农业总产值(当年价)	万元	42394	41943	91244	236412	426901	546383	559280
主要农产品产量								
粮　食	吨	532308	529381	488705	494259	227441	204136	128366
糖　蔗	吨	508976	447318	526033	538712	233803	49359	24768
花　生	吨	14157	29015	20963	13411	3724	1960	1556
水　果	吨	26457	23688	189350	282410	243231	129367	150115
水产品	吨	30900	25471	32641	68508	74778	95076	89599
肉　类	吨	26920	27652	33298	62191	97572	179032	198423
#猪　肉	吨	22790	23461	25759	40130	68649	149648	168353
禽　蛋	吨	425	398	2424	6906	5431	4367	4441
当年造林	亩	25610				15875	13515	38000
森林覆盖率	%			28.6	31.4	29.2	30.6	31.2

注：本部分镇街农村劳动力含部分外来劳动力，下同。

3-1 续表

指　标	单　位	2002年	2003年	2004年	2005年	2006年	2007年	2008年	2009年
镇(街)总户数	户	431459	445001	454605	465008	477046	492510	506357	521190
镇(街)总户籍人口数	人	1561884	1589611	1619690	1656541	1683078	1712593	1748658	1787288
镇(街)总劳动力	人	754294	851484	798954	830705	847361	837283	842933	870156
第一产业	人	151487	130930	119347	110612	92819	85246	82059	77502
第二产业	人	394770	486298	434172	447207	460758	441523	436029	447662
第三产业	人	208037	234256	245435	272886	293784	310514	324845	344992
年末耕地面积	亩	500694	492433	489448	502937	491535	483740	479260	516623
农业机械总动力	千瓦	361552	308159	299152	229297	212312	192990	154344	159010
水利建设总投资	万元	38921	40320	66726	59437	53583	73032	96075	64935
化肥施用量(实物量)	吨	76634	69896	59126	52749	49716	47661	43699	43364
农药施用量	吨	1485	1355	1201	1090	1017	1000	1006	1060
农村用电量	万千瓦时	1927589	2239886	2880220	2970738	2979221	3489058	3373402	3567469
农业总产值(当年价)	万元	536729	490206	441912	420496	212632	199782	255307	253077
主要农产品产量									
粮　食	吨	53732	30500	30374	20004	10040	9864	11902	11912
糖　蔗	吨	15025	2564	1437	450	379	1953	2580	1249
花　生	吨	865	395	216	114	99	73	130	113
水　果	吨	189343	146414	175389	151255	139582	131571	101541	91544
水产品	吨	82361	75756	71526	67381	47059	47292	72282	73323
肉　类	吨	188774	154615	146184	171737	34891	20257	24052	25457
#猪　肉	吨	165344	135344	128286	159169	30199	14862	17946	19095
禽　蛋	吨	4052	3597	3435	1355	371	361	146	515
森林覆盖率	%	31.7	32.2	33.0	33.1	35.1	35.5	36.2	36.5

3-2 主要年份农村经济比例和效益指标

Main Indicators of Proportions and Efficiency in Rural Economy in Main Years

指　　标	单　位	1985年	1990年	1995年	2000年	2005年	2008年	2009年
一、农村各产业劳动力比例								
第一产业	%	52.0	45.0	31.6	26.0	13.3	9.7	8.9
第二产业	%	30.7	38.1	44.2	49.9	53.8	51.7	51.4
第三产业	%	17.3	16.9	24.2	24.1	32.9	38.6	39.7
二、劳动生产条件								
平均每一农业人口用电量	千瓦时	150	826	3778	11666	29762	34398	36676
每亩耕地农业机械总动力	瓦特	691	1138	1122	884	455	322	308
平均每亩耕地化肥施用量	公斤	155	267	175	156	105	91	84
平均每亩耕地农药施用量	公斤	3.05	3.91	2.72	2.77	2.17	2.10	2.10
三、增加值率								
农业增加值率	%			57.8	56.9	51.9	58.1	58.4
四、劳动生产率(平均每个劳动力创造或生产的)								
农业总产值	元	1703	3977	6737	7828	5062	2673	2908
农业增加值	元			3892	4453	2627	1758	1699
粮食产量	吨	0.91	0.83	0.36	0.29	0.02	0.01	0.01
蔬菜产量	吨	0.59	0.75	0.88	0.94	0.55	0.46	0.46
糖蔗产量	吨	0.98	0.91	0.37	0.07			
水果产量	吨	0.35	0.48	0.38	0.19	0.18	0.12	0.11
畜牧总肉产量	吨	0.06	0.10	0.15	0.26	0.21	0.03	0.03
#猪　肉	吨	0.05	0.07	0.11	0.21	0.19	0.02	0.02
水产品产量	吨	0.06	0.12	0.12	0.14	0.08	0.09	0.08

注：劳动生产率中产值部分按当年价计算。

3-3 农村集体(经联社、经济社两级)资产负债及收益分配

Assets，Liabilities and Income Distribution of Rural Collective Economy

单位：亿元

指　　标	2005年	2007年	2008年	2009年
一、资产负债情况				
资产总额	929.60	1088.58	1135.14	1173.48
负债总额	221.56	267.42	275.38	283.25
资产负债率	23.83	24.57	24.25	24.14
净资产	708.04	821.16	859.70	890.23
二、收益分配情况				
经营总收入	120.57	140.19	141.02	136.10
#直接经营收入	12.83	14.31	12.73	12.92
物业出租收入	77.02	86.44	89.79	86.39
管理费收入	13.07	10.30	8.66	7.94
结汇收入		6.41	5.12	3.77
农业发包及上交收入	3.17	2.57	2.25	2.14
投资收益	5.07	6.87	7.43	6.60
其他收入	9.40	13.29	15.05	16.35
经营总费用	48.05	58.39	63.34	63.78
#直接经营费用	6.46	8.11	8.50	8.49
租赁费用	24.05	26.41	28.61	30.47
经营税金		1.37	1.51	1.67
管理费用	9.34	11.50	12.61	12.01
其他支出	7.92	10.99	12.11	11.14
经营纯收入	72.52	81.80	77.68	72.32
收益分配总额	64.57	77.32	82.90	82.39
可弥补分配的收益总额	3.29	7.92	8.71	12.31

3-4 历年农产品人均拥有量

Per Capita Possession of Agricultural Products over Years

单位：公斤

年份	粮食		#稻谷		蔬菜	
	按总人口	按农业人口	按总人口	按农业人口	按总人口	按农业人口
1949	312	378	304	368		
1952	379	463	364	444		
1957	373	463	337	419		
1962	414	514	392	486		
1965	513	632	502	618		
1970	463	562	451	546		
1975	473	565	452	539		
1980	471	570	462	558	111	134
1985	408	510	397	497	260	330
1990	379	495	368	480	337	440
1995	160	211	148	196	388	515
1996	168	224	155	207	411	548
1997	169	225	155	207	436	582
1998	167	224	151	203	450	603
1999	165	222	149	200	443	597
2000	135	181	121	163	431	582
2001	83	113	71	97	459	623
2002	34	54	27	43	418	653
2003	19	30	13	20	352	549
2004	19	30	8	12	329	530
2005	12	20	7	12	278	461
2006	6	10	4	8	212	364
2007	6	10	4	7	200	351
2008	7	12	3	6	224	399
2009	7	12	4	7	224	412

注：本表按户籍人口计算。

3-4 续表

单位：公斤

年份	水果		猪肉		水产品	
	按总人口	按农业人口	按总人口	按农业人口	按总人口	按农业人口
1949					5	6
1952					5	6
1957					5	7
1962					8	10
1965	53	66			12	14
1970	71	87			17	20
1975	34	41			20	24
1980	21	26	21	25	23	27
1985	158	197	21	27	27	34
1990	218	283	31	40	53	69
1995	171	226	48	64	52	70
1996	143	190	58	77	56	76
1997	113	151	68	91	63	84
1998	77	103	84	112	65	88
1999	91	122	87	117	63	84
2000	85	115	97	131	61	82
2001	98	132	109	148	58	79
2002	121	190	106	165	53	82
2003	92	143	85	133	48	74
2004	108	175	79	128	44	71
2005	91	152	96	159	41	68
2006	83	143	18	31	28	48
2007	77	135	9	15	28	48
2008	58	104	10	18	41	74
2009	51	94	11	20	41	75

3-5 主要年份基层组织情况

Conditions of Rural Grassroots Units in Main Years

指 标	单位	1985年	1990年	1995年	2000年	2005年	2008年	2009年
一、农村基层组织								
镇街政府	个	33	33	33	32	32	32	32
社区居委会、村(居)委会	个	528	583	594	593	596	591	598
二、镇街户籍总户数	**户**	**289512**	**327344**	**364273**	**414007**	**465008**	**506357**	**521190**
#农业户	户	219846	238221	263669	299576	275988	282156	280737
三、镇街户籍总人口	**人**	**1208515**	**1318526**	**1436525**	**1526090**	**1656541**	**1748658**	**1787288**
#农业人口	人	953582	1009857	1082703	1130002	998159	980693	972706
四、镇街劳动力（户籍人口）	**人**	**544734**	**598911**	**639985**	**727328**	**830705**	**842933**	**870156**
按性别分								
男性	人	260439	289258	315892	364866	427840	451325	468137
女性	人	284295	309653	324093	362462	402865	391608	402019
按行业分								
农、林、牧、渔业	人	283425	269460	190061	174201	110612	82059	77502
工业	人	133685	194485	254999	335545	414017	402895	413929
建筑业	人	33431	33629	28051	27121	33190	33134	33733
交运仓储和邮政业	人	20142	29005	40032	31291	40619	40827	40299
信息传输、计算机服务和软件业	人					16889	25088	28283
批发与零售业	人					65051	76838	79491
住宿和餐饮业	人					32953	40707	44140
其他行业	人					117374	141385	152779

3-6 历年耕地面积

Area of Cultivated Land over Years

单位：亩

年 份	年末实有耕地面积	当 年新增面积	当 年减少面积	粮食占用耕地面积
1949	1398338			1260357
1952	1445016			1283151
1957	1435861			1199575
1962	1214417	15405	75905	1053985
1965	1199611	4142	11473	956906
1970	1203350	11359	8818	944903
1975	1193180	1246	6402	922916
1978	1183926	288	6515	874967
1979	1182292	120	1754	896347
1980	1177400	177	5069	856824
1981	1159963	279	17716	824166
1982	1146458	1086	14591	834028
1983	1121311	216	25363	837642
1984	1077659	664	44316	784763
1985	966725	1655	112589	691895
1986	889780	2350	79295	624471
1987	887369	1986	22271	618066
1988	877308	12374	22435	609332
1989	885694	13885	5499	626334
1990	882602	6991	10083	621564
1991	878980	962	4584	614994
1992	845159	100	33921	532296
1993	753746	6319	97732	391736
1994	718144	11169	46771	382238
1995	708595	12227	21776	394913
1996	674588	6270	40277	391610
1997	663013	6350	17925	382890
1998	663045	156	124	376133
1999	663122	1684	1607	381933
2000	663304	1632	1450	354980
2001	643648	4410	24066	255771
2002	500694		150	116989
2003	492433	1922	10183	81939
2004	489448	625	3610	85988
2005	502937	291	4302	76037
2006	491535		11403	34366
2007	483740		7795	32314
2008	479260	375	4855	40795
2009	516623	9	1212	41561

3-7 历年耕地面积变动情况

Changes of Area of Cultivated Land over Years

单位：亩

年 份	当年增加耕地面积	#新开荒	围海造田	当年减少耕地面积	#国家基建占用	种果占用	鱼塘占用
"六五"时期累计	**3900**	**1152**		**214575**	**6687**	**148244**	**33462**
1981	279	91		17716	1275	7577	4507
1982	1086	215		14591	505	3345	8073
1983	216	135		25363	788	19590	2152
1984	664	148		44316	1122	31072	7694
1985	1655	563		112589	2997	86660	11036
"七五"时期累计	**33250**	**2507**	**600**	**38017**	**9587**	**9138**	**2698**
1986							
1987							
1988	12374	1199		22435	6971	5379	1871
1989	13885	651	100	5499	1433	330	151
1990	6991	657	500	10083	1183	3429	676
"八五"时期累计	**30777**	**569**	**150**	**204784**	**5339**	**101880**	**44542**
1991	962	95	150	4584	1463	430	57
1992	100	5		33921	1090	17435	3154
1993	6319	270		97732	808	64790	19032
1994	11169	139		46771	645	16031	16162
1995	12227	60		21776	1333	3194	6137
"九五"时期累计	**16092**	**443**	**175**	**61383**	**2824**	**26550**	**9637**
1996	6270	194	19	40277	532	16382	5597
1997	6350			17925	797	10168	4027
1998	156		156	124	85		
1999	1684	148		1607	128		
2000	1632	101		1450	1282		13
"十五"时期累计	**7248**			**42311**	**3114**	**14531**	**5704**
2001	4410			24066	1406	14434	5704
2002				150			
2003	1922			10183	1587		
2004	625			3610	121		
2005	291			4302		97	
"十一五"时期							
2006				11403			
2007				7795			
2008	375			4855			
2009	9			1212			

3-8 历年农村劳动力(按性别、产业分)

Rural Labor Force over Years (by Sex and Industry)

单位：人

年 份	合 计	按性别分		按产业分		
		男	女	第一产业	第二产业	第三产业
1949	329182			281700		
1952	280506			228550		
1957	329204			269365		
1962	328354			267466		
1965	359464			294760		
1970	445768			376585		
1975	451207			427304		
1978	467757			390585	51422	25750
1979	468059			373438		
1980	478599	227496	251103	368322	94576	15701
1981	484346	231033	253313	367225		
1982	502066	239398	262668	360387	106294	35385
1983	512240	262608	249632	305715	145787	60738
1984	526766	253922	272844	248406	178527	99833
1985	544734	260439	284295	283425	167116	94193
1986	557048	265132	291916	277085	187920	92043
1987	571077	272044	299033	269984	204802	96291
1988	582425	281299	301126	270357	216508	95560
1989	589920	281420	308500	273377	215634	100909
1990	598911	289258	309653	269460	228114	101337
1991	601467	286328	315139	261271	232797	107399
1992	612142	298997	313145	239845	253218	119079
1993	625571	311208	314363	219230	267438	138903
1994	627366	313942	313424	200833	245562	180971
1995	639985	315892	324093	202138	283050	154797
1996	639492	316928	322564	206543	286166	146783
1997	643671	320844	322827	208030	284919	150722
1998	661604	329713	331891	205300	297418	158886
1999	668473	333136	335337	207432	300506	160535
2000	727328	364866	362462	189349	362666	175313
2001	743662	377491	366171	174786	383363	185513
2002	754294	384417	369877	151487	394770	208037
2003	851484	439406	412078	130930	486298	234256
2004	798954	412687	386267	119347	434172	245435
2005	830705	427840	402865	110612	447207	272886
2006	847361	445915	401446	92819	460758	293784
2007	837283	446755	390528	85246	441523	310514
2008	842933	451325	390608	82059	436029	324845
2009	870156	468137	402019	77502	447662	344992

注：本表按户籍人口计算。

3-9 历年农村劳动力(按主要行业分)

Rural Labor Force over Years (by Main Sectors)

单位：人

年 份	合 计	农 业	工 业	建筑业	交通仓储邮电通讯业	商饮业
1949	329182	281700				
1952	280506	228550				
1957	329204	269365				
1962	328354	267466				
1965	359464	294760	2626			
1970	445768	376585	9178			
1975	451207	427304	10293			
1978	467757	390585	46651	4771	2515	2441
1979	468059	373438	85306			
1980	478599	368322	94576			
1981	484346	367225	87204			
1982	502066	360387	92860	13434	15580	3158
1983	512240	305715	124791	20996	8129	5916
1984	526766	248406	147324	31203	15804	12808
1985	544734	283425	133685	33431	20142	16970
1986	557048	277085	150136	37784	25049	18417
1987	571077	269984	167354	37448	25832	20919
1988	582425	270357	181234	35274	27280	21698
1989	589920	273377	183107	32527	28491	21582
1990	598911	269460	194485	33629	29005	22652
1991	601467	261271	201152	31645	29787	25813
1992	612142	239845	222722	30496	32777	29991
1993	625571	219230	236994	30444	39612	33629
1994	627366	200833	245562	28425	39479	35798
1995	639985	202138	254999	28051	40032	36974
1996	639492	206543	258227	27939	41092	40166
1997	643671	208030	258432	26487	37375	37702
1998	661604	205300	271099	26319	36939	38880
1999	668473	207432	273914	26592	37323	39284
2000	727328	189349	335545	27121	31291	48088
2001	743662	174786	357527	25836	32153	50512
2002	754294	151487	361418	33352	34919	57997
2003	851484	130930	451920	34378	35517	62978
2004	798954	119347	398596	35576	38406	83901
2005	830705	110612	414017	33190	40619	98004
2006	847361	92819	427500	33258	43295	102259
2007	837283	85246	406910	34613	41687	113141
2008	842933	82059	402895	33134	40827	117545
2009	870156	77502	413929	33733	40299	123631

注：本表按户籍人口计算。

3-10 历年农业总产值及指数

Gross Output Value of Agriculture and Its Indices over Years

年份	农业总产值	种植业			林业	牧业	副业	渔业
			#粮食	水果				
一、农业总产值(万元)								
1978	42394	29425	21006	1404	312	5665	3843	3149
1980	41943	28054	17178	1570	238	6313	4460	2878
1985	91244	57684	19986	1913	759	12652	13930	6219
1986	122988	79251	18869	34831	2425	18078	14294	8940
1987	148414	90502	21593	39295	2330	23324	20328	11930
1988	203685	109531	29776	33939	4732	36915	26007	26500
1989	221079	117464	35488	30276	4316	45313	25491	28495
1990	236412	129032	34543	44268	4324	45405	26202	31449
1991	242587	130986	30256	44250	4038	47839	27084	32640
1992	271293	148412	28551	56967	5307	57163	22384	38026
1993	284539	130666	18519	39505	5489	78919	22728	46737
1994	347451	158315	22426	44798	6735	101117	21020	60263
1995	426901	194921	29030	59567	8850	128089	26494	68547
1996	497161	213018	33620	55763	9149	155112	32890	86992
1997	514373	232721	35329	53483	4383	176254	19442	81573
1998	536047	220614	34338	29852	5472	193404	23467	93090
1999	537442	236429	35549	47159	5640	197474	22404	75495
2000	546383	216318	19893	46423	3649	226293	19006	81118
2001	559280	228740	12895	48496	5309	245444	7655	72132
2002	536729	224452	5680	49790	2346	242928		67003
2003	490206	218039	3377	54346	1414	203477		67276
2004	441912	172481	3489	46992	2247	199912		67272
2005	420496	113577	4194	35130	1746	242534		62639
2006	212632	126923	2232	29801	3101	50638		31968
2007	199782	124627	2446	27434	3238	38354		33562
2008	255307	138205	3326	22551	3585	53221		60296
2009	253077	140221	3170	22986	2232	49982		60642

3-10 续表

年 份	农 业 总产值	种植业	#粮食	水果	林业	牧业	副业	渔业
二、指数(1978=100)								
1978	100.0	100.0	100.0	100.0	100.0	100.0	100.0	100.0
1980	98.0	100.3	98.1	89.0	65.6	81.4	146.7	88.3
1985	138.9	131.3	84.6	719.8	154.2	130.7	411.3	127.5
1986	174.6	158.0	78.8	1159.9	677.2	183.5	470.3	166.7
1987	186.4	160.1	80.0	1354.9	416.9	194.9	637.0	241.0
1988	182.1	143.5	79.8	959.0	476.4	215.1	766.8	262.2
1989	181.9	138.0	84.5	784.5	372.4	225.4	812.9	288.4
1990	195.3	150.6	85.7	1005.4	320.6	238.5	827.4	316.2
1991	199.5	149.4	77.3	961.8	286.4	262.1	859.5	335.9
1992	211.3	163.7	60.0	1255.3	325.7	289.3	697.3	356.7
1993	175.5	115.7	32.9	720.2	281.8	320.1	670.2	332.3
1994	188.4	123.9	32.8	905.8	235.5	364.3	582.0	382.1
1995	207.8	132.8	36.8	1022.0	337.0	410.4	731.1	407.0
1996	216.3	122.6	39.3	791.4	312.7	465.1	900.2	467.4
1997	225.0	129.1	40.0	835.4	167.7	532.0	563.1	540.4
1998	227.3	103.6	39.9	407.7	225.3	612.8	612.0	659.7
1999	242.8	140.2	39.9	981.4	297.4	616.2	52.7	686.0
2000	243.3	111.5	32.9	593.1	214.9	697.5	269.1	769.6
2001	246.3	111.8	20.5	634.6	233.4	750.0	146.4	766.0
2002	263.2	150.9	8.5	1336.5	124.5	730.2		652.5
2003	209.7	105.7	4.6	654.3	62.1	600.5		666.2
2004	213.5	118.0	3.3	899.9	123.9	563.1		647.9
2005	222.2	107.7	2.2	861.4	171.4	662.2		653.8
2006	121.0	108.3	2.4	683.1	246.6	155.2		590.7
2007	105.6	102.7	2.3	667.9	261.7	93.6		584.9
2008	118.3	106.0	3.9	520.6	286.3	109.5		899.5
2009	122.2	109.4	4.3	507.1	178.9	116.9		929.2

注：绝对数按当年价格计算，指数按可比价格计算。从2002年起种植业包含副业产值。

3-11 历年农业增加值

Added Value of Agriculture over Years

年 份	农业增加值	种植业	林业	牧业	副业	渔业
1978	27235	18903	200	3639	2469	2023
1980	26323	17606	149	3962	2799	1806
1985	61475	38864	511	8524	9385	4190
1986	81416	52463	1605	11967	9462	5918
1987	98236	59904	1542	15438	13455	7897
1988	118888	63932	2762	21547	15180	15468
1989	126568	67248	2471	25942	14594	16313
1990	132787	72474	2429	25503	14717	17664
1991	134523	72636	2239	26528	15019	18100
1992	144115	78839	2819	30366	11891	20200
1993	143953	66106	2777	39926	11498	23645
1994	174796	79645	3388	50870	10575	30317
1995	214306	97851	4443	64301	13300	34411
1996	248645	106537	4576	77576	16449	43507
1997	256388	115999	2185	87853	9691	40660
1998	259437	106773	2648	93604	11358	45054
1999	257863	113438	2706	94747	10749	36222
2000	259087	102575	1730	107305	9012	38465
2001	260968	106733	2477	114528	3572	33658
2002	248791	104041	1087	112605		31058
2003	228165	101486	658	94708		31313
2004	227087	88633	1155	102730		34569
2005	218212	84774	1162	97864		34412
2006	123936	88073	1913	17938		16011
2007	118991	86597	1997	13586		16810
2008	148250	96984	2212	18851		30202
2009	147877	98420	1378	17703		30375

注：绝对数按当年价格计算，从2002年起种植业包含副业产值。

3-12 历年农业总产值及增长速度

Gross Output Value of Agriculture and Its Growth Rate over Years

年　份	农　业 总产值	种植业	林业	牧业	副业	渔业
一、农业总产值(万元)						
按1957年可比价格计算						
1949	5400					
1952	6623					
1957	7825	6161	21	724	735	184
1962	7608	6253	42	458	627	228
1965	12792	9434	199	1583	1219	357
1970	14744	11128	50	1761	1235	570
按1970年可比价格计算						
1970	21676	17072	71	2571	1235	727
1975	25320	17927	117	2619	3712	945
1978	26188	18660	129	2800	3039	1560
1979	26215	18344	113	2837	3708	1213
1980	26731	18615	85	2461	4460	1110
按1980年可比价格计算						
1980	33797	23329	162	3648	4460	2198
1981	35910	25221	118	2450	5912	2209
1982	41289	28019	248	4081	6421	2520
1983	41782	26748	244	5013	6999	2778
1984	46277	28524	343	5155	9252	3003
1985	52464	30552	381	5856	12500	3175
1986	65091	36752	1673	8221	14294	4151
1987	72374	37251	1030	8731	19361	6001
1988	74040	33396	1177	9634	23304	6529
1989	75011	32105	920	10099	24705	7182
1990	79531	35033	792	10686	25146	7874

3-12 续表

年份	农业总产值	种植业	林业	牧业	副业	渔业
按1990年可比价格计算						
1990	219801	128547	2882	32509	25789	30074
1991	224549	127525	2575	35720	26790	31939
1992	237766	139763	2928	39423	21735	33917
1993	197475	98819	2533	43627	20890	31606
1994	212051	105798	2117	49655	18141	36340
1995	233836	113373	3030	55938	22787	38708
1996	243361	104643	2811	63394	28059	44454
1997	253217	110259	1508	72509	17553	51388
1998	255820	88460	2025	83521	19076	62738
1999	273198	119657	2674	83985	1642	65240
2000	273806	95233	1932	95061	8387	73193
2001	277203	95474	2098	102224	4564	72843
2002	296185	133497	1119	99520		62049
2003	236014	90261	558	81838		63357
2004	240204	100729	1114	76744		61617
按2005年可比价格计算						
2005	460148	155242	1861	235171		67874
2006	229051	113085	2512	56853		56601
2007	185488	120023	3291	30522		31652
2008	224021	123915	3542	44929		51635
2009	263754	142410	2242	56821		62282
二、年均增长速度(%)						
“一五”时期	2.9					
“二五”时期	-0.3	0.3	14.9	-8.8	-3.1	4.4
1963—1965	18.6	14.7	67.9	51.2	24.8	16.1
“三五”时期	3.0	3.4	-24.2	2.2	0.3	9.8
“四五”时期	1.7	1.0	10.4	0.4	24.6	5.4
“五五”时期	1.0	0.9	-6.3	-2.7	3.7	7.8
“六五”时期	7.2	5.5	18.6	9.9	22.9	7.6
“七五”时期	7.1	2.8	15.8	12.8	15.0	19.9
“八五”时期	1.3	-2.5	1.0	11.5	-2.4	5.2
“九五”时期	1.0	1.0	0.9	1.1	0.8	1.1
“十五”时期	-1.8	-0.7	-13.8	-1.0		-3.2
1979—2000	1.0	1.0	1.0	1.1	1.1	1.1
1991—2000	1.0	1.0	1.0	1.1	0.9	1.1
2001—2009	1.0	1.1	1.0	1.0		1.0

注：1. 2002年起种植业包含副业。
2. 年均增长速度按可比价格计算。

3-13 历年农作物播种面积

Total Sown Area of Farm Crops over Years

单位：亩

年份	农作物总播种面积	粮食	#稻谷	薯类	大豆	甘蔗	#糖蔗	花生	蔬菜(瓜)
1949	2118931	1908828	1783035	100391	40369	32165		39038	30000
1952	2514170	2245205	2035558	170547	37000	60682		47305	32000
1957	2834694	2482883	2015230	303587	53598	87062		53009	41934
1962	2339543	2072742	1795654	222978	31356	70793		67854	36415
1965	2384567	1824562	1681802	105758	24329	102528		113797	48988
1970	2618966	1908766	1752465	102205	31519	116639		118469	56668
1975	3029981	2055514	1739862	82594	43076	129778		141213	68061
1978	2859494	2072184	1715230	66400	36764	131200	130676	155021	68743
1979	2585334	1937441	1676936	62537	37993	110580	110123	185434	63959
1980	2436118	1756854	1624873	49665	39261	92397	91908	232541	58550
1981	2267521	1606926	1525072	48999	32143	131453	131103	264903	63768
1982	2204381	1600137	1511345	57188	35450	125787	124431	217612	82982
1983	2193087	1635344	1530918	71430	32029	110684	109283	152335	119370
1984	2165276	1576777	1468801	77105	31718	98449	96224	173198	153636
1985	1950081	1395692	1293847	70997	28982	96627	91884	159918	139795
1986	1791221	1257126	1174464	54993	31469	67920	63729	152214	159100
1987	1795990	1250934	1165554	57850	28471	63655	59637	130292	184744
1988	1792952	1236359	1151493	55368	27929	69694	66505	113882	208930
1989	1834039	1284184	1199979	55964	26200	85238	82666	101077	211217
1990	1848814	1286028	1194153	61281	26444	85977	83246	97808	229532
1991	1791266	1226573	1138043	60107	22785	90137	87356	85537	238418
1992	1561497	963947	889074	51273	20688	76184	72845	67897	318193
1993	1068053	551155	499223	34449	12843	43720	40594	39062	361826
1994	1009468	536191	482051	32615	7542	36346	34621	25344	367122
1995	1078363	598547	527594	43346	7058	28521	26488	24779	379362
1996	1083418	628347	559499	37989	8276	32620	30880	20805	363331
1997	1082610	624091	560506	32629	8190	41427	40166	18490	369113
1998	1101826	624383	558668	34799	7028	48602	47772	16824	385151
1999	1088854	626481	558508	36329	5597	31641	30889	14305	388173
2000	986022	527689	465616	31754	5290	7566	6775	11969	407304
2001	854229	338467	283351	31214	3947	4610	3290	9405	465659
2002	634205	148184	112388	18265	1983	3193	2299	4746	445447
2003	509504	84782	54970	11154	1550	1879	626	2823	380252
2004	462244	81207	31108	24683	816	868	373	1544	350412
2005	410648	62084	34356	9390	1006	950	55	574	315537
2006	333854	34366	25159	4100	183	575	55	556	241070
2007	320500	32314	19534	5330	253	1676	281	340	236490
2008	352222	40352	18781	4381	443	2330	340	586	287618
2009	370740	41421	18629	5047	140	4144	209	838	306270

3-14 历年农作物产量

Total Output of Farm Crops over Years

单位：吨

年 份	粮食	#稻谷	薯类	大豆	甘蔗	#糖蔗	花生	蔬菜(瓜)
1949	210694	205180	4889		52229	49229	1464	
1952	269458	258860	9641		181901	177696	3545	
1957	288047	260432	22623		170880	160314	3280	
1962	331207	313352	15213		134012	133755	3813	
1965	437106	427809	8165		348519	293622	7232	
1970	450808	438293	9703		397251	395964	9629	
1975	507151	484425	7685		361756	359666	11108	
1978	532308	501074	6458	1948	511492	508976	14157	135603
1979	535342	516263	6568	1982	366424	364084	19100	127918
1980	529381	518591	5432	2245	449907	447318	29015	124859
1981	447540	439534	6318	1722	678160	676074	35506	132846
1982	543349	532998	8430	2162	707764	699174	29930	123117
1983	561246	548073	11345	1875	553174	553105	19662	168878
1984	558216	545548	10946	1980	569225	554919	23076	230454
1985	488705	476399	10304	1771	556983	526033	20963	314539
1986	455243	443760	9422	2050	382608	354759	20056	427138
1987	462830	451032	10058	1920	378094	349749	17019	414261
1988	460929	448923	9950	1965	420391	400045	15119	412436
1989	487648	474476	11052	2023	528463	511031	13746	410879
1990	494259	479350	12452	2184	557102	538712	13411	444377
1991	473663	458425	12998	1838	619884	601734	11510	446204
1992	368083	354298	11070	1763	543657	523271	9323	523806
1993	202097	192018	7366	1035	343133	326389	5594	572376
1994	202356	189688	7929	668	313851	302669	3678	537442
1995	227441	210876	10758	647	246707	233803	3724	557807
1996	243204	224469	11271	806	285732	274531	3120	597732
1997	246901	227163	11487	811	354420	346469	2879	641403
1998	247194	223938	13916	758	411555	406644	2588	668753
1999	247287	223403	14580	566	242773	238774	2204	668822
2000	204136	183485	9730	610	54095	49359	1960	658196
2001	128366	109881	9920	426	33387	24768	1556	706775
2002	53732	42508	5420	244	20224	15025	865	653272
2003	30500	20423	3415	215	8019	2564	395	560523
2004	30374	12230	9803	138	4763	1437	216	532116
2005	20004	11941	2733	147	4433	450	114	460204
2006	10040	7548	1314	31	3167	379	99	356347
2007	9864	6467	1732	48	10834	1953	73	342703
2008	11902	6007	1381	95	15286	2580	130	391192
2009	11912	6560	1437	19	23044	1249	113	400335

3-15 主要年份农作物播种面积、亩产及总产量

Sown Area, Yield Per Acreage and Total Output of Farm Crops in Main Years

单位：亩、公斤、吨

指　标	1978年			1985年			1990年		
	播种面积	亩产	总产量	播种面积	亩产	总产量	播种面积	亩产	总产量
一、粮食作物	**2072184**	**257**	**532308**	**1395692**	**350**	**488705**	**1286028**	**384**	**494259**
按品种分									
稻谷	1715230	292	501074	1293847	368	476399	1194153	401	479350
小麦									
旱粮	290554	85	24776	30848	65	2002	30594	80	2457
薯类	66400	97	6458	70997	145	10304	61281	203	12452
按季节分									
春收				30978	131	4042	33352	174	5790
夏收	1127790	248	279552	649856	377	244755	614059	399	244890
#早稻	814852	309	251907	620409	389	241413	587821	410	241018
秋收	944394	268	252757	714858	336	239907	638617	381	243579
#晚稻	900378	277	249167	673438	349	234985	606332	393	238332
二、大豆	**36764**	**53**	**1948**	**28982**	**61**	**1771**	**26444**	**83**	**2184**
三、经济作物				**306406**			**209120**		
#甘蔗	131200	3899	511492	96627	5765	556983	85977	6480	557102
糖蔗	130676	3895	508976	91884	5725	526033	83246	6471	538712
果蔗	524	4802	2516	4743	6525	30950	2731	6734	18390
油料作物				160186	131	20974	97808	137	13411
#花生	155021	91	14157	159918	131	20963	97808	137	13411
四、其他作物				**219001**			**327222**		
#蔬菜	68743	1973	135603	139795	2250	314539	229532	1936	444377

3-15　续表 1

指　　标	1995年			2000年			2005年		
	播种面积	亩产	总产量	播种面积	亩产	总产量	播种面积	亩产	总产量
一、粮食作物	**598547**	**380**	**227441**	**527689**	**387**	**204136**	**62084**	**322**	**20004**
按品种分									
稻谷	527594	400	210876	465616	394	183485	34356	348	11941
小麦									
旱粮	27607	210	5807	30319	360	10921	18338	291	5330
薯类	43346	248	10758	31754	306	9730	9390	291	2733
按季节分									
春收	17880	224	4008	20787	287	5966	9665	312	3019
夏收	282978	388	109914	245110	392	96015	23286	306	7136
#早稻	255886	405	103592	225985	397	89729	14713	351	5164
秋收	297689	381	113519	261792	390	102155	29133	338	9850
#晚稻	271708	395	107284	239631	391	93756	19643	345	6777
二、大豆	**7058**	**92**	**647**	**5290**	**115**	**610**	**1006**	**146**	**147**
三、经济作物	**62092**			**35221**			**18011**		
#甘蔗	28521	8650	246707	7566	7150	54095	950	4666	4433
糖蔗	26488	8827	233803	6775	7285	49359	55	8182	450
果蔗	2033	6347	12904	791	5987	4736	895	4450	3983
油料作物	24779	150	3724	11969	164	1960	574	199	114
#花生	24779	150	3724	11969	164	1960	574	199	114
四、其他作物	**410666**			**417822**			**329547**		
#蔬菜	379362	1470	557807	407304	1616	658196	315537	1458	460204

3-15 续表 2

单位：亩、公斤、吨

指标	2007年			2008年			2009年		
	播种面积	亩产	总产量	播种面积	亩产	总产量	播种面积	亩产	总产量
一、粮食作物	**32314**	**305**	**9864**	**40352**	**295**	**11902**	**41421**	**288**	**11912**
按品种分									
稻谷	19534	331	6467	18781	320	6007	18629	352	6560
小麦									
旱粮	7197	225	1617	17190	262	4514	17745	221	3915
薯类	5330	325	1732	4381	315	1381	5047	285	1437
按季节分									
春收	6003	301	1805	6629	267	1767	6257	254	1588
夏收	12988	305	3966	16466	306	5039	17314	302	5221
#早稻	8168	346	2826				9117	332	3031
秋收	13323	307	4093	17257	295	5096	17850	286	5103
#晚稻	11366	320	3641				9512	371	3529
二、大豆	**253**	**189**	**48**	**443**	**214**	**95**	**140**	**136**	**19**
三、经济作物	**30299**			**14423**			**16440**		
#甘蔗	1676	6464	10834	2330	6560	15286	4144	5561	23044
糖蔗	281	6950	1953	340	7588	2580	209	5976	1249
果蔗	1395	6366	8881	1990	6384	12706	3935	5539	21795
油料作物	340	215	73	586	221	130	838	135	113
#花生	340	215	73	586	221	130	838	135	113
四、其他作物	**257887**			**297004**			**312739**		
#蔬菜	236490	1449	342703	287618	1360	391192	306270	1307	400335

3-16 主要年份农机总动力、水利、化肥、农药及农村用电量

Statistics on Total Power of Agricultural Machinery, Water Conservancy, Consumption of Chemical Fertilizers and Pesticides, and Electricity Consumed in Rural Areas in Main Years

指 标	单 位	1978年	1985年	1990年	1995年	2000年	2005年	2008年	2009年
一、农业机械总动力	**千瓦**	**248760**	**667750**	**1003980**	**795120**	**586063**	**229297**	**154344**	**159010**
#耕作机械	千瓦	42550	116200	157910	83482	51848	16386	14237	13959
排灌机械	千瓦	104050	149900	178280	112392	91745	36251	22688	26186
收获机械	千瓦	6180	39130	84130	54722	51084	969	625	599
运输机械	千瓦	16930	273270	322950	397735	184949	41678	18437	18423
二、水利建设完成土石方	**万立方米**	**957**	**295**	**737**	**891**	**927**	**682**	**989**	**520**
土方	万立方米	932	266	693	835	864	611	733	445
石方	万立方米	25	29	44	56	63	71	256	75
水利建设总投资	万元	413	886	5428	16900	35550	59437	96075	64935
#各级自筹资金	万元	247	720	4956	14500	33026			
水利建设使用劳动工日	万工日	696	136	994	1019	1200	732	1021	984
三、化肥施用实物量	**吨**	**113296**	**150083**	**235836**	**124263**	**103570**	**52749**	**43699**	**43364**
#氮肥	吨	86371	66846	84642	43441	30214	14439	11387	11024
磷肥	吨	23164	37147	52483	28939	23939	10967	8804	8555
钾肥	吨	3761	13544	26131	16915	14606	6403	5219	5376
复合肥	吨		13117	39098	34968	34811	20940	18289	18409
四、农药施用量	**吨**	**4276**	**2951**	**3453**	**1924**	**1836**	**1090**	**1006**	**1060**
五、农村用电量	**万千瓦时**	**5667**	**14365**	**82545**	**406327**	**1312931**	**2970738**	**3373402**	**3567469**
#农村工业用电量	万千瓦时			70459	386413	1104301	2873735		
平均每一农业人口用电量	千瓦时		150	826	3778	11666	29762	34398	36676

3-17 历年水果面积及产量

Planted Area and Output of Fruits over Years

年 份	年末实有水果面积(亩)	#香(大)蕉	荔 枝	水果总产量(吨)	#香(大)蕉	荔 枝
1949		15659	19300		15911	1391
1952		21827	20050		21633	1976
1957		21827	18242		19469	1976
1962		15547	22844		7766	255
1965		19343	27966	45421	28259	14259
1970		24831	37482	69480	47257	18775
1975		24232	41045	36821	32238	2727
1978	93245	18828	46678	26457	18867	4959
1979	91021	17977	46697	23346	12165	8667
1980	88444	15582	46743	23688	10894	7884
1981	97468	18042	48230	46909	25513	15599
1982	114730	28439	50669	58196	40872	7042
1983	159260	39749	63349	77225	42079	20724
1984	235311	66506	84183	105851	69186	14714
1985	407416	125998	115428	189350	133503	19304
1986	609347	171168	168820	307743	210439	18577
1987	609569	158874	175366	363085	222826	17439
1988	548482	99256	176979	263710	126655	7699
1989	476598	54867	164782	221418	69410	6165
1990	452729	54185	160355	282410	73555	16994
1991	440442	56481	154456	343155	85702	6201
1992	420661	81331	139584	344751	97986	22972
1993	360130	86299	117557	271346	80982	717
1994	325336	67595	121236	264875	92072	12703
1995	322876	62351	142370	243231	86466	23324
1996	326291	59822	159403	206276	77768	14804
1997	319556	57583	188220	165016	80355	22572
1998	310873	46377	208899	114106	78978	2885
1999	285514	48975	198144	136317	82169	35218
2000	297618	71454	189862	129367	108913	9107
2001	275428	86578	156019	150115	132292	7059
2002	209924	76764	109948	189343	135209	45339
2003	199634	82024	95812	146414	130688	9012
2004	183375	84812	80115	175389	150669	18312
2005	176845	75452	83357	151255	123986	21026
2006	173470	73493	81395	139582	124601	8615
2007	163448	66904	80313	131571	116833	10107
2008	178337	64141	94953	101541	86817	8498
2009	177281	52761	103364	91544	75341	10240

3-18 历年林业生产

Statistics on Forestry Production over Years

年　份	林业用地面积(亩)	#杉	松	桉	当年育苗面积(亩)	当年幼林抚育面积(亩)	当年迹地更新面积(亩)	当年四旁植树(万株)
1952					15			3
1957					144			15
1962					333	3740		47
1965					2028			307
1970	711996	20266	596098	8100	531	6783	423	12
1975	711375	59992	572746	35216	693	29200	4343	40
1978	700570	63994	541492	49008	485	32900	5365	44
1979	705764	67104	543210	50439	880	14900	4745	30
1980	740052	70665	568729	56272	316	9500	3924	15
1981	743697	67236	584674	49994	133	12500	931	12
1982	698715	63730	535072	52925	500	11945	2531	19
1983	769893	67423	574171	56724	361	40464	3193	17
1984	739402	66107	552721	58092	501	106982	5120	16
1985	761460				801	120000	4479	150
1986	706823	61438	510042	60581	33231	210540	16908	22
1987	714664	57824	526254	75498	1728	53759	28007	35
1988	729896	59351	512451	90998	3667	70275	34467	37
1989	691944	53293	490370	103887	2101	64950	31241	58
1990	709240	47054	484397	133706	3464	56647	15782	54
1991	709306	44432	459015	148127	609	53827	22294	63
1992	662919	39326	422527	149944	762	60764	28184	49
1993	628612	36213	400816	144346	677	28511	13318	57
1994	1016138	43815	382482	129473	2492	28127	9689	34
1995	1015223	43661	360591	125133	4273	25130	11140	48
1996	1014972	9654	248288	115878	699	21000	23143	133
1997	1014954	8843	235410	113928	823	23745	22462	218
1998	1014876	8367	222147	112005	387	36000	22273	417
1999	1009965	10890	221585	133500	506	29863	29000	522
2000	1009037	29940	526797	280618	625	47145	13515	425
2001	1007298	9678	189930	133464	705	45000	38000	357
2002	900335	8265	187665	138525	516	46500	13700	98
2003	890877	6540	66206	105666	420	38910	10425	147
2004	980942				255	60000	8472	625
2005	934700	3086	2860	100145	195	61005	3383	253
2006	930162	3716	60890	162125	15	25320	3900	480
2007	926760	3870	62363	149440	255	43320	4701	600
2008	923097	3873	59864	145340	255	49571	4548	610
2009	921000	3719	58375	143690	610	56545	6184	60

3-19 历年畜牧业生产及产品产量

Production of Animal Husbandry and Output of Livestock Products over Years

年 份	耕牛年末存栏量(头)	羊年末存栏量(头)	生猪饲养量(头)	生猪存栏量(头)	生猪出栏量(头)	三鸟饲养量(万只)	三鸟出栏量(万只)	畜牧总肉量(吨)	#猪肉	禽蛋总产量(吨)
1949	52475		147266	82266	65000	256	159			
1952	58530		243000	117082	125918	329	205			
1957	62444		300529	154756	145773	400	249			339
1962	47004		185961	103034	82927	339	248			394
1965	53105		640968	369391	271577	421	276			2989
1970	56665		900481	593310	307171	310	163			1614
1975	55292		920100	633527	286573	364	187			1141
1978	53004		1018060	672919	345141	428	219	26920	22790	425
1979	50595		995408	626435	368973	379	187	29209	25647	367
1980	53385		799568	501380	298188	420	209	27652	23461	444
1981	58619		703659	449638	254021	476	252	28011	23387	1284
1982	64067		791518	526106	265412	568	309	33037	27374	679
1983	69117		842198	489887	352311	630	370	35695	28872	1256
1984	70992		784473	458804	325669	652	369	33260	26301	1899
1985	62763		790505	471268	319237	832	414	33298	25759	2424
1986	62874		812102	428545	383557	940	655	43302	30920	5159
1987	58577		781957	396082	385875	1235	862	46120	32588	5478
1988	54723		811945	402035	409910	1400	1020	56125	35067	6734
1989	52713		846598	407317	439281	1565	1136	58563	38270	7109
1990	48760	1559	870782	410875	459907	1592	1188	62191	40130	6906
1991	44121	1396	930377	420919	509458	1806	1336	68844	44702	5924
1992	32259	1068	981698	448586	533112	1889	1419	67983	45492	5845
1993	18688	783	982084	404352	577732	2185	1647	76562	49470	4990
1994	14219	863	1089793	434904	654889	2334	1730	85448	57920	5521
1995	12207	1593	1250597	469355	781242	2501	1881	97572	68649	5431
1996	12945	1806	1407080	490161	916919	2418	1851	116058	83404	5862
1997	12675	2391	1772892	619114	1153778	2608	1863	128992	99300	6295
1998	10522	2159	2217247	776851	1440396	2291	1742	153513	123874	4738
1999	6811	1508	2573310	900285	1673025	2228	1667	159889	130494	4742
2000	5550	1675	2894126	967056	1927070	2362	1784	179032	149648	4367
2001	4618	1851	3255780	1079397	2176383	2226	1683	198423	168353	4441
2002	2919	1931	3075523	927477	2148046	1962	1557	188774	165344	4052
2003	1727	1789	2525252	742101	1783151	1652	1282	154615	135344	3597
2004	1024	1936	2444990	785289	1659701	1396	1048	146184	128286	3435
2005	827	998	2487962	214120	2273842	1314	1072	171737	159169	1355
2006	82	242	530959	110396	420563	485	312	34891	30199	371
2007	399	415	292234	88648	203586	525	341	20257	14862	361
2008	55		454117	195016	259101	758	574	24052	17946	106
2009	94		464727	183904	280823	767	576	25457	19095	515

3-20　历年水产品产量及养殖面积

Output and Cultured Area of Aquatic Products over Years

年　份	水产品产量（吨）	海水产量	海水捕捞	海水养殖	淡水产量	淡水捕捞	淡水养殖	养殖面积（亩）	海水养殖	淡水养殖
1949	3175	1475	1475		1700		1700	27390		27390
1952	3365	1565	1565		1800		1800	26167		26167
1957	4185	2410	2410		1775		1775	36016		36016
1962	6321	3521	3521		2800		2800	100822		100822
1965	9946	5693	5693		4253		4253	93502		93502
1970	16214	10878	10878		5336		5336	72176		72176
1975	21879	15026	15026		6853		6853	83398		83398
1978	30900	23307	23307		7593		7593	89040		89040
1979	22309	13878	13878		8431		8431	94916		94916
1980	25471	17069	17069		8402		8402	95549		95549
1981	24905	15669	15669		9236		9236	104069		104069
1982	27695	16120	16120		11575		11575	112586		112586
1983	30292	17330	17330		12962		12962	116943		116943
1984	32465	18025	18025		14440		14440	119456		119456
1985	32641	15422	15214	208	17219		17219	131350	5301	126049
1986	46534	28439	25918	2521	18095		18095	138651	16078	122573
1987	65679	45214	42793	2421	20465		20465	163225	15036	148189
1988	68087	44111	42926	1185	23976	182	23794	137966	9670	128296
1989	62306	37189	35372	1817	25117	1194	23923	123090	10350	112740
1990	68508	41002	38423	2579	27506	2177	25329	136174	19286	116888
1991	69025	39906	37209	2697	29119	2147	26972	131849	18446	113403
1992	73164	42429	38033	4396	30735	2590	28145	134558	20400	114158
1993	64973	33745	28192	5553	31228	3120	28108	143696	25855	117841
1994	67420	31284	24059	7225	36136	2565	33571	144869	26583	118286
1995	74778	32132	24637	7495	42646	2084	40562	162609	27795	134814
1996	81067	33363	25471	7892	47704	1940	45764	172656	27791	144865
1997	91901	35407	26704	8703	56494	5157	51337	184889	30326	154563
1998	96872	33618	24319	9299	63254	3146	60108	192381	29223	163158
1999	94023	31332	24257	7075	62691	2747	59944	167880	19440	148440
2000	95076	33234	24180	9054	61842	3135	58707	167841	25695	142146
2001	89599	30877	23726	7151	58722	2285	56437	155720	27928	127792
2002	82361	30800	23474	7326	51561	2762	48799	142167	26696	115471
2003	75756	30151	22826	7325	45605	2121	43484	126660	27097	99563
2004	71526	29289	22382	6907	42237	3078	39159	125116	25652	99464
2005	67381	28319	21622	6697	39062	1783	37279	102023	23530	78493
2006	47059	21152	15256	5897	25907	1062	24845	71745	6345	65400
2007	47292	21637	15992	5645	25655	857	24797	71100	5925	65175
2008	72282	21297	14322	6975	50985	512	50473	137718	17559	120159
2009	73323	19034	13205	5829	54289		54289	129136	4197	124939

3-21 主要农产品产量与最高年份比较（2009年）

Output of Main Agricultural Products in Comparison with Peak Year (2009)

指标	单位	2009年	建国以来最高年份		
			年份	产量	2009年为最高年份的%
一、粮食总产量	**吨**	**11912**	**1977**	**563463**	**2.1**
#稻谷	吨	6560	1973	548073	1.2
#早稻	吨		1983	279723	
晚稻	吨		1984	279898	
二、大豆	**吨**	**19**	**1954**	**2790**	**0.7**
三、经济作物					
#甘蔗	吨	23044	1982	707764	3.3
#糖蔗	吨	1249	1982	699174	0.2
花生	吨	113	1981	35506	0.3
四、其他作物					
#蔬菜	吨	400335	2001	706775	56.6
五、水果总产量	**吨**	**91544**	**1987**	**363085**	**25.2**
#香(大)蕉	吨	75341	1987	222826	33.8
荔枝	吨	10240	2002	45339	22.6
六、水产品	**吨**	**73323**	**1998**	**96872**	**75.7**
七、生猪年末存栏量	**头**	**183904**	**2001**	**1079397**	**17.0**
生猪年出栏头数	头	280823	2005	2273842	12.4
猪肉产量	吨	19095	2001	168353	11.3
八、三鸟饲养量	**万只**	**767**	**2000**	**2362**	**32.5**
三鸟出栏量	万只	576	2000	1784	32.3
禽蛋产量	吨	515	1989	7109	7.2

主要统计指标解释

耕地面积 是指可以用来种植农作物、经常进行耕锄的田地面积。耕地分为水田和旱地两类。

农作物播种面积 是指一定生产季节结束时实际播种或移植有农作物的面积。

农作物总产量 是指本年度内生产的各种农作物总产量，不论计划内外，数量多少，耕地上与非耕地上的农作物产量，都应统计在内，不得遗漏。

农业机械总动力 是指主要用于农、林、牧、副、渔业的各种动力机械的动力总和。

农业总产值 是以货币形式表现的一定时期内（通常按日历年度的一年计算）的全部农业产品总量。

农村经济总收入 是指本单位当年经营的收入中可用以抵偿本年度开支并可在国家、集体、农民之间进行分配的农、林、牧、副、渔业、工业、交通运输业、建筑业、商业、餐饮业、服务业等各项经营收入和利息、租金等非生产性收入，但不包括那些不能用来分配、属于借贷性质或暂收性质的收入，如贷款收入、预购定金、国家投资、农民投资等。

农村经济总费用 是指为实现当年各项生产经营收入应由当年负担的各项费用开支，包括生产费用、管理费用和其它费用三项。

农村经济纯收入 是指当年“总收入”减去“总费用”后，当年所得的纯收入部分。

农民人均纯收入 是指农民全年生产经营总收入中，扣除相应的各项费用支出后，最终归农民所有的按农村常住人口平均的收入。

四、工 业

Industry

4-1 主要年份工业主要指标

Main Indicators of Industry in Main Years

指　　标	单位	1998年	2000年	2001年	2005年	2008年	2009年
全市企业单位数	个	16406	16975	18094	21868	25656	30117
全市工业总产值	万元	9877754	15197858	18468234	44700346	73122902	67628037
规模以上工业:							
企业单位数	个	1500	1663	1680	4505	5954	5801
年末固定资产原值合计	万元	6257040	7288486	8259152	18560858	27349214	30799221
年末固定资产净值合计	万元	4392164	4701886	5354719	11052566	16583143	17239987
年末流动资产	万元	3798813	5298239	5629510	18732801	29492879	31652484
年末资产总额	万元	9267121	11225950	11730032	33453291	51144153	52861843
年末负债总额	万元	4752964	5630399	5796530	18580908	29392320	30434568
所有者权益	万元	4514157	5595551	5933502	14872383	21751834	22410155
工业增加值	万元	1687134	2594352	2906664	10624190	16029828	14533667
主营业务收入	万元	6399088	9889058	11312944	39121487	65360828	60077589
利税总额	万元	447544	841047	789734	1830988	2684307	4034721
#利润总额	万元	255715	503589	433640	1243516	1430566	2972487
全员劳动生产率(按增加值计算)	元/人	26688	36101	39438	53340	57535	56766
综合效益指数	%	94.1	114.0	109.5	119.9	116.6	127.2
工业总产值	万元	8162888	12714419	14669051	39420346	66328201	60711098
#轻工业	万元	4807905	5901276	6760814	17339211	29311840	26455424

注：1. 2005年以前数据根据东莞市第一次经济普查取得，2008年数据根据第二次经济普查取得，下同。
2. 规模以上工业企业1997年及以前年份为独立核算工业企业口径，1998-2005年为全部国有工业及年销售收入500万元以上非国有工业企业口径，2006年起为年主营业务收入500万元及以上工业企业口径，下同。

4-2 历年工业企业单位数（按经济成分分）

Number of Industrial Enterprises over Years (by Ownership)

单位：个

年　份	全市工业企　业单位数	国有及国有控股企业	集体企业	港澳台投资企业	外商投资企业	其他类型企业
1949	1	1				
1952	3522	20	3			3499
1957	262	76	186			
1962	280	57	223			
1965	260	61	199			
1970	220	57	163			
1975	324	61	263			
1978	1290	64	1226			
1979	1250	63	1187			
1980	1293	64	1229			
1981	1479	64	1415			
1982	1862	66	1796			
1983	1964	68	1896			
1984	2329	69	2109			151
1985	4187	73	2990	79		1045
1986	5949	81	4263	89		1516
1987	8106	74	5123	175		2734
1988	8408	72	5424	241		2671
1989	8757	76	5835	323		2523
1990	9892	78	6165	521	4	3124
1991	10094	77	6404	754	4	2855
1992	11639	72	6400	932	4	4231
1993	12449	75	7129	1388	24	3833
1994	14086	45	7185	2002	191	4663
1995	15215	70	9345	2631	210	2959
1996	15326	40	8958	2128	253	3947
1997	16857	41	9949	2064	315	4488
1998	16406	29	8814	2050	461	5052
1999	16877	29	10325	2627	731	3165
2000	16975	23	10184	2717	893	3158
2001	18094	20	9978	3605	1186	3305
2002	21313	19	198	10830	907	9359
2003	21935	19	200	10969	958	9789
2004	22156	13	211	9450	1422	11060
2005	21868	10	220	10141	2093	9404
2006	22447	10	211	10271	2190	9765
2007	22587	16	151	10041	2528	9851
2008	25656	25	608	7448	2436	15139
2009	30117	27	607	6724	2402	20357

注：本表2002年起集体企业不包括“三来一补”企业。

4-3 主要年份工业企业单位数（按不同类型分）

Number of Industrial Enterprises in Main Years (by Registration Status)

单位: 个

指　　标	1998年	2000年	2002年	2004年	2005年	2008年	2009年
全市企业单位数	**16406**	**16975**	**21313**	**22156**	**21868**	**25656**	**30117**
轻工业	14389	14440	15193	15270	12651	13498	17995
重工业	2017	2535	6120	6886	9217	12158	12122
在总计中:							
(一)规模以上工业企业	1500	1663	1993	4224	4505	5954	5801
按轻重工业分							
轻工业	1082	1124	1283	2405	2569	3211	3096
重工业	418	539	710	1819	1936	2743	2705
按登记注册类型分							
国有	29	16	12	4	5	9	10
集体	204	248	198	162	162	224	156
私营	24	44	126	557	621	994	1101
联营	5	6	5	4	2	7	4
股份合作	9	6	11		1	2	2
股份有限公司	6	3	6	19	18	20	20
外商投资	134	201	269	787	820	1387	1309
港澳台投资	1082	1119	1315	2367	2481	2700	2571
其他	7	20	51	324	395	611	628
按企业规模分							
大型企业	16	28	24	40	39	80	78
中型企业	27	19	421	592	579	1201	1156
小型企业	1457	1616	1548	3592	3887	4673	4567
(二)规模以下工业企业	14906	15312	19320	20107	17363	19702	24316

4-4 历年工业总产值

Gross Output Value of Industry over Years

年 份	工业总产值	
	绝对值 （万元）	增速 （%）
1978	42046	
1979	48834	10.5
1980	59060	17.7
1981	68611	16.2
1982	82538	18.0
1983	94823	11.1
1984	114237	16.0
1985	173495	48.5
1986	239348	40.1
1987	366859	47.6
1988	617244	54.3
1989	774616	23.8
1990	985847	20.0
1991	1283565	30.5
1992	1866746	44.3
1993	2676691	38.0
1994	3891280	37.0
1995	5225826	32.2
1996	6761860	25.6
1997	7986175	24.2
1998	9877754	23.2
1999	12419007	24.7
2000	15197858	24.4
2001	18468234	23.3
2002	22964444	27.9
2003	28747891	27.5
2004	36836125	26.4
2005	44700346	22.0
2006	55297003	22.8
2007	66678555	18.9
2008	73122902	7.8
2009	67628037	-3.3

注：本表工业总产值绝对值为当年价，增速按可比价计算。

4-5 主要年份工业总产值（按不同类型分）

Gross Output Value of Industry in Main Years (by Registration Status)

单位：万元

指　　标	1998年	2000年	2002年	2004年	2005年	2008年	2009年
全市工业总产值	**9877754**	**15197858**	**22964444**	**36836125**	**44700346**	**73122902**	**67628037**
轻工业	5812217	8012197	11345286	15965813	19661630	32793386	30133426
重工业	4065537	7185661	11619158	20870312	25038716	40329516	37494611
在总计中:							
(一)规模以上工业企业	8162888	12714419	20016645	31454169	39420346	66328201	60711098
按轻重工业分							
轻工业	4807905	5901276	9281826	13594629	17339211	29311840	26455424
重工业	3354983	6813143	10734819	17859540	22081135	37016361	34255674
按登记注册类型分							
国有	313473	452224	485469	154685	2578018	3646301	3483861
集体	734706	1066110	919435	609691	700885	984656	856331
私营	42235	93455	478751	1664066	2404542	5705769	6403588
联营	14408	41781	39528	12012	3848	38089	10443
股份合作	34289	20762	49502		1872	14468	14974
股份有限公司	608956	781168	603166	234344	527772	200267	181502
外商投资	1303037	2918437	6131078	10854409	11431182	21948700	18551925
港澳台投资	5083204	7173595	10472641	16367608	19632981	29684687	26505035
其他	28580	166887	837073	1557354	2139246	4105264	4703440
按企业规模分							
大型企业	1858071	4152216	3578053	6775264	7199762	17147061	14571967
中型企业	260335	536179	10831198	14730599	15837684	28888815	28623984
小型企业	6044482	8026024	5607394	9948306	16382900	20292325	17515148
(二)规模以下工业企业	1714866	2483439	2947799	5381956	5280000	6794701	6916939

4-6 规模以上工业企业单位数（2009年）

Number of Industrial Enterprises above Designated Size (2009)

单位：个

项　　目	工业单位数	按登记注册类型分		
		国有及国有控股工业	集体工业	港澳台及外商投资工业
总　计	**5801**	**27**	**156**	**3880**
按轻重工业分				
轻工业	3096	13	98	2029
重工业	2705	14	58	1851
按企业规模分				
大型企业	78	2		71
中型企业	1156	9	15	967
小型企业	4567	16	141	2842
按工业行业分(大类)				
非金属矿采选业	1			
农副食品加工业	40	2	1	13
食品制造业	48		1	18
饮料制造业	13	2		8
纺织业	333		3	179
纺织服装、鞋、帽制造业	292	2	6	190
皮革、毛皮、羽绒及其制品业	302	1	9	243
木材加工及竹、藤、棕草制品业	49			25
家具制造业	247		1	148
造纸及纸制品业	283		17	112
印刷业、记录媒介的复制	122		5	71
文教体育用品制造业	232	1	5	201
石油加工、及炼焦业及核燃业	7			3
化学原料及化学制品制造业	182	2	1	97
医药制造业	12			6
化学纤维制造业	9			8
橡胶制品业	123		2	97
塑料制品业	623		16	454
非金属矿物制品业	120	1	3	59
黑色金属冶炼及压延加工业	22			14
有色金属冶炼及压延加工业	65			31
金属制品业	392		7	259
通用设备制造业	198	2	4	123
专用设备制造业	255	2	7	175
交通运输设备制造业	53	1		39
电气机械及器材制造业	602		11	429
通信设备、计算机及其他电子设备制造业	860	2	25	654
仪器仪表及文化、办公用机械制造业	118		2	101
工艺品及其他制造业	145		1	113
电力、热力的生产和供应业	13	6	1	8
燃气生产和供应业	4			2
水的生产和供应业	36	3	28	

4-7　规模以上工业总产值和工业增加值（2009年）

Gross Industrial Output Value and Value-added of Industrial Enterprises above Designated Size (2009)

单位：万元

项　　目	工业总产值	按登记注册类型分		
		国有及国有控股工业	集体工业	港澳台及外商投资工业
总　计	**60711098**	**4934803**	**856331**	**45056960**
按轻重工业分				
轻工业	26455424	462311	563552	19649529
重工业	34255674	4472492	292780	25407431
按企业规模分				
大型企业	14571967	538503		13181760
中型企业	28623984	3956953	287586	20843888
小型企业	17515148	439347	568746	11031312
按工业行业分(大类)				
非金属矿采选业	1179			
农副食品加工业	1936283	306823	3296	967944
食品制造业	620354		526	459491
饮料制造业	1174306	26878		1118268
纺织业	2164110		6188	1495351
纺织服装、鞋、帽制造业	2182652	12096	12903	984415
皮革、毛皮、羽绒及其制品业	1900791	15795	61397	1578269
木材加工及竹、藤、棕草制品业	165089			106377
家具制造业	1539859		1092	957955
造纸及纸制品业	3185069		160062	2188523
印刷业、记录媒介的复制	847535		7391	733526
文教体育用品制造业	1467044	4340	7363	1371469
石油加工、及炼焦业及核燃业	108429			43341
化学原料及化学制品制造业	1479320	3434	1730	1118493
医药制造业	95805			28365
化学纤维制造业	27354			19244
橡胶制品业	520001		4413	451456
塑料制品业	3194397		91015	2623489
非金属矿物制品业	1034476	6198	4484	784407
黑色金属冶炼及压延加工业	230060			190545
有色金属冶炼及压延加工业	1107801			427049
金属制品业	1808739		7059	1337053
通用设备制造业	1193064	45451	12671	890327
专用设备制造业	1191061	37585	30245	946824
交通运输设备制造业	898248	241155		833085
电气机械及器材制造业	6079445		188692	4899250
通信设备、计算机及其他电子设备制造业	16712270	12825	125010	14469301
仪器仪表及文化、办公用机械制造业	2082789		6732	2015318
工艺品及其他制造业	975287		2009	885488
电力、热力的生产和供应业	4436225	4134524	2049	1022902
燃气生产和供应业	119126			109432
水的生产和供应业	232931	87699	120002	

4-7 续表

(2009年)

单位：万元

项目	工业增加值	按登记注册类型分		
		国有及国有控股工业	集体工业	港澳台及外商投资工业
总计	**14533667**	**1242830**	**280824**	**10980099**
按轻重工业分				
轻工业	6798568	105116	187100	5105482
重工业	7735099	1137714	93725	5874617
按企业规模分				
大型企业	3104700	173064		2830514
中型企业	7311095	994165	130037	5497259
小型企业	4117872	75602	150788	2652326
按工业行业分(大类)				
非金属矿采选业	702			
农副食品加工业	311432	45196	610	165632
食品制造业	214633		113	173084
饮料制造业	257026	7120		245517
纺织业	543927		4285	370214
纺织服装、鞋、帽制造业	671909	4581	4491	307650
皮革、毛皮、羽绒及其制品业	606280	2413	37942	504918
木材加工及竹、藤、棕草制品业	46048			33184
家具制造业	385739		212	258452
造纸及纸制品业	715041		32760	509910
印刷业、记录媒介的复制	302153		2421	265584
文教体育用品制造业	467407	1354	2221	440486
石油加工、及炼焦业及核燃业	23736			9495
化学原料及化学制品制造业	408025	1171	404	321088
医药制造业	32181			4527
化学纤维制造业	4709			3597
橡胶制品业	127862		3015	112082
塑料制品业	856893		18105	727048
非金属矿物制品业	325811	897	747	263097
黑色金属冶炼及压延加工业	33098			27495
有色金属冶炼及压延加工业	186487			81598
金属制品业	430212		1641	315820
通用设备制造业	250295	6712	3092	191999
专用设备制造业	343777	11451	7539	279694
交通运输设备制造业	238074	51059		223374
电气机械及器材制造业	1440306		68615	1140341
通信设备、计算机及其他电子设备制造业	3392916	3933	39317	2981947
仪器仪表及文化、办公用机械制造业	422523		2921	398525
工艺品及其他制造业	208893		367	189524
电力、热力的生产和供应业	1157068	1064915	309	407428
燃气生产和供应业	29846			26790
水的生产和供应业	98662	42029	49696	

4-8 规模以上工业企业主要财务指标（2009年）

Main Financial Indicators of Industrial Enterprises above Designated Size (2009)

单位：万元

指标	全市总计	按登记注册类型分			按轻重工业分	
		内资企业	港澳台商投资企业	外商投资企业	轻工业	重工业
一、企业单位数(个)	**5801**	**1921**	**2571**	**1309**	**3096**	**2705**
二、年末资产						
流动资产合计	31652484	6755701	14748138	10148645	14733372	16919112
#产成品存货	2577746	537837	1220733	819176	1279031	1298716
固定资产净值	17239987	4703460	8015796	4520731	7460432	9779555
年末资产总额	52861843	12833295	24292977	15735571	24059188	28802656
三、年末负债及所有者权益						
年末负债总额	30434568	8464107	13233980	8736482	13768423	16666145
所有者权益合计	22410155	4368159	11054539	6987457	10285994	12124161
四、损益及分配						
主营业务收入	60077589	15571033	26282948	18223607	26196142	33881447
#主营业务成本	51947873	13754458	22535464	15657952	22226647	29721227
主营业务费用	1260554	343250	500794	416510	783418	477136
主营业务税金及附加	100377	56860	24277	19240	50339	50038
主营业务利润	3443372	686132	1685632	1071607	1487672	1955700
管理费用	3323704	665492	1550454	1107758	1645073	1678631
财务费用	295056	128860	110037	56160	139753	155304
#利息支出	240975	120472	84968	35535	114895	126080
利润总额	2972487	599403	1466392	906692	1289170	1683316
#亏损企业亏损总额	446747	46797	233914	166037	226691	220056
利税总额	4034721	1015050	1830395	1189276	1761761	2272961

4-9 规模以上工业企业主要指标（2009年）

Main Indicators of Industrial Enterprises above Designated Size (2009)

单位：万元

项目	企业单位数（个）	#亏损企业	工业总产值	工业销售产值	工业增加值	全部职工平均人数（人）
总计	**5801**	**1399**	**60711098**	**60238631**	**14533667**	**2560260**
按轻重工业分						
轻工业	3096	754	26455424	26326668	6798568	1441692
重工业	2705	645	34255674	33911964	7735099	1118568
按企业规模分						
大型企业	78	9	14571967	14454196	3104700	340858
中型企业	1156	235	28623984	28421736	7311095	1273143
小型企业	4567	1155	17515148	17362699	4117872	946259
按工业行业分(大类)						
非金属矿采选业	1		1179	1177	702	40
农副食品加工业	40	5	1936283	1936426	311432	5642
食品制造业	48	7	620354	630333	214633	15236
饮料制造业	13	3	1174306	1161654	257026	8778
纺织业	333	60	2164110	2127633	543927	117860
纺织服装、鞋、帽制造业	292	82	2182652	2178259	671909	177112
皮革、毛皮、羽绒及其制品业	302	93	1900791	1880214	606280	257289
木材加工及竹、藤、棕草制品业	49	10	165089	172314	46048	11530
家具制造业	247	60	1539859	1523556	385739	90122
造纸及纸制品业	283	56	3185069	3193619	715041	59427
印刷业、记录媒介的复制	122	25	847535	865270	302153	40672
文教体育用品制造业	232	72	1467044	1464012	467407	169136
石油加工、及炼焦业及核燃业	7	1	108429	113191	23736	638
化学原料及化学制品制造业	182	28	1479320	1498555	408025	25379
医药制造业	12	2	95805	92411	32181	2431
化学纤维制造业	9	3	27354	27475	4709	1229
橡胶制品业	123	36	520001	514013	127862	38943
塑料制品业	623	161	3194397	3170487	856893	240757
非金属矿物制品业	120	35	1034476	1042344	325811	30219
黑色金属冶炼及压延加工业	22	7	230060	225078	33098	1797
有色金属冶炼及压延加工业	65	11	1107801	1098265	186487	12012
金属制品业	392	88	1808739	1777457	430212	98949
通用设备制造业	198	38	1193064	1163502	250295	44378
专用设备制造业	255	60	1191061	1191651	343777	71874
交通运输设备制造业	53	10	898248	899186	238074	20687
电气机械及器材制造业	602	147	6079445	6020322	1440306	268921
通信设备、计算机及其他电子设备制造业	860	217	16712270	16482811	3392916	598235
仪器仪表及文化、办公用机械制造业	118	32	2082789	2072643	422523	78744
工艺品及其他制造业	145	39	975287	956190	208893	45005
电力、热力的生产和供应业	13	1	4436225	4412350	1157068	21909
燃气生产和供应业	4		119126	118536	29846	626
水的生产和供应业	36	10	232931	227697	98662	4683

4-9 续表 1

(2009年)

单位：万元

项目	年末资产合计	#流动资产年合计	#产成品	固定资产净值	年末负债合计	亏损企业亏损总额
总计	**52861843**	**31652484**	**2577746**	**17239987**	**30434568**	**446747**
按轻重工业分						
轻工业	24059188	14733372	1279031	7460432	13768423	226691
重工业	28802656	16919112	1298716	9779555	16666145	220056
按企业规模分						
大型企业	10357616	6293875	536594	3446243	5672520	36222
中型企业	26071027	14376564	1150582	9523408	14520741	198211
小型企业	16433200	10982046	890570	4270336	10241308	212315
按工业行业分(大类)						
非金属矿采选业	2726	1407		1089	350	
农副食品加工业	1204283	908594	63981	223565	946278	2553
食品制造业	655389	388136	31400	209871	267174	1700
饮料制造业	819399	469176	41209	318255	475683	4663
纺织业	2158333	1474834	139298	612864	1244690	10178
纺织服装、鞋、帽制造业	1433028	1060200	87730	252053	819450	16545
皮革、毛皮、羽绒及其制品业	1364289	954182	95610	288143	885357	29512
木材加工及竹、藤、棕草制品业	191585	121937	11339	56406	108050	2022
家具制造业	1338556	894066	121473	340919	744087	13909
造纸及纸制品业	3934966	1599888	215017	2011477	2197154	22301
印刷业、记录媒介的复制	1068023	682878	36985	318838	435056	6009
文教体育用品制造业	1452527	910211	78561	364269	796307	26776
石油加工、及炼焦业及核燃业	74325	62602	9699	8869	55836	19
化学原料及化学制品制造业	1437047	980762	64399	295771	802757	5204
医药制造业	196228	160273	4803	19743	44987	158
化学纤维制造业	24700	18707	990	5381	12504	718
橡胶制品业	517487	354765	43806	112422	322513	5856
塑料制品业	2948793	1965716	174761	805161	1705365	39505
非金属矿物制品业	1427522	707742	73526	617402	815500	10475
黑色金属冶炼及压延加工业	233862	202370	10170	25891	164702	1284
有色金属冶炼及压延加工业	470462	376684	48394	74329	308530	4770
金属制品业	1843203	1250425	102161	485872	1084916	20095
通用设备制造业	1106749	732383	70294	273868	598725	6810
专用设备制造业	1736304	1140538	78681	439948	969083	15019
交通运输设备制造业	899657	591359	81927	267222	512724	1453
电气机械及器材制造业	4575624	3156629	325905	1104562	2577608	38939
通信设备、计算机及其他电子设备制造业	11511021	7574998	476721	3213908	7017890	125282
仪器仪表及文化、办公用机械制造业	1355710	889408	37192	391858	725569	7020
工艺品及其他制造业	930949	635295	40407	221534	513894	9559
电力、热力的生产和供应业	4942158	1097977	11009	3343627	2610014	6906
燃气生产和供应业	125338	40495		55809	63765	
水的生产和供应业	881603	247851	300	479062	608052	11509

4-9 续表 2

(2009年)

单位：万元

项 目	主营业务收入	#主营业务税金及附加	成本费用总额	利润总额	利税总额	本年应交增值税
总 计	**60077589**	**100377**	**56827186**	**2972487**	**4034721**	**961858**
按轻重工业分						
轻工业	26196142	50339	24794890	1289170	1761761	422251
重工业	33881447	50038	32032297	1683316	2272961	539607
按企业规模分						
大型企业	14468812	5581	13372927	862851	1074759	206327
中型企业	28279836	55600	26769134	1492884	2029537	481054
小型企业	17328940	39197	16685125	616752	930426	274477
按工业行业分(大类)						
非金属矿采选业	1007	16	760	232	329	80
农副食品加工业	1926028	1390	1754513	139216	160580	19974
食品制造业	628108	700	535837	101796	133417	30922
饮料制造业	1160047	6661	1033669	72931	123202	43610
纺织业	2121413	3800	2058005	75219	107502	28483
纺织服装、鞋、帽制造业	2141690	3837	2067261	60788	108481	43856
皮革、毛皮、羽绒及其制品业	1869618	2481	1863648	19199	38364	16685
木材加工及竹、藤、棕草制品业	171786	1275	171866	1174	5856	3408
家具制造业	1513015	6392	1472123	60295	83808	17122
造纸及纸制品业	3200338	6525	3029659	186493	278212	85195
印刷业、记录媒介的复制	849895	2357	756085	104782	131751	24612
文教体育用品制造业	1462724	1719	1438364	30124	40945	9102
石油加工、及炼焦业及核燃业	111663	188	107731	3724	5624	1711
化学原料及化学制品制造业	1494650	1328	1398193	106038	152323	44957
医药制造业	91295	571	78429	12915	19212	5725
化学纤维制造业	27539	17	27539	63	1158	1079
橡胶制品业	512315	392	499248	18785	23914	4737
塑料制品业	3153641	3860	3080414	89105	133449	40485
非金属矿物制品业	1028877	895	941794	96161	135835	38779
黑色金属冶炼及压延加工业	224138	60	212873	11790	15104	3254
有色金属冶炼及压延加工业	1097478	897	1050563	39037	45437	5504
金属制品业	1783658	2118	1753860	52726	83369	28525
通用设备制造业	1154618	1092	1020022	51269	77907	25546
专用设备制造业	1185359	1861	1149708	44310	74477	28307
交通运输设备制造业	900451	1661	817983	91570	112487	19255
电气机械及器材制造业	6008904	8678	5527269	402131	460245	49437
通信设备、计算机及其他电子设备制造业	16493169	11717	15747583	608438	759668	139513
仪器仪表及文化、办公用机械制造业	2073368	980	1940869	112449	119875	6446
工艺品及其他制造业	952447	1185	897770	47021	57843	9637
电力、热力的生产和供应业	4394451	17289	4077384	309914	503236	176033
燃气生产和供应业	118185	6537	88853	22796	29333	
水的生产和供应业	225715	1899	227311	-3	11779	9884

4-10 规模以上工业企业主要经济效益指标（2009年）

Main Indicators of Economic Benefit of Industrial Enterprises above Designated Size (2009)

项　　目	工业增加值率 (%)	总资产贡献率 (%)	资产负债率 (%)	流动资产周转率 (次/年)	成本费用利润率 (%)	全员劳动生产率 (元/人)	产品销售率 (%)
总　　计	23.9	8.1	57.6	1.9	5.2	56766	99.2
按轻重工业分							
轻工业	25.7	7.8	57.2	1.8	5.2	47157	99.5
重工业	22.6	8.3	57.9	2.0	5.3	69152	99.0
按企业规模分							
大型企业	21.3	10.6	54.8	2.3	6.5	91085	99.2
中型企业	25.5	8.3	55.7	2.0	5.6	57426	99.3
小型企业	23.5	6.1	62.3	1.6	3.7	43517	99.1
按工业行业分(大类)							
非金属矿采选业	59.6	12.1	12.8	0.7	30.6	175500	99.9
农副食品加工业	16.1	13.6	78.6	2.1	7.9	551988	100.0
食品制造业	34.6	20.6	40.8	1.6	19.0	140872	101.6
饮料制造业	21.9	15.8	58.1	2.5	7.1	292807	98.9
纺织业	25.1	5.3	57.7	1.4	3.7	46150	98.3
纺织服装、鞋、帽制造业	30.8	7.8	57.2	2.0	2.9	37937	99.8
皮革、毛皮、羽绒及其制品业	31.9	2.9	64.9	2.0	1.0	23564	98.9
木材加工及竹、藤、棕草制品业	27.9	3.7	56.4	1.4	0.7	39937	104.4
家具制造业	25.1	6.6	55.6	1.7	4.1	42802	98.9
造纸及纸制品业	22.5	8.2	55.8	2.0	6.2	120323	100.3
印刷业、记录媒介的复制	35.7	12.5	40.7	1.2	13.9	74290	102.1
文教体育用品制造业	31.9	3.0	54.8	1.6	2.1	27635	99.8
石油加工、及炼焦业及核燃业	21.9	8.6	75.1	1.8	3.5	372033	104.4
化学原料及化学制品制造业	27.6	11.0	55.9	1.5	7.6	160773	101.3
医药制造业	33.6	10.2	22.9	0.6	16.5	132377	96.5
化学纤维制造业	17.2	4.8	50.6	1.5	0.2	38318	100.4
橡胶制品业	24.6	4.8	62.3	1.4	3.8	32833	98.9
塑料制品业	26.8	4.7	57.8	1.6	2.9	35592	99.3
非金属矿物制品业	31.5	10.2	57.1	1.5	10.2	107817	100.8
黑色金属冶炼及压延加工业	14.4	7.1	70.4	1.1	5.5	184185	97.8
有色金属冶炼及压延加工业	16.8	10.7	65.6	2.9	3.7	155250	99.1
金属制品业	23.8	4.8	58.9	1.4	3.0	43478	98.3
通用设备制造业	21.0	7.3	54.1	1.6	5.0	56401	97.5
专用设备制造业	28.9	4.5	55.8	1.0	3.9	47830	100.1
交通运输设备制造业	26.5	12.9	57.0	1.5	11.2	115084	100.1
电气机械及器材制造业	23.7	10.3	56.3	1.9	7.3	53559	99.0
通信设备、计算机及其他电子设备制造业	20.3	6.8	61.0	2.2	3.9	56715	98.6
仪器仪表及文化、办公用机械制造业	20.3	9.0	53.5	2.3	5.8	53658	99.5
工艺品及其他制造业	21.4	6.6	55.2	1.5	5.2	46415	98.0
电力、热力的生产和供应业	26.1	11.5	52.8	4.0	7.6	528125	99.5
燃气生产和供应业	25.1	24.4	50.9	2.9	25.7	476773	99.5
水的生产和供应业	42.4	4.1	69.0	0.9		210682	97.8

4-11 国有及国有控股工业企业主要经济指标（2009年）

Main Economic Indicators of State-owned and State-holding Industrial Enterprises (2009)

项目	企业单位数（个）	#亏损企业	工业总产值（万元）	主营业务额（万元）	利润总额（万元）	亏损企业亏损总额（万元）	利税总额（万元）
总计	**27**	**5**	**4934803**	**4873693**	**323303**	**11442**	**512874**
按轻重工业分							
轻工业	13	3	462311	437441	18408	9152	26738
重工业	14	2	4472492	4436252	304895	2290	486136
按企业规模分							
按大中小型企业分							
大型企业	2		538503	537658	73978		95774
中型企业	9		3956953	3918672	231014		394978
小型企业	16	5	439347	417363	18311	11442	22122
按销售收入分							
10亿元以上	7		4628434	4585827	314420		494895
5-10亿元	1		73646	70344	1529		6171
1-5亿元	6	2	163873	154591	7627	8683	10216
1亿元以下	13	3	68851	62931	-272	2759	1592
按工业行业分(大类)							
#非金属矿采选业							
农副食品加工业	2		306823	290080	24066		24230
纺织服装、鞋、帽制造业	2		12096	11672	675		1368
木材加工及竹、藤、棕草制品业							
造纸及纸制品业							
通用设备制造业	2	1	45451	44411	3109	758	3536
通信设备、计算机及其他电子设备制造业	2		12825	12581	689		1043
电力、热力的生产和供应业	6		4134524	4100392	272965		453311

4-12 国有及国有控股工业企业主要经济效益指标（2009年）

Main Indicators on Economic Benefit of State-owned and State-holding Industrial Enterprises (2009)

项　　目	总资产贡献率 (%)	资　产负债率 (%)	流动资产周转率 (次/年)	成本费用利润率 (%)	产　品销售率 (%)
总　计	**10.9**	**53.2**	**3.8**	**7.1**	**99.1**
按轻重工业分					
轻工业	7.5	70.6	3.2	4.5	95.0
重工业	11.3	51.3	3.9	7.4	99.6
按企业规模分					
大型企业	18.9	52.3	2.0	15.8	99.8
中型企业	10.1	52.8	4.5	6.3	99.4
小型企业	9.2	62.4	3.3	4.7	95.4
按工业行业分(大类)					
非金属矿采选业					
农副食品加工业	25.5	62.9	5.6	9.2	93.7
食品制造业					
饮料制造业	8.1	72.7	1.8	4.5	97.5
纺织业					
纺织服装、鞋、帽制造业	8.8	34.0	1.1	6.1	96.6
皮革、毛皮、羽绒及其制品业	7.3	96.0	5.5	-1.6	100.0
木材加工及竹、藤、棕草制品业					
家具制造业					
造纸及纸制品业					
印刷业、记录媒介的复制					
文教体育用品制造业	6.6	15.3	2.2	0.3	109.2
石油加工、及炼焦业及核燃业					
化学原料及化学制品制造业	15.7	66.1	2.5	4.2	104.5
医药制造业					
化学纤维制造业					
橡胶制品业					
塑料制品业					
非金属矿物制品业	-32.5	74.9	1.7	-22.3	100.0
黑色金属冶炼及压延加工业					
有色金属冶炼及压延加工业					
金属制品业					
通用设备制造业	17.7	59.5	3.0	7.6	97.7
专用设备制造业	11.4	49.2	1.3	18.8	95.2
交通运输设备制造业	8.0	71.2	1.1	10.8	99.7
电气机械及器材制造业					
通信设备、计算机及其他电子设备制造业	5.0	49.3	0.6	5.7	97.5
仪器仪表及文化、办公用机械制造业					
工艺品及其他制造业					
电力、热力的生产和供应业	11.5	49.8	4.8	7.2	99.6
燃气生产和供应业					
水的生产和供应业	3.1	76.5	2.0	-8.1	96.2

4-13 规模以上集体工业主要经济指标（2009年）

Main Economic Indicators of Collective-owned Industrial Enterprises above Designated Size (2009)

项　　目	企业单位数（个）	#亏损企业	工业总产值（万元）	主营业务收入（万元）	利润总额（万元）	亏损企业亏损总额（万元）	利税总额（万元）
总　　计	**156**	**31**	**856331**	**849064**	**68858**	**11683**	**83927**
按轻重工业分							
轻工业	98	17	563552	558648	62623	6632	75842
重工业	58	14	292780	290416	6236	5051	8085
按企业规模分							
按大中小型企业分							
大型企业							
中型企业	15	1	287586	288622	51914	2402	57425
小型企业	141	30	568746	560442	16945	9281	26502
按销售收入分							
10亿元以上							
5-10亿元	2		162089	163503	11102		16412
1-5亿元	14	1	300288	299463	41184	69	42628
1亿元以下	140	30	393954	386098	16573	11614	24887
按工业行业分(大类)							
非金属矿采选业							
农副食品加工业	1		3296	2855	178		242
食品制造业	1		526	533	81		97
饮料制造业							
纺织业	3		6188	6188	747		791
纺织服装、鞋、帽制造业	6	1	12903	12903	916	47	1122
皮革、毛皮、羽绒及其制品业	9	2	61397	60699	-1268	2436	-1220
木材加工及竹、藤、棕草制品业							
家具制造业	1		1092	1092	389		390
造纸及纸制品业	17	1	160062	159398	12410	69	19262
印刷业、记录媒介的复制	5	1	7391	7617	393	10	513
文教体育用品制造业	5	2	7363	7210	-586	1263	-530
石油加工、及炼焦业及核燃业							
化学原料及化学制品制造业	1		1730	1846	67		164
医药制造业							
化学纤维制造业							
橡胶制品业	2		4413	4413	154		168
塑料制品业	16	3	91015	90522	11548	234	12066
非金属矿物制品业	3		4484	4212	71		153
黑色金属冶炼及压延加工业							
有色金属冶炼及压延加工业							
金属制品业	7	1	7059	7159	650	12	758
通用设备制造业	4	1	12671	12487	214	198	671
专用设备制造业	7	1	30245	28771	472	474	1055
交通运输设备制造业							
电气机械及器材制造业	11	1	188692	188692	29491	3423	29751
通信设备、计算机及其他电子设备制造业	25	10	125010	124971	5886	1403	6144
仪器仪表及文化、办公用机械制造业	2		6732	6732	428		568
工艺品及其他制造业	1		2009	2009			20
电力、热力的生产和供应业	1		2049	2049	263		285
燃气生产和供应业							
水的生产和供应业	28	7	120002	116706	6356	2114	11459

4-14 规模以上集体工业企业主要经济效益指标（2009年）

Main Indicators on Economic Benefit of Collective-owned Industrial Enterprises above Designated Size (2009)

项　　目	总资产贡献率(%)	资　产负债率(%)	流动资产周 转 率(次/年)	成本费用利 润 率(%)	产　品销售率(%)
总　计	**10.3**	**66.9**	**2.5**	**8.9**	**100.2**
按轻重工业分					
轻工业	11.8	62.7	2.0	12.6	100.5
重工业	4.5	82.7	5.1	2.3	99.7
按企业规模分					
大型企业					
中型企业	25.0	66.8	5.1	21.9	102.6
小型企业	5.4	66.9	2.0	3.2	99.0
按工业行业分(大类)					
非金属矿采选业					
农副食品加工业	17.1	36.9	3.1	6.1	86.6
食品制造业	5.2	89.2	0.6	18.0	90.9
饮料制造业					
纺织业	4.8	15.3	4.1	13.3	100.0
纺织服装、鞋、帽制造业	14.0	87.0	2.7	7.7	100.0
皮革、毛皮、羽绒及其制品业	-1.8	62.0	3.7	-2.0	100.0
木材加工及竹、藤、棕草制品业					
家具制造业	21.6	160.4	5.8	55.4	100.0
造纸及纸制品业	26.5	37.7	3.9	8.5	103.3
印刷业、记录媒介的复制	3.7	71.3	1.6	5.4	97.1
文教体育用品制造业	-9.5	95.6	1.9	-7.5	97.9
石油加工、及炼焦业及核燃业					
化学原料及化学制品制造业	9.2	70.6	1.1	3.8	106.7
医药制造业					
化学纤维制造业					
橡胶制品业	0.7	63.0	2.2	2.7	100.0
塑料制品业	36.7	33.4	9.7	14.9	99.5
非金属矿物制品业	2.5	48.1	0.8	1.7	95.0
黑色金属冶炼及压延加工业					
有色金属冶炼及压延加工业					
金属制品业	5.3	53.5	1.1	9.8	101.4
通用设备制造业	8.9	101.3	3.0	1.7	108.6
专用设备制造业	6.8	83.3	3.7	1.7	95.1
交通运输设备制造业					
电气机械及器材制造业	43.6	71.1	8.7	19.8	100.0
通信设备、计算机及其他电子设备制造业	8.5	112.4	5.9	5.0	100.0
仪器仪表及文化、办公用机械制造业	13.5	115.8	2.6	6.8	100.0
工艺品及其他制造业	2.1	89.7	44.5		100.0
电力、热力的生产和供应业	3.1	101.8	1.5	14.7	100.0
燃气生产和供应业					
水的生产和供应业	4.7	65.8	0.6	5.6	98.4

4-15 规模以上外商投资工业企业主要经济指标（2009年）

Main Economic Indicators of Industrial Enterprises above Designated Size with Foreign Funded (2009)

项　　目	企业单位数（个）	#亏损企业	工业总产值（万元）	主营业务收入（万元）	利润总额（万元）	亏损企业亏损总额（万元）	利税总额（万元）
总　　计	**1309**	**384**	**18551925**	**18223607**	**906692**	**166037**	**1189276**
按轻重工业分							
轻工业	595	189	6602509	6539001	377527	74136	490791
重工业	714	195	11949417	11684606	529165	91901	698485
按企业规模分							
按大中小型企业分							
大型企业	38	5	6287691	6160852	400946	14421	494170
中型企业	364	93	7682821	7558861	304689	93345	414213
小型企业	907	286	4581414	4503895	201058	58270	280893
按销售收入分							
10亿元以上	34	5	7198699	7123877	500184	16322	647747
5-10亿元	36	4	2435565	2397012	196963	14868	226143
1-5亿元	258	53	5385308	5236273	151822	64570	208973
1亿元以下	981	322	3532354	3466445	57722	70276	106413
按工业行业分(大类)							
非金属矿采选业							
农副食品加工业	8	3	608776	589167	28425	2161	39759
食品制造业	4	1	340345	352150	82156	651	104351
饮料制造业	2	1	289195	289195	55331	1251	83447
纺织业	36	9	324604	322917	9636	914	11899
纺织服装、鞋、帽制造业	33	12	222534	221716	-2132	4898	473
皮革、毛皮、羽绒及其制品业	80	28	621736	610611	2762	14745	7133
木材加工及竹、藤、棕草制品业	8	5	14084	13874	-655	911	-156
家具制造业	57	20	403923	406802	37705	5924	38871
造纸及纸制品业	22	9	228080	228329	5941	439	12578
印刷业、记录媒介的复制	21	4	200167	201671	40334	850	47830
文教体育用品制造业	58	20	345387	343254	19042	3785	21825
石油加工、及炼焦业及核燃业	1		15162	15162	2710		3252
化学原料及化学制品制造业	35	7	625330	643926	33490	1595	55495
医药制造业							
化学纤维制造业	2		5544	5424	29		747
橡胶制品业	40	15	225166	216709	6751	2954	8167
塑料制品业	146	48	864286	848257	2255	20895	10081
非金属矿物制品业	17	8	143254	135555	13295	2195	15890
黑色金属冶炼及压延加工业	7	1	99306	97583	7404	136	8085
有色金属冶炼及压延加工业	15	3	267279	264851	14426	1922	16067
金属制品业	78	20	494695	482897	4336	10269	12768
通用设备制造业	39	7	463548	448262	19943	1827	29834
专用设备制造业	68	16	490539	491426	19111	4030	32220
交通运输设备制造业	20	3	427321	427238	59909	444	75364
电气机械及器材制造业	148	38	2176635	2151405	98966	10279	116209
通信设备、计算机及其他电子设备制造业	283	80	7256096	7021694	245605	60911	319467
仪器仪表及文化、办公用机械制造业	36	10	929949	931401	60546	2662	63487
工艺品及其他制造业	40	15	271039	264585	5325	2484	7352
电力、热力的生产和供应业	3	1	88514	88514	12132	6906	18399
燃气生产和供应业	2		109432	109032	21917		28383
水的生产和供应业							

4-16 规模以上外商投资工业企业主要经济效益指标（2009年）

Main Indicators of Economic Benefit of Industrial Enterprises above Designated Size with Foreign Funded (2009)

项　　目	总资产贡献率 (%)	资　产负债率 (%)	流动资产周转率 (次/年)	成本费用利润率 (%)	产　品销售率 (%)
总　计	**7.8**	**55.5**	**1.8**	**5.3**	**98.4**
按轻重工业分					
轻工业	8.2	56.4	1.6	6.1	99.4
重工业	7.6	55.0	1.9	4.8	97.8
按企业规模分					
大型企业	12.1	52.2	2.4	7.1	97.8
中型企业	6.1	55.8	1.7	4.2	98.6
小型企业	6.5	58.0	1.5	4.7	98.7
按工业行业分(大类)					
非金属矿采选业					
农副食品加工业	7.8	75.0	1.5	5.2	98.9
食品制造业	28.0	30.7	1.7	30.3	103.3
饮料制造业	31.1	50.0	1.5	23.7	100.0
纺织业	4.3	62.1	1.7	3.0	100.4
纺织服装、鞋、帽制造业	0.3	66.3	1.9	-1.0	98.7
皮革、毛皮、羽绒及其制品业	1.5	56.9	1.8	0.5	98.5
木材加工及竹、藤、棕草制品业	1.1	52.5	0.5	-4.3	100.4
家具制造业	9.9	48.6	1.7	9.7	99.7
造纸及纸制品业	4.1	35.3	1.5	2.7	101.3
印刷业、记录媒介的复制	15.4	39.2	0.9	24.7	100.8
文教体育用品制造业	5.4	52.8	1.3	5.8	99.3
石油加工、及炼焦业及核燃业	26.8	4.4	1.4	21.8	100.0
化学原料及化学制品制造业	7.8	60.0	1.4	5.5	103.0
医药制造业					
化学纤维制造业	12.5	48.8	1.1	0.5	94.6
橡胶制品业	3.9	61.5	1.6	3.2	96.0
塑料制品业	1.3	59.0	1.6	0.3	98.9
非金属矿物制品业	7.6	39.3	1.8	10.9	94.7
黑色金属冶炼及压延加工业	11.8	63.5	1.6	8.1	98.5
有色金属冶炼及压延加工业	11.0	59.8	2.3	5.8	98.9
金属制品业	2.7	60.3	1.3	0.9	98.0
通用设备制造业	7.5	48.7	1.8	5.9	98.6
专用设备制造业	3.6	59.7	0.8	4.0	100.8
交通运输设备制造业	22.2	46.3	2.1	16.3	99.9
电气机械及器材制造业	7.6	52.3	2.1	4.8	98.8
通信设备、计算机及其他电子设备制造业	6.9	57.0	2.2	3.7	96.7
仪器仪表及文化、办公用机械制造业	10.0	53.6	2.2	6.9	100.0
工艺品及其他制造业	2.8	66.2	1.2	2.1	98.3
电力、热力的生产和供应业	10.2	69.9	0.9	13.4	100.0
燃气生产和供应业	25.1	49.7	2.9	27.2	99.6
水的生产和供应业					

4-17 规模以上港澳台投资工业企业主要经济指标（2009年）

Main Economic Indicators of Industrial Enterprises above Designated Size with Funds from Hong Kong, Macao and Taiwan (2009)

项目	企业单位数（个）	#亏损企业	工业总产值（万元）	主营业务收入（万元）	利润总额（万元）	亏损企业亏损总额（万元）	利税总额（万元）
总计	**2571**	**780**	**26505035**	**26282948**	**1466392**	**233914**	**1830395**
按轻重工业分							
轻工业	1434	446	13047020	12884095	574150	122348	759452
重工业	1137	334	13458014	13398854	892242	111566	1070944
按企业规模分							
按大中小型企业分							
大型企业	33	4	6894069	6895779	406279	21801	489033
中型企业	603	131	13161068	13030808	876725	99678	1068082
小型企业	1935	645	6449899	6356361	183387	112435	273281
按销售收入分							
10亿元以上	37	2	9748782	9721808	793206	12047	943502
5-10亿元	39	4	2524957	2511985	276946	20502	325867
1-5亿元	387	69	7780375	7707787	308876	61722	386463
1亿元以下	2108	705	6450921	6341369	87363	139643	174564
按工业行业分(大类)							
非金属矿采选业							
农副食品加工业	5	1	359168	325241	36799	57	41564
食品制造业	14	4	119146	118297	8249	867	13281
饮料制造业	6	1	829074	818040	13239	3409	34130
纺织业	143	39	1170746	1137583	54724	8484	65607
纺织服装、鞋、帽制造业	157	57	761881	756461	11985	11078	21598
皮革、毛皮、羽绒及其制品业	163	55	956533	936605	11181	11698	18641
木材加工及竹、藤、棕草制品业	17	3	92293	100119	493	852	3139
家具制造业	91	31	554031	546399	4045	6635	9243
造纸及纸制品业	90	24	1960442	1962132	135524	19403	192891
印刷业、记录媒介的复制	50	16	533360	532735	61778	4901	77882
文教体育用品制造业	143	46	1026083	1025054	10016	21267	16224
石油加工、及炼焦业及核燃业	2	1	28178	26451	459	19	1111
化学原料及化学制品制造业	62	18	493163	493933	51612	3572	66674
医药制造业	6	2	28365	26844	1139	158	1940
化学纤维制造业	6	3	13700	14036	-296	718	-146
橡胶制品业	57	19	226290	226420	9234	2731	11117
塑料制品业	308	95	1759203	1741044	49288	17763	72966
非金属矿物制品业	42	13	641153	640258	79101	4762	107403
黑色金属冶炼及压延加工业	7	5	91239	87762	4089	1145	6151
有色金属冶炼及压延加工业	16	5	159770	155624	7683	2433	8945
金属制品业	181	53	842359	833906	28054	8212	37753
通用设备制造业	84	19	426780	406692	19260	4056	26160
专用设备制造业	107	34	456285	457184	15807	9912	25715
交通运输设备制造业	19	5	405764	410346	29288	931	32636
电气机械及器材制造业	281	85	2722616	2689010	221628	23203	236629
通信设备、计算机及其他电子设备制造业	371	109	7213205	7224468	285251	60315	320955
仪器仪表及文化、办公用机械制造业	65	19	1085370	1073510	44968	4111	47175
工艺品及其他制造业	73	18	614448	599161	45863	1222	52618
电力、热力的生产和供应业	5		934389	917632	225930		280397
燃气生产和供应业							
水的生产和供应业							

4-18 规模以上港澳台商投资工业企业主要经济效益指标（2009年）

Main Indicators of Economic Benefit of Industrial Enterprises above Designated Size with Funds from Hong Kong, Macao and Taiwan (2009)

项　　目	总资产贡献率 (%)	资　产负债率 (%)	流动资产周转率 (次/年)	成本费用利润率 (%)	产　品销售率 (%)
总　计	**7.9**	**54.5**	**1.8**	**5.9**	**99.4**
按轻重工业分					
轻工业	6.5	52.6	1.8	4.7	99.2
重工业	9.3	56.4	1.8	7.2	99.6
按企业规模分					
大型企业	9.3	54.4	2.3	6.4	99.7
中型企业	9.3	53.4	1.8	7.2	99.6
小型企业	4.3	56.5	1.4	3.0	98.8
按工业行业分(大类)					
非金属矿采选业					
农副食品加工业	34.2	74.0	3.9	12.8	90.6
食品制造业	9.2	44.7	1.4	7.3	100.1
饮料制造业	7.8	61.8	3.1	1.8	98.6
纺织业	5.3	45.5	1.3	5.1	97.3
纺织服装、鞋、帽制造业	3.5	57.3	1.6	1.6	99.5
皮革、毛皮、羽绒及其制品业	2.8	69.1	1.8	1.2	98.8
木材加工及竹、藤、棕草制品业	3.2	52.9	1.4	0.5	107.7
家具制造业	1.85	53.0	1.4	0.7	98.6
造纸及纸制品业	8.0	53.9	2.0	7.4	100.2
印刷业、记录媒介的复制	12.0	37.2	1.4	12.9	102.9
文教体育用品制造业	1.9	54.2	1.7	1.0	100.1
石油加工、及炼焦业及核燃业	6.2	87.2	1.1	1.8	99.4
化学原料及化学制品制造业	15.5	40.3	1.6	11.5	100.0
医药制造业	6.0	71.9	1.0	4.4	98.5
化学纤维制造业	-1.0	42.1	1.2	-2.0	103.3
橡胶制品业	4.9	59.9	1.3	4.2	101.0
塑料制品业	4.5	54.4	1.5	2.9	99.6
非金属矿物制品业	12.6	54.7	1.6	13.8	101.9
黑色金属冶炼及压延加工业	6.4	69.1	1.0	4.9	96.3
有色金属冶炼及压延加工业	7.8	70.3	1.6	5.2	98.1
金属制品业	4.3	50.2	1.4	3.4	97.8
通用设备制造业	5.9	49.8	1.3	4.9	94.7
专用设备制造业	4.5	45.8	1.2	3.5	100.4
交通运输设备制造业	6.7	62.3	1.2	7.5	100.9
电气机械及器材制造业	11.0	55.3	1.8	9.2	99.3
通信设备、计算机及其他电子设备制造业	6.1	60.9	2.1	4.2	100.1
仪器仪表及文化、办公用机械制造业	7.3	52.3	2.5	4.5	99.0
工艺品及其他制造业	10.1	41.4	1.7	8.4	97.6
电力、热力的生产和供应业	30.7	42.9	2.3	32.7	99.0
燃气生产和供应业					
水的生产和供应业					

4-19 规模以上私营工业企业主要经济指标（2009年）

Main Economic Indicators of Private Industrial Enterprises above Designated Size (2009)

项目	企业单位数(个)	#亏损企业	工业总产值(万元)	主营业务收入(万元)	利润总额(万元)	亏损企业亏损总额(万元)	利税总额(万元)
总计	**1101**	**110**	**6403588**	**6301266**	**239241**	**8474**	**395528**
按轻重工业分							
轻工业	619	59	3826852	3745186	146620	4570	246882
重工业	482	51	2576736	2556079	92622	3904	148647
按企业规模分							
按大中小型企业分							
大型企业	5		527548	543879	38082		61290
中型企业	93	3	2454377	2389515	96027	518	146096
小型企业	1003	107	3421663	3367872	105133	7956	188141
按销售收入分							
10亿元以上	4		816984	829801	21926		43477
5-10亿元	13		941820	904237	43240		58315
1-5亿元	108	2	2025402	2008946	94789	363	138815
1亿元以下	976	108	2619381	2558281	79286	8110	154921
按工业行业分(大类)							
非金属矿采选业							
农副食品加工业	10		240083	235956	7806		11170
食品制造业	19	2	102045	100359	5004	182	7030
饮料制造业	1		793	873	3		35
纺织业	116	7	551250	543147	8615	368	24141
纺织服装、鞋、帽制造业	69	7	1070585	1034958	47309	245	80099
皮革、毛皮、羽绒及其制品业	26	5	98502	98163	1259	416	3859
木材加工及竹、藤、棕草制品业	18	1	39436	39362	1265	27	2140
家具制造业	61	3	369298	357033	11981	284	20287
造纸及纸制品业	94	13	550097	542906	18173	1853	30836
印刷业、记录媒介的复制	26	2	66220	66667	1370	27	3049
文教体育用品制造业	17	3	62759	61432	1153	65	2505
石油加工、及炼焦业及核燃业	2		49107	54068	443		751
化学原料及化学制品制造业	51	3	130056	129258	4910	37	9054
医药制造业	1		1398	692	120		180
化学纤维制造业	1		8110	8078	330		558
橡胶制品业	12	2	21922	22639	221	171	907
塑料制品业	103	9	342497	336427	18772	420	27677
非金属矿物制品业	31	4	182325	189532	5033	62	11827
黑色金属冶炼及压延加工业	4	1	9925	9558	33	3	158
有色金属冶炼及压延加工业	22	2	418285	415733	1689	91	3665
金属制品业	74	7	317457	313303	17182	1014	26140
通用设备制造业	44	5	172500	170446	7103	559	12909
专用设备制造业	48	7	118992	117342	3108	482	6583
交通运输设备制造业	4	2	7760	7201	90	78	508
电气机械及器材制造业	104	11	649962	636955	27453	769	43240
通信设备、计算机及其他电子设备制造业	111	8	725740	712722	44738	797	58839
仪器仪表及文化、办公用机械制造业	9	1	31371	32445	3134	13	4840
工艺品及其他制造业	23	5	65115	64011	944	511	2541
电力、热力的生产和供应业							
燃气生产和供应业							
水的生产和供应业							

4-20 规模以上私营工业企业主要经济效益指标（2009年）

Main Indicators on Economic Benefit of Private Industrial Enterprises above Designated Size (2009)

项目	总资产贡献率(%)	资产负债率(%)	流动资产周转率(次/年)	成本费用利润率(%)	产品销售率(%)
总计	**10.4**	**71.2**	**2.1**	**4.0**	**99.3**
按轻重工业分					
轻工业	10.6	69.4	2.0	4.1	99.3
重工业	10.2	74.1	2.2	3.8	99.4
按企业规模分					
大型企业	17.3	51.2	1.8	7.7	107.2
中型企业	10.5	69.2	2.2	4.2	98.3
小型企业	9.2	75.9	2.0	3.2	98.8
按工业行业分(大类)					
非金属矿采选业					
农副食品加工业	9.6	79.8	2.2	3.6	98.2
食品制造业	10.3	76.7	2.0	5.2	99.4
饮料制造业	2.4	82.0	1.0	0.4	110.2
纺织业	5.8	85.3	1.5	1.6	98.9
纺织服装、鞋、帽制造业	15.7	53.0	2.4	4.8	100.1
皮革、毛皮、羽绒及其制品业	11.0	72.5	4.4	1.3	99.8
木材加工及竹、藤、棕草制品业	9.5	77.9	2.4	3.3	99.6
家具制造业	12.5	74.2	2.5	3.5	98.7
造纸及纸制品业	8.2	70.7	2.1	3.5	99.1
印刷业、记录媒介的复制	8.4	65.9	2.5	2.1	100.6
文教体育用品制造业	7.5	85.5	2.1	1.9	98.4
石油加工、及炼焦业及核燃业	3.4	90.1	2.7	0.8	110.1
化学原料及化学制品制造业	11.2	73.3	1.9	3.9	99.8
医药制造业	8.4	14.1	0.7	20.6	51.3
化学纤维制造业	15.6	89.2	3.6	4.3	99.6
橡胶制品业	8.7	68.0	2.7	1.0	102.8
塑料制品业	11.1	75.6	1.6	5.9	98.3
非金属矿物制品业	8.1	77.6	1.6	2.8	103.5
黑色金属冶炼及压延加工业	1.4	90.5	0.9	0.4	100.3
有色金属冶炼及压延加工业	6.9	78.2	6.4	0.4	99.4
金属制品业	12.3	71.0	1.9	5.8	98.9
通用设备制造业	10.0	63.0	1.9	4.3	99.4
专用设备制造业	7.7	77.0	1.8	2.7	99.4
交通运输设备制造业	13.1	74.3	2.2	1.3	92.8
电气机械及器材制造业	9.5	72.1	1.7	4.5	98.2
通信设备、计算机及其他电子设备制造业	13.8	65.5	2.2	6.7	98.7
仪器仪表及文化、办公用机械制造业	14.5	54.9	1.3	10.6	102.5
工艺品及其他制造业	5.3	76.6	1.5	1.5	100.5
电力、热力的生产和供应业					
燃气生产和供应业					
水的生产和供应业					

4-21 大中型工业企业主要经济指标（2009年）

Main Economic Indicators of Large and Medium-sized Industrial Enterprises (2009)

项　　目	企业单位数（个）	#亏损企业	工业总产值（万元）	主营业务收入（万元）	利润总额（万元）	亏损企业亏损总额（万元）	利税总额（万元）
总　计	**1234**	**244**	**43195951**	**42748649**	**2355734**	**234433**	**3104295**
按轻重工业分							
轻工业	638	131	17339365	17113112	1003233	120532	1316716
重工业	596	113	25856586	25635536	1352501	113901	1787580
按企业规模分							
大型企业	78	9	14571967	14468812	862851	36222	1074759
中型企业	1156	235	28623984	28279836	1492884	198211	2029537
按工业行业分(大类)							
非金属矿采选业							
农副食品加工业	3		564500	511986	41653		55443
食品制造业	10	2	481463	492527	90705	792	118180
饮料制造业	5	1	1098733	1087309	71612	1251	118002
纺织业	49	6	1359957	1334514	59359	3745	75338
纺织服装、鞋、帽制造业	57	10	1537045	1502199	58916	6793	93407
皮革、毛皮、羽绒及其制品业	76	21	1251587	1227069	16240	20699	27840
木材加工及竹、藤、棕草制品业	6		77381	84841	1264		3856
家具制造业	58	19	1007803	991256	51479	9812	65604
造纸及纸制品业	38	7	2277972	2278917	168634	15586	238704
印刷业、记录媒介的复制	31	4	606273	605277	95950	2846	115287
文教体育用品制造业	70	17	1012923	1007261	26637	16704	33718
石油加工、及炼焦业及核燃业							
化学原料及化学制品制造业	17	4	520454	559774	47409	2103	65489
医药制造业	2		57296	55125	11487		16273
化学纤维制造业							
橡胶制品业	14	4	150554	147978	3160	1913	3613
塑料制品业	104	22	1694202	1677796	41462	22687	60846
非金属矿物制品业	17	2	746080	743576	96223	3437	128569
黑色金属冶炼及压延加工业							
有色金属冶炼及压延加工业	7	1	623066	619169	20868	839	22826
金属制品业	53	13	716797	709650	19106	10370	31785
通用设备制造业	32	3	633082	607677	34088	384	47427
专用设备制造业	44	9	631046	635118	23687	5135	38454
交通运输设备制造业	13	2	688003	692047	71394	821	84378
电气机械及器材制造业	151	27	4134827	4087517	350045	17070	382661
通信设备、计算机及其他电子设备制造业	310	64	14753685	14572156	557454	87878	684092
仪器仪表及文化、办公用机械制造业	36	3	1820301	1812155	100183	3147	103610
工艺品及其他制造业	24	3	425240	417509	13922	422	15282
电力、热力的生产和供应业	6		4252036	4217904	281273		467441
燃气生产和供应业							
水的生产和供应业	1		73646	70344	1529		6171

4-22 大中型工业企业主要经济效益指标（2009年）

Main Indicators on Economic Benefit of Large and Medium-sized Industrial Enterprises (2009)

项目	总资产贡献率 (%)	资产负债率 (%)	流动资产周转率 (次/年)	成本费用利润率 (%)	产品销售率 (%)
总计	**9.0**	**55.4**	**2.1**	**5.9**	**99.3**
按轻重工业分					
轻工业	8.9	53.9	1.9	6.3	99.4
重工业	9.0	56.6	2.2	5.6	99.2
按企业规模分					
大型企业	10.6	54.8	2.3	6.5	99.2
中型企业	8.3	55.7	2.0	5.6	99.3
按工业行业分(大类)					
非金属矿采选业					
农副食品加工业	25.3	79.6	3.4	8.9	92.6
食品制造业	22.1	40.2	1.6	22.4	102.2
饮料制造业	17.1	58.1	2.5	7.4	99.0
纺织业	5.5	56.0	1.4	4.6	98.3
纺织服装、鞋、帽制造业	9.7	54.2	2.1	4.1	100.1
皮革、毛皮、羽绒及其制品业	3.3	62.1	2.1	1.3	98.8
木材加工及竹、藤、棕草制品业	4.9	46.3	1.7	1.5	109.7
家具制造业	7.4	52.0	1.7	5.4	99.1
造纸及纸制品业	8.9	53.2	2.2	8.0	100.5
印刷业、记录媒介的复制	15.9	32.1	1.3	18.5	102.4
文教体育用品制造业	3.9	55.5	1.6	2.7	99.5
石油加工、及炼焦业及核燃业					
化学原料及化学制品制造业	11.0	49.3	1.4	9.1	107.7
医药制造业	11.6	7.5	0.4	26.3	96.2
化学纤维制造业					
橡胶制品业	2.1	68.5	1.4	2.1	98.3
塑料制品业	3.9	58.3	1.6	2.5	99.5
非金属矿物制品业	13.8	54.3	1.9	14.7	101.5
黑色金属冶炼及压延加工业					
有色金属冶炼及压延加工业	15.9	65.6	4.8	3.5	99.5
金属制品业	4.4	56.3	1.3	2.7	99.5
通用设备制造业	8.6	47.9	1.7	7.0	96.3
专用设备制造业	3.7	57.6	0.9	3.8	101.5
交通运输设备制造业	12.4	58.5	1.5	11.3	100.4
电气机械及器材制造业	12.6	52.3	2.0	9.5	99.0
通信设备、计算机及其他电子设备制造业	7.2	61.5	2.3	4.0	98.6
仪器仪表及文化、办公用机械制造业	10.0	55.4	2.6	5.9	99.5
工艺品及其他制造业	3.9	41.3	1.5	3.5	98.6
电力、热力的生产和供应业	11.6	49.9	4.4	7.2	99.6
燃气生产和供应业					
水的生产和供应业	5.9	76.4	2.0	2.2	95.5

4-23 主要年份规模以上工业企业经济效益指标

Main Indicators on Economic Benefit of Industrial Enterprises above Designated Size in Main Years

项目	单位	1985年	1990年	1995年	2000年	2004年	2005年	2008年	2009年
产品销售率	%	85.6	94.7	98.7	99.8	99.6	99.5	99.0	99.2
成本费用利润率	%	6.5	1.5	5.0	5.4	3.4	3.3	2.2	5.2
产值利税率	%	6.9	6.4	9.8	9.2	5.6	4.6	4.0	6.6
资金利税率	%	9.0	6.3	6.9	7.5	3.6	5.5	5.2	7.6
销售利税率	%	8.2	6.7	9.1	9.2	5.7	4.7	4.1	6.7
每百元固定资产原值实现的产值	元	174.9	133.6	108.7	125.5	220.3	212.4	242.5	197.1
每百元固定资产原值实现的利税	元	14.2	8.5	10.7	11.5	9.8	9.9	9.8	13.1
每百元固定资产原值实现的利润	元	4.4	1.8	5.5	6.9	6.8	6.7	5.2	9.7
每百元流动资产实现的产值	元	210.2	247.8	169.4	178.6	227.3	216.3	224.9	191.8
每百元流动资产实现的利税	元	17.1	15.7	16.6	16.4	10.2	10.0	9.1	12.7
每百元流动资产实现的利润	元	4.9	3.3	8.6	9.8	7.0	6.8	4.9	9.4
亏损企业亏损面	%	7.2	11.1	25.9	31.3	33.7	30.1	32.7	24.1
全部流动资产周转天数	天	173.7	155.6	201.1	189.0	170.6	169.8	162.0	192.3
增加值全员劳动生产率	元/人	2906	6439	13778	36101	52464	53340	57535	56766
平均每个职工提供利税	元/人	626	1519	5351	11703	12192	9193	9635	15759

注：由于1993年财务会计制度改革，本表中有关财务指标1993年起数字与往年不可比；全员劳动生产率1993年起按增加值计算，以前年份按净产值计算；1993年以前的流动资产按定额资金计算。下同。

4-24 主要年份国有经济工业企业经济效益指标

Main Indicators on Economic Benefit of State-owned and State-holding Industrial Enterprises in Main Years

项目	单位	1985年	1990年	1995年	2000年	2004年	2005年	2008年	2009年
产品销售率	%	89.6	102.0	100.8	98.3	99.9	100.0	96.5	99.1
成本费用利润率	%	8.0	-0.8	15.5	7.0	6.8	5.8	2.9	7.1
产值利税率	%	13.2	9.2	40.6	69.4	98.7	11.3	8.4	10.4
资金利税率	%	20.4	8.3	14.9	21.6	40.8	10.6	8.0	9.8
销售利税率	%	14.8	9.0	20.6	19.2	98.7	11.3	8.7	10.5
每百元固定资产原值实现的产值	元	142.9	85.5	61.1	63.4	44.2	105.0	94.5	73.4
每百元固定资产原值实现的利税	元	21.1	7.8	24.8	44.0	12.2	11.8	7.9	7.6
每百元固定资产原值实现的利润	元	9.6	-0.6	10.8	14.5	8.7	5.6	2.5	4.8
每百元流动资产实现的产值	元	445.1	397.8	96.3	73.4	215.4	443.4	586.2	387.9
每百元流动资产实现的利税	元	65.7	36.4	39.1	50.9	59.3	50.0	49.1	40.3
每百元流动资产实现的利润	元	27.5	-2.4	17.0	16.7	42.3	23.8	15.6	25.4
亏损企业亏损面	%	9.9	16.7	20.9		25.0	20.0	11.1	18.5
全部流动资产周转天数	天	80.9	88.7	299.8	137.7	56.2	83.0	66.0	95.3
增加值全员劳动生产率	元/人	3641	11253	73910	456736	1694891	2320312	1843209	416456
平均每个职工提供利税	元/人	1757	5325	55113	303960	1603751	1197862	637736	171857

4-25 主要年份规模以上集体经济工业企业经济效益指标

Main Indicators on Economic Benefit of Collective-owned Industrial Enterprises above Designated Size in Main Years

项　　目	单位	1985年	1990年	1995年	2000年	2004年	2005年	2008年	2009年
产品销售率	%	85.1	92.2	98.0	97.0	101.2	100.5	98.5	100.2
成本费用利润率	%	5.9	3.3	5.2	2.7	4.5	3.3	5.4	8.9
产值利税率	%	9.3	6.9	9.0	5.1	7.6	5.8	6.9	9.8
资金利税率	%	15.1	9.7	6.0	2.9	5.8	3.2	6.4	9.2
销售利税率	%	11.0	7.5	8.7	5.2	7.6	5.8	7.4	9.9
每百元固定资产原值实现的产值	元	236.7	159.4	128.0	99.3	106.1	98.1	140.4	141.4
每百元固定资产原值实现的利税	元	22.1	11.0	11.5	5.0	7.8	5.7	9.6	13.9
每百元固定资产原值实现的利润	元	10.8	4.5	6.4	2.4	3.8	3.0	6.7	11.4
每百元流动资产实现的产值	元	509.0	225.7	179.5	113.8	194.2	157.7	257.7	249.2
每百元流动资产实现的利税	元	47.5	15.6	16.1	5.7	14.3	9.1	17.7	24.4
每百元流动资产实现的利润	元	23.2	6.4	9.0	2.8	6.9	4.8	12.4	20.0
亏损企业亏损面	%	6.6	8.8	12.8	18.6	19.5	25.9	16.1	19.9
全部流动资产周转天数	天	84.3	175.3	197.4	340.1	207.4	241.7	157.5	147.8
增加值全员劳动生产率	元/人	2664	5437	5820	16344	21711	28414	17949	29447
平均每个职工提供利税	元/人	715	1058	1533	3135	5702	5241	4354	8800

4-26 主要年份大中型工业企业经济效益指标

Main Indicators on Economic Benefit of Large and Medium-sized Industrial Enterprises in Main Years

项　　目	单位	1985年	1990年	1995年	2000年	2004年	2005年	2008年	2009年
产品销售率	%	104.3	103.5	99.7	98.6	99.5	99.5	99.2	99.3
成本费用利润率	%	14.3	2.2	12.9	12.0	3.9	3.8	2.7	5.9
产值利税率	%	16.1	8.7	19.9	21.4	5.2	4.7	4.4	7.2
资金利税率	%	14.8	6.5	14.0	15.3	6.4	6.1	5.8	8.5
销售利税率	%	15.5	8.4	19.8	21.7	5.3	4.7	4.5	7.3
每百元固定资产原值实现的产值	元	106.0	87.1	112.8	98.4	227.2	229.8	226.7	186.3
每百元固定资产原值实现的利税	元	17.1	7.6	22.4	21.1	11.7	10.7	10.0	13.4
每百元固定资产原值实现的利润	元	11.5	1.7	13.1	13.0	8.8	8.4	5.8	10.2
每百元流动资产实现的产值	元	758.8	329.3	174.3	183.4	242.9	227.4	243.1	209.0
每百元流动资产实现的利税	元	122.4	28.6	34.6	39.2	12.5	10.6	10.7	15.0
每百元流动资产实现的利润	元	82.3	6.4	20.2	24.2	9.4	8.3	6.3	11.4
亏损企业亏损面	%		17.2	22.2	12.8	24.6	20.1	33.3	19.8
全部流动资产周转天数	天	46.1	107.1	209.5	210.2	156.7	160.8	152.7	176.3
增加值全员劳动生产率	元/人	6202	16492	81787	280810	65573	72657	63858	64534
平均每个职工提供利税	元/人	2601	7883	52997	165448	14187	11918	11793	19234

4-27 主要年份规模以上港澳台商投资工业企业经济效益指标

Main Indicators on Economic Benefit of Industrial Enterprises with Funds from Hong Kong,Macao and Taiwan above Designated Size in Main Years

项　　目	单位	1990年	1995年	2000年	2004年	2005年	2008年	2009年
产品销售率	%	94.2	99.6	100.8	99.9	99.4	99.2	99.4
成本费用利润率	%	-11.5	2.1	4.6	2.5	3.2	2.4	5.9
产值利税率	%	-9.3	4.9	6.6	3.3	4.0	3.8	6.9
资金利税率	%	-14.3	3.8	5.4	3.5	4.6	4.7	7.5
销售利税率	%	-9.9	4.9	6.5	3.3	4.1	3.9	7.0
每百元固定资产原值实现的产值	元	104.9	114.8	114.5	178.6	198.1	232.5	176.8
每百元固定资产原值实现的利税	元	-9.7	5.6	7.5	8.2	8.0	8.9	12.2
每百元固定资产原值实现的利润	元	-12.6	2.6	5.1	5.5	6.0	5.3	9.8
每百元流动资产实现的产值	元	154.3	165.2	182.2	209.0	192.3	205.6	179.7
每百元流动资产实现的利税	元	-14.3	8.1	12.0	9.5	7.8	7.8	12.4
每百元流动资产实现的利润	元	-18.5	3.7	8.1	6.5	5.8	4.7	9.9
亏损企业亏损面	%	25.0	46.4	36.1	39.9	35.1	34.5	30.3
全部流动资产周转天数	天	251.1	199.1	199.9	207.4	191.1	180.5	205.0
增加值全员劳动生产率	元/人	16962	17478	28933	42634	41933	49631	50040
平均每个职工提供利税	元/人	-8238	4232	7026	5612	6244	7754	13679

4-28 主要年份规模以上外商投资工业企业经济效益指标

Main Indicators on Economic Benefit of Foreign-funded Industrial Enterprises above Designated Size in Main Years

项　　目	单位	1990年	1995年	2000年	2004年	2005年	2008年	2009年
产品销售率	%	94.2	91.0	99.2	98.8	99.4	99.5	98.4
成本费用利润率	%	-11.5	-2.6	4.7	3.2	2.8	1.7	5.3
产值利税率	%	-9.3	-0.6	5.7	3.3	3.2	3.0	6.4
资金利税率	%	-14.3	-0.5	7.4	5.0	4.1	4.0	7.6
销售利税率	%	-9.9	-0.6	5.7	3.3	3.2	3.0	6.5
每百元固定资产原值实现的产值	元	104.9	155.5	231.2	307.9	285.2	273.8	228.6
每百元固定资产原值实现的利税	元	-9.7	-0.9	13.1	9.8	9.2	8.1	14.7
每百元固定资产原值实现的利润	元	-12.6	-1.9	10.3	8.0	7.6	4.5	11.2
每百元流动资产实现的产值	元	154.3	94.3	251.0	252.2	223.6	227.9	182.8
每百元流动资产实现的利税	元	-14.3	-1.5	14.2	8.0	7.2	6.7	11.7
每百元流动资产实现的利润	元	-18.5	5.5	11.1	6.5	5.9	3.8	8.9
亏损企业亏损面	%	25.0	38.2	31.3	29.5	34.5	40.9	29.3
全部流动资产周转天数	天	251.1	174.1	148.4	156.0	164.4	159.0	203.3
增加值全员劳动生产率	元/人	16962	3646	50318	70718	70722	63645	60130
平均每个职工提供利税	元/人	-8238	-700	13714	12328	8288	8049	16693

4-29 主要年份规模以上工业产品产量

Output of Main Industrial Products of Industrial Enterprises above Designated Size in Main Years

产品名称	单位	1985年	1990年	1995年	2000年	2005年	2008年	2009年
木材	立方米	23394	39095	37605	39100			
#原木	立方米	8492	27600	34288	33200			
米制品	吨			47040	28287			
食用植物油	吨	5571	4431	6824	5180	181869	817349	610729
糖	吨	51858	61016	7841	17869			
饼干	吨		45158	26252	21262	38859	119652	131296
罐头	吨	924	1352	5982			9639	10251
饮料酒	吨	4034	2441	1720			161537	281181
软饮料	吨		44061	71566	158599	861853	2851148	2906855
棉纱	吨		321	9902	3048	49383	38823	10368
布	万米		82	31045	28139	65669	18276	13795
针棉织品(折合用线量)	吨		1221	64691	5352	10229		
服装	万件	108	1835	112177	85635	70054	98263	117601
#衬衫	万件			2518	3624	2210	7530	5656
西服	万件			205	1761	555		228
布鞋	万双		101	7086	1948			
轻革	万平方米		5	1076	378	1391	264	374
皮鞋	万双	17	457	27184	23474	31942	30885	36297
锯材	立方米		8263	21619				
人造板	立方米		7100	40666		167088	30799	169446
家具	万件	815	8657	77501	151374	7974	7310	5745
机制纸及纸板	吨	30241	106535	339742	618000	4081761	7147417	8666746
玩具	万元			657936	469792	1354386	588037	677938
合成复合肥料	实物量吨			12079	33837	164724		195103
塑料树脂及共聚物	吨		1451	31802	65226	193515	156015	
磁带(折6.30毫米)	万米			1036199				
火柴	万件	19	22	9				
中成药	吨		216	6268	2354	1759	1596	1836
塑料制品	吨	3089	17335	624476	571900	1265865	1526374	2228984
#塑料薄膜	吨		1928	59128	71394	83954	120462	121923
水泥	万吨	41	140	283	435	305	153	138
石棉制品	吨							
砖	万块	159305	296962	252783		2903	5236	33
釉面砖	万平方米		113	320	95			
墙地砖	万平方米			582	1330			
日用陶瓷	万件	561	480	2414	1860	5745	2600	2005
耐火材料制品	吨	7600	9928	9144			96872	57124
成品钢材	吨	4678	1730	19690	14550	1087242	309053	30185
铝材	吨		881	3536	4080	61510	71161	64973
打火机	万个			22539				
工业锅炉	台	35	12	26	30			
工业锅炉	蒸发量吨	117	42	34	48			
输送机械	米		8622	3736		33200	11654	16368

注：2000年以前家具的计量单位为“万元”，输送机械的计量单位为“吨”。

4-29 续表

产 品 名 称	单 位	1985年	1990年	1995年	2000年	2005年	2008年	2009年
电动工具	万台		1.89	471	357	6	1564	
滚动轴承	万套	36	373	691	594	1333	4465	3331
矿山设备	吨		2898	320	1435			
中小农具	万件	22	24	12	12			
民用钢质船	艘	43	10	16	5			
民用钢质船	综合吨	1916	841	3620	2894			
交流电动机	万千瓦	23	19	43	87		164	155
变压器	千伏安				6730	816409	14850626	4127869
微电机	万台		4	280	141072	101304		91855
电磁线	吨		367	5904	3579			
电力电缆	公里		15091	20694	61996	78266	1075246	260739
原电池(折干电池)	万只	12354	7607	63237	69401	214507	317704	316334
吸尘器	万台	0.13	7.35	483	67	464	914	672
电风扇	万台		106	474	436	964	1286	2011
房间空调器	台	31		26480	39582	4941		1084
排油烟机	台			57551				
电淋浴器	个			7207				
电吹风	万个			137	281			
缝纫机	架			190		504		123
自行车	辆			95439	185608	885211	1392242	1271123
家用电冰箱	台			35336		19360		
灯 泡	万只			5778	8560	45164	32988	23536
灯 具	万件		87	42407	25135	14017	14991	20758
电话单机	万部		17	877	1074	3651	3639	2948
移动电话机	万部				619	639	913	1736
电子计算机	万部				27	180	2	16
彩色显像管	万只			210	394			
电子元件	万只	1422	20487	719259	1039500	46416689	70004541	68920968
电子计算机外部设备	万部			294	757			
半导体分立器件	万只			2484814	32256	2203170		2628605
电视机	万台	1.17	1.72	81	134	135	480	514
#彩色电视机	万台		1.04	81	134	135	480	514
录音机	万台			2706	2538			
收音机	万台			3163	1608	2364	3262	2900
电唱扩音音响播控设备	万部		6.43	60	91			
组合音响	万台			1136	1572	2446	2954	2667
照相机	万架		3	374	122	1355	529	284
手 表	万只		15	8514	954	1370	1131	1367
钟	万只			1986	984	1193	1780	2396
发电量	亿千瓦时	0.29	93	139	269	344	361	337
自来水供应量	万吨			21070	102083	94962	186663	169063
敷铜板	万平方米		63	181	620	1143	3225	2972

4-30 规模以上八大支柱产业总产值和增加值（2009年）

Gross Industrial Output Value and Value-added of Eight Pillar Industries above Designated Size (2009)

单位：万元

项目	总产值	增加值
通信设备、计算机及其他电子制造业	16712270	3392916
电气机械及仪器仪表制造业	8162234	1862828
纺织服装鞋帽制造业	4346762	1215836
造纸及纸制品业	3185069	715041
家具制造业	1539859	385739
玩具制造业	670842	226023
食品饮料制造业	1794660	471659
化工制品制造业	1479320	408025

4-31 规模以上电子信息制造业主要指标（2009年）

Main Economic Indicators of Electronic Information Industry above Designated Size (2009)

指标	单位	2009年
企业单位数	个	1580
#亏损企业单位数	个	396
工业总产值	亿元	2487.45
工业增加值	亿元	525.57
主营业务收入	亿元	2457.54
成本费用总额	亿元	2321.57
#销售成本及费用	亿元	2188.66
管理费用	亿元	127.96
财务费用	亿元	4.95
利税总额	亿元	133.98
#利润总额	亿元	112.30
应交增值税	亿元	19.54
亏损企业亏损总额	亿元	17.12
企业资产总额	亿元	1744.24
#流动资产平均余额	亿元	1162.10
#应收帐款余额	亿元	524.36
产成品存货	亿元	83.98
企业负债总额	亿元	1032.11
企业资产负债率	%	59.17
成本费用利润率	%	4.84

注：本表统计范围为规模以上电子通信类、电气机械及器材类、仪表仪器类制造业。

4-32 规模以上先进制造业企业主要经济指标（2009年）

Main Economic Indicators of Advanced Manufacturing Enterprises above Designated Size (2009)

项　　目	企业单位数(个)	#亏损企业	工业总产值(万元)	主营业务收入(万元)	利润总额(万元)	亏损企业亏损总额(万元)
总　计	**2333**	**551**	**26790829**	**26490446**	**1197375**	**186600**
按企业规模分						
大型企业	45	7	9486408	9406233	439950	32147
中型企业	489	96	10259358	10169357	492540	71935
小型企业	1799	448	7045062	6914856	264885	82517
按工业行业分(大类)						
1. 装备制造业	1999	479	24453019	24147680	1057038	174237
金属制品业	323	72	1462412	1443528	36611	17299
通用机械制造业	198	38	1193064	1154618	51269	6810
专用设备制造业	244	58	1153828	1150121	41626	14719
交通运输设备制造业	45	9	778990	782249	87818	840
电气机械及器材制造业	395	100	4030822	3983874	227123	27493
通信设备、计算机及其他电子设备制造业	755	190	15622014	15420294	591124	105870
仪器仪表及文化办公用品机械制造业	39	12	211890	212997	21467	1205
2. 钢铁冶炼及加工	22	7	230060	224137	11790	1284
炼铁						
炼钢						
钢材加工	21	6	222979	217447	11793	1281
铁合金冶炼	1	1	7081	6690	-3	3
3. 石油及化学	312	65	2107750	2118628	128547	11079
石油和天然气开采业						
石油加工、炼焦及核燃料加工业	7	1	108429	111663	3724	19
化学原料及化学制品制造业	182	28	1479320	1494650	106038	5204
橡胶制品业	123	36	520000	512315	18785	5856

4-32 续表

项目	利税总额(万元)	总资产贡献率(%)	资产负债率(%)	流动资产周转率(次/年)	成本费用利润率(%)	产品销售率(%)
总计	**1535548**	**7.5**	**59.0**	**1.9**	**4.8**	**98.8**
按企业规模分						
大型企业	537556	8.9	62.4	2.3	5.0	98.7
中型企业	604868	7.2	55.9	1.8	5.1	99.3
小型企业	393124	6.4	60.0	1.6	4.0	98.3
按工业行业分						
1. 装备制造业	1338584	7.3	59.0	1.9	4.6	98.7
金属制品业	59728	4.2	60.2	1.4	2.6	98.1
通用机械制造业	77907	7.3	54.1	1.6	5.0	97.5
专用设备制造业	71180	4.5	55.7	1.0	3.7	100.1
交通运输设备制造业	106754	13.5	56.6	1.5	12.5	100.3
电气机械及器材制造业	267485	9.6	58.0	1.9	6.1	98.8
通信设备、计算机及其他电子设备制造业	730515	7.0	60.6	2.2	4.0	98.6
仪器仪表及文化办公用品机械制造业	25015	10.5	46.7	1.3	10.9	100.0
2. 钢铁冶炼及加工	15104	7.1	70.4	1.1	5.5	97.8
炼铁						
炼钢						
钢材加工	15037	7.3	69.8	1.1	5.7	97.8
铁合金冶炼	67	1.2	95.6	1.3		100.0
3. 石油及化学	181861	9.3	58.2	1.5	6.4	100.9
石油和天然气开采业						
石油加工、炼焦及核燃料加工业	5624	8.6	75.1	1.8	3.5	104.4
化学原料及化学制品制造业	152323	11.0	55.9	1.5	7.6	101.3
橡胶制品业	23914	4.8	62.3	1.4	3.8	98.8

4-33 规模以上IT制造业企业主要经济指标（2009年）

Main Economic Indicators of IT Manufacturing Enterprises above Designated Size (2009)

项　　目	企　业单位数（个）	#亏损企业	工　业总产值（万元）	主营业务收入（万元）	利　润总　额（万元）	亏损企业亏损总额（万元）
总　　计	**1248**	**321**	**20321396**	**20063485**	**790673**	**152538**
按企业规模分						
大型企业	40	6	8565430	8501939	438402	29633
中型企业	369	76	8313127	8174999	255870	73124
小型企业	839	239	3442839	3386546	96402	49782
按工业行业分(小类)						
训练健身器材制造	8	1	30358	30655	389	529
玩具制造	129	50	670842	661427	-5744	22682
信息化学品制造	5	2	16764	17110	345	88
医疗诊断、监护及治疗设备制造	1		1075	1253	4	
微电机及其他电机制造	16	4	148610	148996	1806	1154
电线电缆制造	162	45	1654228	1632880	57790	5045
光纤、光缆制造						
电池制造	31	5	620661	620731	101738	2534
通信交换设备制造	1		2109	2109	198	
通信终端设备制造	9	3	314459	320157	1210	1590
移动通信及终端设备制造	9	3	1045872	1043429	76926	1267
电子计算机整机制造	15	3	846390	844413	28524	561
计算机网络设备制造	9	3	599932	595263	33877	361
电子计算机外部设备制造	130	31	2692891	2551737	108007	13652
电子真空器件制造	5	2	308017	313715	13957	144
集成电路制造	15	8	705962	699049	27925	9120
光电子器件及其他电子器件制造	55	13	788999	776785	13052	6230
电子元件及组件制造	320	78	4730944	4745445	133832	50749
印制电路板制造	38	6	630660	608762	40577	6485
家用影视设备制造	37	9	493939	483281	5326	13181
家用音响设备制造	68	18	596317	589594	11988	6231
其他电子设备制造	102	25	1313695	1290290	33823	7075
电子测量仪器制造	9	1	42088	41769	7806	490
照相机及器材制造	16	1	329315	326852	28656	400
复印和胶印设备制造	12	3	867965	861651	47919	1821
计算器及货币专用设备制造	6	1	433709	431987	3693	196
其他未列明的制造业	40	6	435597	424145	17050	952

4-33 续表

项目	利税总额(万元)	总资产贡献率(%)	资产负债率(%)	流动资产周转率(次/年)	成本费用利润率(%)	产品销售率(%)
总计	**958515**	**6.8**	**58.8**	**2.1**	**4.1**	**98.6**
按企业规模分						
大型企业	504826	9.6	59.3	2.5	5.5	98.7
中型企业	313876	5.3	57.8	2.0	3.3	98.7
小型企业	139813	4.7	59.8	1.7	2.9	98.5
按工业行业分(小类)						
训练健身器材制造	532	2.1	68.7	1.4	1.3	100.7
玩具制造	-2259		51.6	1.4	-0.9	99.1
信息化学品制造	584	2.5	12.3	0.9	2.0	101.6
医疗诊断、监护及治疗设备制造	4	0.3	61.3	1.1	0.3	113.6
微电机及其他电机制造	2405	1.8	39.0	1.8	1.2	100.2
电线电缆制造	71792	7.0	68.4	2.0	3.7	98.5
光纤、光缆制造						
电池制造	108139	19.8	48.6	1.8	19.7	99.8
通信交换设备制造	200	42.6		7.7	10.4	100.0
通信终端设备制造	7736	4.0	71.3	1.8	0.4	101.6
移动通信及终端设备制造	86207	15.9	84.5	2.1	8.2	99.9
电子计算机整机制造	50124	15.3	61.7	4.2	3.4	100.6
计算机网络设备制造	34826	17.6	48.3	4.9	6.1	99.3
电子计算机外部设备制造	117433	7.6	62.8	2.3	4.5	94.8
电子真空器件制造	14791	14.3	43.9	3.9	4.7	102.0
集成电路制造	30182	7.0	58.8	2.7	4.2	100.5
光电子器件及其他电子器件制造	15989	3.1	64.7	2.2	1.7	98.5
电子元件及组件制造	168074	4.2	56.7	2.0	2.9	99.3
印制电路板制造	48462	7.8	45.7	1.7	7.0	96.2
家用影视设备制造	11088	3.2	73.3	2.0	1.2	98.9
家用音响设备制造	18065	4.0	60.5	1.8	2.1	99.9
其他电子设备制造	59665	6.3	56.2	1.9	2.7	98.4
电子测量仪器制造	8797	9.8	41.5	0.6	21.7	99.1
照相机及器材制造	29942	13.0	36.8	2.0	9.6	99.7
复印和胶印设备制造	48940	13.5	56.9	3.5	6.0	99.0
计算器及货币专用设备制造	3716	1.5	63.8	2.5	0.9	99.6
其他未列明的制造业	23084	6.3	61.1	1.5	4.3	97.8

4-34　乡镇企业基本情况（2009年）

Basic Conditions of Township Enterprises (2009)

项　　目	企业个数（个）	从业人员（人）	增加值（万元）	总产值（万元）
总　计	**55603**	**2641374**	**10828890**	**44582170**
按登记注册类型分组				
内资企业	42829	758405	2843586	10641222
集体企业	2858	131120	414698	1722580
股份合作企业	296	5813	16127	50320
联营企业	165	3762	44377	164148
有限责任公司	3634	98468	465990	1382285
股份有限公司	182	26152	181136	1042204
私营企业	35694	493090	1721258	6279685
个体独资企业				
其他企业				
港澳台商投资企业	9564	1501663	5470171	21571038
外商投资企业	3210	381306	2515133	12369910
按国民经济行业分组				
农、林、牧、渔业	57	2705	7998	19414
采矿业				
制造业	23110	2243401	9463236	39467845
建筑业	508	43989	189012	867823
交通运输仓储业	643	19913	75625	267474
批发零售业	20621	141787	473070	1731879
住宿及餐饮业	5814	94660	273751	918392
社会服务业	2041	47233	79427	367824
其他	2720	41247	177596	531322

4-34 续表

项　　目	营业收入（万元）	利润总额（万元）	上交税金（万元）	劳动者报酬（万元）
总　计	**40987974**	**1833950**	**1294988**	**3673791**
按登记注册类型分组				
内资企业	10570258	564882	423683	1025214
集体企业	1830228	90689	77397	220728
股份合作企业	55304	2656	7988	9407
联营企业	109411	13078	4450	5613
有限责任公司	1598267	50665	56413	119737
股份有限公司	753719	27941	19490	31670
私营企业	6223329	379853	257945	638059
个体独资企业				
其他企业				
港澳台商投资企业	19773436	874199	621864	1941681
外商投资企业	10644280	394869	249441	706896
按国民经济行业分组				
农、林、牧、渔业	24007	2228	827	3930
采矿业				
制造业	36036216	1391179	1086626	3098569
建筑业	739157	33269	11316	68728
交通运输仓储业	260152	23149	10803	29618
批发零售业	1740523	124828	64606	197427
住宿及餐饮业	950757	81561	47064	129953
社会服务业	367653	103076	19727	59412
其他	639670	49788	23932	73452

4-35 主要年份乡镇工业企业基本情况

Basic Conditions of Township Industrial Enterprises in Main Years

年份	企业单位数(个)	企业从业人数(人)	总收入(万元)	实交国家税金(万元)	纯利润(万元)	工资总额(万元)	总产值(万元)
一、绝对数							
1979	1118	52979	11149				
1980	1116	59776	16236				
1981	1293	69914	19992				
1982	1671	89759	24390				
1983	1781	104786	28773				
1984	1980	125887	37760	1388	4451	10134	72271
1985	3690	173944	70231	2517	8896	20096	77822
1986	5411	211763	105010	2799	12302	26388	110396
1987	7292	268630	166918	3814	16757	40510	169777
1988	7528	316400	253976	5151	25934	63458	268299
1989	7925	343717	291242	5744	28880	82772	312699
1990	8154	381382	347525	7912	30640	106567	384538
1991	8524	442190	428214	10186	35687	127735	489484
1992	10084	529097	622449	16215	49451	172484	729234
1993	10635	643379	922745	25633	70153	214273	1060341
1994	13382	742763	1326140	31902	95236	272952	1517606
1995	12412	840551	1925010	52276	130913	387038	2007671
1996	13583	950809	2191644	46594	129626	407204	2455164
1997	14757	1020894	2664701	36466	163794	487569	2903016
1998	15419	1128837	3166852	61214	178872	582755	3596911
1999	15462	923344	4114722	78107	214017	661972	4595165
2000	15404	928042	5302464	120617	252074	765416	5744679
2001	16255	932243	7145592	171483	343468	963129	7490669
2002	16799	1068233	9406912	231243	468334	1174771	9406912
2003	20429	1192286	11819780	306617	605352	1423123	12480159
2004	22253	2182294	15465583	415727	700898	1773286	16459875
2005	23603	2295900	20696307	509277	611838	2134764	21507908
2006	25103	2498218	30268563	767488	901568	2638652	31713685
2007	24985	2520995	34352988	964854	1675846	2776492	36810285
2008	23811	2389946	37671014	1108627		3227469	40946457
2009	23199	2249840	36266055	1100861	1416051	3111271	39878042

4-35 续表

年　　份	企　业 单位数	企业从 业人数	总收入	实交国 家税金	纯利润	工　资 总　额	总产值
二、指数(以上年为100)							
1980	99.8	112.8	145.6				
1981	115.9	117.0	123.1				
1982	129.2	128.4	122.0				
1983	106.6	116.7	118.0				
1984	111.2	120.1	131.2				
1985	186.4	138.2	186.0	181.3	199.9	198.3	107.7
1986	146.6	121.7	149.5	111.2	138.3	131.3	141.9
1987	134.8	126.9	159.0	136.3	136.2	153.5	153.8
1988	103.2	117.8	152.2	135.1	154.8	156.7	158.0
1989	105.3	108.6	114.7	111.5	111.4	130.4	116.6
1990	102.9	111.0	119.3	137.7	106.1	128.8	123.0
1991	104.5	115.9	123.2	128.7	116.5	119.9	127.3
1992	118.3	119.7	145.4	159.2	138.6	135.0	149.0
1993	105.5	121.6	148.2	158.1	141.9	124.2	145.4
1994	125.8	115.5	143.7	124.5	135.8	127.4	143.1
1995	92.8	113.2	145.2	163.9	137.5	141.8	132.3
1996	109.4	113.1	113.9	89.1	99.0	105.2	122.3
1997	108.6	107.4	121.6	78.3	126.4	119.7	118.2
1998	104.5	110.6	118.8	167.9	109.2	119.5	123.9
1999	100.3	81.8	129.9	127.6	119.7	113.6	127.8
2000	99.6	100.5	128.9	154.4	117.8	115.6	125.0
2001	105.5	100.5	134.8	142.2	136.3	125.8	130.4
2002	103.4	114.6	131.7	134.9	136.4	122.0	125.6
2003	121.6	111.6	125.7	132.6	129.3	121.1	132.7
2004	108.9	183.0	130.8	135.6	115.8	124.6	131.9
2005	115.5	192.6	175.1	166.1	101.1	150.0	172.3
2006	112.8	114.5	195.7	184.6	128.6	148.8	192.7
2007	99.5	100.9	113.5	125.7	185.9	105.2	116.1
2008	95.3	94.8	109.7	114.9		116.2	111.2
2009	97.4	94.1	96.3	99.3	95.2	96.4	97.4

主要统计指标解释

工业 指从事自然资源的开采，对采掘品和农产品进行加工和再加工的物质生产部门。具体包括：对自然资源的开采，如采矿、晒盐、森林采伐等（但不包括禽兽捕猎和水产捕捞）；对农副产品的加工、再加工，如粮油加工、食品加工、轧花、缫丝、纺织、制革等；对采掘品的加工、再加工，如炼铁、炼钢、化工生产、石油加工、机器制造、木材加工等，以及电力、自来水、煤气的生产和供应等；对工业品的修理、翻新，如机器制造设备的修理、交通运输工具（包括小卧车）的修理等。

轻工业 是指主要提供生活消费品和制作手工工具的工业。按其所使用的原料不同，可分为两大类：以农产品为原料的轻工业，是指直接或以农产品为基本原料的轻工业，主要包括食品制造、饮料制造、烟草加工、纺织、缝纫、皮革和毛皮制作、造纸以及印刷等工业；以非农产品为原料的轻工业，是以工业品为原料的轻工业，主要包括文教体育用品、化学药品制造、合成纤维制造、日用化学制品、日用玻璃制品、日用金属制品、手工工具制造、医疗器械制造、文化和办公用机械制造等工业。

重工业 是指为国民经济各部门提供物质技术基础的主要生产资料的工业。按其生产性质和产品用途，可以分为下列三类：采掘（伐）工业，是对自然资源的开采，包括石油开采、煤炭开采、金属矿开采等工业；原材料工业，指向国民经济各部门提供基本材料、动力和燃料的工业，包括金属冶炼及加工、炼焦及焦炭化学、化学原料、水泥、人造板以及电力、石油和煤炭加工等工业；加工工业，是指对工业原材料进行再加工制造的工业。包括装备国民经济各部门的机械设备制造工业、金属结构、水泥制造等工业，以及为农业提供的生产资料如化肥、农药等工业。

工业总产值 是以货币表现的工业企业在报告期内生产的工业产品总量或提供工业性劳务活动的总价值量，它反映一定时间内工业生产的总规模和总水平。它包括：在本企业内不再进行加工，经检验、包装入库（规定不需包装的产品除外）的成品价值；工业性作业价值；自制半成品、在产品期末期初差额价值。工业总产值采用“工厂法”计算，即以工业企业作为一个整体，按工业生产活动的最终成果来计算，企业内部不允许重复计算，不能把企业内部各个车间（分厂）生产的成果相加。但在企业之间、行业之间、地区之间存在着重复计算。

资产总额 是指企业拥有或控制的能以货币计量的经济资源，包括各种财产、债权和其他权利。资产按其流动性（即资产的变现能力和支付能力）划分为：流动资产、长期投资、固定资产、无形资产、递延资产和其他资产，即为企业资产负债表中的资产总计项。

流动资产 是企业资产的重要组成部分，通常是指一年内或超过一年的一个营业周期内可以变现或耗用的资产。其特点是在企业的生产经营或者业务活动中不断地在生产循环中周转，不断改变其形态。其价值一次性消耗、转移或者实现。包括：货币资金、短期投资、应收票据、应收帐款、预付帐款、其他应收款、存货、待摊费用、待处理流动资产损失、一年内到期的本期债券投资及其他流动资产。

流动资产平均余额 指企业在报告期内全部流动资产的平均余额。其计算公式为：

流动资产月平均余额=月初、月末流动资产余额之和÷2

流动资产年平均余额=1 至 12 月各月月初、月末流动资产余额之和÷24

固定资产原价 是指企业在建造、购置、安装、改建、扩建、技术改造某项固定资产时实际支出的全部货币总额。它一般包括买价、包装费、运杂费和安装费等。

固定资产合计 包括固定资产净值、固定资产清理、在建工程、待处理固定资产净损失所占用的资金合计。

固定资产净值 是指固定资产原价减去历年已提折旧额后的净额。

固定资产净值平均余额 指固定资产净值报告期内余额的平均数。

计数公式为：固定资产净值=固定资产原价－累计折旧

固定资产净值月平均余额=月初、月末固定资产净值之和÷2

固定资产净值年平均余额=1 至 12 月各月月初、月末固定资净值之和÷24

负债 是指企业所承担的能以货币计量，将以资产或劳务偿付的债务。其偿还形式可以用货币，也可以用资产或提供劳务的方式进行。包括流动负债、长期负债和递延税款贷项等，即为企业资产负债表的负债合计项。

实收资本 是指企业实际收到的投资人投入的资本。包括有国家资本、集体资本、法人资本、个人资本、外商资本、港澳台资本等。

主营业务收入 是企业在销售商品、提供劳务及让渡资产使用权等日常活动中所产生的收入。

主营业务税金及附加 是指企业日常活动应负担的税金及附加，包括营业税、消费税、城市维护建设税、资源税、土地增值税和教育费附加等。

主营业务成本 是指企业因销售商品、提供劳务或让渡资产使用权等日常活动而发生的实际成本。

营业利润 是企业生产经营活动所取得的利润，包括主营业务利润和其他业务利润。

利润总额 是指企业在一定时期内生产经营活动的最终的财务成果，是企业的收入减去有关成本与费用后的差额，收入大于相关的成本费用，企业就盈利，反之则亏损。包括营业利润、补贴收入、投资净收益、营业外收支净额、以前年度损失调整。

应交增值税 是指企业在报告期内应交纳的增值税额。

从业人员平均人数 从业人员指企业工作并取得劳动报酬的全部人员数。包括在岗职工、再就业的离退休人员、民办教师及在企业工作的外方人员和港澳台方人员、兼职人员、借用的外单位人员和第二职业者。不包括离开本单位但仍保留劳动关系的职工。而从业人员平均人数指报告期内每天平均拥有的从业人员人数。其计算公式为：

月平均人数=报告月内每天实有人数之和÷报告月日历日数

季平均人数=季内各月平均人数之和÷3

年平均人数=全年各月平均人数之和÷12

资产利税率 是在一定时期内已实现的利润、税金总额与同期的资产总额之比。计算公式：

$$资产利税率（\%）= \frac{报告期累计实现利税总额}{资产总额} \times 100\%$$

资产利税率反映每单位（通常是每万元）资产所提供的利税金额。它是考察和评价部门或企业资金运用的经济效益，分析资金投入效果的主要分析指标。

产值利税率 是报告期已实现的利润、税金总额（包括利润总额、产品销售税金及附加和应交增值税）占同期全部工业总产值的百分比，计算公式为：

$$产值利税率（\%）= \frac{利税总额}{工业总产值（现价）} \times 100\%$$

工业经济效益综合指数 是现行综合评价工业经济效益总体水平及工业经济运行质量的指数，它是以若干项代表性经济效益指标，分别除以各项指标的标准值，再乘以各自的权数，加总后除以总权数求得。其计算公式为：

$$工业经济效益综合指数= \Sigma（\frac{某项经济效益指标报告期数值}{该项指标标准值} \times 权数）\div 总权数$$

上式总权数为100。

工业产品销售率 是反映工业产品已实现销售的程度，是分析工业产销衔接情况、研究工业产品满足社会需求的指标。计算公式是：

$$产品销售率（\%）= \frac{现价工业销售产值}{现价工业总产值} \times 100\%$$

总资产贡献率 是指企业一定时期内全部资产获利能力，是企业经营业绩和管理水平的集中体现，是评价和考核企业盈利能力的核心指标。计算公式为：

$$总资产贡献率（\%）= \frac{利润总额+税金总额+利息支出}{平均资产总额} \times 100\%$$

注：税金总额为产品销售税金及附加与应交增值税之和，平均资产总额为期初、期末资产总计的算术平均值。

资本保值增值率 是反映企业净资产变动状况的一个重要指标，是企业发展能力的集中体现。是指期末所有者权益总额与期初所有者权益总额的比率。计算公式为：

$$资本保值增值率（\%）= \frac{期末所有者权益}{期初所有者权益} \times 100\%$$

所有者权益等于资产总计减负债总计。

资产负债率 是指反映企业经营风险的大小，反映企业利用债权人提供的资金从事经营活动的能力。计算公式为：

$$资产负债率（\%）= \frac{负债总额}{资产总额} \times 100\%$$

资产及负债均为报告期期末数。

流动资产周转率 是指一定时期内流动资产完成的周转次数，反映投入工业企业流动资金的周转速度，一般以一年内周转多少次表示。计算公式为：

$$流动资产周转率（次）= \frac{产品销售收入}{流动资产平均余额}$$

成本费用利润率 是指工业企业投入的生产成本及费用的经济效益，同时也反映企业降低成本所取得的经济效益。计算公式为：

$$成本费用利润率（\%）= \frac{利润总额}{成本费用总额} \times 100\%$$

注：成本费用总额为产品销售成本、销售费用、管理费用、财务费用之和。

全员劳动生产率 是指反映企业的生产效率和劳动投入的经济效益。一般用平均每人一年创造的工业增加值表示。计算公式为：

$$全员劳动生产率（元/人）= \frac{工业增加值}{全部职工平均人数}$$

五、固定资产投资与建筑业

Investment in Fixed Assets and Construction

5-1 主要年份固定资产投资与建筑业主要指标

Main Indicators of Investment in Fixed Assets and Construction in Main Years

项 目	单 位	1985年	1990年	1995年	2000年	2005年	2008年	2009年
全社会固定资产投资总额	万元	70600	75052	631355	1028914	5972443	9443426	10940753
#国有单位	万元	16914	50658	106935	197658	686333	667085	1661417
#基本建设	万元	14057	25017	81038	109075	573698	532747	
更新改造	万元	2857	19051	25233	82919	87866	79893	
私营个体经济	万元					1027969	2076386	2378277
港澳台投资经济	万元			10281	130501	1246450	1469186	1114631
外商投资经济	万元			230409	92699	507322	1241212	923601
国有单位新增固定资产	万元	5582	27725	67565	156822	24524	86726	234697
国有单位固定资产交付使用率	%	33.00	54.73	63.18	79.34	3.57	13	14.13
国有单位房屋竣工面积	万平方米	13.17	25.39	35.02	8.87		0.17	0.03
国有单位房屋面积竣工率	%	47.43	47.41	57.38	17.73		5.18	0.06
国有单位计划总投资	万元		317542	179925	489687	2337482	2082620	5219264
国有单位固定资产投资建设周期	年		6.27	1.68	2.96	6.41	3.12	3.14
固定资产投资资金来源	万元	17000	50100	480875	1047861	6717711	12408566	14489422
#国家预算内资金合计	万元	1100	3600	10858	10490	536	396516	117904
国内贷款	万元	2800	2900	27439	122561	651723	1311457	1014574
利用外资	万元		17000	194486	207444	940432	1569279	1189793
自筹资金	万元	13100	25400	163090	587176	3901138	5392425	8697747
房地产开发投资	万元			85163	112498	1444277	2714197	2776623
房地产开发当年房屋施工面积	万平方米			160.74	315.45	1160.17	1998.00	2333.90
房地产开发当年房屋竣工面积	万平方米			76.78	103.20	132.88	477.96	310.22
#住宅	万平方米			68.36	77.97	115.23	395.15	268.08
房地产开发实际销售商品房屋面积	万平方米			25.42	63.21	321.85	511.59	600.27
#住宅	万平方米			20.49	51.02	297.19	467.98	578.82
建筑企业(单位)个数	个		8	8	99	361	379	404
建筑企业平均人数	人		6803	22200	64300	79965	64651	55684
建筑企业总产值	万元		12678	94941	404493	843540	1088107	994007
劳动生产率(按总产值计算)	元/人		18636	42766	60849	108136	174827	184034
建筑业房屋施工面积	万平方米		66.30	278.72	1218.00	1234.98	964.27	730.61
建筑业房屋竣工面积	万平方米		29.95	94.99	53.76	707.77	565.91	351.08

注：1. 本表固定资产投资资金来源1990年前是国有单位数，1995年以后是城镇集体以上单位数；1995年固定资产投资含沙角C厂完成的126374万元，2005年起是全社会固定资产投资单位数。
2. 2005年起农村集体投资划分到基本建设，更新改造，其他投资三部分中，下同。

5-2 历年全社会固定资产投资

Total Investment in Fixed Assets over Years

单位：万元

年份	全社会投资总额	基本建设	更新改造	其他投资	#城镇集体	房地产开发	农村集体	城乡个人
1978	2319	1681	148	193	193		297	
1979	1641	1222	85	234	234		100	
1980	2395	1635	237	415	415		108	
1981	3756	1931	122	669	669		772	262
1982	18102	6908	1002	837	837		1241	8114
1983	18370	3343	1290	1135	1135		1796	10806
1984	30050	7691	1832	1413	1294		5039	14075
1985	70600	14057	2857	10479	10479		17553	25654
1986	115173	40217	3079	7317	7140		35125	29435
1987	141856	20268	5195	7693	7445		69939	38761
1988	165459	23952	5735	8377	7812		82177	45218
1989	50135	27063	5842	12000	12000		1470	3760
1990	75052	25107	19051	25116	18616		1602	4176
1991	137464	77664	7480	40632	28210		2028	9660
1992	188824	98445	7846	57117	30327		10607	14809
1993	327630	160578	20318	46163	35893	52110	24308	24153
1994	1407621	1125660	24045	67400	90219	78392	74316	37808
1995	631355	284300	29228	70762	106821	85163	119420	42482
1996	676185	303061	36141	70990	8091	86258	132409	47326
1997	658941	200428	42723	81348	40710	86662	180207	67573
1998	769953	204575	81640	98142	48897	95451	207068	83077
1999	883201	232876	91716	106743	72893	104411	243263	104192
2000	1028914	280660	112295	120016	76110	112498	283401	120044
2001	1254945	340214	137523	135351	86716	148544	342531	150782
2002	1915741	614846	234872	155544	45946	268350	425521	216608
2003	3193889	976516	445778	467674	129556	551184	500858	251879
2004	4548691	1897424	502923	715717	241303	1144195		288432
2005	5972443	2621391	620438	1027293		1444277		259044
2006	7054511	2911882	720774	1779457		1642398		224483
2007	8412074	3442889	675620	2199378		2094187		333229
2008	9443426	3780194	815274	2133761		2714197		258470
2009	10940753					2776623		

注：1. 1994、1995、1996年全社会投资总额分别含沙角C厂投资额956758万元、126374万元、102760万元。
2. 2005年起取消了城镇集体投资指标。
3. 从2006年起，城乡个人指其他投资中的私人建房投资部分。

5-3 按登记类型和行业分的固定资产投资(2009年)

Total Investment in Fixed Assets by Registration Status and Sector (2009)

项　　目	全市合计	#城镇	#房地产	农村
合　计	**10940753**	**6389747**	**2776623**	**4551006**
按登记注册类型分				
内资	8902521	5782159	2658087	3120362
国有	1661417	1605825		55592
集体	1956472	909188	302939	1047284
股份合作	19747	11394		8353
国有联营				
集体联营	3036			3036
国有与集体联营				
其他联营	8364	8039	8039	325
国有独资公司	99433	99433	58117	
其他有限责任公司	2343158	1496701	1204611	846457
股份有限公司	184850	28100	1550	156750
私营	1876694	1385046	1082831	491648
其他	247767	96707		151060
个体经营：个体户	488244	141726		346518
个人合伙	13339			13339
港澳台商投资	1114631	256776	34620	857855
合资经营	151752	32784		118968
合作经营	65793	37191	154	28602
独资	880029	175856	34466	704173
股份有限	17057	10945		6112
外商投资	923601	350812	83916	572789
合资经营	128730	63143	14353	65587
合作经营	33983	23157	13494	10826
独资	719547	254881	56069	464666
股份有限	41341	9631		31710
按国民经济行业分				
第一产业	6135	1203		4932
第二产业	3965921	1268586		2697335
制造业	3368702	836703		2531999
电力、燃气及水的生产和供应业	595645	431883		163762
建筑业	1574			1574
第三产业	6968697	5119958	2776623	1848739
交通运输、仓储和邮政业	1262742	1015701		247041
信息传输、计算机服务和软件业	207335	205597		1738
批发和零售业	163146	39029		124117
住宿与饮食业	225418	68357		157061
金融业	11242	1969		9273
房地产业	3531113	3043611	2776623	487502
租赁和商务服务业	150643	22367		128276
科学 研究、技术服务和地质勘察业	49643	8810		40833
水利、环境和公共设施管理业	775855	387083		388772
居民服务和其他服务业	19928	11827		8101
教育	140411	85179		55232
卫生、社会保障和社会福利业	212290	132877		79413
文化、体育和娱乐业	74715	54645		20070
公共管理和社会组织	144216	42906		101310

5-4 固定资产投资主要指标（2009年）

Main Indicators of Total Investment in Fixed Assets (2009)

单位：万元

项　　目	计划总投资	本年完成投资	建筑工程	安装工程	设备工器具购置	其他费用
合　计	**16761074**	**8164130**	**4607033**	**414248**	**2476176**	**666673**
按登记注册类型分						
内资	13913646	6244434	4209791	380885	1040853	612905
国有	5219264	1661417	1343534	66761	77905	173217
集体	3755665	1653533	1331019	88239	74062	160213
股份合作	33759	19747	17778	8		1961
国有联营						
集体联营	3388	3036	2174	101	506	255
国有与集体联营						
其他联营	1500	325			325	
国有独资公司	70000	41316	28463	12853		
其他有限责任公司	1964319	1138547	449502	125795	440984	122266
股份有限公司	660598	183300	138034	13477	28466	3323
私营个体	1733982	1295446	739177	49095	368813	138361
其他	471171	247767	160110	24556	49792	13309
港澳台商投资	1719400	1080011	231438	24122	782883	41568
外商投资	1128028	839685	165804	9241	652440	12200
按国民经济行业分						
第一产业	20167	6135	2057	1275	2503	300
第二产业	6829697	3965921	1453209	133485	2191017	188210
制造业	5189922	3368702	1067229	79563	2066406	155504
电力、燃气及水的生产和供应业	1638160	595645	385980	53922	123037	32706
建筑业	1615	1574			1574	
第三产业	9911210	4192074	3151767	279488	282656	478163
交通运输、仓储和邮政业	3519722	1262742	1076292	8347	57552	120551
信息传输、计算机服务和软件业	223382	207335	11406	94631	101028	270
批发和零售业	346844	163146	96411	9066	26694	30975
住宿与饮食业	463354	225418	97111	54833	14428	59046
金融业	38819	11242	9552	128	506	1056
房地产业	1523040	754490	600174	33534	14253	106529
租赁和商务服务业	264437	150643	105984	9857	13665	21137
科学 研究、技术服务和地质勘察业	293371	49643	28565	1000	1028	19050
水利、环境和公共设施管理业	1717162	775855	670527	33384	16240	55704
居民服务和其他服务业	55175	19928	3505	358	1335	14730
教育	368971	140411	121318	2554	2504	14035
卫生、社会保障和社会福利业	483857	212290	158016	19918	26115	8241
文化、体育和娱乐业	346012	74715	49846	4663	2019	18187
公共管理和社会组织	267064	144216	123060	7215	5289	8652
按建设性质分						
新建	10514101	4428950	3325238	195461	399952	508299
扩建	1962974	812130	631472	116512	38914	25232
改建	1626700	839722	564364	99624	125455	50279
单纯建造生活设施	50059	31579	26795	2171	1367	1246
迁建	292617	115871	31270	480	2558	81563
恢复	146213	27948	27894			54
单纯购置	2168410	1907930			1907930	

注：本表不含房地产开发投资。

5-4 续表 1

（2009年）

单位：万元

项　　目	本年新增固定资　产	本年施工房屋面积（万平方米）	本年竣工房屋面积（万平方米）	本年资金来源合　计	#上年末结余资金
合　　计	**4213954**	**1414.89**	**641.26**	**10208401**	**1189665**
按登记注册类型分					
内资	2971595	1196.75	561.43	7870897	953763
国有	234697	52.28	0.03	1810052	329816
集体	954868	347.84	96.48	2106168	114506
股份合作	14123	2.33	1.34	26306	17
国有联营					
集体联营	2412	1.01	0.66	8127	650
国有与集体联营					
其他联营	325			350	
国有独资公司	41315			41315	
其他有限责任公司	660693	199.60	88.92	1529237	95373
股份有限公司	70148	51.55	20.04	619062	301491
私营个体	892734	504.15	332.32	1375044	21485
其他	100280	38.00	21.64	355236	90425
港澳台商投资	650924	157.33	46.80	1314347	131755
外商投资	591435	60.81	33.03	1023157	104147
按国民经济行业分					
第一产业	3389	0.08		10835	1000
第二产业	2505506	646.83	302.85	5152701	664551
制造业	2197484	640.29	301.65	4442316	614789
电力、燃气及水的生产和供应业	306763	6.54	1.21	708776	49682
建筑业	1259			1609	80
第三产业	1705059	767.98	338.41	5044865	524114
交通运输、仓储和邮政业	137667	13.85	2.84	1506897	351310
信息传输、计算机服务和软件业	19585	0.40		209036	
批发和零售业	88685	42.50	25.51	200275	6492
住宿与饮食业	142568	42.68	20.83	316687	5813
金融业	2241	1.33	0.32	24063	1500
房地产业	538085	440.91	233.37	965402	86872
租赁和商务服务业	98793	40.84	20.37	195004	20391
科学 研究、技术服务和地质勘察业	3916	0.02		67627	2500
水利、环境和公共设施管理业	457601	33.53	7.94	880113	27796
居民服务和其他服务业	2612	6.76		35812	4210
教育	75471	31.54	10.64	150508	694
卫生、社会保障和社会福利业	55293	76.06	6.34	267820	10807
文化、体育和娱乐业	19226	2.71	0.83	67023	1392
公共管理和社会组织	63316	34.86	9.42	158598	4337
按建设性质分					
新建	1858321	1248.07	571.30	5340264	599232
扩建	309861	88.53	34.36	1492789	419875
改建	584095	69.73	33.08	1089855	81891
单纯建造生活设施	17605	1.65	1.55	32678	1352
迁建	75042	6.31	0.97	129977	3275
恢复	938	0.60		45268	1936
单纯购置	1368092			2077570	82104

5-4 续表 2

(2009年)

单位：万元

项目	本年资金来源					
	#本年资金来源小计	国家预算内资金	国内贷款	利用外资	自筹资金	其他资金来源
合　计	**9018736**	**117904**	**470405**	**1084396**	**6856994**	**489037**
按登记注册类型分						
内资	6917134	117904	445960	32419	5980835	340016
国有	1480236	9823	150902		1281223	38288
集体	1991662	64966	76350	14025	1664662	171659
股份合作	26289		7500		18789	
国有联营						
集体联营	7477		1500		5881	96
国有与集体联营						
其他联营	350					350
国有独资公司	41315	41315				
其他有限责任公司	1433864	1000	125084	4437	1263020	40323
股份有限公司	317571	800	3713	6138	306345	575
私营个体	1353559		80311	6963	1193728	72557
其他	264811		600	856	247187	16168
港澳台商投资	1182592		8949	559602	536619	77422
外商投资	919010		15496	492375	339540	71599
按国民经济行业分						
第一产业	9835		2563		6069	1203
第二产业	4488150	9180	149318	1059012	3088429	182211
制造业	3827527	9180	91897	1056331	2527001	143118
电力、燃气及水的生产和供应业	659094		57421	2681	559899	39093
建筑业	1529				1529	
第三产业	4520751	108724	318524	25384	3762496	305623
交通运输、仓储和邮政业	1155587	19753	187736	11460	844706	91932
信息传输、计算机服务和软件业	209036				208936	100
批发和零售业	193783	503	12326	6561	165064	9329
住宿与饮食业	310874		53000	5846	250851	1177
金融业	22563	118		680	21765	
房地产业	878530	514	12920		800649	64447
租赁和商务服务业	174613		25900	837	123745	24131
科学 研究、技术服务和地质勘察业	65127	6049			59078	
水利、环境和公共设施管理业	852317	65468	15492		685985	85372
居民服务和其他服务业	31602				31602	
教育	149814	9281			134095	6438
卫生、社会保障和社会福利业	257013	2961	9000		230311	14741
文化、体育和娱乐业	65631	3012	150		55947	6522
公共管理和社会组织	154261	1065	2000		149762	1434
按建设性质分						
新建	4741032	41148	407203	128646	3897422	266613
扩建	1072914	34768	27596	17239	951435	41876
改建	1007964	41928	15003	75948	790583	84502
单纯建造生活设施	31326			1422	19454	10450
迁建	126702				121767	4935
恢复	43332				43332	
单纯购置	1995466	60	20603	861141	1033001	80661

5-5　固定资产投资分类情况(2009年)

Statistics on Total Investment in Fixed Assets by Type (2009)

单位：万元

项　　目	计　划总投资	#本年新开工项目	自开始建设累计完成投资	本年完成投资	#住宅	本年新增固定资　产
固定资产投资总额	**16761074**	**4099534**	**11989024**	**8164130**	**324377**	**4213954**
#基础设施	6833308	1462260	4439425	2747581	240	915564
#基础产业	7095055	2027957	4648537	2855176	240	953500
#城市建设	2352025	580037	1520155	882279		541866
#原材料	418889	135342	363938	246158	1300	138182
#能源	705852	396841	543684	337711		169629
#工业合计	6828082	1484299	5511156	3964347	32076	2504247
#工业九大产业	3560401	563812	2949830	2087845	9894	1279580
#电子信息业	1133228	172879	920091	663149	2676	409799
电气机械及专用设备	647091	106078	532135	483252	5120	338257
石油及化学	105354	37497	96091	85051	598	59789
纺织及服装	333881	32693	310997	263596	200	177846
食品饮料	289042	37351	211836	184283		79435
建筑材料	274334	82132	226623	130973	1300	57671
森工造纸	694495	91384	578726	227628		116794
医药	27345		26626	8061		6847
汽车	55631	3798	46705	41852		33142

注:本表不含房地产开发投资。

5-6　房地产开发主要指标

Main Indicators of Real Estate Development

项　　目	单位	2002年	2003年	2005年	2006年	2007年	2008年	2009年
一、土地开发及购置								
本年土地开发面积	万平方米	111.8	115.6	20.1	63.5	44.3	249.1	66.9
本年土地购置面积	万平方米	93.4	176.5	44.9	73.0	57.7	69.5	92.0
二、本年完成投资额	**万元**	**268350**	**551184**	**1444277**	**1642398**	**2094187**	**2714197**	**2776623**
#住宅	万元	197633	422347	1197154	1475181	1860580	2213498	2513852
三、资金来源	**万元**	**495093**	**676767**	**1632570**	**2120240**	**2900238**	**4049833**	**4281021**
#国内贷款	万元	72221	139527	114755	292488	446710	1079194	544169
利用外资	万元	30213	55616	2075	10140		27053	105397
自筹资金	万元	166636	185201	867824	677095	905912	1067823	1840753
四、房屋建筑面积								
施工面积	万平方米	401.9	689.5	1160.2	1437.6	1521.6	1998.0	2333.9
#住宅	万平方米	340.3	530.0	889.9	1229.4	1371.0	1680.8	2050.1
竣工面积	万平方米	127.7	257.3	132.9	166.3	137.3	478.0	310.2
#住宅	万平方米	117.4	222.0	115.2	114.1	111.9	395.2	268.1
五、商品房屋销售额	**万元**	**282948**	**480189**	**1193991**	**1612449**	**2949939**	**2885975**	**3530040**
#住宅	万元	232269	409037	1091095	1460425	2736729	2461024	3342466
六、商品房屋销售面积	**万平方米**	**95.0**	**165.0**	**321.9**	**382.0**	**573.0**	**511.6**	**600.3**
#住宅	万平方米	82.9	141.9	297.2	353.0	541.1	468.0	578.8

5-7 房地产开发企业主要经济指标（2009年）

Main Economic Indicators of Real Estate Enterprises (2009)

单位：万元

项　目	资产总计	负债总计	主营业务收入	主营业务税金及附加	利润总额	全部从业人员年平均人数（人）
合　计	**133311298**	**110568408**	**33205836**	**2845003**	**2894123**	**10561**
按登记注册类型分						
#内源型经济	119000225	100034549	29849943	2598322	2369581	9211
#民营经济	88985689	73969838	22265153	1806743	1538000	7368
#国有经济	3233561	2780731	1154964	216697	281514	51
集体经济	10128949	8622348	2495158	234412	132681	818
私营个体经济	55968406	48146989	14647466	1186236	1220039	4551
外源型经济	14311073	10533859	3355893	246681	524542	1350
#港澳台商投资	8374591	5971736	2631180	197006	499807	470
外商投资	5936482	4562123	724713	49675	24735	880
控股情况						
国有控股	5945503	5150071	1787309	277928	388333	144
集体控股	13463841	11815778	2552338	238104	106886	897
私人控股	88985689	73969838	22265153	1806743	1538000	7368
港澳台控股	8781858	6084064	2758016	205679	515982	486
外商控股	6657798	5299863	724713	49675	9115	898
资质等级						
一级	9401719	8269171	2516190	196837	512139	559
二级	15613091	12436978	4145844	351531	491627	858
三级	34140082	27436214	8616290	732582	432182	2932
四级	49653616	41859342	13718488	1222296	1256423	4222
暂定	13367474	11571712	2282360	186658	85565	817
其他	11135316	8994991	1926664	155099	116187	1173

5-8 房地产开发投资情况（2009年）

Investment in Real Estate Development (2009)

项　　目	房地产开发投资（万元）	土地开发投资	住宅
合　　计	**2776623**	**47720**	**2513852**
内资	2658087	47600	2409729
国有			
集体	302939	2048	274041
股份合作			
其他联营	8039		8039
国有独资公司	58117	100	53511
其他有限责任公司	1204611	35934	1126273
股份有限公司	1550	200	1450
私营独资	68160		68140
私营合伙			
私营有限责任公司	986068	9318	851791
私营股份有限公司	28603		26484
其他(内资企业)			
港澳台商投资	34620		34620
外商投资	83916	120	69503

5-9 房地产开发企业、房屋建筑面积及价值（2009年）

Floor Space and Value of Buildings in Real Estate Development (2009)

项　　目	房屋建筑面积（平方米）		竣工房屋价值（万元）
	施工面积	竣工面积	
合　　计	**23339013**	**3102151**	**1056370**
内资	21979032	3024401	1020881
国有			
集体	2737018	407238	76188
股份合作			
其他联营	166640		
国有独资公司	400021		
其他有限责任公司	7851303	1161939	382544
股份有限公司	42504	42504	15531
私营独资	133017		
私营合伙			
私营有限责任公司	10584169	1412720	546618
私营股份有限公司	64360		
其他(内资企业)			
港澳台商投资	457058	77750	35489
外商投资	902923		

5-10 商品房屋销售情况（2009年）

Sale of Commercialized Buildings (2009)

项　目	商品房屋销售建筑面积（平方米）	#住宅	商品房屋销售额（万元）	#住宅
合　计	**6002694**	**5788245**	**3530040**	**3342466**
内资	5557683	5364277	3280181	3105120
国有				
集体	655517	634928	341446	317141
股份合作				
其他联营	24496	24496	22028	22028
国有独资公司	153394	153394	107161	107161
其他有限责任公司	2280403	2241711	1412358	1373029
股份有限公司				
私营独资	16887	16887	8339	8339
私营合伙				
私营有限责任公司	2389635	2255510	1365791	1254364
私营股份有限公司	37351	37351	23058	23058
其他(内资企业)				
港澳台商投资	168093	168093	90044	90044
外商投资	276918	255875	159815	147302

5-11 建筑施工企业主要指标（2008-2009年）

Main Indicators of Construction Enterprises (2008-2009)

指　标	单　位	2008年 合　计	2008年 #国有单位	2009年 合　计	2009年 #国有单位
企业单位数	个	379	1	404	1
年平均人数	个	64651	1875	55684	1842
自有固定资产原价	万元	224706	17058	308231	17893
自有固定资产净值	万元	136460	9627	209066	9810
自有施工机械设备年末总台数	台	21172	487	16640	423
自有施工机械设备年末净值	万元	59223	1580	76006	1529
自有施工机械设备年末总功率	万千瓦	21	1	14	1
建筑业总产值	万元	1088107	106125	994007	141397
建筑工程产值	万元	907724	105980	806862	141139
安装工程产值	万元	144669	145	150690	258
其它产值	万元	35714		36455	
建筑业竣工产值	万元	781539	66332	674761	60225
建筑业增加值	万元	823825		815489	
房屋建筑施工面积	万平方米	964	5	731	6
房屋建筑竣工面积	万平方米	566	5	351	
利润总额	万元	34038	514	61495	721
利税总额	万元	74752	4395	99896	6033
劳动生产率(按总产值计算)	元/人	174827	566000	184034	767628
劳动生产率(按增加值计算)	元/人	132365		150983	
技术装备率	元/人	9160	8427	13650	8301
动力装备率	千瓦/人	3.3	5.3	2.5	5.4
房屋建筑面积竣工率	%	58.7	100.0	48	
产值利润率	%	3	0	6	1
产值利税率	%	7	4	10	4

主要统计指标解释

固定资产投资额　是以货币表现的建造和购置固定资产活动的工作量，它是反映固定资产投资规模、速度、比例关系和使用方向的综合性指标。全社会固定资产投资包括国有经济单位投资、城乡集体经济单位投资、其他各项经济类型的单位投资和城乡居民个人投资。按照我国现行计划管理体制，全社会固定资产投资总额分为基本建设投资、更新建设投资、房地产开发投资、其他固定资产投资、私人建房投资和个人投资。

①**基本建设**指列入中央和各级地方本年基本建设计划的建设项目，以及虽未列入本年基本建设计划，但使用以前年度基建计划内结转投资在本年继续施工的建设项目；本年基本建设计划内投资与更新改造计划内投资结合安排的新建项目和新增生产能力达到大中型项目标准的扩建项目，以及为改变生产力布局而进行的全厂性迁建项目；国有单位既未列入基建计划，也未列入更新改造计划的新建、扩建、恢复项目和为改变生产力布局而进行的全厂性迁建项目，以及行政、事业单位增建业务用房和行政单位增建生活福利设施的项目。

②**更新改造**指列入中央和各级地方本年更新改造计划的建设项目以及虽未列入本年更新改造计划，但使用以前年度更新改造计划内结转投资在本年继续施工的项目；本年更新改造计划内投资与基本建设计划内投资结合安排的对企、事业单位原有设施进行技术改造或更新的项目和增建主要生产车间、分厂等其新增生产能力未达到大中型项目标准的项目，以及由于城市环境保护和安全生产的需要而进行的迁建工程；国有企、事业单位既未列入基建计划，也未列入更新改造计划，属于改建或更新改造性质的项目。

③指除上述基本建设和更新改造投资外的**其他投资**，主要有：用油田维护费和石油开发基金进行的油田维护和开发工程；煤炭、铁矿、森工等采掘采伐业用维简费进行的开拓延伸工程；交通部门用公路养路费对原有公路、桥梁进行改建的工程；商业部门用简易建筑费建造的仓库工程；个体户 50 万元以上购置生产性设备投资。

房屋建筑施工面积　指在报告期内施工的全部房屋建筑面积。包括本期内新开工的，上期施工跨入本期继续施工，上期停建本期复工的房屋建筑面积。

房屋建筑本年（季）新开工面积　指在本年（季）内新开工的房屋建筑施工面积。不包上期施工跨入本期继续施工的房屋建筑面积以及上期停建本期复工的面积。

房屋建筑竣工面积　指在报告期内，按照设计所规定的工程内容全部完成，达到了设计规定的交工条件，经有关部门检查验收鉴定合格的房屋建筑面积。

屋建筑面积竣工率　指一定时期内房屋竣工面积占同期房屋施工面积的比率。它是从房屋建筑施工速度的角度反映投资效果和建筑业经济效益的指标。

固定资产交付使用率　指一定时期新增固定资产与同期完成投资额的比率。它反映各个时期固定资产动用速度、衡量建设过程中投资效果的一个综合性指标。

六、运输邮电

Transport, Postal and Telecommunication Services

6-1 主要年份运输邮电主要指标

Main Indicators of Transport, Postal and Telecommunication Services in Main Years

项　　目	单　位	1985年	1990年	1995年	2000年	2005年	2008年	2009年
公路通车里程	公里	1240	1325	2327	2519	2871	4001	4713
#高速公路	公里				89	154	159	207
一级公路	公里		6	679	782	1315	1639	2389
内河通航里程	公里	532	598	598	798	664	643	643
公路桥梁	座	211	267	338	538	826	1014	1065
民用汽车	辆	7897	19394	88311	153684	406577	701600	795554
#载客	辆	1878	7225	25366	69658	268918	557359	653273
载货	辆	5980	12087	52242	80405	129298	136295	137334
摩托车	辆	11786	47881	255591	482636	775838	521118	470818
机动船	艘	2883	5885	5292	806	467	326	293
机动船净载重吨位	吨	80324	186056	259329	152661	148737	199883	203820
邮电局(所)	处	52	53	273	594	702	547	546
邮路长度	公里	790	459	685	3550	6835	5917	6198
长途自动交换机容量	路端		2100	15000	42182	510045	766946	864970
局用交换机容量	万门	1.14	6.98	52.29	103.13	286.25	340.71	347.15
移动电话交换机总容量	万户			4.8	154.2	1059.1	1602.1	1621.6
本地电话用户	万户	0.77	4.90	31.58	78.12	384.52	439.41	378.40
移动电话用户(含充值卡)	万户		0.05	4.77	123.68	1016.41	1454.29	1409.29
互联网用户	万户			0.05	13.78	52.90	96.37	118.02
邮政业务收入	万元						73675	71467
电信业务收入	万元						1650145	1491610
客运量	万人	2072	5758	10237	30697	33551	122468	73324
#公路	万人	1940	5728	10210	30680	33510	122431	73291
旅客周转量	万人公里	95237	322236	446230	1001906	1185290	2248521	1053469
#公路	万人公里	90950	320690	444293	1000492	1182000	2246128	1051324
货运量	万吨	2913	2701	4266	5431	6400	9273	8733
#公路	万吨	1922	1571	2377	3440	4586	8010	6944
货物周转量	万吨公里	171591	184700	264605	404678	424829	1747489	1016490
#公路	万吨公里	113038	72162	128026	246046	272500	462797	452880
港口货物吞吐量	万吨	276	233	201	746	2280	3208	3530

注：2006年起公路通车里程含专用公路和村道，下同。

6-2 历年运输线路长度与公路密度

Length of Transportation Routes and Road Density over Years

年 份	公路通车里程(公里)	#等级公路	#一级	等外公路	高级、次高级路面通车里程(公里)	内河通航里程(公里)	公路密度(公里/百平方公里)
1978	1259	287		972		530	51.08
1979	1225	355		870		603	49.70
1980	1225	355		870		603	49.70
1981	1225	845		380		415	49.70
1982	1225	845		380		115	49.70
1983	1225	872		353		132	49.70
1984	1240	896		344		132	50.30
1985	1240	490		750	488	132	50.30
1986	1248	977		271		274	50.63
1987	1261	991		270		598	51.16
1988	1302	1068	6	234		598	52.82
1989	1325	1091	6	234		598	53.75
1990	1325	1102	6	223	750	598	53.75
1991	1759	1226	6	533	1137	598	71.36
1992	2055	1431	151	624	1442	599	83.37
1993	2260	1673	315	587	1675	598	91.68
1994	2292	1868	599	424	1773	598	92.98
1995	2327	1930	679	397	1650	598	94.40
1996	2330	2087	689	243	1653	598	94.50
1997	2330	2087	690	243	1563	598	94.50
1998	2429	1897	714	480	1958	598	98.52
1999	2467	1935	717	480	2048	798	100.06
2000	2519	2339	782	91	2253	798	102.15
2001	2570	2393	845	78	2321	798	104.26
2002	2641	2464	908	78	2406	798	107.14
2003	2688	2508	967	75	2472	716	109.05
2004	2759	2609	1148	37	2637	798	111.93
2005	2871	2686	1315	31	2774	664	116.47
2006	3891	3619	1585	117	3823	664	157.85
2007	3924	3650	1591	116	3860	535	159.19
2008	4001	3884	1639	117	3864	643	162.31
2009	4713	4598	2389	115	4643	643	191.21

6-3 主要年份运输线路长度

Length of Transport Routes in Main Years

项目	单位	1980年	1985年	1990年	1995年	2000年	2005年	2008年	2009年
一、公路通车里程合计	**公里**	**1225**	**1240**	**1325**	**2327**	**2519**	**2871**	**4001**	**4713**
#按等级分									
等级公路	公里	355	490	1102	1930	2339	2686	3884	4598
高速公路	公里					89	154	159	207
一级	公里			6	679	782	1315	1639	2389
二级	公里		58	65	361	684	703	970	1317
三级	公里		61	60	135	310	297	486	153
四级	公里	355	371	971	755	563	371	631	532
等外公路	公里	870	750	223	397	91	31	117	115
#按路面分									
有路面里程	公里		622	800	1808	2508	2858	3928	4650
#高级、次高级	公里		488	750	1650	2253	2774	3864	4643
无路面里程	公里		618	524	519	11	13	64	63
二、桥梁合计	**座**		**211**	**267**	**338**	**538**	**826**	**1014**	**1065**
	延米					39956	112385	139940	138867
三、公路密度	**公里/百平方公里**	**49.70**	**50.30**	**53.75**	**94.40**	**102.15**	**116.47**	**162.31**	**191.21**
#等级公路密度	公里/百平方公里	14.40	19.88	44.71	78.30	94.89	108.97	157.57	186.54
四、内河通航里程	**公里**	**603**	**532**	**598**	**598**	**798**	**664**	**643**	**643**

6-4 主要年份客货运输量

Passenger and Freight Traffic in Main Years

年份	客运量(万人)	旅客周转量(万人公里)	货运量(万吨)	货物周转量(万吨公里)	港口货物吞吐量(万吨)
1952	86	1350	7	139	
1957	120	2100	10	195	
1962	187	4120	14	293	
1965	193	4725	22	457	
1970	118	2800	36	900	
1975	169	3890	30	694	
1978	403	9425	394	15148	293
1980	572	13584	349	16353	295
1985	2072	95237	2913	171591	276
1990	5758	322236	2701	184700	233
1995	10237	446230	4266	264605	201
1996	10749	477466	4451	267193	289
1997	11300	511592	4644	278649	338
1998	17485	577452	4776	285889	516
1999	25404	804278	5016	300410	654
2000	30697	1001906	5431	404678	746
2001	31220	1031579	5527	406247	883
2002	32100	1091821	5857	420684	1611
2003	32588	1126964	5877	422822	2352
2004	33240	1166262	6054	423669	2600
2005	33551	1185290	6400	424829	2280
2006	35182	1213809	5481	336783	1951
2007	37182	1264982	5676	356677	2017
2008	122468	2248521	9273	1747489	3208
2009	73324	1053469	8733	1016490	3530

6-5 客货运输量

Passenger and Freight Traffic

项　　目	单　位	1980年	1985年	1990年	1995年	2000年	2005年	2008年	2009年
一、客运量	**万人**	**572**	**2072**	**5758**	**10237**	**30697**	**33551**	**122468**	**73324**
公　路	万人	362	1940	5728	10210	30680	33510	122431	73291
水　运	万人	210	132	30	27	17	41	37	33
二、旅客周转量	**万人公里**	**13584**	**95237**	**322236**	**446230**	**1001906**	**1185290**	**2248521**	**1053469**
公　路	万人公里	8285	90950	320690	444293	1000492	1182000	2246128	1051324
水　运	万人公里	5299	4287	1546	1937	1414	3290	2393	2145
三、货运量	**万吨**	**349**	**2913**	**2701**	**4266**	**5431**	**6400**	**9273**	**8733**
公　路	万吨	51	1922	1571	2377	3440	4586	8010	6944
#个体及联户	万吨		1906	1557	2368	3440	4586	1273	1973
水　运	万吨	298	991	1130	1889	1991	1814	1263	1789
#个体及联户	万吨		617	837	1599	1660	1484	86	159
四、货物周转量	**万吨公里**	**16353**	**171591**	**184700**	**264605**	**404678**	**424829**	**1747489**	**1016490**
公　路	万吨公里	1479	113038	72162	128026	246046	272500	462797	452880
#个体及联户	万吨公里		113002	72141	127928	246046	272500	38398	126052
水　运	万吨公里	14874	58553	112538	136579	158632	152329	1284692	563610
#个体及联户	万吨公里		31784	83094	105099	119855	113249	5598	8787

6-6 主要年份运输工具拥有量

Possession of Main Means of Transport in Main Years

项　　目	单　位	1980年	1985年	1990年	1995年	2000年	2005年	2008年	2009年
一、民用车辆拥有量									
(一)汽车	辆	2009	7897	19394	88311	153684	406577	701600	795554
1. 载客汽车	辆	516	1878	7225	25366	69658	268918	557359	653273
	客位	1909	23462	66361	302844	560155	2420591	3994220	4483494
2. 载货汽车	辆	1457	5980	12087	55000	81623	129298	136295	137334
	吨位	3368	20428	38010	133757	332621	243390	236828	234684
3. 其他汽车	辆	36	39	82	7945	2403	8361	7946	4947
(二)摩托车	辆	170	11786	47881	255591	482636	775838	521118	470818
(三)农用运输车	台	3617	12423	21735	7760	1534	1763	551	511
(四)挂车	辆					8	2222	2549	2697
二、民用运输船舶拥有量									
机动船	艘	1948	2883	5885	5292	806	467	326	293
	净载重吨位	42473	80323	186056	259329	152661	148737	199883	203820
	客位	2107	2056	776	1881	1054	604	917	902
#货船	艘		2866	5875	5259	796	465	323	290
	净载重吨位		80285	186038	259314	152661	148431	199422	203360
客船	艘				26	10	2	3	3
	客位				1295	1054	604	917	902
三、期末机动车驾驶员	**人**		**44186**	**118229**	**351947**	**563564**	**798086**	**1003040**	**1144901**
#汽车驾驶员	人		10661	28768	94778	173865	428912	780979	941097

注：2002年起民用汽车拥有量按新的口径分类，部分指标数值与往年不可比。

6-7 历年主要运输工具年末拥有量

Possession of Main Means of Transport at Year-end over Years

年 份	民用汽车（辆）	#客车	#货车	摩托车（辆）	机动船（艘）
1978	623	78	506	134	2169
1979	1115	178	1089	156	2034
1980	2009	516	1457	170	1948
1981	3039	751	2031	517	2107
1982	3419	791	2724	1168	2285
1983	4473	854	3580	1636	2313
1984	6059	1243	4822	7060	2563
1985	7897	1878	5980	11786	2883
1986	8632	2245	6334	18006	4368
1987	9983	2954	6973	21308	4884
1988	13581	3456	8690	26995	4911
1989	16340	4214	10434	36820	4901
1990	19394	7225	12087	47881	5885
1991	20734	5206	15423	65770	4405
1992	32625	5753	25048	106013	4351
1993	48145	8710	35421	153014	4379
1994	61572	11550	43925	200543	4562
1995	88311	25366	55000	255591	5292
1996	90793	29430	54870	249492	5313
1997	103425	40101	62507	287076	5064
1998	113435	47769	64434	382010	456
1999	127007	55715	69470	399324	690
2000	153684	69658	82841	482636	806
2001	183638	89677	91304	560310	536
2002	220134	116783	102253	642034	483
2003	255603	155206	97047	692562	392
2004	319725	210531	105050	687651	417
2005	406577	268918	129298	775838	467
2006	489306	351265	131704	697175	440
2007	608933	466999	134825	567002	393
2008	701600	557359	136295	521118	326
2009	795554	653273	137334	470818	293

6-8 主要年份邮电通信业务基本情况

Basic Conditons of Postal and Telecommunication services in Main Years

项 目	单位	1978年	1985年	1990年	1995年	2000年	2005年	2008年	2009年
一、邮电通信网									
邮电局、所	处	50	52	53	273	594	702	547	546
#设在农村	处	48	50	49	222	539	617	424	478
邮路长度	公里	513	790	459	685	3550	6835	5917	6198
农村投递线路长度	公里	1985	2302	1812	2057	8865	19722	21559	25025
二、邮电通信工具									
邮政汽车	辆		2	7	10	35	192	367	363
长途自动交换机容量	路端			2100	15000	42182	510045	766946	864970
移动电话交换机总容量	万户				4.8	154.2	1059.1	1602.1	1621.6
移动电话用户(含充值卡)	万户					123.68	1016.41	1454.29	1409.29
移动电话用户(不含充值卡)	万户			0.05	4.77	80.97	176.83	91.39	138.14
局用交换机容量	万门		1.14	6.98	52.29	103.13	286.25	340.71	347.15
#市话交换机	万门		0.22	2.10	16.82	21.84	67.68	86.94	90.05
本地电话用户	万户	0.20	0.77	4.90	31.57	78.12	384.52	439.41	378.40
市内电话用户	万户	0.04	0.16	1.50	9.78	19.69	68.30	149.85	113.51
农村电话用户	万户	0.16	0.61	3.40	21.80	58.43	316.22	289.56	264.89
数字数据用户(DDN)	端口					2741	2170	1465	1301
互联网用户	万户				0.05	13.78	52.90	96.37	118.02
三、邮电业务量									
邮电业务收入	亿元							172.38	156.31
#电信业务	亿元							165.02	149.16
#移动通信业务	亿元							106.54	101.29
邮政特快专递	万件						292.17	479.05	557.22
函件	万件		805	3372	10407	8124	9430	6621	4276
长途电话	万次		89	1739	21287	66419	159762	179642	154412

6-9 历年邮电通信业务主要指标

Main Indicators of Postal and Telecommunication Services over Years

年 份	邮电局、所(处)	长途自动交换机容量(路端)	局用交换机容量(万门)	本地电话用户(万户)	移动电话用户(万户)	邮电业务收入(亿元)
1978	50			0.20		
1979	50			0.21		
1980	50		0.50	0.31		
1981	50			0.34		
1982	51			0.35		
1983	51			0.39		
1984	52			0.48		
1985	52		1.14	0.77		
1986	53			0.88		
1987	45			1.63		
1988	48			2.52		
1989	50			4.30	0.02	
1990	53	2100	6.98	4.90	0.05	
1991	60		9.82	7.50	0.11	
1992	91	3510	11.07	9.70	0.30	
1993	161	3510	21.24	14.98	0.72	
1994	216	11410	36.37	23.19	2.41	
1995	273	15000	52.29	31.57	4.77	
1996	310	15000	52.79	36.91	8.24	
1997	339	15000	57.76	42.65	15.29	
1998	397	25000	73.09	50.13	26.17	
1999	458	40000	84.79	60.87	51.01	
2000	594	42182	103.13	78.12	123.68	
2001	689	59000	155.29	98.96	295.76	
2002	696	59000	176.94	127.93	412.39	90.56
2003	846	129000	220.28	206.11	660.86	105.12
2004	854	200985	265.66	281.35	856.09	120.78
2005	702	510045	286.25	384.52	1016.41	132.82
2006	560	563071	299.19	461.31	1216.34	146.69
2007	567	713290	329.50	469.17	1408.23	161.90
2008	547	766946	340.71	439.41	1454.29	172.38
2009	546	864970	347.15	378.40	1409.29	156.31

注：本地电话用户含小灵通用户。

6-10 历年邮电通信企业财务指标

Main Financial Indicators of Postal and Telecommunication Enterprises over Years

单位：万元

指　　标	2002年	2003年	2004年	2005年	2006年	2007年	2008年	2009年
职工人数(人)	5035	5269	9485	10730	10881	11309	10598	10901
#固定工	4038	4277	7941	4803	4498	4528	4389	4459
年末资产总额	1211054	1211056	1342540	1465629	1548349	1623628	1681620	1585605
年末流动资产合计	224550	146908	133768	181039	228697	279043	324775	246591
#应收帐款净额	63042	57368	53062	67608	56478	62631	57927	20441
年末固定资产合计	947924	998057	1151720	1238276	1280974	1258143	1252938	1160814
年末固定资产原值合计	1157237	1402762	1534094	1790159	2018571	2252314	2482921	2694488
#生产用	1122155	1386056	1516466	1770843	2006747	2163153	2474091	2686818
累计折旧	348785	472350	531081	664786	860633	1077754	1281445	1482506
#当年折旧	115935	122390	154417	177293	197314	230146	196217	237351
年末固定资产净值合计	808453	930412	1003012	1125360	1157926	1174540	1201454	1211982
无形资产及递延资产	15635	25839	57051	42582	38777	81176	54555	61802
其它资产	12707	11056		2198	2551	5265	49352	116398
负债及所有者权益总计	1211054	1211056	1342540	1465629	1548349	1623628	1681620	1585605
年末流动资产负债合计	244828	194474	202929	365735	451449	465033	381803	474003
#未交税金	19870	17729	29345	39447	42265	33785	13941	10644
短期借款				3000		8000		
年末长期负债合计	95	14175	9932				52442	64537
期末所有者权益合计	966131	1002408	1129679	1099894	1096900	1158595	1247375	1047065
主营业务收入	890138	1036123	1174265	1326686	1446601	1603151	1760389	1636257
#营业成本	236322	278125	303464	406999	471863	552168	735247	583539
营业税金及附加	26517	34307	36790	41122	41635	48758	50681	46435
其他业务利润	-855	266223	11911	-11316	-15355	1230	4736	2690
管理费用	24375	214051	84868	99425	56157	54236	47383	47008
财务费用	3910	447	37848	539	897	898	2709	1660
营业外收入	874	1088	1676	879	1809	2135	1973	2204
营业外支出	10122	2424	8424	2838	3325	6132	4257	18017
利润总额	548341	580729	676902	716380	805496	877893	911160	738312
利税总额	576501	627697	713700	756757	835548	926720	960285	777806

主要统计指标解释

公路通车里程 指在一定时点上实际达到《公路工程技术标准JTJ01-88》规定的等级公路，并经公路主管部门正式验收交付使用的公路里程数。凡达到交通部《公路工程技术标准JTJ01-88》规定的技术等级的公路，均统计为公路里程。包括大、中城市的郊区公路，以及公路通过城镇（指县城、集镇）街道的里程数和公路桥梁长度、隧道长度、渡口的宽度以及分期修建的公路已验收交付使用的里程。不包括大、中城市街道，国、省干线断头路里程，农业生产用道路以及新建公路尚未进行验收交付使用的路段里程。两条或多条公路共同经由同一路段的重复里程，只计算一次。公路等级分为高速、一、二、三、四级公路。

货（客）运量 在一定时期内，各运输部门实际运送的货物（旅客）数量。货运按吨计算，客运按人计算。货物不论运输距离长短，货物类型，均按实际重量统计；旅客不论行程远近或票价多少，均按一人一次作为客运量统计。半价票，小孩票也按一人统计。货（客）运量反映运输业为国民经济和人民生活服务的数量，也是制定和检查运输生产计划，研究运输发展规模和速度的重要指标。

货物（旅客）周转量 指在一定时期内，由各种运输工具运输业运送的货物（旅客）数量与其相应运输距离的乘积，通常以吨公里和人公里为计算单位。计算货物周转量通常按发出站与到达站之间的最短距离，也就是计费距离计算。它是反映运输业生产总成果的重要指标，也是编制和检查运输生产计划，计算运输效率，劳动生产率以及核算运输单位成本的主要基础资料。

货物吞吐量 是指经由水运运进、运出港区范围，并经过装卸的货物数量。货物吞吐量分别按国内进口（装卸）、出口（装船），外贸进口、出口统计。货物吞吐量按货物实际重量吨统计，以货物交接清单或货单上记载的重量吨为准。如无实际重量吨，可根据船舶装载情况来推算。在本港区内的水运转口分别按进口和出口各计算一次吞吐量。货物吞吐量是衡量港口生产规模的一个主要数量指标。

邮电业务收入 是指邮电营运企业从事邮政、电信、移动及其他邮电业务所取得的营业收入。

局用电话交换机容量 指安装在本地电信运营商内用于接读本地固定电话的电话交换机容量，有倍增设备按倍增后的数量计数。包括现用和备用的人工或自动交换全部容量。

本地电话用户 是指接入本地电信运营商固定电话网上的电话用户。包括：住宅电话、单位用户、公用电话用户等。

移动电话用户 是指在移动通信部门办理登记手续，通过移动电话交换机进入移动电话网，占用移动电话号码的电话用户。

邮电局所 是指对外营业、直接为用户办理邮电业务的服务机构。一个邮电局所，必须同时具备以下三个条件：①有固定的局所地址；②领有上级发给的日戳或戳记；③至少办理出售邮票和收寄挂号信两种邮政业务或办理一种电信业务。凡是具备上述三个条件的，均按邮电局所统计，计量单位为“处”。邮电局所按经营方式分为自办局所和代办所。

邮电服务网点 指为用户进行邮电服务的地点，包括邮电局所、报刊亭等。

七、国内贸易

Domestic Trade

7-1 历年社会消费品零售总额

Total Retail Sales of Consumer Goods over Years

年 份	社会消费品零售总额	
	绝对值（万元）	增速（%）
1978	21269	
1979	24956	17.3
1980	31595	26.6
1981	40201	27.2
1982	48126	19.7
1983	52255	8.6
1984	73930	41.5
1985	93640	26.7
1986	122420	30.7
1987	150511	23.0
1988	246518	63.8
1989	270354	9.7
1990	319738	18.3
1991	364972	14.2
1992	443464	21.5
1993	636882	43.6
1994	851556	33.7
1995	1130081	32.7
1996	1255311	11.1
1997	1460396	16.3
1998	1751551	19.9
1999	2023008	15.5
2000	2351634	16.2
2001	2757143	17.2
2002	3212436	16.5
2003	3697814	15.1
2004	4264704	15.3
2005	5062917	18.7
2006	5993201	18.4
2007	7224491	20.5
2008	8811519	22.0
2009	9590727	8.8

注：本表1979-2003年数据根据东莞市第一次全国经济普查结果重新核定，2005-2008年数据根据东莞市第二次全国经济普查结果重新核定，下同。

7-2 历年批发零售贸易企业与个体户数

Number of Wholesale and Retail Trades Enterprises and Self-employed Individuals over years

单位：个

年 份	单位数合计	国有经济	集体经济	其他经济	#私营个体经济
1979	2459	406	1918	135	135
1980	2613	395	1679	539	537
1981	4603	371	1954	2278	2274
1982	3323	373	1838	1112	1107
1983	8723	401	1539	6783	6783
1984	18917	431	6720	11766	11766
1985	16885	670	4543	11672	11671
1986	18547	823	3063	14661	14660
1987	23468	739	4102	18627	18626
1988	26247	665	4405	21177	21176
1989	28453	695	4196	23562	23561
1990	27931	709	3512	23710	23709
1991	29474	678	3934	24862	24862
1992	34465	803	4193	29469	29469
1993	43511	886	7640	34985	34985
1994	49706	633	11396	37677	37677
1995	56339	745	14492	41102	41101
1996	60078	670	15183	44225	44224
1997	48910	811	8477	39622	39546
1998	52543	1064	4046	47433	46615
1999	55925	1056	3843	51026	50172
2000	57474	1024	3581	5289	51914
2001	68909	866	2960	65083	63760
2002	89246	748	2424	86078	84614
2003	113531	530	2068	110933	109236
2004	149067	539	1941	146587	144304
2005	192525	393	1451	190681	188082
2006	236124	283	1090	234751	231930
2007	284109	268	930	282911	279524
2008	301996	288	833	300875	296613
2009	300088	256	744	299088	294753

7-3 批发零售业商品销售总额（2009）

Total Sales of Commodities in Wholesale and Retail Trades

单位：万元

项目	商品销售总额	#批发额	零售额
合计	**15819073**	**7196598**	**8622475**
按行业分			
批发业	7033257	6665050	368207
零售业	8785816	531548	8254268
按规模分			
限额以上企业	9097281	5399785	3697497
食品、饮料、烟酒类	1115368	854028	261340
粮油类	116030	56038	59992
肉禽蛋类	43222	10037	33185
水产品类	6611	1064	5547
蔬菜类	14378	261	14117
干鲜果品类	17288		17288
饮料类	97806	55274	42532
烟酒类	566233	539587	26646
服装鞋帽、针纺织品类	741007	513984	227023
服装类	380120	260856	119264
鞋帽类	152794	66104	86690
针、纺织品类	208094	187024	21070
化妆品类	43262	5349	37913
金银珠宝类	378743	361085	17659
日用品类	187140	107234	79906
洗涤用品类	83650	35847	47803
儿童玩具类	26076	21186	4890
五金、电料类	83868	69740	14128
体育、娱乐用品类	14323	5162	9160
书报杂志类	20180	10337	9843
电子出版物及音像制品类	6594	4438	2156
家用电器和音像器材类	459330	181061	278269
中西药品类	240372	123019	117354
西药	135624	41670	93954
中草药及中成药	52008	30209	21799
文化办公用品类	58126	22067	36059
家具类	231590	227784	3807
通讯器材类	314721	279014	35706
煤炭及制品类	132988	132983	5
木材及制品类	14977	14977	
石油及制品类	1970865	920296	1050569
化工材料及制品类	582326	582326	
化肥类	481	481	
金属材料类	199077	199077	
建筑及装潢材料类	76840	55802	21038
机电产品及设备类	123171	117541	5631
农机类	272	272	
汽车类	1501012	63818	1437193
种子饲料类	125	125	
棉麻类	197	160	37
其它	601081	548379	52703
限额以下企业和个体户	6721792	1796813	4924978

7-4 星级住宿业和限额以上餐饮业经营情况（2009年）

Business of Star-ranking Hotels and Catering Services above Designated Size (2009)

项目	法人企业（个）	从业人数（人）	营业额（万元）	客房收入	餐费收入	商品销售收入	其它收入
总计	**293**	**66295**	**639244**	**134776**	**419514**	**2358**	**82596**
一、住宿业	**171**	**47601**	**419875**	**131469**	**211204**	**662**	**76541**
（一）按登记注册类型分							
内资企业	156	42317	366510	114558	181096	634	70223
港、澳、台商投资企业	9	3062	29827	9826	16544	20	3437
外商投资企业	6	2222	23538	7085	13564	8	2881
（二）按国民经济行业分							
旅游饭店	140	43978	391788	120352	200590	661	70186
一般旅馆	27	3286	25652	9554	9961	1	6136
其它住宿服务业	4	337	2436	1563	653		219
二、餐饮业	**122**	**18694**	**219369**	**3307**	**208310**	**1696**	**6055**
（一）按登记注册类型分							
内资企业	110	13386	135428	3220	126292	1559	4357
港、澳、台商投资企业	4	814	7617		6601	137	879
外商投资企业	8	4494	76324	88	75417		819
（二）按国民经济行业分							
正餐服务业	104	11927	120498	3187	110167	1696	5447
快餐服务业	9	5803	93534	120	92806		608
饮料及冷饮服务业	1	589	1941		1941		
其他餐饮服务业	8	375	3396		3396		

7-5 限额以上批发和零售企业财务状况（2009年）

Main Financial Indicators of Enterprises above Designated Size in Wholesale and Retail Trade (2009)

单位:万元

项目	法人企业数（个）	年末资产负债 流动资产合计	存货	固定资产原值	累计折旧	本年折旧
总计	**715**	**4202440**	**703499**	**633755**	**212072**	**52717**
一、批发企业	**275**	**2693746**	**423575**	**261122**	**82603**	**19562**
（一）按登记注册类型分						
内资企业	267	2617120	412417	250526	78498	18650
港、澳、台商投资企业	5	56023	7845	4282	799	531
外商投资企业	3	20603	3313	6314	3306	381
（二）按国民经济行业分						
农畜产品批发业						
食品、饮料及烟草制品批发业	32	288109	42983	37295	12801	3734
纺织、服装及日用品批发业	24	190356	6611	38830	12470	1807
文化、体育用品及器材批发业	10	80286	14852	4402	1565	828
医药及医疗器材批发业	11	72646	17626	3954	1756	305
矿产品、建材及化工产品批发业	107	1129081	215803	86379	28393	6756
机械设备、五金交电及电子产品批发业	55	693028	87048	59082	15985	3568
贸易经纪与代理	14	38684	2668	14019	4539	1335
其他批发业	22	201557	35984	17160	5094	1228
二、零售企业	**440**	**1508694**	**279925**	**372634**	**129470**	**33155**
（一）按登记注册类型分						
内资企业	417	1432655	248020	334996	117703	28898
港、澳、台商投资企业	5	20998	11819	10876	2238	688
外商投资企业	18	55041	20086	26761	9529	3569
（二）按国民经济行业分						
综合零售业	85	194100	54259	82567	29878	7312
食品、饮料及烟草制品专门零售业	9	9833	2666	2083	1040	206
纺织、服装及日用品专门零售业	7	8126	5844	8864	8359	4601
文化、体育用品及器材专门零售业	5	11160	5881	314	221	163
医药及医疗器材专门零售业	26	61276	20404	12573	5118	951
汽车、摩托车、燃料及零配件专门零售业	245	1092309	152017	240840	75628	17709
家用电器及电子产品专门零售业	27	86409	28279	5937	1807	924
五金、家具及室内装修材料专门零售业	15	10322	3804	5995	3785	603
无店铺及其他零售业	21	35158	6772	13461	3635	687

7-5 续表 1

(2009年)

单位: 万元

项目	年末资产负债				损益及分配	
	资产总计	负债合计	所有者权益合计	实收资本	营业收入合计	主营业务收入
总计	**5106170**	**3798265**	**1307904**	**472170**	**9119673**	**9031880**
一、批发企业	**3268237**	**2652294**	**615943**	**267579**	**5415981**	**5392470**
(一)按登记注册类型分						
内资企业	3172338	2585508	586831	237669	5200258	5179875
港、澳、台商投资企业	59652	48954	10698	10797	103510	102246
外商投资企业	36247	17833	18415	19113	112212	110349
(二)按国民经济行业分						
农畜产品批发业						
食品、饮料及烟草制品批发业	523625	308212	215413	73566	874918	868376
纺织、服装及日用品批发业	255839	205991	49848	32285	1088126	1085206
文化、体育用品及器材批发业	117897	45168	72729	15666	64494	64394
医药及医疗器材批发业	75329	69268	6061	3596	131990	131980
矿产品、建材及化工产品批发业	1267305	1122425	144879	90356	1929092	1922958
机械设备、五金交电及电子产品批发业	755188	655220	99968	35263	711182	705997
贸易经纪与代理	50647	42604	8044	6071	225814	224179
其他批发业	222408	203407	19001	10776	390366	389381
二、零售企业	**1837933**	**1145971**	**691962**	**204591**	**3703692**	**3639409**
(一)按登记注册类型分						
内资企业	1727223	1062808	664415	177303	3371663	3312177
港、澳、台商投资企业	30894	17287	13608	5843	118425	117444
外商投资企业	79816	65876	13940	21446	213604	209788
(二)按国民经济行业分						
综合零售业	271516	250040	21475	33038	534681	502753
食品、饮料及烟草制品专门零售业	10893	8150	2744	1220	22893	22103
纺织、服装及日用品专门零售业	10168	20783	-10614	960	72099	72028
文化、体育用品及器材专门零售业	12324	10966	1358	3150	11341	11138
医药及医疗器材专门零售业	74512	54757	19755	7325	128084	127676
汽车、摩托车、燃料及零配件专门零售业	1302623	670962	631661	131031	2565891	2550568
家用电器及电子产品专门零售业	92737	74228	18509	10280	274229	261784
五金、家具及室内装修材料专门零售业	13435	19388	-5953	7708	28244	26929
无店铺及其他零售业	49726	36699	13027	9879	66230	64431

7-5　续表 2

(2009年)

单位: 万元

项　目	损益及分配					
	主营业务成本	主营业务税金及附加	主营业务利润	其它业务利润	营业费用	管理费用
总　计	**8225200**	**35610**	**739561**	**67977**	**375512**	**153816**
一、批发企业	**5050810**	**27853**	**317103**	**15397**	**144847**	**70333**
(一)按登记注册类型分						
内资企业	4868017	27829	287325	12866	119132	66321
港、澳、台商投资企业	84454	4	17787	774	18389	1470
外商投资企业	98339	20	11990	1757	7325	2543
(二)按国民经济行业分						
农畜产品批发业						
食品、饮料及烟草制品批发业	730192	18777	118307	6090	30415	16589
纺织、服装及日用品批发业	1061515	357	22038	2423	9383	8563
文化、体育用品及器材批发业	57851	80	5359	101	5880	2190
医药及医疗器材批发业	122398	134	9448	10	4772	2941
矿产品、建材及化工产品批发业	1831292	1062	91440	1826	52277	19349
机械设备、五金交电及电子产品批发业	663123	806	42160	2863	25789	12245
贸易经纪与代理	220256	595	3328	1543	1509	2811
其他批发业	364184	6042	25022	542	14822	5647
二、零售企业	**3174389**	**7757**	**422458**	**52580**	**230665**	**83483**
(一)按登记注册类型分						
内资企业	2883887	7524	386416	48866	206077	76533
港、澳、台商投资企业	106989	23	10432	956	4032	2571
外商投资企业	183513	210	25610	2758	20556	4379
(二)按国民经济行业分						
综合零售业	426231	2825	72066	29749	83770	13175
食品、饮料及烟草制品专门零售业	20579	39	1489	58	848	416
纺织、服装及日用品专门零售业	31670	279	39909	70	24814	13616
文化、体育用品及器材专门零售业	9923	16	648	193	1120	760
医药及医疗器材专门零售业	108591	214	18237	338	10642	6469
汽车、摩托车、燃料及零配件专门零售业	2263533	3311	253183	8248	70698	40933
家用电器及电子产品专门零售业	236480	817	23636	11196	28775	3123
五金、家具及室内装修材料专门零售业	21724	137	4901	1295	5534	1140
无店铺及其他零售业	55658	120	8389	1433	4464	3851

7-5 续表 3

(2009年)

单位: 万元

项目	损益及分配				本年应交增值税	全部从业人员年平均人数(人)
	财务费用	营业利润	利润总额	应交所得税		
总计	**36681**	**259503**	**274590**	**42916**	**114231**	**53370**
一、批发企业	**22902**	**104289**	**122654**	**28754**	**53916**	**18402**
(一)按登记注册类型分						
内资企业	22911	101699	113931	27494	49857	16986
港、澳、台商投资企业	130	-1428	-1503	242	2507	895
外商投资企业	-139	4018	10225	1018	1553	521
(二)按国民经济行业分						
农畜产品批发业						
食品、饮料及烟草制品批发业	4269	74234	81298	21665	23909	3143
纺织、服装及日用品批发业	2433	5375	5815	1406	703	1238
文化、体育用品及器材批发业	51	913	891	171	736	1176
医药及医疗器材批发业	634	1112	1078	306	2854	1020
矿产品、建材及化工产品批发业	11399	12271	21848	2589	16695	4148
机械设备、五金交电及电子产品批发业	2257	6887	7333	1610	4890	5660
贸易经纪与代理	366	185	183	99	466	493
其他批发业	1493	3312	4209	907	3664	1524
二、零售企业	**13779**	**155214**	**151936**	**14161**	**60315**	**34968**
(一)按登记注册类型分						
内资企业	12708	147215	146385	11756	53599	31946
港、澳、台商投资企业	212	4574	4521	1109	2159	411
外商投资企业	859	3425	1031	1297	4557	2611
(二)按国民经济行业分						
综合零售业	1892	4729	2982	2814	10550	10787
食品、饮料及烟草制品专门零售业	14	269	241	46	270	300
纺织、服装及日用品专门零售业	668	398	-596	1053	8461	1287
文化、体育用品及器材专门零售业	163	-660	-659	20	114	182
医药及医疗器材专门零售业	-133	1263	1413	348	2188	3064
汽车、摩托车、燃料及零配件专门零售业	9257	145848	146547	8640	32852	13360
家用电器及电子产品专门零售业	968	2845	3027	960	3451	4014
五金、家具及室内装修材料专门零售业	435	-761	-2328	38	951	670
无店铺及其他零售业	517	1284	1309	243	1478	1304

7-6 限额以上住宿和餐饮企业财务状况（2009年）

Main Financial Indicators of Enterprises above Designated Size in Hotels and Catering Services (2009)

单位:万元

项　　目	法　人 企业数 （个）	年末资产负债				
		流动资产合计	存　货	固定资产原价	累　计 折　旧	本　年 折　旧
总　　计	**293**	**492313**	**27775**	**998658**	**413519**	**64396**
一、住宿业	**171**	**430151**	**22190**	**918210**	**380080**	**56051**
（一）按登记注册类型分						
内资企业	156	359503	18301	721012	264291	44912
港、澳、台商投资企业	9	38168	3129	161570	97983	9381
外商投资企业	6	32481	760	35628	17806	1758
（二）按国民经济行业分						
旅游饭店	140	411644	21113	877444	366929	52889
一般旅馆	27	18186	1039	39755	12704	2982
其它住宿服务业	4	321	38	1010	446	180
二、餐饮业	**122**	**62162**	**5586**	**80449**	**33440**	**8346**
（一）按登记注册类型分						
内资企业	110	49581	3644	45080	16691	5190
港、澳、台商投资企业	4	3816	143	6159	2343	783
外商投资企业	8	8765	1799	29211	14405	2372
（二）按国民经济行业分						
正餐服务业	104	27102	3666	55570	22375	5560
快餐服务业	9	32449	1819	24363	10849	2747
饮料及冷饮服务业	1	408	68	233	23	4
其他餐饮服务业	8	2202	33	283	192	35

7-6 续表 1

(2009年)

单位: 万元

项 目	年末资产负债				损益及分配	
	资产总计	负债合计	所有者权益合计	实收资本	营业收入	主营业务收入
总 计	**1392037**	**1067454**	**324583**	**312183**	**643571**	**638396**
一、住宿业	**1218208**	**986480**	**231729**	**252970**	**425743**	**421179**
(一)按登记注册类型分						
内资企业	1035701	762141	273560	179967	372555	368188
港、澳、台商投资企业	128653	171346	-42693	63310	29395	29239
外商投资企业	53855	52992	862	9692	23793	23752
(二)按国民经济行业分						
旅游饭店	1168652	958972	209680	238873	397283	392954
一般旅馆	48655	26270	22385	13646	26156	25920
其它住宿服务业	902	1238	-336	450	2305	2305
二、餐饮业	**173829**	**80975**	**92854**	**59214**	**217828**	**217217**
(一)按登记注册类型分						
内资企业	123809	67715	56094	36788	133753	133276
港、澳、台商投资企业	9547	7131	2417	4797	7670	7617
外商投资企业	40473	6129	34344	17628	76405	76324
(二)按国民经济行业分						
正餐服务业	67284	45302	21982	28865	118966	118669
快餐服务业	103327	35287	68040	27719	93556	93241
饮料及冷饮服务业	745	54	691	500	1911	1911
其他餐饮服务业	2473	332	2141	2130	3396	3396

7-6 续表 2

(2009年)

单位: 万元

项目	损益及分配					
	主营业务成本	主营业务税金及附加	主营业务利润	其它业务利润	营业费用	管理费用
总计	**234321**	**39003**	**358277**	**3325**	**247715**	**124461**
一、住宿业	**133162**	**26925**	**255851**	**3238**	**166595**	**107939**
(一)按登记注册类型分						
内资企业	116747	23815	225199	3163	144544	88612
港、澳、台商投资企业	8145	1623	16657	34	12458	14044
外商投资企业	8270	1487	13995	41	9593	5282
(二)按国民经济行业分						
旅游饭店	125441	25017	238182	3029	154443	100814
一般旅馆	7149	1772	16073	209	10387	6940
其它住宿服务业	572	137	1595		1765	184
二、餐饮业	**101159**	**12078**	**102426**	**87**	**81120**	**16522**
(一)按登记注册类型分						
内资企业	69563	7760	56175	134	42061	12030
港、澳、台商投资企业	3772	449	1620	11	3285	965
外商投资企业	27824	3869	44631	-57	35774	3528
(二)按国民经济行业分						
正餐服务业	60784	6954	49377	206	40079	10665
快餐服务业	36818	4868	51555	-119	40424	5457
饮料及冷饮服务业	1132	72	707		347	20
其他餐饮服务业	2425	184	787		271	381

7-6 续表 3

(2009年)

单位: 万元

项　　目	损益及分配				全部从业人员年平均人数(人)
	财务费用	营业利润	利润总额	应交所得税	
总　　计	**20327**	**-23910**	**-21952**	**3206**	**66165**
一、住宿业	**18764**	**-28867**	**-27117**	**968**	**47473**
(一)按登记注册类型分					
内资企业	16486	-18765	-16977	881	42189
港、澳、台商投资企业	1276	-8274	-8297	80	3062
外商投资企业	1002	-1829	-1843	7	2222
(二)按国民经济行业分					
旅游饭店	18083	-27792	-26210	831	43820
一般旅馆	666	-707	-536	120	3316
其它住宿服务业	14	-368	-370	17	337
二、餐饮业	**1563**	**4957**	**5165**	**2238**	**18692**
(一)按登记注册类型分					
内资企业	1143	948	1506	1056	13384
港、澳、台商投资企业	108	-951	-951	1	814
外商投资企业	313	4960	4610	1181	4494
(二)按国民经济行业分					
正餐服务业	833	-344	268	719	11927
快餐服务业	720	4836	4477	1435	5801
饮料及冷饮服务业	10	331	283	71	589
其他餐饮服务业	1	135	137	13	375

7-7 历年餐饮企业与个体户数

Number of Enterprises and Self-employed Individuals in Catering Services over Years

单位：个

年　份	单位数合　计	国有经济	集体经济	其他经济	#私营个体经济
1979	147	22	115	10	10
1980	182	23	121	38	38
1981	622	24	283	315	315
1982	308	24	102	182	182
1983	2069	31	98	1940	1940
1984	4012	31	445	3536	3536
1985	2982	36	389	2557	2557
1986	3268	38	270	2960	2956
1987	2281	35	308	1938	1934
1988	2265	31	296	1938	1934
1989	2850	32	276	2542	2538
1990	3387	30	439	2918	2914
1991	3438	44	225	3169	3165
1992	4456	25	320	4111	4106
1993	7119	12	1851	5256	5232
1994	7819	12	1748	6059	6051
1995	8918	26	1802	7090	7082
1996	9708	9	1900	7799	7789
1997	9968	28	606	9334	9210
1998	11069	102	368	10599	10532
1999	11904	80	337	11487	11392
2000	8335	78	361	7896	7831
2001	9776	67	343	9366	9318
2002	15128	74	265	14789	14740
2003	17615	64	229	17322	17276
2004	19802	39	424	19339	19224
2005	25972	28	315	25629	25522
2006	27108	16	247	26845	26747
2007	38435	11	219	38205	38094
2008	40154	9	177	39968	39687
2009	38220	5	130	38085	37795

7-8 历年限额以上企业商品购进、销售、库存总额

Total Purchases, Sales and Stock of Commercial Enterprises above Designated Size over Years

单位：万元

年份	商品购进总额	商品销售总额	批发	零售	年末库存总额
1978	82347	74936	50207	24729	7576
1979	91074	82878	55528	27350	8378
1980	109147	99324	66547	32777	10041
1981	131797	119936	80357	39579	12125
1982	156730	142615	95552	47063	14418
1983	160485	146042	97848	48194	14764
1984	214364	195072	130698	64374	19721
1985	254458	231557	155143	76414	23410
1986	630988	283945	190243	93702	28706
1987	380242	346021	231834	114187	34982
1988	714661	650342	435729	214613	65749
1989	729163	663539	444570	218969	67083
1990	766549	697560	467365	230195	70523
1991	796488	672666	433991	238675	74092
1992	881697	743990	473014	270976	64939
1993	1141163	1063567	725979	337588	92249
1994	1323263	1296363	912457	383906	177377
1995	1584470	1556882	1044334	512548	143404
1996	1694496	1737121	1117111	620010	166267
1997	1857884	1922001	1212399	709602	175715
1998	779319	863214	696921	166293	91640
1999	1064070	1106048	875799	230249	73620
2000	1232026	1354640	1072929	281711	58304
2001	1312924	1405409	1080688	324721	67415
2002	1588853	1682579	1188961	493618	102657
2003	1712564	1805840	1138496	667344	107996
2004		5406921	3479209	1927712	251427
2005	4798504	5683548	3882222	1801326	322445
2006	5324450	6487742	4215562	227179	335108
2007	6706290	8102415	4875668	3226748	485401
2008	8349926	10772768	6604662	4168106	790691
2009	8689984	10167222	6137228	4029994	839175

7-9 市场分类基本情况(2009年)

Basic Statistics on Market Classification (2009)

单位：个

项目	合计	城市	农村
合计	**901**	**228**	**673**
一、消费品市场	**837**	**203**	**634**
（一）消费品综合市场	344	56	288
（二）农副产品市场	399	99	300
1. 农副产品综合市场	390	95	295
2. 农副产品专业市场	9	4	5
（三）工业品消费市场	75	48	27
1. 工业消费品综合市场	30	18	12
2. 工业消费品专业市场	45	30	15
（四）其他消费品市场	19		19
二、生产资料市场	**64**	**25**	**39**
（一）生产资料综合市场	1		1
（二）工业生产资料市场	47	13	34
1. 机动车交易市场	4	2	2
2. 钢材交易市场	2	1	1
3. 煤炭交易市场			
4. 木材交易市场	5	1	4
5. 其他工业生产资料市场	36	9	27
（三）农业生产资料市场			
1. 农业生产资料综合市场			
2. 农业生产资料专业市场			
（四）其他生产资料市场	16	12	4

注：本表数据来源于市工商局。

7-10 历年城乡集市贸易

Statistics on Urban and Rural Trade Fairs over Years

单位：个

年　份	集贸市场 总　数	#城　市	#农　村
1978	35		35
1979	35		35
1980	35		35
1981	38		38
1982	40		40
1983	41		41
1984	43		43
1985	48		48
1986	57	7	50
1987	63	10	53
1988	66	12	54
1989	69	11	58
1990	73	10	63
1991	75	10	65
1992	53	7	46
1993	155	13	142
1994	162	12	150
1995	189	17	172
1996	219	20	199
1997	241	23	218
1998	252	25	227
1999	286	36	250
2000	308	29	279
2001	375	31	344
2002	495	28	467
2003	576	34	542
2004	610	35	575
2005	665	36	629
2006	812	39	773
2007	845	36	809
2008	871	228	643
2009	901	228	673

注：1995年前为工商系统口径，从1996年起为全市口径。2008年以前的城市集贸市场数只包括莞城的集贸市场，2008年起包括莞城、东城、南城和万江四大街道办的市场数。

主要统计指标解释

社会消费品零售总额 指各种经济类型的批发零售贸易业、餐饮业和其他行业对城乡居民和社会集团的消费品零售额总和。

商品购进总额 指从本企业以外的单位和个人购进（包括从国外直接进口）作为转卖或加工后转卖的商品金额（含增值税）。

商品销售总额 指对本企业以外的单位和个人出售的商品金额（包括售给本单位消费用的商品，含增值税。

期末库存 指批发和零售业企业年末已取得所有权的全部商品金额（含增值税）。

批发零售贸易业零售额 指专门从事商品转卖业务的各种经济类型独立核算的批发零售贸易企业、生产活动单位和个体户直接售给居民和社会集团的消费品零售额。

餐饮业零售额 指专门从事食品的烹饪、调制并直接零售给居民饮食的各种饭馆、酒馆、茶馆等餐饮业的商品零售额。

流动资产合计 指可以在一年内或者超过一年的一个营业周期内变现或耗用的资产。

固定资产合计 指使用期限超过一年，单位价值在规定标准以上，并且在使用过程中保持原有物质形态的资产。

无形及递延资产 无形资产：是指企业长期使用但是没有实物形态的资产。递延资产：是指不能全部计入当年损益，应在以后年度内分期摊销的各项费用。包括开办费用，租入固定资产的改良支出等。

所有者权益合计 指所有者在企业资产中享有的经济利益，它等于企业资产减去负债后的余额。包括实收资本（或股本）、资本公积、盈余公积和未分配利润等。

商品销售收入（营业收入） 指批发零售贸易企业商品销售收入、接受其他单位委托代销商品的收入和餐饮企业的营业收入。

营业税金及附加 指与企业营业收入有关的，应由各项经营业务分担的税金及附加，包括营业税、消费税、城市维护建设税、资源税、土地增值税、教育费附加等。

利润总额 指企业在生产经营过程中各种收入扣除各种耗费后的盈余，反映企业在报告期内实现的亏盈总额，包括营业利润、补贴收入、投资净收益和营业外收支净额。

应交增值税 指企业按税法规定，从事货物销售或提供加工、修理修配劳务等增加货物价值的活动本期应交纳的税金。指企业在报告期应交增值税额。

计算公式 本年应交增值税＝销项税额－（进项税额-进项税额转出）

－出口抵减内销产品应纳税额－减免税款＋出口退税

批发零售贸易、餐饮业统计限额标准

行业类别	统计指标名称	计量单位	限额标准
批发业	年主营业务收入	万元	2000及以上
零售业	年主营业务收入	万元	500及以上
住宿业、餐饮业	年主营业务收入	万元	200及以上

说明：

1. 外贸企业包括在批发业中，其年销售额以外币计量的，应折合成人民币，按批发业标准执行。

2. 本限额标准仅对批发企业及其活动单位、零售企业及其活动单位、住宿企业及其活动单位和餐饮企业及其活动单位划分限额，不包括个体户。

八、价格指数

Prices Indices

8-1　历年物价总指数（以上年价格为100）

General Price Indices over Years (Preceding Year=100)

年　份	商品零售价格总指数	#食品	#家用电器及音像器材	居民消费价格总指数	#食品	#服务项目
1978	100.4	101.6				
1979	102.6	107.1				
1980	110.9	114.5				
1981	109.3	110.3				
1982	101.2	100.8				
1983	99.6	99.5				
1984	98.6	97.5		99.3	97.5	102.0
1985	106.9	108.7		106.5	108.7	103.3
1986	104.4	105.0		104.2	105.0	102.3
1987	112.2	113.6		112.0	113.6	109.6
1988	132.8	133.9		136.0	133.9	168.0
1989	122.4	125.7		122.0	127.5	118.8
1990	94.9	92.8		96.6	92.8	111.0
1991	101.4	101.1		102.4	101.1	109.8
1992	107.7	109.0		109.2	109.0	117.9
1993	119.5	123.7		121.8	123.7	134.6
1994	118.4	125.9	99.6	123.5	126.4	141.2
1995	109.7	119.5	95.6	113.9	119.1	128.9
1996	104.7	108.1	94.5	106.8	107.8	115.0
1997	99.7	100.0	92.7	101.5	99.4	113.1
1998	98.7	99.9	93.3	99.9	99.5	108.4
1999	95.9	95.6	94.9	97.9	95.7	109.5
2000	100.1	100.3	97.2	101.5	100.4	112.8
2001	97.8	99.1	97.0	96.6	98.9	101.1
2002	99.1	100.9	98.0	98.1	99.0	98.7
2003	101.7	103.6	99.0	100.7	103.5	97.8
2004	103.2	108.6	98.7	103.0	108.6	99.7
2005	103.0	106.5	101.1	102.4	106.5	100.4
2006	102.8	100.1	100.5	101.2	100.1	101.6
2007	104.2	108.3	98.2	103.1	108.0	100.2
2008	107.9	115.6	100.4	105.5	115.1	100.1
2009	95.3	97.9	95.6	96.9	98.1	96.3

8-2 居民消费价格分类指数(2009年，以上年价格为100)

Consumer Price Indices by Category (2009, Preceding Year=100)

项目	指数
居民消费价格总指数	**96.9**
非食品价格指数	**96.4**
服务项目价格指数	**96.3**
扣除鲜菜鲜果总指数	**97.0**
消费品价格指数	**97.1**
一、食　品	**98.1**
粮食	104.2
大米	105.1
粮食制品	100.4
淀粉	97.9
干豆类及豆制品	99.6
油脂	83.1
肉禽及其制品	94.2
蛋	97.4
水产品	101.0
菜	95.7
鲜菜	95.7
干菜及菜制品	96.1
调味品	99.2
糖	106.4
食糖	103.0
糖果	103.7
茶及饮料	103.1
干鲜瓜果	95.9
鲜瓜果	96.0
糕点饼干	101.9
液体乳及乳制品	101.0
在外用膳食品	100.8
主食	100.7
炒菜	101.0
地方小吃	100.0
其他食品	102.7
二、烟酒及用品	**101.4**
烟草	99.9
酒	104.7
三、衣着	**97.2**
服装	96.5
衣着材料	100.6
棉布	100.8
化纤布	100.3
棉混纺布	101.1
毛线	100.0
鞋袜帽	98.5
鞋	99.7
袜子	91.8
帽子	97.3
衣着加工服务费	100.0
四、家庭设备用品及维修服务	**100.2**
耐用消费品	99.3
家具	100.7
家庭设备	98.2
室内装饰品	99.5
床上用品	105.6
家庭日用杂品	99.2
家庭服务及加工维修服务	100.8
五、医疗保健和个人用品	**98.2**
医疗保健	98.4
中药材及中成药	91.3
西药	101.6
医疗保健服务	100.0
个人用品及服务	97.8
化妆美容用品	95.6
清洁化妆用品	97.5
个人饰品	100.9
个人服务	99.8
六、交通和通信	**98.7**
交通	98.7
交通工具	100.9
市区公共交通费	100.0
城市间交通费	100.5
通信	98.7
通信工具	93.4
通信服务	100.0
七、娱乐教育文化用品及服务	**95.3**
文娱用耐用消费品及服务	96.4
教育	100.3
教材及参考书	100.6
学杂托幼费	100.3
文化娱乐类	99.0
文化娱乐用品	98.8
书报杂志	100.0
文娱费	98.5
旅游	86.1
八、居住	**91.3**
建房及装修材料	98.0
租房	100.0
自有住房	82.1
水、电、燃料	89.3

8-3 居民消费价格分月指数（2009年，以上年同月价格为100）

Consumer Price Indices by Month (2009, Same Month of Preceding Year=100)

项　　目	1 月	2 月	3 月	4 月	5 月	6 月
居民消费价格总指数	**100.2**	**95.5**	**97.0**	**96.5**	**97.1**	**95.9**
非食品价格指数	**97.1**	**95.8**	**96.1**	**96.4**	**96.5**	**95.9**
服务项目价格指数	**98.1**	**94.1**	**96.0**	**96.0**	**97.4**	**97.3**
扣除鲜菜鲜果总指数	**99.9**	**96.6**	**96.8**	**97.0**	**97.0**	**95.9**
消费品价格指数	**100.9**	**95.9**	**97.3**	**96.6**	**97.0**	**95.5**
一、食品	**106.9**	**94.9**	**98.9**	**96.7**	**98.2**	**96.0**
#粮食	108.6	106.3	107.0	106.4	102.8	102.7
肉禽及制品	105.3	92.6	92.0	91.5	90.6	89.6
蛋	105.7	90.9	103.0	101.2	97.1	94.1
水产品	113.3	102.6	99.7	103.6	104.3	95.3
菜	117.0	76.0	106.1	87.6	102.3	93.8
二、烟酒及用品	**103.5**	**103.6**	**103.2**	**101.9**	**100.9**	**101.7**
#烟草	101.7	101.7	101.7	99.9	99.8	99.8
酒	107.3	106.3	105.8	105.8	105.8	105.7
三、衣着	**95.4**	**97.7**	**97.3**	**97.2**	**97.1**	**96.8**
#服装	93.1	96.6	96.6	96.8	96.7	96.2
四、家庭设备用品及维修服务	**105.4**	**103.1**	**101.2**	**101.5**	**100.0**	**99.3**
#耐用消费品	101.8	101.7	99.1	100.1	99.4	100.3
五、医疗保健和个人用品	**97.7**	**97.6**	**98.2**	**98.4**	**98.3**	**97.7**
#医疗保健	98.7	98.4	98.4	98.4	98.0	97.5
个人用品及服务	95.8	96.1	97.9	98.4	98.8	98.1
六、交通和通信	**99.9**	**98.4**	**98.8**	**99.4**	**99.7**	**99.0**
#交通	100.1	97.5	98.2	99.3	99.7	99.9
通信	99.7	99.5	99.4	99.5	99.6	98.1
七、娱乐教育文化用品及服务	**97.8**	**92.7**	**95.6**	**95.4**	**98.0**	**97.8**
#文娱用耐用消费品及服务	98.3	97.9	98.0	97.6	97.2	96.8
教育	100.4	100.4	100.4	100.4	100.4	100.4
文化娱乐类	99.3	99.7	98.9	98.5	98.5	98.4
旅游类	93.8	75.9	85.2	85.3	95.4	94.7
八、居住	**90.1**	**90.4**	**89.2**	**89.8**	**88.6**	**87.5**
#建房及装饰材料	98.2	99.6	95.1	97.4	98.6	97.4
租房	100.0	100.0	100.0	100.0	100.0	100.0
自有住房	79.5	80.0	80.0	80.0	80.0	80.0
水、电、燃料	87.8	87.6	87.2	87.2	84.4	83.0

8-3 续表

项　　目	7 月	8 月	9 月	10 月	11 月	12 月
居民消费价格总指数	**94.8**	**95.8**	**96.3**	**96.4**	**98.0**	**99.9**
非食品价格指数	**95.3**	**94.7**	**95.8**	**96.0**	**97.7**	**99.6**
服务项目价格指数	**95.7**	**93.8**	**95.8**	**95.5**	**97.0**	**99.3**
扣除鲜菜鲜果总指数	**95.7**	**95.2**	**96.0**	**96.7**	**98.2**	**99.6**
消费品价格指数	**94.5**	**96.5**	**96.5**	**96.7**	**98.4**	**100.1**
一、食品	**93.9**	**98.2**	**97.3**	**97.4**	**98.8**	**100.6**
#粮食	102.8	103.0	102.0	102.3	103.2	104.1
肉禽及制品	90.6	90.9	93.8	95.7	100.3	98.7
蛋	97.6	96.9	91.4	96.8	98.0	98.4
水产品	98.1	98.1	95.4	101.7	98.5	102.2
菜	75.7	106.6	102.3	92.7	98.1	108.7
二、烟酒及用品	**102.1**	**100.3**	**100.5**	**100.4**	**99.7**	**99.8**
#烟草	99.8	98.8	98.8	98.8	98.8	98.8
酒	105.8	103.0	103.7	103.3	101.8	102.1
三、衣着	**96.3**	**97.6**	**97.5**	**98.0**	**98.2**	**98.0**
#服装	96.1	96.9	96.8	97.6	97.5	97.4
四、家庭设备用品及维修服务	**99.6**	**99.3**	**99.1**	**97.6**	**97.9**	**98.2**
#耐用消费品	99.2	98.9	98.6	98.2	97.8	97.3
五、医疗保健和个人用品	**97.9**	**97.2**	**98.1**	**98.8**	**98.9**	**99.7**
#医疗保健	97.4	97.4	99.1	99.4	98.8	99.7
个人用品及服务	98.9	96.9	96.5	97.6	99.1	99.8
六、交通和通信	**98.3**	**97.8**	**97.8**	**97.8**	**98.5**	**99.5**
#交通	98.5	97.3	97.4	97.4	98.9	100.6
通信	98.1	98.3	98.2	98.2	98.2	98.2
七、娱乐教育文化用品及服务	**94.6**	**91.1**	**94.5**	**93.6**	**95.5**	**97.8**
#文娱用耐用消费品及服务	96.1	96.3	94.7	94.5	94.5	94.5
教育	100.4	100.4	100.2	100.2	100.2	100.2
文化娱乐类	98.8	98.9	98.8	99.3	99.2	99.6
旅游类	84.6	74.0	84.9	82.4	88.1	95.7
八、居住	**88.3**	**89.5**	**91.0**	**92.5**	**97.4**	**102.5**
#建房及装饰材料	97.4	97.4	98.5	98.2	98.6	99.8
租房	100.0	100.0	100.0	100.0	100.0	100.0
自有住房	80.0	80.0	80.6	83.0	86.8	97.8
水、电、燃料	84.5	86.8	89.2	91.5	99.9	105.9

8-4 居民消费价格分月指数（2009年，以上月价格为100）

Consumer Price Indices by Month (2009, Preceding Month=100)

项　　目	1 月	2 月	3 月	4 月	5 月	6 月
居民消费价格总指数	**101.0**	**98.7**	**100.1**	**99.5**	**99.8**	**100.0**
非食品价格指数	**100.3**	**98.6**	**99.6**	**100.0**	**100.1**	**99.6**
服务项目价格指数	**102.7**	**96.4**	**100.0**	**99.9**	**100.7**	**99.5**
扣除鲜菜鲜果总指数	**100.9**	**99.0**	**99.5**	**99.9**	**99.8**	**99.4**
消费品价格指数	**100.4**	**99.5**	**100.1**	**99.3**	**99.5**	**100.2**
一、食品	**102.4**	**99.0**	**100.9**	**98.3**	**99.2**	**101.0**
#粮食	99.8	101.6	101.9	100.3	99.1	100.3
肉禽及制品	103.6	97.1	98.7	99.9	98.4	99.0
蛋	101.1	99.6	100.0	100.0	99.7	99.6
水产品	107.6	104.6	96.5	97.4	97.5	95.4
菜	105.9	92.3	119.3	87.6	95.8	116.1
二、烟酒及用品	**100.2**	**100.0**	**99.9**	**99.7**	**99.2**	**100.7**
#烟草	100.0	100.0	100.0	99.2	99.6	100.0
酒	100.7	100.0	100.6	100.0	100.0	99.9
三、衣着	**99.7**	**99.9**	**99.8**	**99.4**	**99.6**	**99.9**
#服装	99.5	99.9	99.6	99.2	99.5	99.9
四、家庭设备用品及维修服务	**103.2**	**96.7**	**99.7**	**100.7**	**99.1**	**99.5**
#耐用消费品	99.6	99.7	98.1	101.4	100.0	99.9
五、医疗保健和个人用品	**99.3**	**99.6**	**100.0**	**100.3**	**100.2**	**99.5**
#医疗保健	99.1	99.7	100.0	100.2	100.2	99.8
个人用品及服务	99.8	99.4	100.1	100.5	100.2	99.0
六、交通和通信	**99.5**	**99.0**	**99.9**	**100.4**	**100.2**	**99.7**
#交通	99.2	98.3	99.9	100.7	100.3	100.9
通信	99.9	99.8	100.0	100.0	100.0	98.5
七、娱乐教育文化用品及服务	**102.5**	**95.7**	**99.9**	**99.7**	**101.2**	**98.8**
#文娱用耐用消费品及服务	99.3	99.6	99.9	99.6	99.5	99.6
教育	100.0	100.0	100.0	100.0	100.0	100.0
文化娱乐类	100.0	100.0	99.6	100.0	99.9	99.9
旅游类	110.8	84.0	100.3	99.0	105.9	95.6
八、居住	**99.2**	**100.2**	**98.6**	**99.8**	**99.4**	**99.8**
#建房及装饰材料	100.1	101.3	97.4	101.6	100.3	97.5
租房	100.0	100.0	100.0	100.0	100.0	100.0
自有住房	97.8	100.0	100.0	100.0	100.0	100.0
水、电、燃料	98.9	99.8	98.4	98.8	98.7	100.9

8-4 续表

项　　目	7 月	8 月	9 月	10 月	11 月	12 月
居民消费价格总指数	**100.8**	**99.5**	**100.3**	**99.9**	**100.0**	**100.3**
非食品价格指数	**101.0**	**99.5**	**100.4**	**100.1**	**100.2**	**100.1**
服务项目价格指数	**101.5**	**99.3**	**100.1**	**100.4**	**99.7**	**99.3**
扣除鲜菜鲜果总指数	**100.7**	**99.5**	**100.3**	**100.2**	**100.2**	**100.3**
消费品价格指数	**100.6**	**99.5**	**100.4**	**99.8**	**100.1**	**100.7**
一、食品	**100.3**	**99.3**	**100.1**	**99.5**	**99.6**	**100.8**
#粮食	100.3	100.1	100.6	99.3	100.2	100.5
肉禽及制品	98.9	100.3	101.2	100.2	102.0	99.6
蛋	101.0	99.4	99.8	99.8	99.2	99.0
水产品	102.4	96.6	99.1	102.8	98.4	104.6
菜	101.4	99.6	99.1	98.0	97.9	99.7
二、烟酒及用品	**100.0**	**100.0**	**100.1**	**100.1**	**99.7**	**100.1**
#烟草	100.0	100.0	100.0	100.0	100.0	100.0
酒	100.0	100.0	100.2	100.3	100.0	100.4
三、衣着	**99.7**	**100.0**	**100.0**	**100.0**	**100.1**	**99.9**
#服装	99.9	99.9	100.0	100.0	100.0	99.9
四、家庭设备用品及维修服务	**100.6**	**99.5**	**100.2**	**98.5**	**100.4**	**100.3**
#耐用消费品	99.5	99.2	100.7	99.9	99.5	99.9
五、医疗保健和个人用品	**100.6**	**99.4**	**100.3**	**100.4**	**99.5**	**100.5**
#医疗保健	100.7	100.0	101.0	100.0	98.8	100.2
个人用品及服务	100.6	98.4	99.2	101.2	100.7	100.9
六、交通和通信	**100.6**	**99.6**	**100.3**	**99.8**	**100.4**	**100.1**
#交通	101.3	99.1	100.5	99.7	100.8	100.1
通信	100.0	100.0	100.0	100.0	100.0	100.0
七、娱乐教育文化用品及服务	**102.7**	**98.6**	**99.9**	**100.8**	**99.4**	**98.7**
#文娱用耐用消费品及服务	98.9	99.8	98.4	99.8	100.0	99.9
教育	100.0	100.0	100.2	100.0	100.0	100.0
文化娱乐类	100.4	99.6	99.9	100.1	99.9	100.3
旅游类	112.2	94.9	100.6	103.4	97.7	94.4
八、居住	**101.1**	**100.2**	**101.3**	**100.4**	**101.3**	**101.2**
#建房及装饰材料	101.5	98.7	101.0	99.7	101.7	99.2
租房	100.0	100.0	100.0	100.0	100.0	100.0
自有住房	100.0	100.0	100.0	100.0	100.0	100.0
水、电、燃料	101.5	101.1	102.2	100.9	101.9	103.0

8-5 居民消费价格分月指数(2009年，以上年12月价格为100)

Consumer Price Indices by Month (2009, December of Preceding Year=100)

项　　目	1 月	2 月	3 月	4 月	5 月	6 月
居民消费价格总指数	**101.0**	**99.7**	**99.8**	**99.3**	**99.0**	**99.1**
非食品价格指数	**100.3**	**98.9**	**98.6**	**98.6**	**98.7**	**98.2**
服务项目价格指数	**102.7**	**99.0**	**98.9**	**98.8**	**99.5**	**99.0**
扣除鲜菜鲜果总指数	**100.9**	**99.9**	**99.4**	**99.2**	**99.0**	**98.4**
消费品价格指数	**100.4**	**100.0**	**100.1**	**99.4**	**98.9**	**99.1**
一、食品	**102.4**	**101.4**	**102.4**	**100.6**	**99.8**	**100.9**
#粮食	99.8	101.4	103.4	103.7	102.7	103.1
肉禽及制品	103.6	100.6	99.3	99.1	97.5	96.6
蛋	101.1	100.7	100.7	100.7	100.4	100.0
水产品	107.6	112.6	108.6	105.8	103.2	98.5
菜	105.9	97.7	116.5	102.0	97.7	113.5
二、烟酒及用品	**100.2**	**100.2**	**100.1**	**99.8**	**99.0**	**99.8**
#烟草	100.0	100.0	100.0	99.2	98.8	98.8
酒	100.7	100.7	101.2	101.2	101.2	101.2
三、衣着	**99.7**	**99.6**	**99.4**	**98.7**	**98.3**	**98.3**
#服装	99.5	99.4	99.0	98.2	97.7	97.6
四、家庭设备用品及维修服务	**103.2**	**99.8**	**99.5**	**100.2**	**99.3**	**98.8**
#耐用消费品	99.6	99.2	97.3	98.7	98.7	98.6
五、医疗保健和个人用品	**99.3**	**98.9**	**99.0**	**99.3**	**99.5**	**99.0**
#医疗保健	99.1	98.8	98.8	99.0	99.2	99.0
个人用品及服务	99.8	99.2	99.3	99.8	100.0	98.9
六、交通和通信	**99.5**	**98.6**	**98.5**	**98.9**	**99.0**	**98.7**
#交通	99.2	97.4	97.3	98.0	98.3	99.1
通信	99.9	99.7	99.7	99.8	99.8	98.3
七、娱乐教育文化用品及服务	**102.5**	**98.1**	**98.0**	**97.7**	**98.9**	**97.8**
#文娱用耐用消费品及服务	99.3	98.9	98.7	98.3	97.9	97.5
教育	100.0	100.0	100.0	100.0	100.0	100.0
文化娱乐类	100.0	99.9	99.5	99.5	99.5	99.3
旅游类	110.8	93.1	93.4	92.4	97.9	93.6
八、居住	**99.2**	**99.4**	**97.9**	**97.8**	**97.2**	**97.0**
#建房及装饰材料	100.1	101.4	98.8	100.3	100.6	98.0
租房	100.0	100.0	100.0	100.0	100.0	100.0
自有住房	97.8	97.8	97.8	97.8	97.8	97.8
水、电、燃料	98.9	98.6	97.1	95.9	94.6	95.4

8-5 续表

项目	7月	8月	9月	10月	11月	12月
居民消费价格总指数	**99.9**	**99.3**	**99.6**	**99.6**	**99.6**	**99.9**
非食品价格指数	**99.2**	**98.7**	**99.1**	**99.2**	**99.5**	**99.6**
服务项目价格指数	**100.4**	**99.7**	**99.8**	**100.2**	**99.9**	**99.3**
扣除鲜菜鲜果总指数	**99.1**	**98.6**	**98.9**	**99.2**	**99.3**	**99.6**
消费品价格指数	**99.7**	**99.2**	**99.6**	**99.3**	**99.5**	**100.1**
一、食品	**101.2**	**100.5**	**100.6**	**100.2**	**99.8**	**100.6**
#粮食	103.4	103.6	104.2	103.4	103.6	104.1
肉禽及制品	95.5	95.8	96.9	97.1	99.1	98.7
蛋	101.0	100.5	100.3	100.1	99.3	98.4
水产品	100.8	97.4	96.5	99.3	97.7	102.2
菜	115.1	114.6	113.6	111.3	109.0	108.7
二、烟酒及用品	**99.8**	**99.8**	**99.8**	**99.9**	**99.6**	**99.8**
#烟草	98.8	98.8	98.8	98.8	98.8	98.8
酒	101.2	101.2	101.3	101.7	101.7	102.1
三、衣着	**98.0**	**98.0**	**98.0**	**98.0**	**98.1**	**98.0**
#服装	97.5	97.5	97.5	97.5	97.5	97.4
四、家庭设备用品及维修服务	**99.3**	**98.8**	**99.1**	**97.5**	**97.9**	**98.2**
#耐用消费品	98.1	97.3	98.0	97.9	97.4	97.3
五、医疗保健和个人用品	**99.6**	**99.0**	**99.3**	**99.8**	**99.3**	**99.7**
#医疗保健	99.6	99.6	100.6	100.6	99.4	99.7
个人用品及服务	99.5	97.9	97.1	98.2	98.9	99.8
六、交通和通信	**99.4**	**98.9**	**99.2**	**99.0**	**99.4**	**99.5**
#交通	100.4	99.6	100.1	99.7	100.5	100.6
通信	98.3	98.3	98.3	98.3	98.2	98.2
七、娱乐教育文化用品及服务	**100.4**	**99.0**	**98.9**	**99.7**	**99.1**	**97.8**
#文娱用耐用消费品及服务	96.4	96.2	94.7	94.5	94.5	94.5
教育	100.0	100.0	100.2	100.2	100.2	100.2
文化娱乐类	99.8	99.4	99.3	99.4	99.3	99.6
旅游类	105.0	99.7	100.3	103.7	101.3	95.7
八、居住	**98.0**	**98.2**	**99.5**	**99.9**	**101.2**	**102.5**
#建房及装饰材料	99.5	98.2	99.2	98.9	100.5	99.8
租房	100.0	100.0	100.0	100.0	100.0	100.0
自有住房	97.8	97.8	97.8	97.8	97.8	97.8
水、电、燃料	96.8	97.9	100.1	101.0	102.9	105.9

8-6 商品零售价格分类指数（2009年，以上年价格为100）

Retail Price Indices by Category (2009, Preceding Year=100)

项　　目	指　数	项　　目	指　数
商品零售价格总指数	**95.3**	3. 音像器材类	96.7
一、食品类	**97.9**	**六、文化办公用品**	**98.7**
1. 粮食	104.2	**七、日用品**	**101.5**
2. 淀粉	97.9	1. 日用百货	99.9
3. 干豆类及豆制品	99.6	2. 日用杂品	97.8
4. 油脂	83.1	3. 洗涤用品	104.8
5. 肉禽及其制品	94.2	4. 其他日用品	100.4
6. 蛋	97.4	**八、体育娱乐用品**	**98.6**
7. 水产品	101.0	1. 体育用品	100.1
8. 菜	95.7	2. 娱乐用品	97.2
9. 调味品	99.2	**九、交通、通信用品**	**97.6**
10.糖	106.4	1. 交通运输机械	100.8
11.干鲜瓜果	95.9	2. 通信器材类	94.1
12.糕点饼干面包	101.9	**十、家具**	**100.7**
13.液体乳及乳制品	100.9	**十一、化妆品类**	**97.4**
14.在外用膳食品	100.8	**十二、金银珠宝类**	**91.9**
15.其他食品	102.7	**十三、中西药品及医疗保健用品类**	**97.8**
二、饮料、烟酒	**102.4**	1. 医疗器具及用品	100.0
1. 茶及饮料	103.1	2. 中药材及中成药	91.3
2. 烟草	99.9	3. 西药	101.6
3. 酒	104.7	4. 保健器具及用品	100.3
三、服装、鞋帽类	**97.4**	**十四、书报杂志及电子出版物类**	**100.2**
1. 服装	96.5	1. 教材及参考书	100.6
2. 鞋袜帽	98.5	2. 书报杂志	100.0
3. 其他	99.1	3. 电子音像制品	99.5
四、纺织品类	**104.4**	**十五、燃料类**	**83.2**
1. 衣着材料	100.6	1. 煤炭及制品类	100.0
2. 床上用品	105.6	2. 石油及制品类	83.1
五、家用电器及音像器材	**95.6**	**十六、建筑材料及五金电料类**	**96.1**
1. 家庭设备	98.2	1. 建筑装璜材料	95.2
2. 文娱用耐用消费品	91.3	2. 五金电料类	98.6

8-7 主要年份食品全社会综合平均价格

Comprehensive Average Prices of Food in Main Years

项　目	规格等级	单位	价格(元)						
			1985年	1990年	1995年	2000年	2005年	2008年	2009年
大　米	标　　二	千克	0.39	0.85	2.93	2.16	2.90	3.31	3.43
面　粉	南　　方	千克	0.74	1.70	3.11	3.65	2.53	5.60	5.82
豆　类	一等大豆	千克	1.07	2.94	3.77	3.99	5.57	8.26	7.38
植物油	一级花生油	千克	3.55	7.36	12.53	10.62	11.95	21.85	16.95
猪　肉	鲜 上 肉	千克	3.55	9.50	15.98	13.78	18.53	26.18	21.97
瘦猪肉	鲜　　肉	千克	7.20	13.35	23.73	18.04	25.00	32.65	30.08
牛　肉	去骨统肉	千克	5.60	11.22	22.40	18.61	25.73	41.65	45.43
白条鸡	开　　膛	千克		9.21	13.80	14.61	21.82	25.83	26.11
鸡	上等竹丝鸡	千克	7.20	13.04	22.31	15.77	14.99	17.79	17.10
鸭	上等番鸭	千克	3.17	5.81	11.65	14.28	14.33	17.44	17.51
鸡　蛋	新鲜鸡蛋	千克	3.63	6.70	7.91	6.21	7.73	12.27	12.42
再制蛋	皮　　蛋	千克	2.40	4.52	6.40	5.85	7.05	8.52	8.59
香　肠	本地产中等	千克	11.60	23.75	52.13	53.67	31.67	88.50	90.00
烧　鹅	本 地 产	千克	8.53	14.41	32.54	30.67	44.49	56.28	55.25
胖头鱼	中等0.5公斤以上一条	千克	2.91	4.81	9.56	8.80	11.79	14.66	14.53
红三鱼	冰　　鲜	千克			9.13	16.20	24.85	29.07	28.33
虾	罗 氏 虾	千克				40.06	37.18	53.63	65.20
草　鱼	中等1公斤以上一条	千克	2.69	6.67	13.30	10.18	14.25	20.86	20.76
精　盐	再 制 盐	千克		0.49	1.20	1.60	1.27	1.85	1.23
白砂糖	国家机制一级	千克	1.36	2.71	6.10	4.32	5.23	6.40	6.50
红　糖	一级冰片糖	千克		2.95	6.55	4.95	5.70	9.50	9.50
卷　烟	广州双喜	盒	1.12	1.40	4.87	5.92	6.62	6.50	6.50
白　酒	0.5千克装	瓶	2.30	2.40	5.55	6.58	7.25	8.48	6.25
啤　酒	热 12 度	瓶		1.60	6.40	4.92	4.66	5.00	5.00
红　茶	一　　级	千克	3.98	12.76	28.95	64.68	6.91	127.92	129.58
绿　茶	一　　级	千克	8.00	10.34	15.40	59.21	27.40	123.30	123.00
苹　果	一　　级	千克	2.14	4.89	6.54	5.80	6.44	8.07	8.61
梨	一　　级	千克	1.86	4.40	5.46	3.99	3.74	4.58	4.40
柑	一　　级	千克	1.75	1.97	3.28	3.27	3.54	5.34	3.92
香　蕉	一　　级	千克	1.24	2.22	3.90	3.18	3.04	4.35	4.02
荔　枝	桂味/糯米糍	千克	2.57	7.95	20.50	14.93	11.75	15.30	12.70
面　包	中　　等	千克	2.00	5.09	4.39	15.25	7.39	16.70	16.70
饼　干	一　　级	千克	2.48	7.88	9.03	22.97	8.80	24.17	22.00
奶　粉	国　　产	千克	4.80	5.27	25.12	24.55	22.33	44.22	32.00

注：2000年起茶叶的档次提高。

8-8 工业品出厂价格总指数(2003－2009年，以上年价格为100)

General Producer Price Index (PPI) for Manufactured Goods (2003-2009,Preceding Year=100)

项　　目	2003年	2004年	2005年	2006年	2007年	2008年	2009年
工业品价格总指数	98.3	101.4	100.4	100.7	101.4	101.7	96.8
#轻工业	98.2	100.2	99.9	100.2	101.4	102.6	97.7
重工业	101.7	105.4	100.6	101.1	101.5	101.0	96.1
#非金属矿采选业	95.6	96.5	97.0	100.1	101.3	101.7	103.9
农副食品加工业	92.4	107.7	107.5	99.2	106.8	119.1	93.2
食品制造业	99.1	100.9	100.3	100.2	101.5	101.7	97.2
饮料制造业	99.4	98.6	99.2	100.8	99.9	103.0	102.2
纺织业	100.6	103.5	101.5	102.2	101.5	104.2	99.3
纺织服装、鞋、帽制造业	100.5	109.8	100.9	100.5	100.9	100.5	98.3
皮革、皮毛、羽毛(绒)及其制品业	103.7	101.4	101.1	101.0	105.6	103.7	100.8
木材加工及木、竹、藤、棕、草制品业	98.7	100.8	100.5	102.6	101.6	106.3	100.4
家具制造业	99.6	99.9	100.7	102.2	101.8	103.1	100.9
造纸及纸制品业	96.8	97.4	100.8	101.8	101.4	104.3	94.3
印刷业和记录媒介的复制	103.3	102.9	99.6	98.2	100.4	103.7	100.4
文教体育用品制造业	100.2	100.1	101.8	103.9	103.3	101.6	100.4
石油加工、炼焦及核燃料加工业	115.8	113.7	122.8	117.0	104.6	120.1	88.5
化学原料及化学制品制造业	102.5	110.3	103.5	101.2	106.7	104.8	92.7
医药制造业	101.6	96.9	101.1	100.4	105.7	102.3	97.5
化学纤维制造业	102.9	105.0	104.4	101.0	101.6	95.1	87.1
橡胶制品业	96.4	98.5	101.0	104.1	99.8	100.2	97.5
塑料制品业	99.9	104.3	107.4	101.7	101.0	102.0	96.7
非金属矿物制品业	99.8	112.4	96.7	100.3	102.2	104.7	99.0
黑色金属冶炼及压延加工业	108.3	123.8	101.2	94.2	113.4	130.1	79.1
有色金属冶炼及压延加工业	102.0	118.7	106.8	136.6	110.0	98.7	87.3
金属制品业	97.6	102.8	100.8	103.0	104.9	105.9	96.2
通用设备制造业	100.5	101.3	104.0	102.8	100.1	103.8	99.2
专用设备制造业	96.7	99.1	101.6	100.9	99.7	103.6	99.1
交通运输设备制造业	97.2	102.1	99.2	96.7	95.7	99.7	100.2
电气机械及器材制造业	98.4	101.4	103.7	106.6	104.3	99.7	93.0
通信设备、计算机及其他电子设备制造业	96.7	98.4	96.9	95.9	98.3	97.6	96.1
仪器仪表及文化、办公用机械制造业	95.3	98.4	100.6	102.2	100.4	100.5	99.1
工艺品及其他制造业	101.6	100.2	101.6	106.0	102.2	103.9	103.0
电力、热力的生产和供应业	97.5	101.1	102.3	101.7	101.4	103.4	102.4
水的生产和供应业	103.2	101.7	100.8	103.4	104.1	102.8	101.3

主要统计指标解释

居民消费价格指数　是度量消费商品及服务项目价格水平随着时间而变动的相对数，反映居民家庭购买的消费品及服务价格水平的变动情况。它是宏观经济分析、决策、调控和价格总水平监测以及国民经济核算的重要指标。其按年度计算的变动率通常被用来作为反映通货膨胀(或紧缩)程度的指标。

商品零售价格指数　是度量市场商品零售价格水平变动趋势和变动程度的相对数，反映商品在流通过程中最后一个环节的价格即工业、商业、餐饮业和其他零售企业向城乡居民、机关团体出售生活消费品和办公用品价格水平的变动趋势。它可以为国家宏观调控和国民经济核算提供参考依据，并在此基础上派生其他价格指数。

九、对外经济贸易与旅游

Foreign Economy, Trade and Tourism

9-1　主要年份对外经济与旅游业主要指标

Main Indicators of Foreign Trade and Economic Cooperation and Tourism in Main Years

指　　标	单 位	1979年	1985年	1990年	1995年	2000年	2005年	2008年	2009年
进出口总额	万美元			108229	1539112	3204526	7437150	11329947	9415458
出口总额	万美元	5382	17545	56828	779867	1715927	4092905	6553738	5516861
进口总额	万美元			51401	759245	1488599	3344245	4776209	3898597
新签利用外资协议(合同)数	宗	184	625	1267	3077	1276	992	588	601
#增资项目	宗						1138	815	484
#“三来一补”项目	宗	184	514	1075	2094	871	219	35	22
“三资”项目	宗		111	192	983	405	773	553	579
合同规定外商投资额	万美元	476	6815	30180	330920	183633	475238	393701	203040
#增资项目	万美元						187422	170446	66735
#“三来一补”项目	万美元	476	1870	12346	97428	69302	166363	134952	41420
“三资”项目	万美元		4945	17834	233492	114331	308875	258749	161620
实际利用外资(不含对外借款)	万美元	173	2894	24319	105665	164712	375139	322570	294157
“三来一补”项目	万美元	173	1511	14309	38418	55975	93023	77902	34758
“三资”项目	万美元		1383	10010	67247	108737	282116	244668	259399
本年止累计“三来一补”企业投产宗数	宗	140	1592	3880	8447	9917	8997	7128	6757
年末“三来一补”企业从业人员	万人	1.15	9.82	21.48	59.44	72.89	126.49	108.00	91.24
本年止累计“三资”企业投产数	宗		51	454	2629	3908	6657	7647	7940
年末“三资”企业从业人员	万人		0.64	3.81	25.01	87.17	145.50	162.00	150.00
当年来料加工企业转为三资或民营企业	家							197.00	339.00
合同规定外商投资额(新口径)	万美元						298029	258749	161620
实际利用外资(新口径)	万美元						146796	244668	259399
全年接待旅游人数	万人次			125	89	291	1156	1872	2037
#国际及港澳台旅游者	万人次			27	27	106	169	268	286
#外国人	万人次			1	6	15	70	103	104
国内旅客	万人次			98	62	185	987	1604	1751
国际旅游收入	万美元			1025	5679	7617	28189	45614	51756
三星级以上宾馆酒店客房数	间			3793	7568	18024	18258	19510	16332
宾馆酒店客房开房率	%			60.19	68.80	61.88	58.90	58.90	57.96

注：1. 对外经济部分除有注明新口径的以外均为旧口径，旧口径包括“三资”和“三来一补”，新口径不含“三来一补”且以验资作为统计标准，后同。
2. 2008年起对外经济各项指标为新口径，与往年数不可比。
3. 2002年起旅游业指标采用旅游局口径，与往年数不可比。

9-2 主要年份进出口贸易

Total Imports and Exports in Main Years

单位：万美元

项　　目	1995年	2000年	2001年	2002年	2003年	2004年	2005年	2008年	2009年
进出口总额	**1539112**	**3204526**	**3445457**	**4424706**	**5210623**	**6451775**	**7437150**	**11329947**	**9415458**
出口总额	**779867**	**1715927**	**1898924**	**2373646**	**2800227**	**3519237**	**4092905**	**6553738**	**5516861**
按贸易方式分									
#一般贸易	23180	20937	25945	34848	48988	85056	175502	487193	571682
来料加工装配	434646	834347	940908	1171688	1257934	1503757	1611676	2428365	1823160
进料加工	320186	858409	931766	1167047	1492723	1929967	2304325	3585619	3055047
其他	1855	2234	305	63	582	457	1402	52561	66971
按经济类型分									
#国有企业	474304	867501	972541	1189726	991762	1086698	1139776	1590416	1112383
三资企业	305061	835611	908388	1153178	1498993	1948473	2353253	3801299	3345624
集体企业	122	12259	17584	25798	27072	30229	37893	107400	93853
民营企业			143	4905	282079	453457	561650	1052746	961892
进口总额	**759245**	**1488599**	**1546533**	**2051060**	**2410396**	**2932538**	**3344245**	**4776209**	**3898597**
按贸易方式分									
#一般贸易	5394	72475	68392	83522	144235	222262	236133	455447	456075
来料加工装配	353138	645562	684323	922916	962367	1090197	1216566	1712939	1297315
进料加工	259397	616319	656910	886699	1127404	1402413	1625629	2206139	1820882
其他	141316	154243	5513	4112	5551	217666	265917	401684	324325
按经济类型分									
#国有企业	419827	764945	795407	1019994	832593	855107	987421	1377786	994470
三资企业	329164	706145	733492	1002467	1308831	1655308	1882393	2573134	2159599
集体企业	243	10267	12101	17930	19408	24151	32167	55317	56164
民营企业			21	6521	244005	391706	439521	766724	681737
贸易顺差	**20622**	**227328**	**352391**	**322586**	**389831**	**586699**	**748660**	**1777529**	**1618264**

9-3 历年进出口总额

Total Value of Imports and Exports over Years

单位：万美元

年 份	进出口总额	出口总额	#一般贸易	来料加工装配	进料加工	进口总额	#一般贸易	来料加工装配	进料加工
1978		3938							
1979		5382							
1980		7737							
1981		9173							
1982		10879							
1983		11890							
1984		12966							
1985		17545							
1986		23280							
1987		26755							
1988		31781							
1989		34868							
1990	108229	56828				51401			
1991	317463	165159				152304			
1992	509007	260272				248735			
1993	675647	321137				354510			
1994	882997	429416				453581			
1995	1539112	779867	23180	434646	320186	759245	5394	353138	259397
1996	1784222	918683	16377	496833	405066	865539	8956	383988	309710
1997	2129885	1136768	18020	582863	535708	993117	7598	445237	420014
1998	2327324	1306055	15409	652853	636822	1021269	10406	462194	463450
1999	2846291	1515391	16347	759638	738191	1330900	51726	584224	582721
2000	3204526	1715927	20937	834347	858409	1488599	72475	645562	616319
2001	3445457	1898924	25945	940908	931766	1546533	68392	684323	656910
2002	4424706	2373646	34848	1171688	1167047	2051060	83522	922916	886699
2003	5210623	2800227	48988	1257934	1492723	2410396	144235	962367	1127404
2004	6451775	3519237	85056	1503757	1929967	2932538	222262	1090197	1402413
2005	7437150	4092905	175502	1611676	2304325	3344245	236133	1216566	1625629
2006	8422107	4737640	265784	1661399	2806910	3684467	259709	1265725	1879233
2007	10687290	6023212	357941	2235125	3398212	4664078	371073	1702595	2196521
2008	11329947	6553738	487193	2428365	3585619	4776209	455447	1712939	2206139
2009	9415458	5516861	571682	1823160	3055047	3898597	456075	1297315	1820882

注：出口总额1990年以前为外经贸口径，1990年起为海关口径。

9-4 分国别(地区)进出口总值（2008-2009年）

Total Value of Imports and Exports by Country (Region) (2008-2009)

单位：亿美元

国别(地区)	实际出口		进口到货	
	2009年	2008年	2009年	2008年
亚洲	273.35	303.47	340.64	415.31
东南亚联盟	17.78	20.99	54.38	64.69
非洲	2.95	2.93	1.26	1.64
欧洲	96.30	131.07	19.71	25.20
欧洲共同体	92.56	125.03	18.38	23.48
拉美洲	13.24	17.25	9.26	10.82
北美洲	157.70	190.71	16.38	21.17
大洋洲	8.13	9.90	2.44	3.55
美国	149.26	177.27	14.40	19.38
香港	174.49	194.94	4.65	7.07
日本	46.95	48.30	71.70	88.32
荷兰	17.49	27.67	1.63	2.19
德国	23.21	26.47	5.41	8.21
英国	15.96	22.18	1.88	2.37
韩国	14.13	16.05	32.49	39.08
台湾	7.12	9.31	73.39	90.63
法国	7.83	9.29	1.13	1.54
加拿大	8.43	13.44	1.98	1.78
澳大利亚	7.56	9.26	1.79	3.03
新加坡	5.53	7.16	7.56	9.07
马来西亚	3.14	3.16	14.39	17.52

9-5 主要商品类别出口总值（2007–2009年）

Total Export Value by Category of Main Commodities (2007-2009)

单位：亿美元

商品名称	2007年	2008年	2009年
机电产品	436.87	483.66	387.52
高新技术产品	197.82	201.49	159.39
自动数据处理设备及其部件	75.93	65.86	42.26
服装及衣着附件	29.30	31.92	28.11
录、放像机	11.73	11.64	8.41
自动数据处理设备的零件	30.63	31.97	26.68
纺织纱线、织物及制品	16.57	14.69	13.68
玩具	15.24	14.69	12.28
鞋类	23.07	27.06	24.57
家具	27.44	27.79	24.26
录音机及收录(放)音组合机(包括整套散件)	11.07	10.62	7.46
塑料制品	11.76	10.74	9.10
静止式变流器	21.63	26.71	23.14
旅行用品及箱包	9.43	10.91	11.43
灯具、照明装置及类似品	7.64	8.87	7.84
电线和电缆	11.76	14.03	10.81
通断及保护电路装置	10.90	12.36	10.37
有线电话机	15.69	15.37	14.84
电视、收音机及无线电讯设备的零附件	11.94	16.21	12.59

9-6 主要商品进口数量与金额(海关口径，2007-2009年)

Main Import Commodities in Volume and Value (Customs Statistics) (2007-2009)

单位：万美元

商品名称	数量单位	2007年		2008年		2009年	
		数量	金额	数量	金额	数量	金额
谷物及谷物粉	万吨	1.48	691	1.31	691	3.18	1205
#小麦粉	吨	800	26	60	2	12	2
食用植物油	万吨	40.20	29769	22.26	23839	3.50	2218
食糖	万吨	5.88	1740	0.23	112	6.63	2187
配制的动物饲料	吨	0.29	0.16	0.04	0.01		
天然橡胶(包括胶乳)	万吨	2.71	3802	2.22	3737	2.30	3612
合成橡胶(包括胶乳)	万吨	15.26	24689	11.31	21892	9.49	17575
原木	万立方	3.19	1338	4.30	1900	5.50	2664
锯材	万立方	53.84	14838	41.42	11827	32.17	8082
羊毛(包括羊毛条)	吨	1840	810	1737	899	1348	818
纺织用合成纤维	万吨	2.72	4566	1.85	3244	1.81	3082
#聚脂纤维	万吨	2.98	5988	2.00	4136	1.15	1829
纺织用人造纤维	吨	173	46	103.40	31	40.92	13
成品油	万吨	0.98	1544	0.43	1092	0.36	835
合成有机染料	吨	3720	1928	2384.71	1577	1471.71	1053
初级形状的塑料	万吨	257.68	401392	210.78	366351	191.68	308584
#初级形状的聚乙烯	万吨	21.69	30584	17.99	27214	16.66	21793
初级形状的聚丙烯	万吨	37.49	48726	32.14	47116	29.74	39425
初级形状的苯乙烯聚合物	万吨	91.19	140287	73.66	122337	63.05	99175
初级形状的氯乙烯聚合物	万吨	28.52	26580	45.87	81013	24.08	21237
初级形状的聚酯	万吨	20.41	47341	27.79	41324	15.15	39344
牛皮革及马皮革	万吨	11.34	58721	6.91	47354	5.38	42245
纸及纸板(未切成形的)	万吨	75.39	44893	60.74	39163	59.26	34709
毛纱线	万吨	0.99	5851	0.89	5964	0.67	4483
合成纤维纱线	万吨	7.40	19957	5.44	16151	4.86	15035
棉机织物	万米	20697.89	26388	15848.24	22938	13525.38	19178
涂覆浸渍塑料的织物	万吨	5.90	12185	4.58	11596	3.16	9184
针织或钩编织物	万米		39048		35766	25197.31	27452
鞋靴零件	万吨	0.42	3029	0.42	3332		
钢材	万吨	197.47	171401	155.84	168061	110.17	109430
#钢铁板材	万吨	177.02	149259	143.10	147777	100.54	94963
铜	万吨	38.03	235941	31.25	214850	24.12	130340
#铜材	万吨	26.99	162869	22.23	151154	17.24	96339
铝	万吨	12.89	38524	10.03	34795	8.92	29377
#铝材	万吨	6.12	24032	4.82	22431	4.41	20253

9-6 续表

单位：万美元

商品名称	数量单位	2007年		2008年		2009年	
		数量	金额	数量	金额	数量	金额
钢材或铝制结构体及其部件	吨	428	103	867	210	934	285
蒸汽锅炉及过热水锅炉	台	18	82	6	23	7	18
液泵及液体提升机	台	2018336	1727	1958356	1134	1362113	1155
冷冻机和制冷设备	台		420		407		90
机械装卸设备	台		3295		3405		2892
制造纸及纸制品用机械	金额		20867		11477		11023
印刷、装订机械	金额		50930		59061		44739
纺织机械	金额		19858		26378		8668
#针织机及缝编机	台	4719	16598	6418	23494	1764	5834
花边绣品饰带织机、簇绒机	台	165	451	359	1068		
纱线织物等后整理机器	台	1866	1631	490	1147	974	690
工业用缝纫机	台	8849	1883	7225	1563	2262	343
制革、制鞋机器	台	1346	945	602	519		
金属加工机床	台	6460	27322	4834	20192	1635	7283
橡胶或塑料加工机械及零件	金额		17035		11989		5487
型模及金属铸造用型箱	吨	437	5042	229	4732		4547
自动数据处理设备及其部件	万台	3358	115830	4080	104516	2744	59580
自动数据处理设备的零件	吨	15255	65225	17536	69482	17967	73356
电动机及发电机	万台	32762	23834	33202	24974	32351	22938
发电机组及旋转式变流机	台	219	1885	175	2284	80	961
旋转式电力设备的零件	吨	21054	14797	17831	13926		
焊接机器及零件	金额		5475		3343		
电视、收音机及无线电讯设备	吨	7520	56182	8677	70241	8153	60863
通断及保护电路装置	万吨		98427		109681		89996
电视显像管	万只	31.72	273	30.40	184	2.98	23
#彩色显像管	万只	10.01	198	5.58	119	0.75	19
二极管、晶体管及类似半导体	亿个	496.91	166972	471.88	176757	419.24	147379
电线和电缆	吨	40745	33191	38492	35692	28328	27093
计量检测分析自控仪器及器具	金额		30798		27297		19697
钟表机芯及钟表零件	金额		7677		8660		
塑料制品	吨	32991	13037	30749	13271	22961	10870
玩具	金额		1868		1627		

9-7 主要商品出口数量与金额（海关口径，2007-2009年）

Main Export Commodities in Volume and Value (Customs Statistics) (2007-2009)

单位：万美元

商品名称	数量单位	2007年		2008年		2009年	
		数 量	金 额	数 量	金 额	数 量	金 额
活猪(种猪除外)	万头	1.49	224	1.40	268	1.13	217
活家禽	万只	21.06	60	18.86	64		
水海产品	万吨	0.10	223	0.60	155	0.04	253
谷物及谷物粉	万吨	0.06	31				1
蔬菜	万吨	0.05	42		13	0.02	19
#鲜蔬菜	万吨	0.02	16		2		
鲜、干水果及坚果	万吨	0.05	50	0.21	188		2
食用植物油(包括棕榈油)	吨	0.79	0.25	9.58	3	24.75	9
药材	吨	30.95	7				
锯材	立方米	951	34	250	12	200	10
成品油	万吨		15		17	0.03	50
合成有机染料	吨	69.46	81	282.92	426	319.02	315
医药品	吨	4220.70	2254	5570.22	3005	2480.77	1425
美容化妆品及护肤品	吨	2742.41	880	3274.45	1072	2888.88	1226
洗衣粉	吨	8209.96	486	8165.15	553	11106.46	687
烟花、爆竹	吨	5652.87	555	1460.68	132	998.44	95
初级形状的聚氯乙烯	吨	4863.92	454	6479.68	914	3500.00	533
家用或装饰用木制品	吨	22004.70	2500	13297.37	1651	8900.00	1321
纸及纸板(未切成形的)	万吨	35.39	17216	15.15	7717	5.09	2773
纺织纱线、织物及制品	金额		165703		146949		136789
#棉纱线	吨	29769.97	11285	24549.17	9197	25499.61	9265
亚麻及苎麻纱线	吨	407.77	175	208.33	82		
人造纤维短纤纱线(缝纫线)	万米	1.45	0.84				
棉机织物	万米	3144.41	3815	3716.00	4728	2093.69	2870
玻璃制品	金额		2972		2618		2616
家用陶瓷器皿	吨	29807.40	2816	24723.98	2481	20900.00	2335
装饰用陶瓷制品	吨	26963.55	3082	17375.97	2000		
钢材	万吨	2.66	2785	3.27	4184	2.39	2839
未锻造的铜及铜材	吨	31425.89	25160	33181.98	26575	24790.85	15726
未锻造的铝及铝材	吨	11448.21	4165	9517.93	3675	4800.00	1874
手用或机用工具	吨	16688.02	9403	12456.81	8385	9200.00	6544

9-7 续表

单位：万美元

商品名称	数量单位	2007年		2008年		2009年	
		数量	金额	数量	金额	数量	金额
锁	吨	8351	3310	6861	3512		
电扇	万台	11326.2	27119	10600.7	28595	9316.9	25552
纺织机械及零件	金额		1065		1564		1928
金属加工机床	万台	2.0	1197	2.4	1524	0.8	1068
电子计算器	亿台	0.6	16947	0.6	17698	0.4	11829
电动机及发电机	亿台	8.7	45391	8.1	46148	6.1	41501
静止式变流器	亿个	4.4	216311	5.2	267124	4.4	231369
原电池	亿个	13.4	11544	12.9	12902	11.5	11942
蓄电池	亿个	2.4	46104	2.5	49461	2.2	27656
有线电话机	万个	6188.5	157558	4965.9	153716	4240.1	148365
扬声器	亿个	2.2	44545	2.0	45902	1.4	34594
录音机及收录(放)音组合机	万台	5965.5	110670	4494.4	106267	3337.9	74636
电视机	万台	472.8	68114	451.1	79805	568.7	101880
#彩色电视机	万台	472.8	68114	451.1	79805	568.7	101880
电视、收音机及无线电讯设备	万吨	10.3	119781	9.7	162116	6.9	125973
电容器	吨	14576	46500	13049	44385	11598	49340
通断及保护电路装置	亿个		109062		123618		103732
二极管、晶体管及类似半导体	亿个	350.9	34942	358.0	42912	350.8	36080
电线和电缆	万吨	26.0	117631	23.0	140256	17.5	108069
照相机	万架	206.5	1024	208	159	2144	127230
医疗仪器及器械	金额		8941		10557		8573
手表	亿只	0.6	8366	0.6	9826	0.6	8562
#电动手表	亿只	0.6	8037	0.6	9384	0.6	8306
家具	金额		274441		277855		242625
灯具、照明装置及类似品	金额		76327		88680		78441
旅行用品及箱包	金额		94304		109052		114374
服装及衣着附件	金额		292959		319244		281057
#织物制服装	金额		245988		268855		242454
裘皮服装	吨	213	2542	190	2444	157	2013
帽类	万个	19473.4	8108	15416.3	7993	9939.9	8992
鞋	亿双	6.0	224025	5.5	261248	2.4	237001
塑料制品	万吨	67.6	117618	54.5	107390	44.6	90913
玩具	金额		152464		146857		122821
贵金属或贵金属的首饰	金额		1591		2435		5934
人造花	吨	25010	5643	22103	5145		

9-8 历年新签利用外资协议(合同)宗数

Number of Signed Agreements or Contracts of Utilization of Foreign Capital over Years

单位：宗

年　份	新签协议(合同)数	“三来一补”企业	“三资”企业
1979	184	184	
1980	415	415	
1981	555	553	2
1982	470	468	2
1983	454	447	7
1984	551	508	43
1985	625	514	111
1986	618	559	59
1987	824	729	95
1988	2048	1839	209
1989	939	779	160
1990	1267	1075	192
1991	1636	1268	368
1992	2232	1374	858
1993	3118	1773	1345
1994	2678	1521	1157
1995	3077	2094	983
1996	1678	1343	335
1997	1685	1492	193
1998	1383	1051	332
1999	1362	1135	227
2000	1276	871	405
2001	1395	705	690
2002	1391	524	867
2003	1524	392	1132
2004	1423	391	1032
2005	992	219	773
2006	786	177	609
2007	790	82	708
2008	588	35	553
2009	601	22	579

9-9 历年新签利用外资协议(合同)规定外商投资额

Amount of Signed Agreements or Contracts of Utilization of Foreign Capital over Years

单位：万美元

年　份	协议(合同)规定外商投资额	"三来一补"企业	"三资"企业
1979	476	476	
1980	1055	1055	
1981	806	784	22
1982	787	771	16
1983	1616	841	775
1984	3217	1013	2204
1985	6815	1870	4945
1986	3398	1593	1805
1987	18513	14082	4431
1988	62173	42507	19666
1989	23365	9268	14097
1990	30180	12346	17834
1991	64483	19348	45135
1992	208825	29720	179105
1993	355515	54823	300692
1994	349703	47700	302003
1995	330920	97428	233492
1996	208861	62811	146050
1997	121351	62114	59237
1998	163677	58709	104968
1999	147247	69756	77491
2000	183633	69302	114331
2001	209779	56833	152946
2002	248914	47285	201629
2003	325633	59538	266095
2004	413216	124089	289127
2005	475238	166363	308875
2006	552758	197836	354922
2007	625088	176903	448185
2008	393701	134952	258749
2009	203040	41420	161620

9-10 历年实际利用外资

Foreign Capital Actually Utilized over years

单位：万美元

年　份	累计实际利用外资	当年实际利用外资	“三来一补”企业	“三资”企业	当年对外借款发生额
1979	173	173	173		
1980	1107	934	934		
1981	1642	535	528	7	
1982	2357	715	668	47	
1983	3258	901	871	30	
1984	5175	1917	1233	684	
1985	8668	3493	1511	1383	599
1986	13209	4541	1553	1489	1499
1987	26422	13213	9185	2074	1954
1988	56310	29888	17717	6409	5762
1989	83563	27253	16559	8390	2304
1990	109173	25610	14309	10010	1291
1991	137493	28320	11478	14676	2166
1992	185568	48075	13716	32876	1483
1993	290487	104919	14181	79247	11491
1994	409946	119459	26938	77874	14647
1995	525788	115842	38418	67247	10177
1996	656821	131033	38061	69503	23469
1997	808384	151563	33467	87960	30136
1998	963140	154756	40780	93033	20943
1999	1142063	178923	48620	97112	33191
2000	1337487	195424	55975	108737	30712
2001	1540416	202929	66841	114721	21367
2002	1775260	234844	68980	145868	19996
2003	2052473	277213	80936	175400	20877
2004	2387187	334714	89555	213875	31284
2005	2812036	424849	93023	282116	49710
2006	3312468	500432	98543	335230	66659
2007	3913207	600739	94365	410030	96344
2008	4384117	470910	77902	244668	148340
2009	4805275	421158	34758	259399	127001

9-11 主要年份“三资”企业利用外资

Utilization of Foreign Capital of Enterprises with Foreign Investment in Main Years

项目	计量单位	1985年	1990年	1995年	2000年	2005年	2008年	2009年
一、全部“三资”企业利用外资情况								
当年新签协议宗数	宗	111	192	983	405	773	553	579
本年止累计执行宗数	宗	51	591	2807	4012	6657	7647	7940
#已投产	宗	47	454	2629	3908	5870	7094	7282
项目(协议)终止宗数	宗	3	24	48	338	193	356	286
实际投资总额	万美元	2565	18642	75853	115801	290553	249688	264549
境内资金总额	万美元	1182	8632	8606	7064	8437	5020	5150
中方实际投资	万美元	1182	5515	6448	4445	8337	5020	5150
企业境内借款	万美元		3117	2158	2619	100		
境外资金总额	万美元	1383	10010	67247	108737	282959	244668	259399
外商实际投资	万美元	1383	8934	65416	108468	282116	244668	259399
企业境外借款	万美元		1076	1831	269	842		
引进设备价值	万美元	995	6619	50267	80215	118401	68197	37922
出口总值	万美元	799	13439	178351	835600	2353253	3801299	3345624
期末职工人数	万人	0.54	3.81	25.01	87.17	145.50	162.00	150.00
二、中外合作企业利用外资情况								
当年新签协议宗数	宗	86	72	195	19	2		2
本年止累计执行宗数	宗	43	237	730	705	337	286	281
#已投产	宗	41	177	682	700	299	286	279
项目(协议)终止宗数	宗	3	15	12	130	25	13	7
实际投资总额	万美元	1301	5072	15159	10045	13529	14300	4563
境内资金总额	万美元	423	1427	176	1731	860	510	328
中方实际投资	万美元	423	651	136	1486	860	510	328
企业境内借款	万美元		776	40	245			
境外资金总额	万美元	878	3645	14983	8314	12669	13790	4235
外商实际投资	万美元	878	3642	14981	8314	12669	13790	4235
企业境外借款	万美元		3	2				
引进设备价值	万美元	290	2411	9320	5033	4060	935	509
出口总值	万美元	534	2423	35718	92100	116157	134057	117228
期末职工人数	万人	0.33	1.02	5.82	13.57	10.38	6.12	5.70

注：本表2000年起出口总值是海关口径。

9-11 续表

项目	计量单位	1985年	1990年	1995年	2000年	2005年	2008年	2009年
三、中外合资企业利用外资情况								
当年新签协议宗数	宗	25	93	378	29	31	20	15
本年止累计执行宗数	宗	8	338	1590	1690	712	671	663
#已投产	宗	6	251	1498	1650	668	651	648
项目(协议)终止宗数	宗		9	31	159	53	32	23
实际投资总额	万美元	1264	13070	39659	23966	25672	37229	40650
境内资金总额	万美元	759	7199	8345	5333	7477	4510	4822
中方实际投资	万美元	759	4864	6312	2959	7477	4510	4822
企业境内借款	万美元		2335	2033	2374			
境外资金总额	万美元	506	5871	31314	18633	18195	32719	35828
外商实际投资	万美元	506	4798	29496	18364	18195	32719	35828
企业境外借款	万美元		1073	1818	269			
引进设备价值	万美元	705	3920	25557	14365	4060	18334	15742
出口总值	万美元	265	10934	90357	248800	289344	346152	265929
期末职工人数	万人	0.20	2.69	13.51	24.68	17.95	14.15	13.07
四、外商独资企业利用外资情况								
当年新签协议宗数	宗		27	410	357	740	533	562
本年止累计执行宗数	宗		16	487	1614	5607	6690	6996
#已投产	宗		8	449	1555	4903	6157	6263
项目(协议)终止宗数	宗			5	49	115	311	256
实际投资总额	万美元		500	21035	79113	252194	198159	218703
境内资金总额	万美元		6	85		100		
中方实际投资	万美元							
企业境内借款	万美元		6	85		100		
境外资金总额	万美元		494	20950	79113	252094	198159	218703
外商实际投资	万美元		494	20939	79113	251252	198159	218703
企业境外借款	万美元			11		842		
引进设备价值	万美元		288	15390	58140	91288	48927	21670
出口总值	万美元		82	52276	494700	1947751	3321090	2962467
期末职工人数	万人		0.10	5.67	48.92	117.17	141.73	131.23

9-12 主要年份分方式、分国别（地区）实际利用外资

Foreign Capital Actually Utilized by Type and Country(Region) in Main Years

单位：万美元

项　　目	1990年	1995年	2000年	2001年	2003年	2005年	2008年	2009年
一、按引进方式分								
总　　计	**10167**	**68438**	**164712**	**181562**	**256336**	**375139**	**322570**	**294157**
外商直接投资	10010	67247	108737	114721	175400	282116	244668	259399
合资经营企业	5871	31314	18865	16413	12938	18195	33145	35828
合作经营企业	3645	14983	8305	6798	8608	12669	13790	4235
外资(独资)经营企业	494	20950	78890	88413	153854	251252	197701	218703
外商投资股份公司			2677	3097			32	633
外商其他投资	157	1191	55975	66841	80936	93023	77902	34758
国际租赁								
补偿贸易								
加工装配	157	1191	55975	66841	80936	93023	77902	34758
二、按国家和地区分								
总　　计	**10167**	**67247**	**164712**	**181562**	**256336**	**375139**	**322570**	**294157**
香　　港	10167	58333	88950	89559	122639	185214	188173	169794
澳　　门		13				44		824
台　　湾		3016	23722	32130	30005	130682	84397	81208
日　　本		391	7476	6994	11037	25253	18398	13556
泰　　国		96	33	108		20		
新 加 坡		822	3511	5595	5003	3994	10405	6121
德　　国		3	1884	1210	5265	487	1553	494
法　　国			89			20	2618	542
瑞　　士			546	426			23	41
加 拿 大		46	15	142	56	99	4089	195
美　　国		3230	2391	2576	5987	8122	3345	6054
澳大利亚		56	14	118	252	48	215	193
韩　　国			2362	2792	5012	6958	3053	4962
利 比 亚			153					
英　　国		79		570	194	12	380	2576
其　　他		1162	33566	39342	70886	14186	5921	7597

注：1995年分国别地区的外商投资额是外商直接投资额。

9-13 外商直接投资分行业情况（2009年）

Foreign Direct Investment by Sector (2009)

单位：万美元

行　　业	项目个数（个）	合同外资金额	实际投资金额
总　计	**579**	**161620**	**259399**
农、林、牧、渔业		13	35
制造业	465	136926	234131
#纺织业	30	5457	8067
化学原料及化学制品制造业	12	1915	5001
医药制造业		50	134
通用设备制造业	14	2994	7105
专用设备制造业	21	6230	13276
通信设备、计算机及其他电子设备制造业	66	36972	63052
电力、燃气及水的生产和供应业			3223
建筑业	1	1285	1339
交通运输、仓储和邮政业	2	254	4195
信息传输、计算机服务和软件业	4	235	571
批发和零售业	86	12403	7596
住宿和餐饮业	1	149	997
金融业			
房地产业	5	8305	3128
#房地产开发经营	1	7969	2929
租赁和商务服务业	12	1575	3433
科学研究、技术服务和地质勘查业	3	477	184
居民服务和其他服务业			107
卫生、社会保障和社会福利业			435
文化、体育和娱乐业			

9-14 主要年份宾馆酒店接待能力和接待人数

Capacity and Number of Tourists Received by Hotels in Main Years

项　　目	单 位	1990年	1995年	2000年	2005年	2008年	2009年
一、三星级以上宾馆(酒店)	家	3	16	30	63	77	80
三星级	家	3	16	23	27	32	35
四星级	家			6	22	25	26
五星级	家			1	14	20	19
二、客　房	间	3793	7568	18024	18258	19510	16332
床　位	张	8531	15136	30895	25014	26864	24389
开房率	%	60.2	68.8	61.9	58.9	58.9	58.0
三、全年接待人数	万人次	125	89	291	1156	1872	2037
(一) 国际及港澳台旅游者	万人次	27	27	106	169	268	286
#外国人	万人次	1	6	15	70	103	104
港澳台同胞	万人次	26	21	89	99	165	182
(二) 国内旅客	万人次	98	62	185	987	1604	1751

注：客房数、床位数2002年起是指三星级以上的宾馆和酒店。

9-15 历年国际旅游外汇收入

Foreign Exchange Earnings from International Tourism over Years

单位：万元(外汇券)、万美元

年　份	外汇收入合　计	商品性收入	商品销售	饮食销售	劳务性收入
1986	554	295	294	1	259
1987	453	320	251	69	133
1988	710	278	157	121	432
1989	504	152	111	41	352
1990	1025	268	86	182	757
1991	2443	590	28	562	1853
1992	2473	510	6	504	1963
1993	2888	365	27	338	2523
1994	3464	435	6	429	3029
1995	5679	2322			3357
1996	6464	2560			3904
1997	6778	2085			4693
1998	6601	1848	1228	620	4753
1999	7055	1411			5644
2000	7617				
2001	8200				
2002	11847				
2003	13825				
2004	23437				
2005	28189				
2006	33180				
2007	42702				
2008	45614				
2009	51756				

注：1995年起外汇收入计量单位为万美元。

9-16 历年旅游业情况

Statistics on Tourism over Years

年份	三星级以上宾馆(酒店)(家)	客房(间)	床位(张)	开房率(%)	全年接待人数(万人次)	国际旅游者	外国人	港澳台同胞	国内游客	国际旅游外汇收入(万元、外汇券/万美元)
1978										
1979										
1980										
1981										
1982										
1983										
1984										
1985										
1986					80	11		10	69	554
1987					107	19	1	18	87	453
1988		6435	7641	65.8	125	20		19	105	710
1989		3324	7376	64.8	115	18		18	97	504
1990		3793	8531	60.2	125	27	1	26	98	1025
1991		4004	8701	64.9	155	37	1	36	118	2443
1992		4042	8770	72.6	172	47	2	46	125	2473
1993		4258	8517	75.1	169	52	2	50	117	2888
1994		3542	7443	77.6	119	44	4	40	75	3464
1995	16	7568	15136	68.8	89	27	6	21	62	5679
1996	16	13409	26818	50.3	175	36	6	29	139	6464
1997	19	10420	19142	50.6	171	59	5	54	112	6778
1998	20	17428	31987	53.3	216	75	11	63	141	6601
1999	20	17931	25482	63.5	253	97	17	77	156	7055
2000	30	18024	30895	61.9	291	106	15	89	185	7617
2001	48	20572	32789	62.0	327	110	22	88	217	8200
2002	53	9427	14652	69.0	930	108	22	86	822	11847
2003	52	8170	12599	65.0	1086	80	24	56	1006	13825
2004	60	10530	14934	61.2	1131	149	66	83	982	23437
2005	63	18258	25014	58.9	1156	169	70	99	987	28189
2006	71	18258	25014	60.1	1363	193	81	112	1170	33180
2007	74	19023	26132	63.4	1725	248	102	146	1477	42702
2008	77	19510	26864	58.9	1872	268	103	165	1604	45614
2009	80	16332	24389	58.0	2037	286	104	182	1751	51756

注：1. 客房数、床位数2002年起是指三星级以上的宾馆和酒店。
2. 国际旅游外汇收入1995年以前单位为万元(外汇券)，1995年起为万美元。

9-17 外出旅游情况（2008-2009年）

Statistics on Domestic and Outbound Tourism （2008-2009）

项　　目	单位	2008年	2009年
外出旅游人数	万人次	108.32	127.1
(一)国内旅游人数	万人次	97.78	114.45
(二)出国(境)游人数	万人次	10.54	12.65
#旅行社组团出境旅游合计	人	105400	126500
香港游	人	42350	35507
澳门游	人	11986	53952
香港、澳门	人	7981	5154
泰国	人	2981	2055
泰港	人	1954	1790
泰港澳	人	4800	112
新马港	人	3596	4631
新泰港	人	5874	2209
新马泰港	人	3618	1355
韩国	人	5875	1853
韩港	人	3873	2583
菲律宾	人	2516	1218
澳大利亚	人	1079	207
日本	人	3936	4521
其他	人	2981	9353

主要统计指标解释

海关进出口总额 指实际进出我国国境的货物（包括贸易和非贸易）的价值总和。主要包括对外贸易实际进出口货物，来料加工装配、补偿贸易、进料加工进出口货物，国家间及国际组织无偿援助物资和赠送品，华侨、港澳台同胞和外籍华人捐赠品，租赁期满归承租人所有的租赁货物，边境地方贸易及边境地区小额贸易进出口货物（边民互市贸易除外），中外合资、合作经营企业、外商独资经营企业进出口货物和公用物品，到、离岸价格在规定限额以上的进出口货样和广告品（无商业价值、无使用价值和免费提供出口的除外），从保税仓库提取在中国境内销售的进出口货物，以及其他进出口货物。海关进出口总额反映一个国家在对外经济贸易方面实际进出口货物的总规模。

创汇总额 包括一般贸易出口、"三来一补"出口应收工缴费、三资企业出口和非贸易。

贸易出口 指由外贸进出口公司、工农贸易进出口公司和地方性的进出口公司由国家统一安排的出口、代理出口和自营、联营出口，其中包括进料加工出口，以及各进出口公司在国内以外汇结算方式售给友谊商店、华侨商店、出国人员服务公司和中外合资、合作经营和外资企业等的出口商品。

"三来一补"出口： 指来料加工装配出口按工缴费计算，中小型补偿贸易按金额计算。

"三资"企业出口： 指三资企业自己出口的本企业产品。不包括委托外贸进出口公司出口的商品。

利用外资 指我国各级政府、部门、企业和其他经济组织通过对外借款、吸收外商直接投资以及向境外发行债券、股票等方式筹措的境外资金。

外资的形式可以是现汇、实物、工业产权或专有技术等有形资本和无形资本。

我国自有外汇如国家外汇、中国银行等金融机构用自有资金发放的外汇贷款等，华侨、港澳同胞的捐赠，联合国或其他国际组织的无偿赠送资金、无偿援建的项目均不属于外资范围。

利用外资的方式有：对外借款，外国（或港澳地区）企业和经济组织或个人在我国境内开办独资企业，与我国境内的企业或组织共同开办合资企业合作经营（企业）项目或合作开发资源，以及补偿贸易、国际租赁等。

对外借款 指我国政府、部门、企业和中国银行等单位向国际金融组织、外国政府、企业等借用的长期、短期资本，到期需还本付息。借款按不同渠道划分为：1. 外国政府贷款；2. 国际金融组织贷款；3. 外国银行贷款；4. 出口信贷；5. 发行债券、股票。

外商直接投资 指外国企业和经济组织或个人（包括华侨、港澳同胞以及我在境外注册的企业）按我国有关政策、法规，在我国境内开办外商独资企业，与我国境内的企业或经济组织共同举办中外合资企业、合作经营企业或合作开发资源的投资以及外商从企业得到收益的再投资。

国际旅游（外汇）收入 指国内各部门为来我国旅游的外国人、华侨、港澳和台湾同胞提供商品和劳务而得到的外汇收入。包括供应商品、饮食和提供住宿、交通、邮电、文化娱乐、导游等各项服务所得的全部外汇收入。

十、财政、金融与保险

Government Finance, Banking and Insurance

10-1 主要年份财政收支主要指标

Main Indicators of Government Revenue and Expenditure in Main Years

单位：万元

项　　目	1978年	1980年	1985年	1990年	2000年	2005年	2006年
一、财政收入							
来源于东莞的财政收入(含关税)					1035562	3319079	4065412
中央财政收入					617151	1935069	2323977
#关税和海关代征税					273972	483327	526251
省级财政收入					113681	344330	451990
市财政一般预算收入					304730	1039680	1289445
来源于东莞的财政收入(不含关税)	6604	6710	11118	35719	761590	2835752	3539161
中央财政收入					343179	1451742	1797726
省级财政收入					113681	344330	451990
市财政一般预算收入	6604	6710	11118	35719	304730	1039680	1289445
各项税收	6595	6699	10998	33544	265565	879653	1077152
工商税收	5826	5785	9708	31911	248159	797038	990029
农业税类	769	914	1290	1633	17406	82615	87123
专项收入				686	14709	36423	49285
其他收入	9	11	120	1489	24456	123604	163008
二、工商税收							
工商税收总额					867584	2923001	3593704
国税（不含关税）					607216	1849818	2208722
地税					260368	1073183	163008
三、财政支出							
市财政一般预算支出	1792	2015	4999	22779	336102	1170427	1478955
#基本建设支出					27426	276646	242829
企业挖潜改造支出		88	15	37	1584	9107	9691
科技三项费用支出		7		140	9963	31572	87397
农林水气部门事业费支出		304	1154	3261	40097	62181	64911
工交部门事业费支出		2	7	180	192	20499	18552
城市维护费支出		31	219	1350	41267	162370	205426
科教文卫体事业费支出		1051	2139	7357	86737	210620	291467
#科学事业费				404	936	3956	3874
教育事业费		760	1504	3786	68194	171055	244113
卫生事业费		185	262	743	12083	11469	12826
体育事业费		18	50	827	1517	2860	3266
抚恤和社会福利救济支出		75	132	368	2888	8335	34050
行政管理费支出		293	320	1324	29817	102296	119034
公检法司支出			92	740	46446	166055	225382

注：从2007年起财政收支按新的分类项目，在10-2表中反映。

10-2 财政收支主要指标（2006-2009年）

Main Indicators of Government Revenue and Expenditure (2006-2009)

单位：万元

指　　标	2006年	2007年	2008年	2009年
来源于东莞的财政收入（含关税）	4065412	5395362	6010642	6278199
财政总收入	3358095	4574778	5234746	5389799
#中央	1638195	2151906	2476902	2380580
省级	430455	558404	665596	697658
市财政一般预算收入	1289445	1864468	2092248	2311556
#增值税	347153	474288	552515	534382
营业税	291122	380958	422427	446884
企业所得税	145739	173566	184478	176786
个人所得税	60518	75765	87895	87313
房产税	51622	63228	65560	75806
契税	80793	355039	113509	157533
罚没收入	75238	81766	79104	72888
市财政一般预算支出	1478955	1930968	2182626	2326216
#一般公共事务	161657	220367	234172	259865
公共安全	233413	324714	365387	367266
教育	293000	412347	499978	553429
科学技术	10593	91232	93518	112506
社会保障和就业	27100	104264	232742	194637
农林水事务	77188	116452	143695	131828
交通运输	14439	54144	49759	73635
工商税收总额	3593704	4709341	5361733	5475100
#国税(不含关税)	2208722	3057525	3390812	3384667
地税	1384982	1651816	1970921	2090433

10-3 历年财政收入

Government Revenue over Years

单位：万元

年份	来源于东莞的财政总收入（含关税）	来源于东莞的财政总收入（不含关税）	中央财政收入	省级财政收入	市财政一般预算收入	各项税收	工商税收	专项收入	其他收入
1978		6604			6604	6595	5826		9
1979		6634			6634	6625	5725		9
1980		6710			6710	6699	5785		11
1981		6823			6823	6805	5942		18
1982		8103			8103	8068	7184		35
1983		8578			8578	8501	7599		77
1984		8469			8469	8385	7442		84
1985		11118			11118	10998	9708		120
1986		16053			16053	15865	14574	45	143
1987		20221			20221	19989	18551	50	182
1988		27076			27076	26837	25309	76	163
1989		31888			31888	30997	29331	116	775
1990		35719			35719	33544	31911	686	1489
1991		44374			44374	41659	39302	913	1802
1992		56204			56204	52620	48272	1351	2233
1993		93828			93828	88920	83462	1947	2961
1994		130531	53591		76940	70451	60889	2697	3792
1995		180051	64433		115618	106388	95463	4070	5160
1996	283506	201579	78403	26635	96541	85648	74323	4470	6423
1997	335044	237391	94320	29002	114069	96980	85245	4794	12295
1998	472422	342792	133803	57977	151012	123816	106700	5693	21503
1999	717847	438761	182160	74024	182577	159873	134852	8759	13945
2000	1035561	761590	343179	113681	304730	265565	248159	14709	24456
2001	1259961	1100212	477826	172223	450163	402668	381660	18356	29139
2002	1678848	1510978	710391	247654	552933	489780	467998	26438	36715
2003	2064052	1811345	864349	272535	674461	575342	536390	30710	68409
2004	2591086	2232480	1099129	306962	826389	707954	655571	35273	83162
2005	3319079	2835752	1451742	344330	1039680	879653	797038	36423	123604
2006	4065412	3539161	1797726	451990	1289445	1077152	990029	49285	163008
2007	5395362	4738885	2316013	558404	1864468	1652620	1291335	55863	155985
2008	6010642	5376839	2476902	665596	2092248	1682270	1555499	60590	10085
2009	6278199	5533570	2380580	697658	2311556	1822650	1618514	60007	40700

10-4 历年财政支出

Government Expenditure over Years

单位：万元

年 份	预算内地方财政支出总 额	#基本建设支出	#科技三项费用	#农林水气等部门事业费	#城市维护费	#科教文卫体育事业费	#教育事业费	#行政管理费
1978	1792							
1979	1908		20	451	74	852	618	202
1980	2015		7	304	31	1051	760	293
1981	2139		4	341	36	1182	818	246
1982	2612		1	359	141	1346	912	336
1983	2804		1	413	28	1672	1004	287
1984	3013			264	48	1868	1309	340
1985	4999			1154	219	2139	1504	320
1986	9916			2541	1431	2887	1793	330
1987	12512			3479	1624	4759	1871	510
1988	17475		100	4094	1614	6950	3339	888
1989	21623		103	3509	2286	7958	3733	1159
1990	22779		140	3261	1350	7357	3786	1324
1991	27499		30	4938	866	7956	4720	1484
1992	38162		50	5637	567	17505	7682	2348
1993	72910	5400	1289	8882	5737	25716	14427	4002
1994	88984	14575	1496	12835	5254	20725	13552	6158
1995	124173	13736	441	15798	9947	31021	23110	8433
1996	124059	17285	1332	14962	5199	28927	21237	10384
1997	148510	16923	1479	15349	6258	36614	23262	11691
1998	179064	26144	1164	19255	7264	36710	25578	11082
1999	212641	40681	1429	26648	12994	40863	30631	12979
2000	336102	27426	9963	40097	41267	86737	68194	29817
2001	478646	119692	4113	28957	43706	105990	85544	28961
2002	649606	165283	28013	37348	64483	143225	120195	43678
2003	765190	201077	30062	41164	44240	193138	163390	50022
2004	941554	179039	27110	53855	164770	162573	139337	84798
2005	1170427	276646	31572	62181	162370	210620	171055	102296
2006	1478955	242829	87397	64911	205426	291467	244113	119034
2007	1930968							
2008	2182626							
2009	2326216							

注：从2007年起财政支出按新的分类项目，在10-2表中反映。

10-5 税务登记情况及税种征收情况（2008-2009年）

Statistics on Tax registration and Tax Collection（2008-2009）

指　　标	国税		地税	
	2008年	2009年	2008年	2009年
税务登记情况（户）	**195204**	**205588**	**251779**	**237858**
#国有企业	418	360	627	874
集体企业	6624	5742	9020	7122
私营企业	27024	29684	22691	24244
港澳台投资企业	5152	5445	7683	5783
外商投资企业	3813	3850	3516	3170
个体经营	124041	127726	164132	148353
工商税收总额（万元）	**3390811**	**3384667**	**1970921**	**2090433**
#国有企业	9894	10420	50459	56759
集体企业	45496	37186	233839	237882
私营企业	293421	300923	203999	203804
港澳台投资企业	770615	787927	257835	256827
外商投资企业	621472	641713	291406	282171
个体经营	391038	276327	199239	190681
#增值税	2821013	2859992		
消费税	7293	22848		
营业税			783093	875821
企业所得税	407616	374517	465384	438967
个体所得税	23592	7825	366230	363805
房产税			65560	75806
印花税			23453	37672
城镇土地使用税			36266	79479
土地增值税			120075	100970
车船税			26748	27410
车辆购置税	131297	117778		
#第一产业	657	968	946	848
第二产业	2089391	2054904	786232	779784
#采矿业	209	745	624	808
制造业	1880232	1859444	496818	499247
农副食品加工业	16792	8965	5170	6482
食品制造业	62421	56991	27119	26221
饮料制造业	30958	34716	6162	10055
纺织业	82347	91797	11247	11067
纺织服装、鞋、帽制造业	124317	126588	22057	21183
皮革、毛皮、羽绒及其制品业	65206	48555	10238	11473
木材加工及竹、藤、棕草制品业	9031	9986	1628	1683
家具制造业	98824	67214	10746	11217
造纸及纸制品业	106761	103606	15605	12176

注：2009年国税的工商税收总额中含代地税征收的城市维护建设税共1707万元。

10-5 续表

单位：万元

指标	国税		地税	
	2008年	2009年	2008年	2009年
印刷业、记录媒介的复制	37429	41117	9770	9772
文教体育用品制造业	46797	36737	16413	14150
石油加工、及炼焦业及核燃业	1266	1868	555	1934
化学原料及化学制品制造业	60839	61011	12961	12406
医药制造业	8328	11303	3316	2920
化学纤维制造业	2902	2723	253	105
橡胶制品业	18297	17312	6144	5716
塑料制品业	139891	128595	32976	34944
非金属矿物制品业	46011	47204	5794	5860
黑色金属冶炼及压延加工业	229	170	1849	1429
有色金属冶炼及压延加工业	3398	3263	10225	1626
金属制品业	108843	101350	26930	25235
通用设备制造业	51998	52259	21365	17815
专用设备制造业	64924	58774	14347	13963
交通运输设备制造业	29753	35556	4909	21366
电气机械及器材制造业	146669	135985	33775	34476
通信设备、计算机及其他电子设备制造业	362903	419887	151058	149515
仪器仪表及文化、办公用机械制造业	30659	37341	6293	6484
其他制造业	122439	118571	27910	27974
电力、热力的生产和供应业	181436	167255	46159	58666
建筑业	8082	6248	242631	221063
房屋和土木工程建筑业	1168	773	50126	44822
建筑安装业	3190	2413	153237	145732
建筑装饰业	2189	1645	20587	14751
其他建筑业	1535	1417	18681	15758
第三产业	1300763	1328795	1183743	1309801
#交通运输、仓储及邮政业	2968	3681	72778	67782
信息传输、计算机服务和软件业	10475	2494	82380	70474
批发和零售业	360790	361715	91249	97468
住宿和餐饮业	1882	1013	76194	74341
金融业	135427	91444	126851	187363
房地产业	83405	79321	439831	480420
租赁和商务服务业	8036	11156	68192	79964
居民服务和其他服务业	19949	12915	126698	157730
教育	800	112	2593	4728
卫生、社会保险和社会福利业	262	351	7244	6662
文化、体育和娱乐业	352	210	17420	21558
公共管理和社会组织	1883	1	18166	21696
其他行业	674534	764382	54147	39615

10-6 历年金融机构各项人民币存款余额

Deposits Balance in Renminbi in Various Forms of Financial Institutions over Years

单位：万元

年　份	各项存款余额	#企业存款余额	#城乡居民储蓄存款余额	#财 政 性存款余额
1978	10497	1431	5409	963
1979	14875	2319	7184	1028
1980	26093	5107	11718	1481
1981	38003	6546	20339	1503
1982	45120	8169	27650	1937
1983	60547	10190	38597	3343
1984	110265	22510	61823	5060
1985	134867	23367	91941	3488
1986	195948	35422	131352	5801
1987	284819	49618	189654	5321
1988	380511	73733	249134	6724
1989	468203	75491	325670	9202
1990	680696	116074	455140	7953
1991	949713	164519	614737	10313
1992	1473354	319933	815404	19926
1993	1798346	423791	1071715	33016
1994	2497834	616328	1515445	60551
1995	3836761	895021	2329685	83933
1996	4896463	1114040	3180215	56860
1997	6711687	1595280	4258238	48923
1998	8640053	2515686	5337482	49729
1999	10408377	3268530	6163430	35166
2000	12286706	4385202	6720704	39949
2001	14586491	5032045	7991768	57056
2002	17901799	5775722	10016909	78673
2003	21267775	6378486	12310616	110077
2004	24628693	7546584	14316777	164648
2005	29334026	8558552	17282760	259771
2006	33656508	10111005	20133979	298793
2007	37518345	11624537	21207413	568912
2008	43545340	11839005	26380433	495375
2009	49866108	14199448	29045704	524501

10-7 历年金融机构各项人民币贷款余额及现金收支

Loans Balance in Renminbi, Cash Income and Expenditure in Various Forms of Financial Institutions over Years

单位：万元

年份	各项贷款余额	#短期贷款	#中长期贷款	现金收入合计	#商品销售收入	现金支出合计	现金净投放(+)净回笼(-)
1978	19607	19607		20774	14102	22122	1348
1979	21301	21301		24534	16526	26866	2332
1980	30797	29669	403	31479	20608	35825	4346
1981	40243	38365	765	46686	27780	56128	9442
1982	45525	44081	690	61297	33398	69210	7913
1983	57618	56063	837	70482	35539	92040	21558
1984	121891	114522	3365	88743	36275	143081	54338
1985	142437	130716	6230	140341	48661	173190	32849
1986	206813	193501	9486	176408	57195	231184	54776
1987	312431	292104	7162	286438	75083	346268	59830
1988	415818	381957	12351	547812	136849	577049	29237
1989	493737	456504	12338	843887	181085	856946	13059
1990	630355	570324	13427	1209730	195286	1258795	49065
1991	783957	714848	17385	1798653	247206	1923571	124918
1992	1059794	935064	23000	3038847	369975	3445508	406661
1993	1343103	923157	237985	4901078	562202	5403709	502631
1994	1734350	1246772	250806	6808963	636843	7217477	408504
1995	2548512	1645696	274157	8584483	752404	8974313	389830
1996	3128076	2053343	353298	11245241	764331	11935860	690619
1997	3826560	2737916	205486	13909740	852965	14381835	472095
1998	4427394	3666563	155295	24885265	1963439	25150137	264872
1999	5243735	4628058	328875	29970415	2541776	30985960	1015545
2000	6308405	5313933	469249	35945777	3277631	37187782	1242005
2001	7501801	5341925	1436127	38494378	3451596	38583059	88681
2002	9334054	5731973	2312883	45085355	4071749	44611686	-473669
2003	12067237	6918877	3730104	55556021	5374491	54193508	-1362513
2004	14052461	7118671	5222504	68687707	5675223	67287198	-1400509
2005	15005217	7341939	7007138	73752467	5532266	71784959	-1967507
2006	17305554	7792175	8684306	78759519	6057902	77137021	-1622498
2007	21547660	9245906	11427676	90319897	6045894	89760923	-558973
2008	23803585	10132902	12052974	91343779	5997521	90710505	-633274
2009	29037984	12604957	14519686	84494728	5218187	84862223	367496

注：现金收入与支出1997年及以前年份为国家银行口径，1998年起为金融机构口径。

10-8 历年各项人民币存贷款余额与现金收支增加额

The Balance of Deposits and Loans in Renminbi and the Increase of Cash Income and Expenditure over Years

单位：万元

年 份	各项存款余额		各项贷款余额		现金收入		现金支出	
	年末数	年增加额	年末数	年增加额	合 计	年增加额	合 计	年增加额
1978	10497		19607		20774		22122	
1979	14875	4378	21301	1694	24534	3760	26866	4744
1980	26093	11218	30797	9496	31479	6945	35825	8959
1981	38003	11910	40243	9446	46686	15207	56128	20303
1982	45120	7117	45525	5282	61297	14611	69210	13082
1983	60547	15427	57618	12093	70482	9185	92040	22830
1984	110265	49718	121891	64273	88743	18261	143081	51041
1985	134867	24602	142437	20546	140341	51598	173190	30109
1986	195948	61081	206813	64376	176408	36067	231184	57994
1987	284819	88871	312431	105618	286438	110030	346268	115084
1988	380511	95692	415818	103387	547812	261374	577049	230781
1989	468203	87692	493737	77919	843887	296075	856946	279897
1990	680696	212493	630355	136618	1209730	365843	1258795	401849
1991	949713	269017	783957	153602	1798653	588923	1923571	664776
1992	1473354	523641	1059794	275837	3038847	1240194	3445508	1521937
1993	1798346	324992	1343103	283309	4901078	1862231	5403709	1958201
1994	2497834	699488	1734350	391247	6808963	1907885	7217477	1813768
1995	3836761	1338927	2548512	814162	8584483	1775520	8974313	1756836
1996	4896463	1059702	3128076	579564	11245241	2660758	11935860	2961547
1997	6711687	1815224	3826560	698484	13909740	2664499	14381835	2445975
1998	8640053	1928366	4427394	600834	24885265	10975525	25150137	10768302
1999	10408377	1768324	5243735	816341	29970415	5085150	30985960	5835823
2000	12286706	1878329	6308405	1064670	35945777	5975362	37187782	6201822
2001	14586491	2299785	7501801	1193396	38494378	2548601	38583059	1395277
2002	17901799	3315308	9334054	1832253	45085355	6590977	44611686	6028627
2003	21267775	3365976	12067237	2733183	55556021	10470666	54193508	9581822
2004	24628693	3360918	14052461	1985224	68687707	13131686	67287198	13093690
2005	29334026	4705333	15005217	952756	73752467	5064760	71784959	4497761
2006	33656508	4322482	17305554	2300337	78759519	5007052	77137021	5352062
2007	37518345	3861837	21547660	4242106	90319897	11560378	89760923	12623902
2008	43545340	6026995	23803585	2255925	91343779	1023882	90710505	949582
2009	49866108	6320768	29037984	5234399	84494728	-6849051	84862223	-5848282

注：现金收入与支出1998年以前是国家银行口径，1998年起是金融机构口径。

10-9 保险行业主要指标（2006-2009年）

Main Indicators of Insurance (2006-2009)

	单位	2006年	2007年	2008年	2009年
保险公司	家	26	30	35	37
保险业从业人员	人	11714	17846	24771	27386
保费收入	万元	473835	676062	902986	1150795
寿险类	万元	277769	397962	583983	797192
#传统寿险	万元	51772	57890	61255	63681
分红险	万元	157264	190521	355674	572703
万能险	万元	34050	51114	73233	85142
投连险	万元	1750	60993	38195	18481
意外险	万元	12382	14490	17188	17143
健康险	万元	20477	22954	38438	40043
财险类	万元	196066	278100	319010	353602
#机动车险	万元	155067	231073	270082	301526
企财险	万元	17160	21254	22626	24276
家财险	万元	3228	3393	1373	1113
货运险	万元	1985	2514	2819	3648
责任险	万元	4179	5477	6571	7273
短健险	万元	1448	271	759	8058
短意险	万元	10536	12945	13145	6184
农业险	万元	23	43	17	

主要统计指标解释

财政收入 国家财政参与社会产品分配所取得的收入，是实现国家职能的财力保证,主要包括：

（1）各项税收 包括增值税、营业税、消费税、土地增值税、城市维护建设税、资源税、城市土地使用税、印花税、个人所得税、企业所得税、关税、农牧业税和耕地占用税等。

（2）专项收入 包括征收排污费收入、征收城市水资源费收入，教育费附加收入等。

（3）其他收入 包括基本建设贷款归还收入、基本建设收入、捐赠收入等。

（4）国有企业计划亏损补贴这项为负收入，冲减财政收入。

财政支出 国家财政将筹集起来的资金进行分配使用，以满足经济建设和各项事业的需要，主要包括：基本建设支出、企业挖潜改造资金、地质勘探费用、科技三项费用、支援农村生产支出、农林水利气象等部门的事业费用、工业交通商业等部门的事业费、文教科学卫生事业费、抚恤和社会福利救济费、国防支出、行政管理费、价格补贴支出等项目。

银行信贷存款 指企业、机关、团体或居民把货币资金存入银行或其他信用机构保管并取得一定利息的一种信用活动形式。根据存款对象的不同可划分为：企业存款、财政存款、机关团体存款、基本建设存款、城镇居民储蓄存款、农村存款等科目。它是银行信贷资金的主要来源。

银行信贷贷款 银行或其他信用机构根据必须归还的原则，按一定利率，为企业、个人等提供资金的一种信用活动形式。我国银行贷款，分流动资金贷款、固定资产贷款、城乡个体工商户贷款以及农业贷款等科目。

十一、人民生活

People's Live Conditions

11-1 主要年份人民生活主要指标

Main Indicators of People's Living Conditions in Main Years

指　　　标	单 位	1985年	1990年	1995年	2000年	2005年	2008年	2009年
城镇职工年平均工资	元	1456	3552	9682	14051	28253	39516	42585
国有单位	元	1400	3600	9390	16371	37919	51441	56129
城镇集体单位	元	1501	3507	7507	10475	15958	20833	22077
其他各种单位	元	1571	3525	7891	14218	20882	28838	31195
城市居民家庭每一就业者负担人口	人	1.58	1.70	1.50	1.54	1.58	1.69	1.54
城市居民家庭人均可支配收入	元	791	2508	9588	14142	22882	30275	33045
城市居民家庭人均总支出	元	718	2152	10049	14193	25822	26656	29647
城市居民家庭人均消费性支出	元	689	2038	9220	12529	21768	23208	24270
食品	元	493	1295	3644	4048	6035	7778	7972
衣着	元	28	95	604	487	1285	1349	1492
家庭设备用品及服务	元	48	153	694	623	1165	1539	1616
医疗保健	元	14	42	258	431	811	1332	1400
交通和通讯	元	4	25	1562	3309	7482	4462	5456
娱乐教育文化服务	元	21	113	991	1517	3205	3464	3326
居住	元	58	184	1084	1218	1242	2585	2232
杂项商品和服务	元	23	131	383	896	543	699	776
城市居民家庭人均非消费性支出	元		12	829	1664	4054	3448	5377
农民人均纯收入	元	746	1359	3988	6731	9842	12328	13064
全市职工年平均工资	元				7765	10639	13523	14416

注：1.职工年平均工资从2000年起是城镇在岗职工工资,不含乡镇及以下办企业职工，下同。
2.全市职工年平均工资统计是根据中央、省、市属各类企事业机关单位，各镇街、村及村以下非农企业,个体私营非农企业以及“三资”、“三来一补”非农企业的在岗从业人员劳动报酬抽样调查计算所得。
3.本表城市居民人均可支配收入1997年以前是生活费收入口径，1997年起是可支配收入口径。
4.城市居民家庭每一就业者负担人口已扣除离退休人口。

11-2 历年城镇职工工资总额与平均工资

Total Wages and Average Wage of Staff and Workers in Urban Areas over Years

项 目	工资总额(万元)	国有单位	城镇集体单位	其他单位	平均工资(元)	国有单位	城镇集体单位	其他单位
1978	4485	2911	1574		474	630	325	
1979	5869	3611	2258		650	708	574	
1980	7255	4210	3045		750	867	632	
1981	9416	5000	4416		887	979	801	
1982	11839	6440	5399		1095	1089	1102	
1983	12808	6834	5974		1197	1138	1273	
1984	14963	7002	7961		1383	1333	1431	
1985	17260	7619	9238	403	1456	1400	1501	1571
1986	20980	10336	10026	618	2616	1698	1525	1940
1987	27610	12300	14159	1151	2067	2028	2094	2166
1988	35007	17931	14854	2222	2757	2942	2588	2574
1989	42947	20340	20808	1799	3320	3355	3295	3236
1990	46780	22321	21012	3447	3552	3600	3507	3525
1991	54002	24456	23268	6278	3777	3841	3674	3933
1992	68360	30469	28886	9005	4531	4610	4404	4696
1993	107088	47088	40171	19829	6228	7007	5583	6044
1994	131160	61869	49323	19968	8360	9390	7507	7891
1995	171543	75157	51398	44988	9682	10802	8007	10367
1996	178968	83372	52581	43015	10382	11623	8658	10775
1997	175156	87890	47185	40081	10691	12160	8774	10610
1998	187636	98109	50302	39225	11422	13123	9362	10959
1999	204550	109437	52217	42896	12557	14601	9966	12062
2000	229404	125711	53903	49790	14051	16371	10475	14218
2001	261645	152564	52645	56436	16183	19869	11001	15238
2002	291778	165611	58907	67260	17804	22228	11640	17348
2003	362935	230464	55866	76605	22598	29773	12940	19140
2004	432893	282512	62898	87483	25326	35163	13954	19223
2005	518216	349572	70872	97772	28253	37919	15958	20882
2006	608670	413718	74637	120315	31135	41457	17174	23032
2007	707007	487826	74408	144773	35284	46197	18807	26218
2008	809893	570134	82432	157327	39516	51441	20833	28838
2009	944243	639161	76001	229081	42585	56129	22077	31195

注：2000年起本表统计口径为城镇在岗职工工资总额和平均工资。

11-3 城镇在岗职工工资总额及平均工资(2009年，按经济类型、行业分)

Total Wages and Average Wage of Fully Employed Staff and Workers in Urban Areas (2009,by Status of Registration and Sector)

项目	工资总额(万元)	国有单位	城镇集体单位	其他单位	平均工资(元)	国有单位	城镇集体单位	其他单位
总计	**944243**	**639161**	**76001**	**229081**	**42585**	**56129**	**22077**	**31195**
一、按企业、事业和机关分								
企业	487994	186239	72674	229081	38522	94653	21650	31195
事业	255696	252369	3327		44369	44453	38782	
机关	200553	200553			53588	53588		
二、按国民经济行业分								
农、林、牧、渔业	3364	3364			70827	70827		
工业	232336	24738	43724	163874	25401	71188	19112	25168
建筑业	3610	3225	358	27	25787	26875	18963	24364
交通运输、仓储及邮政业	27493	12971	11944	2578	40725	58298	30586	41313
信息传输、计算机服务和软件业	29702	27912	60	1730	117960	124774	13378	73309
批发和零售业	20879	4623	5264	10992	37224	33941	28544	45745
住宿和餐饮业	1380		441	939	21035		22273	20500
金融业	174846	116141	10259	48446	97728	126254	24258	108549
房地产业	2219	1742	477		47933	57125	30190	
租赁和商务服务业	9144	6259	2390	495	41545	45091	34845	38976
科学研究、技术服务和地质勘查业	9093	8899	194		49231	49686	34679	
水利、环境和公共设施管理业	2986	2721	265		49269	54849	24109	
居民服务和其他服务业	544	544			52269	52269		
教育	96261	96261			37639	37639		
卫生、社会保障和社会福利业	119564	119180	384		49246	49220	59092	
文化、体育和娱乐业	8928	8687	241		49378	49753	38806	
公共管理和社会组织	201894	201894			53017	53017		
国际组织								

11-4 主要年份各种分组的城镇职工平均工资

Average Wage of Staff and Workers in Urban Areas by Various Items in Main Years

单位：元

项目	1980年	1985年	1990年	1995年	2000年	2005年	2008年	2009年
职工平均工资	**750**	**1456**	**3552**	**9682**	**14051**	**28253**	**39516**	**42585**
一、按企业事业和机关分								
企　业				9316	13501	24152	35781	38522
事　业				10872	15485	32203	42399	44369
机　关				12171	15383	38441	46647	53588
二、按经济类型分								
国有单位	867	1400	3600	10802	16371	37919	51441	56129
城镇集体单位	632	1501	3507	8007	10475	15958	20833	22077
其他单位		1571	3525	10367	14218	20882	28838	31195
三、按国民经济行业分								
农、林、牧、渔业	694	1312	3639	12412	14000	37046	46701	70827
工　业	769	1450	3481	8945	12316	18371	23136	25401
建筑业	1018	2052	3813	9125	9820	18385	22639	25787
交通运输、仓储及邮政业						31989	40115	40725
信息传输、计算机服务和软件业						71801	105472	117960
批发和零售业						28565	31328	37224
住宿和餐饮业						18257	20308	21035
金融业	685	1500	3303	13254	20560	40655	83125	97728
房地产业	577	1779	4414	11184	17993	34805	47825	47933
租赁和商务服务业						29824	37002	41545
科学研究、技术服务和地质勘查业						37423	46433	49231
水利、环境和公共设施管理业						34573	47458	49269
居民服务和其他服务业						44853	43462	52269
教　育						27255	37626	37639
卫生、社会保障和社会福利业						37991	46480	49246
文化、体育和娱乐业						37710	46982	49378
公共管理和社会组织	695	1519	3666	12347	15424	37888	46011	53017
国际组织								

注：2000年起本表统计口径为城镇在岗职工工资总额和平均工资。

11-5 各种经济类型分行业职工工资总额、平均工资(2008-2009年)

Total Wages and Average Wage of Staff and Workers by Status of Registration and Sector (2008-2009)

项　　目	国有经济		城镇集体经济		其他经济类型	
	2008年	2009年	2008年	2009年	2008年	2009年
一、职工工资总额(万元)	**570134**	**639161**	**82432**	**76001**	**157327**	**229081**
农、林、牧、渔业	2762	3364				
工业	22203	24738	50654	43724	105506	163874
建筑业	2780	3225	363	358	27	27
交通运输、仓储及邮政业	11957	12971	9833	11944	2070	2578
信息传输、计算机服务和软件业	27924	27912	60	60	799	1730
批发和零售业	3836	4623	6590	5264	10067	10992
住宿和餐饮业			441	441	983	939
金融业	100839	116141	9724	10259	37284	48446
房地产业	1449	1742	359	477		
租赁和商务服务业	5434	6259	2225	2390	592	495
科学研究、技术服务和地质勘查业	7800	8899	194	194		
水利、环境和公共设施管理业	2720	2721	246	265		
居民服务和其他服务业	452	544				
教育	93979	96261				
卫生、社会保障和社会福利业	107934	119180	346	384		
文化、体育和娱乐业	7997	8687	150	241		
公共管理和社会组织	170068	201894	1248			
国际组织						
二、职工平均工资(元)	**51441**	**56129**	**20833**	**22077**	**28838**	**31195**
农、林、牧、渔业	60570	70827				
工业	63930	71188	18780	19112	22617	25168
建筑业	23168	26875	19180	18963	24364	24364
交通运输、仓储及邮政业	55151	58298	30748	30586	35574	41313
信息传输、计算机服务和软件业	114630	124774	13378	13378	32230	73309
批发和零售业	28497	33941	20966	28544	49057	45745
住宿和餐饮业			22273	22273	19535	20500
金融业	109894	126254	22793	24258	85829	108549
房地产业	60133	57125	26175	30190		
租赁和商务服务业	39549	45091	32296	34845	35461	38976
科学研究、技术服务和地质勘查业	46828	49686	34679	34679		
水利、环境和公共设施管理业	54849	54849	19039	24109		
居民服务和其他服务业	43462	52269				
教育	37626	37639				
卫生、社会保障和社会福利业	46457	49220	54952	59092		
文化、体育和娱乐业	47602	49753	27685	38806		
公共管理和社会组织	46207	53017	29168			
国际组织						

注：本表统计口径为城镇在岗职工工资总额和平均工资。

11-6 国有企、事业和机关单位从业人员工资总额及平均工资(2009年)

Total Wages and Average Wage of Employed Persons in State-owned Enterprises, Institutions and Government Agencies (2009)

项　目	单位从业人员劳动报酬(万元)	在岗职工工资总额	其他从业人员工资总额	在岗职工平均工资(元)
总　计	**964401**	**944243**	**20159**	**42585**
一、按企事业机关分				
企　业	501946	487994	13952	38522
#地　方				
事　业	259028	255696	3332	44369
#地　方				
机　关	203427	200553	2875	53588
#地　方				
二、按行业分				
农、林、牧、渔业	3875	3364	511	70827
工　业	242192	232336	9856	25401
建筑业	3612	3610	2	25787
交通运输、仓储及邮政业	27514	27493	21	40725
信息传输、计算机服务和软件业	29702	29702		117960
批发和零售业	21754	20879	875	37224
住宿和餐饮业	1380	1380		21035
金融业	177530	174846	2684	97728
房地产业	2237	2219	18	47933
租赁和商务服务业	9264	9144	120	41545
科学研究、技术服务和地质勘查业	9589	9093	496	49231
水利、环境和公共设施管理业	3009	2986	23	49269
居民服务和其他服务业	650	544	106	52269
教　育	96384	96261	123	37639
卫生、社会保障和社会福利业	121275	119564	1711	49246
文化、体育和娱乐业	9042	8928	114	49378
公共管理和社会组织	205392	201894	3498	53017
国际组织				

11-7 主要年份工业、建筑业职工工资总额和平均工资

Total Wages and Average Wage of Staff and Workers in Industrial and Construction Units in Main Years

项目	2000年		2005年		2009年	
	工资总额(万元)	平均工资(元)	工资总额(万元)	平均工资(元)	工资总额(万元)	平均工资(元)
一、工业总计	**85303**	**12316**	**142060**	**18371**	**232336**	**25401**
(一) 按经济类型分						
国有单位	18184	17409	21272	61692	24738	71188
城镇集体单位	26612	9021	44574	13593	43724	19112
其他各种单位	40507	13815	76214	18548	163874	25168
(二) 按工业行业分(大类)						
非金属矿采选业	95	15557	212	36586	301	60240
木材及竹材采运业						
食品加工业	4074	12987	410	17172	1030	26536
食品制造业	357	10037	256	15172	312	18707
饮料制造业	600	9367	576	10105	1631	12035
烟草加工业						
纺织业	2045	10137	2411	12947	1904	13146
服装及其他纤维制品制造业	4566	10761	6759	14469	8137	13388
皮革、毛皮、羽绒及其制品	74	7500	217	10757	10707	20091
木材加工及竹、藤、棕、草制品业	488	12728	57	10942		
家具制造业	21	6118	7424	17079	12973	26704
造纸及纸制品业	1099	11458	1406	12281	1793	17880
印刷业、记录煤介的复制	709	9275	1270	12423	1474	15536
文教、体育用品制造业	6	7111	254	9922	1440	13795
石油加工及炼焦业						
化学原料及化学制品制造业	961	10934	648	9336	1606	15695
医药制造业	3707	13695	3189	17351	5984	33771
化学纤维制造业						
橡胶制品业	60	4082				
塑料制品业	1244	9228	1959	11793	6479	19266
非金属矿物制品业	1487	9124	4621	13149	1670	25219
黑色金属冶炼及压延加工业						
有色金属冶炼及压延加工业	130	15140	105	13513	110	13568
金属制品业	4812	20636	1055	12964	707	13388
普通机械制造业	1768	12832	1768	20583	3686	34197
专用设备制造业	719	12703	309	13214	678	13723
交通运输设备制造业	490	12519	965	32163	7999	32125
电气机械及器材制造业	13773	8039	16399	11894	21898	20897
电子及通信设备制造业	22371	16436	35289	20038	61378	28136
仪器、仪表及文化办公用品制造业	6123	8418	16175	11973	34564	20537
其他制造业	1445	9846	173	13872	1088	14737
电力蒸汽热水生产和供应业	10342	22136	34588	53575	35366	61006
煤气生产和供应业	755	28614				
自来水生产和供应业	982	14496	3507	28861	7356	45326
二、建筑业总计	**7689**	**9820**	**2261**	**18385**	**3610**	**25787**
国有单位	1911	12418	1693	17603	3225	26875
城镇集体单位	5778	9184	542	21235	358	18963
其他各种单位			26	20308	27	24364

注：2000年起本表劳动工资统计口径为城镇在岗职工工资总额和平均工资。

11-8 历年居民收支、农民收入

Income and Expenditure of Urban Households and Net Income of Rural Households over Years

年 份	城市居民人均可支配收入(元)	城市居民人均消费性支出(元)	农民人均纯收入(元)
1978			149
1979			186
1980			266
1981			449
1982			544
1983			586
1984			649
1985	791	689	746
1986	1033	883	874
1987	1247	1174	1039
1988	1778	1583	1193
1989	2282	1980	1268
1990	2508	2038	1359
1991	3068	2481	1459
1992	4026	3901	1976
1993	5970	5533	2479
1994	8270	7270	3185
1995	9588	9220	3988
1996	10824	8585	7596
1997	11032	8309	5021
1998	11506	8644	5534
1999	12954	11348	6177
2000	14142	12529	6731
2001	16938	14669	7366
2002	16949	15157	7907
2003	18471	15446	8481
2004	20526	18426	9083
2005	22882	21768	9842
2006	25320	18995	10661
2007	27025	21545	11606
2008	30275	23208	12328
2009	33045	24270	13064

注：本表可支配收入1997年以前是生活费收入口径，1997年起是可支配收入口径，下同。

11-9 历年城市居民家庭户基本情况

Basic Conditions of Urban Households over Years

年 份	平均每户家庭人口(人)	平均每户家庭就业人口(人)	平均每户住房使用面积(平方米)	平均每户家庭可支配收入(元)	平均每户家庭消费性支出(元)
1985	3.89	2.30	42.79	3077	2680
1986	4.01	2.13	48.12	4142	3541
1987	4.02	2.09	52.26	5013	4719
1988	4.08	2.17	61.20	7254	6459
1989	3.88	2.01	65.96	8854	7682
1990	4.06	2.09	64.96	10182	8274
1991	4.08	2.14	65.28	12517	10122
1992	4.06	2.06	69.02	16346	15838
1993	3.86	2.68	77.20	23044	21357
1994	3.86	2.26	88.78	31922	28062
1995	3.94	2.18	78.80	37777	36327
1996	4.07	2.31	85.47	44054	34941
1997	4.02	2.30	84.42	44349	33402
1998	3.92	2.17	101.92	45104	33884
1999	4.05	2.38	120.29	52464	45959
2000	3.89	2.69	121.10	55012	48738
2001	3.75	2.30	149.59	63518	55009
2002	3.66	2.47	152.99	62033	55475
2003	3.57	2.11	147.73	65941	55142
2004	3.50	2.17	145.53	71841	64491
2005	3.38	2.14	144.26	77341	73576
2006	3.68	2.31	166.23	93178	69902
2007	3.41	2.09	147.11	92155	73468
2008	3.43	1.81	138.06	103843	79603
2009	3.38	2.00	136.59	111692	82033

注：平均每户住房使用面积2002年以前为平均每户居住面积口径。

11-10 历年人均总收入分类

Categories of Total Income Per Capita over Years

单位：元

年 份	年人均总收入	#可支配收入	工资性收入	经营净收入	财产性收入	转移性收入
1985	837	791	603			
1986	1111	1033	974			
1987	1364	1247	989			
1988	1889	1778	1097			
1989	2439	2282	1185			
1990	2678	2508	1459	46	30	417
1991	3343	3062	2160	226	55	534
1992	4520	4026	2560	411	175	709
1993	6623	5969	3684	749	889	319
1994	9131	8270	5758	840	553	994
1995	10491	9588	6260	1210	659	1329
1996	11640	10824	8428	1127	455	1273
1997	11063	11032	8024	625	349	1544
1998	11551	11506	8334	884	319	1207
1999	13009	12954	7910	1799	357	1541
2000	14231	14142	8702	2740	895	720
2001	17062	16938	11037	2643	895	1879
2002	17711	16949	13050	1662	1076	1923
2003	19478	18471	15282	1598	1210	1388
2004	21875	20526	17153	1634	1553	1535
2005	24663	22882	18524	2709	1894	1536
2006	27157	25320	18318	4389	2504	1946
2007	29335	27025	18930	3359	4849	2101
2008	31967	30275	20872	4521	3527	3047
2009	35750	33045	23723	4724	4209	3094

注：1. 本表2007年以前采用50户抽样调查的统计口径,2007年起采用250户抽样调查的统计口径，下同。
2. 本表年人均总收入指标2002年以前采用年人均实际收入统计口径， 2002年起采用年人均总收入统计口径，下同。

11-11 历年人均消费性支出分类

Categories of Per Capita Living Expenditure over Years

单位：元

年 份	年人均消费性支出	食 品	衣 着	家庭设备用品及服务	医疗保健	交通与通讯	娱乐教育文化服务	居 住	杂项商品和服务	恩格尔系数(%)
1985	689	493	28	48	14	4	21	58	23	71.6
1986	883	588	43	84	15	6	46	66	35	66.6
1987	1174	709	64	128	55	9	106	79	24	60.4
1988	1583	977	64	171	22	12	124	136	77	61.7
1989	1980	1235	101	196	55	24	115	156	98	62.4
1990	2038	1295	95	153	42	25	113	184	131	63.5
1991	2481	1476	188	122	47	47	211	254	136	59.5
1992	3901	1834	259	263	94	587	331	369	164	47.0
1993	5533	2615	373	583	133	855	389	333	252	47.3
1994	7270	3172	420	925	192	850	714	761	236	43.6
1995	9220	3644	604	694	258	1562	991	1084	383	39.5
1996	8585	3682	706	660	225	990	847	674	802	42.9
1997	8309	3681	594	435	415	916	939	880	449	44.3
1998	8644	3785	457	612	455	1025	1074	659	577	43.8
1999	11348	3712	400	601	371	3398	1043	898	923	32.7
2000	12529	4048	487	623	431	3309	1517	1218	896	32.3
2001	14669	4572	648	746	513	4258	1429	1173	1330	31.2
2002	15157	4818	748	611	529	4303	2660	1060	428	31.8
2003	15446	4804	921	1093	693	2062	2512	2966	395	31.1
2004	18426	5041	1134	925	811	4973	2673	2517	352	27.4
2005	21768	6035	1285	1165	811	7482	3205	1242	543	27.7
2006	18995	6321	1238	1229	809	3531	3001	2341	525	33.3
2007	21545	6966	1213	1342	860	5208	3515	1903	538	32.3
2008	23208	7778	1349	1539	1332	4462	3464	2585	699	33.5
2009	24270	7972	1492	1616	1400	5456	3326	2232	776	32.8

注：本表中的各项人均支出按全部调查人口计算。

11-12 不同收入等级年人均可支配收入与消费性支出水平

Annual Disposable Income and Consumption Expenditure Per Capita by Level of Income

单位：元

年份	年人均可支配收入水平	#最低收入户	低收入户	高收入户	最高收入户	年人均消费性支出水平	#最低收入户	低收入户	高收入户	最高收入户
1985	791					689				
1986	1033					883				
1987	1247					1174				
1988	1778					1583				
1989	2282					1980				
1990	2508	1391	1744	3774	4546	2038	1170	1539	2099	4156
1991	3068	1665	2286	4092	4592	2481	1725	1877	2699	3784
1992	4026	2053	2650	5988	7275	3901	1966	2648	4690	6070
1993	5970	2977	4203	8484	9852	5533	3046	3685	6691	6956
1994	8270	4157	5248	12217	14265	7270	4477	5762	10839	8378
1995	9588	4539	5867	13828	18771	9220	4362	6912	12194	19353
1996	11639	5627	7142	15377	19224	8585	5152	6278	11496	10498
1997	11032	5778	7214	16496	22069	8309	5298	5963	15265	12323
1998	11506	6136	7853	16660	21591	8644	4888	6259	11774	14733
1999	12954	5998	7944	18951	23447	11348	4777	7755	18118	26001
2000	14142	6826	7806	19104	28769	12529	6706	7211	10297	25896
2001	16938	7174	10365	25167	33526	14669	6990	7425	18880	29834
2002	16949	6374	9398	23342	45001	15157	7224	8974	29735	21807
2003	18471	4535	9146	27000	48849	15446	6436	7990	25065	26683
2004	20526	8548	11658	31923	39058	18426	8047	9190	30530	45944
2005	22882	9590	13348	35885	43010	21768	10038	8908	31542	31498
2006	25320	13551	15633	37559	51957	18995	8841	11781	32568	39862
2007	27025	12073	16207	39071	55821	21545	12862	14547	31653	36732
2008	30275	11172	17340	46744	66034	23208	10927	14275	37741	53404
2009	33045	13642	19311	47680	71031	24270	12793	13654	27597	42949

11-13 主要年份城市居民家庭基本情况

Basic Conditions of Urban Households in Main Years

项　　　目	单 位	1985年	1990年	1995年	2000年	2005年	2008年	2009年
一、调查户数	**户**	**50**	**50**	**50**	**50**	**50**	**250**	**250**
二、平均每户家庭人口	**人**	**3.90**	**4.06**	**3.94**	**3.89**	**3.38**	**3.43**	**3.38**
三、平均每户家庭就业人口	**人**	**2.30**	**2.09**	**2.18**	**2.69**	**2.14**	**1.81**	**2.00**
四、平均每一就业者负担人口	**人**	**1.58**	**1.70**	**1.50**	**1.54**	**1.58**	**1.69**	**1.54**
五、平均每人每年可支配收入	**元**	**791**	**2508**	**9588**	**14142**	**22882**	**30275**	**33045**
#工薪收入	元	603	1459	6260	8702	18524	20872	23723
六、平均每人每年消费性支出	**元**	**689**	**2038**	**9220**	**12529**	**21768**	**23208**	**24270**
(一)食　品	元	493	1295	3644	4048	6035	7778	7972
(二)衣　着	元	28	95	604	487	1285	1349	1492
(三)家庭设备用品及服务	元	48	153	694	623	1165	1539	1616
#耐用消费品	元	21	93	368	18	425	681	522
(四)医疗保健	元	14	42	258	431	811	1332	1400
(五)交通与通讯	元	4	25	1562	3309	7482	4462	5456
(六)娱乐教育文化服务	元	21	113	991	1517	3205	3464	3326
#文化娱乐用品	元	13	36	521	532	610	759	734
文化娱乐服务	元	5	37	173	286	1112	1511	1603
教　育	元	3	40	297	699	1482	1194	989
(七)居　住	元	58	184	1084	1218	1242	2585	2232
(八)杂项商品和服务	元	23	131	383	896	543	699	776
七、平均每人住房使用面积	**平方米**	**10.98**	**16.61**	**20.00**	**31.13**	**42.68**	**40.25**	**40.41**
八、平均每人每年购买商品								
1.粮　食	公斤	106	109	74	66	65	408	393
2.油脂类	公斤	5	5	7	8	8	177	141
3.肉禽及其制品	公斤	37	48	40	50	72	1849	1694
4.蛋　类	公斤	6	6	10	9	8	94	81
5.水产品	公斤	23	29	25	29	22	663	644
6.鲜　菜	公斤	90	100	117	116	114	558	529
7.烟草类	元	3	18	52	94	53	156	168
8.酒和饮料	元	16	25	48	78	132	191	286
9.干鲜瓜果	元	11	84	258	298	344	454	564
10.奶及奶制品	元		13	42	105	264	180	301
11.服　装	元	28	95	434	356	944	1007	1108
12.衣着材料	元	2	11	30	11	4	1.82	1.16

注：1. 工薪收入2002年以前为基本工资收入口径，2002年起为工薪收入口径。
2. 平均每人住房使用面积2002年以前为平均每人居住面积口径。
3. 粮食、油脂类、肉禽及其制品、蛋类、水产品、鲜菜2008年起以元为计量单位。
4. 平均每一就业者负担人口已扣除离退休人口。

11-14 主要年份城市居民消费性支出及构成

Living Expenditure of Urban Households and Its Composition in Main Years

项　　目	单 位	1985年	1990年	1995年	2000年	2005年	2008年	2009年
一、年消费性支出	**元**	**689**	**2038**	**9220**	**12529**	**21768**	**23208**	**24270**
(一)食　品	元	493	1295	3644	4048	6035	7778	7972
(二)衣　着	元	28	95	604	487	1285	1349	1492
(三)家庭设备用品及服务	元	48	153	694	623	1165	1539	1616
#耐用消费品	元	21	93	368	18	425	681	522
(四)医疗保健	元	14	42	258	431	811	1332	1400
#药品费	元			109	240	276	432	442
滋补保健品	元			46	178	207	485	544
(五)交通与通讯	元	4	25	1562	3309	7482	4462	5456
交通	元	4	25	1245	2154	6381	3208	4153
通讯	元			317	1155	1101	1253	1303
(六)娱乐教育文化服务	元	21	113	991	1517	3205	3464	3326
文化娱乐用品	元	13	36	521	532	610	759	734
文化娱乐服务	元	5	37	173	286	1112	1511	1603
教　育	元	3	40	297	699	1482	1194	989
(七)居　住	元	58	184	1084	1218	1242	2585	2232
#住房	元	7	92	725	455	34	1205	837
水电燃料	元	51	92	358	763	972	1222	1188
(八)杂项商品和服务	元	23	131	383	896	543	699	776
二、消费性支出构成								
(一)食　品	%	71.55	63.54	39.52	32.31	27.72	33.51	32.85
(二)衣　着	%	4.06	4.66	6.55	3.89	5.90	5.81	6.15
(三)家庭设备用品及服务	%	6.97	7.51	7.53	4.97	5.35	6.63	6.65
#耐用消费品	%	43.76	60.78	53.03	2.89	1.95	2.93	2.15
(四)医疗保健	%	2.03	2.06	2.80	3.44	3.73	5.74	5.77
(五)交通与通讯	%	0.58	1.23	16.94	26.41	34.37	19.23	22.48
(六)娱乐教育文化服务	%	3.05	5.54	10.75	12.11	14.72	14.93	13.70
(七)居　住	%	8.42	9.03	11.76	9.72	5.71	11.14	9.20
(八)杂项商品和服务	%	3.34	6.43	4.15	7.15	2.50	3.01	3.20

11-15 历年城市居民家庭平均每百户主要耐用消费品拥有量

Number of Durable Consumer Goods Owned per 100 Urban Households over Years

年 份	汽车 (辆)	电冰箱 (台)	洗衣机 (台)	空调器 (台)	组合音响 (套)	彩色电视机 (台)	电话机 (部)	移动电话 (部)	电脑 (台)
1985		22	56			22			
1986		26	66			40			
1987		42	72			52			
1988		52	86			66			
1989		72	96		4	84			
1990		84	54	16	14	92			
1991		98	106	16	14	100			
1992		96	112	12	18	98	64		
1993		108	108	28	34	102	60		
1994		110	114	60	52	114	72		
1995		110	108	82	54	138	82		
1996		104	110	128	68	132	98		
1997		106	108	100	68	116	98		22
1998	2	110	112	122	64	146	96	28	28
1999	10	116	118	130	84	178	100	72	34
2000	12	108	114	150	88	178	100	126	68
2001	16	118	110	184	76	176	100	186	98
2002	24	126	112	204	76	192	100	200	102
2003	26	134	108	226	82	194	104	224	96
2004	32	132	118	258	80	192	112	264	108
2005	42	124	110	264	72	200	112	294	114
2006	44	130	112	280	80	218	116	255	90
2007	54	115	110	271	82	206	115	272	111
2008	47	110	103	200	59	180	108	248	100
2009	63	113	105	233	69	184	105	261	112

11-16　按收入等级分的城市居民家庭基本情况(2009年)

Basic Conditions of Urban Households by Level of Income (2009)

项　　目	单 位	总平均	最　低 收入户	低　收 入　户	中　等 偏下户	中　等 收入户	中　等 偏上户	高　收 入　户	最　高 收入户
调查户数	户	250	20	26	50	50	52	26	26
平均每户家庭人口	人	3.38	3.72	3.99	3.36	3.23	3.35	3.15	3.13
平均每户家庭就业人口	人	2.00	1.54	1.78	1.90	2.08	2.07	2.19	2.24
平均每一就业者负担人口	人	1.54	2.00	1.97	1.64	1.42	1.48	1.34	1.31
平均每户就业面	%	65.10	50.00	50.76	60.98	70.42	67.57	74.63	76.34
平均每人总收入	元	35750	15231	20793	26702	33639	42169	51058	76223
平均每人可支配收入	元	33045	13642	19311	24816	30700	38789	47680	71031
平均每人总支出	元	29647	14928	16014	22156	27276	39834	35875	52706
平均每人消费性支出	元	24270	12793	13654	19279	22171	32009	27597	42949
平均每一就业者总收入	元	60418	36792	46609	47220	52237	68245	73440	100735
平均每人住房建筑面积	平方米	53.75	42.37	46.71	50.16	56.94	57.18	62.34	61.99
平均每百户家庭年末主要									
耐用消费品拥有量									
家用汽车	辆	63	26	26	45	62	63	85	104
洗衣机	台	105	98	100	102	107	106	107	127
电冰箱	台	113	100	104	102	115	117	111	150
彩色电视机	台	184	156	157	170	172	204	178	254
家用电脑	台	112	79	92	104	100	138	119	138
组合音响	套	69	63	57	60	72	74	67	88
照相机	架	68	37	48	57	62	62	81	123
钢琴	架	4	4		4	2	6	4	8
空调器	台	233	170	183	207	200	285	263	319
淋浴热水器	台	128	107	119	119	128	126	141	158
消毒碗柜	台	74	56	70	62	60	81	85	100
健身器材	套	9	7	11		4	11	17	8
固定电话	部	105	96	104	96	96	111	104	123
移动电话	部	261	248	270	257	243	274	248	281

11-17 按收入等级分的城市居民家庭平均每人全年现金收入(2009年)

Per Capita Annual Cash Income of Urban Households by Level of Income (2009)

项目	单位	总平均	最低收入户	低收入户	中等偏下户	中等收入户	中等偏上户	高收入户	最高收入户
一、平均每户家庭就业人口	**人**	**2.00**	**1.54**	**1.78**	**1.90**	**2.08**	**2.07**	**2.19**	**2.24**
国有单位职工人数	人	0.31	0.24	0.29	0.14	0.32	0.33	0.23	0.75
集体单位职工人数	人	0.48	0.24	0.26	0.58	0.59	0.34	0.68	0.62
其它各类经济类型单位职工人数	人	0.35	0.34	0.30	0.39	0.24	0.50	0.40	0.23
个体雇主与自营者人数	人	0.27	0.20	0.19	0.19	0.21	0.39	0.38	0.32
个体被雇人员数	人	0.39	0.37	0.56	0.51	0.43	0.30	0.31	0.25
其他就业人员人数	人	0.15	0.15	0.19	0.07	0.26	0.19	0.12	
二、家庭总收入	**元**	**35750**	**15231**	**20793**	**26702**	**33639**	**42169**	**51058**	**76223**
#可支配收入	元	33045	13642	19311	24816	30700	38789	47680	71031
(一)工薪性收入	元	23723	9309	13262	19260	23481	27728	33690	41291
工资及补贴收入	元	23690	9292	13206	19245	23384	27725	33682	41283
其他劳动收入	元	32	17	56	15	97	3	8	8
(二)经营净收入	元	4724	1545	2052	2418	3944	6416	9841	14093
(三)财产性收入	元	4209	860	2733	2404	3964	4608	4663	12032
#股息与红利收入	元	1788	904	1490	1265	1980	1662	1996	4166
租金收入	元	2142	385	1187	971	1839	2626	2439	6637
(四)转移性收入	元	3094	3517	2746	2620	2250	3418	2863	5373
#离退休金	元	2060	3142	2007	1696	1318	2350	1529	3304
赠送收入	元	524	71	406	447	450	569	768	1049

11-18 城市居民家庭平均每人全年消费性支出（2009年）

Per Capita Annual Living Expenditure of Urban Households (2009)

项目	单位	总平均	最低收入户	低收入户	中等偏下户	中等收入户	中等偏上户	高收入户	最高收入户
平均每人年消费性支出	**元**	**24270**	**12793**	**13654**	**19279**	**22171**	**32009**	**27597**	**42949**
（一）食　品	**元**	**7972**	**4948**	**5716**	**7328**	**7631**	**8840**	**9440**	**12279**
粮油类	元	602	467	505	634	587	626	697	663
肉禽蛋水产品类	元	2418	1760	2144	2564	2313	2467	2892	2685
蔬菜类	元	586	444	527	627	554	591	698	642
调味品	元	62	48	48	66	63	61	73	75
糖烟酒饮料类	元	540	384	451	506	467	629	703	657
干鲜瓜果类	元	564	376	469	592	535	589	685	681
糕点、奶及奶制品	元	420	266	321	404	476	427	444	568
其他食品	元	87	54	74	78	77	92	115	132
饮食服务	元	2694	1151	1176	1857	2559	3358	3132	6176
（二）衣　着	**元**	**1492**	**622**	**957**	**951**	**1462**	**1749**	**1917**	**3160**
#服　装	元	1108	448	708	691	1035	1312	1389	2503
衣着材料	元	1.16	1.13	0.57	3.30	0.35		0.44	2.37
（三）居　住	**元**	**2232**	**1076**	**1215**	**2058**	**1787**	**3564**	**2096**	**3130**
#住房	元	837	2	61	867	467	2111	362	1031
水电、燃料及其它	元	1191	979	1068	1092	1187	1154	1480	1539
（四）家庭设备用品及服务	**元**	**1616**	**857**	**860**	**1114**	**1451**	**1945**	**1824**	**3723**
#耐用消费品	元	522	244	219	328	434	781	681	1026
（五）医疗保健	**元**	**1400**	**775**	**982**	**1094**	**1268**	**2041**	**1513**	**1927**
#药品费	元	442	247	410	402	423	489	492	630
滋补保健品	元	544	325	211	461	413	861	606	867
（六）交通与通讯	**元**	**5456**	**2928**	**1548**	**4180**	**5035**	**8320**	**5636**	**9965**
#交通	元	4152	2091	565	3058	3640	6986	4015	8029
通讯	元	1303	837	983	1123	1395	1335	1621	1936
（七）教育文化娱乐服务	**元**	**3326**	**1310**	**2125**	**2194**	**2817**	**4772**	**3973**	**6314**
文化娱乐用品	元	734	381	314	427	555	1354	846	1156
文化娱乐服务	元	1603	234	583	1081	1461	2012	1983	4259
教育	元	989	695	1228	686	802	1406	1144	899
（八）杂项商品和服务	**元**	**776**	**277**	**251**	**360**	**720**	**778**	**1198**	**2451**

11-19 按收入等级分的城市居民平均每人全年主要食品购买量（2009年）

Per Capita Annual Purchases of Main Food Commodities of Urban Households by Level of Income (2009)

项　　目	单位	总平均	最低收入户	低收入户	中等偏下户	中等收入户	中等偏上户	高收入户	最高收入户
粮　食	元	393.33	306.11	324.32	420.53	382.52	416.18	443.15	427.33
#大　米	公斤	52.60	41.48	44.29	59.01	47.95	54.98	60.68	56.13
其它粮食及制品	元	143.93	116.19	116.52	143.70	152.95	153.12	149.13	161.92
淀粉及薯类	元	21.25	15.05	16.91	21.59	22.17	24.38	22.79	21.65
干豆类及豆制品	元	46.54	39.35	39.52	46.51	47.34	50.27	53.31	45.81
油脂类	元	140.71	106.32	124.05	145.51	135.18	135.61	177.36	168.13
#食用植物油	公斤	7.32	6.03	6.57	7.58	7.23	6.86	9.02	8.40
猪牛羊	公斤	33.97	23.97	30.16	36.44	31.46	36.35	40.70	35.96
肉制品	元	187.81	157.58	166.57	193.81	169.05	176.53	242.89	235.84
禽　类	元	537.98	420.48	478.04	574.89	523.77	515.83	658.21	598.95
#鸡	公斤	16.48	12.93	14.66	17.90	15.98	16.01	20.13	17.44
禽制品	元	119.46	103.53	101.30	118.09	121.13	113.51	145.41	143.24
蛋　类	元	80.64	60.18	81.89	81.12	82.32	75.76	97.57	86.36
鱼	公斤	19.42	13.86	17.79	21.28	17.50	20.15	23.16	21.20
虾	公斤	1.68	1.21	1.35	1.83	1.68	1.66	1.99	1.97
鲜　菜	公斤	110.20	87.31	97.58	121.08	103.18	111.68	132.58	112.93
调味品	元	62.08	47.80	48.14	65.64	62.85	60.81	73.31	75.39
糖　类	元	86.36	73.37	79.05	76.82	86.22	90.37	97.95	107.20
烟草类	元	167.50	119.67	143.91	169.77	120.74	180.19	296.55	172.43
白　酒	元	8.91	5.56	6.17	10.91	6.23	8.72	8.52	17.51
果　酒	元	24.56	13.98	20.07	19.01	39.87	27.99	20.69	17.36
啤　酒	元	7.00	5.34	5.09	5.88	6.39	6.07	12.74	10.71
瓶装饮用水	公斤	8.04	5.59	6.19	8.91	5.52	9.05	9.15	12.60
鲜　果	公斤	47.96	31.43	40.35	51.89	45.85	50.32	57.21	54.40
奶及奶制品	元	300.59	186.68	231.78	288.90	359.52	293.94	306.59	406.31
在外饮食	元	2693.37	1150.53	1176.21	1856.44	2559.10	3357.71	3131.97	6176.22

11-20 按收入等级分的城市居民平均每人(每户)全年主要非食品购买量（2009年）

Per Capita or Per Household Annual Purchases of Main Non-food Commodities of Urban Households by Level of Income (2009)

项　　目	单位	总平均	最低收入户	低收入户	中等偏下户	中等收入户	中等偏上户	高收入户	最高收入户
衣　着	元/人	1492	622	957	951	1462	1749	1917	3160
服　装	件/人	13.66	6.16	8.64	9.13	12.60	16.79	15.48	29.80
衣着材料	元/人	1.16	1.13	0.57	3.30	0.35		0.44	2.37
鞋　类	双/人	3.59	2.18	2.67	2.71	4.03	3.80	4.34	5.81
其它衣着用品	元/人	39.05	11.76	5.31	16.96	35.32	77.10	24.76	93.57
金银珠宝饰品	元/人	152.44	31.02	27.49	40.73	144.14	122.69	153.23	732.05
化妆品	元/人	205.67	78.33	86.79	85.37	195.62	252.14	296.05	551.80
床上用品	元/人	118.98	35.45	50.21	151.64	65.57	90.41	110.80	390.70
家庭日用杂品	元/人	695.42	420.07	517.79	566.24	745.03	756.13	777.52	1127.62
水　费	元/人	222.31	180.32	209.47	227.34	225.96	198.52	265.54	265.90
电　费	元/人	673.02	511.25	584.38	576.29	656.28	691.03	888.48	910.24
液化石油汽	元/人	291.64	287.34	273.20	287.35	304.44	247.80	324.55	362.62
微波炉	台/百户	1.68		3.04	0.20	2.78	0.97	1.15	4.23
洗衣机	台/百户	9.04	2.54	6.08	7.80	8.15	16.65	6.92	8.08
淋浴热水器	台/百户	3.20	6.10	2.66	0.20	4.17	3.10		8.85
空调器	台/百户	13.52	12.71	2.66	8.80	9.93	19.16	13.85	29.62
彩色电视机	台/百户	7.44	4.07	3.04	3.40	6.16	13.55	8.85	11.15
家用电脑	台/百户	13.40	2.03	9.87	9.40	8.74	24.00	20.00	14.62
移动电话	部/百户	38.04	15.76	89.62	24.80	39.93	29.81	30.77	48.08
汽　车	台/百户	2.68			1.99	2.90	3.85	4.00	4.62

11-21　农村居民人均实际收入与实际支出（2006-2009年）

Per Capita Actual Income and Expenditure of Rural Households (2006-2009)

单位：元/人

年　份	家庭现金收入	可支配收入	家庭现金支出	生活消费现金支出	食品消费支出
2006	17676	13663	12173	9370	3380
2007	19945	16373	13078	10771	3805
2008	20622	18038	13154	10887	3823
2009	22077	19241	14643	11598	4061

11-22　农村居民人均实际收入（2006-2009年）

Per Capita Actual Income of Rural Households (2006-2009)

单位：元/人

年　份	家庭现金收　入	#工资性收入	#家庭经营收入	财产性收入	转移性收入
2006	17676	8522	4195	4171	789
2007	19945	9446	4388	5191	920
2008	20622	9876	4326	5531	889
2009	22077	10442	4517	6210	908

注：农村居民数据由农村住户抽样调查1195户样本户推算得出，下同。

11-23 农村居民人均消费支出（2006-2009年）

Per Capita Consumption Expenditure of Rural Households (2006-2009)

单位：元/人

年份	生活消费现金支出	#食品	衣着	家庭设备及服务	医疗保健	交通通讯	教育文化娱乐服务	居住	杂项商品和服务
2006	9370	3380	448	474	510	1543	932	1458	625
2007	10771	3805	602	581	494	1953	1029	2001	306
2008	10887	3823	691	622	545	1799	1198	1500	709
2009	11598	4061	692	515	618	1931	1338	1626	817

11-24 每百户农村居民家庭主要耐用消费品拥有量（2006-2009年）

Number of Durable Consumer Goods Owned per 100 Rural Households (2006-2009)

项目	单位	2006年	2007年	2008年	2009年
洗衣机	台	101	105	107	103
电冰箱	台	108	111	111	109
空调机	台	210	223	234	209
微波炉	台	37	45	50	46
热水器	台	137	143	142	129
摩托车	辆	134	95	84	83
生活用汽车	辆	49	59	67	53
固定电话机	部	139	137	137	122
移动电话	部	240	251	261	257
彩色电视机	台	175	178	183	160
影碟机	台	92	95	95	74
摄像机	台	15	17	21	13
照相机	架	54	59	64	53
家庭计算机	台	84	97	107	98
中高档乐器	件	8	9	10	10

主要统计指标解释

城市居民家庭可支配收入 指调查户可用于最终消费支出和其它非义务性支出以及储蓄的总和，即居民家庭可以用来自由支配的收入。它是家庭总收入扣除交纳的所得税、个人交纳的社会保障费以及调查户的记帐补贴后的收入。计算公式为：可支配收入=家庭总收入-经营性支出-交纳所得税-个人交纳的社会保障支出-记帐补贴

城市居民家庭消费性支出 指调查户用于本家庭日常生活的全部支出，包括食品、衣着、家庭设备用品及服务、医疗保健、交通和通讯、娱乐教育文化服务、居住、杂项商品和服务八大类等，均按商品（服务）的用途分类。

农村居民家庭总收入 是指农村住户年内从各种来源得到的全部实际收入（包括现金收入和实物收入）。由基本收入、转移性收入和财产性收入三部分组成。

农村居民家庭纯收入 是农村常住居民家庭总收入扣除相应的各项费用性支出后，归农民所有的收入。它既可以用于生产、非生产投资、改善物质和文化生活，以及用于再分配的支出和结余的收入。这个指标用来观察农民实际收入水平，以及农民扩大再生产和改善生活的能力。

农村居民家庭生活费支出 是指农民住户年内用于物质生活和精神生活方面的实际支出，直接反映农民的生活水平、研究农民消费结构变化的基本指标。生活消费支出包括食品，衣着、居住，家庭设备，用品及服务，医疗保健，交通和通讯，文化教育娱乐用品及服务，其他商品和服务等消费支出。

单位从业人员劳动报酬 指各单位在一定时期内直接支付给本单位在岗职工的工资总额和其他从业人员的劳动报酬。

在岗职工工资总额 指各单位在一定时期内直接支付给本单位在岗职工的劳动报酬总额。

不在岗职工（离岗职工）生活费 指各单位在一定时期内按政策直接支付给本单位中离开本单位仍保留劳动关系的这部分不在岗职工的最低生活保障费。

职工工资总额 指各单位在一定时期内直接支付给本单位在岗职工的工资总额和不在岗职工（离岗职工）的生活费。

单位从业人员劳动报酬和职工工资总额的计算原则应以直接支付给职工的全部劳动报酬为根据。各单位支付给职工的劳动报酬以及其他根据有关规定支付的工资，不论是计入成本的还是不计入成本的，不论是按国家规定列入计征奖金税项目的，还是未列入计征奖金税项目的，不论是以货币形式支付的还是以实物形式支付的，均包括在内。

职工平均工资 指企业、事业、机关单位的职工在一定时期内平均每人所得的货币工资额。它表明一定时期职工工资收入的高低程度，是反映职工工资水平的主要指标。计算公式为：职工平均工资=报告期实际支付全部职工工资总额/报告期全部职工平均人数

职工平均实际工资 指扣除物价变动因素后职工平均工资。计算公式为：
职工平均实际工资=报告期职工平均工资÷报告期城镇居民消费价格指数

十二、社会事业

Social Undertakings

12-1 主要年份社会事业主要指标
Main Indicators of Social Undertakings in Main Years

项　　　　目	单 位	1985年	1990年	1995年	2000年	2005年	2008年	2009年
国有企事业单位科学技术人员数	人	9166	11629	16856		42593	51729	55097
三种专利申请量	件		34	325	1653	6694	14406	19106
三种专利授权量	件		30	262	1399	3114	8093	12918
各类技术合同签订项目数	项		5	46	110	50	54	60
各类技术合同签订项目金额	万元		12	1804	3469	4058	12838	6996
教育现代化发展指数	%						97.3	
在校学生数								
普通高等学校	人			1628	3241	16645	28656	33992
成人高等学校	人	403	531	1254	3642	12665	18658	21464
中等职业技术学校	人	3363	8919	18737	23144	29487	45419	46538
普通中学	人	46596	61188	92481	112418	191044	248442	249464
小学	人	134421	162664	195063	272793	480923	528644	511160
学龄儿童入学率	%	99.8	99.9	100.0	100.0	100.0	100.0	100.0
小学毕业生升学率	%	79.5	95.4	99.2	99.8	99.9	100.0	100.0
初中毕业生升学率	%	38.5	43.6	85.4	90.3	94.1	96.6	97.0
普通高中毕业生升学率	%	26.5	31.2	64.9	70.5	96.5	91.0	87.5
高考省线入围人数	人	285	224	809	2646	11196	9987	12569
电影放映单位	个	60	114	218	192	70	40	40
艺术表演团体	个	1	7	2	1		1	4
文化馆	个	1	1	1	1	1	1	1
公共图书馆(室)	个	3	5	15	18	473	387	504
博物馆	个	2	2	2	3	16	23	31
档案馆	个	1	1	1	1	1	1	1
《东莞日报》发行量	万份		177	987	1578	2751	4380	4745
广播电台	座		1	1	1	1	1	1
电视台	座	1	1	1	1	1	1	1
病床床位数	张	2323	3866	5798	7081	11688	16778	18080
卫生技术人员数	人	3305	3902	5290	6915	16608	33113	35766
#医生	人	1201	1721	2299	3309	6901	11869	12884
平均每千人口医院床位数	张	2	3	4	5	7	10	10
平均每千人口卫生技术人员数	人	3	3	4	5	10	19	20
举办镇街级及以上体育运动会	次	72	114	14	5	8	7	5
参加运动会的运动员人数	万人次	3.60	6.38	5.15	1.70	1.36	0.21	0.30
执业律师人数	人	6	12	85	130	625	1056	1223
公证人员数	人	6	10	19	20	48	82	90
人民调解委员会调解人员数	人	3603	3664	3664	3644	4556	19547	16248
优抚收养单位收养人数	人		19	11	7	8	8	7
每万元工业产值工业废水排放量	吨/万元	154.82	41.83	10.55	7.73	4.78	5.32	
工业固体废物利用率	%	37.5	17.9	18.2	63.8	86.5	94.3	95.0
城市环境空气质量优良天数	天						344	

注：1. 中等职业技术学校不含一般成人中专，下同。
　　2. 2004年起，卫生方面包含诊所、卫生所、医务室及村卫生室的数据，与往年数不可比；其中平均每千人口医院床位数及卫生技术人员数是按户籍人口计算。
　　3. 由于工业废水排放量2007年起统计口径变更，因此2007年起每万元工业产值工业废水排放量与往年数不可比。

12-2 科技活动基本情况(2009年)

Basic Statistics on Scientific and Technological Activities (2009)

项　　目	单位	2009年	项　　目	单位	2009年
一、科技企业			专利申请数	件	403
企业数	个	2863	获专利授权数	件	238
#国家高新技术企业	个	246	营业收入	万元	305400
省创新型试点企业	个	6	四、科技园区和基地		
省创新型企业	个	5	国家级高新区	个	
省民营科技企业	个	562	省级高新区	个	1
重点培育上市后备科技企业	个	41	专业镇	个	13
市民营科技企业	个	2003	#工业总产值	万元	30196665
二、科技合作			专业镇科技投入	万元	106305
国际合作项目立项数	项	11	国家高新技术企业数	家	132
#国家立项数	项	2	火炬计划特色产业基地	个	8
省级立项数	项	9	#工业总产值	万元	14125800
国际科技合作示范基地	个	1	国家高新技术企业数	家	77
#国家级基地	个		科技企业孵化器/加速器	个	3
省级基地	个	1	#建筑场地面积	万平方米	7.4
产学研项目立项数	项	99	在孵企业数	个	209
#省部合作	项	83	毕业企业数	个	53
省院合作	项	16	五、工程中心		
总投入	万元	25892	国家级工程中心	个	1
新增产值	万元	53200	省级工程中心	个	34
新增利税	万元	5640	#工程中心职工总数	人	9199
省部产学研示范基地	个	24	经费收入	万元	209939
省部产学研创新联盟	个	4	研究开发课题(项目)	项	241
三、科技机构			专利授权数	项	126
机构数	个	76	研究与发展(R&D)人员	人	4473
从业人员	人	7791	研究与发展经费	万元	63054
#科技活动人员	人	3030	市级工程中心	个	69
#本科及以上	人	2279	#工程中心职工总数	人	7142
#中级及以上职称	人	741	经费收入	万元	100665
科技经费筹集额	万元	58903	研究开发课题(项目)	项	967
#政府拨款	万元	12372	专利授权数	项	502
企业自筹	万元	8510	研究与发展(R&D)人员	人	4579
科技经费内部支出	万元	46163	研究与发展经费	万元	79459
项目(课题)数	项	293	六、科技金融		
项目(课题)经费支出额	万元	29084	科技贷款机构	个	
论文数	篇	445	上市后备企业	个	41
科技专著数	篇	8	创业风险机构	个	3

12-3 主要年份企事业单位科学技术人员及研究(开发)活动基本情况

Number of Scientific and Technical Personnel and Basic Statistics on R&D Activities in Enterprises and Institutions in Main Years

项　　目	单 位	1990年	1995年	2000年	2002年	2004年	2005年	2008年	2009年
一、国有企事业单位科技人员数	**人**	**11629**	**16856**		**28154**	**39398**	**42593**	**51729**	**55097**
#工程技术人员	人	1084	1718		1651	1752	1839	2375	2302
农业技术人员	人	432	230		183	276	290	343	284
卫生技术人员	人	1430	1988		6155	14541	16188	20955	21679
科学研究人员	人	21	52		19	141	77	50	43
教学人员	人	7524	11553		18599	20905	21717	24063	26741
经济人员	人	278	329		555	561	636	1048	1129
财会人员	人	581	484		500	613	1299	1827	1940
统计人员	人	170	77		70	74	82	100	122
二、科技活动情况									
科技活动机构数	个		604	1450	1482	1810	1950	2466	
科技活动人员数	人		93542	107321	116496	125250	144448	152433	
科技活动经费筹集总额	万元		13248	44885	58086	71867	95486	901683	
科技活动经费使用总额	万元		12109	44773	50901	40553	87565	573407	
科技活动项目数	个		3811	2072	2091	3405	3523	3509	
三、全部科学研究及开发机构情况									
机构数	个	6	12	40	51	117	127	79	
职工总数	人	158	314	473	533	2216	2412	4278	
科研开发经费筹集总额	万元	591	2527	4826	5010	16951	26402	45234	
科研开发经费支出总额	万元	557	2036	4568	4723	11842	18406	42518	
四、县级及以上政府部门属研究与开发基本情况									
机构数	个	5	5	5	5	4	4	4	
职工总数	人	158	245	242	237	256	281	290	
#科学家(工程师)	人	18	23	44	27	39	87	131	
其他科技人员	人	40	55	63	128	82	82	92	
经费收入	万元	591	2052	2956	2155	2895	4100	9416	
#政府拨款	万元	428	658	774	1121	1938	2269	9268	
经费支出	万元	557	2035	2748	1918	2740	3352	6338	
基本建设投资实际完成额	万元	279	570	415	249	424	343	2489	
五、接收大中专毕业生									
大学本科及以上	人	445	735	1805	2673	5922	6029	6169	6440
大专	人	478	936	1226	1177	3608	3838	8817	8085
中专	人	456	1118	1331		2213	1990	8	

12-4　主要年份三种专利申请量与授权量

Number of Three Kinds of Patents Applications Accepted and Granted in Main Years

单位：件 单位：件

项　　目	1990年	1995年	1999年	2000年	2002年	2004年	2005年	2008年	2009年
一、申请量	**34**	**325**	**1221**	**1653**	**3100**	**4325**	**6694**	**14406**	**19106**
发　明	1	5	15	35	90	185	245	1188	1593
实用新型	5	70	305	386	937	1523	1971	4606	6557
外观设计	28	250	901	1232	2073	2617	4478	8612	10956
二、授权量	**30**	**262**	**819**	**1399**	**2680**	**3167**	**3114**	**8093**	**12918**
发　明	1	8	16	4	10	26	24	115	254
实用新型	4	41	157	344	669	919	1116	3616	4370
外观设计	25	213	646	1051	2001	2222	1974	4362	8294

12-5　主要年份各类技术合同签订情况

Statistics on Technical Contracts Signed by Type in Main Years

项　　目	1990年	1995年	1999年	2000年	2002年	2004年	2005年	2008年	2009年
一、技术合同项目数(项)	**5**	**46**	**20**	**110**	**91**	**69**	**50**	**54**	**60**
#技术开发合同	3			1	5	62	41	48	46
技术咨询合同							2		
技术转让合同	2	44	20	78	81	6	1	2	3
技术服务合同		2		31	5	1	6	4	11
二、技术合同金额(万元)	**12**	**1804**	**1124**	**3469**	**766**	**4278**	**4058**	**12838**	**6996**
#技术开发合同				1000	110	4175	1888	11145	6031
技术咨询合同			1124				80		
技术转让合同	12	1656		2007	637	91	2000	1428	270
技术服务合同		148		1362	19	13	90	265	695
三、技术合同实现金额(万元)	**7**	**1623**	**1077**	**2398**	**730**	**2726**	**2522**	**3694**	**6264**
#技术开发合同				700	110	2623	1427	2111	5299
技术咨询合同							35		
技术转让合同	7	1535	1077	1260	601	91	1000	1428	270
技术服务合同		88		438	19	13	60	155	695

12-6 主要年份高新科技发展情况

Statistics on High-tech Development in Main Years

项　　目	单 位	1995年	1999年	2000年	2002年	2004年	2005年	2008年	2009年
一、高新技术企业									
企业数	个	11	53	66	102	201	247	382	246
总产值	亿元	30.55	215.00	274.41	405.32	690.00	925.07	1471.74	780.97
总收入	亿元	26.76	213.00	266.49	409.93	691.00	927.72	1454.28	797.10
出口总额	亿美元	0.54	14.40	7.34	20.16	45.00	71.59	127.82	58.26
从业人员数	人	6400	29840	36304	50955	107541	171812	294412	171813
#科技活动人员	人	832	6424	8663	14426	26885	34448	49459	56478
二、高新技术产品									
产品	个	27	159	177	619	668	947	1558	1828
总产值	亿元	31.43	144.00	186.00	430.23	711.11	1062.40	2028.44	1778.97
#电子与信息技术	亿元				289.99	355.63	726.92	1412.38	1351.58
生物技术	亿元				3.63	8.45	8.20	16.83	17.79
新材料技术	亿元				22.80	34.48	51.43	135.89	213.39
光机电一体化技术	亿元				54.05	91.36	146.94	100.32	101.16
新能源高效节能技术	亿元				4.80	11.40	32.71	78.38	61.94
环保技术	亿元				0.53	1.07	6.58	30.35	33.11
其他	亿元				54.43	208.71	89.63	254.29	
三、国家级计划项目									
火炬项目	项		3	7	3	16	14	23	
总投资	万元		5680	24162	360	38000	21580	37206	
总产值	万元		2240	17677	2867	33253	15976	129450	
利税总额	万元		675	2690	604	6635	1637	9639	
星火项目	项	1	5	3	7	4	3		
总投资	万元	1000	8000	2405	35640	3300	700		
总产值	万元	250	26333	2084	24263	550	1340		
利税总额	万元	30	5946	1078	274	95	152		
新产品计划项目	项		7						
四、省级计划项目									
火炬项目	项	1	6	5	2	29	13	11	
总投资	万元	1485	20215	6166	720	60000	13248	14474	
总产值	万元	2250	67000	6545	2067	31428	51631	43363	
利税总额	万元	410	1423	3143	584	6910	9648	3665	
星火项目	项	5	8	9	3				
总投资	万元	2910	10050	5321	524				
总产值	万元	6500	28933	10494	1362				
利税总额	万元	950	6462	3840	103				
新产品计划项目	项		18						

注：高新技术企业情况2009年以前为省级高新技术企业情况，2009年起为国家级高新技术企业情况。

12-7 主要年份科学技术成果项数

Number of Achievements for Scientific and Technological Research in Main Years

单位：项

项　目	1985年	1990年	1995年	1999年	2000年	2002年	2004年	2005年	2008年	2009年
获省级科技进步奖		**1**	**4**	**9**	**6**	**3**	**6**	**3**	**10**	**19**
市级科技进步奖	**68**	**31**	**22**	**39**	**47**	**47**	**60**	**75**	**83**	**85**
1. 农业方面	**30**	**8**	**3**	**11**	**13**	**4**	**10**	**9**	**9**	**8**
一等奖	1	4		1	2		1	1	2	2
二等奖	3	3		3	5	3	2	3	3	2
三等奖	18	1	3	6	6	1	7	5	4	4
四等奖	8									
2. 工业方面	**32**	**18**	**14**	**19**	**24**	**23**	**27**	**42**	**57**	**62**
特等奖					1		1	2		
一等奖	1	3		3	5	4	4	7	15	19
二等奖	8	11	5	8	8	6	11	19	21	16
三等奖	10	4	9	8	10	13	11	14	21	27
四等奖	13									
3. 医药卫生方面	**6**	**5**	**5**	**5**	**10**	**20**	**22**	**25**	**17**	**15**
特等奖										
一等奖			1	1		3	1		2	1
二等奖		1			2	6	6	4	4	6
三等奖	2	4	4	4	8	11	15	19	11	8
四等奖	4									
市长奖										**5**
技术成果类										1
荣誉类										4
创新企业奖										**8**

12-8 主要年份民营科技活动情况

Statistics on Scientific and Technological Activities in Private Enterprises in Main Years

项　目	单 位	1995年	1998年	1999年	2000年	2002年	2004年	2005年	2008年	2009年
企业数	个	30	105	160	232	500	900	1100	1797	2003
科技活动人员	人	209	856	1653	2937	5060	14267	16143	24061	30521
工业总产值	亿元	1.19	8.25	25.92	34.83	140.00	247.50	294.00	506.55	615.43

12-9　科技创新平台情况（2009年）

Statistics on Technology Innovation Platform (2009)

项　　目	单位	2009年
科技创新平台合计	个	156
#公共科技创新平台	个	9
行业性科技创新平台	个	26
#行业性科技创新平台（企业研究院）	个	9
专业镇技术创新平台	个	11
科技行业技术联盟	个	6
企业创新平台	个	104
#企业工程技术研究开发中心	个	104
#国家级	个	1
省级	个	34
市级	个	69
实验室	个	17
#国家级	个	4
#资助获中国合格评定国家认可委员会认可实验室	个	4
省级	个	2
市级	个	11

12-10　民营科技企业情况（2009年）

Statistics on Private Scientific and Technology Enterprises (2009)

指　标　名　称	单位	2009年
企业数	个	2003
年末从业人员数	人	170126
#科技活动人员	人	30521
#研究开发人员	人	15019
具有中高级职称人员	人	9802
具有本科及以上学历人员	人	15034
产品数	个	1860
工业总产值	万元	6154322
工业增加值	万元	1610923
总收入	万元	5064587
#技术收入	万元	98172
产品销售收入	万元	452436
出口总额	万元	152316
上缴税费总额	万元	204423
当年科技活动支出总额	万元	221876
#研究与实验发展经费(R&D)	万元	133421

12-11 历年企事业单位科学技术人员数

Number of Scientific and Technical Personnel in Enterprises and Institutions over Years

单位：人

年 份	科学技术人员	工程技术人员	农业技术人员	卫生技术人员	科学研究人员	教学人员	经济人员	财会人员	统计人员
1980	6619	370	190	1076	19	4282		564	99
1981	7473	463	217	1166	23	4978		501	109
1982	7547	468	243	1241	28	4954		509	101
1983	8453	525	315	1699		5257		109	109
1984	9033	615	307	1791		5534		261	201
1985	9166	663	318	2319	6	5129		491	214
1986	9490	768	358	2398	5	5222		501	203
1987	10945	797	378	2426	6	6495		583	222
1988	12495	1014	359	3093	24	7064	72	590	197
1989	11306	960	388	1393	19	7394	281	632	181
1990	11629	1084	432	1430	21	7524	278	581	170
1991	15004	2170	405	3347	13	7843	308	558	153
1992	16809	2522	375	3690	18	8659	313	613	153
1993	18491	2871	264	4074	112	9511	290	916	141
1994	20198	3490	272	4513	57	9949	300	657	112
1995	23104	3944	255	4878	66	11613	329	750	171
1996	24693	4037	263	5356	51	12287	360	740	143
1997	26103	4258	294	5504	48	13371	418	882	280
1998	26582	4321	310	4862	48	14316	376	894	171
1999	28789	4620	288	5246	48	15604	416	946	152
2000									
2001	24677	795	121	5493	31	17309	252	273	40
2002	34168	5261	246	6538	28	18756	555	1319	184
2003	33070	996	159	11145	44	19614	314	741	57
2004	39398	1752	276	14541	141	20905	561	613	74
2005	42593	1839	290	16188	77	21717	636	1299	82
2006	46371	1913	462	18401	70	22434	763	1512	93
2007	49032	2037	492	19528	71	23364	892	1832	92
2008	51729	2375	343	20955	50	24063	1048	1827	100
2009	55097	2302	284	21679	43	26741	1129	1940	122

注：本表是国有企事业单位口径。

12-12 历年三种专利与技术合同签订情况

Statistics on Three Kinds of Patents and Technical Contracts Signed by Type over Years

年　份	三种专利申请量（件）	#发明	三种专利授权量（件）	#发明	技术合同签订项目数（项）	技术合同签订金额（万元）	技术合同实现金额（万元）
1990	34	1	30	1	5	12	7
1991	70	3	50	1	4	10	10
1992	102	5	78	2	3	23	10
1993	100	3	90	1	2	24	2
1994	104	4	100	2	14	2537	1756
1995	325	5	262	8	46	1804	1623
1996	333	3	312	4	133	4839	3756
1997	725	1	321		78	2036	800
1998					62	3048	2398
1999					20	1124	1077
2000	1653	35	1399	4	110	3469	2398
2001	2914	71	1753	5	89	1335	953
2002	3100	90	2680	10	91	766	730
2003	3865	93	2858	14	58	700	680
2004	4325	185	3167	26	69	4278	2726
2005	6694	245	3114	24	50	4058	2522
2006	9879	553	4872	28	25	13644	13402
2007	13842	876	6752	44	53	8510	8138
2008	14406	1188	8093	115	54	12838	3694
2009	19106	1593	12918	254	60	6996	6264

12-13　历年科学技术成果项数

Number of Scientific and Technological Achievements Projects over Years

单位：项

年　份	获国家级科技进步奖	获省级科技进步奖	获市级科技进步奖	特等奖	一等奖	二等奖	三等奖	四等奖
1979			25			5	4	16
1980			27			2	11	14
1981			35		2	4	11	18
1982			62		1	3	21	37
1983			38		2	6	11	19
1984			35			11	11	13
1985			68		2	11	30	25
1986			86		5	14	27	40
1987			59		2	19	25	13
1988		1	37		6	10	16	5
1989		1	32		4	6	22	
1990		1	31		7	15	9	
1991		4	35	1	3	18	13	
1992		3	19		4	7	8	
1993			18	1	3	8	6	
1994		6	23		4	9	10	
1995		4	22		1	5	16	
1996		3	32		7	6	19	
1997		4	32		7	6	19	
1998		6	38	1	2	11	24	
1999		9	39		6	11	22	
2000		6	47	1	7	15	24	
2001		4	51		4	23	24	
2002		3	47		7	15	25	
2003		4	50		7	14	29	
2004		6	60	1	6	19	34	
2005		3	75	2	10	25	38	
2006		3	70	1	8	24	37	
2007		4	83	1	18	26	38	
2008		10	83		19	28	36	
2009		19	85		22	24	39	

12-14　主要年份各类学校情况

Statistics on Schools by Type in Main Years

项　　　目	单位	1985年	1990年	1995年	2000年	2005年	2008年	2009年
一、普通高等专业学校								
学校数	所			1	1	4	4	5
毕业生数	人			395	985	1439	6486	7292
招生数	人			576	1440	7273	10218	12863
在校学生数	人			1628	3241	16645	28656	33992
教职工数	人			262	293	1761	2592	3068
#专任教师	人			119	161	1081	1691	1890
二、中等职业技术学校								
学校数	所	3	17	20	23	21	26	26
毕业生数	人	234	2210	4641	9554	9062	10728	11927
招生数	人	1508	3866	8697	8759	10971	17475	15767
在校学生数	人	3363	8919	18737	23144	29487	45419	46538
教职员工数	人	217	619	1134	1608	2230	3013	3112
#专任教师	人	150	434	859	1221	1621	2218	2321
三、普通中学								
学校数	所	106	64	69	77	134	180	186
毕业生数	人	12317	18688	24165	30261	48935	66594	71811
#高中生	人	2055	2527	3231	7120	12233	19315	20550
招生数	人	16978	20441	33086	41488	70843	89808	88325
#高中生	个	2915	3389	6099	9048	19540	22313	23631
在校学生数	人	46596	61188	92481	112418	191044	248442	249464
#高中生	人	6304	8572	13653	24677	52283	63962	66750
教职员工数	人	3266	4001	5900	6012	12177	16677	17212
#专任教师	个	2420	2963	4381	5027	9640	12995	13598
四、小　学								
学校数	所	583	570	595	552	414	352	337
毕业生数	人	17901	18262	27257	33684	61173	78037	78027
招生数	人	20264	26158	36702	53786	84784	94641	92281
在校学生数	人	134421	162664	195063	272793	480923	528644	511160
教职员工数	人	7009	7797	9560	9131	21964	27235	26605
#专任教师	人	6017	6785	8060	7946	17478	21203	21130

12-14 续表

项目	单位	1985年	1990年	1995年	2000年	2005年	2008年	2009年
五、成人高等专业教育								
当年招生人数	人				1697	6387	7029	8092
在校学生数	人	403	531	1254	3642	12665	18658	21464
#广播电视大学	人	403	531	1254	1362	4169		
六、学龄儿童入学								
学龄儿童总数	人	103460	133011	177791	247555	423058	459145	441557
已入学学龄儿童数	人	103282	132934	177787	247539	423058	459145	441557
学龄儿童入学率	%	99.8	99.9	100.0	100.0	100.0	100.0	100.0
七、小学毕业生升学								
小学毕业生人数	人	17901	18262	27257	33684	61173	78037	78027
已升学人数	人	14235	17413	27166	33627	61095	78037	78027
小学毕业生升学率	%	79.5	95.4	99.2	99.8	99.9	100.0	100.0
八、初中毕业生升学								
初中毕业生人数	人	10262	16161	20933	23141	36702	47279	51261
已升学人数	人	3955	7134	17876	20896	34536	45671	49723
初中毕业生升学率	%	38.5	43.6	85.4	90.3	94.1	96.6	97.0
九、普通高中毕业生升学								
高考省线入围人数	人	285	224	809	2646	6455	9987	12569
高考录取人数	人	543	759	2095	5017	12461	16702	18767
#高考升本科人数	人	274	250	697	1678	5161	8080	9571
普通高中毕业生升学率	%	26.5	31.2	64.9	70.5	96.5	91.0	87.5
十、幼儿园								
幼儿园数	所	83	86	258	452	511	617	680
在园幼儿数	人	31382	47040	84263	111763	111330	156362	176249
幼教职工数	人	984	1387	1427	7517	12567	18973	21347
#专任教师	人	841	1160	1160	4618	7002	11072	12419
十一、全国各类大中专院校招生人数								
国家各大(学)专院校在我市招生人数	人				11680	35831	38364	38364
国家各中专学校在我市招生人数	人				3359	2768		
全市教育经费投入总额	亿元				15.5	50.2	71.1	78.8

12-15 历年各类学校在校学生数

Number of Students Enrollment by Type of School over Years

单位：人

年 份	普通高等学校	中等职业技术学校	#技工学校	普通中学	#高中	小 学	幼儿园
1949		151		1960	318	52781	
1952		543		3394	296	70359	
1957		561		6652	848	88001	
1962		380		9736	1513	119998	
1965		358		10469	1397	160931	
1970				60150	9873	118128	
1975		689		49569	10847	168236	
1978		595		76025	12092	161114	18228
1979		450		62292	7010	158008	12774
1980		386		54829	6909	154871	7630
1981		450		43514	5755	150857	8103
1982		661		41683	4654	144754	14650
1983		967		42777	4798	135440	15436
1984		1070		46488	5766	134567	23702
1985		3363		46596	6304	134421	31382
1986		3891	60	49445	7880	140700	38195
1987		5847	117	54435	8367	144287	42569
1988		7120	229	59268	8201	150097	42845
1989		7878	293	61955	7687	155852	44110
1990		8919	582	61188	8572	162664	47040
1991		10938	915	60146	8725	170064	51051
1992		13161	1277	65171	9711	175203	57537
1993	1079	14176	1516	75305	10297	180114	65310
1994	1451	16084	2025	85827	11409	186244	72552
1995	1628	18737	2404	92481	13653	195063	84263
1996	1771	22614	2567	95150	16887	205957	85709
1997	2025	24821	2598	98005	20609	221838	100059
1998	2171	25588	2291	101202	22490	235787	103585
1999	2241	25073	2001	105518	23084	248759	109773
2000	3241	23144	1746	112418	24677	272793	111763
2001	3802	23638	2039	122115	28232	295384	112963
2002	5144	25363	2152	135256	32398	342804	108898
2003	6884	27664	2564	149656	38143	386890	104832
2004	9104	28487	2559	171336	45050	448296	112538
2005	16645	29487	2618	191044	52283	480923	111330
2006	22005	35403	2905	214638	57662	496828	118683
2007	25178	40429	3063	234578	61151	520684	130932
2008	28656	45419	3238	248442	63962	528644	156362
2009	33992	46538	3268	249464	66750	511160	176249

12-16 历年各类学校当年招收学生数

Number of New Students Enrollment by Type of School over Years

单位：人

年 份	普通高等学校	中等职业技术学校	#技工学校	普通中学	#高中	小 学
1949		102				
1952		285		1666	190	
1957		80		2516	259	
1962		45		3716	566	
1965		134		3656	476	
1970				45069	7919	
1975		188		28329	5930	
1978		250		29788	3436	30152
1979		200		25364	3900	28315
1980		186		24083	3906	26857
1981		266		16808	2594	26461
1982		162		17492	2317	23970
1983		573		18111	2344	19604
1984		1964		16609	2477	17644
1985		1508		16978	2915	20264
1986		1977	60	17944	2781	25867
1987		2883	64	21720	2665	28926
1988		2832	112	23280	2925	29437
1989		2966	124	21877	2686	27539
1990		3866	343	20441	3389	26158
1991		5008	445	21430	3266	27539
1992		5696	487	26161	3751	28804
1993	567	5835	633	29948	3944	31841
1994	569	7064	952	32229	4440	34495
1995	576	8697	996	33086	6099	36702
1996	711	10119	978	33576	7385	39689
1997	750	9718	798	35140	8273	42066
1998	750	9664	852	36423	8118	43802
1999	802	9060	665	38400	8199	47715
2000	1440	8759	527	41488	9048	53786
2001	1597	8850	1116	44729	10727	56521
2002	2190	9417	1153	49881	11852	65066
2003	3104	9809	874	55564	15147	71476
2004	3804	10618	1044	63085	17467	80525
2005	7273	10971	1100	70843	19540	84784
2006	8032	13357	1250	79985	20866	89663
2007	8519	16491	1297	85816	21146	92860
2008	10218	17475	1163	89808	22313	94641
2009	12863	15767	1598	88325	23631	92281

12-17 历年各类学校当年毕业生数

Number of Graduates by Type of School over Years

单位：人

年 份	普通高等学校	中等职业技术学校	#技工学校	普通中学	#高中	小 学
1949				414	83	
1952		48		588	44	14349
1957		87		1365	203	59056
1962		209		2680	468	28418
1965		44		2363	393	32508
1970				15081	1954	26187
1975		374		20842	4937	25009
1978		244		43035	8533	30480
1979		244		33554	8004	28925
1980		250		19578	3096	27294
1981		191		13308	3046	27215
1982				10483	3004	27348
1983		260		10752	1940	26723
1984		230		10969	1404	17870
1985		234		12317	2055	17901
1986		660		13527	1271	17533
1987		819		13895	2296	23183
1988		1323		15322	2966	23054
1989		1960	60	15310	2716	20315
1990		2210	57	18688	2527	18262
1991		2634	112	19820	2559	19186
1992		2126	123	19323	2643	23308
1993	30	2915	390	18363	3020	26893
1994	197	5035	445	20360	2787	28500
1995	395	4641	541	24165	3231	27257
1996	560	5813	753	27675	3483	27156
1997	484	6745	691	28729	3834	27992
1998	556	8316	918	29839	5448	29794
1999	714	9044	796	30109	6585	31426
2000	985	9554	634	31291	7120	33684
2001	1019	7748	684	32409	7553	37077
2002	753	7171	542	34204	8277	40611
2003	1350	7217	509	39031	8784	45599
2004	1506	8630	917	43471	10676	51831
2005	1439	9062	777	48935	12233	61173
2006	2269	9422	677	55856	15486	70474
2007	5096	10061	754	60436	17354	74681
2008	6486	10728	821	66594	19315	78037
2009	7292	11927	962	71811	20550	78027

12-18 历年各级各类学校专任教师数

Number of Full-time Teachers by Level and Type of School over Years

单位：人

年份	普通高等学校	中等职业技术学校		普通中学		小学	幼儿园
			技工学校		高中		
1978		34		3641	638	5641	
1979		31		3367	369	6136	
1980		29		2996	370	6022	
1981		32		2343	344	6433	
1982		38		2210	284	6186	
1983		61		2361	296	5830	
1984		63		2352	309	5971	
1985		150		2420	354	6017	841
1986		168	5	2463	407	6515	720
1987		208	7	2709	490	6878	941
1988		306	9	3007	540	7112	967
1989		422	11	2949	462	6743	980
1990		434	12	2963	488	6785	1160
1991		513	15	3019	500	6831	1470
1992		600	17	3198	479	7164	1569
1993	99	737	16	3583	610	7314	1773
1994	113	767	26	4001	710	7610	1920
1995	119	859	34	4381	733	8060	1160
1996	119	924	40	4310	886	7410	2175
1997	123	1151	89	4404	991	7518	2753
1998	125	1338	93	4632	1065	7912	3247
1999	133	1205	92	4699	1149	7198	3715
2000	161	1221	84	5027	1310	7946	4618
2001	231	1286	121	5348	1411	8693	4701
2002	290	1445	125	6373	1769	10880	5351
2003	312	1548	124	7069	1976	12490	5505
2004	560	1531	134	8437	2367	15512	6218
2005	1081	1621	150	9640	2817	17478	7002
2006	1357	1801	122	10953	3215	18717	7919
2007	1569	1965	156	12272	3678	20511	9279
2008	1691	2218	161	12995	3976	21203	11072
2009	1890	2321	160	13598	4178	21130	12419

12-19 历年各类学校入(升)学率与高考入围人数

Number of Passing College Entrance Examination and Percentage of Graduates of Entering Secondary School by Type of School over Years

年 份	学龄儿童入学率(%)	小学毕业生升学率(%)	初中毕业生升学率(%)	高中毕业生升学率(%)	高考入围人数(人)	
						省线入围人数
1978	98.36	85.80	14.30	8.14	846	250
1979	98.70	76.00	16.00	6.71	566	166
1980	98.85	73.40	25.40	7.15	222	140
1981	98.72	50.56	27.40	8.64	239	154
1982	99.06	54.40	34.40	8.04	252	115
1983	99.75	57.60	37.40	12.34	245	150
1984	99.65	70.80	29.86	43.32	619	220
1985	99.83	79.52	38.54	26.50	534	285
1986	99.90	84.71	33.89	43.69	595	228
1987	99.94	83.60	40.10	27.09	644	297
1988	99.93	89.88	42.00	30.63	925	315
1989	99.92	96.18	43.30	32.92	977	284
1990	99.94	95.35	43.60	31.20	759	224
1991	99.92	96.18	45.20	26.22	861	268
1992	99.94	97.58	56.00	35.59	994	312
1993	99.95	97.79	68.50	39.23	1102	423
1994	99.96	98.94	79.02	62.75	1823	586
1995	99.99	99.16	85.40	64.90	2095	809
1996	99.98	96.45	86.70	66.80	2160	1093
1997	99.99	99.90	87.35	60.00	2212	1215
1998	99.99	99.86	88.25	47.69	2348	1315
1999	99.99	99.87	89.80	53.15	3501	1790
2000	99.99	99.83	90.30	70.50	5017	2646
2001	100.00	99.77	90.50	74.82	5651	3225
2002	100.00	99.80	91.10	83.00	6873	3759
2003	100.00	99.80	92.10	93.60	9167	4509
2004	100.00	99.90	93.30	96.70	10756	5452
2005	100.00	99.90	94.10	96.50	11196	6455
2006	100.00	100.00	94.80	82.90	11359	7652
2007	100.00	100.00	95.20	89.10	13275	9185
2008	100.00	100.00	96.60	91.00	15047	9987
2009	100.00	100.00	97.00	87.50	17487	12569

12-20 历年文化艺术、文物事业机构数

Number of Institutions in Culture and Cultural Relics over Years

年　份	电影放映单位(个)	#影剧院(座)	艺术表演团体(个)	群　众艺术馆(个)	镇街级文化站(个)	公　共图书馆(座)	公共图书馆藏书量(万册)	博物馆(座)	档案馆(座)
1949	5	2							
1952	8	3							
1957	14	5							
1962	28	4	2	1	4	1		2	1
1965	28	4	2	1	4	1		2	1
1970	28	4	3	1	33	1		2	1
1975	33	4	3	1	33	1		2	1
1978	167	5	1	1	33	1	11	2	1
1979	157	5	1	1	33	1	15	2	1
1980	65	5	1	1	33	1	16	2	1
1981	75	6	1	1	33	1	17	2	1
1982	53	6	1	1	33	1	19	2	1
1983	49	6	1	1	33	1	19	2	1
1984	65	6	1	1	33	1	24	2	1
1985	60	7	1	1	33	3	30	2	1
1986	61	9	2	1	33	3	30	2	1
1987	70	13	4	1	33	8	30	2	1
1988	78	15	5	1	33	3	30	2	1
1989	102	26	6	1	33	3	30	2	1
1990	114	26	7	1	33	5	30	2	1
1991	126	36	5	1	33	6	31	2	1
1992	150	50	2	1	33	8	37	2	1
1993	163	53	2	1	33	11	47	2	1
1994	193	63	2	1	33	14	58	2	1
1995	218	97	2	1	33	15	68	2	1
1996	225	111	4	1	33	16	73	2	1
1997	229	130	4	1	33	26	84	2	1
1998	233	147	4	1	32	26	106	3	1
1999	210	87	4	1	32	20	133	3	1
2000	192	87	1	1	32	18	97	3	1
2001	145	84	1	1	32	21	99	3	1
2002	162	81	2	1	32	24	109	3	2
2003	107	55	2	1	32	346	289	3	2
2004	88	78		1	32	397	631	6	2
2005	70	31		1	32	473	660	16	2
2006	51	34		1	33	1222	771	21	2
2007	51	34		1	33	1271	896	23	2
2008	40	34	1	1	33	387	515	23	1
2009	40		4	1	33	504	599	31	1

12-21 主要年份广播电视事业发展情况

Basic Statistics on Radio and Television Industry in Main Years

项 目	单位	1985年	1990年	1995年	1999年	2000年	2004年	2005年	2008年	2009年
广播电台	座		1	1	1	1	1	1	1	1
电视台	座	1	1	1	1	1	1	1	1	1
镇街文化广电服务中心	个								28	28

12-22 主要年份安全生产事故中火灾事故情况

Basic Statistics on Fires Accidents of Production Accidents in Main Years

项 目	单位	1995年	1998年	1999年	2000年	2002年	2004年	2005年	2008年	2009年
一、发生起数	起	24	24	33	60	25	13	13	11	5
二、受伤人数	人	8	15	22	34	15	7	7	1	1
三、死亡人数	人	12	18	40	31	24	18	18	11	6
四、损失折款	万元	1596	1111	1016	1022	592	208	22	7	6
五、平均每起事故损失	万元	66.50	46.29	30.79	17.03	23.68	15.98	1.67	0.64	1.20

注：本表按安全生产委员会统计口径。

12-23 主要年份交通事故发生情况

Basic Statistics on Traffic Accidents in Main Years

项 目	单位	1995年	1998年	1999年	2000年	2002年	2004年	2005年	2008年	2009年
一、发生起数	起	2015	4248	6619	7386	9393	8029	7124	5380	5039
二、受伤人数	人	2061	4681	6843	8217	10410	9655	8642	5985	5560
三、死亡人数	人	692	858	902	903	1263	978	921	591	546
四、损失折款	万元	685	1213	1418	1759	1538	1038	934	933	670
五、平均每起事故损失	元	3400	2855	2142	2382	1637	1293	1312	1733	1330

12-24 各类卫生事业机构及床位、人员数（2009年）

Number of Health Care Institutions, Beds and Employed Personnel by Type of Institution (2009)

项目	机构数（个）	实有床位数（张）	人员数（人）		
				卫生技术人员	
					医生
总计	**2106**	**18080**	**43561**	**35766**	**12884**
医疗机构	2101	18080	43141	35427	12773
县及县以上及其他医院	65	17685	31021	25219	8807
#综合医院	52	15996	28464	23214	8093
中医医院	2	666	1172	1063	383
专科医院	11	1023	1385	942	331
社区卫生服务中心	348		4457	3235	1176
村(社区)卫生站	1206		3892	3892	1511
门诊部	222		2089	1598	639
诊所、卫生所、医务室	257		848	781	420
妇幼保健院	1	326	601	525	178
专科疾病防治院	1	69	204	154	42
急救中心(站)	1		29	23	
采供血机构	1		119	86	9
疾病预防控制中心	1		166	151	88
卫生监督所	1		91	67	
健康教育所	1				
其他卫生机构	1		44	35	14

注：医生包含执业医师、执业助理医师。

12-25 主要年份卫生事业机构各类人员数

Number of Personnel in Health Institutions in Main Years

单位：人

项目	1980年	1985年	1990年	1995年	2000年	2002年	2005年	2008年	2009年
总计	**3599**	**3945**	**4503**	**6149**	**9289**	**10692**	**22127**	**40449**	**43561**
一、卫生技术人员	2960	3305	3902	5290	6915	9011	16608	33113	35766
医生	980	1177	1724	2326	2819	3523	5981	11869	12884
注册护士	584	643	1164	1751	2673	3462	6303	12001	13638
药剂人员	236	572	546	602	706	794	1281	1891	2001
检验人员	120	147	152	216	367	476	781	1151	1257
其他	1040	766	316	395	350	756	2262	6201	5986
二、其他技术人员	8		13	96	174	215	786	1047	1065
三、管理人员	299	282	243	432	597	745	1080	2225	2416
四、工勤人员	332	358	345	331	453	721	1504	4064	4314
五、每千人口卫生技术人员数	3	3	3	4	5	7	10	19	20
#每千人口医生数	1	1	1	2	2	2	4	7	7

注：1. 从2002年起卫生技术人员按新口径分类。
2. 2004年起，卫生方面包含诊所、卫生所、医务室及村卫生室的数据，与往年数不可比；每千人卫生技术人员数是按户籍人口计算。

12-26 妇幼保健和疾病控制情况

Statistics on Maternal and Child Health Care and Disease control

指标名称	单位	2006年	2007年	2008年	2009年
婴儿死亡率	‰	5.99	4.63	4.02	3.91
5岁以下儿童死亡率	‰	7.27	6.26	6.07	5.91
孕产妇死亡率	1/10万	12.21		15.44	5.28
5岁以下儿童中、高度营养不良患病率	%	1.46	1.49	1.57	1.53
出生缺陷发生率	‰	26.96	26.99	25.87	30.92
低出生体重儿发生率	%	4.94	4.17	3.96	4.91
卡介苗接种率	%	99.47	99.75	99.73	99.85
脊髓灰质炎疫苗接种率	%	99.25	98.99	98.88	98.72
百白破疫苗接种率	%	98.81	98.67	98.57	98.35
麻疹疫苗接种率	%	97.71	97.74	98.02	97.48
乙肝疫苗接种率	%	98.78	98.79	98.56	98.75
住院分娩率	%	90.5	99.36	100	100
农村孕产妇住院分娩率	%	99.5	99.34	100	100
农村高危孕产妇住院分娩率	%	100	99.83	99.94	100
孕妇产前医学检查率	%	97.15	96.7	94.4	94.97
孕产妇系统管理率	%	49.65	50.97	50.79	53.03
7岁以下儿童保健管理率	%	84.51	86.24	85.7	89.69
婚前医学检查率	%	0.84	10.68	11.45	11.71
0-4个月婴儿母乳喂养率	%	88.45	87.46	88.4	84.71
妇科病检查率	%	25.74	25.87	1.74	
乙肝疫苗全程接种率	%	98.78	98.79	98.56	98.75
传染病发病总例数(甲、乙)	例	11607	12960	14130	12875
发病率	1/10万	154.63	171.64	193.81	177.01
传染病死亡总人数	人	53	21	26	30
死亡率	1/10万	0.71	0.28	0.36	0.41
结核病登记病例数	例	3973	1548	1366	3158
登记患病率	‰	0.53	0.23	0.21	0.43
结核病新发病例数	例	1439	3878	1345	3143
登记新发病率	1/万	1.9	5.7	2.05	4.32
结核病死亡人数	人	6		4	
死亡率	1/10万	0.08		0.06	

12-27 医疗机构服务情况（2009年）

Services in Medical Institutions (2009)

指标名称	诊疗人数(人次)	门、急诊	入院人数(人)	治愈率(%)	病死率(%)	健康检查人数(人次)
总计	**51585463**	**51342522**	**685223**	**67.67**	**0.52**	**3795826**
医院	30926143	30689505	665681	67.48	0.53	3186201
#综合医院	29092781	28864022	629680	67.57	0.54	3114612
中医医院	1285742	1284102	20540	52.01	0.54	28325
专科医院	547620	541381	15461	84.38	0.07	43264
#民营医院	3970466	3961844	131595	72.78	0.48	814249
社区卫生服务中心(站)	7751050	7749610				573979
村卫生站	8448064	8448064				
门诊部(所)	3496368	3491782				13777
妇幼保健院(所、站)	784474	784197	18710	76.92	0.03	3861
专科疾病防治院(所、站)	179364	179364	832	10.1	0.25	18008

12-28 历年卫生事业机构、床位、人员数

Number of Health Care Institutions, Beds and Personnel over Years

年 份	机 构 (个)	床 位 (张)	卫生工作人员 (人)	#卫生技术人员	#医生
1949	5	219	170	156	
1952	6	179	124	109	
1957	26	403	287	252	
1962	37	1376	1572	1262	
1965	38	1308	1932	1618	
1970	39	1476	2135	1678	
1975	40	1970	2840	2282	
1978	82	2257	3242	2636	768
1979	81	2271	3466	2863	971
1980	83	2207	3599	2960	1167
1981	83	2210	3724	3091	1102
1982	83	2292	3886	3253	1097
1983	83	2098	3985	3335	1088
1984	83	2231	4005	3351	1132
1985	87	2323	3945	3305	1201
1986	88	3054	4084	3454	1179
1987	88	3393	4475	3490	1304
1988	87	3640	4582	3829	1537
1989	87	3677	4522	3874	1620
1990	85	3866	4503	3902	1721
1991	85	4085	4578	3946	1755
1992	83	4517	4705	4127	1832
1993	99	4940	5247	4524	2023
1994	98	5365	5689	4930	2221
1995	99	5798	6149	5290	2299
1996	99	5288	6712	5766	2449
1997	151	5505	7286	6283	2605
1998	171	5892	8306	7139	2955
1999	176	6241	8697	7575	3080
2000	174	7081	9289	8065	3309
2001	173	7474	9323	8064	3429
2002	178	8641	10692	9011	3523
2003	172	9820	11584	9807	3758
2004	944	10797	15058	13053	4870
2005	874	11972	22127	18757	6901
2006	1210	13293	27128	22904	8629
2007	1649	15227	34151	28758	10446
2008	2106	16778	40449	33113	11869
2009	2106	18080	43561	35766	12884

注：2004年起此表包含诊所、卫生所、医务室及村卫生室的数据，与往年数不可比。

12-29 历年体育运动情况

Statistics on Sports over Years

年份	破(超)世界纪录(次)	破(超)亚洲纪录(次)	破(超)全国纪录(次)	在国际比赛中获得金牌总数(枚)	在全国比赛中获得金牌总数(枚)	在省级比赛中获得金牌总数(枚)	市级运动会参赛运动员人数(人)	为国家省输送运动员(人)
1978			9	1	7	26	2500	11
1979	2		2	1	7		2250	18
1980			12		2		2400	14
1981			11	4	19		2500	13
1982			14	4	30	15	2650	9
1983	1		7	5	6		2420	7
1984			1	16	5		2500	33
1985		2	1	5	2		1960	7
1986		7	4	7	4	52	2420	16
1987	1	1	8	35	9		2130	19
1988	3	1	4	14	25		2540	15
1989			27	5	43	92	6430	18
1990	13	5		4	6		2370	25
1991	2	1	8	12	14		4800	16
1992	2	3	21	10	6		15000	30
1993	2	8	5	12	9		10350	16
1994	34	2	24	6	23	157	2720	14
1995	10	1		5	37		1500	14
1996				3	16		7800	13
1997	10	9		1	6	36	6000	74
1998	2	4	28	4	28	87	1560	74
1999				4	33		6000	6
2000			3	4	91		4000	6
2001				13	22	48	8000	5
2002				2	35	58		11
2003		7		2	31	82		6
2004	3	4	4	49	34			18
2005				2	13	46	8564	44
2006				20	21	32	16000	
2007				3	25	46	2740	9
2008				3	16	49	630	17
2009		1	3	8	20	94	1550	17

注：2007年镇街级运动会含单项比赛。

12-30 主要年份体育比赛成绩

Statistics on Sports Achievements in Main Years

项　　目	单位	1980年	1985年	1990年	1995年	2000年	2002年	2005年	2006年	2008年	2009年
破世界纪录	次			13	10						
获得国际赛冠军	个		5	4	5	4			20	3	8
破亚洲纪录	次		2	5	1						1
破全国纪录	次	12	1			3					3
获国际比赛奖牌											
金牌	枚		5	4	5	4	2	2	20	3	8
银牌	枚			4	3	2	2	1	18		3
铜牌	枚							2	7		4
获全国比赛金牌	枚	2	2	6	37	91	35	13	21	16	20

注："获得国际赛冠军"及"国际赛中获奖牌"含地区赛。

12-31 主要年份群众体育活动情况

Statistics on Activities of Mass Sports in Main Years

项　　目	单位	1980年	1985年	1990年	1995年	2000年	2002年	2005年	2006年	2008年	2009年
举办市级运动会	次	5	4	9	4	2		4	7	2	1
市级运动会参赛运动员人数	人	2400	1960	2370	1500	4000		8564	3100	630	1550
举办镇街级运动会	次	57	68	105	10	3		4	10	5	4
镇街级运动会参赛运动员人数	人	17100	34300	61500	50000	13000		5000	4000	1500	1437
为国家和省输送运动员	人	14	7	25	14	6	11	47		17	17

12-32 历年治安案件情况

Statistics on Public Security Cases over Years

项　　目	2000年	2001年	2002年	2003年	2004年	2005年	2006年	2007年	2008年	2009年
治安案件发现受理数(起)	13805	37759	17279	10338	11514	13760	17537	32293	42270	64506
扰乱社会秩序	444	773	754	308	183	2816	1525	741	645	514
危害公共安全	122	118	81	77	71	243	445	496	598	592
侵犯人身、财产权利	6336	12861	9300	6241	4518	6044	9328	20171	25446	25157
#偷窃财物	1683	3284	2417	1912	1623	2599	2984	6229	11633	10192
妨害社会管理秩序	2665	3792	2687	2017	3301	4296	6239	10885	15581	38243
#吸食、注射毒品	1171	1716	1472	1296	2264	2697	3214	4180	3850	4164
卖淫、嫖宿暗娼	479	442	190	105	131	153	376	351	386	481
赌博	663	1157	571	427	616	942	1431	3123	6312	30416
治安案件查处数(起)	12748	34815		7827	9704	12490	16711	29533	36081	58868
扰乱社会秩序	411	653	636	265	150	2797	1523	729	623	503
危害公共安全	120	114	71	51	60	237	418	476	592	569
侵犯人身、财产权利	5478	10200	6403	4057	3377	4865	8538	17504	19438	19706
#偷窃财物	1440	2244	1395	1154	1260	2007	2479	4559	7416	6241
妨害社会管理秩序	2627	3734	2589	1968	3199	4246	6232	10824	15428	38090
#吸食、注射毒品	1168	1700	1459	1278	2203	2665	3211	4179	3805	4059
卖淫、嫖宿暗娼	471	432	180	104	130	147	376	349	382	481
赌博	657	1133	545	416	570	938	1430	3113	6260	30402
查处违法人员数(人)	32951	73118	32989	13996	15225	20692	24539	36382	36081	65351
扰乱社会秩序	1026	1364	1254	471	300	4486	1696	909	1118	457
危害公共安全	201	201	130	78	76	218	477	565	641	573
侵犯人身、财产权利	8790	16285	9413	5079	4574	6769	12010	19598	19353	15748
#偷窃财物	1915	2798	1692	1277	1695	2676	2969	4222	5967	4448
妨害社会管理秩序	8115	8956	5746	4121	5703	8201	10356	15310	19736	48573
#吸食、注射毒品	2589	2545	2191	1734	3069	3922	3842	4675	4145	4442
卖淫、嫖宿暗娼	1536	1130	523	312	288	415	850	737	814	1143
赌博	3258	4373	2034	1724	1883	3179	4089	6395	9672	39732

12-33 历年刑事案件情况

Statistics on Criminal Cases over Years

项　　目	2005年	2006年	2007年	2008年	2009年
刑事案件立案数(起)	44641	35528	33837	33880	33309
危害公共安全	264	293	263	205	348
破坏市场经济秩序	451	373	531	418	492
侵犯公民人身权利	3748	3328	3658	3634	3365
#杀人	87	70	72	52	67
伤害	3071	2703	2873	2840	2509
强奸	266	229	293	263	270
侵犯财产	39657	31045	28909	29120	28298
#抢劫	9144	7862	7380	7331	6704
抢夺	3736	2563	2343	2181	2364
入室盗窃	4150	3038	3327	5804	6834
盗窃机动车	16050	10588	7876	7264	4962
诈骗	897	953	1136	1587	2513
妨害社会管理秩序	571	488	458	503	805
#毒品犯罪	215	258	261	257	424
刑事案件破案数(起)	13682	13477	12729	8342	12525
危害公共安全	161	191	131	103	301
破坏市场经济秩序	439	283	243	273	239
侵犯公民人身权利	2037	1896	2077	1732	1748
#杀人	73	52	65	40	60
伤害	1586	1472	1527	1282	1231
强奸	171	147	192	152	165
侵犯财产	10598	10672	9870	5856	9543
#抢劫	3582	3707	3527	2474	3136
抢夺	1525	1328	1113	610	929
入室盗窃	1081	864	891	796	2422
盗窃机动车	1880	1717	703	526	761
诈骗	202	278	285	154	572
妨害社会管理秩序	490	429	387	378	693
#毒品犯罪	210	247	239	243	412

12-34 历年道路交通违法情况

Statistics on Traffic Offenses over Years

项　　目	2005年	2006年	2007年	2008年	2009年
处理违法起数(万起)	61.04	92.71	94.95	266.96	294.27
#机动车		90.29	92.05	263.86	291.69
非机动车		1.04	1.88	1.9	1.11
行人和乘车人		1.15	1.03	1.19	1.48
教育人次(万人次)		10.76	13.05	15	24.37
#机动车		8.76	11.17	13.27	22.51
非机动车		0.93	0.98	0.79	0.62
行人和乘车人		1.07	0.90	0.93	1.24
罚款总额(万元)	9991.7	19072.80	19705.00	43761.11	24534.65
#机动车		19069.10	19689.00	43744.65	24531.19
非机动车		2.00	16.00	17.14	2.98
行人和乘车人				0.32	0.48

12-35 主要年份律师、公证、基层司法及普法教育

Basic Statistics on Lawyers, Notarization, Grassroots Judicial Work and Law Education in Main Years

项　　目	单位	1990年	1995年	2000年	2002年	2005年	2008年	2009年
一、律师工作								
律师事务所	个	2	8	22	27	46	76	90
执业律师	人	12	85	221	333	625	1056	1223
担任常年法律顾问	家	102	364	416	993	1426	2339	2316
民事代理	件	145	343	1203	2600	6543	16096	13172
非诉讼事件	件	110	1162	2079	7981	13391	23858	22427
刑事辩护	件	295	235	438	996	2496	2808	2447
国内经济法律事务	件	107	348	1100	1973	1801	2148	790
涉外法律经济事务	件	165	11	27	108	160	234	615
二、公证工作								
公证处	个	1	1	1	1	1	3	3
公证人员	人	10	19	20	30	48	82	90
办结公证总数	件	5347	11377	28910	36932	60685	29410	41055
#国内民事公证	件	113	2795	19607	27615	19627	16553	27808
国内经济公证	件	236	898	1776	1870	34015	3181	2474
涉外民事经济公证	件	4998	7684	4809	5321	4607	9676	10773
三、基层司法工作								
法律服务所	个	24	29	32	32	32	32	32
法律服务人员	人	70	115	117	131	191	285	285
担任法律顾问	家	62	482	695	783	1208	717	830
民事诉讼代理	件	26	568	1221	1223	1790	1650	1364
非诉讼代理	件	129	1045	3016	3584	3837	2859	2537
人民调解委员会	个	904	813	750	826	814	1596	1586
调解人员	人	3664	3466	3644	3846	4556	19547	16248
调解纠纷总数	件	2005	2632	2642	5100	15210	20009	16042
四、参加普法教育人数	**万人**	**80**	**170**	**79**	**513**	**571**	**747**	**154.3**

12-36 历年计划生育情况

Statistics on Family Planning over Years

年 份	已婚育龄妇女人数(人)	女性初婚人数(人)			落实各种节育措施	
			23周岁及以上	不足20周岁	育龄夫妇(对)	节育率(%)
1978	130438	10974			103414	79.3
1979	134483	11914			104612	77.8
1980	136742	9270	8920		101190	74.0
1981	141079	13714			112956	80.1
1982	142324	8729			115302	81.0
1983	149928	12664			129035	86.1
1984	156444	9579			138785	88.7
1985	159985	11208			142974	89.4
1986	168611	13983	11899		150545	89.3
1987	176868	13492	11252		158857	89.8
1988	183022	12419	10072		164889	90.1
1989	196042	13691	10228	15	172799	88.2
1990	202505	13264	9670	29	177425	87.6
1991	211544	13790	10834	12	184254	87.1
1992	224624	15295	10375	13	190151	84.7
1993	235150	13932	9793	6	200673	85.3
1994	243456	13213	9833	9	208234	85.5
1995	252627	13921	10430	26	215339	85.2
1996	258873	13556	10114	20	221805	85.7
1997	263646	12968	9623	9	226674	85.98
1998	267982	12366	9260	7	233007	86.95
1999	280455	12114	8999	4	249368	88.92
2000	285244	11122	7050	14	249741	87.55
2001	295395	10903	6755	14	260077	88.04
2002	303134	11635	7082	8	268243	88.49
2003	306157	12441	7767	5	266832	87.16
2004	312941	13957	9318	2	273387	87.36
2005	317062	13251	9057	5	275685	86.95
2006	323479	12460	9117	3	279246	86.33
2007	331556	13621	10333	1	293733	85.29
2008	343051	14485	11053	1	291049	84.84
2009	352115	14450	11157	5	297559	84.51

12-36 续表

年份	领取独生子女证		人口出生率（‰）		计划生育率（%）	多孩率（%）
	累计（人）	领证率（%）	省计划指标	实际完成		
1978			13.0	18.73		
1979			12.0	24.13		
1980	423	1.84	13.0	24.41	69.72	23.38
1981			11.9	21.86		
1982			18.1	19.07		
1983			17.0	16.74		
1984			15.5	15.54		
1985	1954	1.22	15.3	15.37	88.94	4.27
1986	2029	1.20	16.5	16.44	92.45	2.93
1987	2257	1.28	16.0	16.11	93.16	1.97
1988	2408	1.32	17.0	16.75	93.58	2.14
1989	2116	1.10	17.0	17.06	92.35	2.54
1990	2288	1.13	17.5	17.07	89.08	3.71
1991	2514	1.19	20.0	17.91	89.55	3.65
1992	2335	1.04	19.8	19.31	86.08	4.44
1993	2905	1.24	20.0	18.38	87.29	4.50
1994	3245	1.33	19.2	17.88	86.50	4.71
1995	3389	1.34	19.3	17.76	85.09	4.33
1996	4028	1.63	18.3	17.05	83.83	4.87
1997	4514	1.71	18.0	16.50	83.98	4.68
1998	4971	1.85	16.6	15.31	90.01	2.92
1999	21228	7.57	15.8	14.55	89.31	2.92
2000	30921	10.84	15.3	12.11	90.17	1.77
2001	41636	14.10	14.9	11.16	91.75	1.57
2002	49188	16.23	14.3	10.35	91.80	1.31
2003	51814	16.92	12.5	10.34	92.45	1.24
2004	55425	17.71	12.5	10.86	93.48	1.14
2005	60426	19.06	11.5	10.62	94.32	0.80
2006	69507	21.49	11.6	10.14	94.69	0.71
2007	73766	22.25	11.0	10.39	95.48	0.63
2008	77919	22.71	11.0	10.77	96.28	0.54
2009	80738	22.93	11.0	10.67	96.75	0.75

注：领证率是期末已领取独生子女证人数除以全市已婚育龄妇女人数。

12-37 主要年份优抚和社会救济、福利事业

Statistics on Special Care, Social Relief and Welfare in Main Years

项　　目	单位	1990年	1995年	2000年	2002年	2004年	2005年	2008年	2009年
一、优抚事业									
优抚收养性事业单位数	个	1	1	1	1	1	1	1	1
#民政部门办	个	1	1	1	1	1	1	1	1
优抚收养性单位收养人数	人次	19	11	7	9	8	8	8	7
优抚事业费用	万元	340	213	412	949	2112	2400	3918	4258
二、社会救济									
社会困难救济人数	人次	4433	7273	19914	17202	21552	23886	39677	40438
年末社会散居孤老残幼人数	人	2026	2444	1596	460	765	875	443	379
#国家定期定量救济	人	142	569	29	19	20	18		379
社会救济福利事业费	万元		190	993	3068	4296	6955	21364	23729
自然灾害救济费	万元	4.6	70	50	673	30	744	2564	235
三、社会福利									
社会福利事业单位数	个	1	1	3	36	36	36	34	36
#民政部门办	个	1	1	3	4	4	4	3	3
社会福利事业单位收养人数	人	363	351	406	1370	2028	2240	2586	2570
#民政部门办	人	363	351	406	426	649	893	1110	1106
社会福利企业单位	个	9	15	20	18	19	20	9	10
安排“四残”人员就业数	人	199	239	393	398	469	351	252	247
集体单位安排人数	人		7	10	398	469	351		
社会福利事业单位费用支出	万元							8942	9129
四、敬老院情况									
全市敬老院个数	个			32	32	31	31	31	33
年末敬老院供养人数	人			833	1453	1379	1347	1476	1464
五、“五保户”情况									
年末列入“五保户”户数	户			1545	1936	1538	1575	1438	1364
年末列入“五保户”人数	人			1587	1553	1561	1575	1441	1364
全年“五保户”费用支出	万元			2198	1430	1943	1594	954	999
六、城乡基层社会保障									
农村建立社会保障网络乡镇数	个	33	24	32	32	32	32	32	32
城镇社会服务设施数	个	215	225	342	48	48	48	639	398

注：“五保户”人数及费用支出含敬老院供养人数及费用支出。

12-38 主要年份婚姻登记情况

Statistics on Marriage Registration in Main Years

项　　目	单位	1985年	1990年	1995年	2000年	2002年	2004年	2005年	2008年	2009年
准予登记结婚	对	11870	13668	14170	10535	11800	15814	14293	16390	18604
#涉外、华侨、港澳台同胞	对	638	709	510	213	169	134	113	115	116
准予登记离婚	对				448	475	1120	1319	1928	2277
#涉外、华侨、港澳台同胞	对								26	19
计划生育率	%								96.3	96.8

12-39 主要年份环境保护基本情况

Basic Statistics on Environmental Protection in Main Years

项　　目	单 位	1985年	1990年	1995年	2000年	2002年	2004年	2005年	2008年	2009年
一、废水										
废水排放总量	万吨	3100	5259	9681	40703	71047	68541	69049	82225	74612
#工业废水	万吨	2686	4124	5511	11753	25587	22501	21355	33359	29960
工业废水排放达标率	%	55.0	46.1	85.4	72.0	90.6	90.1	92.1	94.6	97.8
每万元工业产值工业废水排放量	吨/万元	1955	302	144	29	63	43	58		
城镇生活污水处理率	%								81	67
二、废气										
工业废气排放量	亿标立方	34	307	556	1318	1492	1675	1695	2150	2135
三、工业固体废物										
固体废物产生量	万吨	16	112	108	149	169	267	284	349	318
固体废物处置量	万吨	8	2	1	5	5	10	12	20	15
固体废物处理率	%	48.2	1.8	0.9	66.9	99.3	98.9	99.8	5.6	4.8
固体废物利用率	%	37.5	17.9	18.2	63.8	90.5	82.6	86.5	94.2	95.0
主要污染物总量减排完成率	%								100.0	
四、城市环境质量及污染控制										
空气污染指数	范围值				21-87	68-86	30-147	24-123	14-109	57
交通干线噪声平均值	db(A)				68.4	68.0	68.0	67.9	63.6	63.8
烟尘控制区覆盖率	%				98.0	100.0	100.0	100.0		
环境噪声达标区覆盖率	%				53.4	70.0	60.0	55.4		
汽车尾气达标率	%				81.2	81.8	85.1	88.1	89.9	83.5
城市生活垃圾无害化处理率	%								100.0	100.0

12-40　主要年份社会保险事业情况

Statistics on Social Insurance in Main Years

项　　目	单 位	1995年	1999年	2000年	2002年	2004年	2005年	2008年	2009年
一、社会保险									
参加各种社会保险人数	万人次	149.33	167.73	338.33	427.75	479.25	804.71	1909.67	2397.83
#失业保险人数	万人	6.49	8.68	17.84	67.91	100.00	177.78	256.33	259.15
养老保险人数	万人	8.46	8.35	82.95	103.19	104.44	182.49	262.63	315.81
地方养老保险人数	万人							257.90	310.87
医疗保险人数	万人	7.60	9.95	88.21	105.19	105.95	189.40	513.25	536.57
工伤保险人数	万人	126.78	136.23	136.53	136.56	150.46	235.10	419.47	438.87
社会保险基金总收入	万元	18155	36220	127964	248199	383308	491540	1035476	1201283
#失业保险基金收入	万元	60	1512	2732	5159	23406	28954	21684	25488
养老保险基金收入	万元	7697	10556	85245	174649	267473	343429	640632	714507
地方养老保险基金收入	万元							110394	122869
医疗保险基金收入	万元	2057	4323	23488	47560	64595	82138	189845	281366
工伤保险基金收入	万元	8341	15051	15891	19855	26392	35073	69327	57053
社会保险待遇总支出	万元	10520	24321	40454	91555	172852	217413	443285	604796
#失业保险待遇支出	万元	16	42	440	1371	4486	6676	13715	17388
养老保险待遇支出	万元	7450	14710	24130	58771	107845	135958	227840	241649
地方养老保险待遇支出	万元							37775	43190
医疗保险待遇支出	万元	1436	3356	3694	17491	37116	51021	122147	267092
工伤保险待遇支出	万元	1618	5982	11703	12910	21989	22220	39287	35477
二、农民基本养老保险									
实际参保人数	万人			58.51	59.42	59.74	51.55	46.03	45.83
实际申领人数	万人			16.45	17.05	18.09	18.63	24.76	24.48
保费征缴金额	万元				32146	34038	33845	63612	175470
养老支付金额	万元			2467	30293	32194	33411	71656	74542

注：1997年起养老保险因口径调整，与以前年份不可比。

12-41　主要年份最低生活保障情况

Statistics on Minimum Income Relief in Main Years

项　　目	单 位	2000年	2001年	2002年	2003年	2004年	2005年	2008年	2009年
居民最低生活保障线	元/人月	273	300	300	300	320	320	400	400
村民最低生活保障线	元/人月	234	260	260	260	300	300	400	400
居民最低生活保障户数	户	918	1028	1319	1392	1725	1911	1531	1606
居民最低生活保障人数	人	1825	2003	2711	2876	4968	4885	3653	3770
居民最低生活保障金发放额	万元						789.5	1052.0	726.7
村民最低生活保障户数	户	3997	4571	5772	6146	6469	6705	12125	13106
村民最低生活保障人数	人	9156	10601	14491	15616	16584	17426	33384	33549
村民最低生活保障金发放额	万元						2318	9747	6295.3

12-42 主要年份市政建设情况

Statistics on Municipal Construction in Main Years

项　　目	单 位	1995年	1999年	2000年	2004年	2005年	2008年	2009年
水厂综合生产能力	万吨/日	66	182	187	430	480	650	700
年末供水管道总长度	公里	1580	2011	2106	3580	3680	9551	12668
全年供水量	万吨	18802	66268	70046	140100	155100	173550	160782
#生活用水量	万吨	7361	29530	21433	43200	51100		46099
年末实有铺装道路长度	公里	1148	1106	1157	3774			
年末实有铺装道路面积	万平方米	1829	1794	1884	7824	8961		
园林绿地面积	公顷	800	1229	1396	11404	10298	27938	29497
#公园绿地面积	公顷						10254	10266
建成区绿化覆盖面积	公顷	1885	1556	1364	6317	9436	30173	31865
建成区土地面积	平方公里	82.00	126.14	147.68	649.67	657.17		
公园数	个		249	273	678	931		777
公园面积	公顷		827	1423	1489	2887		5919
城市人均公园绿地面积	平方米						14.75	16.17

注：1. 1999年公园数含小游园数；1999年实有铺装道路面积因口径调整，与以往年份数据不可比。
　　2. 城市人均公园绿地面积按常住人口计算。

12-43 主要年份液化石油气及天然气供应情况

Statistics on Supply of Liquefied Petroleum Gas and Natural Gas in Main Years

项　　目	单 位	1995年	1999年	2000年	2004年	2005年	2008年	2009年
年末液化石油气用户数	户	63419	150000	110172	121087	144797	912026	892874
#家庭用气户数	户	62246	120000	106910	120160	144035	876622	873246
全年液化石油气供应量	吨	25935	56000	58287	127578	161930	394510	351893
#家庭用量	吨	18948	44800	22104	29937	24354	233183	215357
年末天然气用户数	户				253	5027	82916	112230
#家庭用气户数	户				250	5000	82303	111501
全年天然气供应量	万立方米				12	350	18808	29255
#家庭用量	万立方米				1	45	924	1078

注：本表2000-2006年为市喜威液化石油气有限公司与市中液石油气有限公司的业务量，2007年起调整为市城市管理局统计口径。

12-44 历年环境保护基本情况

Basic Statistics on Environmental Protection over Years

年　份	全市降水PH均值(范围值)	全市酸雨PH均值(范围值)	全市酸雨频率(%)	全市酸雨占总降水量(%)	交通干线噪声平均值(db)	工业废水排放量(万吨)	工业废水排放达标量(万吨)	工业废水排放达标率(%)
1982						1842	1381	74.97
1983						2068	1564	75.63
1984	6.53					2127	1203	56.56
1985						2686	1483	55.21
1986					76.8	2416	596	24.67
1987	6.64	5.38		38.4	78.9	3501	1843	52.64
1988	4.85	4.72	63.6	75.1	77.6	3029	2349	77.55
1989	5.44	5.21	31.0	31.8	74.1	3976	2473	62.21
1990	6.15	5.30	29.5	43.3	75.9	4124	1900	46.07
1991	5.24	4.78	35.4	30.4	72.2	5506	3560	64.70
1992	5.10	4.71	36.8	35.9	76.0	5849	3501	59.90
1993	4.93	4.41	22.5	29.1	75.8	6500	4175	64.23
1994	5.33	4.81	23.2	25.5	72.6	7057	5361	75.97
1995	5.89	5.49	9.2	13.7	70.3	5511	4706	85.40
1996	5.83	5.40	14.7	10.9	70.4	6033	4790	79.40
1997	4.94	4.84	56.6	76.4	70.6	8930	5697	63.80
1998	4.79	4.70	60.3	80.4	70.3	7989	3683	46.10
1999	4.97	4.68	40.0	50.5	69.1	11719	6258	53.40
2000	4.90	4.67	50.7	56.6	68.7	11753	8468	72.00
2001	5.06	4.74	31.6	43.9	68.2	11694	8168	69.90
2002	5.47	5.09	29.3	28.8	68.0	25587	23179	90.60
2003	4.55	4.44	60.5	77.2	67.9	23389	19761	84.49
2004	4.47	4.41	69.6	85.7	68.0	22501	20274	90.10
2005	4.07	4.00	65.7	86.2	67.9	21355	19667	92.10
2006	3.57-6.57	4.70	50.0	42.4	68.0	24134	22344	92.58
2007	5.21	4.36-7.59	54.2	59.2	67.9	91260	88072	96.51
2008	4.83	4.65	60.1	63.6	63.6	33359	31560	94.61
2009	5.03	4.88	51.8	67.3	63.8	29960	29309	97.82

注：2007年工业废水排放量和工业废水排放达标量两个指标统计口径变更，与往年不可比。

主要统计指标解释

工程技术人员 指在国民经济各行业从事工程技术工作的自然科学技术专业人员，包括：高级工程师、工程师、助理工程师、技术员和未评定职称的技术人员。

农业技术人员 指在国民经济各行业从事农业技术工作的自然科学技术专业人员，包括：高级农艺师、农艺师、助理农艺师、技术员和未评定职称的技术人员。

科学研究人员 指在国民经济各行业从事科学技术活动的科学技术专业人员，包括：正副研究员、助理研究员、研究实习员、技术员和未评定职称的技术人员。

发明 专利法及其实施细则所称的发明是指对有关产品、方法或其改进所提出的新的技术方案。

实用新型 专利法及其实施细则所称的实用新型是指对产品的形状、构造或者其结合所提出的适于实用的新的技术方案。

外观设计 专利法及其实施细则所称的外观设计是指对产品的形状、图案、色彩或者其结合所作出的富有美感并适于工业上应用的新设计。

在校学生数 是指具有学籍的注册学生总数。

学龄儿童入学率 指调查范围内已入小学学习的学龄儿童占校内外学龄儿童总数（包括弱智儿童在内，但不包括盲聋哑儿童）的比重。

电影放映单位 指具有放映机器设备、固定或不固定的放映场所与专职或兼职的放映技术人员，经有关部门登记批准，经常为一定的观众对象放映电影的机构。包括经批准对外开放进行营业，并与电影发行放映管理机构分帐的专用放映单位和军委系统租片单位。

医院 指设有固定床位能收容病人住院并能为病人提供医疗、护理服务的医疗机构。包括县及县以上医院、农村乡卫生院、其他医院三部分。按所属性质分为卫生部门、工业及其他部门、集体经济单位三类。其中县及县以上医院按业务性质分为综合医院和专科医院。

卫生技术人员 指卫生事业机构支付工资的全部固定职工和合同制职工中现任职务为卫生技术工作的专业人员。包括中医师、西医师、中西医结合高级医师、护师、中药师、西药师、检验师、其他技师、中医士、西医士、护士、助产士、中药剂士、西药剂士、检验士、其他技士、其他中医、护理员、中药剂员、西药剂员、检验员，其他初级卫生技术人员。

医生 指经卫生部门审查合格，从事医疗工作的专业人员。分为中医医生和西医医生。包括卫生技术人员中的中医师、西医师、中西结合高级医师、中医士、西医士和其他中医。

律师 指受聘参加法律顾问处工作，提任法律顾问、刑（民）事代理人、刑事辩护人，办理非诉讼事件、解答法律询问，代写法律事务文书等主要从事律师业务的专职法律工作者和兼职律师。

公证人员 指在国家公证机关依法办理公证事务的司法人员。包括公证员、助理公证员和在公证处工作的其他人员。

调解人员 在人民调解委员会担负调解民间一般民事纠纷和轻微违法行为所引起的纠纷的工作人员。包括调解委员会的委员和调解小组的调解员。

社会福利事业单位 指集中收养社会孤老、残、幼的机构。包括由民政部门管理的社会福利院、儿童福利院、精神病人福利院和城镇集体办的福利院，以及农村集体举办的敬老院。

社会福利事业单位收养人数包括民政部门管理的和城镇及农村集体举办的社会福利事业单位中收养的老人、少年儿童、缺乏生活自理能力的残疾人员和精神病人。

废水排放总量 包括工业废水和生活污水。工业废水指工业企业在生产、科研过程中向企业外部排放的所有排放口的废水量总和。生活污水指居民或职工在饮用、洗涤、烹饪、清洁卫生等过程中排放的污水量。

十三、能　源

Energy

13-1 能源主要指标

Main Indicators of Energy

项　　目	单　位	2005年	2006年	2007年	2008年	2009年
地区能源消费总量(等价值)	万吨标准煤	1885.78	2138.97	2393.92	2589.66	2603.52
地区能源消费总量(当量值)	万吨标准煤	1800.14	2010.20	2154.52	2280.31	2311.86
电力消耗	亿千瓦时	419.83	472.01	515.40	514.16	495.58
单位GDP能耗(等价值，2005年可比价)	吨标准煤/万元	0.864	0.822	0.778	0.738	0.705
单位GDP能耗(当量值，2005年可比价)	吨标准煤/万元	0.825	0.772	0.700	0.650	0.626
单位GDP电耗(2005年可比价)	千瓦小时/万元	1923.00	1813.46	1674.45	1465.25	1341.26
规模以上工业综合能源消费量(当量值)	万吨标准煤	1203.77	1329.05	1437.94	1452.85	1367.94
规模以上工业增加值能耗(当量值,2005年可比价)	吨标准煤/万元	1.14	1.02	0.92	0.82	0.82
规模以上工业发电量	万千瓦时	378.81	410.54	402.54	362.53	342.29
全社会用电量	万千瓦时	419.83	472.01	515.40	514.16	495.58
火力发电转换效率	%	37.05	36.97	36.68	37.59	39.24
供热转换效率	%				87.75	89.74
能源消费比上年增长	%		13.43	11.92	8.18	0.54
电力消费比上年增长	%		12.43	9.19	-0.24	-3.61
GDP比上年增长	%		19.22	18.26	14.00	5.25
能源消费弹性系数			0.70	0.65	0.58	0.10
电力消费弹性系数			0.65	0.50		

13-2 综合能源平衡表

Overall Energy Balance Sheet

单位：万吨标准煤

项　　目	2005年	2006年	2007年	2008年	2009年
可供本地区消费的能源量	**1885.78**	**2138.97**	**2393.92**	**2589.66**	**2603.52**
年初库存量	77.54	67.21	77.91	87.19	158.56
一次能源生产量					
回收能	1.31	5.51	13.81	13.67	13.31
外省调入量	1866.72	2139.88	2328.67	2537.65	2493.23
进口量	9.31	1.71	60.72	100.59	83.79
我国轮、机在外国加油量					
本省调出量(-)					
出口量(-)					
外国轮、机在我国加油量(-)					
年末库存量(-)	-69.11	-75.35	-87.19	-149.43	-145.37
加工转换投入(-)产出(+)量	**-0.08**				
火力发电					
供热					
洗选煤					
炼焦					
炼油					
制气					
损失量	**63.74**	**63.40**	**84.93**	**65.64**	**34.59**
运输和输配损失	63.74	63.40	84.93	65.64	33.77
终端消费量	**1821.96**	**2075.57**	**2308.98**	**2524.02**	**2568.93**
第一产业	5.04	6.61	6.46	4.74	6.17
农、林、牧、渔业	5.04	6.61	6.46	4.74	6.17
第二产业	1334.30	1491.65	1654.16	1782.54	1790.15
工业	1305.42	1459.54	1617.24	1742.08	1749.90
#用作原材料、燃料					
建筑业	28.88	32.11	36.92	40.46	40.25
第三产业	304.16	366.00	409.89	459.67	475.19
交通运输仓储及邮电通信业	84.47	97.27	114.30	129.63	134.83
批发和零售贸易业、餐饮业	137.35	172.82	178.02	193.99	200.60
其他	82.34	95.91	117.57	136.05	139.76
生活消费	178.45	211.31	238.48	277.07	297.42
城镇	178.45	211.31	238.48	277.07	297.42
乡村					
平衡差额					
消费量合计	**1885.78**	**2138.97**	**2393.92**	**2589.66**	**2603.52**

13-3　石油平衡表

Petroleum Balance Sheet

单位：万吨

项　　目	2005年	2006年	2007年	2008年	2009年
一、可供量	413.06	461.36	444.13	460.89	445.10
生产量					
外省(区、市)调入量	408.02	462.31	448.20	472.40	442.12
进口量	1.82	1.20			
我轮、机在外国加油量					
本省(区、市)调出量(–)					
出口量(–)					
外轮、机在我国加油量(–)					
年初年末库存差额	3.22	-2.15	-4.07	-11.51	2.98
年初库存量	18.64	15.42	17.57	21.64	33.15
年末库存量(–)	15.42	17.57	21.64	33.15	30.17
二、消费量	413.06	461.36	444.13	460.89	445.10
消费量分组一	413.06	461.36	444.13	460.89	445.10
农林牧渔业	1.23	2.36	2.22	1.10	2.21
工业	249.88	269.49	227.73	196.77	172.29
建筑业	14.49	16.17	16.18	14.89	16.69
交通运输、仓储和邮政业	54.93	63.34	73.81	83.33	85.93
批发、零售业和住宿、餐饮业	28.76	33.17	37.70	55.53	52.47
其他	21.91	25.00	27.44	34.45	33.86
生活消费	41.86	51.83	59.05	74.82	81.65
消费量分组二	413.06	461.36	444.13	460.89	445.10
终端消费	266.62	286.63	320.59	381.24	414.02
#工业	103.76	95.08	104.24	117.23	141.34
加工转换损失	146.12	174.41	123.49	79.54	30.93
火力发电	146.12	174.41	123.49	79.54	30.85
供热					0.08
炼油损耗					
制气					
损失量	0.32	0.32	0.05	0.11	0.15
三、平衡差额					

13-4 煤炭平衡表

Coal Balance Sheet

单位：万吨

项　　目	2005年	2006年	2007年	2008年	2009年
一、可供量	1596.99	1738.97	1849.66	1924.57	1916.83
生产量					
外省(区、市)调入量	1582.15	1746.25	1769.23	1847.82	1906.10
进口量	9.40		85.00	140.82	
本省(区、市)调出量(-)					
出口量(-)					
年初年末库存差额	5.44	-7.28	-4.57	-64.07	10.73
年初库存量	70.80	65.36	72.64	77.21	141.28
年末库存量(-)	65.36	72.64	77.21	141.28	130.55
二、消费量	1596.99	1738.97	1849.66	1924.57	1916.83
消费量分组一	1596.99	1738.97	1849.66	1924.57	1916.83
农林牧渔业					
工业	1596.99	1738.97	1849.66	1924.57	1914.73
建筑业					
交通运输、仓储和邮政业					
批发、零售业和住宿、餐饮业					2.10
其他					
生活消费					
消费量分组二	1596.99	1738.97	1849.66	1924.57	1916.83
终端消费	132.22	184.22	233.99	441.92	481.42
#工业	132.22	184.22	233.99	441.92	479.32
用于加工转换	1464.76	1554.75	1615.67	1482.65	1434.21
火力发电	1464.76	1554.75	1615.67	1459.21	1335.14
供热				23.44	101.71
洗煤损耗					
炼焦					
制气					
型煤加工损耗					-2.64
损失量	0.01				1.20
三、平衡差额					

13-5 全社会用电量

Consumption of Electricity

单位：万千瓦时

项　　目	2005年	2006年	2007年	2008年	2009年
全社会用电量总计	**4198289**	**4720112**	**5154025**	**5141578**	**4955750**
#各行业用电量合计	3855742	4329080	4718336	4651348	4409908
#第一产业	9761	9514	9643	9584	9354
第二产业	3397588	3761186	4101528	4019849	3724455
第三产业	448393	558380	607165	621915	676099
城乡居民生活用电量合计	342547	391032	435689	490230	545842
各行业用电分类					
一、农、林、牧、渔业	9761	9514	9643	9584	9354
二、工业	3374306	3735651	4061784	3962669	3673716
#轻工业	1357858	1502077	1656565	1675707	1590781
重工业	2016448	2233574	2405219	2286962	2082935
#采矿业	8112	6024	8796	8607	6865
制造业	3044575	3381692	3625554	3567232	3382129
#电力、燃气及水的生产和供应业	321619	347935	427434	386830	284722
#电力、热力的生产和供应业	240737	272067	328413	268378	173866
#电厂生产全部耗用电量	41656	75606	75090	68094	67286
线路损失电量	190736	189347	253318	200284	106573
燃气生产和供应业	654	845	895	917	1433
水的生产和供应业	80228	75023	98126	117535	109423
三、建筑业	23282	25535	39744	57180	50739
四、交通运输、仓储、邮政业	14425	15508	19789	22453	23358
#交通运输业	8614	9387	12512	13868	13997
仓储业	2084	2300	3122	3890	4459
邮政业	3727	3821	4155	4695	4902
五、信息传输、计算机服务和软件业	15277	17376	22259	26429	31172
六、商业、住宿和餐饮业	282238	364478	356196	337296	364374
#批发和零售业	148555	193891	177435	162736	177608
住宿和餐饮业	130153	170587	178761	174560	186766
七、金融、房地产、商务及居民服务业	65223	79917	101327	110630	114305
#金融业	16158	16225	16870	16178	15073
房地产业	21976	25083	25846	23986	23111
租赁和商务服务、居民服务和其他服务	27089	38609	58611	70466	76121
八、公共事业及管理组织	71230	81101	107594	125107	142890
#科学研究、技术服务和地质勘查业	4550	3206	3012	2691	2675
#地质勘查业	248	23	17	15	30
水利、环境和公共设施管理业	26633	30069	33736	38338	49440
#水利管理业	12157	11650	6618	2443	4127
教育、文化、体育和娱乐业	13596	15417	21112	24582	27728
#教育	4793	4871	5988	6295	7208
卫生、社会保障和社会福利业	12151	15088	7522	4012	5889
公共管理和社会组织、国际组织	14300	17321	42212	55484	57158

13-6 规模以上工业综合能源消费量

Overall Energy Consumpiton of Industrial Enterprises above Designated

单位：吨标准煤

指　　标	2005年	2006年	2007年	2008年	2009年
合　计	**12037714**	**13290543**	**14379411**	**14528511**	**13679420**
(一)采矿业	769	675	706	361	160
煤炭开采和洗选业					
石油和天然气开采业					
黑色金属矿采选业					
有色金属矿采选业					
非金属矿采选业	769	675	706	114	160
其他采矿业				247	
(二)制造业	5273612	6365772	7492792	8140697	7848902
农副食品加工业	59666	94383	139017	146621	169496
食品制造业	51949	75174	84197	85670	89657
饮料制造业	34764	48904	60046	59173	54740
烟草制品业					
纺织业	876658	842201	932175	856952	758755
纺织服装、鞋、帽制造业	165413	144783	138591	99994	83779
皮革、毛皮、羽毛(绒)及其制品业	92086	183236	203600	160892	142298
木材加工及木、竹、藤、棕、草制品业	8684	11324	12470	17024	17524
家具制造业	106972	105694	100380	99529	75372
造纸及纸制品业	1452027	2246173	2889078	3477439	3708558
印刷业和记录媒介的复制	38855	41457	49755	63425	58184
文教体育用品制造业	150581	138360	136963	143387	108321
石油加工、炼焦及核燃料加工业	67	29939	92308	56016	696
化学原料及化学制品制造业	149516	156848	162108	174693	165849
医药制造业	4950	6075	6443	7111	6932
化学纤维制造业	17288	25988	22388	4378	4179
橡胶制品业	42554	41997	41964	61100	51890
塑料制品业	326872	320924	342762	424140	383414
非金属矿物制品业	333262	409912	539683	612137	657556
黑色金属冶炼及压延加工业	22399	27459	28448	20815	10287
有色金属冶炼及压延加工业	26412	34052	41856	55869	33015
金属制品业	180098	171235	180663	138760	115815
通用设备制造业	45760	48845	57133	81424	57777
专用设备制造业	104801	80444	89690	112887	103566
交通运输设备制造业	14488	13571	16419	51812	38347
电气机械及器材制造业	283994	305746	318329	301393	252323
通信设备、计算机及其他电子设备制造业	578746	659829	702659	697227	585042
仪器仪表及文化、办公用机械制造业	78158	69880	72045	65574	62713
工艺品及其他制造业	26474	31338	31624	65255	52816
废弃资源和废旧材料回收加工业	117				
(三)电力、燃气及水的生产和供应业	6763334	6924096	6885913	6387453	5830358
电力、热力的生产和供应业	6728304	6859857	6817766	6323666	5775585
燃气生产和供应业				21	184
水的生产和供应业	35030	64238	68147	63766	54589

主要统计指标解释

能源生产总量　指一定时期内全国（地区）一次能源生产量的总和，是观察全国（地区）能源生产水平、规模、构成和发展速度的总量指标。一次能源生产量包括原煤、原油、天然气、水电、核能及其他动力能（如风能、地热能等）发电量。不包括低热值燃料生产量、生物质能、太阳能等的利用和由一次能源加工转换而成的二次能源产量。

能源消费总量　指一定时期内全国（地区）生产和生活消 费的各种能源的总和，是观察能源消费水平、构成和增长速度的总量指标，能源消费总量包括原煤和原油及其制品、天然气、电力。不包括低热值燃料、生物质能和太阳能等的利用 。能源消费总量分为三部分，即终端能源消费量、能源加工转换损失量和损失量。

(1)终端能源消费量　指一定时期内全国（地区）生产和生活消费的各种能源在扣除了用于加工转换二次能源消费量和损失量以后的数量。

(2)能源加工转换损失量　指一定时期内全国（地区）投入加工转换的各种能源数量之和与产出各种能源产品之和的差额。它是观察能源在加工转换过程中损失量变化的指标。

(3)能源损失量　指一定时期内能源在输送、分配、储存过程中发生的损失和由客观原因造成的各种损失量。不包括各种气体能源放空、放散量。

能源生产弹性系数　是研究能源生产增长速度与国民经济增长速度之间关系的指标。计算公式：

$$能源生产弹性系数=\frac{能源生产总量增长速度}{国民经济增长速度}$$

国民经济增长速度，可根据不同的目的或需要，用国民生产总值，国内生产总值等指标来计算，本资料是采用国内生产总值指标计算的。

电力生产弹性系数　是研究电力生产增长速度与国民经济增长速度之间关系的指标。一般来说，电力的发展应当快于国民经济的发展，也就是说电力应超前发展。计算公式：

$$电力生产弹性系数=\frac{电力生产量增长速度}{国民经济增长速度}$$

能源消费弹性系数　是反映能源消费增长速度与国民经济增长速度之间比例关系的指标。计算公式：

$$能源消费弹性系数=\frac{能源消费量增长速度}{国民经济增长速度}$$

电力消费弹性系数　是反映电力消费增长速度与国民经济增长速度之间比例关系的指标。计算公式：

$$电力消费弹性系数=\frac{电力消费量增长速度}{国民经济增长速度}$$

能源加工转换效率　指一定时期内能源经过加工、转换后，产出的各种能源产品的数量与同期内投入加工转换的各种能源数量的比率。它是观察能源加工转换装置和生产工艺先进与落后、管理水平高低等的重要指标。计算公式：

$$能源加工转换效率=\frac{能源加工、转换产出量}{能源加工、转换投入量}\times 100\%$$

十四、镇街主要指标

Main Indicatory of Towns

14-1 镇街生产总值

Gross Domestic Product by Town

单位：万元

镇街	(1991年)				(1992年)			
	生产总值	第一产业	第二产业	第三产业	生产总值	第一产业	第二产业	第三产业
全市	**959073**	**134523**	**503220**	**321330**	**1108922**	**144115**	**592701**	**372106**
莞城	22046	174	16612	5260	28881	108	22263	6510
石龙	25154	907	17669	6578	29467	1026	21163	7278
虎门	44900	10059	16412	18429	56539	10336	24781	21422
东城	23500	7179	13793	2528	32770	7362	21392	4016
万江	18518	3874	11653	2991	27997	3968	18928	5102
南城	13339	2219	8181	2939	18147	1973	12681	3493
中堂	14889	3300	9065	2524	19902	4360	10669	4873
望牛墩	11950	2794	7394	1762	13789	2854	8683	2252
麻涌	24449	10489	11478	2482	26907	9797	14294	2816
石碣	12556	2686	7660	2210	16967	2888	11140	2939
高埗	11546	3352	5163	3031	14295	4017	6503	3775
道滘	15659	4540	9542	1577	19009	4805	12003	2201
洪梅	6492	3879	1872	741	6906	2441	3435	1030
沙田	12616	6467	4552	1597	16779	6511	7850	2417
厚街	31303	5679	22403	3221	38272	6064	28528	3680
长安	24850	7961	13185	3704	36298	8980	21883	5435
寮步	23700	9030	8979	5691	30083	9256	12627	8200
大岭山	10557	5918	3123	1516	16175	6342	4928	4905
大朗	19481	11277	4870	3334	24694	10104	9836	4754
黄江	20403	2765	15888	1750	28355	3244	22864	2247
樟木头	10515	10515	2107	6426	13972	2212	8536	3224
清溪	8673	2076	4428	2169	12742	2405	6936	3401
塘厦	17826	6128	9049	2649	30454	6300	19988	4166
凤岗	8676	2698	5550	428	12119	3257	8146	716
谢岗	9472	2019	5197	2256	7178	2339	4236	603
常平	38008	13134	14511	10363	45046	11625	20103	13317
桥头	14030	4083	8114	1833	22099	5429	10336	6334
横沥	11125	2499	6349	2277	15673	2710	9342	3621
东坑	16245	3544	11393	1308	22332	3368	17294	1670
企石	16155	3731	9575	2849	21159	4699	13097	3363
石排	16123	2350	10727	3046	18091	2704	11839	3548
茶山	13328	3385	7146	2797	16377	4160	8782	3435

注：各镇街合计不等于全市数，下同。

14-1　续表 1

单位：万元

镇　街	(1993年)				(1994年)			
	生产总值	第一产业	第二产业	第三产业	生产总值	第一产业	第二产业	第三产业
全　市	**1570491**	**143953**	**873114**	**553424**	**2170340**	**174796**	**1194928**	**800616**
莞　城	41307		32838	8469	55021		43120	11901
石　龙	34182	582	21188	12412	48891	216	32738	15937
虎　门	74808	11281	37710	25816	103070	14350	51597	37123
东　城	37567	4379	25901	7287	44963	5223	30065	9675
万　江	39317	4818	26939	7561	45953	5499	31186	9268
南　城	23341	2767	16312	4262	46416	2811	38511	5094
中　堂	31352	7282	16982	7089	34819	6271	19472	9076
望牛墩	15717	2642	10196	2879	18449	2796	11974	3679
麻　涌	34553	9305	22223	3025	42676	9160	27917	5599
石　碣	23877	2542	16311	5024	34401	2816	24582	7003
高　埗	17843	4751	8347	4745	22368	5495	10877	5996
道　滘	24306	5086	15471	3749	37062	5698	27835	14072
洪　梅	8069	2265	4292	1512	9020	2406	4756	1858
沙　田	24446	6574	14434	3438	31950	6196	20646	5107
厚　街	57912	6707	44408	6796	101289	7615	77637	16037
长　安	49862	9995	31962	7905	68914	11024	46939	10951
寮　步	46311	9423	21926	14962	63089	12428	30205	20456
大岭山	22611	6717	7660	8234	27722	6725	11258	9739
大　朗	32720	10237	15152	7331	46550	13958	21052	11540
黄　江	37008	3021	30171	3816	47096	3254	39031	4811
樟木头	18265	1361	13994	2910	23438	1680	18008	3750
清　溪	19533	3299	12076	4158	30510	4230	20391	5889
塘　厦	41635	4353	31001	6281	80870	6396	65620	8854
凤　岗	16961	3282	12778	901	24520	4166	19054	1300
谢　岗	12063	2367	8997	699	16093	3365	11143	1585
常　平	67921	12564	34518	20839	100294	13561	62109	24624
桥　头	27654	5023	15085	7546	40632	6225	22445	11962
横　沥	23825	23825	2604	13815	33565	3922	17444	12198
东　坑	33565	4073	25007	4485	36161	4245	26665	5251
企　石	28573	5167	17684	5722	34915	6545	21854	6516
石　排	25462	2992	17949	4521	31920	3699	21172	7049
茶　山	21196	4908	12096	4192	30233	6017	18221	5995

14-1 续表 2

单位：万元

镇街	(1995年)				(1996年)			
	生产总值	第一产业	第二产业	第三产业	生产总值	第一产业	第二产业	第三产业
全市	**2962892**	**214306**	**1669723**	**1078863**	**3617502**	**248645**	**1994826**	**1374031**
莞城	69318		52710	16608	72335		50523	21812
石龙	70501	318	46550	23633	72190	303	36303	35584
虎门	130282	18388	68784	43110	158257	25193	85444	47620
东城	85114	6208	57257	21649	100581	6744	66136	27701
万江	55648	6705	37884	11059	63649	8488	40934	14227
南城	83707	2938	63407	17362	103785	3667	79347	20771
中堂	41537	6593	23358	11585	50533	7418	28908	14206
望牛墩	21961	3197	14061	4703	25963	3440	16512	6011
麻涌	47340	11783	28584	6973	49764	15494	26884	7386
石碣	46831	3332	33206	10293	66081	3495	45532	17054
高埗	28324	6213	14403	7708	36274	6945	19348	9981
道滘	47605	5698	27835	14072	55596	6031	35931	13634
洪梅	15209	2667	6923	5619	16733	2908	7657	6168
沙田	42922	7741	29376	5806	49023	10655	32354	6015
厚街	118353	9670	90642	18041	140036	10906	83151	45979
长安	93323	12505	65233	15585	131672	12882	97066	21724
寮步	75398	14727	32311	28360	85876	15651	37022	33203
大岭山	39228	8485	17265	13478	49383	9773	21083	18527
大朗	66807	17319	25844	23644	78506	16982	29641	31883
黄江	61098	3708	46392	10998	63391	3929	46558	12904
樟木头	31914	2662	24710	4543	41323	3443	32232	5647
清溪	52550	5721	35627	11202	82953	6083	55419	21451
塘厦	112158	6909	90588	14661	139903	9900	112916	17087
凤岗	37051	4767	30135	2149	48015	5521	39670	2824
谢岗	18872	4356	12655	1861	25536	5213	18242	2081
常平	135315	18444	87856	29015	146594	19303	86033	41258
桥头	54012	7206	30626	16180	64694	8418	38393	17883
横沥	44663	4484	23559	16620	54922	4717	29045	21161
东坑	34654	5179	19727	9748	50965	5274	32218	13473
企石	44588	7760	28861	7967	54066	8947	35535	9584
石排	34349	4898	20547	8904	37946	5718	21459	10769
茶山	41484	6017	18221	5995	51339	7159	24892	9433

14-1 续表 3

单位：万元

镇街	(1997年)				(1998年)			
	生产总值	第一产业	第二产业	第三产业	生产总值	第一产业	第二产业	第三产业
全市	**4485981**	**256388**	**2432816**	**1796777**	**5579965**	**259437**	**3056779**	**2263749**
莞城	80298		49962	30336	110076		49677	60399
石龙	95560	293	48361	46906	133953	116	77910	55927
虎门	246823	25799	130963	90061	362826	29535	176729	156562
东城	125730	5850	78959	40921	161819	5246	105142	51431
万江	69516	8749	42333	18434	82239	9424	50075	22922
南城	130392	3490	103126	23776	160524	3933	128850	27741
中堂	61741	7610	35991	18140	76980	7727	45359	23894
望牛墩	30854	3780	19390	7684	36531	3941	22769	9821
麻涌	52217	15965	29345	6907	62531	16443	35485	10603
石碣	85990	3782	54674	27534	109255	3852	70872	34531
高埗	46630	7586	26579	12465	60242	8235	36383	15624
道滘	69424	6383	47525	15516	80887	6756	54039	20092
洪梅	20052	4501	7602	7949	23134	4607	9569	8958
沙田	54881	11342	36602	6936	71203	16829	42167	12207
厚街	184205	11448	96880	75877	247177	12150	146229	88798
长安	180377	13111	134235	33031	245676	13562	183031	49083
寮步	103656	17341	45112	41203	129731	18768	60452	50511
大岭山	65246	10538	31884	22824	83268	9134	45040	29094
大朗	95301	19093	38996	37212	122409	15008	53085	54316
黄江	67618	4139	47073	16406	83585	4244	58492	20849
樟木头	55682	4725	43020	7936	71299	5333	51615	14351
清溪	120961	7519	84276	29166	160483	7802	115314	37367
塘厦	178757	11467	140870	26420	230580	12121	177569	40890
凤岗	63066	5925	51486	5655	79286	6187	65440	7659
谢岗	29488	6379	20521	2588	34881	6958	24888	3035
常平	185390	20195	98068	67127	231059	19811	131252	79995
桥头	79685	8523	51919	19243	96661	9712	61140	25809
横沥	67894	6411	34892	26591	81263	5364	45427	30472
东坑	63718	4810	44682	14226	78576	5726	54359	18491
企石	62625	9562	42240	10823	72065	9827	47551	14687
石排	43477	6463	23530	13484	53842	6606	28932	18304
茶山	63955	9321	39524	15110	77319	9878	47785	19656

14-1 续表 4

单位：万元

镇 街	(1999年)				(2000年)			
	生产总值	第一产业	第二产业	第三产业	生产总值	第一产业	第二产业	第三产业
全 市	**6672386**	**257863**	**3670519**	**2744004**	**8202531**	**259087**	**4507072**	**3436372**
莞 城	131005		58104	72901	184225		67030	117195
石 龙	157715	349	86171	71195	184256	189	98240	85827
虎 门	442633	31013	213607	198014	532946	30479	263928	238539
东 城	207432	4126	125159	78147	262854	4233	153667	104954
万 江	97379	9435	59636	28308	138724	11604	85526	41594
南 城	198820	2756	149678	46386	233013	3119	171413	58481
中 堂	94412	7001	57217	30194	123213	7032	76571	39610
望牛墩	43303	4012	26738	12553	51516	4072	31399	16045
麻 涌	75449	12466	44768	18215	90816	12213	45965	32638
石 碣	137148	3866	88152	45130	175180	4021	111038	60121
高 埗	78709	8792	50131	19786	102516	9155	67888	25473
道 滘	93751	7151	61687	24913	109999	7569	67841	34589
洪 梅	26118	4162	11872	10084	29921	4383	14095	11443
沙 田	86339	12167	53505	20667	109128	12714	71503	24911
厚 街	300721	12412	171495	116814	405317	12705	221947	170665
长 安	332335	13820	240690	77825	419347	14256	299650	105441
寮 步	161782	19944	82582	59256	202379	20732	110577	71070
大岭山	108469	9238	67662	31569	138789	9742	89991	39056
大 朗	156427	16699	69193	70535	201504	17826	94065	89613
黄 江	97621	4410	67206	26005	123331	5243	83748	34340
樟木头	94385	4225	64138	26021	147697	4639	71921	71138
清 溪	206524	8790	151219	46515	303131	9984	231303	61844
塘 厦	288110	12783	217897	57430	363971	13486	272234	78251
凤 岗	100753	6267	61392	33094	128298	6336	79138	42824
谢 岗	42142	3610	29017	9515	50174	3975	35779	10420
常 平	302805	15703	166347	120755	395318	16116	218229	160974
桥 头	111892	9062	69595	33235	130380	9093	82261	39026
横 沥	97209	6178	55276	35756	116749	8593	62314	45842
东 坑	101287	5363	65010	30913	118430	6241	76250	35940
企 石	85313	10000	51789	23524	99467	11339	58897	29231
石 排	69030	6772	37874	24384	87817	6913	48532	32372
茶 山	90250	9514	55468	25268	105432	10712	64726	29994

14-1 续表 5

单位：万元

镇街	(2001年)				(2002年)			
	生产总值	第一产业	第二产业	第三产业	生产总值	第一产业	第二产业	第三产业
全市	**9918905**	**260968**	**5405092**	**4252845**	**11869374**	**248791**	**6488109**	**5132474**
莞城	222233		80203	142030	312742		76890	235852
石龙	215738	150	115691	99897	248664	144	135163	113357
虎门	618557	30469	304781	283307	717425	26838	350636	339951
东城	342044	3785	188628	149631	466960	2110	232502	232348
万江	175693	13015	90857	71821	213919	11026	106945	95948
南城	286473	2929	211622	71922	350029	2711	262431	84887
中堂	153366	7155	95677	50533	194263	5908	122819	65536
望牛墩	60921	3540	36872	20509	73104	3591	43299	26214
麻涌	127061	12298	74806	39957	173557	1002	120426	43079
石碣	243163	4139	150613	88411	340162	4141	209830	126191
高埗	133362	9477	90730	33155	173004	9701	120415	42888
道滘	128327	8011	76692	43624	153201	8479	87039	57683
洪梅	34245	4587	16543	13115	41756	4793	21676	15287
沙田	142060	13641	92266	36153	182363	13912	119778	48673
厚街	483117	13088	253149	216880	583689	13976	297707	272006
长安	529219	14496	371263	143460	679022	14622	469032	195368
寮步	252526	21246	143824	87456	314871	20276	182688	111907
大岭山	194021	10089	133489	50443	251078	5741	178811	66526
大朗	264929	17764	128283	118882	341930	15525	181234	145171
黄江	154595	5176	98438	50981	199781	5288	122001	72492
樟木头	176062	4460	84195	87407	210845	5545	101237	104063
清溪	393471	10517	302613	80341	501941	11106	382584	108251
塘厦	457175	13796	335872	107507	573947	13603	425078	135266
凤岗	162854	6400	97540	58914	205006	2035	126903	76068
谢岗	58323	4115	41585	12623	71092	5665	40790	24637
常平	493419	16451	272983	203985	557039	16077	310537	230425
桥头	151979	8366	98054	45559	179442	7245	118564	53633
横沥	140251	9252	74148	56851	168932	9380	90576	68976
东坑	132805	6013	84256	42535	149147	5438	92587	51122
企石	115314	12403	63421	39490	127616	9088	68807	49721
石排	107585	6925	61859	38801	131394	6967	75798	48629
茶山	123931	9801	75341	38789	153215	9801	91916	51498

14-1 续表 6

单位：万元

镇 街	(2003年)				(2004年)			
	生产总值	第一产业	第二产业	第三产业	生产总值	第一产业	第二产业	第三产业
全 市	**14525187**	**228165**	**7981954**	**6315068**	**18060258**	**227087**	**10160382**	**7672789**
莞 城	415993		80802	335191	552370		94035	458335
石 龙	287713	116	167126	120471	317521	51	186652	130820
虎 门	905165	27106	462105	415954	1139827	27168	598000	514659
东 城	652408	1657	314094	336657	897727	900	411172	485655
万 江	269593	9622	129625	130346	329849	5617	156431	167801
南 城	452911	2743	314752	135416	741609	1869	349496	390244
中 堂	256251	7013	162945	86292	338808	5956	206693	126159
望牛墩	87872	3520	50846	33506	106086	3550	59709	42827
麻 涌	234612	8769	177540	48303	292911	8664	226131	58116
石 碣	463023	4253	290495	168275	590604	3649	381862	205093
高 埗	224078	9891	157949	56238	282716	9943	202317	70456
道 滘	178954	8975	100566	69413	217400	9499	119688	88213
洪 梅	53960	5113	29668	19179	76686	4770	41140	30776
沙 田	236769	13944	155438	67387	310921	13975	202383	94563
厚 街	721188	12275	374482	334431	878666	12341	454284	412041
长 安	887947	14863	603308	269776	1162826	15040	759582	388204
寮 步	394322	13167	234806	146349	498253	5327	303435	189491
大岭山	322872	4937	226565	91370	447412	4571	313857	128984
大 朗	443891	10640	240983	192268	574604	6986	325826	241792
黄 江	258682	4567	152903	101212	331432	3294	187369	140769
樟木头	250877	4863	119145	126869	291893	4350	139729	147814
清 溪	645553	11218	495035	139300	848426	9610	660589	178227
塘 厦	710030	13565	526730	169735	882099	13700	653816	214583
凤 岗	284608	2048	170574	111986	373309	2015	220434	150860
谢 岗	91482	4266	51312	35904	119007	4328	69024	45655
常 平	657385	12627	377679	267079	796109	10792	468642	316674
桥 头	213712	5419	134937	73356	264849	4495	144282	116072
横 沥	205872	9602	117554	78716	253887	9075	153884	90928
东 坑	181394	8423	113270	59701	230057	7943	145998	76116
企 石	142717	5216	72284	65217	167279	3848	80461	82970
石 排	157729	7144	92020	58565	190127	7259	109953	72915
茶 山	195098	8607	118895	67596	268473	7413	161070	99990

14-1 续表 7

单位：万元

镇街	(2005年)				(2006年)			
	生产总值	第一产业	第二产业	第三产业	生产总值	第一产业	第二产业	第三产业
全市	**21831961**	**205546**	**12278624**	**9347791**	**26279791**	**120089**	**15065985**	**11093717**
莞城	617849		153367	464482	712319		230144	482174
石龙	349301	141	194749	154411	384329	35	213392	170902
虎门	1283052	22937	668632	591483	1492628	11446	763086	718096
东城	1049758	480	473888	575389	1264850	427	571728	692694
万江	375471	4209	164099	207164	440346	4711	187932	247702
南城	1016644	1900	440431	574313	1229016	1995	508223	718798
中堂	424212	6122	276399	141691	507968	6428	332766	168774
望牛墩	126751	3511	73191	50049	156949	3480	87638	65831
麻涌	387211	8588	310275	68348	494018	7106	398466	88445
石碣	728816	3782	491498	233535	868731	3091	588622	277018
高埗	366593	10020	254017	102556	456695	6552	320225	129918
道滘	255589	8753	143285	103551	301036	9568	174820	116648
洪梅	102660	3939	61138	37583	123863	4082	77274	42507
沙田	364800	13695	240822	110283	442784	12585	293854	136345
厚街	1033929	11722	531019	491188	1199117	6929	609223	582965
长安	1339428	9492	917732	412204	1539236	7505	1042139	489592
寮步	598969	7765	364261	226943	739610	1136	451671	286803
大岭山	547734	4102	370108	173524	675091	2329	431260	241502
大朗	707369	14112	411161	282096	850356	1491	499588	349277
黄江	364377	3065	220654	140658	441152	741	276062	164349
樟木头	330537	3463	157434	169640	393688	600	185556	207532
清溪	984943	9036	761281	214626	1097986	8012	828219	261755
塘厦	1057175	13661	771724	271790	1186644	12312	830537	343794
凤岗	517427	1762	320177	195488	623929	1750	373375	248804
谢岗	148917	4467	91026	53424	192841	4795	118714	69332
常平	951464	10062	556932	384470	1119659	6338	644544	468777
桥头	287240	4495	168473	114271	388604	1387	210763	176454
横沥	304870	8593	195659	100619	373304	7274	242406	123624
东坑	261238	11543	165441	84254	295233	5703	194653	94877
企石	200581	3129	102183	95269	244027	2266	129255	112506
石排	234709	7268	128132	99308	294009	7283	154259	132467
茶山	305183	6652	190620	107911	384988	3215	245078	136695

14-1 续表 8

单位：万元

镇 街	(2007年)				(2008年)			
	生产总值	第一产业	第二产业	第三产业	生产总值	第一产业	第二产业	第三产业
全 市	**31600489**	**118991**	**17546573**	**13934924**	**37036004**	**148251**	**19016068**	**17871685**
莞 城	897597		298250	599347	1015311		294311	721000
石 龙	427216	10	235821	191385	475742	7	239943	235792
虎 门	1846638	10373	936639	899626	2153489	11940	1093014	1048535
东 城	1559123	377	699730	859017	1816793	339	773623	1042831
万 江	520636	3405	221314	295917	604659	3702	262498	338459
南 城	1425257	2015	583496	839747	1632407	1285	618209	1012913
中 堂	588085	6553	379181	202351	659949	6760	419455	233734
望 牛 墩	193635	3462	105983	84190	236495	3359	127759	105377
麻 涌	651344	5985	537412	107947	834681	7564	693959	133158
石 碣	994532	3096	670790	320646	1082524	2795	694349	385380
高 埗	568276	6530	384637	177109	690604	6526	442377	241701
道 滘	362268	8202	211240	142826	439328	7218	240510	191600
洪 梅	163384	4281	110958	48145	206785	4381	147969	54435
沙 田	515106	12403	327706	174997	588063	12863	337140	238060
厚 街	1420026	7270	719643	693113	1616483	7971	797404	811108
长 安	1770272	7746	1152474	610052	2029075	4979	1158887	865209
寮 步	886584	1118	531815	353650	1038493	2141	584767	451585
大 岭 山	822554	2241	502679	317634	960138	2248	554712	403178
大 朗	1025864	2098	592111	431655	1100875	877	688340	411658
黄 江	556305	740	347972	207593	721414	724	438204	282486
樟 木 头	461719	505	228647	232567	507743	311	253050	254382
清 溪	1266762	6207	924401	336153	1417816	5170	966538	446108
塘 厦	1365736	11206	903107	451422	1602945	10447	980030	612468
凤 岗	747757	1752	409163	336843	901696	1725	472782	427189
谢 岗	239771	5178	143093	91500	273944	9273	160217	104454
常 平	1311744	6665	747353	557726	1495652	6058	796227	693366
桥 头	467790	1326	242928	223536	536868	2692	254438	279737
横 沥	443014	4350	275399	163265	522130	6972	300380	214778
东 坑	320991	4532	204804	111654	372361	4017	231268	137076
企 石	291765	2868	150052	138844	320630	2314	159252	159064
石 排	360806	7308	187787	165711	417073	7313	216033	193727
茶 山	476010	3131	293991	178888	593265	4327	353036	235902

14-1 续表 9

单位：万元

镇街	(2009年)			
	生产总值	第一产业	第二产业	第三产业
全市	**37639142**	**147877**	**18230836**	**19260428**
莞城	1054949		318447	736502
石龙	502973	6	249848	253119
虎门	2437582	13180	1213679	1210723
东城	1989067	386	742171	1246510
万江	611916	3578	241005	367333
南城	1841809	1235	706141	1134433
中堂	662727	6965	396592	259170
望牛墩	288697	3395	162960	122342
麻涌	932351	8332	788621	135398
石碣	1094432	2667	641983	449782
高埗	609392	6228	387053	216111
道滘	449115	8024	234381	206710
洪梅	253003	4612	186637	61754
沙田	614104	12894	360064	241146
厚街	1695963	8373	880274	807316
长安	2083662	4532	1196987	882143
寮步	1120641	1866	630705	488070
大岭山	975717	2255	505238	468224
大朗	1160519	1242	675946	483331
黄江	768073	720	419897	347456
樟木头	524759	378	251340	273041
清溪	1363307	5410	873074	484823
塘厦	1713803	11448	1059192	643163
凤岗	1013446	1220	513090	499136
谢岗	294969	9452	166712	118805
常平	1516942	6725	799850	710367
桥头	535223	3546	251952	279725
横沥	538610	6294	326010	206306
东坑	387579	2118	237522	147939
企石	318197	1974	172565	143658
石排	438939	7500	243190	188249
茶山	620174	4327	360862	254985

14-2 镇街第三产业增加值（2009年）

Value-added of the Tertiary Industry by Town (2009)

单位：万元

镇街	第三产业增加值总计	#交通运输及仓储业	批发和零售业	住宿和餐饮业	金融业	房地产业
全市	**19260428**	**799116**	**3605753**	**1473255**	**1540408**	**2830855**
莞城	736502	62587	168129	25737	142162	160742
石龙	253119	14807	54463	25441	33946	45857
虎门	1210723	48343	335232	104227	78813	114315
东城	1246510	56490	141899	98657	119996	368187
万江	367333	20537	57692	35438	28062	67695
南城	1134433	24350	139035	58727	121043	251342
中堂	259170	10746	63011	27465	20769	28666
望牛墩	122342	19888	16626	8421	11932	10840
麻涌	135398	18524	17406	9119	14678	13805
石碣	449782	26303	82636	39115	41611	60024
高埗	216111	25161	37260	23753	15159	35595
道滘	206710	9648	26520	17399	14910	67539
洪梅	61754	7348	9667	7054	4296	9088
沙田	241146	26987	41105	24611	16755	34188
厚街	807316	24502	108952	85934	59325	130234
长安	882143	15868	222014	103475	63569	96331
寮步	488070	34593	76661	45446	33599	90799
大岭山	468224	10580	158730	32078	26226	72556
大朗	483331	7468	81343	57927	40764	95083
黄江	347456	14932	64038	40866	26960	78465
樟木头	273041	6922	60487	25634	25723	57880
清溪	484823	12266	52487	45921	30371	110443
塘厦	643163	18632	89111	77958	47390	111397
凤岗	499136	8885	68832	58658	35065	116014
谢岗	118805	6101	21427	11627	9737	27416
常平	710367	26801	109298	101089	54212	148388
桥头	279725	8490	43360	30805	15385	34934
横沥	206306	3301	32894	21987	16042	47922
东坑	147939	1253	23563	16053	13586	33015
企石	143658	7744	16580	12431	9120	28633
石排	188249	6063	33749	23623	17117	38439
茶山	254985	20833	36023	25928	20421	57748

14-3 镇街户籍户数与人口数(2009年)

Number and Population of Household Registration by Town (2009)

镇街	户数(户)	农业户	非农业户	人口数(人)	按性别分 男	按性别分 女	按农业、非农业分 农业人口	按农业、非农业分 非农业人口	总人口中未落户籍的人口数(人)
全市总计	**521190**	**280737**	**240453**	**1787288**	**907747**	**879541**	**972706**	**814582**	**4055**
莞城	37664	1	37663	170359	87904	82455	2345	168014	125
石龙	20981	2387	18594	70331	34958	35373	8928	61403	685
虎门	34548	22566	11982	126120	63601	62519	81282	44838	2
东城	23057		23057	83605	42709	40896		83605	3
万江	23183		23183	75404	38368	37036		75404	280
南城	18270		18270	68166	35879	32287		68166	9
中堂	21537	15034	6503	74261	37772	36489	55158	19103	102
望牛墩	11758	10023	1735	45475	22672	22803	39330	6145	748
麻涌	21668	17497	4171	71809	36042	35767	61864	9945	689
石碣	14668	11010	3658	43333	22167	21166	36937	6396	69
高埗	11700	10616	1084	37648	19025	18623	34918	2730	168
道滘	16891	12318	4573	55635	27808	27827	43956	11679	31
洪梅	6328	5795	533	21592	10954	10638	20399	1193	198
沙田	12540	11414	1126	40149	20267	19882	36055	4094	80
厚街	28926	23290	5636	95975	48163	47812	83714	12261	47
长安	13227		13227	42469	21828	20641		42469	4
寮步	19778	12808	6970	67223	34063	33160	42597	24626	2
大岭山	13008	11469	1539	43642	21906	21736	38645	4997	
大朗	18225	16068	2157	69239	35738	33501	61612	7627	22
黄江	7728	5778	1950	24079	12266	11813	18149	5930	3
樟木头	7754		7754	26835	13634	13201		26835	6
清溪	11318	9117	2201	35209	17590	17619	29304	5905	
塘厦	16664		16664	44079	22246	21833		44079	96
凤岗	6729	4938	1791	23362	11367	11995	17422	5940	13
谢岗	5276	4131	1145	20232	10082	10150	17001	3231	176
常平	24627	17943	6684	72481	37251	35230	57456	15025	3
桥头	11773	4970	6803	35569	17795	17774	16304	19265	167
横沥	11570	8836	2734	36284	18547	17737	30339	5945	18
东坑	10728	8987	1741	29964	15372	14592	27006	2958	161
企石	12823	10779	2044	41346	21109	20237	36240	5106	4
石排	12804	11448	1356	42193	21249	20944	38798	3395	116
茶山	13392	11514	1878	44401	22387	22014	36947	7454	28

14-4 镇街户籍人口自然变动情况（2009年）

Natural Changes of Population Household Registration by Town (2009)

镇 街	出 生		死 亡		自然增长	
	人 数 (人)	出生率 (‰)	人 数 (人)	死亡率 (‰)	人 数 (人)	自然增长率 (‰)
全市总计	**18584**	**10.67**	**7587**	**4.36**	**10997**	**6.31**
莞 城	1372	8.34	668	4.06	704	4.28
石 龙	529	7.62	282	4.06	247	3.56
虎 门	1166	9.36	523	4.20	643	5.16
东 城	884	11.30	305	3.90	579	7.40
万 江	769	10.44	302	4.10	467	6.34
南 城	1088	17.06	164	2.57	924	14.48
中 堂	803	11.01	356	4.88	447	6.13
望 牛 墩	430	9.59	188	4.19	242	5.40
麻 涌	673	9.52	350	4.95	323	4.57
石 碣	427	10.08	175	4.13	252	5.95
高 埗	370	9.90	148	3.96	222	5.94
道 滘	481	8.69	251	4.54	230	4.16
洪 梅	210	9.81	75	3.51	135	6.31
沙 田	483	11.99	204	5.06	279	6.93
厚 街	1030	10.82	285	2.99	745	7.83
长 安	419	10.12	191	4.61	228	5.51
寮 步	836	12.69	328	4.98	508	7.71
大 岭 山	497	11.72	130	3.07	367	8.65
大 朗	707	10.36	279	4.09	428	6.27
黄 江	315	13.52	89	3.82	226	9.70
樟 木 头	307	12.30	87	3.49	220	8.82
清 溪	433	12.36	167	4.77	266	7.59
塘 厦	482	11.32	192	4.51	290	6.81
凤 岗	273	11.80	57	2.46	216	9.33
谢 岗	277	13.94	97	4.88	180	9.06
常 平	734	10.26	576	8.05	158	2.21
桥 头	478	13.48	180	5.07	298	8.40
横 沥	419	11.66	173	4.81	246	6.84
东 坑	309	10.30	169	5.63	140	4.67
企 石	466	11.26	208	5.03	258	6.24
石 排	456	10.94	177	4.25	279	6.69
茶 山	461	10.43	211	4.78	250	5.66

注：本表按户籍人口统计。

14-5 镇街人口迁移变动情况（2009年）

Changes of Population Migration by Town (2009)

单位：人

镇　　街	迁移总计	省　内	省　外	迁入总计	省内迁入	省外迁入	迁出总计	迁往省内	迁往省外
全市总计	**43768**	**16041**	**27727**	**36387**	**13373**	**23014**	**7381**	**2668**	**4713**
莞　　城	6071	1535	4536	3962	1273	2689	2109	262	1847
石　　龙	901	470	431	698	377	321	203	93	110
虎　　门	1757	838	919	1565	757	808	192	81	111
东　　城	6124	2037	4087	5748	1753	3995	376	284	92
万　　江	1880	527	1353	1785	499	1286	95	28	67
南　　城	7679	2391	5288	6703	1938	4765	976	453	523
中　　堂	443	229	214	370	202	168	73	27	46
望 牛 墩	181	101	80	166	94	72	15	7	8
麻　　涌	601	227	374	480	187	293	121	40	81
石　　碣	830	375	455	685	311	374	145	64	81
高　　埗	161	71	90	138	61	77	23	10	13
道　　滘	180	86	94	135	68	67	45	18	27
洪　　梅	140	70	70	117	63	54	23	7	16
沙　　田	542	189	353	508	183	325	34	6	28
厚　　街	718	231	487	615	205	410	103	26	77
长　　安	1426	460	966	1264	413	851	162	47	115
寮　　步	1297	375	922	1171	358	813	126	17	109
大 岭 山	853	384	469	778	364	414	75	20	55
大　　朗	973	356	617	888	344	544	85	12	73
黄　　江	778	388	390	738	372	366	40	16	24
樟 木 头	904	352	552	772	323	449	132	29	103
清　　溪	662	327	335	503	299	204	159	28	131
塘　　厦	1978	823	1155	1589	736	853	389	87	302
凤　　岗	1094	476	618	1003	449	554	91	27	64
谢　　岗	200	121	79	165	117	48	35	4	31
常　　平	1349	494	855	1198	448	750	151	46	105
桥　　头	357	155	202	305	139	166	52	16	36
横　　沥	456	167	289	388	153	235	68	14	54
东　　坑	216	70	146	139	62	77	77	8	69
企　　石	384	136	248	302	125	177	82	11	71
石　　排	334	103	231	246	91	155	88	12	76
茶　　山	412	140	272	305	132	173	107	8	99

注：本表按户籍人口统计。

14-6 镇街土地面积和人口密度（2009年）

Land Area and Population Density by Town (2009)

镇街	土地面积（平方公里）	人口密度（人/平方公里）	
		户籍人口	常住人口
莞城	11.2	15211	21063
石龙	13.8	5096	9877
虎门	166.5	757	3229
东城	105.1	795	3451
万江	48.5	1555	3373
南城	56.6	1204	3645
中堂	59.9	1240	2100
望牛墩	31.6	1439	2576
麻涌	87.2	823	1226
石碣	36.2	1197	4823
高埗	34.6	1088	4691
道滘	54.3	1025	2414
洪梅	33.2	650	1446
沙田	78.8	510	1419
厚街	125.7	764	3347
长安	89.4	475	6202
寮步	72.5	927	3331
大岭山	95.5	457	1770
大朗	97.5	710	2510
黄江	92.9	259	2097
樟木头	118.8	226	1077
清溪	140.1	251	1575
塘厦	128.2	344	2995
凤岗	82.4	284	2001
谢岗	91.0	222	867
常平	103.3	702	2447
桥头	56.0	635	1793
横沥	44.7	812	3177
东坑	23.7	1264	3806
企石	58.2	710	1515
石排	48.7	866	2686
茶山	45.4	978	2762

14-7 镇街常住人口和人均GDP（2006-2009年）

Permanent Population and Per Capita Gross Domestic Product by Town(2006-2009)

镇　街	常住人口(万人)				人均GDP(元)		
	2006年	2007年	2008年	2009年	2007年	2008年	2009年
全市总计	**674.88**	**694.72**	**694.98**	**635.00**	**46146**	**53301**	**56601**
莞　城	22.69	24.08	23.83	23.59	38383	42384	44494
石　龙	13.59	14.06	14.35	13.63	30902	33491	35952
虎　门	57.06	61.42	54.82	53.76	31172	37052	44899
东　城	27.70	30.03	43.38	36.27	54014	49497	49945
万　江	16.23	16.93	17.21	16.36	31401	35422	36456
南　城	14.35	17.77	20.60	20.63	88746	85088	89343
中　堂	12.90	13.41	12.61	12.58	44704	50726	52618
望牛墩	7.70	7.84	8.12	8.14	24921	29636	35510
麻　涌	10.56	11.21	11.16	10.69	59839	74625	85341
石　碣	19.86	21.21	20.46	17.46	48431	51957	57723
高　埗	11.43	12.31	16.60	16.23	47875	47776	37124
道　滘	13.03	13.78	13.58	13.11	27025	32115	33654
洪　梅	4.62	4.80	4.86	4.80	34689	42813	52382
沙　田	10.68	11.87	11.96	11.18	45686	49355	53077
厚　街	48.58	50.98	53.16	42.07	28526	31044	35618
长　安	63.91	69.25	69.09	55.28	26589	29335	33507
寮　步	22.25	24.18	24.32	24.15	38190	42824	46241
大岭山	18.99	21.37	23.08	16.90	40761	43201	48810
大　朗	22.81	24.64	25.68	24.47	43240	43755	46282
黄　江	20.70	21.92	20.85	19.48	26105	33735	38089
樟木头	16.52	15.25	14.80	12.80	29066	33793	38026
清　溪	30.61	33.33	27.36	22.07	39623	46723	55161
塘　厦	33.79	34.88	33.29	38.57	39777	47028	47698
凤　岗	31.30	16.51	15.61	16.49	31280	56145	63143
谢　岗	7.92	9.27	8.59	7.89	27897	30677	35797
常　平	38.62	32.55	30.87	25.28	36862	47167	54032
桥　头	12.55	12.45	10.94	10.04	37423	45906	51022
横　沥	16.20	16.51	15.17	14.20	27087	32963	36678
东　坑	9.10	8.68	8.54	9.02	36107	43248	44143
企　石	8.94	9.51	9.66	8.82	31628	33451	34437
石　排	11.57	13.09	13.26	13.08	29262	31656	33329
茶　山	16.25	17.13	13.66	12.54	28521	38536	47342

14-8 镇街新莞人人口数（2008-2009年）

Migrant Population by Town (2008-2009)

单位：人

镇　　街	2008年			2009年		
	新莞人	男	女	新莞人	男	女
全市总计	**5525022**	**2657712**	**2867310**	**4299615**	**2093055**	**2206560**
莞　　城	75571	37567	38004	64884	32270	32614
石　　龙	78436	34090	44346	63193	29035	34158
虎　　门	450333	210562	239771	426320	212155	214165
东　　城	378923	193460	185463	229981	131924	98057
万　　江	104806	52695	52111	84867	43202	41665
南　　城	152836	75984	76852	141752	68240	73512
中　　堂	55645	27877	27768	53967	27489	26478
望 牛 墩	38452	22205	16247	37873	17901	19972
麻　　涌	42877	22340	20537	32805	19013	13792
石　　碣	172095	78852	93243	113228	47335	65893
高　　埗	136572	76115	60457	128976	78766	50210
道　　滘	85365	38132	47233	75937	33625	42312
洪　　梅	28935	15453	13482	27437	13687	13750
沙　　田	85278	42611	42667	68777	35191	33586
厚　　街	463685	218047	245638	297107	138679	158428
长　　安	690106	337778	352328	542680	250483	292197
寮　　步	188391	94162	94229	182566	94938	87628
大 岭 山	199893	85736	114157	109817	60343	49474
大　　朗	200347	108974	91373	175068	82722	92346
黄　　江	196923	78870	118053	168781	82890	85891
樟 木 头	129540	64798	64742	113253	56654	56599
清　　溪	253800	84625	169175	151264	54283	96981
塘　　厦	308458	184755	123703	199882	93729	106153
凤　　岗	142116	73312	68804	141798	73150	68648
谢　　岗	70051	34914	35137	56013	25685	30328
常　　平	252377	112730	139647	142572	67152	75420
桥　　头	78904	35031	43873	60891	26512	34379
横　　沥	123141	59379	63762	103502	53847	49655
东　　坑	59104	25448	33656	68027	29817	38210
企　　石	59152	28305	30847	42256	20856	21400
石　　排	96458	44403	52055	92178	43825	48353
茶　　山	98289	43351	54938	76048	33836	42212
其他单位	28163	15151	13012	25915	13821	12094

14-9 镇街计划生育情况（2009年）

Statistics on Family Planning by Town (2009)

镇街	已婚育龄妇女人数(人)	女性初婚人数(人)	#23周岁及以上	落实各种节育措施育龄夫妇(对)	节育率(%)	领取独生子女证累计(人)	领证率(%)	计划生育率(%)	多孩率(%)
全市总计	**352115**	**14450**	**11157**	**297559**	**84.51**	**80738**	**22.93**	**96.75**	**0.75**
莞城	34934	1065	940	29825	85.38	10064	28.81	96.72	0.66
石龙	14050	517	426	12004	85.44	4133	29.42	96.03	0.57
虎门	24151	991	795	19620	81.24	5688	23.55	96.83	1.54
东城	17201	544	464	14518	84.40	3224	18.74	97.40	0.90
万江	14240	604	485	12343	86.68	3989	28.01	96.88	0.39
南城	15111	1040	918	12108	80.13	3043	20.14	96.88	0.28
中堂	13741	638	488	11648	84.77	2819	20.52	96.89	0.25
望牛墩	7994	361	285	6719	84.05	1633	20.43	97.44	1.16
麻涌	12546	650	486	10297	82.07	2661	21.21	97.47	0.30
石碣	8262	358	244	6805	82.37	2037	24.66	96.25	0.70
高埗	6626	263	196	5699	86.01	1233	18.61	97.03	
道滘	10465	403	303	8982	85.83	2158	20.62	96.05	0.62
洪梅	3934	167	123	3360	85.41	945	24.02	96.67	
沙田	8285	408	298	6942	83.79	1794	21.65	97.72	0.83
厚街	18709	748	590	15558	83.16	3538	18.91	96.41	0.78
长安	8499	377	308	7061	83.08	1627	19.14	97.85	1.43
寮步	13646	525	356	11666	85.49	3012	22.07	95.81	1.91
大岭山	9260	484	348	7853	84.81	1704	18.40	97.59	1.01
大朗	13488	502	350	11322	83.94	3112	23.07	96.46	0.57
黄江	5217	196	148	4529	86.81	1339	25.67	96.19	0.95
樟木头	6060	298	226	5065	83.58	1099	18.14	97.39	0.33
清溪	7841	293	201	6776	86.42	1462	18.65	97.00	0.46
塘厦	8065	375	292	6661	82.59	2070	25.67	97.10	0.83
凤岗	5206	236	193	4383	84.19	846	16.25	97.07	0.73
谢岗	4223	166	120	3625	85.84	886	20.98	96.39	0.72
常平	14815	538	408	12901	87.08	3935	26.56	96.59	0.54
桥头	7324	270	190	6229	85.05	2087	28.50	96.44	1.05
横沥	7588	314	211	6476	85.35	1915	25.24	95.70	1.91
东坑	5646	196	129	4846	85.83	1379	24.42	96.76	0.65
企石	8280	328	213	7238	87.42	1673	20.21	96.35	0.21
石排	7970	303	220	6786	85.14	1631	20.46	96.93	0.44
茶山	8738	292	203	7714	88.28	2002	22.91	95.88	0.43

14-10 镇街农村劳动力(按主要行业分)(2009年)

Labor Force by Town (by Main Sectors) (2009)

镇　　街	劳动力总计(人)	农业	工　业	建筑业	运输仓储邮电通讯业	商饮业
石　　龙	35381	113	11132	979	2011	8756
虎　　门	62237	4928	15986	3568	4813	15212
东　　城	40538	1544	21425	1773	2610	5524
万　　江	40261	873	21131	1630	1454	7838
南　　城	31773	428	10571	1459	2648	6779
中　　堂	38349	4244	21944	2300	1728	3901
望 牛 墩	24359	5029	11528	1536	720	1800
麻　　涌	44549	15009	15715	1823	1693	4748
石　　碣	25017	1921	15852	957	858	1592
高　　埗	19000	3487	7103	1500	836	2129
道　　滘	32516	3154	17429	1719	1819	3836
洪　　梅	12919	4821	4814	504	286	965
沙　　田	29592	8569	12727	983	1194	2769
厚　　街	53537	1826	38553	1825	1208	7794
长　　安	19344	242	5706	242	396	2456
寮　　步	36634	1683	17281	832	1869	5831
大 岭 山	25359	1167	11614	615	899	3704
大　　朗	38392	2247	22615	613	861	4478
黄　　江	13754	1715	5075	235	759	2003
樟 木 头	13625	520	3993	297	752	4100
清　　溪	19078	1114	9475	440	870	2419
塘　　厦	22001	2220	7941	1847	1118	4302
凤　　岗	11633	226	5297	131	216	1335
谢　　岗	12670	1697	6427	299	461	2403
常　　平	36914	1120	18590	827	1941	3880
桥　　头	17053	308	10043	372	2592	1400
横　　沥	21912	1036	9365	887	873	2077
东　　坑	17065	938	10173	483	499	1835
企　　石	26878	1946	15228	1352	721	2205
石　　排	23234	2346	14527	940	752	2547
茶　　山	24582	1031	14669	765	842	3013

注：本表含部分外来劳动力。

14-11 镇街农村劳动力（按性别、产业分）(2009年)

Labor Force by Town (by Sex and Industry) (2009)

镇街	劳动力总计（人）	按性别分		按三次产业分		
		男	女	第一产业	第二产业	第三产业
石龙	35381	19112	16269	113	12111	23157
虎门	62237	33080	29157	4928	19554	37755
东城	40538	21631	18907	1544	23198	15796
万江	40261	21140	19121	873	22761	16627
南城	31773	18076	13697	428	12030	19315
中堂	38349	20552	17797	4244	24244	9861
望牛墩	24359	12867	11492	5029	13064	6266
麻涌	44549	22862	21687	15009	17538	12002
石碣	25017	13120	11897	1921	16809	6287
高埗	19000	10526	8474	3487	8603	6910
道滘	32516	16823	15693	3154	19148	10214
洪梅	12919	6565	6354	4821	5318	2780
沙田	29592	14961	14631	8569	13710	7313
厚街	53537	31879	21658	1826	40378	11333
长安	19344	10331	9013	242	5948	13154
寮步	36634	19507	17127	1683	18113	16838
大岭山	25359	13977	11382	1167	12229	11963
大朗	38392	20476	17916	2247	23228	12917
黄江	13754	7155	6599	1715	5310	6729
樟木头	13625	7489	6136	520	4290	8815
清溪	19078	10349	8729	1114	9915	8049
塘厦	22001	11341	10660	2220	9788	9993
凤岗	11633	6588	5045	226	5428	5979
谢岗	12670	6307	6363	1697	6726	4247
常平	36914	20065	16849	1120	19417	16377
桥头	17053	8831	8222	308	10415	6330
横沥	21912	11445	10467	1036	10252	10624
东坑	17065	9367	7698	938	10656	5471
企石	26878	16124	10754	1946	16580	8352
石排	23234	12218	11016	2346	15467	5421
茶山	24582	13373	11209	1031	15434	8117

注：本表含部分外来劳动力。

14-12 镇街农业总产值（2009年，按当年价格计算）

Gross Output Value of Agriculture by Town (2009, at Current Prices)

单位：万元

镇街	农业总产值	种植业产值	林业产值	牧业产值	渔业产值	服务业产值
石龙	26				26	
虎门	26958	5827	94	8546	12492	
东城	2477	1797			681	
万江	6065	5395	4		667	
南城	2436	2290	13	15	118	
中堂	12176	9489	2	1376	1308	
望牛墩	5326	3668		1242	416	
麻涌	14525	10090	5	664	3766	
石碣	3971	2965			429	578
高埗	10621	9351			979	290
道滘	13275	6187	2	4302	2725	59
洪梅	7841	2483		3467	1890	
沙田	25629	8311	1	2735	14583	
厚街	14705	11619	17	200	2869	
长安	6875	761	11	6	6098	
寮步	3849	1899	28	234	1688	
大岭山	4072	2737	32	11	1254	38
大朗	2142	1376	1	103	661	
黄江	913	507	46		360	
樟木头	741	403	15	254		68
清溪	8042	7583	62		247	150
塘厦	16244	9776	73	4710	685	1000
凤岗	2140	1992	5		143	
谢岗	15992	3924	8	7477	4584	
常平	18352	8306	3	8362	1680	
桥头	6057	2884	5	1640	1529	
横沥	10668	4181	76	4154	2256	
东坑	3762	3325			437	
企石	3138	1080	11	500	1548	
石排	10657	3573	1	3600	3283	199
茶山	7713	1867		3222	2625	

14-13 镇街主要农产品生产及产品产量（2009年）

Production and Output of Main Agricultural Products by Town (2009)

镇 街	粮食播种面积（亩）	粮 食总产量（吨）	稻谷播种面积（亩）	稻 谷产 量（吨）	蔬菜播种面积（亩）	蔬 菜产 量（吨）	水 果总面积（亩）	水 果总产量（吨）
石 龙								
虎 门	1900	460	487	181	19330	18360	5320	2686
东 城	1436	639	1436	639	3232	5886	235	145
万 江	627	236	439	155	12568	20632	151	260
南 城					38	3	84	13
中 堂	1833	624	1431	526	19779	32112	6100	5997
望牛墩	569	177	480	159	3036	4296	8356	12848
麻 涌	6335	1231	1071	373	7931	9840	24223	37811
石 碣	500	165	200	83	10900	13097	301	446
高 埗	1900	710	1520	610	26444	40285	45	130
道 滘	3200	1183	3200	1183	12706	25933	91	150
洪 梅	3291	696	3203	674	246	316	7216	11131
沙 田	3201	1197	3169	1190	14986	20021	5821	6243
厚 街	1400	345			42063	46087	11642	2377
长 安					801	712	2000	469
寮 步	288	149			4592	5949	2158	235
大岭山	686	262			6681	7402	6753	969
大 朗	716	174			4055	3444	9386	598
黄 江					810	817	4920	462
樟木头	80	17			960	1358	5301	159
清 溪	1000	242			12500	13500	11684	782
塘 厦	941	256	6	3	27364	34491	19661	2242
凤 岗	700	174			5151	5434	13283	864
谢 岗	3214	847	1004	403	5000	7500	9841	2825
常 平	1167	290			16280	26045	9130	286
桥 头	1176	252			6121	8724	2034	400
横 沥	851	220	11	3	11251	13900	4217	137
东 坑	665	272	665	272	9104	11357	1279	72
企 石	1745	386	307	106	1842	3223	2643	33
石 排	1000	447			13396	12948	215	344
茶 山	1000	261			7103	6663	3191	290

14-13 续表 1

(2009年)

镇 街	香(大)蕉面积(亩)	香(大)蕉产量(吨)	荔 枝 面 积(亩)	荔 枝 产 量(吨)	林业用地面积(亩)	当年种植面积(亩)	生猪年末存栏(头)	肉 猪 出 栏(头)
石 龙					150			
虎 门	321	190	3169	734	32055	830	35000	40000
东 城			57	6	10958			
万 江	117	236	9	2				
南 城	3	4	68	3	15659			
中 堂	6005	5967					3427	5837
望 牛 墩	8351	12843					6065	7220
麻 涌	23240	36915					2598	2195
石 碣	250	438	51	8				
高 埗								
道 滘	91	150					23960	30771
洪 梅	7216	11131					11752	27190
沙 田	5323	5889	50	10	500	141	20	212
厚 街	296	133	9235	2032	55721	500		
长 安			1802	391	19356	225		
寮 步	35	65	1717	103	14931	800		
大 岭 山			5812	658	54684	1700		
大 朗			8904	518	34889			
黄 江			4230	450	72045	1000		
樟 木 头			4470	48	54123	1244	600	1701
清 溪	80	3	9140	600	72264	1000		
塘 厦			18042	2059	36780	1150	12000	26500
凤 岗	30	7	9937	709	42209	2000		
谢 岗	1050	840	8000	1500	61814	700	41080	51014
常 平	94	11	7505	140	30375		18018	26036
桥 头	40	40	970	42	10446		2520	12640
横 沥	51	51	4000	61	6395		15000	25300
东 坑	23		948	33	5459			
企 石			2323	18	9441	750	2314	3924
石 排	100	250	59	7	767			
茶 山	45	38	2866	108	9980		9550	20283

注：林业用地面积、当年种植面积指标采用林业局数据。

14-13 续表 2

(2009年)

镇街	三鸟年末存栏量(只)	三鸟出栏量(只)	畜牧总肉量(吨)	#猪肉	禽蛋产量(吨)	淡水养殖面积(亩)	水产品产量(吨)	#淡水产量
石龙						67	30	30
虎门	130231	214891	3542	3207	18	568	12241	4516
东城						2505	835	835
万江						1999	970	970
南城	1389	5480	6		1	480	144	144
中堂			654	408		3622	1354	993
望牛墩	41250	140500	676	500	13	1398	491	491
麻涌	70788	86000	249	153	152	3397	2378	2360
石碣						900	561	561
高埗						3013	1350	1350
道滘	50125	89627	2273	2148	90	7819	3185	3185
洪梅	22245	35125	1863	1816		3749	1821	1821
沙田	266714	1170285	1119	14	15	18105	14763	7178
厚街						6036	1850	1850
长安	8698					2636	3783	434
寮步	890	54270	78			3014	2033	2033
大岭山						2120	1609	1609
大朗	18384	40546	42			1973	818	818
黄江						4545	378	378
樟木头	10000	12518	132	119				
清溪						870	301	301
塘厦	489053	970864	2283	1838	37	5740	1133	1133
凤岗						1574	220	220
谢岗	118789	948500	4200	2656		18700	8850	8850
常平	611721	1733208	3652	1923	179	3894	2329	2329
桥头	25529	38724	879	855	2	3976	2278	2278
横沥	20500	68000	1849	1771	8	4230	2546	2546
东坑						3120	720	720
企石			268	268		3090	1854	1854
石排						7494	4090	4090
茶山	24210	153254	1690	1419		4305	2896	2896

14-14 镇街农机总动力、机耕面积及农村用电量（2009年）

Statistics on Total Power of Agricultural Machinery,Area of Tractor Ploughing and Electricity Consumption in Rural Areas by Town (2009)

镇　　街	农　机 总动力 (千瓦)	#耕作机械	排灌机械	农　　村 用 电 量 (万千瓦时)	化肥施用 实 物 量 (吨)	农　药 使用量 (吨)
石　　龙				1562		
虎　　门	33819	144	1031	353210	2062	136
东　　城	10000	154		55130	212	2
万　　江	588	26	160	107257	1019	18
南　　城				8337	95	1
中　　堂	9672	716	2872	109900	2605	28
望 牛 墩	2204	119	407	58063	1715	19
麻　　涌	4315	992	354	9639	7944	105
石　　碣	2327	222	1554	141371	1112	29
高　　埗	13059	4161	2003	117113	1505	81
道　　滘	2166	487	237	109678	1984	75
洪　　梅	588	129	90	955	1746	13
沙　　田	50234	1479	1260	51349	5940	121
厚　　街	2904	376	255	282486	2911	115
长　　安	605		119	468040	181	5
寮　　步	148	10	138	18748	705	11
大 岭 山	2172	398	502	23142	538	19
大　　朗	1793	730	258	175773	1329	36
黄　　江	142	45	2	51748	242	29
樟 木 头				82898	81	6
清　　溪	2441	1127	1118	200402	966	78
塘　　厦	725	94	97	267253	1505	17
凤　　岗	394	110	195	160655	267	12
谢　　岗	2512	1098	1330	4163	573	6
常　　平	273	15	58	164847	814	12
桥　　头	2515	175	1921	115835	1339	10
横　　沥	8805	600	7745	102320	373	12
东　　坑	25		25	69526	707	4
企　　石	435	360	75	58205	323	3
石　　排	3258	493	1346	94069	1595	49
茶　　山	1229	37	1034	114743	976	8

14-15 镇街农村集体(经联社、经济社两级合计)经济收益分配(2009年)

Income Distribution of Rural Collective Economy by Town (2009)

单位：万元

镇 街	经营总收入	经营总费用	经营纯收入
全市总计	**1361017**	**637782**	**723235**
莞 城	14871	4485	10386
石 龙	15532	8238	7294
虎 门	133835	63391	70444
东 城	94528	46429	48100
万 江	50962	23169	27792
南 城	52099	22926	29173
中 堂	41855	14662	27193
望牛墩	7430	3029	4401
麻 涌	16131	7526	8605
石 碣	58184	28621	29563
高 埗	22329	8547	13782
道 滘	20727	8707	12021
洪 梅	5054	2706	2348
沙 田	20189	8694	11496
厚 街	103080	56864	46216
长 安	145694	65402	80292
寮 步	59462	31771	27691
大岭山	35582	14835	20748
大 朗	50045	21227	28818
黄 江	21569	8451	13118
樟木头	19014	17026	1988
清 溪	43701	18650	25051
塘 厦	52366	22992	29374
凤 岗	60223	21592	38631
谢 岗	7779	2901	4878
常 平	65085	30451	34634
桥 头	28144	13916	14228
横 沥	22092	13135	8957
东 坑	20371	11454	8917
企 石	12950	8768	4182
石 排	27080	11244	15836
茶 山	33056	15977	17080

14-16 镇街规模以上工业企业主要经济指标（2009年）

Main Economic Indicators of Industrial Enterprises above Designated Size by Town (2009)

单位：万元

镇街	企业单位数（个）	亏损企业	工业总产值	工业销售产值	工业增加值（生产法）
莞城	54	17	723803	722924	202153
石龙	70	19	1181935	1169958	227280
虎门	384	77	4263344	4209195	1194000
东城	270	52	2257333	2262466	639285
万江	152	23	656479	652221	154618
南城	79	12	1763234	1750325	475274
中堂	117	28	1329572	1417004	285755
望牛墩	107	32	500619	507783	131592
麻涌	85	17	3672947	3566982	802122
石碣	185	35	2716302	2760905	527987
高埗	121	29	1166165	1165583	406668
道滘	164	20	778173	782428	185946
洪梅	68	15	1034063	1056397	213647
沙田	148	29	1252890	1208671	320078
厚街	290	91	3221451	3188008	702795
长安	392	132	4199336	4164881	1043110
寮步	228	57	2830840	2782012	596062
大岭山	235	69	1710088	1696888	403009
大朗	324	48	1869580	1843451	460634
黄江	161	49	1415690	1443490	362771
樟木头	124	28	681998	678435	186345
清溪	308	55	3554564	3455120	787618
塘厦	402	117	3368121	3280223	762456
凤岗	215	67	1330900	1324002	330067
谢岗	91	30	383302	373768	91138
常平	271	77	2505359	2513667	591651
桥头	139	37	701317	696951	155394
横沥	110	24	753302	741124	200047
东坑	75	25	797001	792947	150882
企石	102	21	438814	430400	92926
石排	127	25	442698	438628	113292
茶山	157	32	967260	944167	226074

14-16 续表 1

(2009年)

单位：万元

镇　　街	资产总额	流动资产年合计	#产成品存货	固定资产净值	负债总额
莞　城	856415	323309	28180	385759	486738
石　龙	822578	574968	31989	202407	383940
虎　门	3198815	2029924	178192	862611	1789154
东　城	2284719	1508764	130566	614723	1315792
万　江	581099	409942	37669	128587	402709
南　城	1361785	923396	59924	327962	713543
中　堂	1396029	779086	103630	535871	826043
望牛墩	447527	290581	26296	126000	302601
麻　涌	3987658	1863320	185173	1751500	2419458
石　碣	1726581	1237349	57337	411689	928097
高　埗	973510	620151	36349	305175	634510
道　滘	585868	381933	41796	170460	323512
洪　梅	1270674	658801	58435	547633	687304
沙　田	999417	622786	48947	296914	605639
厚　街	2074415	1482289	140944	486194	1316188
长　安	3732617	2181306	192013	1283226	2284752
寮　步	1875081	1329777	105163	447998	1175624
大岭山	1706535	1084771	103224	472570	1016339
大　朗	1692133	1154502	82955	416093	1046693
黄　江	1184730	778621	47044	346740	699976
樟木头	650723	390024	39500	234354	356581
清　溪	2802681	1944503	116185	727375	1497126
塘　厦	2819846	1915519	186795	661256	1634198
凤　岗	1459607	807030	77813	461519	696872
谢　岗	392147	259468	29711	120946	231156
常　平	2340660	1674175	96132	558010	1428943
桥　头	715040	487910	40967	190048	436945
横　沥	656964	440694	43180	186945	427213
东　坑	599030	416397	82241	168456	385852
企　石	455951	343512	20142	91022	279323
石　排	380232	264240	16671	95710	225511
茶　山	961017	597618	57005	292782	549379

14-16 续表 2

(2009年)

单位：万元

镇街	主营业务收入	#主营业务税金及附加	利润总额	亏损企业亏损总额	利税总额	本年应交增值税	职工平均人数(人)
莞城	721476	7305	56663	13524	83255	19287	22048
石龙	1169278	997	71874	4149	83177	10305	34790
虎门	4160928	8057	184374	20737	265154	72723	214048
东城	2254943	7615	194765	10412	255513	53133	103644
万江	650464	1618	25541	8729	40456	13297	32040
南城	1744405	1408	174824	1536	209688	33456	53819
中堂	1408286	9807	21368	18878	67472	36297	36218
望牛墩	521840	725	37911	7683	52145	13509	21643
麻涌	3557013	1448	284565	17958	349823	63809	39130
石碣	2792071	1274	93713	6654	123470	28483	97500
高埗	1164368	932	59966	10075	73017	12118	122411
道滘	777637	2142	27377	2608	42887	13368	38919
洪梅	1054605	379	80640	2950	100861	19842	18357
沙田	1226780	554	47138	11668	64832	17140	43762
厚街	3164700	5011	87690	25056	114546	21845	177594
长安	4164900	3591	120090	87442	185731	62050	248530
寮步	2784901	3342	134347	26213	172924	35234	101295
大岭山	1687477	2990	18377	15837	45359	23992	95794
大朗	1841360	5524	61775	5594	95559	28260	90921
黄江	1425104	665	70575	9360	89272	18033	78057
樟木头	668868	1793	44695	4983	54488	8001	44745
清溪	3449069	2207	221471	12454	241010	17333	144210
塘厦	3273210	2808	119998	44044	154909	32104	169122
凤岗	1317788	544	33028	16597	54885	21313	89798
谢岗	371090	236	9411	4325	13389	3742	25404
常平	2505481	3731	159550	12341	192278	28998	115819
桥头	689904	854	7369	6316	14212	5989	47478
横沥	741765	511	21868	8253	30117	7737	58253
东坑	791373	276	19562	7252	30504	10667	41839
企石	423882	412	10745	2010	17311	6154	23427
石排	437394	496	9357	3430	14927	5075	37785
茶山	938261	1402	38022	6778	59396	19972	42724

14-17 镇街规模以上工业企业主要经济效益指标（2009年）

Main Indicators of Economic Benefit of Industrial Enterprises above Designated Size by Town (2009)

镇　街	工业增加值率 (%)	总资产贡献率 (%)	资产负债率 (%)	流动资产周转率 (次/年)	成本费用利润率 (%)	全员劳动生产率 (元/人)	产品销售率 (%)
莞　城	27.9	11.5	56.8	2.2	8.6	91688	99.9
石　龙	19.2	10.4	46.7	2.0	6.6	65329	99.0
虎　门	28.0	8.6	55.9	2.1	4.7	55782	98.7
东　城	28.3	11.6	57.6	1.5	9.4	61681	100.2
万　江	23.6	8.0	69.3	1.6	4.1	48258	99.4
南　城	27.0	15.9	52.4	1.9	11.5	88310	99.3
中　堂	21.5	6.1	59.2	1.8	1.5	78899	106.6
望牛墩	26.3	12.3	67.6	1.8	7.9	60801	101.4
麻　涌	21.8	9.5	60.7	1.9	8.7	204989	97.1
石　碣	19.4	7.2	53.8	2.3	3.5	54153	101.6
高　埗	34.9	8.2	65.2	1.9	5.4	33221	100.0
道　滘	23.9	7.7	55.2	2.0	3.7	47778	100.6
洪　梅	20.7	8.3	54.1	1.6	8.3	116384	102.2
沙　田	25.6	7.1	60.6	2.0	3.9	73141	96.5
厚　街	21.8	5.8	63.5	2.1	2.8	39573	99.0
长　安	24.8	5.2	61.2	1.9	3.0	41971	99.2
寮　步	21.1	9.7	62.7	2.1	5.1	58844	98.3
大岭山	23.6	2.8	59.6	1.6	1.1	42070	99.2
大　朗	24.6	6.0	61.9	1.6	3.5	50663	98.6
黄　江	25.6	7.7	59.1	1.8	5.2	46475	102.0
樟木头	27.3	9.4	54.8	1.7	7.2	41646	99.5
清　溪	22.2	8.7	53.4	1.8	7.0	54616	97.2
塘　厦	22.6	5.6	58.0	1.7	3.9	45083	97.4
凤　岗	24.8	4.0	47.7	1.6	2.7	36757	99.5
谢　岗	23.8	3.9	59.0	1.4	2.6	35875	97.5
常　平	23.6	8.5	61.1	1.5	6.9	51084	100.3
桥　头	22.2	2.4	61.1	1.4	1.1	32730	99.4
横　沥	26.6	5.0	65.0	1.7	3.0	34341	98.4
东　坑	18.9	5.3	64.4	1.9	2.5	36063	99.5
企　石	21.2	4.7	61.3	1.2	2.6	39666	98.1
石　排	25.6	4.5	59.3	1.7	2.2	29983	99.1
茶　山	23.4	6.8	57.2	1.6	4.2	52915	97.6

14-18 镇街乡镇企业基本情况（2009年）

Basic Conditions of Township Enterprises by Town (2009)

单位：万元

镇街	企业单位数（个）	从业人员（人）	总产值	增加值	营业收入	上交税金	利润总额	工资总额
总计	**55603**	**2641374**	**44582170**	**10828890**	**40987974**	**1294988**	**1833950**	**3673791**
东城	2310	92932	1124665	334923	1002638	33515	84349	116934
万江	2205	88029	868113	267211	790254	31022	67325	83757
南城	764	93793	1844095	632863	1805756	42789	139531	184906
中堂	1489	42795	1497947	373246	1479023	38278	18894	50844
望牛墩	473	50488	410734	138988	400708	28765	37500	69673
麻涌	736	41515	3796630	757478	3675901	54357	191859	53233
石碣	1633	137628	3123289	687881	3078625	114849	161217	247730
高埗	888	132314	1036477	278325	978953	57438	31172	146730
道滘	5225	63817	901433	206756	900927	31663	19967	62492
洪梅	132	26586	1049151	230810	1075598	26564	51847	35124
沙田	1145	71860	1728465	417049	1688673	80959	144042	134402
厚街	3160	193019	1171235	325599	1170937	70317	77088	311520
长安	2193	170237	4735221	943097	2281696	77867	71217	314099
寮步	723	95680	1279520	344230	1182640	34952	63295	155249
大岭山	1260	91507	943176	270495	914881	44329	28295	105636
大朗	916	90705	1292510	371845	1292115	38150	49838	106123
黄江	7665	93215	1114459	251867	1086597	28782	12367	118441
樟木头	1851	91899	862790	240995	836621	9125	22090	106401
清溪	2616	197144	3209351	546966	2783408	130071	259456	289561
塘厦	1741	193929	3254288	682566	3206833	42125	56447	188629
凤岗	2032	133862	1831707	477018	1820307	45452	58569	164588
谢岗	578	24363	370664	80374	360092	3950	1735	22511
常平	2588	62350	1590317	240226	1668828	51812	52739	135770
桥头	550	54760	848940	239910	802250	10540	9760	61168
横沥	2781	71880	1150356	326548	1135849	54458	18899	92032
东坑	4930	79536	879125	410454	1102172	39277	51632	126344
企石	1282	31023	560969	116156	372460	5537	10112	34210
石排	1129	77305	1047124	370385	1042967	43079	25926	90460
茶山	608	47203	1059419	264629	1050265	24966	16782	65224

14-19 主要年份镇街乡镇工业企业单位数

Number of Township Industrial Enterprises by Town in Main Years

单位: 个

镇　　街	1985年	1990年	1995年	2000年	2004年	2005年	2008年	2009年
东　　城	205	452	573	566	658	663	652	649
万　　江	278	456	567	623	1055	1264	1126	1138
南　　城	79	161	308	276	222	767	688	689
中　　堂	85	205	268	242	735	821	1486	1489
望 牛 墩	63	158	155	218	335	399	389	436
麻　　涌	60	381	128	138	267	289	325	335
石　　碣	110	202	250	856	1236	1322	1011	1005
高　　埗	148	282	345	237	336	512	484	429
道　　滘	244	431	313	272	508	520	576	573
洪　　梅	15	48	69	58	114	127	132	132
沙　　田	16	141	297	245	420	490	496	481
厚　　街	332	619	935	1019	1856	1007	1056	877
长　　安	60	440	1064	1000	1597	1650	1773	1681
寮　　步	69	233	529	814	942	853	711	523
大 岭 山	14	103	270	444	652	765	756	746
大　　朗	472	495	856	1256	705	515	595	625
黄　　江	75	185	424	514	863	906	921	976
樟 木 头	109	279	272	430	421	425	442	442
清　　溪	53	210	407	402	754	746	1046	1029
塘　　厦	166	314	491	862	1314	1421	1588	1214
凤　　岗	108	471	849	923	1238	1252	1243	1242
谢　　岗	27	218	231	299	364	494	551	542
常　　平	217	522	686	1348	1495	1719	2091	1882
桥　　头	55	146	268	381	450	460	560	550
横　　沥	87	225	412	361	652	687	731	726
东　　坑	143	178	263	366	507	615	478	439
企　　石	95	176	300	345	1065	1322	542	973
石　　排	83	232	360	387	689	750	861	856
茶　　山	133	854	423	522	803	842	501	520

14-20 镇街固定资产投资总额（2008-2009年）

Total Investment in Fixed Assets by Town(2008-2009)

单位：万元

镇　街	2008年	2009年	镇　街	2008年	2009年
莞　城	249452	176232	寮　步	285164	222382
石　龙	163393	173226	大岭山	271931	299124
虎　门	567682	621214	大　朗	283995	383551
东　城	383431	493153	黄　江	216509	234778
万　江	263088	297823	樟木头	89356	92971
南　城	782269	1016714	清　溪	156600	194943
中　堂	162007	181538	塘　厦	248588	308828
望牛墩	109014	132344	凤　岗	168842	253263
麻　涌	217584	238321	谢　岗	63561	71238
石　碣	185872	154241	常　平	263055	291712
高　埗	134275	142932	桥　头	101044	101442
道　滘	121519	106584	横　沥	79298	87432
洪　梅	248162	189294	东　坑	65855	87590
沙　田	182523	216753	企　石	20307	50917
厚　街	291820	333477	石　排	271386	187225
长　安	499810	500547	茶　山	155164	175391

14-21 镇街邮电局、所通信能力及服务网点（2009年）

Communication Capacity and Number of Postal and Telecommunication Offices by Town (2009)

镇　街	邮电局（所、综合营业厅）(处)		服务网点（含报刊亭）(处)		固定电话用户（含小灵通）(户)	
	2008年	2009年	2008年	2009年	2008年	2009年
全市总计	**546**	**546**	**2792**	**2772**	**4394143**	**3783993**
市　区	65	68	476	481	1467532	1068619
石　龙	12	13	48	48	97159	88613
虎　门	37	35	230	225	254885	234892
中　堂	9	9	53	54	70968	60311
望牛墩	6	5	24	22	35618	31460
麻　涌	6	4	19	17	49641	41759
石　碣	26	26	90	86	99315	88743
高　埗	11	12	51	51	49904	43436
道　滘	6	7	35	37	56396	49467
洪　梅	4	4	13	13	24070	22331
沙　田	9	10	44	44	52803	46892
厚　街	34	30	157	158	207078	184767
长　安	39	41	245	245	258670	234830
寮　步	19	19	94	89	119356	110901
大岭山	18	19	90	89	80021	74564
大　朗	18	19	117	113	148318	138082
黄　江	17	14	80	77	95023	91769
樟木头	15	16	79	80	87074	75931
清　溪	23	20	113	110	115295	106105
塘　厦	32	33	135	140	165136	150228
凤　岗	25	26	81	84	106721	95527
谢　岗	6	7	41	41	37719	34095
常　平	34	34	164	162	187986	172123
桥　头	13	13	63	64	72705	65064
横　沥	14	16	54	53	77611	66433
东　坑	13	11	36	35	50173	42630
企　石	9	9	43	43	52962	45987
石　排	12	12	64	62	67059	61139
茶　山	14	14	53	49	86337	76501

注：市区指莞城、南城、东城、万江四个街道。

14-22 镇街社会消费品零售总额（2008-2009年）

Total Retail Sales of Consumer Goods by Town (2008-2009)

单位：万元

镇　　街	2008年	2009年	镇　　街	2008年	2009年
莞　城	908795	995207	寮　步	862000	972500
石　龙	246417	280601	大岭山	255268	315256
虎　门	855300	1038334	大　朗	209018	238699
东　城	836510	961987	黄　江	138405	156362
万　江	204123	221620	樟木头	186109	212138
南　城	775522	835410	清　溪	172197	191270
中　堂	92116	106625	塘　厦	206884	240254
望牛墩	21485	25483	凤　岗	178304	214780
麻　涌	51430	48935	谢　岗	66735	75465
石　碣	169948	176888	常　平	472213	537743
高　埗	159350	160960	桥　头	240690	285950
道　滘	51587	58584	横　沥	151028	176258
洪　梅	70356	82408	东　坑	56589	46805
沙　田	79828	84274	企　石	77735	81665
厚　街	419920	483205	石　排	109311	120384
长　安	356698	411073	茶　山	113351	128744

14-23 镇街注册工商企业及个体户数（2009年）

Number of Registered Industrial and Commercial Enterprises and Self-employed Individuals by Town (2009)

单位：户

镇街	企业总户数	国有集体	三资企业	三来一补	私营企业	个体户
市属	45	3	26		16	7
莞城	4591	759	205	22	3605	12851
石龙	1143	267	110	33	733	7107
虎门	6771	699	706	333	5033	41910
东城	8798	1067	602	180	6949	24817
万江	3797	333	200	51	3213	11212
南城	7900	881	460	44	6515	11220
中堂	1511	293	97	34	1087	8085
望牛墩	782	156	102	28	496	2480
麻涌	837	187	77	25	548	3557
石碣	2380	306	185	177	1712	9503
高埗	1312	208	156	53	895	5695
道滘	1467	180	168	57	1062	4200
洪梅	398	80	68	13	237	1658
沙田	1487	265	186	31	1005	5712
厚街	4969	413	539	226	3791	25265
长安	10675	826	891	738	8220	38352
寮步	4800	527	404	175	3694	16152
大岭山	3258	342	326	104	2486	18112
大朗	3547	530	336	239	2442	16526
黄江	2768	283	305	204	1976	7549
樟木头	2376	333	204	144	1695	10190
清溪	2585	218	499	323	1545	10417
塘厦	5514	452	800	478	3784	17287
凤岗	3066	357	375	540	1794	11840
谢岗	986	125	174	129	558	4278
常平	4406	623	527	367	2889	28675
桥头	1851	274	276	171	1130	7141
横沥	2108	284	305	217	1302	8378
东坑	1129	238	118	124	649	3802
企石	1296	243	144	115	794	4801
石排	1843	311	205	177	1150	9899
茶山	1868	332	183	154	1199	7441
松山湖	399	116	49		234	107

注:本表数据来源于市工商局。

14-24 镇街集市贸易市场数及私营个体户注册资金额(2008-2009年)

Number of Fair Trades and Registered Capital of Private Enterprises and Self-employed Individuals by Town (2008-2009)

镇街	集市贸易市场数(个)		个体工商户注册资金额(万元)		私营企业注册资金额(万元)	
	2008年	2009年	2008年	2009年	2008年	2009年
市属			15	15	20766	53266
莞城	40	41	22865	23337	802380	833668
石龙	15	15	13895	10834	129355	135396
虎门	95	95	95390	86049	649132	678679
东城	70	72	78813	47243	1141998	1205057
万江	40	41	31524	24237	376136	406859
南城	29	31	22151	20664	1509778	1585654
中堂	25	26	25124	19037	150419	182020
望牛墩	6	8	6338	6349	65179	71589
麻涌	17	17	18010	7133	98828	112191
石碣	27	28	23132	21313	122416	130666
高埗	13	14	12020	11877	130100	144425
道滘	12	12	13272	12029	115342	130511
洪梅	3	3	2878	3045	43080	60562
沙田	19	22	13126	12098	165759	176957
厚街	51	53	50592	50605	483549	510579
长安	49	51	79536	79310	577018	628921
寮步	40	41	25621	29157	406911	454272
大岭山	21	22	41658	43309	177550	197154
大朗	29	29	53174	43093	242514	287323
黄江	27	29	20441	19122	152371	170843
樟木头	30	30	21036	21570	112689	120164
清溪	22	22	22226	19039	111388	131484
塘厦	29	32	36794	37397	374356	417246
凤岗	21	21	31202	25748	147244	161983
谢岗	8	8	10211	10693	47063	51673
常平	39	42	81061	85514	289709	321045
桥头	21	21	29039	19220	145731	151088
横沥	15	20	20129	19893	103571	115676
东坑	15	16	10555	11014	61278	85573
企石	13	15	15498	15142	118129	132718
石排	25	25	30758	28640	79016	88434
茶山	21	21	23037	21037	103277	127506
松山湖			125	197	115279	154576

注:本表数据来源于市工商局。

14-25 镇街来料加工装配签约宗数、出口值及引进设备价值（2009年）

Number of Contracts of Processing and Assembling of Imported Materials, Export Value and Imported Value of Equipments by Town (2009)

镇　街	新签协议宗数 (宗)	累计投产宗数 (宗)	出口值 (万美元)	引进设备价值 (万美元)
莞　城		18	5199	176
石　龙	1	26	9160	398
虎　门	1	248	15355	58
东　城	1	149	14671	402
万　江		55	2896	25
南　城		33	69310	9256
中　堂		26	2399	4
望牛墩		19	2339	113
麻　涌		20	1227	
石　碣	1	150	17641	444
高　埗		46	67808	743
道　滘		41	5370	67
洪　梅		9	6100	173
沙　田		18	535	3
厚　街		183	173052	995
长　安	1	650	201553	11984
寮　步	1	175	154596	1798
大岭山	1	76	76717	2323
大　朗		213	25651	208
黄　江		190	267708	3419
樟木头		120	37622	448
清　溪	1	285	198016	1977
塘　厦	5	409	62019	835
凤　岗	5	462	68397	924
谢　岗	1	107	7527	356
常　平		274	40048	1259
桥　头	1	136	135920	2493
横　沥		196	27053	169
东　坑		104	20888	357
企　石		78	4694	52
石　排		138	8584	93
茶　山	1	113	15826	164

注：本表为外经贸局口径。

14-26 镇街“三资”企业签约、实际利用外资及出口值(新口径)(2009年)

Contracts, Amount of Foreign Capital Actually Utilized and Export Value of Enterprises with Foreign Investment by Town (2009)

镇街	签约宗数(宗)	投产企业宗数	协议(合同)规定外商投资总额(万美元)	外商实际投资总额(万美元)	出口值(万美元)
莞城	7	59	915	1989	20073
石龙	7	51	9510	4446	120873
虎门	37	479	9462	10595	175918
东城	24	311	4298	10131	125845
万江	10	149	1373	3618	16683
南城	22	175	3177	6117	34242
中堂	2	80	1650	1668	15835
望牛墩	5	70	2211	1871	9772
麻涌	11	45	12046	24114	112320
石碣	5	130	939	4688	236540
高埗	8	129	2772	5203	31501
道滘	7	122	2911	1547	27473
洪梅	2	54	2634	10825	13618
沙田	6	125	1247	6769	59998
厚街	24	358	4320	9917	237897
长安	48	550	8668	16062	288452
寮步	19	250	7672	6488	195130
大岭山	8	257	2350	10636	102848
大朗	30	274	3680	7709	60107
黄江	14	256	6054	10493	129188
樟木头	11	165	1756	4070	35329
清溪	40	454	8693	15594	295256
塘厦	32	617	9946	14705	247625
凤岗	26	326	8498	10369	82212
谢岗	14	144	4540	4062	24606
常平	32	272	5241	13167	249162
桥头	20	251	3352	5934	45046
横沥	38	213	9064	8038	67624
东坑	7	105	3118	4796	70049
企石	16	100	2459	2333	19733
石排	14	168	2225	4101	28089
茶山	16	144	4480	6330	21012

注：本表为外经贸局口径。

14-27 镇街进出口总额（2009年，海关口径）

Total Value of Exports and Imports by Town (2009, Customs Statistics)

单位：万美元

镇街	进出口总额	进口	出口	镇街	进出口总额	进口	出口
莞城	85582	40686	44896	寮步	654579	272451	382128
石龙	194629	63959	130670	大岭山	300518	117480	183038
虎门	295900	102666	193234	大朗	215453	89158	126296
东城	241425	84012	157413	黄江	650028	250790	399238
万江	37851	11650	26201	樟木头	122033	47877	74156
南城	396951	255365	141587	清溪	842272	344308	497963
中堂	64313	37801	26512	塘厦	511018	194792	316226
望牛墩	23724	9494	14230	凤岗	264985	105032	159953
麻涌	279163	160068	119095	谢岗	49514	17324	32191
石碣	407283	150471	256812	常平	516360	221717	294643
高埗	158594	54513	104081	桥头	293935	110268	183668
道滘	59679	24857	34822	横沥	149721	54713	95009
洪梅	106517	86428	20089	东坑	161084	67420	93664
沙田	133146	67872	65273	企石	35088	10260	24827
厚街	632162	217617	414546	石排	58601	16515	42086
长安	856901	357322	499579	茶山	70211	30612	39599

14-28 镇街实际利用外资（2008-2009年）

Amount of Foreign Capital Actually Utilized by Town (2008-2009)

单位：万美元

镇　街	2008年	2009年	镇　街	2008年	2009年
莞　城	3374	1989	寮　步	7285	6488
石　龙	4128	4446	大岭山	9025	10636
虎　门	9849	10595	大　朗	7215	7709
东　城	9130	10131	黄　江	10290	10493
万　江	3096	3618	樟木头	3693	4070
南　城	4877	6117	清　溪	15352	15594
中　堂	4110	1668	塘　厦	13195	14705
望牛墩	1940	1871	凤　岗	9022	10369
麻　涌	22989	24114	谢　岗	3942	4062
石　碣	4227	4688	常　平	13540	13167
高　埗	4775	5203	桥　头	5468	5934
道　滘	2973	1547	横　沥	5643	8038
洪　梅	9938	10825	东　坑	3918	4796
沙　田	7307	6769	企　石	2201	2333
厚　街	9245	9917	石　排	4328	4101
长　安	13170	16062	茶　山	5254	6330

14-29　镇街工商税收总额（2008-2009年）

Total Taxes by Town (2008-2009)

单位：万元

镇　　街	2008年	2009年	镇　　街	2008年	2009年
莞　　城	314243	283194	寮　　步	160191	165236
石　　龙	86075	90648	大 岭 山	110989	116655
虎　　门	316570	294917	大　　朗	107248	108582
东　　城	374706	409819	黄　　江	84876	89158
万　　江	89317	90481	樟 木 头	62633	60170
南　　城	351649	403738	清　　溪	146664	121867
中　　堂	84777	80296	塘　　厦	248896	231760
望 牛 墩	30306	33077	凤　　岗	123877	125419
麻　　涌	120512	141902	谢　　岗	23500	26452
石　　碣	138570	115017	常　　平	166532	176827
高　　埗	78016	65630	桥　　头	53661	54685
道　　滘	70244	62168	横　　沥	56589	54509
洪　　梅	27253	37022	东　　坑	42151	39418
沙　　田	77519	70505	企　　石	34425	34949
厚　　街	211445	196626	石　　排	43744	43170
长　　安	268165	297627	茶　　山	68053	70053

注:本表数据来源于市财政局。

14-30 镇街本级可支配财政收入（2008-2009年）

Local Government Disposable Revenue by Town (2008-2009)

单位：万元

镇　　街	2008年	2009年	镇　　街	2008年	2009年
莞　　城	58708	62678	寮　　步	70538	79610
石　　龙	40318	46016	大 岭 山	66902	70502
虎　　门	118839	143368	大　　朗	56433	59843
东　　城	107766	120067	黄　　江	45912	48715
万　　江	47494	50204	樟 木 头	47931	38265
南　　城	237893	129219	清　　溪	56570	50467
中　　堂	42139	50262	塘　　厦	90930	97842
望 牛 墩	28739	30595	凤　　岗	50109	52001
麻　　涌	44936	49852	谢　　岗	24590	27543
石　　碣	39005	40184	常　　平	88110	89126
高　　埗	33433	35842	桥　　头	38343	35626
道　　滘	48128	48323	横　　沥	36922	40429
洪　　梅	18860	21541	东　　坑	35049	41362
沙　　田	44915	41230	企　　石	24993	23806
厚　　街	77820	79103	石　　排	45300	36078
长　　安	114080	123864	茶　　山	36547	40174

14-31 镇街本级财政支出（2008-2009年）

Local Government Expenditure by Town (2008-2009)

单位：万元

镇　街	2008年	2009年	镇　街	2008年	2009年
莞　城	54406	58854	寮　步	70537	79235
石　龙	40300	45683	大岭山	68594	70128
虎　门	117769	140236	大　朗	56336	60311
东　城	104095	115288	黄　江	45411	48633
万　江	46693	54592	樟木头	48393	67533
南　城	210082	115052	清　溪	53831	51415
中　堂	42120	50245	塘　厦	90326	97614
望牛墩	28575	30459	凤　岗	51639	48012
麻　涌	44923	49843	谢　岗	24214	26351
石　碣	42067	40589	常　平	84819	90722
高　埗	32873	35596	桥　头	38537	48521
道　滘	48354	48102	横　沥	36914	41604
洪　梅	18882	21564	东　坑	35023	41099
沙　田	47262	41557	企　石	24969	23791
厚　街	78514	79101	石　排	46489	35603
长　安	117622	124335	茶　山	38468	40001

14-32　镇街资产负债总额（2008-2009年）

Total Assets and Liabilities by Town (2008-2009)

单位：万元

镇　　街	资产总额		负债总额	
	2008年	2009年	2008年	2009年
莞　　城	432996	479675	139224	153561
石　　龙	316609	301583	165696	153871
虎　　门	453341	826800	60823	64956
东　　城	238500	242500		
万　　江	217564	261766	71846	99694
南　　城	387591	498392	52607	135739
中　　堂	270500	330849	142291	164836
望 牛 墩	133966	169113	69172	100863
麻　　涌	167862	209375	74430	96992
石　　碣	230159	353126	84893	182181
高　　埗	134298	183016	71412	94860
道　　滘	161617	197778	55804	64277
洪　　梅	117161	156272	66782	92982
沙　　田	255463	270128	78981	95044
厚　　街	301172	377148	66455	118648
长　　安	504998	546912	52319	53005
寮　　步	271642	277494	95293	88847
大 岭 山	257760	281317	93557	94226
大　　朗	153021	206610	35818	34826
黄　　江	208305	253963	63872	79312
樟 木 头	230610	248885	121220	149188
清　　溪	273859	290077	116117	122940
塘　　厦	414401	606634	100527	182578
凤　　岗	312955	354382	126125	158325
谢　　岗	104815	136487	52587	71750
常　　平	480748	535082	130172	163922
桥　　头	175570	177880	84095	79300
横　　沥	201808	206051	95719	104282
东　　坑	160509	202954	92013	113876
企　　石	147962	154620	57648	59848
石　　排	184790	208932	64756	75590
茶　　山	137913	140001	56648	53561

14-33 镇街农民人均纯收入（2008-2009年）

Per Capital Net Income of Rural Households by Town (2008-2009)

单位：元

镇　街	2008年	2009年	镇　街	2008年	2009年
莞　城	11588	11430	寮　步	10382	11118
石　龙	12568	13045	大岭山	12156	12769
虎　门	14391	15195	大　朗	14720	15286
东　城	14939	15688	黄　江	10821	11340
万　江	12197	12769	樟木头	13620	13698
南　城	11704	16240	清　溪	13718	14541
中　堂	10973	11751	塘　厦	16079	16795
望牛墩	8112	8659	凤　岗	14099	14908
麻　涌	8739	9011	谢　岗	9598	10079
石　碣	12462	12975	常　平	12262	12868
高　埗	11872	12464	桥　头	12140	12761
道　滘	10616	11143	横　沥	12202	12767
洪　梅	8452	8853	东　坑	10792	11342
沙　田	8895	8995	企　石	9926	9976
厚　街	14660	15393	石　排	11484	12173
长　安	23127	24282	茶　山	11185	11753

14-34 镇街各项人民币存贷款余额与城乡居民储蓄存款余额(2008-2009年)

The balance of Deposits and Loans in Renminbi in Various Forms and that of Savings Deposits by Urban and Rural Residents by Town(2008-2009)

单位：万元

镇　街	年末各项存款余额		年末各项贷款余额		城乡居民储蓄存款余额	
	2008年	2009年	2008年	2009年	2008年	2009年
莞　城	6106216	6413744	4736198	5314985	1917542	2087825
石　龙	967440	1190569	412430	488305	754728	808199
虎　门	3755206	4084004	1409514	1690341	2951072	3213867
东　城	4255190	3849488	2640760	2508767	1996967	2188415
万　江	902768	1020666	667232	758795	651829	725482
南　城	4382924	7028632	3905236	5790360	1469005	1858000
中　堂	659159	714301	375076	436289	470779	494051
望牛墩	303286	349813	89031	126699	227871	245156
麻　涌	595487	567709	219294	262127	280718	302623
石　碣	1143627	1293160	292360	427950	784860	846502
高　埗	552798	621829	137788	146334	409584	432531
道　滘	471562	518720	161254	170566	349438	375379
洪　梅	152798	182227	53389	98322	100525	111857
沙　田	616067	727804	158552	265791	349542	383528
厚　街	2222878	2567309	1526305	1838245	1716149	1894020
长　安	2886050	3285949	1107932	1463433	2075406	2253195
寮　步	983741	1150222	410799	574138	695043	781796
大岭山	832629	880373	340844	433206	586891	622434
大　朗	1228426	1492982	574546	768526	988068	1105730
黄　江	759068	876372	331854	360363	568969	619018
樟木头	788812	844491	500809	566392	641044	664447
清　溪	897733	1049565	362967	407992	649549	710980
塘　厦	1525545	1813651	735434	976916	1064546	1180713
凤　岗	1078965	1215656	422745	557951	721104	786894
谢　岗	275937	324139	71909	97656	210749	228236
常　平	1821519	2074004	798645	994423	1360895	1478324
桥　头	561835	612109	324028	283866	453981	499079
横　沥	551122	618282	206986	247083	430187	484785
东　坑	401330	455310	138882	166085	304779	337088
企　石	373491	398386	186159	243495	281096	309910
石　排	534395	619247	161937	199583	402967	456423
茶　山	709357	743269	210541	225654	495217	530999

注：本表是按人民银行东莞市分行口径。

14-35 镇街普通中学情况（2009年）

Statistics on Regular Secondary Schools by Town (2009)

镇街	学校数（所）	毕业生数（人）	#普通高中	招生数（人）	#普通高中	在校学生数（人）	#普通高中	教职工数（人）	#专任教师
全市总计	**186**	**71811**	**20550**	**88325**	**23631**	**249464**	**66750**	**17212**	**13598**
莞城									
石龙	4	1390		1526		4676		303	266
虎门	7	3052		3906	358	12025	955	861	748
东城	9	2777		3544		9443		538	478
万江	7	3255	548	3826	864	11193	2275	760	574
南城	6	1867	232	3141	714	8308	1977	539	452
中堂	7	2270	115	2297	165	6873	440	474	370
望牛墩	2	1540		1490		4487		222	206
麻涌	3	1605	374	1531	355	4769	983	306	275
石碣	8	1725	323	2251	308	5959	738	369	313
高埗	5	1046		1273		3627		225	194
道滘	4	1649	447	2108	493	5861	1464	363	285
洪梅	1	354		325		1044		84	64
沙田	3	1012	130	1247	318	3853	923	420	260
厚街	8	2126		2722		7382		403	348
长安	5	1587		2683		6563		399	327
寮步	7	2351	353	3684	466	9806	1315	590	465
大岭山	6	1616	282	2007	344	5906	958	364	295
大朗	7	2339	429	3127	521	8190	1473	497	420
黄江	3	834		1013		2941		179	157
樟木头	3	1077	324	1293	283	3955	899	264	200
清溪	5	1361	326	1361		3968	190	288	237
塘厦	4	1123		2496	161	6256	161	364	282
凤岗	7	1536	439	2330	273	6334	1050	494	404
谢岗	3	680		888		2435		185	127
常平	11	2364		2625		7245		477	383
桥头	5	1247	344	1938	487	4927	1023	401	292
横沥	4	786	122	1090		3125	90	233	184
东坑	4	900		1240		3372		205	169
企石	3	1429	356	1448	324	4245	1003	279	258
石排	4	1128		1248		3565		214	187
茶山	7	1794	465	2443	703	6480	1676	459	378

14-36 镇街中等职业技术学校情况（2009年）

Statistics on Secondary Vocational Schools by Town (2009)

镇　街	学校数（所）	毕业生数（人）	招生数（人）	在校学生数（人）	教职工数（人）	#专任教师
全市总计	**26**	**11927**	**15767**	**46538**	**3112**	**2321**
莞　城						
石　龙						
虎　门	1	515		2359	171	127
东　城	1		258	918	55	50
万　江		274	200	585	46	34
南　城	1	250	691	2125	128	92
中　堂						
望牛墩						
麻　涌						
石　碣	2		718	1828	111	71
高　埗	1		548	1695	110	60
道　滘		146	180	458	16	14
洪　梅		73				
沙　田						
厚　街						
长　安						
寮　步						
大岭山						
大　朗						
黄　江						
樟木头						
清　溪						
塘　厦						
凤　岗						
谢　岗						
常　平						
桥　头						
横　沥						
东　坑						
企　石						
石　排						
茶　山						

14-37 镇街小学情况（2009年）

Statistics on Primary Schools by Town (2009)

镇　街	学校数（所）	毕业生数（人）	招生数（人）	在校学生数（人）	教职工数（人）	#专任教师
全市总计	**337**	**78027**	**92281**	**511160**	**26605**	**21130**
莞　城	9	2582	2133	13400	687	648
石　龙	6	1710	1530	9921	466	430
虎　门	26	5556	5425	35080	1794	1293
东　城	14	4524	5518	29056	1517	1224
万　江	16	3380	3635	22212	1148	974
南　城	10	2628	3503	18474	935	803
中　堂	9	2245	2247	13305	964	680
望牛墩	4	1307	859	6289	369	327
麻　涌	8	1316	1152	7025	470	426
石　碣	8	2588	3314	17167	774	645
高　埗	6	1391	1741	9357	524	428
道　滘	6	1852	1581	9791	497	418
洪　梅	3	459	273	2068	124	109
沙　田	4	1202	1041	6445	369	306
厚　街	15	3187	3842	22765	1091	889
长　安	21	3510	6159	29366	1441	1100
寮　步	18	3629	4237	22514	1101	882
大岭山	9	2101	2751	14444	672	553
大　朗	18	3395	4799	24142	1048	892
黄　江	9	1536	2036	10434	537	438
樟木头	8	1774	2108	11538	581	437
清　溪	9	2121	2723	14605	734	585
塘　厦	12	3293	4852	24366	1244	920
凤　岗	17	2882	4342	21663	1099	814
谢　岗	3	943	907	5471	324	245
常　平	18	3970	4693	26716	1209	1021
桥　头	7	1551	2137	11384	647	487
横　沥	7	1760	2535	12663	736	563
东　坑	7	1655	2051	10848	460	424
企　石	10	1460	1627	9547	496	386
石　排	9	1809	2055	11596	563	499
茶　山	7	2270	2481	14185	802	665

14-38 镇街卫生事业机构、床位及人员数（2009年）

Number of Health care Institutions, Beds and Personnel by Town (2009)

镇街	机构数（个）	#医院	病床床位（张）	卫生工作人员（人）	#卫生技术人员	#医生	注册护士	药剂人员	检验人员
全市总计	**2106**	**65**	**18080**	**43561**	**35766**	**12884**	**13638**	**2001**	**1257**
莞城	60	6	2606	4801	4073	1311	1778	251	123
石龙	26	3	1400	1809	1497	512	620	91	42
虎门	178	7	1424	4061	3441	1214	1326	219	143
东城	159	5	1827	3853	3207	1156	1243	198	161
万江	62	3	260	993	777	297	270	41	28
南城	82	4	1419	3049	2169	853	811	74	67
中堂	50	1	271	674	623	204	204	24	16
望牛墩	32	1	80	342	276	73	67	22	5
麻涌	37	1	135	438	367	124	133	25	12
石碣	40	1	265	869	743	298	293	67	25
高埗	57	2	210	520	419	194	145	19	14
道滘	64	1	80	484	397	131	109	33	18
洪梅	12	1	50	241	203	55	62	6	5
沙田	32	1	135	441	357	134	112	20	9
厚街	119	2	952	2313	1936	684	805	83	60
长安	89	5	979	2289	1848	657	764	106	65
寮步	111	2	784	1730	1365	505	511	79	37
大岭山	82	1	150	873	765	299	268	56	30
大朗	95	2	572	1302	1085	407	399	62	34
黄江	47	1	408	1085	857	320	308	64	36
樟木头	34	2	430	981	786	279	338	36	24
清溪	74	1	395	1160	915	368	318	44	42
塘厦	75	2	641	1645	1374	536	472	79	49
凤岗	58	2	720	1542	1218	468	442	61	54
谢岗	21	1	80	263	221	93	82	8	8
常平	124	1	356	1480	1219	452	465	58	43
桥头	52	1	300	759	653	221	222	35	19
横沥	64	1	305	777	630	226	210	23	20
东坑	49	1	130	538	468	179	153	22	16
企石	35	1	338	715	583	177	234	38	15
石排	39	1	250	819	686	235	251	19	14
茶山	43	1	128	627	538	196	199	28	18

注：本表不含省、市属医疗机构。

14-39 镇街专利申请与授权数（2009年）

Statistics on Patents Application Accepted and Granted by Town (2009)

单位：件

指标名称	专利申请数	#发明	实用新型	外观设计	专利授权数	#发明	实用新型	外观设计
全市总计	**19106**	**1593**	**6557**	**10956**	**12918**	**254**	**4370**	**8294**
莞　城	211	37	92	82	166	11	55	100
石　龙	145	28	64	53	105	3	52	50
虎　门	914	58	314	542	589	9	263	317
东　城	3769	169	599	3001	2543	25	469	2049
万　江	467	52	195	220	402	10	181	211
南　城	743	148	363	232	531	18	230	283
中　堂	134	20	48	66	97	6	23	68
望牛墩	61	7	22	32	63	4	19	40
麻　涌	191	59	105	27	68	2	24	42
石　碣	347	28	206	113	272	8	134	130
高　埗	221	49	74	98	168	5	46	117
道　滘	342	18	93	231	204	4	63	137
洪　梅	59	5	22	32	35		6	29
沙　田	141	7	69	65	121	1	64	56
厚　街	1975	60	320	1595	1712	6	205	1501
长　安	2313	155	806	1352	730	15	474	241
寮　步	772	77	334	361	400	15	212	173
大岭山	581	29	134	418	645	3	76	566
大　朗	412	40	221	151	504	10	166	328
黄　江	427	18	244	165	179	8	115	56
樟木头	319	25	101	193	233	4	66	163
清　溪	577	31	243	303	283	7	168	108
塘　厦	664	50	357	257	434	18	190	226
凤　岗	232	15	110	107	142	3	60	79
谢　岗	76	15	39	22	38		24	14
常　平	564	71	240	253	485	26	215	244
桥　头	233	29	94	110	146	1	49	96
横　沥	244	20	129	95	154	2	47	105
东　坑	528	35	328	165	378	3	193	182
企　石	280	31	117	132	161	3	93	65
石　排	346	19	78	249	258	2	72	184
茶　山	430	58	207	165	423	3	153	267
松山湖	375	125	184	66	240	17	158	65
其　他	13	5	5	3	9	2	5	2

14-40 镇街总用电量（2008-2009年）

Total Electricity Consumption by Town (2008-2009)

单位：万千瓦时

镇　街	2008年	2009年	镇　街	2008年	2009年
莞　城	48746	47942	寮　步	189268	189748
石　龙	67936	65765	大 岭 山	150688	145699
虎　门	359566	352310	大　朗	170974	175774
东　城	231910	166402	黄　江	129204	140385
万　江	107938	107257	樟 木 头	76390	82898
南　城	83840	88056	清　溪	217652	200401
中　堂	209719	232846	塘　厦	277086	270126
望 牛 墩	52531	58063	凤　岗	163420	167916
麻　涌	81563	92288	谢　岗	58296	55300
石　碣	152880	141371	常　平	237500	232874
高　埗	118283	117113	桥　头	116388	113423
道　滘	110624	104837	横　沥	104349	102224
洪　梅	41949	46272	东　坑	73074	69358
沙　田	88010	92370	企　石	63029	62449
厚　街	329671	282486	石　排	98493	94567
长　安	500030	473889	茶　山	114935	114743

14-41 镇街总供水量（2008-2009年）

Total Water Consumption by Town (2008-2009)

单位：万吨

镇　街	2008年	2009年	镇　街	2008年	2009年
莞　城	16836	18154	寮　步	4981	4410
石　龙	2660	2464	大岭山	4375	3884
虎　门	13408	12023	大　朗	8076	7384
东　城	9899	7710	黄　江	5836	5354
万　江	5259	4746	樟木头	1789	1772
南　城	869	1028	清　溪	7054	5966
中　堂	2596	2721	塘　厦	9900	9225
望牛墩	1796	1762	凤　岗	4802	4734
麻　涌	2354	2278	谢　岗	2282	1939
石　碣	4597	3795	常　平	11318	10732
高　埗	3254	2961	桥　头	3610	3336
道　滘	3481	3096	横　沥	3913	3435
洪　梅	1415	1400	东　坑	2579	2222
沙　田	3538	3235	企　石	1940	1625
厚　街	12806	11079	石　排	3253	2985
长　安	14393	12631	茶　山	4738	4202

十五、村（居）委会主要指标

Main Indicatory of Villagers' (Neighborhood) Committees

15　村(居)委会主要指标（2009年）

村(居)委会	土地面积(平方公里)	总人口数(人)	户籍人口	外来暂住人口	户籍人口从业人数(人)	全部企业及个体户数(个)	#工业企业
莞　城							
市　桥	0.9	32447	31145	1302	10154	2701	3
东　正	1.7	25642	21009	4633	12605	739	23
罗　沙	1.8	17764	14341	3423	5490	1864	24
西　隅	0.6	11915	11280	635	3424	243	2
北　隅	1.1	33875	28863	5012	18152	1596	4
博　厦	1.0	8781	8781		3110	208	10
兴　塘	2.6	22620	12368	10252	7484	4261	13
创　业	1.5	21784	17408	4376	9672	2326	20
罗沙联合社							
博厦联合社							
细村联合社							
石　龙							
忠维村	0.8	4984	981	4003	464	102	10
林屋村	0.7	1894	644	1250	292	104	29
新维村	0.6	2135	548	1587	316	478	38
蒲溪村	0.7	995	624	371	162	10	1
西湖村	3.5	7336	2776	4560	1450	580	85
王屋洲村	3.2	4121	1561	2560	535	256	16
黄家山村	2.5	4057	1925	2132	477	168	6
中山东	0.5	32531	16403	16128	9445	305	25
中山西	0.5	24247	20352	3895	9510	685	68
兴　龙		26281	17981	8300	9004	1260	15
虎　门							
树　田	4.0	10646	1461	9185	716	339	339
怀　德	13.8	33779	6195	27584	3690	895	168
居　歧	1.8	25286	1286	24000	776	672	76
村　头	1.3	8754	808	7946	419	190	52
陈　村	1.3	4774	774	4000	200	35	35
黄　村	0.9	4659	559	4100	336	81	26
大　宁	5.4	22713	2713	20000	1193	600	200
北　栅	5.8	39378	4378	35000	2967	2023	325
龙　眼	3.0	39712	2712	37000	1067	905	242
赤　岗	7.5	8952	4352	4600	2676	203	80
博　涌	5.9	31789	6789	25000	3498	3420	306
新　联	0.6	11155	1155	10000	560	430	36
白　沙	7.8	16965	6965	10000	3550	1320	195
镇　口	1.8	15620	3120	12500	1381	180	250
金　洲	4.8	28717	3717	25000	1051	2035	60

Main Indicators of Villagers'(Neighborhood) Committees (2009)

规模以上工业总产值（当年价，万元）	农业		当年可支配财政收入（万元）	资产总额（万元）	负债总额（万元）	资产负债率（%）	农民人均纯收入（元）
	粮食（吨）	肉类总产量（吨）					
			415	595	82	13.8	
6883			321	481	61	12.7	
62433			445	231	30	13.0	
			272	973	249	25.6	
998			761	845	179	21.2	
26516			328	305	57	18.7	
1748			216	335	111	33.1	
119114			390	304	71	23.4	
			1772	23383	816	3.5	11391
			322	6105	1054	17.3	9716
			1721	14933	688	4.6	19245
			1472	11327	7551	66.7	5933
			1161	5951	1601	26.9	14519
			2116	11627	1002	8.6	18978
			885	3458	414	12.0	10994
5500			5758	79293	6187	7.8	17621
			985	13875	525	3.8	12427
			665	8466	3272	38.7	8953
			224	1761	1187	67.4	
1517			296	5731	3925	68.5	
			282	1759	1008	57.3	
49799		15	1733	11983	3646	30.4	11793
441521		2248	5636	30473	1969	6.5	9839
244001			2316	12089	776	6.4	38846
33176			1883	13225	5478	41.4	16417
33561		2	703	5610	1585	28.3	12021
5882			604	2930	1787	61.0	7750
296033		6	9594	64520	9323	14.5	19689
414734	42		3978	35183	9556	27.2	17913
340434		12	10727	92831	4093	4.4	40769
			3298	25529	9323	36.5	11180
139043			1344	8830	5016	56.8	15380
43800			1293	6088	714	11.7	12007
146871	43	705	3218	28403	10501	37.0	12793
302705			3453	14405	737	5.1	11511
30500			2638	20868	12452	59.7	23673

15 续表 1

(2009年)

村(居)委会	土地面积(平方公里)	总人口数(人)	户籍人口	外来暂住人口	户籍人口从业人数(人)	全部企业及个体户数(个)	#工业企业
小捷滘	2.0	5005	883	4122	553	461	107
南　栅	8.2	42428	5228	37200	4168	1580	310
东　风	2.8	8229	1749	6480	918	500	52
宴　岗	1.3	9981	1117	8864	621	173	35
路　东	5.6	20580	3080	17500	2047	902	197
沙　角	11.5	27965	5665	22300	3060	1310	325
虎门寨	2.0	17419	7419	10000	3882	6900	35
九门寨	2.6	5511	1411	4100	673	31	31
南　面	7.3	6269	2749	3520	1480	140	18
北　面	5.5	6092	2492	3600	1609	80	75
武山沙	2.9	6544	2240	4304	822	185	60
东　方	0.7	12360	9510	2850	6182	712	9
则　徐	1.2	24234	13884	10350	7200	2012	65
新　湾	1.0	11662	9642	2020	4100	200	47
东　城							
温　塘	11.6	33510	9510	24000	5690	605	63
桑　园	4.0	45676	3676	42000	2407	445	135
周　屋	2.8	12308	2308	10000	1391	364	60
余　屋	2.0	5035	1635	3400	992	329	104
鳌峙塘	2.0	5527	1027	4500	510	220	80
峡　口	1.6	5015	1215	3800	665	370	86
柏洲边	1.0	4925	1075	3850	682	217	58
上　桥	1.0	3180	1380	1800	781	228	40
下　桥	2.0	9501	2401	7100	1521	867	47
樟　村	3.0	5887	2999	2888	1683	528	43
梨　川	1.0	5671	1641	4030	1180	564	90
堑　头	1.5	7445	3025	4420	1994	255	30
主　山	6.6	36103	5943	30160	3662	595	
石　井	6.7	4945	1997	2948	940	145	145
同　沙	4.6	7399	2399	5000	1665	395	125
光　明	1.9	3995	1395	2600	910	132	28
牛　山	11.0	21661	4075	17586	3046	472	
立　新	2.5	7576	2976	4600	1380	472	54
火炼树	1.2	7135	1285	5850	770	460	405
岗　贝	1.2	20852	17952	2900	2662	98	1806
花园新村	0.8	2612	1212	1400	820	742	
东　泰	1.4	16755	11555	5200	4750	568	
万　江							
万　江	2.6	8215	4166	4049	2150	88	65
石　美	2.5	7684	3988	3696	1480	218	68
莫　屋	1.0	4119	1449	2670	865	155	83
拔蛟窝	1.3	4310	2018	2292	973	242	64

规模以上工业总产值（当年价，万元）	农业		当年可支配财政收入（万元）	资产总额（万元）	负债总额（万元）	资产负债率（%）	农民人均纯收入（元）
	粮食（吨）	肉类总产量（吨）					
22018		10	2249	16102	6418	39.9	
355636			9779	94530	30083	31.8	16720
3107			1453	10103	5015	49.6	10218
38873		3	860	5935	1737	29.3	9529
437037		30	7245	43441	5038	11.6	25153
285108		39	4157	38530	17329	45.0	13820
5286			3796	21779	1773	8.1	41393
28689			1269	8737	2066	23.7	8246
58630	17		4638	19292	1821	9.4	9948
	153	3	409	9600	5896	61.4	8610
3208	95	3	770	7061	4232	59.9	8967
13018			263	462	93	20.1	
30087			537	1244	130	10.5	
12690			1013	4032	3570	88.5	7075
			2884	19885	3075	15.5	16035
23930			1654	11718	165	1.4	14540
21600	455		1080	6852	339	5.0	16046
			622	5376	254	4.7	15125
			579	2607	358	13.7	13845
			837	4498	811	18.0	12504
6826		102	1279	5996	118	2.0	18194
			2486	3735	479	12.8	17778
31870			959	6759	1213	18.0	20702
36415			2314	14924	639	4.3	20980
			1548	5966	638	10.7	17307
			2043	8815	464	5.3	14260
101193			1996	13311	645	4.9	13414
			1091	12838	5027	39.2	12660
23000			1029	11123	595	5.4	14159
			1837	9417	73	0.8	18505
33614			1461	14602	4462	30.6	15086
			1178	5718	2556	44.7	15538
66070			1402	7899	3682	46.6	15289
			981	1167	246	21.1	
			994	2002	315	15.7	
			773	4074	209	5.1	
195048			3570	13332	2434	18.3	13455
23330			2713	15414	1707	11.1	15561
17601			603	5525	1466	26.5	11482
10503			3936	20680	3124	15.1	13560

15 续表 2

(2009年)

村(居)委会	土地面积(平方公里)	总人口数(人)	户籍人口	外来暂住人口	户籍人口从业人数(人)	全部企业及个体户数(个)	#工业企业
黄粘洲	0.3	2133	783	1350	486	35	23
蚬涌	2.0	4815	1969	2846	1280	241	97
谷涌	2.0	5342	2937	2405	1496	168	27
小享	3.8	9932	4942	4990	3338	159	120
滘联	2.1	5981	3381	2600	1836	72	36
金泰	1.0	4597	2022	2575	1097	128	30
曲海	1.2	2563	1542	1021	960	35	3
牌楼基	1.6	2979	1606	1373	1010	153	39
大莲塘	0.8	2050	1025	1025	665	81	37
水蛇涌	1.5	3750	2014	1736	965	144	39
共联	1.3	9112	1912	7200	1034	170	50
新谷涌	1.4	4139	2139	2000	1256	85	40
坝头	1.4	3052	1540	1512	983	18	13
胜利	0.9	9386	930	8456	469	28	26
官桥滘	1.9	4105	1605	2500	712	54	51
简沙洲	1.6	5691	1691	4000	850	126	115
新和	3.7	7962	2604	5358	1195	151	114
上甲	1.4	4492	2424	2068	1092	50	69
严屋	0.7	1744	1067	677	665	15	31
大汾	2.6	5282	3362	1920	2018	178	66
新村	5.9	10939	7963	2976	5562	153	167
流涌尾	2.5	4720	2294	2426	1346	27	49
万江墟	1.0	7255	5369	1886	2280	239	23
新城		10899	3639	7260	2198	350	
南城							
胜和	4.0	21773	6503	15270	4365	2639	8
亨美	0.5	4261	1761	2500	1005	23	21
三元里	0.4	1905	1080	825	559	28	8
篁村	1.0	9478	2978	6500	1935	668	12
新基	2.0	8027	2680	5347	1669	1292	37
周溪	5.0	8838	3853	4985	2143	154	25
袁屋边	2.0	4880	1880	3000	981	300	28
白马	4.0	10374	3272	7102	2151	826	42
石鼓	2.0	8562	1742	6820	911	247	24
蛤地	8.0	8280	2720	5560	1458	111	26
西平	3.9	6565	3313	3252	1848	722	11
水濂	6.0	3011	1990	1021	1017	71	16
雅园	1.8	3541	1188	2353	620	127	127
元美	0.4	4958	2578	2380	1146	97	14
鸿福		6689	6689				
宏远	1.0	13284	5361	7923	3515	735	8
新城	4.5	2959	1920	1039	678	1609	

规模以上工业总产值（当年价，万元）	农业		当年可支配财政收入（万元）	资产总额（万元）	负债总额（万元）	资产负债率（%）	农民人均纯收入（元）
	粮食（吨）	肉类总产量（吨）					
12101			545	3525	793	22.5	13386
69731			1736	6184	1668	27.0	13124
76896	44		2390	21707	681	3.1	12461
7054	9		3435	15965	440	2.8	12245
14270	51		830	6857	3955	57.7	10795
4031			1002	5981	1966	32.9	15261
767			876	14480	114	0.8	11996
2514			1665	18718	1836	9.8	12839
8959			1052	8957	740	8.3	12410
4499	7		2034	16181	1364	8.4	11650
14974			1242	6033	530	8.8	15582
32209	2		1686	14663	1264	8.6	12024
5147	4		1521	15581	5354	34.4	14555
1186	34		769	3141	452	14.4	13278
18421			1360	9253	800	8.7	12668
46675			571	5473	3516	64.2	12660
147018	3		1644	9634	1245	12.9	11521
28623			1293	8104	2341	28.9	12004
23424			550	5113	1416	27.7	10498
64938	59		2071	13131	593	4.5	12042
15934	16		1583	14148	1931	13.7	12032
34537	7		795	4792	1242	25.9	14553
5609			727	4669	2684	57.5	
			517	692	43	6.2	
42781			2622	37204	26948	72.4	16205
1647			2325	28277	10883	38.5	13373
8832			1688	31002	7536	24.3	16952
			1287	28750	2477	8.6	20025
42948			3448	78326	16629	21.2	20197
115299	72		4339	44339	8411	19.0	17579
2446			4842	32553	3357	10.3	18757
64047			4987	38862	5906	15.2	14939
120622			3457	33124	8019	24.2	16084
29893			2055	26235	7939	30.3	14960
48190			2385	67775	48435	71.5	12160
			1168	17803	11589	65.1	14681
13809			2932	20551	974	4.7	15032
			725	12535	10790	86.1	14860
132996							
			298	298	181	60.7	

15 续表 3

(2009年)

村(居)委会	土地面积(平方公里)	总人口数(人)	户籍人口	外来暂住人口	户籍人口从业人数(人)	全部企业及个体户数(个)	#工业企业
中 堂							
潢涌村	9.3	17509	9114	8395	6206	936	69
三涌村	4.0	5916	3711	2205	2657	380	50
湛翠村	1.8	4078	2300	1778	1502	171	32
袁家涌村	4.0	8364	5554	2810	3515	511	88
吴家涌村	3.4	5479	2661	2818	1354	447	68
凤冲村	1.3	2605	1628	977	1025	94	38
鹤田村	2.2	5324	2194	3130	1391	444	78
东泊	2.9	8215	3700	4515	1810	729	130
中堂村	1.1	3001	1914	1087	1131	151	32
一村	0.7	8009	1714	6295	962	398	31
东向村	2.4	5121	3241	1880	2084	395	72
斗朗	2.5	4103	2533	1570	1668	160	45
江南	2.1	6303	2396	3907	1788	731	126
蕉利村	4.6	8869	4893	3976	2888	528	102
槎滘村	9.4	12326	9916	2410	6343	643	122
下芦村	1.3	1647	1166	481	656	67	24
马沥村	1.9	2381	1946	435	1405	62	11
四乡村	4.2	3490	3150	340	1904	47	14
红锋	0.1	861	765	96	493	60	7
居民	0.7	13349	8642	4707	3982	1595	19
望牛墩							
李屋村	0.6	2197	626	1571	340	80	33
望东村	1.7	4144	2044	2100	942	85	21
扶冲村	0.5	2085	885	1200	470	72	11
赤滘村	2.0	6018	2918	3100	1805	45	38
五冲村	1.6	3321	1521	1800	788	69	35
下漕村	2.9	8139	4183	3956	2362	98	42
上合村	1.7	4830	2880	1950	1156	46	34
聚龙江村	0.6	3227	937	2290	460	220	18
望联村	3.0	7724	5059	2665	2998	424	24
洲湾村	1.3	3548	1898	1650	983	45	16
洲涡村	1.5	3030	2498	532	1007	20	22
寮厦村	1.0	2232	1420	812	570	23	12
官桥涌村	0.7	1613	941	672	555	22	14
芙蓉沙村	0.6	1479	1029	450	635	15	15
杜屋村	1.5	3833	2325	1508	1402	92	30
横沥村	1.7	2540	2190	350	1478	36	7
福安村	0.6	1372	1052	320	609	6	5
官洲村	0.6	1502	1046	456	626	40	13
石排村	0.3	1024	604	420	326	16	7
朱平沙村	4.5	6176	3286	2890	2052	50	14
锦涡村	1.1	2239	1509	730	938	39	7
居民		4624	4624		1985		

规模以上工业总产值（当年价，万元）	农业		当年可支配财政收入（万元）	资产总额（万元）	负债总额（万元）	资产负债率（%）	农民人均纯收入（元）
	粮食（吨）	肉类总产量（吨）					
605139	229		19782	189638	16898	8.9	14589
26786	116		1729	8269	4441	53.7	10500
18852	91		562	3717	1385	37.3	10734
40240	80		1528	7180	2401	33.4	10110
84791			1352	9190	3059	33.3	12334
5248	135		408	1653	796	48.2	10983
23156	4		561	3378	1526	45.2	10633
112813			2009	20819	6932	33.3	12649
8828			342	967	175	18.1	11697
36973	48		1309	5360	153	2.9	12824
12634	15		561	3044	558	18.3	11755
3863			1384	8850	3811	43.1	10663
12228			3026	12440	204	1.6	13813
16469	20	246	965	5911	2187	37.0	11172
67259	136	408	3067	25993	2782	10.7	11550
25745			540	1420	951	67.0	10111
11479			2509	5579	1684	30.2	9486
836			460	2358	1316	55.8	10673
			212	1253	878	70.1	11279
5206			143	1751	1420	81.1	
26143	8		299	1627	661	40.6	9473
		56	232	2757	1618	58.7	8038
	9		415	3058	1124	36.8	8470
	5		982	9302	2578	27.7	9511
	1	6	530	2405	1310	54.5	7991
37622	42	94	570	4375	3323	76.0	7378
17580	2		474	7216	4088	56.7	8083
			976	7742	1651	21.3	8730
	18		724	4027	1351	33.6	9496
	10	55	315	2611	1636	62.7	8672
	20	91	649	3113	1125	36.1	9528
	8	101	325	4168	2796	67.1	8860
		28	461	3589	371	10.3	9022
	5		400	4655	2161	46.4	8538
	1	1	448	4688	1682	35.9	8790
	2	28	449	3240	1569	48.4	9059
			978	5493	3425	62.4	8308
	6	58	256	2148	1418	66.0	8432
			212	1925	1018	52.9	9060
23100	3	106	766	4221	4099	97.1	8394
12069	37	52	600	4498	2698	60.0	8323

15 续表 4

(2009年)

村(居)委会	土地面积(平方公里)	总人口数(人)	户籍人口	外来暂住人口	户籍人口从业人数(人)	全部企业及个体户数(个)	#工业企业
麻　涌							
麻一村	4.0	6331	4081	2250	2836	237	14
麻　二	6.8	4467	3587	880	2221	821	4
麻三村	3.7	5242	3747	1495	2215	716	15
麻四村	4.5	5780	4753	1027	2800	183	17
大步村	10.7	12564	7137	5427	3798	490	66
东太村	4.8	5837	4491	1346	2631	172	9
新基村	4.4	10146	5620	4526	3368	343	37
川槎村	3.0	5965	3907	2058	2248	222	49
鸥涌村	2.8	8765	3765	5000	2280	176	11
黎滘村	1.3	1700	1308	392	689	33	9
华阳村	5.5	6097	5295	802	3226	110	9
南洲村	3.4	4923	2743	2180	1648	181	20
大盛村	6.9	6881	2764	4117	1791	350	21
漳澎村	29.6	13523	12218	1305	8343	189	7
居　民		6349	6349		4437		
石　碣							
唐洪村	1.0	5681	1791	3890	811	452	35
水南村	2.8	10725	3496	7229	1543	1082	152
石碣村	4.6	13946	5186	8760	2936	1644	216
刘屋村	4.9	9109	4434	4675	2557	506	102
横滘村	1.6	6182	1926	4256	1038	589	92
鹤田厦村	2.5	11331	1874	9457	1145	278	22
四甲村	4.0	11785	4578	7207	2663	810	132
沙腰村	4.0	6784	3501	3283	2249	249	54
梁家村	1.9	4021	2421	1600	1305	246	68
桔洲村	1.2	10973	1443	9530	867	494	80
单屋村	2.3	4407	1309	3098	778	173	92
涌口村	1.6	6332	1732	4600	956	489	140
西南村	2.6	8790	2040	6750	1073	1035	83
黄泗围村	1.2	2964	709	2255	385	321	79
居　民		12029	6893	5136	4711	1267	32
高　埗							
冼沙村	7.5	29527	7296	22231	4302	428	130
卢溪村	2.3	11987	1646	10341	785	48	35
宝莲村	0.7	2714	1047	1667	741	41	17
塘厦村	2.7	16932	1850	15082	1230	99	17
草墩村	0.8	1988	802	1186	463	23	20
护安围村	1.9	2018	1093	925	603	40	40
保安围村	2.3	4873	2265	2608	1410	70	30

规模以上工业总产值（当年价，万元）	农业		当年可支配财政收入（万元）	资产总额（万元）	负债总额（万元）	资产负债率（%）	农民人均纯收入（元）
	粮食（吨）	肉类总产量（吨）					
6896	55	7	1042	3776	3162	83.7	9140
		3	1378	13672	317	2.3	10400
5031	14	6	1048	9084	884	9.7	9445
25066	12	12	1569	11301	1432	12.7	10389
55091	8	9	4400	16650	1747	10.5	9410
1398	181	2	724	4043	1246	30.8	8270
31534		1	1717	6329	315	5.0	7966
18643			62	573	540	94.2	8124
33032		10	305	594	292	49.2	7965
		1	416	1268	595	46.9	7951
10712	186	1	3064	7295	935	12.8	8347
4033	6	6	1883	13425	584	4.4	9462
35988	4	1	3014	19966	2600	13.0	9982
1208	1396	17	2665	27586	2279	8.3	9101
2537			2200	11221	2290	20.4	12928
34339			1767	19813	5465	27.6	13236
66401			3528	20208	6871	34.0	13618
8068	26		1997	9560	3285	34.4	11916
23667			2028	11006	5335	48.5	13326
20813			1930	11717	4026	34.4	12499
177144	11		2860	15350	3961	25.8	11651
44243	51		2087	12801	1293	10.1	11285
4274	39		1315	11656	4332	37.2	9900
359114			5286	33285	1571	4.7	17797
10675	38		1408	11824	2404	20.3	14252
56841			2730	21330	7568	35.5	13631
69614			6609	42188	6180	14.7	16812
23547			1815	11219	1659	14.8	13372
1759			934	8035	8369	104.2	
85650	84		1536	13641	9437	69.2	12871
44000	51		727	3922	283	7.2	12025
5706	69		274	1509	279	18.5	11592
134965	21		343	2010	236	11.7	12253
19032	22		592	3474	1294	37.3	11035
9670	42		1068	4385	556	12.7	11065
44197	120		3040	23759	15811	66.6	14292

15　续表 5

(2009年)

村(居)委会	土地面积(平方公里)	总人口数(人)	户籍人口	外来暂住人口	户籍人口从业人数(人)	全部企业及个体户数(个)	#工业企业
三联村	2.1	2319	1385	934	850	20	5
横滘头村	0.9	1908	1086	822	749	17	9
低涌村	2.2	11389	2837	8552	1686	395	21
朱磡村	1.0	2289	1459	830	892	25	15
欧邓村	0.7	1751	939	812	585	15	9
芦　村	1.3	2084	1709	375	745	55	19
高埗村	2.1	17065	3228	13837	1981	280	53
凌屋村	1.2	3047	1257	1790	716	38	8
上江城村	1.9	12391	2277	10114	1188	119	13
下江城村	1.5	10830	1419	9411	862	130	28
新联村	1.3	3142	1623	1519	976	146	9
居　民		28370	2430	25940	1231	315	1
道　滘							
南城村	7.1	9105	4356	4749	2664	605	77
闸口村	5.2	12276	2804	9472	1702	444	42
北永村	6.3	8605	3680	4925	2259	245	118
永庆村	3.1	5078	1673	3405	1136	145	94
厚德村	4.2	9440	2453	6987	1590	185	36
蔡白村	5.5	9780	4694	5086	2886	290	60
南丫村	6.8	22010	4096	17914	2750	395	95
九曲村	4.6	6326	3066	3260	1978	162	48
大罗沙村	4.5	6518	2857	3661	1728	55	20
小河村	6.1	11188	5676	5512	3546	206	64
昌平村	3.8	6531	3350	3181	2357	166	34
大岭丫村	4.1	9198	3523	5675	2138	289	76
大鱼沙村	1.7	3838	1728	2110	1083	213	33
居　民		11679	11679		6034		
洪　梅							
洪屋涡村	14.1	9610	6584	3026	4205	148	145
新庄村	1.7	1386	846	540	488	33	20
梅沙村	3.5	6402	3952	2450	2461	63	25
金鳌沙村	1.8	1707	1337	370	677	25	8
乌沙村	3.8	4418	2118	2300	1200	34	5
尧均村	1.0	2111	598	1513	390	47	11
夏汇村	2.1	807	687	120	413	7	3
氹涌村	1.6	4855	1865	2990	931	66	9
黎洲角村	2.1	5209	2624	2585	1461	11	10
居　民	1.0	7050	900	6150	693		
沙　田							
中围村	0.9	1793	1691	102	912	19	1
和安村	0.7	3406	3134	272	1857	59	4
大流村	0.5	2550	1997	553	1248	45	1

规模以上工业总产值（当年价，万元）	农业		当年可支配财政收入（万元）	资产总额（万元）	负债总额（万元）	资产负债率（%）	农民人均纯收入（元）
	粮食（吨）	肉类总产量（吨）					
	80	530	420	2930	1193	40.7	11424
13590	30		1009	4841	2152	44.5	10847
15560	28		758	5686	1893	33.3	13731
3125			255	1196	596	49.8	9020
			497	2958	1644	55.6	11433
			262	1264	556	44.0	11471
202337	46		1270	8072	4330	53.6	13591
14354	9		829	5382	1898	35.3	10868
8524			868	7813	2935	37.6	13211
			567	4759	2384	50.1	13376
			272	2731	1294	47.4	12680
52264			246	1393	1814	130.2	
52563	11	394	2480	15801	858	5.4	11693
16600	842	88	1966	11690	1185	10.1	12176
39250	330	497	4183	20631	3278	15.9	11788
17183		27	1763	7702	384	5.0	11650
		319	1250	12222	1625	13.3	11743
30537		298	1199	16824	6162	36.6	11236
216789		29	4037	28896	7878	27.3	11260
52200		352	862	5973	1308	21.9	11513
42312		115	1393	6786	1502	22.1	9097
54339		38	820	5626	1421	25.3	9826
36010		63	734	2314	2569	111.0	10815
79175		9	3503	25700	6722	26.2	11068
19126		44	659	4087	873	21.4	12691
			125	335	59	17.6	
19263	150	738	1889	14623	2832	19.4	8545
16703	66	8	393	3314	1734	52.3	9140
11500	245	85	520	6135	2018	32.9	9096
1668	238	9	671	3653	2063	56.5	8551
5520	397	147	689	7990	948	11.9	8526
1770			256	2078	1151	55.4	8528
	1	261	288	1897	1355	71.4	9012
4800	122	51	566	3082	2620	85.0	8645
1728	13	230	1237	9645	2882	29.9	9790
			75	25			
		7	1061	7835	1683	21.5	8213
	235	11	1186	8819	1834	20.8	7917
	72	6	578	7401	4672	63.1	8427

15 续表 6

(2009年)

村(居)委会	土地面积(平方公里)	总人口数(人)	户籍人口	外来暂住人口	户籍人口从业人数(人)	全部企业及个体户数(个)	#工业企业
泥洲村	0.3	4098	3728	370	2350	30	2
杨公洲村	3.9	6863	1863	5000	1203	460	231
阁西村	4.7	12430	2180	10250	1079	402	53
民田村	4.8	9524	2524	7000	1290	651	110
大泥村	4.3	6507	1852	4655	731	783	204
福禄沙村	3.2	4579	1915	2664	1150	152	48
西大坦村	0.3	2361	2061	300	1079	18	1
穗丰年村	5.6	4363	2698	1665	1750	228	90
齐沙村	3.8	9878	2065	7813	1250	789	120
稔洲村	4.3	12538	2472	10066	1545	1207	204
义沙村	4.4	7243	1893	5350	1134	310	105
西太隆村	4.1	10523	1984	8539	1244	422	250
横流	0.2	8061	4061	4000	2176	1238	40
先锋村	0.2	2209	2031	178	1205	35	6
厚街							
厚街村	8.0	18815	8986	9829	5800	2192	69
珊美村	2.1	7583	2418	5165	1378	469	12
寮厦村	2.5	8055	2297	5758	1400	740	25
河田村	9.1	23171	6110	17061	3398	718	
汀山村	4.3	12118	1934	10184	1234	769	55
环冈村	4.2	8692	2052	6640	1432	222	39
三屯村	4.5	18768	2641	16127	1698	906	72
宝屯村	3.0	10425	2536	7889	1405	429	106
陈屋村	2.0	5103	1508	3595	998	568	53
赤岭村	5.3	20385	3583	16802	2390	810	61
桥头村	10.0	19322	7794	11528	4396	887	56
南五村	1.6	4629	1465	3164	531	115	29
溪头村	4.1	14825	3676	11149	1210	938	103
沙塘村	1.5	5007	2055	2952	1340	170	29
宝塘村	1.7	7055	1535	5520	962	295	27
下汴村	2.2	5448	1738	3710	1051	400	58
白濠村	5.3	16451	5241	11210	2611	973	118
新塘村	4.4	13208	5644	7564	3371	701	55
双岗村	4.2	10977	6846	4131	4408	781	49
涌口村	4.0	15395	5534	9861	3388	856	84
大迳村	11.8	4838	3600	1238	1968	156	14
新围村	15.1	6982	4521	2461	2723	143	15
居民		17341	12261	5080	5677	3421	115
长安							
涌头	4.1	21464	1729	19735	684	1393	115
霄边	7.6	50005	3441	46564	1917	2275	113
咸西	4.0	15263	1253	14010	587	1123	80

规模以上工业总产值（当年价，万元）	农业		当年可支配财政收入（万元）	资产总额（万元）	负债总额（万元）	资产负债率（%）	农民人均纯收入（元）
	粮食（吨）	肉类总产量（吨）					
6915		22	791	3417	2744	80.3	8300
17481	28	3	1192	5787	4699	81.2	8309
166678		7	1579	18320	8377	45.7	9377
21048	249		1458	10383	2241	21.6	9796
68816			1358	6244	897	14.4	8911
248777	585	4	687	8995	3674	40.8	8462
1635			437	8525	2444	28.7	8251
49663	28	995	2128	16763	4355	26.0	9334
202906		25	1674	15421	2880	18.7	10562
266039		5	1936	8455	2750	32.5	9955
122512		35	2074	9906	1266	12.8	10027
31632			1515	7593	3011	39.7	9304
39973			651	6938	2208	31.8	9050
662			362	5383	2454	45.6	9263
101945	30		2788	25917	13593	52.5	16389
182666			757	9717	2796	28.8	17184
43473	11		2005	15629	2828	18.1	17771
33948	36		2106	19466	8073	41.5	13269
97781	15		1801	14906	4816	32.3	15655
100957	17		2348	23216	8687	37.4	15739
234665			1863	25416	7630	30.0	19883
114570			3002	22818	10885	47.7	14705
41265	2		2844	18496	3492	18.9	15590
257369	79		3980	41453	25107	60.6	15226
124436	38		4336	33220	7014	21.1	20872
31136			1455	7448	2726	36.6	15776
112947	30		4579	29919	4360	14.6	16020
19053	4		2595	16497	6398	38.8	16115
106395			4280	28318	9050	32.0	15954
56012	4		2554	20267	4304	21.2	13567
101585	45		3291	20569	5327	25.9	14543
57203			4707	26921	4707	17.5	14165
80835	63		1488	14323	3114	21.7	14696
144520	4		3686	31322	7897	25.2	14053
94850	170		698	5180	1851	35.7	11123
6352	64		686	5142	2828	55.0	10205
3589			372	5193	336	6.5	
89202			2828	29061	13919	47.9	24991
532730			12196	123284	7071	5.7	23171
67323			13258	79723	23623	29.6	36573

15 续表 7

(2009年)

村(居)委会	土地面积(平方公里)	总人口数(人)	户籍人口	外来暂住人口	户籍人口从业人数(人)	全部企业及个体户数(个)	#工业企业
锦厦	9.7	62794	4250	58544	2220	2867	212
新安	8.6	61533	3381	58152	1736	2156	257
乌沙	7.3	82586	3830	78756	2054	3923	506
新民	1.5	18737	915	17822	395	965	155
沙头	9.9	51240	6139	45101	3380	3668	355
上沙	5.2	44175	2823	41352	1500	2660	360
厦岗	5.3	58500	3171	55329	1531	2510	328
厦边	4.4	26521	2461	24060	1301	2351	288
上角	3.2	31704	1298	30406	711	1136	198
长盛	0.7	60627	7778	52849	5319	1242	10
寮步							
塘边	0.7	4614	1614	3000	850	250	30
西溪村	4.5	12066	4566	7500	2156	314	110
凫山村	4.0	12287	5907	6380	3555	471	301
石步村	4.7	8186	4386	3800	1930	210	58
良边村	2.7	7008	3208	3800	1927	400	245
富竹山村	3.5	4409	1909	2500	1009	72	34
塘唇村	3.4	4866	2266	2600	1056	109	54
向西村	2.9	6055	2535	3520	1032	108	26
下岭贝村	1.8	9666	1499	8167	886	212	11
岭厦	0.9	5519	1019	4500	588	110	110
新旧围	1.4	2978	978	2000	629	285	210
霞边村	1.3	1735	835	900	420	44	19
横坑	5.9	22731	4766	17965	2757	465	452
竹园村	1.5	1973	873	1100	450	129	31
上屯村	4.5	6245	3287	2958	1904	144	41
石龙坑村	1.9	8629	3629	5000	2294	210	201
牛杨	1.2	6874	1474	5400	755	117	62
泉塘	2.3	6520	1532	4988	876	51	
坑口	1.6	3358	1158	2200	659	200	30
浮竹山村	3.4	4031	1471	2560	928	140	30
上底村	2.0	2652	1452	1200	735	85	11
刘屋巷村	1.6	2267	567	1700	317	41	29
药勒村	2.4	3608	1108	2500	618	111	37
陈家埔村	1.6	3847	847	3000	379	65	18
缪边	1.6	4183	1183	3000	742	165	36
居民	1.7	13862	8906	4956	5901	2600	18
小坑村	1.5	3751	801	2950	395	20	20
长坑村	1.0	1211	911	300	403		10
井巷村	1.1	1982	882	1100	483	20	20

规模以上工业总产值（当年价，万元）	农业		当年可支配财政收入（万元）	资产总额（万元）	负债总额（万元）	资产负债率（%）	农民人均纯收入（元）
	粮食（吨）	肉类总产量（吨）					
322561			17297	115378	16552	14.4	28314
2549876			4453	56036	564	1.0	19892
795048			9001	52244	3548	6.8	41505
96766			9200	31850	14560	45.7	29539
455178	12	332	24548	127318	54148	42.5	18837
211102			14321	63501	13270	20.9	24901
171861			17620	44621	1398	3.1	24614
96717			3208	24867	6154	24.8	19599
306162			8578	60092	26600	44.3	30974
			2286	12322	9933	80.6	17116
7700			671	8732	5034	57.7	13661
14030			2050	16492	2387	14.5	8671
23180			1305	13596	6511	47.9	11567
234484	75		2123	24893	15368	61.7	13944
40500			940	5982	339	5.7	8803
75040			1816	12943	2188	16.9	10455
71150			1910	15914	2773	17.4	11147
			871	10029	3972	39.6	7613
			1760	10800	483	4.5	9300
56050			2552	20339	3390	16.7	19819
			1273	7123	541	7.6	8514
54300	9		1023	6113	982	16.1	7784
			7406	90981	90981	100.0	16413
8080			857	6817	2585	37.9	10392
35300			1855	12319	359	2.9	10563
15624			1538	6422	577	9.0	12394
44900		4	1855	9037	2677	29.6	9274
3265			1086	7364	2267	30.8	12977
12000			1452	14474	1993	13.8	9221
12250	2		3250	15963	4941	31.0	13738
4000			237	3405	1287	37.8	7686
	4		489	5314	1503	28.3	9037
12000	15		2155	11280	3323	29.5	9371
			1101	4840	3484	72.0	8897
24532			1517	12443	3747	30.1	15672
			863	1786	1094	61.3	10264
	44		975	4733	201	4.3	8350
			716	6125	336	5.5	8529
			1855	6308	1370	21.7	8798

15 续表 8

(2009年)

村(居)委会	土地面积(平方公里)	总人口数(人)	户籍人口	外来暂住人口	户籍人口从业人数(人)	全部企业及个体户数(个)	#工业企业
大岭山							
马蹄岗村	0.8	5973	2173	3800	1418	113	34
大塘朗村	3.0	3728	1580	2148	1053	230	238
新塘村	2.0	8228	2140	6088	1387	269	91
元岭村	0.3	1595	967	628	450	20	1
金桔村	4.3	10086	3556	6530	2390	540	62
鸡翅岭村	4.5	4316	1316	3000	701	173	14
大沙村	3.0	3801	1801	2000	1021	150	50
旧飞鹅村	3.1	951	451	500	245	10	10
连平村	7.2	20860	2860	18000	1080	275	21
梅林村	1.5	8035	535	7500	286	138	138
下高田村	0.5	953	473	480	310	62	44
大环村	2.0	1267	579	688	299	15	15
太公岭村	2.2	6657	1657	5000	915	150	49
百花洞村	4.8	7269	1269	6000	633	46	41
大片美村	2.6	7010	1010	6000	303	178	18
矮岭冚村	5.5	14805	3560	11245	2032	849	96
大岭村	7.0	3207	2347	860	1450	80	90
农场	1.0	4230	730	3500	333	518	14
水朗村							
大塘村	8.5	13202	3202	10000	2056	186	90
杨屋村	12.0	19796	4796	15000	3602	550	135
颜屋村	3.0	7050	750	6300	358	145	68
居民	10.0	37030	4466	32564	2424	530	13
大朗							
竹山	1.3	5308	1651	3657	750	286	136
高英村	1.7	5977	1827	4150	1031	301	87
巷头	3.5	23812	4312	19500	2476	2352	473
巷尾	1.6	8749	1988	6761	1153	924	227
求富路	1.4	7788	1427	6361	838	481	99
长塘	2.7	23125	4690	18435	2710	1441	176
大井头	4.1	17505	5589	11916	2967	2288	304
圣堂	0.9	7380	1580	5800	907	1220	38
蔡边村	6.1	12059	4149	7910	2241	1012	291
水口村	3.3	11427	2941	8486	1522	834	266
洋乌村	2.1	5547	1682	3865	892	446	195
洋坑塘村	1.1	5411	1061	4350	621	335	135
松柏朗村	2.5	10248	4118	6130	2265	543	108
黄草朗	1.5	8810	2310	6500	1047	770	344
黎贝岭村	1.9	4164	2240	1924	1400	409	173
佛子凹村	1.1	4063	2390	1673	1210	111	44
佛新	0.6	2489	868	1621	419	236	119
松木山村	2.7	19690	2579	17111	1570	708	298
犀牛陂村	8.0	10502	3202	7300	1792	942	548

规模以上工业总产值（当年价，万元）	农业		当年可支配财政收入（万元）	资产总额（万元）	负债总额（万元）	资产负债率（%）	农民人均纯收入（元）
	粮食（吨）	肉类总产量（吨）					
32675			562	6390	1938	30.3	11412
			1037	4527	389	8.6	12190
27549			1547	10098	1810	17.9	13806
11237			3380	15627	294	1.9	12689
122221			3245	23155	5168	22.3	14952
25883			1311	5651	1718	30.4	11952
4036			1299	8215	2869	34.9	10389
12025			785	3995	194	4.9	11991
8865			1504	5611	1960	34.9	12479
59221			865	4420	1114	25.2	12368
1897			458	2187	587	26.8	11670
3669		2	542	3266	1159	35.5	11396
60840			549	3430	1267	36.9	11409
67264		2	1380	12194	3309	27.1	11602
82802			1034	3519	168	4.8	11849
254921			1975	14603	7364	50.4	14679
122640			604	4001	204	5.1	11957
74031			653	3916	509	13.0	16695
							12163
76712			1705	10713	2862	26.7	13804
73261			1546	10667	1499	14.1	11978
11372			834	5498	723	13.2	12693
32202			317	735	481	65.4	12976
59141			701	11318	930	8.2	14101
60691		1	1600	14326	1268	8.9	17943
206101	45		4037	45399	9328	20.6	20561
101623			2512	28760	7349	25.6	17562
53219			2390	19384	2229	11.5	18797
116240			6766	57826	12777	22.1	20808
73331	12	1	5244	56298	20044	35.6	15870
10167			2344	20763	695	3.4	21083
49886	8		1591	32239	7496	23.3	17973
48066		2	2443	25090	3130	12.5	18055
95588			486	5594	2802	50.1	14678
27927		1	1208	11542	782	6.8	13355
11797	6	4	1636	15710	6945	44.2	11634
38328			1529	16812	7232	43.0	9385
32129		1	1178	12811	994	7.8	11474
9728			1223	7980	862	10.8	10122
7325			459	11750	4959	42.2	9076
72297			2173	20926	2543	12.2	14661
543232	33	12	1611	15600	1081	6.9	13493

15 续表 9

(2009年)

村(居)委会	土地面积(平方公里)	总人口数(人)	户籍人口	外来暂住人口	户籍人口从业人数(人)	全部企业及个体户数(个)	#工业企业
水平村	7.9	8178	1888	6290	1231	375	134
屏山	2.3	652	509	143	281	36	19
宝陂村	0.5	816	698	118	253	29	6
石厦村	8.0	11152	2941	8211	1725	658	306
杨涌村	1.5	6406	1346	5060	712	381	114
沙步村	3.1	8433	2253	6180	1268	565	297
新马莲村	6.6	6218	1598	4620	1168	284	135
大朗	0.3	7853	6857	996	3941	648	16
长富	1.5	545	545		352	10	
黄江							
社贝村	4.0	18435	1077	17358	583	523	71
鸡啼岗村	3.0	8818	1403	7415	853	85	54
合路村	1.4	8092	892	7200	412	125	125
袁屋围村	0.6	1313	363	950	228	54	10
北岸村	3.5	9498	1547	7951	963	201	58
田心村	4.0	12617	1617	11000	953	655	65
大冚村	6.4	3029	779	2250	485	68	68
龙见田村	3.0	5442	873	4569	329	52	52
长龙村	18.0	10464	2464	8000	1400	250	55
星光村	3.3	4307	1107	3200	690	64	15
新市	3.0	11066	5566	5500	3726	480	
旧村	1.5	2661	281	2380	161	41	35
田美	7.4	29140	3327	25813	1827	573	304
三新	16.0	15375	2783	12592	1503	682	130
樟木头							
墟镇	4.3	22123	9179	12944	5876	2510	134
樟罗	6.8	19328	3459	15869	1892	2691	68
百果洞	2.4	5656	879	4777	540	1504	25
樟洋	13.5	33517	2402	31115	1106	1541	21
石新	7.3	12998	2286	10712	1072	1692	130
柏地	6.6	8789	1366	7423	691	856	88
官仓	3.0	3951	1097	2854	651	349	32
裕丰	10.0	16196	1972	14224	895	577	57
金河	14.0	15039	1704	13335	902	798	125
清溪							
罗马村	7.0	8732	1840	6892	1154	332	48
长山头村	4.3	7119	1119	6000	730	75	32
荔横村	3.4	5302	1502	3800	810	240	57
浮岗村	3.0	7441	1941	5500	891	725	61
松岗村	3.9	5917	1267	4650	493	75	43
上元村	4.3	969	926	43	648	223	29
重河村	8.4	17663	2663	15000	1313	362	32

规模以上工业总产值（当年价，万元）	农业		当年可支配财政收入（万元）	资产总额（万元）	负债总额（万元）	资产负债率（%）	农民人均纯收入（元）
	粮食（吨）	肉类总产量（吨）					
50231	49	9	1551	14001	4959	35.4	14110
17463		2	336	1966	152	7.7	11161
23113			761	12452	4911	39.4	10545
94669	6	4	2275	12914	1816	14.1	15058
19399	4	1	763	4316	338	7.8	12775
22326	11	1	341	1161	863	74.3	11798
45265		1	445	1922	1373	71.4	10375
612			348	2015	569	28.2	
6313			1237	7999	197	2.5	14906
121064			1948	10635	1420	13.4	12546
472561			1609	10588	613	5.8	17850
			1467	7963	3129	39.3	17464
17930			1378	7612	563	7.4	10832
56630			1622	11525	749	6.5	13154
			563	3539	191	5.4	9431
126930							12333
118000			1375	8849	3322	37.5	6911
55238			468	3406	1334	39.2	7289
			316	1045	162	15.5	13699
6035			362	4710	808	17.2	13899
25817			2658	24138	4143	17.2	11834
34773			1225	13409	1391	10.4	
33957		1	7707	22515	14072	62.5	13961
73227		1	6322	38719	13746	35.5	15793
30110		1	2137	19979	7611	38.1	14232
91055	13	73	2096	18879	5283	28.0	11919
56124		3	5260	48939	30435	62.2	12835
48168		1	1671	23574	7402	31.4	16709
6805	8	1	1504	8506	3234	38.0	11969
64420	4	50	3117	9642	5500	57.0	12941
50071		1	1949	10389	3985	38.4	11878
15271			570	3580	1240	34.6	14421
62000	36		2301	12238	5277	43.1	15855
80000			1111	11712	10975	93.7	14503
55594			1331	12779	5550	43.4	18477
16756	16		634	2356	777	33.0	14404
14153	14		743	3241	1010	31.2	13631
48880	35		770	10414	3947	37.9	16270

15 续表 10

(2009年)

村(居)委会	土地面积(平方公里)	总人口数(人)	户籍人口	外来暂住人口	户籍人口从业人数(人)	全部企业及个体户数(个)	#工业企业
清厦村	2.3	9025	1525	7500	878	575	39
铁松村	5.6	12529	2529	10000	1103	168	85
铁场村	7.4	931	779	152	429	13	
九乡村	7.5	4699	1699	3000	1051	200	62
大埔村	1.8	3702	702	3000	350	97	29
大利村	9.6	18329	2646	15683	1661	1012	70
渔梁围村	2.5	17569	1059	16510	535	292	63
三星村	2.5	4407	1082	3325	522	99	24
厦坭村	1.7	6719	885	5834	475	353	28
土桥村	1.2	7493	573	6920	322	325	50
谢坑村	3.2	13759	759	13000	506	72	88
三中村	9.0	66767	1767	65000	990	700	177
青皇村	6.5	4816	1116	3700	652	63	29
居民	7.0	18840	6830	12010	3565	1860	16
塘厦							
林村	21.0	38295	5295	33000	3696	1816	243
莲湖	9.0	21870	2160	19710	542	450	215
石潭埔	6.8	1592	1592		1189	140	65
横塘	4.0	8192	1092	7100	700	96	96
莆心湖	6.1	9128	2028	7100	920	150	75
诸佛岭	2.4	13698	1098	12600	695	296	50
振兴围	2.4	9955	955	9000	646	164	
四村	4.0	12554	1054	11500	499	438	290
蛟乙塘	4.9	11306	1408	9898	710	327	
沙湖	4.0	5820	584	5236	222	89	74
大坪	13.0	12490	1331	11159	745	61	55
田心	4.5	7933	833	7100	430	95	95
龙背岭	8.2	8933	937	7996	520	250	67
石鼓	6.4	13486	2486	11000	1276	298	92
石马	2.7	6286	486	5800	309	167	42
清湖头	4.1	17179	1347	15832	829	215	148
平山	4.8	7893	759	7134	485	92	92
桥陇	2.8	8263	1013	7250	668	140	148
凤凰岗	3.5	9674	1322	8352	733	309	86
塘厦	0.9	13240	13240		6187	2200	360
三局							
凤岗							
雁田村	22.0	40634	3586	37048	1650	3443	522
官井头村	10.1	18132	1863	16269	1116	600	175
油甘埔村	7.4	20680	1997	18683	955	620	350
凤德岭村	3.3	8359	1255	7104	541	343	89

规模以上工业总产值（当年价，万元）	农业		当年可支配财政收入（万元）	资产总额（万元）	负债总额（万元）	资产负债率（%）	农民人均纯收入（元）
	粮食（吨）	肉类总产量（吨）					
27166			1341	8406	5537	65.9	12595
45225	33		1619	15623	8071	51.7	12299
	51		641	3001	630	21.0	6336
15800	32		426	6351	5143	81.0	12933
33566	20		590	3334	1111	33.3	14497
79756	5		2026	12629	3174	25.1	15038
29859			1764	11509	3374	29.3	11754
36016			496	3989	3143	78.8	14069
22386			853	7113	1763	24.8	17273
38350			1481	10442	5647	54.1	17811
59180			977	3120	1635	52.4	16451
48000			1290	9637	4888	50.7	17419
25000			745	1926	484	25.1	8502
21355			1310	4316	2616	60.6	17399
467026	170	229	10834	56917	4605	8.1	14559
75000	38	60	2285	19617	6071	31.0	18423
45100		240	2482	17091	3507	20.5	20077
38650		74	1503	7620	2317	30.4	17124
27513	35	70	3407	20292	3605	17.8	16308
35744			2948	27197	6733	24.8	20082
30120		1	1641	13152	3058	23.3	17653
21580		35	1818	15086	5418	35.9	17971
196238		19	2014	20445	7177	35.1	15845
25405		13	1675	14265	3550	24.9	15823
12339		602	5215	18165	4296	23.7	17330
5700		1	1445	19112	3029	15.9	16671
31853		100	1533	10737	2311	21.5	16779
72000		335	3322	27720	7073	25.5	14694
31200		71	870	5768	1957	33.9	17924
29826		40	3748	21083	4237	20.1	16876
68450		12	1712	13934	1106	7.9	18128
35260	9	142	1591	11900	6199	52.1	18286
41756	4	198	2210	13528	3564	26.4	16086
33000			365	1879	589	31.4	20354
366989	114		14376	237725	22225	9.4	17762
75865			6040	94741	5752	6.1	15892
76336			3987	38372	11209	29.2	14844
46865			1536	11086	2579	23.3	14319

15 续表 11

(2009年)

村(居)委会	土地面积(平方公里)	总人口数(人)	户籍人口	外来暂住人口	户籍人口从业人数(人)	全部企业及个体户数(个)	#工业企业
塘沥村	6.5	17384	1903	15481	824	250	62
黄洞村	11.9	10546	2245	8301	1290	225	54
竹塘村	5.6	11960	1289	10671	499	345	125
竹尾田村	1.6	7020	730	6290	274	133	14
三联村	3.3	9742	1527	8215	768	792	41
五联村	5.6	6682	1321	5361	560	141	139
天堂围村	4.1	7672	1094	6578	670	106	106
居民	1.3	6349	4552	1797	2486	430	7
谢岗							
黎村	11.0	7419	3699	3720	1700	95	20
南面村	39.6	3535	1478	2057	930	36	13
窑山村	11.3	2151	521	1630	363	25	19
大龙村	5.6	2700	999	1701	602	54	23
大厚村	5.6	4522	1004	3518	570	116	55
谢山村	4.0	5692	563	5129	315	123	53
谢岗村	14.0	6180	2932	3248	1880	70	70
赵林村	3.8	9540	1680	7860	673	128	63
曹乐村	6.6	8429	2136	6293	1258	208	105
五星村	1.6	5746	1269	4477	834	48	20
稔子园村	2.5	2006	635	1371	370	52	30
泰园		18325	3316	15009	1835	620	4
常平							
居民	4.0	35200	15025	20175	8540	877	42
下墟村	0.4	2816	816	2000	437	224	34
岗梓村	2.7	11035	2535	8500	1395	122	65
桥梓村	2.0	7818	2492	5326	1512	201	83
塘角村	1.1	9934	947	8987	502	130	150
苏坑村	4.0	8787	3567	5220	1373	184	148
袁山贝村	5.0	12748	3538	9210	1238	623	295
金美村	3.0	13407	2407	11000	1301	308	145
还珠沥村	5.5	19598	2746	16852	1636	397	157
朗贝村	4.0	7938	1938	6000	650	450	98
板石村	3.4	13417	1917	11500	1103	738	47
桥沥村	9.8	43426	3426	40000	1500	746	198
卢屋村	3.0	4722	832	3890	458	165	118
土塘村	8.7	30252	2802	27450	1537	1095	144
麦元村	2.4	4256	1056	3200	372	122	22
九江水村	9.0	7955	1415	6540	713	336	68
朗洲村	4.1	1734	614	1120	390	108	29
陈屋贝村	2.2	6482	1102	5380	695	178	40
司马村	8.0	17420	2770	14650	1447	511	75

规模以上工业总产值（当年价，万元）	农业		当年可支配财政收入（万元）	资产总额（万元）	负债总额（万元）	资产负债率（%）	农民人均纯收入（元）
	粮食（吨）	肉类总产量（吨）					
238049			1021	6265	2092	33.4	14211
63534		3	1049	11987	1604	13.4	13547
99048			1243	7187	1875	26.1	14308
53310			1301	8003	363	4.5	14426
77468			705	3613	2087	57.8	13724
88588			1667	16090	8110	50.4	13402
76112			2019	20070	3875	19.3	14163
			67	499	63	12.6	13463
3990	664	1870	1270	7275	1205	16.6	9611
1758		8	560	2545	608	23.9	7727
1250		1	306	2089	446	21.4	8839
5250	1	3	339	2866	1678	58.6	9780
8505	21	124	570	3600	370	10.3	10996
9120		107	495	2889	355	12.3	11413
11600		2633	816	7409	965	13.0	11027
9895	23	866	871	4918	1452	29.5	10792
20158		130	848	5190	987	19.0	9668
1468			390	1560	1205	77.2	11190
		65	463	2201	156	7.1	10063
320			245	674	757	112.3	
7715			387	1560	1141	73.1	
23924		1	330	4091	2778	67.9	27488
18180	28	315	1442	10518	6220	59.1	9700
52859	3	50	2737	23716	5798	24.5	14196
35238		2	1875				14171
	20	32	1065	8061	2352	29.2	10751
87800	22	194	2459	20133	5283	26.2	10647
38771	10	181	4327	28002	5631	20.1	18604
19825	27	6	2036	15490	6743	43.5	12062
31700	26	2	1018	6016	245	4.1	15831
15469	1	9	887	5181	539	10.4	15125
184640	29	470	1915	13428	2388	17.8	13754
20245	2	22	314	1911	1417	74.2	7687
1480356	5	11	4500	25365	1236	4.9	17555
67708	34	6					10806
101489	7	6	2686	15255	621	4.1	13231
	13	1523	731	3319	880	26.5	8322
26246	31	39	1231	9988	1073	10.7	11468
200617	10	280	3825	21801	3635	16.7	14448

15 续表 12

(2009年)

村(居)委会	土地面积(平方公里)	总人口数(人)	户籍人口	外来暂住人口	户籍人口从业人数(人)	全部企业及个体户数(个)	#工业企业
霞坑村	1.6	4544	728	3816	363	216	28
澉旧村	2.0	5225	1125	4100	691	132	28
澉新村	2.4	7296	1246	6050	697	527	160
黄泥塘村	1.0	3403	903	2500	447	119	55
元江元村	1.9	7488	1488	6000	898	138	43
横江厦村	5.0	7495	2779	4716	1283	232	90
田尾村	2.1	5756	1556	4200	825	56	36
白花沥村	1.0	699	695	4	163	10	10
沙湖口村		4621	1021	3600	672	100	28
白石岗村	5.0	9299	3699	5600	1556	106	104
松柏塘村	3.8	8019	2326	5693	1069	83	36
上坑村	1.3	3320	920	2400	516	145	49
木棆村	3.5	6650	2050	4600	935	505	49
桥　头							
东江村	4.8	4268	2365	1903	1535	182	39
山和村	2.5	3524	974	2550	503	22	24
屋厦村	2.0	2091	691	1400	438	101	36
岗头村	0.6	3302	485	2817	302	51	30
李屋村	2.3	3455	1565	1890	770	50	39
邓屋村	2.7	10640	1840	8800	998	58	38
朗厦村	4.1	7591	1591	6000	842	77	77
邵岗头村	1.3	2247	862	1385	493	36	34
桥　头	1.0	3812	1312	2500	472	275	
迳　联	1.5	4938	1738	3200	815	108	46
田　新	2.2	5993	2193	3800	966	360	220
岭　头	1.3	4596	1143	3453	545	259	65
石水口村	7.0	11457	4477	6980	2380	578	110
大　洲	4.6	6832	3212	3620	1521	139	55
禾坑村	1.5	2092	992	1100	600	72	21
田头角村	1.0	2014	753	1261	427	40	40
居　民	15.6	59510	9376	50134	4759		
横　沥							
石涌村	3.9	10547	1761	8786	1056	629	103
隔坑村	1.8	8687	2677	6010	1703	761	69
半仙山村	1.5	4346	1597	2749	785	1215	30
横沥村	3.5	7155	2896	4259	1807	672	51
田头村	4.0	10078	2489	7589	1470	786	52
田坑村	5.0	7621	2813	4808	1966	1154	132
村头村	4.0	6343	2240	4103	693	540	75
长巷村	2.4	2463	1641	822	935	64	23
田饶步村	2.4	3468	1818	1650	800	167	53

规模以上工业总产值（当年价，万元）	农业		当年可支配财政收入（万元）	资产总额（万元）	负债总额（万元）	资产负债率（%）	农民人均纯收入（元）
	粮食（吨）	肉类总产量（吨）					
48047		4	679	4821	401	8.3	11126
	28	76	806	4272	204	4.8	7929
51141	4	90	1019	6600	2084	31.6	12873
20400	4	28	526	2683	1470	54.8	9203
16375		8	1169	8261	1491	18.1	10981
58712	95	236	925	7267	2953	40.6	9986
	1	100	711	3310	1271	38.4	9170
3685	1	25	393	1954	1374	70.3	8906
	3	36	528	4556	2716	59.6	13425
33280	51	96	1051	6900	4280	62.0	10867
21213	33	42	656	6519	2915	44.7	9712
47036	2	2	1460	12408	5271	42.5	15952
10649	2		4362	24560	1902	7.7	20576
11438		30	1421	8149	3878	47.6	13116
13192		106	1020	6600	1557	23.6	11507
16050			1663	5869	2102	35.8	11566
9521		51	650	3348	1069	31.9	11755
9526		1	1269	15654	3688	23.6	11681
33860	320	260	3709	26441	10271	38.8	12059
35000	250	710	2341	12775	4475	35.0	11311
5700	71	81	916	5620	2427	43.2	11457
23000			2189	20373	2383	11.7	14497
16503	140	120	3743	18770	936	5.0	11499
29900			2863	23042	7933	34.4	13419
18900		10	2174	15361	2866	18.7	14626
14050		205	4899	30476	7112	23.3	13847
13409	7	422	2510	21490	4254	19.8	13093
4200			1024	6021	1789	29.7	11108
			1047	5801	1631	28.1	12749
			73				
12869			1906	16602	5841	35.2	15023
19953		136	2187	15186	7822	51.5	14780
18417			2047	20918	14572	69.7	14327
7260			1237	16043	6661	41.5	14168
64829		422	1981	13248	8304	62.7	14002
11643	15	51	1191	7242	1864	25.7	13171
26560		138	2387	10274	3976	38.7	11670
432		45	631	4174	1678	40.2	10141
325		57	1721	14068	8394	59.7	12563

15 续表 13

(2009年)

村(居)委会	土地面积(平方公里)	总人口数(人)	户籍人口	外来暂住人口	户籍人口从业人数(人)	全部企业及个体户数(个)	#工业企业
六甲村	1.5	4405	1090	3315	663	152	45
村尾村	2.3	5061	1461	3600	948	423	41
水边村	5.0	7239	2709	4530	1774	263	35
新四村	3.8	9219	2038	7181	1220	459	120
山厦村	2.7	3748	1066	2682	631	214	38
月塘村	2.8	2317	1083	1234	548	178	22
张坑村	1.0	1935	612	1323	360	108	35
居民	1.0	7506	6163	1343	3626	1789	25
东坑							
东坑村	2.0	3025	3025		1823	233	68
黄麻岭村	0.7	3890	1078	2812	743	46	46
长安塘村	1.2	2755	1855	900	1039	115	90
寮边头村	0.8	3743	1597	2146	737	25	25
塔岗村	1.7	5731	1751	3980	900	74	60
坑美村	1.8	5530	1954	3576	930	120	63
新门楼村	1.4	8752	1702	7050	864	143	
井美村	1.9	5628	2508	3120	1535	532	50
初坑村	3.0	10575	2451	8124	1286	385	39
凤大村	0.3	3624	724	2900	506	310	14
丁屋村	1.1	4179	1079	3100	502	15	7
彭屋村	2.3	1887	1887		1225	8	8
黄屋村	1.8	6737	1941	4796	1140	518	35
角社村	5.7	8377	3377	5000	2070	171	71
居民	0.1	3248	2948	300	1798	95	4
企石							
铁岗村	5.8	4806	2430	2376	1460	35	17
深巷村	4.1	4259	2209	2050	1221	127	48
湖美村	1.0	1251	806	445	380	34	15
博夏村	6.7	4023	3497	526	1637	48	15
上洞村	5.3	5196	2646	2550	1896	105	28
清湖村	4.6	3385	1995	1390	856	35	22
江边村	5.0	5331	2945	2386	1626	73	23
旧围村	3.8	2941	1859	1082	910	43	
东平村	1.5	3374	720	2654	470	208	28
上截村	0.8	2403	1135	1268	497	53	10
下截村	1.2	2254	1424	830	771	45	18
东山村	6.2	10195	4256	5939	1452	406	83
铁炉坑村	3.4	5247	2999	2248	1598	130	90
企石村	1.5	2072	1350	722	742	40	18
杨屋村	0.8	1059	636	423	325	40	10
莫屋村	1.0	2700	1195	1505	590	63	26
霞朗村	1.0	4488	865	3623	172	253	32
新南村	2.8	3601	2081	1520	1376	308	40
南坑村	2.1	2413	1192	1221	811	90	26

规模以上工业总产值（当年价，万元）	农业		当年可支配财政收入（万元）	资产总额（万元）	负债总额（万元）	资产负债率（%）	农民人均纯收入（元）
	粮食（吨）	肉类总产量（吨）					
6701		2	690	6848	3421	50.0	11722
15925		13	1167	8802	3635	41.3	12576
31390	8		1154	6385	2968	46.5	10122
7866		77	225	2622	2054	78.3	12749
5732		11	2462	11470	836	7.3	10957
			10307	13430	428	3.2	11858
15757			602	6639	1196	18.0	10375
991			183	1339	893	66.7	
12589			1898	16344	8635	52.8	11150
			1045	6791	3755	55.3	10649
9220			1316	7878	5637	71.6	10599
19371			1463	6864	3218	46.9	11686
17195			1144	6673	2444	36.6	10829
			986	4939	1520	30.8	10853
26893			1233	9934	5866	59.1	12214
21500			2718	10014	4616	46.1	11596
32791		7	656	2565	1548	60.4	11690
			502	1782	1478	82.9	11213
			504	3451	1495	43.3	11378
			647	4337	1281	29.5	10890
23240			2129	9500	2668	28.1	11267
			1625	29618	1987	6.7	11957
	21	52	1796	11052	3546	32.1	10407
	51	40	720	6128	2596	42.4	9357
	41		418	3750	2053	54.8	9743
	83		774	6365	915	14.4	8537
		106	1073	4952	870	17.6	9271
			655	5392	1811	33.6	8813
			1073	4525	908	20.1	8574
	18		1916	4841	1167	24.1	9624
			581	3590	2470	68.8	11011
			1889	5737	4327	75.4	9568
			955	5759	2401	41.7	9807
	2		5788	25108	8065	32.1	11073
	12		1276	9764	3176	32.5	11903
	2		638	7112	2257	31.7	9735
			335	3394	1446	42.6	9119
			492	2207	1180	53.5	10537
			2008	13161	5424	41.2	13634
		162	1236	8646	3180	36.8	10596
		43	1353	7135	569	8.0	9748

15 续表 14

(2009年)

村(居)委会	土地面积(平方公里)	总人口数(人)	户籍人口	外来暂住人口	户籍人口从业人数(人)	全部企业及个体户数(个)	#工业企业
居民	0.5	12604	5106	7498	3610	435	
石排							
石排村	2.4	7793	3578	4215	1525	1269	56
下沙村	3.4	5900	2586	3314	970	592	64
庙边王村	3.7	9925	2353	7572	1213	1069	189
福隆村	5.6	16334	5739	10595	3253	813	295
沙角村	3.4	6845	2548	4297	1596	562	30
黄家壆村	2.4	5099	1905	3194	996	150	30
赤坎村	3.2	3487	1386	2101	478	470	53
向西村	2.0	7050	1177	5873	334	642	44
水贝村	3.5	7732	3198	4534	1571	653	72
田寮村	3.3	2953	1944	1009	942	452	41
横山村	3.8	6118	2003	4115	1122	512	45
谷吓村	3.1	4719	1863	2856	777	660	61
埔心村	2.2	12124	1541	10583	848	889	689
塘尾村	1.6	5380	1072	4308	437	632	76
李家坊村	0.9	3961	923	3038	468	437	68
田边村	4.2	5207	2093	3114	789	545	69
中坑村	3.2	5809	2295	3514	1356	478	29
燕窝村	4.3	9240	1698	7542	760	918	87
太和		3564	2291	1273	1216		
茶山							
上元村	4.5	8131	3131	5000	1820	107	107
茶山村	1.3	6294	1724	4570	1093	71	43
下朗村	1.0	4390	1390	3000	897	68	29
横江村	3.7	8307	3047	5260	2125	118	58
卢边村	3.3	3893	2713	1180	1686	78	74
寒溪水村	1.3	3083	946	2137	545	45	41
增埗村	6.0	18607	7028	11579	4055	308	170
南社村	6.9	16822	3522	13300	2038	146	97
塘角村	4.7	12349	2899	9450	1500	155	135
京山村	3.5	7163	2413	4750	1370	328	40
博头村	1.2	1482	630	852	375	44	15
冲美村	0.8	2332	736	1596	429	75	
粟边村	3.2	5546	1966	3580	1029	49	46
刘黄村	0.8	5818	998	4820	593	258	71
孙屋村	0.6	1815	715	1100	471	42	25
超朗村	8.2	5002	2933	2069	1728	65	65
茶山墟		10482	7609	2873			

规模以上工业总产值（当年价，万元）	农业		当年可支配财政收入（万元）	资产总额（万元）	负债总额（万元）	资产负债率（%）	农民人均纯收入（元）
	粮食（吨）	肉类总产量（吨）					
			177	132	49	37.1	
11983			757	2226	959	43.1	12543
5507			569	3945	2277	57.7	11945
20258	108		876	4632	1070	23.1	12337
27526	96		1836	23629	12386	52.4	12613
38222			716	3122	631	20.2	12008
6311			3901	11766	637	5.4	11422
20598	84		1497	7749	1211	15.6	11710
51989			1129	6635	1542	23.2	10584
18189	50		939	6070	771	12.7	13254
537			1042	4320	1924	44.5	10637
23713			563	3300	2664	80.7	10277
11009			433	3964	1769	44.6	11739
64918			1638	8762	370	4.2	16169
23689			727	8111	418	5.2	11143
11685			613	4618	1439	31.2	11567
38486	20		583	3228	2044	63.3	11716
12709	50		882	10844	324	3.0	12598
25238			1721	7073	1179	16.7	12533
3318			154	1396	969	69.4	12222
37269			469	2853	1635	57.3	12099
33743			1293	12609	5422	43.0	13980
			1207	12382	2876	23.2	11511
55308			1135	9244	2575	27.9	10554
8334		80	1592	9732	2229	22.9	11014
31820		15	850	3877	858	22.1	11004
40265	213		1296	11246	6618	58.9	12356
151201	10	350	2289	32118	3357	10.5	10874
51393			1168	11251	1837	16.3	12113
10899			2043	14519	5029	34.6	14038
13080			679	4727	652	13.8	10032
4892			1667	7066	1041	14.7	11079
12879		4	1560	7320	1202	16.4	9391
27985			1184	7592	2959	39.0	10101
6573	13	3	255	2240	647	28.9	10127
35729		335	1012	24260	587	2.4	12825

十六、建国以来
国民经济和社会发展主要指标

Main Indicators on National Economy and Social Development from the Founding of the PRC

16 建国以来国民经济和社会发展主要指标

Main Indicators on National Economy and Social Development from the Founding of the PRC

年　份	户籍人口(万人)	常住人口(万人)	新莞人人口(万人)	人口自然增长率(‰)	户籍从业人员(万人)	新莞人从业人员(万人)	城镇在岗职工人数(万人)	城镇在岗职工平均工资(元)
1949	68.24							
1952	71.68							
1957	77.48				37.57		3.90	400
1962	79.64				36.78		2.93	552
1965	86.46			29.60	40.56		3.17	524
1970	98.56			20.60	49.97		3.29	534
1975	107.94			14.51	51.44		3.80	577
1978	111.23			13.81	54.97		8.20	474
1979	112.04			19.00	56.51		9.68	650
1980	112.70			19.31	57.86		9.86	750
1981	114.46			16.57	59.42		10.66	887
1982	116.19			14.14	61.76		11.41	1095
1983	117.59			11.53	63.25		11.59	1197
1984	118.95			10.60	65.51		11.76	1383
1985	120.85			10.83	67.35		12.30	1456
1986	123.01		15.62	11.56	69.68	10.41	13.27	2616
1987	124.86		25.29	11.67	71.63	18.03	13.67	2067
1988	126.76		36.89	12.09	71.99	29.25	12.71	2757
1989	128.76		47.19	12.39	73.95	40.53	13.10	3320
1990	131.85	175.62	65.59	12.31	75.10	57.20	13.16	3552
1991	133.65	200.01	80.58	13.34	76.99	70.20	14.59	3777
1992	136.06	227.78	114.48	14.50	77.55	107.10	15.47	4531
1993	138.92	259.41	121.70	13.41	79.36	112.68	17.66	6228
1994	141.40	295.43	139.09	13.37	81.02	124.18	16.09	8360
1995	143.65	336.45	142.18	12.75	82.40	126.54	17.87	9682
1996	145.25	383.17	143.32	11.97	83.52	127.66	17.50	10382
1997	147.12	436.38	144.68	12.09	84.78	130.73	16.50	10691
1998	148.77	496.97	199.11	10.86	85.98	183.19	16.40	11422
1999	150.82	565.98	244.81	10.22	87.82	216.15	16.39	12557
2000	152.61	644.84	254.72	7.52	88.62	244.84	16.41	14051
2001	153.89	654.43	457.82	7.01	90.80	449.68	16.42	16183
2002	156.19	654.84	433.65	5.91	92.93	426.01	16.42	17804
2003	158.96	655.25	440.45	5.65	95.64	432.73	16.60	22598
2004	161.97	655.66	486.95	5.96	98.36	473.39	17.54	25326
2005	165.65	656.07	584.98	6.02	101.30	553.42	18.86	28253
2006	168.31	674.88	586.76	5.86	103.76	566.98	19.99	31135
2007	171.26	694.72	557.80	5.98	106.65	538.95	20.56	35284
2008	174.87	694.98	552.50	6.23	109.67	530.30	20.72	39516
2009	178.73	635.00	429.96	6.31	112.18	413.46	22.60	42585

注：城镇在岗职工人数与平均工资1952－1975年是全所有制单位资料，1978－1999年为城镇职工资料，2000年起为城镇在岗职工资料。

16 续表 1

年 份	地区生产总值(亿元)	第一产业	第二产业	工 业	建筑业	第三产业	人均地区生产总值(元)
1949							
1952							
1957							
1962							
1965							
1970							
1975							
1978	6.11	2.72	2.68			0.71	553
1979	6.62	2.65	2.92			1.05	593
1980	7.22	2.63	3.33			1.26	643
1981	9.11	3.28	4.30			1.54	802
1982	11.43	3.73	5.81			1.89	991
1983	13.03	3.98	6.90			2.15	1115
1984	15.96	4.57	7.81			3.59	1350
1985	22.60	6.15	11.66			4.80	1885
1986	30.02	8.14	13.57	10.54	3.03	8.30	2462
1987	39.29	9.82	17.72	14.24	3.49	11.74	3170
1988	55.46	11.89	28.28	25.05	3.23	15.29	4408
1989	60.92	12.66	27.97	27.22	0.75	20.29	4768
1990	80.44	13.28	40.53	39.18	1.34	26.63	6173
1991	95.91	13.45	50.32	48.34	1.98	32.13	5095
1992	110.89	14.41	59.27	56.63	2.64	37.21	5038
1993	157.05	14.40	87.31	82.89	4.42	55.34	5850
1994	217.03	17.48	119.49	110.77	8.72	80.06	6357
1995	296.29	21.43	166.97	154.19	12.78	107.89	7421
1996	361.75	24.86	199.48	187.85	11.63	137.40	8444
1997	448.60	25.64	243.28	230.79	12.50	179.68	9747
1998	558.00	25.94	305.68	290.69	14.99	226.37	11265
1999	667.24	25.79	367.05	349.53	17.52	274.40	12494
2000	820.25	25.91	450.71	430.45	20.25	343.64	13679
2001	991.89	26.10	540.51	517.03	23.48	425.28	15268
2002	1186.94	24.88	648.81	621.86	26.96	513.25	18131
2003	1452.52	22.82	798.20	757.18	41.01	631.51	22174
2004	1806.03	22.71	1016.04	968.01	48.03	767.28	27554
2005	2183.20	20.55	1227.86	1173.23	54.63	934.78	33287
2006	2627.98	12.01	1506.60	1441.69	64.91	1109.37	39490
2007	3160.05	11.90	1754.66	1681.83	72.83	1393.49	46146
2008	3703.60	14.83	1901.61	1819.22	82.38	1787.17	53301
2009	3763.91	14.79	1823.08	1741.53	81.55	1926.04	56601

注：1. 本表按当年价格计算。
2. 人均生产总值1990年及以前年份按年平均户籍人口计算，1991年起按年平均常住人口计算。

16 续表 2

上年＝100

年 份	地区生产总值指数	第一产业	第二产业	工业	建筑业	第三产业	人均地区生产总值指数
1949							
1952							
1957							
1962							
1965							
1970							
1975							
1978							
1979	99.5	86.5	107.0			146.4	98.6
1980	102.7	90.3	117.3			113.9	102.0
1981	116.6	115.0	122.1			110.8	115.4
1982	116.9	105.3	131.0			117.6	115.1
1983	110.4	104.8	115.7			111.3	108.9
1984	114.2	109.0	107.0			140.9	112.9
1985	132.3	118.9	144.5			132.7	130.5
1986	126.1	111.9	110.3			174.7	124.0
1987	122.5	111.6	127.7	125.8	147.0	126.0	120.5
1988	115.7	90.6	143.7	151.4	77.9	103.0	114.0
1989	107.1	99.8	106.2	106.4	103.7	113.7	105.5
1990	123.2	104.4	127.6	130.6	76.4	128.0	120.8
1991	117.5	103.1	121.5	121.8	113.2	118.6	108.8
1992	108.3	100.0	112.6	113.7	78.0	105.1	92.6
1993	127.9	79.4	139.2	138.5	168.1	129.0	104.8
1994	122.5	107.2	124.7	124.3	138.5	122.3	96.3
1995	127.4	110.5	135.1	135.3	128.3	116.8	108.9
1996	117.5	109.4	115.5	116.2	91.2	123.5	109.5
1997	119.6	104.5	119.8	120.1	106.1	121.8	111.3
1998	121.8	100.9	122.1	122.2	115.1	124.5	113.1
1999	119.7	102.3	120.6	120.7	115.2	120.3	111.0
2000	119.7	99.8	120.7	120.9	110.5	120.0	106.6
2001	119.9	103.0	121.6	122.0	113.0	118.9	110.7
2002	120.5	97.6	122.6	123.0	114.1	119.1	119.6
2003	120.5	90.2	122.3	121.4	143.5	119.7	120.4
2004	121.0	90.0	125.6	126.5	106.8	115.8	120.9
2005	119.5	102.3	120.0	120.2	113.5	119.3	119.4
2006	119.2	58.9	121.9	122.0	118.7	117.1	117.5
2007	118.3	89.9	114.8	115.0	108.7	123.3	114.9
2008	114.0	110.6	106.1	106.4	100.9	124.0	112.4
2009	105.3	102.3	99.7	99.4	104.7	111.4	110.0

注：本表按可比价格计算。

16 续表 3

年 份	全社会固定资产投资(亿元)	地方财政一般预算收入(亿元)	地方财政一般预算支出(亿元)	居民消费价格指数(上年=100)	商品零售价格指数(上年=100)	农林牧渔总产值(亿元)	农林牧渔总产值指数(1952年=100)
1949						0.54	
1952		0.28	0.02			0.66	122.6
1957		0.32	0.04			0.78	118.1
1962		0.31	0.07			0.76	97.2
1965		0.47	0.07			1.28	168.1
1970		0.48	0.08			1.47	115.3
1975		0.65	0.11			2.53	116.8
1978	0.23	0.66	0.18		100.4	4.24	103.4
1979	0.16	0.66	0.19		102.6	4.15	100.1
1980	0.24	0.67	0.20		110.9	4.19	97.9
1981	0.38	0.68	0.21		109.3	5.04	106.3
1982	1.81	0.81	0.26		101.2	5.59	115.0
1983	1.84	0.86	0.28		99.6	5.64	101.2
1984	3.01	0.85	0.30	99.3	98.6	7.02	110.8
1985	7.06	1.11	0.50	106.5	106.9	9.12	103.5
1986	11.52	1.61	0.99	104.2	104.4	12.30	125.7
1987	14.19	2.02	1.25	112.0	112.2	14.84	106.8
1988	16.55	2.71	1.75	136.0	132.8	20.37	97.7
1989	5.01	3.19	2.16	122.0	122.4	22.11	99.8
1990	7.51	3.57	2.28	96.6	94.9	23.64	107.4
1991	13.75	4.44	2.75	102.4	101.4	24.26	102.2
1992	18.88	5.62	3.82	109.2	107.7	27.13	105.9
1993	32.76	9.38	7.29	121.8	119.5	28.45	83.1
1994	140.76	7.69	8.90	123.5	118.4	34.75	107.4
1995	63.14	11.56	12.42	113.9	109.7	42.69	110.3
1996	67.62	9.65	12.41	106.8	104.7	49.72	104.1
1997	65.89	11.41	14.85	101.5	99.7	51.44	104.1
1998	77.00	15.10	17.91	99.9	98.7	53.60	101.0
1999	88.32	18.26	21.26	97.9	95.9	53.74	106.8
2000	102.89	30.47	33.61	101.5	100.1	54.64	100.2
2001	125.49	45.02	47.86	96.6	97.8	55.93	101.2
2002	191.57	55.29	64.96	98.1	99.1	53.67	106.8
2003	319.39	67.45	76.52	100.7	101.7	49.02	79.7
2004	454.87	82.64	94.16	103.0	103.2	44.19	101.8
2005	597.24	103.97	117.04	102.4	103.0	42.05	104.1
2006	705.45	128.94	147.90	101.2	102.8	21.26	54.5
2007	841.21	186.45	193.10	103.1	104.2	19.98	87.2
2008	944.34	209.22	218.26	105.5	107.9	25.53	112.1
2009	1094.08	231.16	232.62	96.9	95.3	25.31	103.3

注：农林牧渔总产值1952-1970年按1957年不变价计算，1975年按1970年不变价计算，1978年起按当年价计算。

16　续表 4

年　份	农作物总播种面积(千公顷)	#粮食	粮食产量(万吨)	油料产量(万吨)	水果产量(万吨)	肉类产量(万吨)	水产品产量(万吨)
1949	141.26	127.26	21.07	0.15			0.32
1952	167.61	149.68	26.95	0.35			0.34
1957	188.98	165.53	28.80	0.33			0.42
1962	155.97	138.18	33.12	0.38			0.63
1965	158.97	121.64	43.71	0.72	4.54		0.99
1970	174.60	127.25	45.08	0.96	6.95		1.62
1975	202.00	137.03	50.72	1.11	3.68		2.19
1978	190.63	138.15	53.23	1.42	2.65	2.69	3.09
1979	172.36	129.16	53.53	1.91	2.33	2.92	2.23
1980	162.41	117.12	52.94	2.90	2.37	2.77	2.55
1981	151.17	107.13	44.75	3.55	4.69	2.80	2.49
1982	146.96	106.68	54.33	2.99	5.82	3.30	2.77
1983	146.21	109.02	56.12	1.97	7.72	3.57	3.03
1984	144.35	105.12	55.82	2.31	10.59	3.33	3.25
1985	130.01	93.05	48.87	2.10	18.94	3.33	3.26
1986	119.41	83.81	45.52	2.01	30.77	4.33	4.65
1987	119.73	83.40	46.28	1.70	36.31	4.61	6.57
1988	119.53	82.42	46.09	1.51	26.37	5.61	6.81
1989	122.27	85.61	48.76	1.37	22.14	5.86	6.23
1990	123.25	85.74	49.43	1.34	28.24	6.22	6.85
1991	119.42	81.77	47.37	1.15	34.32	6.88	6.90
1992	104.10	64.26	36.81	0.93	34.48	6.80	7.32
1993	71.20	36.74	20.21	0.56	27.13	7.66	6.50
1994	67.30	35.75	20.24	0.37	26.49	8.54	6.74
1995	71.89	39.90	22.74	0.37	24.32	9.76	7.48
1996	72.23	41.89	24.32	0.31	20.63	11.61	8.11
1997	72.17	41.61	24.69	0.29	16.50	12.90	9.19
1998	73.46	41.63	24.72	0.26	11.41	15.35	9.69
1999	72.59	41.77	24.73	0.22	13.63	15.99	9.40
2000	65.73	35.18	20.41	0.20	12.94	17.90	9.51
2001	56.95	22.56	12.84	0.16	15.01	19.84	8.96
2002	42.28	9.88	5.37	0.09	18.93	18.88	8.24
2003	33.97	5.65	3.05	0.04	14.64	15.46	7.58
2004	30.82	5.41	3.04	0.02	17.54	14.62	7.15
2005	27.38	4.14	2.00	0.01	15.13	17.17	6.74
2006	22.26	2.29	1.00	0.01	13.96	3.49	4.71
2007	21.37	2.15	0.99	0.01	13.16	2.03	4.73
2008	23.48	2.72	1.20	0.01	10.15	2.41	7.23
2009	24.72	2.77	1.19	0.01	9.15	2.55	7.33

年 份	工业企业单位数(个)	工业总产值(亿元)	工业总产值指数(上年=100)	规模以上工业增加值(亿元)	总供电量(亿千瓦时)	总售电量(亿千瓦时)	建筑业总产值(亿元)	建筑业增加值(亿元)
1949	1	0.29						
1952	3522	0.40						
1957	262	0.70						
1962	280	0.75			0.08	0.07		
1965	260	1.10			0.36	0.32		
1970	220	1.58			0.71	0.60		
1975	324				1.24	1.11		
1978	1290	4.20			1.64	1.49		
1979	1250	4.88	110.5		1.93	1.73		
1980	1293	5.91	117.7		2.17	1.97		
1981	1479	6.86	116.2		2.22	1.99		
1982	1862	8.25	118.0		2.69	2.35		
1983	1964	9.48	111.1		3.15	2.75		
1984	2329	11.42	116.0		3.26	2.84		
1985	4187	17.35	148.5		3.82	3.39		
1986	5949	23.93	140.1	6.96	3.93	3.51		3.03
1987	8106	36.69	147.6	8.68	6.43	5.71		3.49
1988	8408	61.72	154.3	15.03	9.48	8.47		3.23
1989	8757	77.46	123.8	15.54	12.09	10.84	1.03	0.75
1990	9892	98.58	120.0	23.76	18.01	16.15	1.27	1.34
1991	10094	128.36	130.5	31.54	24.05	21.67	2.19	1.98
1992	11639	186.67	144.3	38.21	32.00	28.87	3.19	2.64
1993	12449	267.67	138.0	59.08	43.62	39.40	5.39	4.42
1994	14086	389.13	137.0	78.43	58.58	53.02	7.99	8.72
1995	15215	522.58	132.2	111.02	68.00	61.68	9.49	12.78
1996	15326	676.19	125.6	140.89	80.03	72.71	9.66	11.63
1997	16857	798.62	124.2	177.71	94.93	86.65	28.73	12.50
1998	16406	987.78	123.2	240.22	109.48	100.91	35.92	14.99
1999	16877	1241.90	124.7	292.58	132.78	123.42	40.73	17.52
2000	16975	1519.79	124.4	360.11	178.03	169.06	40.45	20.25
2001	18094	1846.82	123.3	410.67	207.72	196.59	50.13	23.48
2002	21313	2296.44	127.9	542.03	258.55	246.97	65.84	26.96
2003	21935	2874.79	127.5	673.59	321.65	283.54	76.48	41.01
2004	22156	3683.61	126.4	826.58	372.84	350.28	77.01	48.03
2005	21868	4470.03	122.0	979.34	415.66	396.59	84.35	58.61
2006	22447	5529.70	122.8	1186.20	464.45	445.52	94.58	64.91
2007	22587	6667.86	118.9	1388.34	507.89	482.56	112.87	72.83
2008	25656	7312.29	107.8	1602.98	507.35	487.32	108.81	82.38
2009	30117	6762.80	96.7	1453.37	488.85	478.19	99.40	81.55

注：工业总产值1952－1970年按1957年不变价格计算，1971－1980年按1970年不变价格计算，1981－1989年按1980年不变价格计算，1990年及以后按当年价格计算；指数按可比价格计算。

16 续表 6

年　份	公路通车里程（公里）	民用汽车拥有量（万　辆）	旅　客周转量（万人公里）	货　物周转量（万吨公里）	邮电业务收入（万元）	本地电话用户（万户）	移动电话用户（万户）
1949	204	0.002					
1952	219	0.002	1350	139			
1957	373	0.005	2100	195			
1962	598	0.007	4120	293			
1965	882	0.010	4725	457			
1970	1134	0.012	2800	900			
1975	1173	0.025	3890	694			
1978	1259	0.06	9425	15148	686	0.20	
1979	1225	0.11	11162	15290	790	0.21	
1980	1225	0.20	13584	16353	927	0.31	
1981	1225	0.30	13845	15606	962	0.34	
1982	1225	0.34	16026	17185	940	0.35	
1983	1225	0.45	54075	108634	1018	0.39	
1984	1240	0.61	62107	140113	1263	0.48	
1985	1240	0.79	95237	171591	1560	0.77	
1986	1248	0.86	127458	126898	2015	0.88	
1987	1261	1.00	159117	174942	3410	1.63	
1988	1302	1.36	173335	169112	5728	2.52	
1989	1325	1.63	240999	186626	9620	4.30	0.02
1990	1325	1.94	322236	184700	17555	4.90	0.05
1991	1759	2.07	373284	194101	27733	7.50	0.11
1992	2055	3.26	503973	232752	42155	9.70	0.30
1993	2260	4.81	577800	248230	65699	14.98	0.72
1994	2292	6.16	595134	273053	102238	23.19	2.41
1995	2327	8.83	446230	264605	152761	31.57	4.77
1996	2330	9.08	477466	267193	207573	36.91	8.24
1997	2330	10.34	511592	278649	284278	42.65	15.29
1998	2377	11.34	577452	285889	376708	50.13	26.17
1999	2467	12.70	804278	300410	515916	60.87	51.01
2000	2518	15.37	1001906	404678	724593	78.12	123.68
2001	2570	18.36	1031579	406247	1225474	98.96	295.76
2002	2641	22.01	1091821	420684	1816802	127.93	412.39
2003	2688	25.56	1126964	422822	1051220	206.11	660.86
2004	2759	31.97	1166262	423669	1207778	281.35	856.09
2005	2871	40.66	1185290	424829	1328172	384.52	1016.41
2006	3891	48.93	1213809	336783	1466871	461.31	1216.34
2007	3924	60.89	1264982	356677	1619048	469.17	1408.23
2008	4001	70.16	2248521	1747489	1723829	439.41	1454.29
2009	4713	79.56	1053469	1016490	1563077	378.40	1409.29

注：1. 公路通车里程2006年起含专用公路和村道。
　　2. 邮电业务收入2003年以前为邮电业务总量，按1990年不变价计算，2003年起为邮电业务收入。

年 份	社会消费品零售总额(亿元)	进出口总额(亿美元)	出口额	进口额	协议(合同)规定外商投资额(亿美元)	实际利用外资(亿美元)	#外商直接投资
1949							
1952							
1957			0.02				
1962			0.04				
1965			0.08				
1970			0.10				
1975			0.25				
1978	2.13		0.39				
1979	2.50		0.54		0.05	0.02	
1980	3.16		0.77		0.11	0.09	
1981	4.02		0.92		0.08	0.05	0.001
1982	4.81		1.09		0.08	0.07	0.005
1983	5.23		1.19		0.16	0.09	0.003
1984	7.39		1.30		0.32	0.19	0.07
1985	9.36		1.75		0.68	0.35	0.14
1986	12.24		2.33		0.34	0.45	0.15
1987	15.05		2.68		1.85	1.32	0.21
1988	24.65		3.18		6.22	2.99	0.64
1989	27.04		3.49		2.34	2.73	0.84
1990	31.97	10.82	5.68	5.14	3.02	2.56	1.00
1991	36.50	31.75	16.52	15.23	6.45	2.83	1.47
1992	44.35	50.90	26.03	24.87	20.88	4.81	3.29
1993	63.69	67.56	32.11	35.45	35.55	10.49	7.92
1994	85.16	88.30	42.94	45.36	34.97	11.95	7.79
1995	113.01	153.91	77.99	75.92	33.09	11.58	6.72
1996	125.53	178.42	91.87	86.55	20.89	13.10	6.95
1997	146.04	212.99	113.68	99.31	12.14	15.16	8.80
1998	175.16	232.73	130.61	102.13	16.37	15.48	9.30
1999	202.30	284.63	151.54	133.09	14.72	17.89	9.71
2000	235.16	320.45	171.59	148.86	18.36	19.54	10.87
2001	275.71	344.55	189.89	154.65	20.98	20.29	11.47
2002	321.24	442.47	237.36	205.11	24.89	23.48	14.59
2003	369.78	521.06	280.02	241.04	32.56	27.72	17.54
2004	426.47	645.18	351.92	293.25	41.32	33.47	21.39
2005	506.29	743.72	409.29	334.42	47.52	42.48	14.68
2006	599.32	842.21	473.76	368.45	55.28	50.04	18.08
2007	722.45	1068.73	602.32	466.41	62.51	60.07	21.18
2008	881.15	1132.99	655.37	477.62	39.37	47.09	24.47
2009	959.07	941.55	551.69	389.86	20.30	42.12	25.94

注：1. 出口总额1990年起为海关口径，1990年以前为外经贸口径。
2. 实际外商直接投资2004年起为新口径，是以验资作为统计标准，与往年数不可比。

16 续表 8

年 份	入境旅游人数(万人次)	国际旅游外汇收入(万美元)	接待国内游客人次(万人次)	旅 游总收入(亿元)	各项人民币存款余额(亿元)	城乡居民储蓄存款余额(亿元)	各项人民币贷款余额(亿元)
1949							
1952						0.003	0.004
1957						0.02	0.26
1962					0.08	0.04	0.75
1965					0.16	0.09	0.81
1970					0.39	0.16	0.87
1975					0.96	0.41	1.39
1978					1.05	0.54	1.96
1979					1.49	0.72	2.13
1980					2.61	1.17	3.08
1981					3.80	2.03	4.02
1982					4.51	2.77	4.55
1983					6.05	3.86	5.76
1984					11.03	6.18	12.19
1985					13.49	9.19	14.24
1986	80	554	69		19.59	13.14	20.68
1987	107	453	87		28.48	18.97	31.24
1988	125	710	105		38.05	24.91	41.58
1989	115	504	97		46.82	32.57	49.37
1990	125	1025	98		68.07	45.51	63.04
1991	155	2443	118		94.97	61.47	78.40
1992	172	2473	125		147.34	81.54	105.98
1993	169	2888	117		179.83	107.17	134.31
1994	119	3464	75		249.78	151.54	173.44
1995	89	5679	62		383.68	232.97	254.85
1996	175	6464	139		489.65	318.02	312.81
1997	171	6778	112		671.17	425.82	382.66
1998	216	6601	141		864.01	533.75	442.74
1999	253	7055	156		1040.84	616.34	524.37
2000	291	7617	185		1228.67	672.07	630.84
2001	327	8200	217	39.80	1458.65	799.18	750.18
2002	930	11847	822	72.51	1790.18	1001.69	933.41
2003	1086	13825	1006	79.92	2126.78	1231.06	1206.72
2004	1131	23437	982	85.70	2462.87	1431.68	1405.25
2005	1156	28189	987	90.72	2933.40	1728.28	1500.52
2006	1363	33180	1170	96.01	3365.65	2013.40	1730.56
2007	1725	42702	1477	118.88	3751.83	2120.74	2154.77
2008	1872	45614	1604	128.69	4354.53	2638.04	2380.36
2009	2037	51756	1751	151.49	4986.61	2904.57	2903.80

16　续表 9

年　份	在校学生数（万人）				学龄儿童入学率（%）	高考入围人数（人）	#省线入围人数	医院、卫生院床位数（张）
	普通高等学校	普通中等学校	#普通中学	小学				
1949		0.21	0.20	5.28				219
1952		0.39	0.34	7.04				179
1957		0.72	0.67	8.80				403
1962		1.01	0.97	12.00				1376
1965		1.08	1.05	16.09				1308
1970		6.02	6.02	11.81				1476
1975		5.03	4.96	16.82				1970
1978		7.66	7.60	16.11	98.36	846	250	2257
1979		6.27	6.23	15.80	98.70	566	166	2271
1980		5.52	5.48	15.49	98.85	222	140	2207
1981		4.40	4.35	15.09	98.72	239	154	2210
1982		4.23	4.17	14.48	99.06	252	115	2292
1983		4.37	4.28	13.54	99.75	245	150	2098
1984		4.76	4.65	13.46	99.65	619	220	2231
1985		5.00	4.66	13.44	99.83	534	285	2323
1986		5.33	4.94	14.07	99.90	595	228	3054
1987		6.03	5.44	14.43	99.94	644	297	3393
1988		6.64	5.93	15.01	99.93	925	315	3640
1989		6.98	6.20	15.59	99.92	977	284	3677
1990		7.01	6.12	16.27	99.94	759	224	3866
1991		7.11	6.01	17.01	99.92	861	268	4085
1992		7.83	6.52	17.52	99.94	994	312	4517
1993	0.11	8.95	7.53	18.01	99.95	1102	423	4940
1994	0.15	10.19	8.58	18.62	99.96	1823	586	5365
1995	0.16	11.12	9.25	19.51	99.99	2095	809	5798
1996	0.18	11.78	9.52	20.60	99.98	2160	1093	5288
1997	0.20	12.28	9.80	22.18	99.99	2212	1215	5505
1998	0.22	12.68	10.12	23.58	99.99	2348	1315	5892
1999	0.22	13.06	10.55	24.88	99.99	3501	1790	6241
2000	0.32	13.56	11.24	27.28	99.99	5017	2646	7081
2001	0.38	14.58	12.21	29.54	100.00	5651	3225	7474
2002	0.51	16.06	13.53	34.28	100.00	6873	3759	8641
2003	0.69	17.73	14.97	38.69	100.00	9167	4509	9820
2004	0.91	19.98	17.13	44.83	100.00	10756	5452	10797
2005	1.66	22.05	19.10	48.09	100.00	11196	6455	11972
2006	2.20	25.00	21.46	49.68	100.00	11359	7652	13293
2007	2.52	27.50	23.46	52.07	100.00	13275	9185	15227
2008	2.87	29.39	24.84	52.86	100.00	15047	9987	16778
2009	3.40	29.60	24.95	51.12	100.00	17487	12569	18080

16　续表 10

年　份	卫生机构技术人员数(万人)	#医生	每万人口拥有 床位数(张)	每万人口拥有 医生数(人)	年末参加基本养老保险人数(万人)	年末参加基本医疗保险人数(万人)
1949	0.02		3.21			
1952	0.01		2.50			
1957	0.03		5.20			
1962	0.13		17.28			
1965	0.16		15.13			
1970	0.17		14.98			
1975	0.23		18.25			
1978	0.26	0.08	20.29	6.90		
1979	0.29	0.10	20.27	8.67		
1980	0.30	0.12	19.58	10.35		
1981	0.31	0.11	19.31	9.63		
1982	0.33	0.11	19.73	9.44		
1983	0.33	0.11	17.84	9.25		
1984	0.34	0.11	18.76	9.52		
1985	0.33	0.12	19.22	9.94		
1986	0.35	0.12	24.83	9.58		
1987	0.35	0.13	27.17	10.44		
1988	0.38	0.15	28.72	12.13		
1989	0.39	0.16	28.56	12.58		
1990	0.39	0.17	22.01	9.80		
1991	0.39	0.18	20.42	8.77		
1992	0.41	0.18	19.83	8.04		
1993	0.45	0.20	19.04	7.80		
1994	0.49	0.22	18.16	7.52	7.55	7.77
1995	0.53	0.23	17.23	6.83	8.46	7.60
1996	0.58	0.24	13.80	6.39	9.16	7.65
1997	0.63	0.26	12.62	5.97	7.53	8.29
1998	0.71	0.30	11.86	5.95	7.84	9.05
1999	0.76	0.31	11.03	5.44	8.35	9.95
2000	0.81	0.33	10.98	5.13	82.95	88.21
2001	0.81	0.34	11.42	5.24	83.01	84.99
2002	0.90	0.35	13.20	5.38	103.19	105.19
2003	0.98	0.38	14.99	5.74	104.13	105.90
2004	1.31	0.49	16.47	7.43	104.44	105.95
2005	1.88	0.69	18.25	10.52	182.49	189.40
2006	2.29	0.86	19.70	12.79	204.08	212.16
2007	2.88	1.04	21.92	15.04	227.98	236.32
2008	3.31	1.19	24.14	17.08	262.63	513.25
2009	3.58	1.29	28.47	20.29	315.81	536.57

注：本表按常住人口计算。

16 续表 11

年份	科技活动机构数(个)	科技活动人员(人)	专利申请量(件)	专利授权量(件)	城市居民人均可支配收入(元)	农民人均纯收入(元)	城镇人均住房使用面积(平方米)	农村人均生活用房使用面积(平方米)
1949								
1952								
1957								
1962								
1965								
1970								
1975								
1978						149		
1979						186		
1980						266		
1981						449		
1982						544		
1983						586		
1984						649		
1985					791	746	11	
1986					1033	874	12	
1987					1247	1039	13	
1988					1778	1193	15	
1989					2282	1268	17	
1990			34	30	2508	1359	16	
1991			70	50	3068	1459	16	
1992			102	78	4026	1976	17	
1993			100	90	5970	2479	20	
1994			104	100	8270	3185	23	
1995	604	93542	325	262	9588	3988	20	
1996	706	88012	333	312	10824	7596	21	20
1997	816	95859	725	321	11032	5021	21	41
1998	987	103624	890	709	11506	5534	26	43
1999	1149	106586	1221	819	12954	6177	29.7	46
2000	1450	107321	1653	1399	14142	6731	31.1	47
2001	1461	115519	2914	1753	16938	7366	39.9	48
2002	1482	116496	3100	2680	16949	7907	41.8	55
2003	1670	124850	3865	2858	18471	8481	41.4	58
2004	1810	125250	4325	3167	20526	9083	41.6	65
2005	1950	144448	6694	3114	22882	9842	42.7	65
2006	1982	151621	9879	4872	25320	10661	45.2	60
2007	2182	158536	13842	6752	27025	11606	43.1	59
2008	2466	152433	14406	8093	30275	12328	40.3	55
2009			19106	12918	33045	13064	40.4	56

十七、东莞与全国、全省及三角洲城市主要指标比较

Comparison of Main Indicators between Dongguan and China Guangdong Province, the Cities, of the Pearl River Delta

17-1 主要年份全国国民经济与社会发展指标

Main Indicators of National Economic and Social Development of China

指　　标	单 位	1980年	1985年	1990年	1995年	2000年	2005年	2008年	2009年
一、人口与劳动力									
年末总人口	万人	98705	105851	114333	121121	126743	130756	132802	133474
年末从业人员人数	万人	42361	49873	64749	68065	72085	75825	77480	77995
#城镇从业人员	万人	10525	12808	17041	19040	23151	27331	30210	31120
二、经济总量									
生产总值	亿元	4518	8964	18548	60794	99215	182321	300670	335353
第一产业增加值	亿元	1359	2541	5017	12020	14716	22718	34000	35477
第二产业增加值	亿元	2192	3867	7717	28679	45556	86208	146183	156958
第三产业增加值	亿元	967	2556	5814	20094	38942	73395	120487	142918
人均国内生产总值	元	460	853	1634	5046	7858	13985	22698	24673
三、农业									
农林牧渔业总产值	亿元	1923	3619	7662	20341	24916	39337		
主要农产品产量									
粮食	万吨	32056	37911	44624	46662	46218	48402	52850	53082
水果	万吨	679	1164	1874	4215	6225	16120		
肉类	万吨		1927	2857	5260	6125	7743	7269	7642
水产品	万吨	450	705	1237	2517	4278	5106	4895	5120
四、工业									
主要工业产品产量									
机制纸及纸板	万吨	535	911	1372	2812	2487	5404	8391	9389
彩电	万台	3	435	1033	2058	3936	8283	9033	9899
发电量	亿千瓦时	3006	4107	6212	10070	13556	24747	34669	37147
成品钢材	万吨	2716	3693	5153	8980	13146	39692	58488	69626
水泥	亿吨	0.80	1.46	2.10	4.76	5.97	10.64	14.00	16.50
五、运输邮电									
货运量	亿吨	54.65	74.58	97.06	123.48	135.81	183.70	249.00	274.43
货物周转量	亿吨公里	12026	18365	26207	35730	44452	78330	105513	119189
客运量	亿人	34.18	62.02	77.27	117.26	147.86	184.20	239.70	297.74
旅客周转量	亿人公里	2281	4437	5628	9002	12261	17473	23372	24765
邮电业务总量	亿元	13	30	82	989	4793	12199	23841	27313
年末固定电话用户	万户		312	685	4071	14483	35043	34081	31369
年末移动电话用户	万户			1.8	363	8453	39343	64123	74738

注：1. 城镇从业人员1998年起为城镇在岗职工人数。
2. 邮电业务总量1999年及以前年份按1990不变价计算，2000年起按2000年不变价计算。

17-1 续表

指　　标	单　位	1980年	1985年	1990年	1995年	2000年	2005年	2008年	2009年
六、固定资产投资									
全社会固定资产投资总额	亿元	911	2543	4517	20019	32918	88604	172291	224846
#房地产开发	亿元			253	3149	4984	15759	30580	36232
七、商业									
社会消费品零售总额	亿元	2140	4305	8300	20620	34153	67177	108488	125343
八、物价总指数									
商品零售价格指数	上年=100	106.0	108.8	102.1	114.8	98.5	100.8	105.9	98.8
居民消费价格指数	上年=100		109.3	103.1	117.1	100.4	101.8	105.9	99.3
九、外贸外经									
海关进出口总额	亿美元	381	696	1154	2809	4743	14221	25616	22072
进口额	亿美元	200	423	533	1321	2251	6601	11331	10056
出口额	亿美元	181	273	621	1488	2492	7620	14285	12017
实际利用外资	亿美元		20	38	378	494	603	924	900
十、财政、金融									
财政收入	亿元	1160	2005	2937	6242	13395	31649	61317	68477
财政支出	亿元	1229	2004	3084	6824	15887	33930	62427	76300
各项人民币存款余额	亿元				53882	123804	287163	466203	597740
各项人民币贷款余额	亿元				50544	99371	194690	303468	399684
十一、人民生活									
在岗职工人均工资	元	762	1148	2140	5500	9371	18405	29229	32736
城市居民人均可支配收入	元	478	739	1510	4283	6280	10493	15781	17175
农民人均纯收入	元	191	398	686	1578	2253	3255	4761	5153
城乡居民人民币储蓄存款余额	亿元	400	1623	7120	29662	64332	141051	217885	264761
十二、教育									
在校学生数									
普通高等学校	万人	114	170	206	291	556	1562	2021	2145
普通中学	万人	5508	4706	4586	5371	7369	8624	8051	7875
小学	万人	14627	13370	12241	13195	13013	10864	10332	10072
十三、卫生									
医院床位数	万张	198	223	262	284	295	307	369	396
卫生技术人员	万人	280	341	390	426	449	446	492	522
#医生	万人	115	141	176	192	208	194	205	216

注：实际利用外资不含对外借款，2005年起为实际使用外商直接投资口径。

17-2 主要年份广东省国民经济与社会发展指标

Main Indicators of National Economic and Social Development of Guangdong Province

指　　标	单　位	1980年	1985年	1990年	1995年	2000年	2005年	2008年	2009年
一、人口与劳动力									
年末户籍人口	万人	5228	5656	6246	6789	7499	7900	8267	8366
年末从业人员人数	万人	2368	2731	3118	3551	3989	5023	5554	5652
#城镇从业人员	万人	564	661	785	912	759	904	1008	1055
二、经济总量									
生产总值	亿元	250	577	1559	5933	10741	22367	36797	39483
第一产业增加值	亿元	83	172	385	864	986	1428	1973	2010
第二产业增加值	亿元	103	230	616	2900	5000	11440	18502	19420
第三产业增加值	亿元	64	176	559	2168	4755	9598	16321	18053
人均生产总值	元	481	1026	2484	8129	12736	24438	38748	41166
三、农业									
农林牧渔业总产值	亿元	126	245	601	1445	1701	2448	3293	3338
主要农产品产量									
粮食	万吨	1682	1604	1896	1803	1822	1395	1243	1315
水果	万吨	29	116	329	415	644	832	983	1062
肉类	万吨	63	128	202	305	324	384	261	427
水产品	万吨	63	109	208	354	593	695	680	703
四、工业									
工业总产值	亿元	249	535	1902	8850	16904	41662	74415	75887
主要工业产品产量									
机制纸及纸板	万吨	31	53	104	288	260	691	1154	1316
彩电	万台	1	79	262	764	1532	4090	4086	4093
发电量	亿千瓦时	109	167	344	821	1293	2163	2663	2666
成品钢材	万吨	45	79	134	247	406	1366	2040	2286
水泥	万吨	387	1120	2071	5318	5872	8032	9484	10029
五、运输邮电									
货运量	万吨	14201	58726	85809	111063	119216	134101	176279	179722
货物周转量	亿吨公里	1413	1608	2214	4643	3065	3919	4520	4943
客运量	万人	21444	49848	78046	130998	164791	161357	238375	428705
旅客周转量	亿人公里	114	270	453	936	1219	2043	2845	2853
邮电业务总量	亿元	2	4	26	205	602	2177	3565	3938
年末程控电话用户	万户		24	113	591	1415	3443	3573	3367
年末移动电话用户	万户			1	99	1357	6407	8395	8939
六、固定资产投资									
全社会固定资产投资总额	亿元	38	185	381	2327	3234	7164	11165	13353
#基本建设投资	亿元	22	94	175	906	1164	3661	5232	
更新改造投资	亿元	4	32	59	256	435	967	1397	
房地产开发	亿元			33	564	859	1592	2932	2961

注：邮电业务总量1999年及以前年份按1990不变价计算，2000年起按2000年不变价计算。

17-2 续表

指标	单位	1980年	1985年	1990年	1995年	2000年	2005年	2008年	2009年
#国有经济投资	亿元	25	131	272	1123	1287	2062	2755	4199
集体经济投资	亿元	2	24	54	364	449	397	552	696
私营个体经济投资	亿元	11	29	55	250	424	1403	2575	2700
房屋建筑施工面积	万平方米			9164	21365	23521	38352	44752	49419
房屋建筑竣工面积	万平方米			6821	10689	13493	17054	18056	18737
七、商业									
社会消费品零售总额	亿元	118	289	667	2478	4380	7883	12772	14892
八、物价总指数									
商品零售价格指数	上年=100	108.5	113.6	95.6	111.6	99.9	101.8	106.0	96.8
居民消费价格指数	上年=100		114.8	97.5	114.0	101.4	102.3	105.6	97.7
九、外贸外经									
海关进出口总额	亿美元	26	54	419	1040	1701	4280	6835	6111
进口额	亿美元	4	24	197	474	782	1898	3793	2522
出口额	亿美元	22	30	222	566	919	2382	4042	3590
实际利用外资总额	亿美元	2	9	20	121	146	152	213	203
十、财政、金融									
地方财政一般预算收入	亿元	38	69	131	382	911	1807	3310	3650
地方财政一般预算支出	亿元	27	67	151	526	1070	2289	3779	4334
各项人民币存款余额	亿元				7090	16908	35784	53591	66766
各项人民币贷款余额	亿元				5496	11717	20745	30273	38893
十一、人民生活									
在岗职工人均工资	元	789	1393	2929	8250	13823	23959	33110	35965
城市居民人均可支配收入	元	473	954	2303	7439	9762	14770	19733	21575
农民人均纯收入	元	274	495	1043	2699	3654	4690	6400	6907
城乡居民人民币储蓄存款余额	亿元	30	155	752	3885	8667	19051	27418	32136
十二、教育									
在校学生数									
#普通高等学校	万人	4	7	10	15	30	87	122	133
中等职业教育学校	万人	6	18	45	67	66	71	100	120
普通中学	万人	252	236	234	339	461	612	680	696
小学	万人	749	671	747	883	930	1067	956	888
十三、卫生									
医院床位数	万张	8	10	11	14	16	19	23	25
卫生技术人员	万人	14	18	19	23	27	30	38	41
#医生	万人	6	7	8	10	11	12	14	16

注：海关进出口总额1985年及以前年份为外贸部门统计数字。

17-3 主要经济指标东莞占全国、全省的比重（2009年）

Proportion of Main Economic Indicators of Dongguan to China and Guangdong Province (2009)

指　　标	单 位	绝 对 值			东莞占全国的比重(%)	东莞占全省的比重(%)
		全 国	全 省	东 莞		
一、人口						
年末户籍人口	万 人	133474	8366	178.73	0.13	2.14
二、经济总量						
生产总值	亿 元	335353	39483	3763.91	1.12	9.53
第一产业增加值	亿 元	35477	2010	14.79	0.04	0.74
第二产业增加值	亿 元	156958	19420	1823.08	1.16	9.39
第三产业增加值	亿 元	142918	18053	1926.04	1.35	10.67
三、工业						
规模以上工业总产值	亿 元			6071.11		
主要工业产品产量						
发电量	亿千瓦时	37147	2666	337.00	0.91	12.64
机制纸及纸板	万 吨	9389	1316	866.67		65.88
彩　电	万 台	9899	4093	514.00	5.19	12.56
四、农业						
农林牧渔业总产值	亿 元		3338	25.31		0.76
主要农产品产量						
粮　食	万 吨	53082	1315	1.19		0.09
水　果	万 吨		1062	9.15		0.86
肉　类	万 吨	7642	427	2.55	0.03	0.60
水产品	万 吨	5120	703	7.33	0.14	1.04
五、固定资产投资额						
全社会固定资产投资额	亿 元	224846	13353	1094.08	0.49	8.19
六、运输邮电						
货物周转量	亿吨公里	119189	4943	101.65	0.09	2.06
旅客周转量	亿人公里	24765	2853	105.35	0.43	3.69
年末固定电话用户	万 户	31369	3367	272.03	0.87	8.08
年末移动电话用户	万 户	74738	8939	1409.29	1.89	15.77
七、财政、金融						
地方财政收入	亿 元	68477	3650	231.16	0.34	6.33
财政支出	亿 元	76300	4334	225.94	0.30	5.21
各项人民币存款余额	亿 元	597740	66766	4986.61	0.83	7.47
各项人民币贷款余额	亿 元	399684	38893	2903.80	0.73	7.47
八、外经外贸						
进出口总额	亿美元	22072	6111	941.55	4.27	15.41
进口总额	亿美元	10056	2522	389.86	3.88	15.46
出口总额	亿美元	12017	3590	551.68	4.59	15.37
实际利用外商直接外资	亿美元	900	203	25.94	2.88	12.78
九、商业、物价						
社会消费品零售总额	亿 元	125343	14892	956.25	0.76	6.42
商品零售价格指数	上年=100	98.8	96.8	95.3		
居民消费价格指数	上年=100	99.3	97.7	96.9		
十、人 民 生 活						
在岗职工人均工资	元	32736	35965	42585		
城市居民人均可支配收入	元	17175	21575	33045		
农村人均纯收入	元	5153	6907	13064		
城乡居民人民币储蓄存款余额	亿 元	264761	32136	2904.57	1.10	9.04

17-4 主要经济指标东莞占全国、全省的比重（2008年）

Proportion of Main Economic Indicators of Dongguan to China and Guangdong Province (2008)

指　　标	单 位	绝对值			东莞占全国的比重(%)	东莞占全省的比重(%)
		全 国	全 省	东 莞		
一、人口						
年末户籍人口	万 人	132802	8267	175	0.13	2.12
二、经济总量						
生产总值	亿 元	300670	36797	3702.53	1.23	10.10
第一产业增加值	亿 元	34000	1973	12.30	0.04	0.62
第二产业增加值	亿 元	146183	18502	1954.17	1.34	10.56
第三产业增加值	亿 元	120487	16321	1736.06	1.44	10.64
三、工业						
规模以上工业总产值	亿 元		74415	6372.28		
主要工业产品产量						
发电量	亿千瓦时	34669	2663	361	1.04	13.55
机制纸及纸板	万 吨		1154	715		61.94
彩　电	万 台	9033	4086	480	5.31	11.75
四、农业						
农林牧渔业总产值	亿 元		3293	25.53		0.78
主要农产品产量						
粮　食	万 吨	52850	1243	1.20		0.10
水　果	万 吨		983	10.15		1.03
肉　类	万 吨	7269	261	2.41	0.03	0.92
水产品	万 吨	4895	680	7.23	0.15	1.06
五、固定资产投资额						
全社会固定资产投资额	亿 元	172291	11165	943	0.55	8.45
六、运输邮电						
货物周转量	亿吨公里	105513	4520	37.44	0.04	0.83
旅客周转量	亿人公里	23372	2845	137.86	0.59	4.85
年末固定电话用户	万 户	34081	3573	444.23	1.30	12.43
年末移动电话用户	万 户	64123	8395	1454.29	2.27	17.32
七、财政、金融						
地方财政收入	亿 元	61317	3310	209.22	0.34	6.32
财政支出	亿 元	62427	3779	218.26	0.35	5.78
各项人民币存款余额	亿 元	466203	53591	4354.53	0.93	8.13
各项人民币贷款余额	亿 元	303468	30273	2380.36	0.78	7.86
八、外经外贸						
进出口总额	亿美元	25616	6835	1132.99	4.42	16.58
进口总额	亿美元	11331	3793	477.62	4.22	12.59
出口总额	亿美元	14285	4042	655.37	4.59	16.22
实际利用外商直接外资	亿美元	924	213	24	2.65	11.49
九、商业、物价						
社会消费品零售总额	亿 元	108488	12772	838	0.77	6.56
商品零售价格指数	上年=100	105.9	106.0	107.9		
居民消费价格指数	上年=100	105.9	105.6	105.5		
十、人民生活						
在岗职工人均工资	元		33110	39516		
城市居民人均可支配收入	元	15781	19733	30275		
农村人均纯收入	元	4761	6400	12328		
城乡居民人民币储蓄存款余额	亿 元	217885	27418	2638	1.21	9.62

17-5 主要经济指标人均水平东莞与全国、全省的比较(2009年)

Comparison of Per Capita Level of Main Economic Indicators between Dongguan and China, Guangdong Province (2009)

指 标	单 位	人 均 水 平			东莞相当于全国(%)	东莞相当于全省(%)
		全 国	全 省	东 莞		
生产总值	元	24673	41166	56601	229.4	137.5
财政收入	元	5143	3805	3476	67.6	91.4
出口总额(海关口径)	美元	903	3743	8296	919.1	221.6
各项人民币存款余额	元	44896	69613	78529	174.9	112.8
居民储蓄存款余额	元	19886	33343	45741	230.0	137.2
固定资产投资额	元	16888	13923	16453	97.4	118.2
社会消费品零售总额	元	9415	15527	14422	153.2	92.9
实际利用外资	美元	68	212	390	577.1	184.0
在岗职工人均工资	元	32736	35965	42585	130.1	118.4
城市居民可支配收入	元	17175	21575	33045	192.4	153.2
农民人均纯收入	元	5153	6907	13064	253.5	189.1
粮食产量	公斤	399	137	2	0.4	1.3
水产品产量	公斤	38	73	11	28.7	15.0
水果产量	公斤		111	14		12.6
工业发电量	千瓦时	2790	2780	5068	181.6	182.3
医院卫生院床位数	张/千人	2.97	2.61	2.72	91.4	104.2
卫生技术人员数	人/千人	3.92	4.31	5.38	137.2	124.8

注：本表人均指标时点数按常住人口计算，时期数按平均常住人口计算。

17-6 主要经济指标人均水平东莞与全国、全省的比较(2008年)

Comparison of Per Capita Level of Main Economic Indicators between Dongguan and China, Guangdong Province (2008)

指 标	单 位	人 均 水 平			东莞相当于全国(%)	东莞相当于全省(%)
		全 国	全 省	东 莞		
生产总值	元	22698	38748	53285	234.8	141.8
财政收入	元	4629	3485	3011	65.0	86.4
出口总额(海关口径)	美元	1078	4255	9432	874.6	221.7
各项人民币存款余额	元	35194	56152	62657	178.0	111.6
居民储蓄存款余额	元	16448	29582	37959	230.8	128.3
固定资产投资额	元	13006	11774	13591	104.5	115.4
社会消费品零售总额	元	8190	13449	12681	154.8	94.3
实际利用外资	美元	70	259	352	504.9	157.0
在岗职工人均工资	元	29229	33073	39516	136.7	119.5
城市居民可支配收入	元	15781	19733	30275	191.8	153.4
农民人均纯收入	元	4761	6400	12328	258.9	192.6
粮食产量	公斤	399	131	2	0.4	1.3
水产品产量	公斤	37	83	10	28.2	14.5
水果产量	公斤		104	15		14.1
工业发电量	千瓦时	2617	3243	5194	198.4	185.2
医院卫生院床位数	张/千人	2.79	2.80	2.41	86.7	99.7
卫生技术人员数	人/千人	3.71	4.63	4.77	128.3	119.1

注：本表人均指标时点数按常住人口计算，时期数按平均常住人口计算。

17-7 珠江三角洲国民经济和社会发展主要指标（2009年）

指　　标	单 位	广州市	深圳市	珠海市
一、人口、综合				
行政区域土地面积	平方公里	7287	1953	1654
年末常住人口	万人	1033.45	891.23	149.12
年末户籍人口	万人	794.62	245.96	102.65
地区生产总值	亿元	9138.21	8201.32	1038.66
第一产业增加值	亿元	172.28	6.69	28.82
第二产业增加值	亿元	3405.16	3827.08	543.96
#工业增加值	亿元	3117.34	3593.05	506.76
第三产业增加值	亿元	5560.77	4367.55	465.88
人均生产总值(按常住人口计算)	元	89082	92772	69889
二、农村经济				
农业总产值	亿元	295.62	15.48	51.62
粮食总产量	万吨	43.00	0.01	4.12
水果总产量	万吨	42.29	0.39	11.76
水产品总产量	万吨	43.70	3.03	19.09
三、工业				
规模以上工业企业数	个	7023	8413	1386
规模以上工业总产值	亿元	11376.76	15416.24	2405.04
规模以上工业企业主营业务收入	亿元	11214.09	14981.25	2328.11
规模以上工业企业利润总额	亿元	779.12	1087.42	129.27
规模以上工业产品销售率	%	98.6	96.8	92.6
四、固定资产投资				
全社会固定资产投资总额	亿元	2455.65	1709.15	410.51
#基本建设投资额	亿元	1290.26	1043.63	200.16
更新改造投资额	亿元	541.72	166.96	30.79
房地产开发投资额	亿元	703.44	437.46	168.44
商品房屋销售面积	万平方米	1082.75	762.16	289.73
商品房屋销售额	亿元	1127.65	1113.88	214.60
五、交通、邮电				
民用汽车拥有量	万辆	103.30	108.36	13.08
年末固定电话用户数	万户	633.31	469.20	79.60
年末移动电话用户数	万户	1629.10	1879.58	213.70
全年总用电量	亿千瓦时	511.60	585.68	91.72
#工业用电量	亿千瓦时	278.90	323.75	57.45

Main Indicators of National Economic and Social Development of the Pearl River Delta Economic Zone (2009)

佛山市	惠州市	肇庆市	江门市	东莞市	中山市
3849	11356	14822	9541	2465	1800
599.68	397.21	388.83	420.14	635.00	251.74
367.63	324.36	413.69	391.52	178.73	147.86
4820.90	1414.70	862.00	1340.88	3763.91	1566.41
95.77	90.29	165.73	100.75	14.79	45.26
3037.69	776.62	320.65	777.40	1823.08	904.42
2933.15	738.31	283.69	745.07	1741.53	859.61
1687.44	535.45	376.98	459.08	1926.04	616.73
80686	35819	22415	32140	56601	62304
195.03	147.91	256.81	193.09	25.31	77.77
9.75	58.64	110.41	87.12	1.19	7.30
5.76	51.82	95.69	20.99	9.15	19.20
54.91	14.06	31.84	65.39	7.33	32.98
7807	1870	1065	3246	5801	5036
11711.28	3005.14	1179.01	2933.26	6071.11	4057.97
11262.92	2975.25	1136.53	2754.63	6007.76	3677.28
629.90	115.26	62.34	148.13	297.25	195.96
97.0	99.0	97.3	94.8	99.2	95.2
1470.56	564.95	176.43	211.85	1094.08	545.61
441.69	226.53	195.77	262.88	464.07	247.82
305.71		53.78	94.11	212.88	61.41
358.25	149.01	35.58	57.61	277.66	192.37
779.51	564.95	168.98	177.29	604.11	563.53
487.64	207.04	63.79	69.40	353.17	259.41
65.11	16.57	9.63	18.49	79.56	25.99
269.46	152.20	84.85	97.49	378.40	92.15
641.94	336.65	197.81	261.65	1409.29	393.95
416.77	95.97	27.58	74.14	478.19	161.58
313.56	62.34	17.88	50.25	376.10	109.91

17-7 续表

(2009年)

指标	单位	广州市	深圳市	珠海市
六、金融、贸易、财政				
年末金融机构人民币存款余额	亿元	20142.08	16938.19	2105.20
#城乡居民储蓄存款余额	亿元	7745.78	5723.76	828.04
年末金融机构人民币贷款余额	亿元	13474.82	11646.34	1062.44
全社会消费品零售总额	亿元	3430.19	2567.94	404.46
预算内地方财政收入	亿元	655.66	880.82	101.41
预算内地方财政支出	亿元	734.71	1000.84	121.29
七、对外经济				
海关进口总额	亿美元	393.32	1081.75	196.57
海关出口总额	亿美元	374.05	1619.79	177.83
外商直接投资项目	个	843	1498	198
合同利用外资金额	亿美元	37.23	35.58	4.60
实际利用外商直接投资	亿美元	37.73	41.60	11.80
八、人民生活、物价				
在岗职工年平均工资	元	49519	46723	31764
城市居民年人均可支配收入	元	27610	29244	22859
城市居民年人均消费支出	元	22821	21526	17948
农民人均纯收入	元	11667		8552
居民消费价格总指数(以上年为100)	%	97.5	98.7	97.0
九、教育、卫生				
学校数				
高等学校	所	76	8	10
中等职业技术学校	所	93	13	9
普通中学	所	471	285	60
小学	所	1022	346	130
在校学生数				
高等学校	万人	7.96	6.70	10.16
中等职业技术学校	万人	24.70	2.86	2.28
普通中学	万人	57.53	31.60	9.39
小学	万人	82.89	58.95	12.56
医院医疗机构数	个	2341	2486	486
#医院	个	224	107	31
医院床位数	张	50367	20011	4870
医生数	人	32926	21524	4260

注：江门市的医院床位数为卫生机构床位数。

佛山市	惠州市	肇庆市	江门市	东莞市	中山市
7211.14	1317.09	444.52	1090.00	4986.61	2159.59
3945.01	565.93	221.15	667.57	2904.57	1220.95
4101.97	758.73	307.54	535.27	2903.80	1142.53
1408.78	302.78	98.87	241.14	959.07	549.76
254.70	78.64	23.58	49.74	231.16	110.44
266.99	88.57	42.59	62.86	225.94	117.12
137.62	120.92	12.34	30.91	389.86	67.34
245.78	171.49	20.30	79.49	551.68	177.36
162	279	82	178	579	155
10.13	14.04	15.20	11.34	16.16	4.05
18.74	13.95	8.88	10.37	25.94	6.08
34106	25786	26174	24304	42585	36165
24578	21278	15063	19004	33045	23088
19296	17914	11030	14263	24270	17415
10699	7583	6291	7534	13064	12288
98.4	98.5	97.8	98.0	96.9	97.1
3	1	4	3	5	5
49	40	20	17	26	13
178	209	182	221	186	99
429	785	1056	417	337	212
3.70	1.20	4.82	2.17	3.40	3.46
9.68	7.66	5.48	4.47	4.65	2.88
32.31	30.59	32.24	26.97	24.95	14.77
43.42	40.13	39.65	31.66	51.12	23.68
1051	680	605	899	2106	442
57	42	41	33	65	44
12578	6673	9186	11734	17685	8822
11386	5852	4724	6381	12884	4915

17-8 长江三角洲国民经济和社会发展主要指标（2009年）

指　　标	单 位	上海市	南京市	苏州市	无锡市	常州市	镇江市
一、人口、综合							
行政区域土地面积	平方公里	6341	6582	8488	4788	4375	3847
年末常住人口	万人	1921.32	771.31		619.57	445.20	306.90
年末户籍人口	万人	1379.23	629.77	633.29	465.65	359.80	269.90
地区生产总值	亿元	14900.93	4230.26	7740.20	4992.00	2518.70	1672.08
第一产业增加值	亿元	113.82	129.18	142.82	593.92	91.60	75.92
第二产业增加值	亿元	5939.96	1930.67	4547.12	2336.38	1429.70	972.21
第三产业增加值	亿元	8847.15	2170.42	3050.26	2061.70	997.30	623.95
人均生产总值(按常住人口计算)	元		55290	122565	81151	56861	54732
二、农村经济							
农业总产值	亿元	283.13	223.66	213.14	152.70	160.80	113.20
三、工业							
规模以上工业总产值	亿元	23873.08	6756.15	20235.95	10917.83	5978.70	3211.21
规模以上工业企业主营业务收入	亿元		6674.49	19800.00	10595.78	5862.05	3003.40
规模以上工业企业利润总额	亿元	1405.74	318.34	1024.59	693.27	273.90	148.11
四、固定资产投资							
全社会固定资产投资总额	亿元	5273.33	2668.03	2967.35	2387.56	1704.77	1010.57
#房地产开发投资额	亿元	1464.18	595.68	724.34	463.37	306.20	95.47
五、交通、邮电							
民用汽车拥有量	万辆	147.30	67.10	101.57	60.07	35.90	15.70
年末固定电话用户数	万户	935.48	300.10	382.00	234.34		114.80
年末移动电话用户数	万户	2106.32	801.06	1136.00	668.81	424.60	231.00
六、金融、贸易、财政							
年末金融机构本外币存款余额	亿元	44620.27	11088.39	11450.54	7405.68	3854.89	1814.16
#城乡居民储蓄存款余额	亿元	14357.65	3125.00	4004.87	2733.12	1773.74	855.39
年末金融机构本外币贷款余额	亿元	29684.10	9444.48	9032.28	5474.94	2568.93	1348.25
全社会消费品零售总额	亿元	5172.88	1961.58	1846.30	1651.37	901.40	488.50
预算内地方财政收入	亿元	2540.30	434.51	745.18	415.91	215.89	101.57
预算内地方财政支出	亿元	2989.65	461.31	681.04	401.27	217.31	120.74
七、对外经济							
海关进口总额	亿美元	1358.17	152.86	873.61	179.33	42.13	24.96
海关出口总额	亿美元	1419.14	184.59	1140.87	260.12	108.62	35.41
实际利用外商直接投资	亿美元	105.38	23.92	82.27	32.03	22.61	14.41
八、人民生活、物价							
城市居民年人均可支配收入	元	28838	25504	26320	25027	23751	20949
城市居民年人均消费支出	元	20992	16339	16402	15619	15961	13031
农民人均纯收入	元		9858	12987	12403	11198	9642
居民消费价格总指数(以上年为100)	%	99.6	100.1	99.8	99.5	99.5	99.6

注：1. 杭州民用汽车拥有量为机动车拥有量。

Main Indicators of National Economic and Social Development of the Yangtze River Delta Economic Zone(2009)

南通市	扬州市	泰州市	杭州市	宁波市	嘉兴市	湖州市	绍兴市	舟山市	台州市
8001	6634	5793	16596	9817	3915	5818	8256	1440	9411
		466.61	810						
762.66	458.80	503.98	683.38	571.00	339.60	259.17	437.34		578.47
2872.80	1856.39	1651.02	5098.66	4214.60	1917.96	1111.50	2375.46	533.26	2025.47
236.46	144.88	133.70	190.25	183.80	107.01	89.74	124.45	51.41	131.91
1607.50	1042.03	936.56	2434.89	2247.80	1111.74	617.76	1379.50	248.25	1069.01
1028.80	669.48	580.76	2473.52	1783.00	699.21	404.00	871.51	233.60	854.55
40231	41406	35498	63471	73998	44896	39206	54309	55106	35148
420.80	256.42	223.36	288.84	268.40	182.97	153.09	190.06		227.40
6042.35	4460.20	3723.74	9367.79	8152.45	3876.39	2186.86	5460.58	796.17	2968.17
5897.37	4240.30	3569.33	9015.91	7704.18	3595.18	2071.13	5349.52		
391.71	186.50	244.25	495.99	452.73	195.82	100.27	288.94	27.07	118.82
1802.38	1063.90	1166.20	2291.65	2004.22	1233.34	637.84	1055.03	400.66	834.10
200.79	129.50	123.88	704.68	374.51	187.18	110.47	210.46	48.99	152.27
25.82		17.42	157.89			16.77	78.24	4.68	45.48
273.04			390.64		170.21	112.52	226.28	56.82	189.95
510.16	331.91	300.64	1028.93		424.67	245.50	378.52	107.96	567.19
4006.23	2101.21	1916.30	14284.21	8241.40	2904.21	1397.69	4139.54	943.93	2935.61
2285.89	1103.88	1001.90	4286.92	2901.76	1385.62	688.33	1707.01	356.36	1449.72
2431.98	1236.17	1204.99	13113.30	7715.90	2278.65	1150.71	3296.95	854.02	2518.06
1086.11	618.97	469.89	1804.93	1434.40	694.30	442.57	717.90	181.69	817.88
198.99	128.08	138.62	520.79	432.77	141.70	80.01	160.43	48.78	136.02
236.12	151.48	168.86	490.40	506.10		108.51	169.54	82.74	175.95
50.79	14.20	16.04	132.37	221.62	48.64	7.57	47.29	32.84	19.65
111.80	40.13	42.15	271.80	386.51	123.41	40.76	157.61	37.39	100.67
20.05	15.19	10.56	40.14	21.96	13.35	8.11	8.11	1.06	1.88
19469	19416	18079	26864	27368	24693	23280	26874	24082	24429
13103	12888	12163	18595	18203	15361	14561	16607		
8696	8295	8180	11822	12641	12685	11745	12026	12561	10006
98.7	99.9	99.7	98.6	99.4	101.6	99.2	99.2	99.2	103.6

2. 苏州、绍兴、舟山、台州人均生产总值按户籍人口计算。

第三部分　基本单位情况

Part Three　Basic Units

1-1 按行业分的法人单位、产业活动单位数（2009年）

Number of Corporate Units and Industrial Establishments by Sector (2009)

项　　目	法　人单位数（个）	单产业法人单位	多产业法人单位	产业活动单位数（个）	多产业法人单位的产业活动单位数
合　计	**65477**	**63829**	**1648**	**76421**	**10944**
采矿业	**11**	**11**		**11**	
煤炭开采和洗选业	1	1		1	
石油和天然气开采业	2	2		2	
黑色金属矿采选业	1	1		1	
有色金属矿采选业	1	1		1	
非金属矿采选业	5	5		5	
其他采矿业	1	1		1	
制造业	**30869**	**30685**	**184**	**31131**	**262**
农副食品加工业	171	166	5	184	13
食品制造业	243	235	8	252	9
饮料制造业	64	60	4	68	4
烟草制品业					
纺织业	1497	1486	11	1516	19
纺织服装、鞋、帽制造业	1680	1664	16	1704	24
皮革、毛皮、羽毛(绒)及其制品业	1290	1287	3	1297	7
木材加工及木、竹、藤、棕、草制品业	278	276	2	283	5
家具制造业	980	975	5	991	11
造纸及纸制品业	1615	1609	6	1619	4
印刷业和记录媒介的复制	1118	1115	3	1120	2
文教体育用品制造业	1025	1019	6	1032	7
石油加工、炼焦及核燃料加工业	29	28	1	31	2
化学原料及化学制品制造业	778	769	9	790	12
医药制造业	40	39	1	41	1
化学纤维制造业	50	50		50	
橡胶制品业	657	655	2	659	2
塑料制品业	3745	3738	7	3759	14
非金属矿物制品业	553	551	2	557	4
黑色金属冶炼及压延加工业	128	126	2	128	
有色金属冶炼及压延加工业	257	254	3	259	2
金属制品业	3414	3406	8	3429	15
通用设备制造业	1484	1472	12	1494	10
专用设备制造业	2094	2084	10	2105	11

1-1 续表 1

(2009年)

项　　目	法人单位数（个）	单产业法人单位	多产业法人单位	产业活动单位数（个）	多产业法人单位的产业活动单位数
交通运输设备制造业	237	234	3	247	10
电气机械及器材制造业	2314	2298	16	2338	24
通信设备、计算机及其他电子设备制造业	3538	3509	29	3576	38
仪器仪表及文化、办公用机械制造业	477	472	5	485	8
工艺品及其他制造业	1092	1088	4	1094	2
废弃资源和废旧材料回收加工业	21	20	1	23	2
电力、燃气及水的生产和供应业	**131**	**127**	**4**	**159**	**28**
电力、热力的生产和供应业	25	25		27	2
燃气生产和供应业	24	24		26	2
水的生产和供应业	82	78	4	106	24
建 筑 业	**2085**	**2067**	**18**	**2312**	**227**
房屋和土木工程建筑业	348	347	1	461	113
建筑安装业	580	573	7	636	56
建筑装饰业	884	876	8	921	37
其他建筑业	273	271	2	294	21
交通运输、仓储和邮政业	**1080**	**1039**	**41**	**1683**	**603**
铁路运输业	3	3		3	
道路运输业	359	339	20	513	154
城市公共交通业	73	72	1	76	3
水上运输业	46	45	1	49	3
航空运输业	7	7		10	3
管道运输业	1	1		1	
装卸搬运及其他运输服务业	413	402	11	520	107
仓储业	98	96	2	101	3
邮政业	80	74	6	410	330
信息传输、计算机服务和软件业	**1282**	**1262**	**20**	**1558**	**276**
电信和其他信息传输服务业	261	252	9	475	214
计算机服务业	794	787	7	838	44
软件业	227	223	4	245	18
批发和零售业	**12855**	**12598**	**257**	**15959**	**3104**
批发业	6197	6109	88	7065	868
零售业	6658	6489	169	8894	2236
住宿和餐饮业	**987**	**873**	**114**	**1674**	**687**
住宿业	521	432	89	646	125
餐饮业	466	441	25	1028	562
金 融 业	**187**	**142**	**45**	**1739**	**1552**
银行业	24	13	11	1151	1127
证券业	8	6	2	43	35
保险业	60	31	29	374	314

1-1 续表 2

(2009年)

项目	法人单位数（个）	单产业法人单位	多产业法人单位	产业活动单位数（个）	多产业法人单位的产业活动单位数
其他金融活动	95	92	3	171	76
房地产业	**2190**	**2117**	**73**	**2519**	**329**
房地产业	2190	2117	73	2519	329
租赁和商务服务业	**7358**	**7230**	**128**	**8533**	**1175**
租赁业	67	67		69	2
商务服务业	7291	7163	128	8464	1173
科学研究、技术服务和地质勘查业	**759**	**754**	**5**	**813**	**54**
研究与试验发展	158	157	1	162	4
专业技术服务业	478	474	4	524	46
科技交流和推广服务业	117	117		120	3
地质勘查业	6	6		7	1
水利、环境和公共设施管理业	**304**	**298**	**6**	**346**	**42**
水利管理业	54	54		58	4
环境管理业	82	79	3	106	24
公共设施管理业	168	165	3	182	14
居民服务和其他服务业	**1478**	**1454**	**24**	**1700**	**222**
居民服务业	534	525	9	669	135
其他服务业	944	929	15	1031	87
教　育	**1475**	**1441**	**34**	**1850**	**375**
教育	1475	1441	34	1850	375
卫生、社会保障和社会福利业	**498**	**443**	**55**	**912**	**414**
卫生	454	400	54	864	410
社会保障业	3	3		3	
社会福利业	41	40	1	45	4
文化、体育和娱乐业	**310**	**302**	**8**	**383**	**73**
新闻出版业	13	13		14	1
广播、电视、电影和音像业	51	51		53	2
文化艺术业	82	81	1	85	3
体育	32	32		33	1
娱乐业	132	125	7	198	66
公共管理与社会组织	**1618**	**986**	**632**	**3139**	**1521**
中国共产党机关	54	54		56	2
国家机构	573	524	49	1344	771
人民政协和民主党派	11	11		11	
群众团体、社会团体和宗教组织	349	341	8	466	117
基层群众自治组织	631	56	575	1262	631
国际组织					
国际组织					

1-2 按注册类型分的法人单位、产业活动单位数（2009年）

Number of Corporate Units and Industrial Establishments by Registration Status(2009)

项目	法人单位数（个）	单产业法人单位	多产业法人单位	产业活动单位数（个）	多产业法人单位的产业活动单位数
合计	**65477**	**63829**	**1648**	**76421**	**10944**
内资企业	**54338**	**52807**	**1531**	**64520**	**10182**
国有	1435	1327	108	3123	1688
集体	2174	2075	99	2990	816
股份合作	149	143	6	697	548
国有联营	9	9		9	
集体联营	45	44	1	52	7
国有与集体联营	16	15	1	52	36
其他联营	34	32	2	44	10
国有独资公司	34	34		40	6
其他有限责任公司	12477	12222	255	14589	2112
股份有限公司	642	597	45	1699	1057
私营独资	8424	8370	54	8652	228
私营合伙	2116	2103	13	2163	47
私营有限责任公司	19483	19178	305	20982	1499
私营股份有限公司	799	785	14	850	51
其他内资	6501	5873	628	8578	2077
港澳台投资企业	**8083**	**8018**	**65**	**8489**	**406**
与港澳台商合资经营	396	387	9	483	87
与港澳台商合作经营	419	415	4	445	26
港澳台商独资	7043	6992	51	7329	286
港澳台商投资股份有限公司	225	224	1	232	7
外商投资企业	**3056**	**3004**	**52**	**3412**	**356**
中外合资经营	249	234	15	338	89
中外合作经营	122	119	3	149	27
外资企业	2570	2537	33	2801	231
外商投资股份有限公司	115	114	1	124	9

1-3 按地域分的法人单位、产业活动单位数（2009年）

Number of Corporate Units and Industrial Establishments by District (2009)

项目	法人单位数（个）	单产业法人单位	多产业法人单位	产业活动单位数（个）	多产业法人单位的产业活动单位数
全市	**65477**	**63829**	**1648**	**76421**	**10944**
东城街道	4335	4214	121	5105	770
南城街道	3948	3819	129	4584	636
万江街道	2204	2145	59	2530	326
莞城街道	3029	2889	140	3618	589
石碣镇	1836	1786	50	2161	325
石龙镇	845	801	44	1155	310
茶山镇	1536	1505	31	1775	239
石排镇	1429	1396	33	1658	229
企石镇	1035	1003	32	1215	180
横沥镇	1386	1358	28	1628	242
桥头镇	1397	1368	29	1672	275
谢岗镇	900	882	18	1038	138
东坑镇	744	711	33	961	217
常平镇	2857	2774	83	3450	593
寮步镇	2831	2760	71	3165	334
樟木头镇	1624	1580	44	1986	362
大朗镇	2980	2925	55	3458	478
黄江镇	1448	1418	30	1671	223
清溪镇	1942	1875	67	2223	281
塘厦镇	3467	3425	42	3821	354
凤岗镇	2103	2074	29	2340	237
大岭山镇	2056	2017	39	2320	264
长安镇	5651	5566	85	6379	728
虎门镇	4735	4656	79	5472	737
厚街镇	2443	2392	51	2970	527
沙田镇	1367	1331	36	1585	218
道滘镇	986	957	29	1173	187
洪梅镇	393	372	21	503	110
麻涌镇	779	751	28	964	185
望牛墩镇	671	646	25	799	128
中堂镇	1293	1257	36	1560	267
高埗镇	892	853	39	1090	198
松山湖	299	290	9	350	51
虎门港	36	33	3	39	3
东莞生态园				3	3

1-4 营业收入超5000万元的内资企业（2009年）

Domestic-funded Enterprises with Business Revenue over RMB 50 Million (2009)

单位名称	负责人	联系电话	主要产品(或服务)
农副食品业			
东莞中纺粮油工业有限公司	张德友	88235183	豆油
东莞市华南油脂工业有限公司	苗秀清	88235666	棕榈油
东莞市永益食品有限公司	王侃群	85811111	食用油
东莞市樟木头食品有限公司	吴育光	87718596	牲猪
东莞市富之源饲料蛋白开发有限公司	李福官	88436096	豆粕
东莞市湘大骆驼饲料有限公司	陶一山	23175022	饲料
东莞市东美食品有限公司	罗明昌	88872108	淀粉
东莞市海大饲料有限公司	徐传万	88237100	畜禽饲料
东莞市太粮米业有限公司	王秩西	87703313	大米
东莞市虎门日隆食品厂	单志超	85564450	豆制品糕点
东莞市沙田顺发畜禽实业有限公司	许爱顺	88686610	饲料
东莞市制糖厂有限公司	李锦生		制糖
东莞市康达尔饲料有限公司	谢永东	22236928	零售饲料
东莞市穗丰食品有限公司	陈茂玲	88224098	小麦粉
东莞市中储粮粮油有限公司	刘建民	88236688	豆油
食品制造业			
内蒙古伊利实业集团股份有限公司东莞分公司	靳志刚	88835173	冰淇淋
内蒙古伊利实业集团股份有限公司东莞茶山分公司	靳志刚		冷冻食品
广东丹宝利酵母有限公司	肖可见	88812123	高活性干酵母
东莞市百味佳食品有限公司	钟焕新	83285888	鸡精
东莞市金娃食品工业有限公司	谢立平	87636739	果冻
广东一品鲜生物科技有限公司	陈尧燊	22613911	酵母抽提物
东莞市金富士食品有限公司	曾浩贤	22621998	饼干
东莞市广利饲料有限公司	袁建康	83352060	混合饲料
东莞市华美食品有限公司	袁旭培	86643036	饼干
东莞日之泉蒸馏水有限公司	林志伟	88815015	蒸馏水
东莞爱维蒸馏水有限公司	何　祥	85519666	蒸馏水
东莞市福地纯水有限公司	安　海	22404191	饮用水
纺织业			
东莞市宝丰服装实业有限公司	尹耀林	83216003	毛织品
东莞市科纺纺织有限公司	张　熠	88115588	牛仔布
东莞市信远无纺布有限公司	谢铁冬	88951008	无纺布
东莞市盈邦针织有限公司	陈瑞娟	83482998	针织服装
东莞市兴锋毛纺织有限公司	李德锋	83317439	毛针织服装
东莞市精英针织有限公司	夏崇光	86262888	毛针织品
东莞市圣旗路时装有限公司	陈观福	89851115	针织品
东莞市民生纺织有限公司	黄伟强	88188870	气流纺纱
东莞市建盛针织有限公司	叶浩海	83110188	针织服装
东莞市拓展实业有限公司	刘宇星	86485888	化学纤维
东莞市入世丰针织有限公司	李浩强	88905668	针织衫
东莞市英伟实业有限公司	关　伟	83102266	针织服装
东莞市兴业针织有限公司	陈锡培	83311479	针织服装
东莞市颖祺实业有限公司	陈伟波	83180838	针织服装
东莞市众圣针织有限公司	钟秋明	83111739	毛衫

1-4 续表 1

(2009年)

单位名称	负责人	联系电话	主要产品(或服务)
东莞市环宇织造有限公司	吴小溪	83112688	毛织服装
东莞市广昌隆毛织时装有限公司	周飞洪	83197153	毛织服装
东莞市凯纳德针织服饰有限公司	薛文秀	83110775	毛衣
东莞市金凌印刷有限公司	陈培忠	87881585	丝印染精
东莞市辉骏针织时装有限公司	陈巧娥	83183029	针织时装
东莞市众达针织制衣有限公司	钟达光	83109181	毛衫
东莞市颖和祺服饰有限公司	曾祥谦	81125303	毛衣
东莞市和辉针织有限公司	李少芬	83133988	针织品
东莞市瑞锋服饰有限公司	陈　俊	86260003	针织毛衣
东莞市东林制衣有限公司	翟向东	83238080	毛织品
东莞市大朗民源生毛织制衣有限公司	黄旭忠	83186260	针织服装
东莞市稳丰纺织有限公司	卢楚东		纺织品
东莞市富士达针织有限公司	陈锐球	83319826	毛衫
东莞市大朗和利达针织制衣厂	李书和	83133988	针织毛衫
纺织服装、鞋、帽制造业			
东莞市中玲制衣有限公司	钟凤群	22175828	纺织品服装
东莞市永豪制衣实业有限公司	陈灼豪	83327589	针织服装
东莞市东城嘉文制衣厂	张耀祥	22267333	梳织服装
东莞市由美制衣有限公司	黄浩泉	88562339	服装
东莞市斌斌时装有限公司	张耀先	88923858	服装
东莞市源源制衣有限公司	佟永叶	88126801	裤
东莞市原野服装有限公司	陈楚荣	85226693	纺织服装
东莞市中堂稳发制衣厂	袁志稳	88881891	棉制梳织服装
东莞市鸿锦服饰有限公司	张钦宋	86091828	制衣
东莞市搜于特服装股份有限公司	马　鸿	88320269	设计服装
东莞市时艺时装制衣有限公司	王穗生	85260068	针梳织服装
东莞市圣隆制衣有限公司	王锦灵	81638100	牛仔服装
东莞市新虎威实业有限公司	叶兰芳	85198313	鞋及鞋材
东莞市百思特服饰有限公司	陈玉玲	85709002	服装
东莞市卓越实业有限公司	胡镇泰	86550111	针织服装
广东金盾服装公司	刘海平	22404168	警察服装
东莞市鸿越服装有限公司	叶桂强	89036522	纺织服装
东莞市成功针织制衣厂	尹灿耀	22265157	纺织服装
东莞市极奇制衣有限公司	杜照荣	86664648	衣服
东莞市松鹰实业有限公司	王国宾	85561999	棉织服装
东莞市盛丰制衣有限公司	张少媚		服装
东莞市惠琪针织有限公司	简玉光	88909698	毛衣制品
东莞市尚景服装有限公司	邓晓东		纺织服装
东莞市凫山新兴发针织有限公司	尹雪祖	83321465	毛衫
东莞市业联制衣有限公司	宁　塄	81069908	牛仔服装
东莞市以纯集团有限公司	郭东林	85520146	纺织服装
皮革、毛皮、羽毛(绒)及其制品业			
东莞市新虎威鞋厂	叶兰芳	85198313	皮鞋
东莞黄江宝泰鞋材厂	曾锦昌	83363017	鞋材制品
东莞市琪胜鞋业有限公司	尹积琪	88632999	皮鞋

1-4　续表 2

(2009年)

单位名称	负责人	联系电话	主要产品(或服务)
东莞市江顺箱包袋配件有限公司	江汉辉	87912965	箱包袋配件
东莞市中盛针织实业有限公司	潘梅香	83716818	毛衫
东莞市龙运鞋业有限公司	李柏臣	85933911	鞋类制品
东莞黄江裕成制鞋厂	曾锦昌	83363017	运动鞋
东莞长安霄边兴鹏鞋厂	蔡文斌	85531541	男女装皮鞋
东莞长安乌沙宝业皮具厂	戴永全	85417333	皮制品
东莞市振国皮革制品有限公司	江　川	85825356	皮革制品
东莞市莎米特箱包有限公司	许文宝	87712545	旅行包袋
木材及木、竹、藤、棕、草制品业			
东莞市黄江华业卡板厂	钟　鸣	83629886	卡板
东莞市德曼木业有限公司	付少东	81037666	木门
东莞市凯旋木器制品有限公司	黄朝兵	81300168	胶合卡板
东莞市南兴木工机械有限公司	林旺南	89982033	木工机械木工刀具
东莞市森宝康木业有限公司	陈旭文	88439626	中密度竹斑板
家具制造业			
东莞市慕思寝室用品有限公司	詹善平	85058288	沙发
东莞市兆生家具实业有限公司	陈少生	85921466	家具
东莞市远大家具有限公司	朱佛章	85617870	木制家具
东莞英记夹万家私厂有限公司	侯伟富	89160200	沙发
东莞市元宗家具有限公司	任作辉	85610588	家具
东莞市星港家具有限公司	何建良	22901327	家具
东莞市美迪家具有限公司	黄孔伦	88843128	木质家具
东莞市荣圣家具有限公司	何　梅	87842272	办公椅
东莞市东品家具有限公司	何　梅	87842343	软体家私
东莞市明晟家具有限公司	郭淦波	22653163	实木家具
东莞市城市之窗家具有限公司	王东平	85980355	家具
东莞市华晟家具制造有限公司	郭万权	22653163	家具
东莞市利普家具有限公司	刘日武	83082222	家具居配套用品
东莞市好好家具有限公司	申　迅	81120825	木器家具
东莞市广纳家具制造有限公司	陈宋孟	83136198	家具
东莞市富宝沙发制造有限公司	黄进宝	85611985	家具
东莞市千顺五金有限公司	林丽雪	87313028	铁制家具
东莞市逸欧家具有限公司	李三宝	85652269	家具配件
东莞润丰金属塑胶有限公司	张颖懿	83320898	五金家具
东莞市时兴家具制造有限公司	黄炳辉	88872168	家具
东莞市大宇家具有限公司	陈　应	88180888	办公椅、办公桌
东莞市卓之神家具厂	彭润平	88704226	木家具
东莞市银通家具有限公司	黄锡基	88686466	玻璃家具
东莞市鸿福家具有限公司	陈旭标	88663836	木质家具
东莞市佳森家具有限公司	何少卿	85611222	咖啡桌
东莞市桥新家私有限公司	罗锦耀	88343337	木制家具
东莞市嘉梦家具有限公司	蔡明生	83826528	床垫床上用品
造纸及纸制品业			
东莞市凤岗新达纸品有限公司	张国雄	87750288	机制纸及纸板
东莞市雄东纸业有限公司	李舜超	88844928	造纸

1-4　续表 3

(2009年)

单位名称	负责人	联系电话	主要产品(或服务)
东莞市华利纸品有限公司	李建军	88703832	纸板
东莞市永安造纸有限公司	陈荷标	88818068	瓦楞纸
东莞市顺丰纸品制造有限公司	刘沛堆	86176968	纸板
东莞市宝华造纸有限公司	周汉洪	88336328	双灰纸张
东莞市达成纸品有限公司	孔少松	88289898	纸制品
东莞市天荣纸品有限公司	许南兮	85631665	纸板
东莞市大田包装有限公司	袁树枢	85269998	纸板
东莞市天赐纸品有限公司	黎连枝	88734233	纸板
东莞市顺通纸品有限公司	卢志成	88328608	纸板
广东玉兰装饰材料有限公司	万庆棠	22652789	墙纸
东莞市银兴纸品厂	刘伟民	87816636	纸板
东莞市易创实业有限公司	郭　财	81118021	纸制品
东莞市潢涌银洲纸业有限公司	黎伟儿	88899113	挂面箱板纸
东莞市伟联纸业有限公司	吴桂忠	88382688	纸浆
东莞市骏业纸业有限公司	吴炯泰	88830822	中卡纸
东莞市中联纸业有限公司	吴浩炳	88811357	包装用纸
东莞东兴纸品厂	李庆全	86228785	瓦楞纸板、瓦楞纸箱
东莞市道滘东发纸品有限公司	方叙贤	88839018	灰板纸
东莞市金桦纸业有限公司	黎惠华	88557698	瓦楞纸
东莞市宝建纸业有限公司	胡宝明	22270703	卷纸
东莞市盈泰纸品厂	许小光	88552289	生活用纸
东莞市珠江特种纸业有限公司	陈树芬	88889080	瓦楞纸
东莞市建桦造纸有限公司	黎灿辉		箱板纸
东莞市泰昌纸业有限公司	杜学英	88852607	仿牛卡纸
东莞市天全纸品有限公司	郭广全	81338828	纸板
东莞市道窖东发造纸厂	方叙贤	88839018	瓦楞纸
东莞市振兴造纸有限公司	张玉其	88949288	高强芯纸
东莞市莞桦纸品有限公司	何少锋	81200332	纸板
东莞市华深包装材料有限公司	潘明河	81197702	木质包装箱
东莞市旗峰纸业有限公司	黄惠锋	88328212	纸
东莞市强安造纸有限公司	邓锦波	88876118	造纸
东莞市永顺纸品有限公司	黄阶争	88551655	纸制品
东莞市中堂镇吴家涌有利造纸厂	吴全浩	88412438	瓦楞纸
东莞市高埗东保纸品厂	黎连枝	88734233	纸板
东莞市白天鹅纸业有限公司	卢宝祥	22172128	纸制品
东莞市东保纸业有限公司	黎康仔	88786298	瓦楞纸挂面纸
东莞市恒伟纸业有限公司	黄善权	88323168	纸板
东莞市高埗横滘头纸箱厂	张全恩	88873883	纸制品
东莞市瑞安纸品实业有限公司	刘美娇	22660198	纸箱
东莞市双洲纸业有限公司	吴祐银	88182618	瓦楞纸
东莞市贝辉装饰材料有限公司	贝友能	83199339	装饰材料
东莞市鸿晖实业有限公司	邱玉萍	86382008	纸制品
东莞市深联造纸有限公司	陈锐良	88818778	瓦楞芯纸
东莞市鸿业造纸有限公司	吴业恩	88814848	瓦楞纸
东莞市同力纸业有限公司	袁顺德	88881892	瓦楞芯纸

1-4 续表 4

(2009年)

单位名称	负责人	联系电话	主要产品(或服务)
东莞市大步纸业有限公司	李佐荣	88286883	机制纸及纸制品
东莞市裕杨纸品实业有限公司	刘智聪	86411555	纸箱
东莞市伟虹纸业有限公司	冯克伟	88558198	造纸
东莞市中堂东江造纸厂	吴浩炳	88812598	机制纸
东莞市龙腾纸业有限公司	张成明	88826898	纸制品
东莞市高埗镇保安围福利纸箱厂	黎日权	88787838	纸品
东莞市横通纸品有限公司	陈见新	83378968	纸板
东莞市厚威包装有限公司	马仁杰	82228320	纸箱
东莞市新富发纸业有限公司	陈志东	22711928	灰纸板
东莞市裕元纸品包装有限公司	方日和	82270888	纸箱
东莞市宝力造纸厂	梁树荣	88846388	造纸
东莞市银桦纸品有限公司	梁仲佳	81163388	包装材料纸箱
东莞市明丰纸品厂	黄月娇	88322388	纸板
东莞市金田纸业有限公司	欧阳忠	22280688	灰板纸
东莞市华通包装有限公司	黎永棠	81332988	纸制品
印刷业和记录媒介的复制			
东莞市二轻包装彩印厂有限公司	尹锡标	22699213	各类包装彩盒
东莞市天华创展印刷有限公司	陈永华	87862122	出版物印刷
文教体育用品制造业			
东莞伟易达电子厂	陈放韶	85581806	电子玩具
东莞市丰泽文具有限公司	钟磅兴	85506636	文件夹
东莞大岭山高资玩具制品厂	欧阳万福	83350001	纸制品玩具
东莞市天宇玩具制品有限公司	邓林光	83429729	塑胶玩具
东莞市智乐堡儿童玩具有限公司	王志光	86550188	玩具
东莞市智高文具有限公司	梁佛南	86634176	彩泥
石油、炼焦及核燃料业			
东莞市佐川润滑科技有限公司	汪小龙	83213232	环保清洗溶剂和润滑材料
东莞市荣高废油处理有限公司	冯国峰	88221178	润滑油
东莞市晔联道路改性沥青有限公司	殷　力	88439822	储存改性石油沥青
东莞市安美化学有限公司	汪小龙	83210707	润滑油
化学原料及化学制品制造业			
东莞市瑞德丰生物科技有限公司	高焕森	83359225	农药复配
东莞市竣成化工有限公司	陈惠斌	85595702	胶水
东莞市威亮实业有限公司	陈家富	88886988	合成洗衣服
东莞市友邦新材料科技有限公司	钟灵觉	86332327	聚酯树脂
东莞市三联科技实业有限公司	叶满芳	83215622	颜料
东莞市英科水墨有限公司	刘润林	86481155	水性墨
东莞市贝特利新材料有限公司	王　全	88283198	油墨
东莞市爱粤金属粉末有限公司	熊跃军	88385804	环氧聚酯型粉末涂料
东莞市合裕粘贴制品有限公司	严慧梅	83369560	胶粘剂
东莞市广华化工有限公司	刘锦婵	88328668	酸性蚀刻液
东莞市芙蓉沙化工有限公司	胡相义	88857923	分散松香胶
东莞市同兴涂料有限公司	陈锡光	88739118	二甲苯
广东省福利龙复合肥有限公司	王书新	88739816	复合肥料
东莞市盛和化工有限公司	王怀业	87132012	苯酐
东莞市大众农业科技有限公司	赵小云	88438227	土壤调试剂

1-4 续表 5

(2009年)

单位名称	负责人	联系电话	主要产品(或服务)
医药制造业			
广东众生药业股份有限公司	张绍日		众生丸
广东华南药业集团有限公司	张绍日		中西药产品
橡胶制品业			
东莞市伟捷包装实业有限公司	苏柱良	22172183	包装材料封箱胶带
东莞市建东橡胶制品有限公司	耿晓东	83050888	橡胶制品
东莞市石碣东英塑胶制品厂	单庆秋	86631490	塑胶鞋底
东莞清溪旺普登电子厂	李云光	86816688	液晶用背光板
塑料制品业			
东莞市百分百科技有限公司	安 波	88754800	塑胶塑胶开关
东莞市巨祺包装有限公司	赵 峰	81093697	塑料瓶盖
东莞市博美包装制品有限公司	陈楚斌	86255725	小型包装制品
东莞市冠宏包装实业有限公司	陈淦和	88518756	BOPP封箱皮
东莞市天宝五金塑胶制品有限公司	杨思娜	87914500	五金铁钗
东莞市港源胶粘带制品有限公司	丘水泉	81111360	胶粘带
东莞市安历电子有限公司	周淑娟	83420011	塑胶制品
东莞市泰至塑料五金有限公司	陈泰明	81821668	pvc管材
东莞市铭丰包装品制造有限公司	赖沛铭	22171188	首饰盒
东莞市华源包装有限公司	党令军	86646996	塑料包装袋
东莞市华瀚儿童用品有限公司	万润华	87867129	婴儿车
东莞市朝阳实业有限公司	沈庆凯	86722142	其他塑料制品
东莞市合鑫电子厂	叶锦标	86537079	塑胶
东莞新航包装材料有限公司	汉斯·莱辛奈克		发泡胶(泡沫)包材
东莞市丸万塑料包装有限公司	阮锡均	22024286	塑料制品
深圳市航天远东实业有限公司东莞分公司	李瑞征	82100375	塑胶制品
东莞市兄奕塑胶制品有限公司	罗新勇	87792188	塑胶制品
东莞嘉汇塑胶制品厂	祁浩林	83352643	电器塑胶壳
东莞市钜仕尔五金制品有限公司	谢斌周	86481766	橱柜拉手配件
东莞市富利时塑胶制品有限公司	林 彬	22653193	塑胶
东莞市晓铭实业有限公司	王贵东	85390608	塑胶制品
东莞市荣辉塑料粒有限公司	谭伟良	85154933	塑料粒
东莞市泰和塑胶制品有限公司	梁凤珍	83450238	塑料制品
东莞市华立实业股份有限公司	谭洪汝	83333239	塑料板
东莞市汇美实业有限公司	蔡顺利	85412223	DVD VCD塑胶面壳
东莞市晟美包装制品有限公司	邓君迪	86228778	塑料制品
东莞市惠德丽实业有限公司	韩凤志	86728338	塑料杂品
非金属矿物制品业			
东莞市茶山和兴粉磨站	吴灿均	86404633	粉磨水泥
东莞市建东水泥制品有限公司	袁志稳	88121288	预制桩
东莞市银通玻璃有限公司	万永宁	88868988	其他玻璃制品
东莞市唯美陶瓷工业园有限公司	黄建平	81133333	瓷砖
东莞市千色有机玻璃有限公司	蒋素珍	81611738	有机玻璃
东莞市虎门摩天建材实业公司	许银堂	85561768	加气混凝土
东莞市东成石材有限公司	陈润林	85596328	大理石花岗的切割
东莞市通州预制件有限公司	张润柏	88733388	预制件水泥管桩
东莞市唯美装饰材料有限公司	黄建平	22650006	陶瓷制品

1-4 续表 6

(2009年)

单位名称	负责人	联系电话	主要产品(或服务)
黑色金属冶炼及压延业			
东莞市佳瑞金属制品有限公司	赵晓鸣		铁带、铁板等五金制品
东莞市东上钢材有限公司	吴锦满	88815968	钢材
东莞市锦上钢材有限公司	吴贺贞	88186778	PC钢棒
有色金属冶炼及压延业			
东莞市宏顺金属材料有限公司	姚小明	86764001	电镀锌钢板
东莞市永铖铝业有限公司	曹柱深	22175338	铝挤型材
东莞市恒兴电子五金有限公司	叶德良	86321888	铝材板
元生有色金属(东莞)有限公司	许美珍	83281886	铝合金管材
东莞市金龙珠宝首饰有限公司	刘旺枝	85832107	黄金饰品
东莞市华昌铝合金制品厂	余锐春	22265108	铝材
东莞市华雨金属材料有限公司	纪春雨	83131757	铝棒延压
东莞市宏发钢铁结构材料有限公司	姚旭权	86737153	钢结构材料
东莞市亿鑫钢业有限公司	邱启光	86768769	钢结构材料
金属制品业			
东莞市坚朗五金制品有限公司	白宝鲲	87943311	点支撑幕墙配件
东莞市冠辉五金有限公司	汪卫星	85413848	五金配件
东莞市东钰五金塑胶有限公司	张　侠	87338371	办公椅底盘
东莞长安上沙金鑫金属制品厂	孙旺高	85379422	五金配件
东莞市金翔电器设备有限公司	周沛池	22704478	电脑机箱
东莞市志兴电子五金有限公司	王兴立	85619268	五金制品电子配件
东莞市旺明纺织服装有限公司	何　明	87980777	金属制品
东莞市宏力实业有限公司金属结构厂	梁志强	88861110	空心导轨
东莞市汇雅实业有限公司	王敏超	85830032	五金制品
东莞寮步岭下五腾五金厂	钟润湖	83302522	五金制品
东莞市广成五金塑胶实业有限公司	张志雄	81023992	五金塑胶制品
东莞市千岛金属锡品有限公司	黄守友	87880129	锡线
东莞市扬明精密塑胶五金电子有限公司	覃太明	85338940	塑胶五金电子制品
东莞市精丽制罐有限公司	王炳效	81702261	日用不锈钢制品
东莞市中意厨房设备有限公司	赵永利	82061888	厨柜
东莞市石碣展辉五金制品厂	何顺全	86320111	矽钢片
东莞展茂塑胶五金模具有限公司	罗意忠	86985888	五金
东莞市汇昌金属制品厂	余庆华	83307988	铝制品
东莞市东兴铝材制造有限公司	何旭坤	88813671	铝合金型材
东莞科力钢铁线材有限公司	沈德才	88557276	金属丝绳
东莞市通旺达五金制品有限公司	庄瑞莲	87561911	金属制品
通用设备制造业			
东莞市宝特模具钢有限公司	傅建国	88516020	金属制品
东莞市TR轴承有限公司	张顺成	22461784	滚动轴承
东莞市庆新安制冷设备配件有限公司	李姚暖	83341457	制冷空调器
东莞厚街科技电业厂	王应权		电钻电锯工具
东莞市百利电器有限公司	周锦波	88858916	商用冷柜

1-4 续表 7

(2009年)

单位名称	负责人	联系电话	主要产品(或服务)
东莞市优富利电子有限公司	周明波	85784995	风扇
东莞市石龙万通实业有限公司	王苏仔		屉滑轨
东莞市快意施耐德电梯有限公司	罗爱文	87736443	电梯
东莞市三联机械有限公司	罗镜湖	83321381	铸铁件
东莞市台冠起重机械设备有限公司	唐来森	83019666	桥式起重机
东莞市快意电梯有限公司	罗爱文	87731075	电梯
东莞市勤上金属制品有限公司	李淑贤	83395678	铁线
东莞市三和兴模具钢材有限公司	郭碧山	82016100	模具钢材
东莞市熙晟实业投资有限公司	李云妹	88883710	铸件
东莞市富士电梯有限公司	钟重庆	23062593	电梯
东莞市石排同利五金厂	廖柱成	86659735	锌合金
东莞市东城永强弹簧厂	何浩坚	22261357	弹簧
东莞市莱钢钢结构有限公司	刘衍敏	83666666	钢结构件
东莞市寮步兆峰轴承有限公司	陈灿华	83328819	轴承
东莞市有同电器有限公司	徐锡强	22401688	电子变压器用铁心电
东莞市得鑫五金有限公司	刘晓惠	81124006	螺丝
东莞市建华机械制造有限公司	何建华	85636311	工程机械零配件
专用设备制造业			
东莞科威医疗器械有限公司	王安勤	21985698	膜式氧合器
东莞市大朗安富塑料机械厂	何越赋		塑料机械
东莞市道滘兴隆造纸厂	叶锐锋	88381933	制浆
东莞市隆泰实业有限公司	梁少龙		煤矿机械
东莞市新盛电子有限公司	袁效新	85639728	电线
东莞百汇塑胶五金厂	尤景涛	85602838	塑胶模具五金模具
东莞市东力电器设备有限公司	林月芳	83307608	高低合成奎开关设备
东莞市泰康电子科技有限公司	方建斌	85322066	电子连接器
东莞市雄丰配电设备有限公司	魏润族	86647816	高压配电柜
东莞市康达机电工程有限公司	沈剑山		制造业
东莞市方达实业有限公司	卢润田	85338842	PVC排水器材
东莞市虎门机械厂	姚信青	85711932	B24小型拉伸机
东莞市嘉利五金电器厂	袁汝根	86416228	光管支架
交通运输设备制造业			
东莞市旗丰消声器有限公司	张　福	22658795	汽车及摩托车消声器
东莞市永强汽车制造有限公司	陈达强	83307688	罐式车
电气机械及器材制造业			
东莞市迈科新能源有限公司	李中延	83197555	锂离子电池
东莞市理士奥电源核技术有限公司	董　李	87925180	阀控式蓄电池
东莞市杉杉电池材料有限公司	李智华	22035233	锂离子电池材料
广东五星太阳能有限公司	胡广良	22176388	太阳能热水器
东莞市大忠电子有限公司	李正中	22630563	电子产品
东莞市蓝冠环保节能科技有限公司	申卫红	83309068	太阳能热水设备
东莞樟木头津地本电子厂	蔡运基	87707507	电线连接头
东莞市华达电缆厂	曾环坤	85617836	电缆
东莞清溪光荣电业制品厂	黄恩球	87300000	吸尘器

1-4 续表 8

(2009年)

单位名称	负责人	联系电话	主要产品(或服务)
东莞市瑞桥电器有限公司	白建明	81358668	电器产品及连接线
东莞市石碣志业电子有限公司	陈健钊	86318226	电线制品
东莞市凌力电池有限公司麻涌电池厂	莫炳森	88822642	干电池
东莞市稳畅电子制品有限公司	郑灼坤	85521148	电线
东莞华旭电线电缆有限公司	王丽香	85526356	电线电缆、插头
东莞市奇声电子实业有限公司	钟海亮	88231648	音响
东莞勤上光电股份有限公司	李旭亮	83395678	LED路灯
广东领亚电子科技有限公司	白建功	85510688	电线
东莞市联升电线电缆有限公司	张玉良	85253317	电线、铜线、电源线、插头电源线
东莞市中亚电缆有限公司	沈煜郷	88111000	电线、电缆
东莞市石龙富华电子有限公司	黄子田		电源适配器
东莞市绿雅家用电器有限公司	朱鹏晖	88991088	电扇
东莞市益达实业有限公司	谢松登	86412628	漆包绕组线
东莞市梅兰电器有限公司	李文杰	83300022	高压开关板
东莞联盈电业有限公司	张玉良	85152115	电线及电源线
东莞市祺龙电业有限公司	宁建华	85152798	电线
东莞市欧雷玛电源有限公司	张武生	87865169	铅酸蓄电池
东莞市亿丰电池有限公司	陈伟基	22179288	干电池
东莞市勤上企业有限公司	温　琦	81107158	烧烤炉
广东康菱动力科技有限公司	赵　敏	22032222	发电机及发电机组
东莞市迈科科技有限公司	李中延	83015380	镍氢电池
东莞市凯晟灯头实业有限公司	姚利民	86787878	铜灯头
广东省东莞电机有限公司	黄进安	22810778	交流电动机
高达粤电安信电力检修安装有限公司	饶苏波	85561893	机电设备
东莞市石碣东诚电子有限公司	黄旺珍	86319827	电子材料
东莞塘厦新联电器厂	冯国强	87910170	电器制品风筒
东莞市康尔信电力系统有限公司	吴保良	22713999	柴油发电机组
东莞市雷洋电子科技有限公司	倪春红	85391369	电子设备
东莞市锐升电线电缆有限公司	黄荣海	86092388	电线
东莞市民兴电缆有限公司	吴惠明	87510316	电线电缆
东莞市瑞柯电机有限公司	杨　琪		空压机
东莞市奥维漆包线有限公司	谢锐钦	81810183	漆包绕线组
东莞市东阳光电容器有限公司	吕文进	85315188	电容器
东莞市石碣德昌电子制品厂	夏健德	88488080	电源线插头
东莞市开关厂有限公司	陆少雄	83225258	高低压配电设备
东莞市昶泰五金制品有限公司	樊　慧	83107188	灯饰制品
东莞市星锐灯饰有限公司	王玉如	83218568	灯饰
广东科旺电源设备有限公司	方旺福	22900009	稳压器
东莞市凌力电池有限公司	莫福聪	22271791	干电池
东莞市西伦电器实业有限公司	柯　航	83984308	草地灯
东莞市三友联众电器有限公司	宋朝阳	85914551	继电器
东莞市东伟漆包线有限公司	林炯邦		漆包线
广东明家科技股份有限公司	周建林	87061828	插座
广东钜龙电力设备有限公司	龚玉生		油浸式电力变压器

1-4 续表 9

(2009年)

单位名称	负责人	联系电话	主要产品(或服务)
东莞市高能电气股份有限公司	罗素芳	22291876	绝缘体制品
东莞道滘镇协益电子厂	梁伯沂	88831848	电气机械
东莞市光华实业有限公司	陈锦麟		电源变压器
广东美林电线电缆有限公司	陈志辉	88920098	电线、电缆
通信设备、计算机及其他电子设备制造业			
郡懋电子(东莞)有限公司	朱政权	87282000	微晶合金
广东志成冠军集团有限公司	韩妹平	87722374	不间断电源
东莞市步步高通信设备有限公司	周顺翔	85540688	有绳电话机
东莞市嘉田五金塑胶制品有限公司	赖少忠	87774386	电脑机箱
东莞石龙华南电子五金制品厂	李志波	86624941	电子元件
东莞市旭田电子有限公司	王肖鹏	86300036	键盘
东莞田渊电机厂	方健文	85832800	电机器件
东莞黄江达裕科技电子厂	曾锦昌	83531877	液晶显示器
东莞市塘厦克琛达塑胶电子厂	吴东海	86851777	电子元件
东莞市欧珀电子工业有限公司	金乐亲	86670688	影碟机
东莞市煜弘电子制造有限公司	邓慧燕	85014888	音箱电脑
东莞市天皓电子有限公司	范玉田		电子计算机设备
东莞市德生通用电器制造有限公司	梁 伟	23167118	收音机
东莞市亿达音响制造有限公司	刘恩海	22665300	组合音箱
东莞市金正数码科技有限公司	刘会来	81111299	DVD
东莞市龙光电业有限公司	陈乐孟	85338787	机箱
东莞市横沥金叶实业有限公司	宋幔林	83731747	电子元件
东莞市金锐显数码科技有限公司	方江涛	86858666	液晶电视主板
东莞市大朗涌韵音膜厂	刘庆佳		振动膜
东莞市数字印数码科技有限公司	邓运南	87510868	数码音乐播放器
东莞市洋湖电子有限公司	孟尧天	88977999	彩色电视机
东莞市方达电子工业有限公司	卢润田	85410922	电子产品
东莞市时唛特电器有限公司	陈 彬	87987070	电子设备
东莞市盈聚电子有限公司	赵星宝	86327382	电子配件
东莞市佰利电子有限公司	黎锦洪	88708002	发光二极管
东莞市新泰粮食有限公司	黄启东	87123620	粮食
东莞伟易达电子元器件制造厂	陈放韶	85581806	电子元件
东莞伟易达电子通讯设备厂	陈放韶	85581806	室内无线电话
东莞市东方雷豹电子有限公司	陈云秀	88973333	电子产品
东莞市粤林电脑科技有限公司	邓会英	87890888	电脑机箱
东莞市森特电子有限公司	林永泰	86329018	电脑机箱
东莞市飞尔液晶显示器有限公司	邓 宏	83106619	电子元器件
东莞市奕联实业有限公司	黄 磊	86064988	连接线连接器
东莞嘉财电业制造厂	黎任荪	83359040	
东莞海益机械配件有限公司	林正盛	83220188	传感器零件
东莞市前锋电子有限公司	袁灿荣	86633990	电磁炉
东莞市大朗迅田视讯设备厂	陈如辉	83482898	锌合金分路线
东莞市金业电子科技有限公司	黄剑忠	83261111	VCD机
东莞南城添迪制品厂	殷锐潮	22417969	电脑磁头臂

1-4　续表 10

(2009年)

单位名称	负责人	联系电话	主要产品(或服务)
东莞市东方科技有限公司	方敬湖	85586389	电脑周边设备
东莞市众誉电子有限公司	陈伟贤	85554168	鼠标键盘
东莞市芊和电子有限公司	陈章妹	81803262	耳机
东莞市奥莱克电子有限公司	莫启旭	88226006	组合音响
东莞市步步高视听电子有限公司	戴永乐	85545555	影碟机
东莞市步步高教育电子产品有限公司	邹文高	85540888	语言复读机
东莞市宇阳科技发展有限公司	陈伟荣	87507868	电子产品
东莞市金河田实业有限公司	方植宁	85585691	电脑外部设备
广东步步高电子工业有限公司	金志江	85545555	手机
东莞市铭基电子有限公司	王彩晓	83096688	电脑连接线
东莞市金铭电子有限公司	刘立荣	85656666	手机
东莞市金盈电子有限公司	苏福钦	86326328	电源变压器
东莞宇球电子有限公司	倪孟尧	83529888	电子插接件
东莞清溪欣冠电子厂	汪日新	87311298	调制解调器
东莞市光普实业发展有限公司	王志哲	87339849	电脑机箱
东莞厚街下汴电子厂	陈灿平	85591388	CD电唱盘及收音机
东莞佳汇电子厂	袁永坚	85602828	电脑显示器及家用电
东莞市铭普实业有限公司	杨先进	81701560	网络变压器
东莞市茵莉电子有限公司	彭　日		变压器
东莞市康祥电子有限公司	曾利琼	85261575	电脑连接器
仪器仪表及文化、办公用机械制造业			
东莞市华兰海电子有限公司	伍　敏	88823105	便携式轴重台
广东正业科技有限公司	徐地华	86279158	电子材料耗材
东莞寮步铨讯电子厂	陈永乐	83527668	数码相机
东莞市邦泽电子有限公司	李　霁	89191288	碎纸机
工艺品及其他制造业			
东莞太平电镀元件厂	文永畴	85511047	拉链
东莞市昌晖印染器材有限公司	邓志坚	85555020	印刷、印染机械
东莞市钮成服装辅料有限公司	林元隆	22625327	钮扣
东莞市宝山地毡有限公司	田　梅	83361594	羊毛地毡
东莞市雅居乐日用制品有限公司	刘承发	86598000	PVC台布
东莞市日月不锈钢有限公司	周亚金	83606259	不锈钢
东莞市阳光树脂制品有限公司	张晓光	86633666	胶粘剂
东莞市华辉玻璃制品有限公司	莫瑞娟		玻璃镀银镀铝
东莞市冠炜塑胶五金制品有限公司	吴　嵘	83981763	塑胶制品
电力、热力的生产和供应业			
广深沙角B电力有限公司沙角B火力发电厂	刘燕航		火力发电
东莞市三联热电有限公司	李锦生	88812123	火力发电
东莞市基宁发电有限公司	陈锡活	85136442	火力发电
广东电力发展股份有限公司沙角A电厂	饶苏波	85136679	火力发电
广东省粤电集团有限公司沙角C电厂	朱志飞	85165698	发电
水的生产和供应业			
东莞市东城自来水公司	祁水炳	22612699	自来水
东莞市自来水股份有限公司	罗伟权	22214443	自来水

1-4　续表 11

(2009年)

单位名称	负责人	联系电话	主要产品(或服务)
东莞市清溪自来水有限公司	黄托坤	87733362	自来水
东莞市常平镇自来水公司	周庆宗	83335588	自来水
东莞市寮步自来水公司	陈炯球	83328899	自来水
东莞市大朗镇自来水公司	梁绍堂	83318306	自来水
东莞市长安镇自来水公司	陈绍熙	85535689	自来水
东莞市虎门自来水有限公司	黄集辉	85525510	自来水
东莞市东江水务有限公司	罗沛强	22609238	自来水
东莞市沙田自来水厂	黎淦钊	88862620	自来水
东莞市横沥镇自来水公司	叶旭志	83375146	自来水
东莞市黄江镇镇中自来水有限公司	袁成强		自来水
东莞市塘厦自来水公司	罗应深	87724614	自来水
东莞市厚街镇自来水公司	叶汉高	85832348	自来水
东莞市茶山自来水公司	谢庆春	86412848	自来水
房屋和土木工程建筑业			
东莞市骏鹏建筑工程有限公司	罗成昌	87727708	房屋建筑工程
东莞市沙田镇建筑工程公司	黎锐坚	88663738	房屋工程建筑
东莞市东城建筑公司	谢锦平	22319001	房屋建筑
东莞市中厚建筑工程公司	董伟乐	85582766	房屋工程建筑
东莞市腾飞建筑工程有限公司	何任荣	22425528	建筑房屋住宅
东莞市凤岗建筑工程公司	叶汉雄	87860335	房屋工程建筑
东莞市瑞安建筑工程有限公司	何永康	22386908	建筑工程
东莞市恒泰建筑工程有限公司	刘德文	83378981	房屋建筑工程
东莞市道滘建筑工程有限公司	余　强	81332333	房屋工程建筑
东莞市方中建筑工程有限公司	骆柏谦	86222001	建筑工程施工
东莞市建工集团有限公司	陈炽辉	22427888	房屋建筑工程施工
东莞市健升建筑工程有限公司	陈健新	22302222	房屋建筑工程施工
东莞市华源建筑工程有限公司	林平能	85596888	建筑工程
广东省东莞市石龙建筑工程公司	何荣坚	86116908	房屋建筑
东莞市天源建筑工程有限公司	张学勤	22496099	房屋建筑
广东省东莞市莞城建筑工程公司	尹锦培	22229020	工业和民用建筑工程施工
东莞市正大建筑工程有限公司	郑启杨	22278818	建筑工程
东莞市鸿高建设工程有限公司	刘镇庭	86664882	房屋工程建筑
东莞市南城区建筑工程有限公司	罗沛林	22413912	房屋建筑
东莞市横沥镇建筑工程公司	叶庆辉	83373808	房屋工程建筑
东莞市南粤建筑工程有限公司	胡政斌	22020079	房屋建筑施工
东莞市宏达建设工程有限公司	袁　斌	22380008	房屋建筑工程
东莞市凤安电力工程有限公司	刘送庆	82082968	电力设施工程
广东省水利水电第三工程局	蔡旗高	87721441	水利水电工程
东莞市盛帆建筑工程有限公司	黄照南	87722638	房屋工程建筑
建筑安装业			
东莞市建安集团有限公司	陈润光	22986086	房屋建筑
东莞市昌晖电气工程有限公司	钟燕红	85835768	电气设备安装
东莞市高宝电气安装工程有限公司	梁孖贵	88786869	安装电力设备
广东集明电力工程有限公司	李文杰	22492728	建筑装饰业

1-4　续表 12

(2009年)

单位名称	负责人	联系电话	主要产品(或服务)
东莞市粤发电气安装有限公司	黄振华	86118998	承修电力设施
东莞市安利来电气安装有限公司	叶秀英	83010013	电力设施承装
东莞市石龙第二建筑工程有限公司	郑焕泉	86600222	房屋工程建筑
东莞市广安电器安装工程有限公司	张新连	82266666	电器工程安装
东莞市虎门建设发展有限公司	何锐军	85188631	建筑
东莞市协力钢构工程有限公司	万任齐	85919838	钢购件
东莞市景安电器安装工程有限公司	彭春梅	81762299	电器安装
湖南望新建设集团股份有限公司东莞分公司	郭卫峰	22999910	建筑
其他建筑业			
东莞市国贸水电安装工程有限公司	梁红娣	22760555	水电安装
东莞市东塘电气安装有限公司	何　河	87905273	承装电力设施
东莞市岭南园林建设有限公司	尹洪卫	22450507	园林绿化工程
东莞市力丰钢结构有限公司	王建强	85916822	钢结构安装
东莞市黄江镇建筑工程有限公司	温伟光	83363938	房屋工程建筑
东莞市福华建筑工程有限公司	霍福祥	88866688	房屋建筑
道路运输业			
东莞市万隆华禹运输有限公司	程秀峰	85922143	普通货运
东莞市交通集团有限公司	赵道平	22701663	交通运输服务
东莞市嘉达快运服务有限公司	曾治平	22981833	货物快递
东莞市汽车运输有限公司	邓建民	22463079	道路旅客运输
东莞市正泰运输服务有限公司	林钟龙	88222278	货物中转
东莞市玖龙运输有限公司	张成飞	88234888	公路货运运输
东莞市飞马物流有限公司	黄国喜	86916838	普通货运
东莞市三和物流有限公司	韩爱香	83214617	普通货运
东莞市长城客运有限公司	邓炽光	22461975	公路客运
城市公共交通业			
东莞市城巴运输有限公司	赵道平	22492259	交通运输
东莞市华悦客运集团有限公司	邢文文	27231596	小汽车
东莞市公共汽车有限公司	赵道平	22211806	交通运输
水上运输业			
东莞市海昌船务有限公司	袁小玲	86018810	货物运输
东莞市丰海海运有限公司	韩月明	87926329	港澳航线运输
广州港集团新沙港务有限公司	苏兴旺	82159033	货物装卸堆存
装卸搬运及其他运输服务业			
东莞市南城南方物流有限公司	沈宝跃	22986935	运输
东莞市德邦货运有限公司	崔维星	22907828	货运代理
仓储业			
东莞市百安石化仓储有限公司	黎庆恺	88666030	化工品仓储
东莞市金明商贸发展有限公司	彭金耀	88688692	石油化工仓储库
中央储备粮广东新沙港直属库	茹秀观	88231111	粮食储备
邮政业			
东莞市邮政局	陈明志	22330782	函件

1-4　续表 13

(2009年)

单位名称	负责人	联系电话	主要产品(或服务)
电信和其他信息传输服务业			
中国铁通集团有限公司东莞分公司	倪平波	86272388	电信固定电话
中国铁通集团有限公司东莞分公司长安营业厅	樊桂玲	86249800	电信业务
东莞广电网络传媒发展股份公司虎门分公司	孟穗东	85518836	广播电视传输
中国电信股份有限公司东莞分公司	杨一鸣	22808888	固定电话服务
中国网络通信集团公司东莞市分公司	罗　翼	89826085	通讯服务
中国电信股份有限公司东莞道滘新城客户服务中心	梁健民	88832000	电信服务
东莞市海铭诺信息科技有限公司	胡晓敏	86810828	计算机产品
软件业			
东莞市泰阳实业有限公司	文革萍	85136389	计算机网络工程
批发业			
东莞市康盈贸易有限公司	陈艳珍	22784583	食糖
东莞市鑫泉石油化工有限公司	吴锦鹏		化工产品
东莞市日之泉贸易有限公司	林　洁	88815015	钢材
东莞市利兴糖业贸易有限公司	邓汝洪	22784583	糕点、糖果及糖
东莞市朝阳药业有限公司	陆　晓	88327952	中成药、中药材
东莞市华江石油化工有限公司	吴汉清	82119266	石油化工
广东省东莞国药集团仁济堂药业有限公司	罗永球	22484521	中药材
东莞市精骏包装材料有限公司	郑金生	88180800	电镀锡薄钢板
东莞市东江石油化工有限公司	张金锡	87076081	石油及制品
东莞市洋通饮料贸易有限公司	赖禹铭	86110722	啤酒
广东省东莞市海东石油有限公司	方寺卿	88232325	油品
东莞市润泰纸业有限公司	叶国华	85499268	纸张
东莞市东塑进出口有限公司	卢亮坤	83862338	货物进出口贸易
东莞市中彦进出口有限公司	叶淦波	83315888	服装
东莞市伟伦贸易有限公司	叶伟华	86223358	化工产品
东莞市辉明石化产品有限公司	周子明	23183527	石油
东莞市欢盈投资有限公司	李葵璋		空调
东莞市日之泉物流有限公司	林　勤	88815015	钢材
东莞市东安石油化工有限公司	韩月明	88865128	汽油
东莞市金鹏塑料原料有限公司	郭　明	87126666	化学产品
东莞市真映切削工具有限公司	付国新	83111711	螺纹切削工具
东莞市中堂废旧物资回收有限公司建桦分公司	莫志江	88120732	废纸收购
东莞市泽通贸易有限公司	张少君	22224050	电器
东莞市世发贸易有限公司	周志博	22800368	化工原料
广东省东莞市虎门供销社	梁建平	85513008	家用电子类
东莞市常平好必来塑胶贸易有限公司	刘国芬	86992038	塑胶原料
东莞市中堂废旧物资回收有限公司有利分公司	罗庆辉	88120732	废纸收购
东莞市德凯经贸有限公司	莫如熊	23027769	服装出口贸易
东莞市电力燃料有限公司	林建军	22475222	石油及制品
东莞市同汇贸易有限公司	黎　明	23360488	化工产品
东莞市糖酒集团美宜佳便利店有限公司	张国衡	22465830	小食品
东莞市麒麟机械有限公司	陈海燕	22473938	轴承
东莞市科虹金属有限公司	吴伟东	86309328	铜材
东莞市佳森能源有限公司	林增群	88235233	煤炭
广东省东莞盐业总公司	陈耀嘉	22380236	盐产品

1-4 续表 14

(2009年)

单位名称	负责人	联系电话	主要产品(或服务)
广东省东莞市谢岗食品公司	赵寿天	87687328	生猪
东莞市年丰饮料有限公司	袁炳坤	22256391	饮料
东莞市溢安贸易有限公司	陈桂恒	88280993	重油
市糖酒集团东方配销有限公司	祁伟标	22184011	小食
东莞市中堂废旧物资回收有限公司	王炯森	88811203	收购废品
东莞市东孚商贸有限公司	黄罗发	22772277	化妆品及卫生用品
东莞市中堂废旧物资回收有限公司建晖分公司	罗　锐	88120732	废纸收购
东莞市溢源对外贸易有限公司	郭　美	22201203	代理进出口
东莞市伟力地坪材料有限公司	陈三喜		地称材料
东莞市利士石油化工有限公司	田育旺	88731368	石油
东莞市东普贸易有限公司	余杏莲	86604338	钢材
东莞市创丰科技发展有限公司	张民生	22855300	自动化设备
东莞市美德石化产品有限公司	邹　萍	87682025	溶剂油
东莞市科大贸易有限公司	周健海	88867777	钢材
东莞市名加石油有限公司	陈惠平	81823808	汽油
东莞市长安利源石油有限公司	陈启平	85416068	石油
东莞市银洲燃料有限公司	黎葵明	88181366	煤炭
东莞市东益实业投资有限公司	李锡柱	88815898	钢材
东莞中茂石油化工贸易有限公司	温成表		甲醇
东莞市天锐贸易有限公司	李青松	85545555	电子元件
广东省东莞机械进出口有限公司	陈海生	22222040	进出口机电产品
广东省东莞市厚街供销社	方毓明	85581485	日用百货建材
东莞市中堂废旧物资回收有限公司深联分公司	黎艳平	88120732	废纸收购
东莞市中堂废旧物资回收有限公司汇达分公司	梁沛昌	88120732	废纸收购
东莞市百业进出口有限公司	董海光	22421328	一般贸易
中铝洛阳铜业有限公司东莞分公司	刘　冶	85562885	有色金属
广东大地通讯连锁服务有限公司	梁沛棠	23066666	通讯设备
东莞市星辰塑胶有限公司	莫小兰	86991286	塑胶原料
东莞市广联通信器材有限公司	黎国志		手机
广东省东莞包装进出口有限公司	尹梓伟	22802861	纺织品进出口
东莞市三方贸易有限公司	何应章	23051611	其他食品
东莞市百维食品化工原料实业有限公司	陈辉霞	83263989	食品添加剂
东莞市华润涂料有限公司	丁志民	22363331	油漆
东莞市金仙峰实业有限公司	沈　宏	22416577	白砂糖
东莞市卓远发展经贸有限公司	周祖俊	87132056	苯酐
东莞市鸿甲五金材料有限公司	彭春红	87517744	五金材料
东莞市环球工艺进出口贸易有限公司	朱丰儿	22802312	出口家具
东莞市彬源塑胶贸易有限公司	刘兰英		塑胶
东莞市华发纸张有限公司	丁耀辉	86313868	白纸板
东莞市豪景商贸有限公司	袁树洪	86118181	机电产品
中国石油天然气股份有限公司广东东莞销售分公司	佟福财	22022155	成品油
东莞市瑞腾贸易有限公司	温玉奇	22223639	农副产品
东莞市瑞峰纸业有限公司	袁雪峰	22623952	纸张
东莞市东物剧毒化学物品有限公司	彭方龙	22383672	物流流通

1-4　续表 15

(2009年)

单位名称	负责人	联系电话	主要产品(或服务)
东莞市成泰化工有限公司	刘婉嫦	22884548	EVA
东莞市泓海贸易有限公司	彭锐刚	22340699	纺织品染料
东莞市中堂废旧物资回收有限公司东江分公司	罗建洪	88120732	废纸收购
东莞市嘉宝石油化工有限公司	王敏康	87711087	甲基苯
东莞市恒生进出口有限公司	陈柱良	23181991	泡棉机进出口
东莞市合联进出口贸易有限公司	吴仁和	83125556	出口毛衣
广东烟草东莞市有限公司	刘恒建	22210936	烟草
东莞市同舟化工有限公司	谢文勇	22365733	甲苯
东莞市鼎鑫贸易有限公司	姚伟文	22314016	贸易
东莞市恒利达贸易有限公司	陈广堂	83721778	五金材料
东莞市彩虹塑胶颜料有限公司	季德虎	87777113	塑胶颜料
东莞市中堂废旧物资回收有限公司振桦分公司	莫志江	88120732	废纸收购
东莞市顺盈钢材贸易有限公司	黄辉云	88188790	钢材、五金
东莞市瑞展皮革贸易有限公司	李志平	85825996	皮革
东莞市莞晟贸易有限公司	吴湛林	88110155	煤炭
东莞市东源投资实业有限公司	洪素兰	22855416	煤炭
东莞市达明发展有限公司	黄广明	22363006	出口家具
东莞市翔顺妇幼用品有限公司	李淦辉	88281327	奶粉
东莞市源源钢铁贸易有限公司	刘玉明	83130830	钢材材料
东莞市广利食品进出口有限公司	杜锡坤	22223344	食品
东莞市超捷实业有限公司	周文胜	88228979	重油
东莞市海华五金矿产进出口有限公司	刘建钧	22243170	进出口代理
东莞峻晟鞋材有限公司	蔡忠周	85529190	鞋材
东莞市中信化工有限公司	莫春南	86918388	塑胶粒
东莞市信立实业有限公司	蒋秀梅	85633333	农产品贸易
东莞市乘风实业有限公司	林绮云	86615001	购销包
东莞市亿丰行洗涤产品有限公司	袁富杨	86311487	洗涤用品
东莞市昱方钢材有限公司	黄剑鸿	85349788	模具钢材
东莞市健宇塑胶原料有限公司	邓文辉	86991001	塑胶原料
东莞市金叶珠宝有限公司	王志伟	85822216	珠宝首饰
东莞市广通贸易有限公司	袁日明	22407968	汽车轮胎
东莞市南洋计算机软件有限公司	李　莉	22505550	计算机应用软件
东莞市伟业石油化工有限公司	胡玉培	88850666	柴油
广东省东莞市新华书店有限公司	张康玉	22115138	教材图书
东莞市德利石油化工有限公司	潘俊琪	85516299	石油及制品
东莞市桥供废品回收有限公司	尹日林	83341037	废旧物资回收
东莞市力丰燃料油有限公司	卢　冲	85479318	燃料油
广东省东莞轻工业品进出口有限公司	黎少刚	22212413	各类电器
东莞市中泰纸业有限公司	郭伟璇	85415136	纸张
东莞市万通化工有限公司	张成枝	22187777	聚氯乙烯
东莞市万红贸易有限公司	罗苑琳	22316751	进出口贸易
东莞市隆兴纸业有限公司	李炳成	86088777	文化用纸
东莞市荣兴纸业有限公司	单伟荣	86013903	纸类
广东省东莞纺织品进出口有限公司	梁大钧		服装进出口

1-4 续表 16

(2009年)

单位名称	负责人	联系电话	主要产品(或服务)
广东省东莞医药保健品进出口有限公司	罗志全	22802920	出口服装
东莞市创兴糖业贸易有限公司	邓汝洪	22784583	糕点、糖果及糖
东莞市冠中信息技术有限公司	王玉祥	88754891	电脑
东莞市广济医药器械有限公司	黄柱谋	22906161	药品
东莞市一君医药有限公司	聂有根	81306988	中成药
东莞市锦茂进出口有限公司	刘小斌	22339829	国内商业服务
东莞市惠顺贸易有限公司	欧阳生		建材
东莞市汇众进出口有限公司	陈汉枢	83209503	针织制品
东莞市诚昌纸业有限公司	卢明记	85311598	文具
东莞市正诚贸易有限公司	曾海帆	22680808	进出口业务
东莞市百业兴经贸有限公司	温锦坤	22421328	一般贸易
东莞市厚龙燃气有限公司	陈秋荣	85817336	液化石油气
东莞市先锋特殊钢有限公司	何德兆	87777097	钢材
东莞市糖酒集团丰裕贸易有限公司	龚鉴铭	22481231	食品
东莞市鸿越实业有限公司	张振胜		粉煤灰渣
东莞市文一实业有限公司	杜　章	88327025	文具
东莞市长成纸张有限公司	石玉凤		纸张
东莞市巨树食品有限公司	周巧璋	22422166	副食
东莞市东辉贸易有限公司	梁尹琦	83364788	化工原料
东莞市金马经贸有限公司	黄汇滔	22307188	进出口代理
东莞市凯盈贸易有限公司	王佛禧	23188808	机电产品
东莞市信佳贸易有限公司	陈万科	23186737	热轧卷板
东莞市天泰控股集团有限公司	刘克伟	23138888	成品油
东莞市君科进出口贸易有限公司	张少君	22299128	货物及技术出口
东莞市汇鸿纸业有限公司	丁耀光	86010920	纸张
东莞市泰昌石油化工贸易有限公司	肖志庄	87710980	罐装润滑油
东莞市海川进出口有限公司	李慧玲	83113663	服装
东莞市华银贸易有限公司	王汉能	88311866	煤炭
东莞市对外贸易发展有限公司	陈永强		代理进出口
东莞市宇兴贸易有限公司	陈锡强	83109968	毛衣
东莞市鸿基煤炭有限公司	刘建鹏	88280186	煤炭
东莞市顺安废纸回收有限公司	蔡绍和	88851243	废纸回收
东莞市美星塑胶材料有限公司	余学超	23120868	塑胶原料
东莞市永椿净化设备工程有限公司	袁建明	81107819	净化设备工程
东莞市东伟石油化工有限公司	谭继贤	88855108	油
东莞市宏川化工有限公司	林海川	22893998	其他化工产品
东莞市雄峰特殊钢有限公司	何德雄	87559810	模具钢材
东莞市振东医药有限公司	戴伟生	22323888	药品
东莞市寮步根记五金贸易部	邝亮枝	83219698	铜制品
东莞市旗峰对外贸易有限公司	李舜超	22633592	进出口业务
东莞市明盛能源有限公司	朱日明	86313666	煤炭
东莞市中凯进出口有限公司	付慧仪	83101855	出口毛衫
东莞市友华机电工程有限公司	邓文光	23050801	中央空调
东莞市永祥贸易有限公司	陈文龙		燃料油

1-4　续表 17

(2009年)

单位名称	负责人	联系电话	主要产品(或服务)
东莞市兴峰化工贸易有限公司	张旭强	22287666	其他化工产品
东莞市建筑材料进出口有限公司	欧创仔	22816022	鞋帽
东莞市东糖集团有限公司	陈尧燊	22613931	成品糖
东莞市中堂废旧物资回收有限公司金洲分公司	罗　锐	88120732	废纸收购
广东省东莞国药集团药材有限公司	邓沛棠	22239530	中药材
东莞市南腾贸易有限公司	黎锦南	88122189	有机溶剂
广东省东莞畜产进出口有限公司	张　博	22206023	五金
东莞市中堂废旧物资回收有限公司鸿业分公司	张庆菘	88120732	废纸收购
东莞市华辉金属材料有限公司	邓　清	22468979	金属材料
东莞市汇富进出口贸易有限公司	方广华	22389322	家具
东莞市道滘珠洲石油气有限公司	孙洪德	88389233	液化石油气
东莞市华闽金属材料有限公司	苏承碚	83792951	金属贸易
东莞市富励贸易有限公司	杨品煌		化工产品
东莞市澳洁贸易有限公司	陈绍培	83750888	日用百货
上海凯群贸易有限公司东莞分公司	方妙芳	85750312	零售塑胶、塑样原料及制品
东莞市萃华商贸有限公司	邓永洪	83342322	贸易管理
广东省东莞五金矿产进出口有限公司	霍树根	22227420	进出口代理
广东省东莞国药集团有限公司	尹沛全	22337200	药品
东莞市大通电脑有限公司	仇延生	23071386	计算机软硬件
东莞市建晖燃料有限公司	谢裕祥	22348877	煤炭
东莞市银河废纸回收有限公司	王振滔	88188108	废纸回收
东莞市金汇废纸回收有限公司	黎金成		废纸回收
东莞主致医药有限公司	林心养	22036911	医药
东莞市拓顺贸易有限公司	陈国勇	23032773	五金配件
东莞市建森废纸回收有限公司	梁树全	88121098	废纸回收
东莞市津盈实业有限公司	邵志雄	85121693	钢材
东莞市东达汽车有限公司	陈彩兰	85935999	汽车
东莞市双丰废纸回收有限公司	邓少和	88182628	废纸回收
东莞市源来废纸回收有限公司	吴志荣	88117972	废纸
东莞市明泰贸易有限公司	黎三明	22824398	国际商业贸易
东莞市东建浆纸有限公司	袁建辉	22623930	纸张
东莞市中堂废旧物资回收有限公司中联分公司	张庆菘	88120732	废纸收购
东莞市天牛塑胶原料有限公司	梁海燕	86998877	塑胶原料
广东鸿程油库有限公司	潘鸿飞		石油及制品
东莞市中堂废旧物资回收有限公司银洲分公司	罗　锐	88120732	废纸收购
东莞市新技术进口有限公司	陈伟斌	22428678	各类商品和技术的进出口
深圳市庆鹏石油化工经销有限公司东莞分公司	黄俊雄	88864889	成品油
东莞市宝信实业有限公司	赖锡胤	88731100	服装
东莞市恒泰石油制品贸易有限公司	伍锡莲	85322068	重油
东莞市天昌塑胶原料有限公司	赵　平	86992933	塑胶原料
东莞市大洲进出口有限公司	佘楚瑜	83032998	服装
东莞市仲源化工有限公司	苏俊超		甲醇
东莞市兴富石油产品有限公司	卢淦全	85338225	燃料油
东莞市天泰石油化工有限公司	陈雪琴	22028726	润滑油

1-4 续表 18

(2009年)

单位名称	负责人	联系电话	主要产品(或服务)
东莞市永信药业有限公司	郭章才		中成药
东莞市祥兴针车有限公司	梁佛祥	86882006	缝纫设备
广东省东莞化工进出口有限公司	袁翔光	22231118	进出口代理
广东洛贝电子科技有限公司	张宏志		电磁炉
东莞市伟明贸易有限公司	苏丽明	23033918	泡棉全棉涂色布
东莞市文成酒业有限公司	邓伟文	22111386	酒类
东莞市东悦机电设备有限公司	刘　俭	88188200	钢材
东莞市银图贸易有限公司	廖树波	88412888	塑料
东莞市创维电器发展有限公司	林大光	22292742	家用电器
广东省东莞丝绸进出口有限公司	何伟基	22482892	服装
东莞市中堂废旧物资回收有限公司同力分公司	黎满华	88120732	废纸收购
东莞市港源贸易有限公司	雷天保	22488703	工艺品进出口
东莞市中堂废旧物资回收有限公司双洲分公司	梁沛昌	88120732	废纸收购
东莞市中堂废旧物资回收有限公司珠江分公司	罗建洪	88120732	废纸收购
广东省东莞快宜外经发展有限公司	卢建超	22421003	商品进出口
东莞市智丰贸易有限公司	卢红花	83015809	服装
东莞市永联化工贸易有限公司	陈钟茬	83112349	过氧化氢
东莞市建安贸易有限公司	梁礼萍	22321232	轻纺产品服装
东莞市永盛燃料有限公司	余燕儿	22287225	石油及制品
零售业			
东莞市华升汽车有限公司	肖楚盛	85246601	汽车
东莞市宏宝汽车销售服务有限公司	梁　女	81106028	汽车
东莞市江铃汽车销售有限公司	卢沛锋	83220527	汽车
东莞市福丰汽车有限公司	叶　帆	22850001	长安福特品牌汽车
东莞市大新商贸有限公司清溪大新第二商场	程志坚	87301882	日用百货
东莞市东升汽车有限公司	任　军	85089656	汽车
东莞市南城丰田汽车销售服务有限公司	李国宏	22987090	汽车
东莞市南城周溪英油加油站	梁煖溢	22403634	汽油
东莞市中油迅兴实业有限公司	任禹绩	88412338	柴油
东莞市永佳丰田汽车销售服务有限公司	叶志荣	81691185	丰田汽车
东莞市中昌贸易有限公司	张柱海	81123383	汽车
上海大众汽车东莞销售服务有限公司	郭庆丰	22337006	汽车
东莞市森和纸业有限公司	陈兆成	85588818	纸制品
东莞市塘厦林村加油站	陈云娇	87902608	成品油
东莞市龙成汽车销售服务有限公司	李宝柱	22779999	汽车
东莞市广物正通达汽车贸易有限公司	石新琦	83269019	长安品牌汽车
东莞市合信汽车销售服务有限公司	王淦权	23188228	汔车
东莞市安信丰田汽车销售服务有限公司	韦松根	81870333	汽车
东莞市博雅贸易有限公司	李鎧彤	81090360	长安福特品牌汽车
东莞市立诚立信贸易有限公司	燕　妹	86919417	塑胶批发
东莞市盈顺石油有限公司	江瑞艮	88888656	汽油
东莞市东城加成加油站有限公司	钟国仁	22489229	汽油柴油灌装润滑油
东莞市虎门煤气有限公司	张泽新	85111140	燃气
东莞市桥南加油站有限公司	林广金	85882970	汽油

1-4 续表 19

(2009年)

单位名称	负责人	联系电话	主要产品(或服务)
东莞市百力恒丰田汽车销售服务有限公司	苏 葳	81603800	汽车
东莞市常平石油供应有限公司	尹国辉	83022221	汽油煤油
中域电讯连锁集团股份有限公司	李健明	22888888	手机通讯产品
东莞市万威水上加油站有限公司	卢伟民	88823882	柴油
东莞市永奥汽车贸易有限公司	陈祖永	83261895	汽车
东莞东风南方东益汽车销售服务有限公司	任 军	85133806	汽车
东莞市凯润东成汽车销售服务有限公司	李琬瑜	82223988	广州本田品牌汽车
东莞市聚成汽车技术服务有限公司	叶 帆	22406200	汽车
东莞市南方汽车博览有限公司	蔡玉李	87707666	汽车
东莞市骏鸣汽车销售服务有限公司	陈就泉	81112813	汽车
广东省东莞市医药有限公司	叶达球	22507881	西药批发
上海嘉定乐购生活购物有限公司东莞市常平分公司	陈永忠	81896969	百货
东莞市汇福轮胎有限公司	王连富	86180598	汽车轮胎
中国石油天然气股份有限公司广东东莞东城中旲加油站	褚东虹	22297999	成品油
东莞市丰华汽车销售服务有限公司	伦瑞祥	87193088	汽车
广东省东莞国药集团虎门医药有限公司	陈建智	85511364	药品
东莞市新元素能源有限公司	吴育武	22763444	重油
东莞市常平供销社	叶振辉	83331117	超级市场
东莞市东神贸易有限公司寮步分公司	任 军	83523042	汽车
东莞市南城区农机服务站宏伟加油站	陈建志	22404202	汽油
东莞市天虹商场有限公司	赖伟宣	23164880	百货
东莞市合禾汽车销售服务有限公司	刘晓风	82201168	丰田汽车
东莞市常平石油供应有限公司陈屋贝加油站	刘国柱	83391105	机动车燃料
中国石油化工股份有限公司广东东莞石油分公司	吴征燃	22506200	汽油批发
东莞市永怡汽车贸易有限公司	陈祖永	22904057	汽车
东莞市粤美特加油站有限公司	许锦潮	83351331	汽油、柴油
东莞市华树电脑有限公司	李华严	22313954	电子计算机及其配件
东莞市金美汽车销售服务有限公司	卢惠朝	83553927	汽车
东莞市合宝汽车销售服务有限公司	梁 女	22851228	宝马轿车
东莞市励骏实业有限公司	卢锦祥	21123920	皮鞋
东莞市东奥汽车服务有限公司	梁浩森		汽车
东莞市东神贸易有限公司樟木头分公司	任 军	83841312	品牌汽车
东莞市顺昌贸易有限公司	黄庆贤		机动车燃料
东莞市寮步横坑加油站有限公司	袁达生	83520080	汽油
东莞市志祥汽车销售服务有限公司	黄志超	83226599	汽车
东莞市南城海雅百货有限公司	涂乔轶	23027222	服装
东莞市大岭山联英加油站	马晓平	83351606	柴油
东莞市冠丰汽车有限公司	叶 帆	83525630	汽车
东莞市东富实业有限公司	张 义	83220559	汽车
东莞市黄江镇江南加油站有限公司	钟国仁	83629433	汽油
东莞市正欣科技有限公司	马文科	22023588	软件设计
东莞市东鑫汽车销售服务有限公司	叶 帆	82089077	汽车
东莞市大参林连锁药店有限公司	潘雪艳	22884901	药品
东莞市虎门石油公司虎威加油站	方旭芳	85109138	柴油

1-4 续表 20

(2009年)

单位名称	负责人	联系电话	主要产品(或服务)
东莞市大兴汽车贸易有限公司	邓益民	22662646	汽车
上海嘉定乐购生活购物有限公司东莞市虎门分公司	陈永忠	81613268	百货
东莞市东城中油柏洲边加油站	任禹绩	22263969	汽油
东莞市中油国威油品销售有限公司	佟福财	85503019	汽油
东莞市人人乐商业有限公司	李嘉伟	81633337	食品
东莞市冠骏汽车销售服务有限公司	袁　星	83230777	汽车
东莞市三益汽车有限公司	陆　勇	83526653	汽车
东莞市华美汽车销售服务有限公司	肖楚盛	85017927	汽车
东莞东风南方汽车销售有限公司	周先鹏	22985916	东风日产品牌汽车
东莞市嘉荣超市有限公司	胡近泰	22808810	家用百货
东莞市英利数控设备有限公司	黄光瑛	85317431	数控设备
东莞市万昌燃气有限公司	王　琪	88751011	生活用燃料
东莞市骏标汽车销售有限公司	刘绍学	22850962	小轿车
东莞市捷达通贸易有限公司	郑子先		汽车
东莞市鸿鹰汽车销售服务有限公司	尹灿洪	22981108	汽车
东莞市大朗镇长塘加油站	叶瑞麟	83319244	柴油、汽油、润滑油
东莞市石步加油站有限公司	陈广权	83218292	汽油
东莞市南城区加油站	陈建志	22417222	汽油
东莞市新东联汽车贸易有限公司	苗舜泽	83527292	汽车
东莞市中维商贸有限公司	阮秀莲	83887138	西装
深圳市国美电器有限公司东莞市分公司	王俊洲	22807391	家用电器
东莞市常平木抡加油站	刘国柱	83988331	机动车燃料
东莞市永升汽车贸易有限公司	周　鹏	81128180	汽车
东莞市渝庆汽车销售服务有限公司	罗添培	83300138	汽车
广东省东莞市万江供销社	叶伟明	22271856	批发
东莞市金良稻丰米业有限公司	邓　琪	87709579	粮油
广东省东莞国药集团长安医药有限公司	钟　路	85308840	药品
东莞市新大地汽车贸易有限公司	梁浩权		汽车
广州市好又多(天利)百货商业有限公司世博分公司	严文志	22763201	百货超市
东莞市厚街涌口加油站有限公司	袁达生	85050598	柴油
东莞市悦海实业投资有限公司	刘宇雄	81254225	服装
东莞市骏丰汽车有限公司	叶耀雄	83229371	汽车
东莞市骐骏汽车销售服务有限公司	谭新潮	87798302	汽车
东莞东美丰田汽车销售服务有限公司	叶　帆	82087662	汽车
东莞市苏宁电器有限公司	鲍东N	22320266	家用电器
东莞市时尚电器有限公司	李铸诚	22342220	家用电器
东莞凯润丰田汽车销售服务有限公司	李琬瑜	85133988	汽车
东莞市国贸超级市场有限公司	王健勇	22117591	副食品
东莞市华锐塑胶实业投资有限公司	王晓斌	83608800	塑胶原料
东莞华多利汽车有限公司	张　粤	83523000	汽车
东莞市海雅百货有限公司	冯　峰	22031333	百货
东莞市桥头加桥加油站有限公司	钟国仁	22367236	机动车燃料
东莞市世纪骏丰频谱科技有限公司	王淑萍		频谱仪
广东钻石世家国际珠宝有限公司	陈小凤	22028888	钻石

1-4　续表 21

(2009年)

单位名称	负责人	联系电话	主要产品(或服务)
东莞市天和商贸有限公司	邬志新	22508941	百货
东莞市恒波商业有限公司	杨乾坤	83018679	通讯产品
东莞市新日水果食品有限公司	陆爱章	22489993	水果、食品
东莞市石排燕窝加油站	钟国仁	86524520	汽油
东莞市恒信汽车销售服务有限公司	赵冬宇	22767228	汽车
东莞市佳华百货有限公司	庄陆坤	83841861	百货
东莞市华美乐建材超市有限公司	郑晓利	22901188	瓷砖
东莞市中堂镇东泊加油站	陈松茂	88885838	柴油
东莞市汇天源汽车销售服务有限公司	李瑞勤	83528753	汽车
深圳市海王星辰健康药房连锁有限公司东莞分公司	王少棠	22366079	药品
东莞市长久汽车贸易有限公司	博世久	22663933	汽车
东莞市天下行丰田汽车销售服务有限公司(常平)	陆新薇	83558216	汽车
东莞市彩怡百货有限公司	卢成通	22497688	百货
东莞龙华丰田汽车销售服务有限公司	李宝柱	22773388	汽车
东莞市羚丰汽车贸易有限公司	黄卫东	22981618	汽车
东莞市骏捷汽车贸易有限公司	吴沃川	83080019	东风本田汽车
东莞市星高达汽车销售服务有限公司	张风品	81105588	斯柯达品牌汽车
东莞市兴隆汽车贸易有限公司	赵少飞	82315618	汽车
东莞市愉康超市有限公司	陈锡光	85536488	百货
东莞市遂通汽车销售服务有限公司	伦瑞祥	22850555	汽车
东莞市华康空调电器有限公司	钟镇尧	22348888	空调
东莞市君通汽车贸易有限公司	张巧华	83226599	汽车
东莞市锦亚汽车贸易有限公司	杜　茗	81117637	进口现代品牌汽车
东莞市同庆汽车贸易有限公司	何庆同	83300188	汽车
东莞市广物君豪实业投资有限公司	李民毅	22703999	汽车
东莞市华顺汽车贸易有限公司	王　玲	85909050	东南牌汽车
东莞市东部丰田汽车销售服务有限公司	叶　帆	83285989	汽车丰田品牌车
东莞市志达汽车销售服务有限公司	万凤晶	85226333	汽车
东莞市黄江农机管理服务站	叶小红	83634377	柴油
东莞市中科能源有限公司	吴楚金	83600900	润滑油
东莞市明丰贸易有限公司	刘旺枝	81633278	百货
东莞市东盛超市有限公司	贝多拉	23139067	日用百货
东莞市骏宇汽车贸易有限公司	李伟洪	22851778	汽车及配件
上海嘉定乐购生活购物有限公司东莞市厚街分公司	陈永忠	88913888	百货
东莞市大新汽车贸易有限公司	李洪光	22672268	汽车
东莞市万江国威加油站	方　挺	22275846	机动车燃料
东莞中汽南方汽车销售服务有限公司	黎木金	86225930	汽车
东莞市银星实业发展有限公司	黄华精	87737539	柴油
东莞市中油西溪加油站有限公司	肖锡洪	83328508	汽油
东莞市塘厦镇诸佛岭加油站	刘宁安	87926329	成品油
东莞市永成加油站有限公司	王爱慈	85588949	汽油
东莞市常平液化石油气供应有限公司	陈锦新	83337820	液化石油气
东莞市华安加油站有限公司	董树轩	22298698	成品油
东莞市新天地汽车销售服务有限公司	张龙阁	83523008	汽车

1-4 续表 22

(2009年)

单位名称	负责人	联系电话	主要产品(或服务)
东莞市黄江镇飞龙加油站	曾锦昌	83363017	汽油
东莞市锦华汽车贸易有限公司	吴根亮	85990730	小汽车
东莞市大朗镇松木山加油站	黄柱辉	83128021	汽油
东莞市昊安汽车有限公司	苗舜泽	85223818	汽车
东莞市锦多宝能源有限公司	吴锦福	87780788	汽油、重油、润滑
东莞市永濠汽车销售服务有限公司	刘润红	22904888	汽车
东莞市东仁汽车销售服务有限公司	崔　毅	86228588	汽车
住宿业			
东莞市松山湖酒店有限公司凯悦酒店分公司	卢淦波	22891234	住宿
东莞宾馆有限公司	胡焕文	22222222	正餐服务
东莞市会展国际大酒店	梁志文	22889999	旅游饭店
东莞市塘厦三正半山酒店有限公司	莫浩棠	87299333	旅游饭店
东莞市华尔登国际酒店有限公司	李建忠	81028888	住宿餐饮
东莞市美怡登酒店	刘柏林	83028888	旅游饭店
东莞市汇华饭店	刘柏全	83938888	旅游饭店
东莞市丰泰花园酒店有限公司	苏志江	85708888	旅业
东莞市宏远酒店有限公司	陈树德	22418888	餐饮
东莞市石龙名冠金凯悦大酒店有限公司	莫冠良	86188888	酒店住宿
东莞市汇景酒店有限公司	张玉昆	88848888	餐饮
东莞市长安国际酒店有限公司	陈灿球	85333333	餐饮服务
东莞市嘉华酒店有限公司	林干能	85928888	餐饮
东莞市太子酒店有限公司	梁灶暖	83363333	住宿
东莞市昌明实业有限公司喜来登酒店	陈润昌	85988888	饮食服务
东莞市富盈酒店有限公司	邓华昭	85888888	餐饮
东莞市东城国际酒店有限公司	祁炜锦	82268888	星级酒店
东莞市名冠金凯悦大酒店有限公司	莫冠良	87759888	饭店服务
东莞市龙泉国际大酒店	张佛思	85188688	餐饮
东莞市蒂豪花园酒店有限公司	梁永雄	83122222	提供住宿服务
东莞市中汇文华酒店有限公司	熊毅文	88788888	餐饮服务
餐饮业			
东莞市万豪酒店有限公司	王弟坤	87898888	旅业
东莞市花园粥城服务有限公司	零宝生	22612051	餐饮服务
真功夫餐饮管理有限公司	蔡达标	38792952	快餐饮食服务
东莞市长安广城海鲜酒家	麦少波	81627666	中餐服务
银行业			
东莞市农村信用合作联社	何沛良	22103131	办理金融业务
东莞农村商业银行股份有限公司沙田支行	陈伟贤	88867203	金融业
招商银行股份有限公司东莞分行	王耀球	22303888	办理金融业务
中国银行股份有限公司东莞分行	刘　劲	22819888	金融业务
兴业银行股份有限公司东莞分行	刘永革	22809988	金融业务
中国建设银行股份有限公司东莞市分行	李洪茂	22816118	金融业务
中信银行股份有限公司东莞分行	彭周福	22667876	金融业务
中国工商银行股份有限公司东莞分行	吴传武	22481728	办理金融业务
广东发展银行股份有限公司东莞分行	卢少斌	22477888	金融业务
中国农业银行东莞分行	何绍成	23305742	金融业务
交通银行股份有限公司东莞分行	朱木森	22505643	办理金融业务

1-4 续表 23

(2009年)

单位名称	负责人	联系电话	主要产品(或服务)
证券业			
东莞证券有限责任公司	游锦辉	22119350	证券经纪业务
广发证券股份有限公司东莞虎门证券营业部	李志文	85521178	证券经纪
中国人寿保险股份有限公司东莞分公司	李秋文	22488488	人寿保险业务
太平人寿保险有限公司东莞中心支公司	乔振刚	23188161	经营人寿保险业务
中国太平洋财产保险股份有限公司东莞中心支公司	郭振雄	22807699	金融保险
中国平安财产保险股份有限公司东莞分公司	李培义		办理财产保险业务
中华联合财产保险股份有限公司东莞中心支公司	杨佛华	22605888	财产保险经营业务
东莞市南枫佳誉保险代理有限公司	兀云岗	22995003	代理保险产品
中国人民人寿保险股份有限公司东莞市中心支公司	黄日球	22306285	人寿保险
永安财产保险股份有限公司东莞中心支公司	叶 青	22996100	企业财产损失保险
中国人民财产保险股份有限公司东莞市分公司	潘振雄	22313601	办理财产保险业务
泰康人寿保险股份有限公司东莞中心支公司	李春辉	22994019	办理人寿保险
中国大地财产保险股份有限公司东莞中心支公司	张沛森	22361158	财产保险
天平汽车保险股份有限公司东莞中心支公司	杨庆苏	22992063	车辆保险
阳光人寿保险股份有限公司东莞中心支公司	黄贤辉	88981959	人寿保险
中国太平洋人寿保险股份有限公司东莞中心支公司	叶学辉	22321518	承保各种人身保险业务
中国平安人寿保险股份有限公司东莞中心支公司	何 毅	21683205	人寿保险
太平保险有限公司东莞中心支公司	邱惠坤	22476688	财产保险业务
中国人民健康保险股份有限公司东莞中心支公司	伍世强	22328887	健康保险业务
新华人寿保险股份有限公司东莞中心支公司	唐鹤飞	22498243	寿险营销
其他金融活动			
东莞信托有限公司	何锦成	22366101	信托业务
中国邮政储蓄银行有限责任公司东莞分行	王毅燕	22116366	办理金融业务
房地产业			
东莞市高田房地产开发有限公司	欧阳忠	22386908	房地产开发
东莞市康联房地产开发有限公司	王梓洪	85753088	房地产开发
东莞市佳驹实业有限公司	赖洪中	22679733	房地产开发
东莞景天房地产开发有限公司	袁德宗	22667836	开发建设
东莞市鑫伯房地产投资有限公司	方植宁	81636821	房地产开发
东莞市天诚房地产开发有限公司	李金培		房地产开发
东莞市石龙镇房地产公司	叶淇光	86116822	镇域房地产监管
东莞市富盈房地产开发有限公司	刘学斌	81226161	房地产开发
东莞市横沥镇房地产开发公司	温国福	83371828	房地产开发
东莞市东城区房地产开发公司	李民立	22470531	商品房零售
东莞华美新村建造有限公司	卢贺华		房地产开发经营
东莞新世纪房地产开发有限公司	张应旋	22382251	房地产开发
东莞市恒盈房地产开发有限公司	陈静峰	22265062	房地产开发
东莞市松山居置业有限公司	周 彤		房地产开发
东莞市华建物业投资有限公司	陈立新	22820769	房地产开发
广东宏远集团房地产开发有限公司	钟振强		城市综合开发
东莞市中信康华房地产有限公司	林瑞明	22482388	房地产

1-4 续表 24

(2009年)

单位名称	负责人	联系电话	主要产品(或服务)
东莞市翠云轩房地产开发有限公司	赖洪中	22679733	其它房地产活动
东莞市建工集团房地产开发有限公司	陈炽辉	22427888	房地产开发
东莞市阳光房地产开发有限公司	刘福利	83916852	房地产经营
东莞市金众房地产有限公司	冯向东	22820205	房地产开发
东莞市三正房地产开发有限公司	莫浩棠	87299333	房地产开发
中信华南东莞有限公司	林瑞明	22482388	其他房地产
东莞市三元盈晖投资发展有限公司	胡桂容		房地产项目经营
东莞市广盈服务有限公司企石分公司	李楚敏		服务业
广东三正集团有限公司	莫浩棠	82470333	房地产开发
东莞市新世纪怡岛花园商住开发有限公司	李晓明	88638888	房地业开发
东莞市中惠香樟绿洲房地产开发有限公司	叶惠全	22360398	房地产开发
东莞市金盛房地产开发有限公司	张金胜		房地产开发经营
东莞市兴裕商贸中心开发有限公司	朱旭基	85166008	房地产开发
东莞市塘盛房地产开发有限公司	周炳辉	87917238	房地产开发
东莞市粤海村(单项)开发有限公司	侯庆虎	22611621	房地产开发
东莞市新世纪丽江豪园商住开发有限公司	周凯婴	86409800	房地产开发经营
中信华南(集团)东莞有限公司	林瑞明	22482388	房地产开发
东莞市大步花园房地产开发有限公司	史学新	88283478	房地产开发
东莞市万科房地产有限公司(万科高尔夫)	周　彤	23013500	房地产开发
东莞市新世纪润城实业投资有限公司	黄俊灿	88991899	房地产开发
东莞市阳光海岸实业有限公司	王赞新	81615333	房地产
广东南峰房地产有限公司	谭金荣	22383796	房地产经营
东莞市富鹏置业有限公司	许志雄	87862310	房地产开发经营
东莞市莞深长城地产有限公司	宋　扬	22891428	房地产开发
东莞市碧湖花园有限公司	李少明	83981809	房地产开发经营
东莞市凯东实业投资有限公司	方武权	85609718	实业投资
东莞市铭可达商住中心开发有限公司	赵武豪	22309112	房地产开发
东莞市塘厦镇房地产开发公司	黎润祥	87722361	房地产开发
东莞市深国投房地产开发有限公司	李南峰		房地产开发
东莞市东沙港建设发展有限公司	霍福华	88661823	房地产开发
东莞市松山湖房地产有限公司	张志毅	22892337	房地产开发
东莞市樟木头镇物业管理公司	蔡运明	87713517	物业管理
东莞市同方房地产开发有限公司	王启荣	22483998	房地产开发
东莞市新世纪明上居商住开发有限公司	周　彤	23013547	房地产开发
东莞市鼎峰房地产开发有限公司	麦彦桐	86666016	房地产开发
东莞市丰泰建设房地产有限公司	何淑芳	85221133	房地产开发
东莞市丰泰建设房地产有限公司(丰泰城)	何淑芳	85188701	房地产开发
东莞市阳龙房地产有限公司	梁晖林		房地产开发
东莞市锋尚公寓房地产开发有限公司	伦瑞祥	23183571	房地产开发
东莞市君怡豪园建造有限公司	叶惠全		房地产开发经营
东莞市龙泉房地产开发有限公司长安商业广场项目	张佛恩	85112323	房地产开发区
东莞市中惠沁林山庄房地产开发公司	廖桂源	83716088	实业项目开发投资
东莞市御鹿华庭建造有限公司	谭金荣	87293176	产地产开发
东莞市濠兴逸苑商住开发有限公司	卢光远		濠兴逸苑项目房地产开发

1-4 续表 25

(2009年)

单位名称	负责人	联系电话	主要产品(或服务)
东莞市光大房地产开发有限公司	陈润光	22986086	房地产开发
东莞市樟木头房地产开发总公司	蔡汉雄	87711310	土地开发商品房
东莞市大绿地房地产开发有限公司	殷洪庆	87388810	房地产开发
东莞市石排镇房地产公司	黄耀强	86656011	房地产开发
东莞市美居广场建造有限公司	邓学勤	22777795	房地产开发经营
东莞市龙城房地产开发有限公司	刘树昌	86111268	房地产开发
东莞市广源房地产开发有限公司	赵智谋		房地产开发经营
东莞市篁城开发有限公司	叶向明	22113388	房地产项目开发
东莞市盈丰房地产开发有限公司	王文城	85873818	房地产开发
东莞百事威房住开发有限公司	江清波	83639979	房地产开发
东莞市桃源商住建造有限公司	陈润光		房地产开发
东莞市金田实业投资有限公司	孙桂新	83555838	房地产项目投资
东莞市富怡房地产开发有限公司	郭锦桃	85832206	房地产开发经营
东莞市新世纪房地产开发有限公司(领居)	叶向荣	83053693	其他房地产
东莞市瀚森投资集团有限公司	陈伟洪	22333488	房地产投资
东莞市丽水佳园开发有限公司	陈　昕	88318806	房地产开发
东莞市合盛房地产开发有限公司	王迪勋	85705222	房地产开发
东莞市山水雅居房地产开发有限公司	张京生	82206266	房地产业 房地产开发经营
东莞市神鹰塑料有限公司	胡松柏	86991888	物业管理
东莞市鹏程物业投资有限公司	莫应忠	81667958	房地产开发
东莞市田禾房地产投资有限公司	王晓梅	23030787	房地产开发
东莞市东城区房地产开发公司	周日佳	22483788	房地产开发
东莞市万盛房地产开发有限公司	刘学斌	88561185	房地产开发
东莞市长佳长安花园开发有限公司	孙志中	85338777	房地产项目开发
东莞市丰泰华园山庄建造有限公司	何锐平	85188896	房地产开发
东莞市东田丽园房地产开发有限公司	刘向荣	83989677	开发经营
东莞市明康家园商住开发有限公司	陈树德	83752565	房地产开发
东莞市鸿景房地产有限公司	王基才	22821111	房地产开发
东莞市宝田实业有限公司	冼七妹	88689966	厂房出租
东莞市永江集团有限公司	胡永添	87840888	实业投资
东莞市致富物业管理有限公司	陈浩森	88868218	物业管理
东莞市聚豪名轩商住开发有限公司	何志鹏	86088001	房地产投资
东莞市康湖房地产开发有限公司	谭伟雄	87633333	房地产开发与管理
东莞市玉泉投资开发有限公司	朱国和	87508188	土地开发
东莞宏远工业区股份有限公司	周明轩	22414228	开发经营工业区
东莞市中惠沁林山庄房地产开发有限公司	叶惠全	22360398	其他房地产
东莞市汇景房地产开发有限公司	伦瑞祥	85923777	房地产开发
东莞市富麟实业有限公司	杨志茂	87568889	房地产开发
东莞市星河传说商住区有限公司	廖卓强	22031328	房地产开发
东莞市新世纪房地产有限公司	张应旋	88237666	房地产开发
东莞市新世纪科教拓展有限公司	朱凤廉	87773222	其他房地产活动
东莞市万科物业服务有限公司	周　彤	88013333	物业管理
东莞市陶然居房地产开发有限公司	麦谦和		房地产开发
东莞市东逸物业管理有限公司	陈炳林	85883333	房地产开发
东莞市捷利物业投资有限公司	陈硕生	85124488	房地产开发经营
东莞市丰华房地产开发有限公司	卢淦波	22629333	房地产开发
东莞市信义房地产开发有限公司	李贤义	81888880	房地产开发经营

1-4 续表 26

(2009年)

单位名称	负责人	联系电话	主要产品(或服务)
商务服务业			
东莞市虎门永丰鞋业个体商场	黄果荣	85107836	市场管理
富盈集团有限公司	刘学斌	81568888	综合
东莞市长安供电公司	苏志刚	85313828	电力供应管理
东莞市长安镇锦厦经济联合社	李学军	85301960	企业管理
东莞市大朗供电公司	李雄峰	83316187	电力供应管理
东莞市厚街供电公司	黄满林	85585368	电力供应管理
东莞市桥头镇邓屋股份经济联合社	邓满容	83341073	合作社经济管理
东莞市虎门镇路东经济联合社	黄广基	85567032	合作经济管理
东莞市南城区工业发展公司	吕庆鸿	22415322	办理开办T场业务
东莞市塘厦镇林村股份经济联合社	李茂云	87721501	企业管理咨询
东莞市智能市场管理服务有限公司	刘美强	87738170	市场管理
东莞市建华贸易有限公司	王建华	87733209	日用品批发
东莞市东城实业发展总公司	何照棠	22331385	实业投资
东莞市中国旅行社有限公司	叶沛新	22218288	旅游业
东莞市寮步镇经济联合总社	罗军文	83323805	企业管理咨询
东莞市长安镇沙头经济联合社	陈柏安	85544888	经济管理工作
东莞市天纬通信有限公司	莫　侨	22482678	劳务派遣
广东宏远集团有限公司	陈　林	22414228	经营和代理各类商品的进出口业务
广东智通人才连锁股份有限公司	叶　菁	87078157	人才信息咨询服务
东莞市东城供电公司	周　粤	22669826	电力供应管理
东莞市长安镇长实发展总公司	林光辉	85310368	企业管理
东莞市黄江供电公司	江　峰	83361290	电力供应管理
东莞市常平镇资产经营管理有限公司	袁庆华	83331431	企业资产管理
东莞市中堂镇潢涌股份经济联合社	黎锡康	88881002	合作社经济管理
东莞市粤龙物业发展有限公司	叶汉泉	86181222	企业管理咨询
东莞市国际旅行社有限公司	陈冀凯	22458168	旅行社
东莞市清溪对外经济发展有限公司	黄沛林	87732058	外引内联企业咨询
东莞市景鸿物业管理有限公司	王晓冬	22381011	劳务派遣
东莞市新远高速公路发展有限公司	尹锦容	22083200	投资开发东莞高速公路网
东莞市明煜管理咨询有限公司	张鹤杰	22408845	企业管理服务
东莞市鸿弋进出口有限公司	李凤池	85037999	货物进出口
东莞市黄河集团房地产开发有限公司	郑任辉	85222222	实业投资
东莞市群策外商投资服务有限公司	刘祖全	22813652	企业登记代理咨询服务
东莞市凤岗供电公司	李洁明	87756877	电力供应
东莞市麻涌镇经济发展总公司	郑玉艮	88239336	企业管理服务
东莞市南城供电公司	陈乃昊	22414348	电力供应管理
东莞市虎门镇龙眼股份经济联合社	张国平	85553988	投资和资产投资
东莞市中堂资产经营管理有限公司	陈俭良	88811116	镇属资产经营管理
东莞市石碣供电公司	李富强	86317627	电力供应管理
东莞市高埗供电公司	黎达祺	88781518	电力供应管理

1-4 续表 27

(2009年)

单位名称	负责人	联系电话	主要产品(或服务)
东莞市石排供电公司	刘志阳	86550387	电力供应
东莞市电化集团公司本部	龙　伟	22461466	实业投资
东莞市石龙镇工业总公司	梁耀光	86103661	企业管理咨询
东莞市虎门镇南栅股份经济联合社	王惠文	85561938	合作社经济管理
东莞市清溪经济发展公司	王冠清	87366293	企业管理服务
东莞市塘厦供电公司	莫汉培	87727425	电力供应管理
东莞市石碣镇发展实业公司	陈启桃	86631030	企业咨询
东莞市东城资产经营管理有限公司	卢润江	22331385	资产管理
东莞市松山湖控股有限公司	陈建枝	22898178	第一产业投资
东莞市大岭山镇资产经营管理有限公司	黄庆辉	85788362	经济管理
东莞市寮步经济发展总公司	尹学思	83328387	经济贸易咨询
东莞市长安镇综合市场	许春树	85535310	农贸市场管理
东莞市青年国际旅行社有限公司	李钦源	22239388	旅游
东莞市宏图工业开发公司	张耀平	22415322	宏图工业区内土地开发
东莞市虎门城郊供电公司	李　耘	85527786	电力供应管理
东莞市塘厦镇资产经营有限公司	叶锦河	82087792	资产经营管理
东莞市桥头镇资产经营管理有限公司	邓沃辉	83342135	企业管理服务
东莞市桥头供电公司	莫林波	83341212	电力供应
东莞市华源集团有限公司	林干能	85928888	酒店
东莞市沙田对外经济开发总公司	冼七妹	88689966	对外资用地办理立项
东莞市丰华集团有限公司	卢淦波	22629333	酒店投资
上沙股份经济联合社	孙锡明	85547208	合作社经济管理
东莞市中之进出口有限公司	尹梓伟	23182111	自营和代理各类商品和技术的进出口
东莞市桥头镇石水口股份经济联合社	莫锦伦	83428823	企业管理咨询
东莞市石龙粤龙实业公司	叶汉泉	86181222	电机、金属机械
东莞市厚街经济发展总公司	陈海平	85990333	物业租赁
东莞市虎门镇资产经营管理有限公司	张勇江	85522409	镇属资产产权的管理
东莞市大岭山供电公司	何平稳	83350287	电力供应管理
东莞市桥头镇桥头股份经济联合社	邓金焕	83342308	合作经济管理
东莞市常平镇土塘股份经济联合社	黄沛龙	83553233	合作社经济管理
东莞市京盟实业投资有限公司	叶景坤	85589878	实业投资
东莞市桥头镇田新股份经济联合社	罗春林	83341032	合作社经济管理
东莞市长安镇霄边经济联合社	蔡伟权	81882222	合作社经济管理
东莞市大莹物业管理有限公司	程明华	85151566	市场管理
东莞市昌明实业有限公司	陈润昌	85598888	实业投资
东莞市广晟商贸发展有限公司	何一平	22301668	物业投资
东莞市石碣镇经济发展总公司	王伟东	86631048	进出口服务
东莞市樟木头资产经营管理有限公司	黄少雄	87188978	镇属资产产权管理
东莞市寮步镇横坑股份经济联合社	钟满棠	83301024	其他企业管理服务
东莞市东坑镇经济联合总社	张耀洪	83889698	企业管理机构
东莞市横沥镇经济联合总社	杨永存	83717663	企业管理咨询
东莞市方达集团有限公司	麦校勋	85330098	兴办实业
东莞市万江供电公司	袁单光	22788971	企业管理机构
城区资产办	萧健峰	22102722	政府内资产物业管理
东莞市长安镇咸西经济联合社	麦全意	85533868	合作社经济管理
东莞市常平供电公司	周黄球	83399778	电力供应管理

1-4 续表 28

(2009年)

单位名称	负责人	联系电话	主要产品(或服务)
东莞市凤岗镇官井头股份经济联合社	卓金华	87771352	其他企业管理服务
东莞市合鑫膳食管理服务有限公司	王　清	23111916	膳食管理
东莞市清溪供电公司	蓝汉清	87314148	电力供应
东莞市石碣镇桔洲股份经济联合社	黄加仔	86332030	经联社经济管理
东莞市石龙镇西湖股份经济联合社	张应海	86113078	合作社经济管理
东莞市鸿信实业有限公司	黄志辉	83383786	投资实业
东莞市沙田经济发展总公司	梁治平	88861003	机构商务代理服务
东莞市虎门名铺城	何福祥	85113665	商铺管理
东莞市集源资产经营管理有限公司	杨德良	83633322	出租房屋服务
东莞市光华医院有限公司	邝华仔	22668152	医疗卫生
东莞市南城区资产经营管理有限公司	刘林宏	22417250	管理区属资产
东莞市凤岗镇资产经营有限公司	朱国和	87759398	资产管理
东莞市寮步供电公司	尹植滔	81113608	全镇电力供应
东莞市虎门镇北栅经济联合社	陈树培	85551481	资产管理
东莞市松山湖工业发展有限公司	练　刚	22891044	房产管理
东莞市中堂供电公司	吴柱坚	88893288	电力供应
东莞市清溪镇经济联合总社	黄沛林	87733292	咨询服务
东莞康辉国际旅行社有限公司	李继烈	22001168	国内旅游服务
东莞市望牛墩资产经营管理有限公司	叶孔新	88853008	镇居资产产权管理
东莞市桥光实业集团公司	罗锦海	83341012	主营办理外引内联企业的咨询业务
东莞市虎门镇虎门寨股份经济联合社	王洪亮	85509032	合作经济管理
东莞市万江区资产经营管理有限公司	刘沛林	22273273	投资与资产管理
东莞市企石振华开发总公司	谢耀光	86765688	外引内联企业咨询洽谈、签约及办厂
东莞市虎门富民服务有限公司	孙俊才	85111883	市场管理
东莞市谢岗供电公司	黄汉良	87761224	电力供应管理
东莞市大朗镇长塘股份经济联合社	叶惠光	83318030	合作社经济管理
东莞市厚街镇溪头股份经济联合社	方巨希	85599061	合作社经济管理
东莞市凤岗镇雁田经济联合社	邓泽荣	87774631	合作社经济管理
研究与试验发展			
东莞市万科建筑技术研究有限公司	张纪文	22890188	建筑技术开发
专业技术服务业			
东莞市大族粤铭激光科技有限公司	张建群	22771433	激光雕刻机
东莞市公路桥梁开发建设总公司	尹锦容	22083269	规划建设公路桥梁
东莞市清溪工业开发有限公司	王冠清	87732058	工业开发
科技交流和推广服务业			
东莞市方达环宇环保科技有限公司	许志榕	89998656	环保技术的开发转让服务培训
公共设施管理业			
东莞市松山湖公用事业有限公司	刘清涛	23306078	园林绿化维护
居民服务业			
东莞市东保押运有限公司	刘沛声	83528016	贵重物品押运
东莞市美升达市政工程有限公司	王美始	85831187	市政工程
其他服务业			
东莞市大洋电机工程有限公司	谢光华	82061188	电机设备维修
东莞市虎门大宁企业发展公司	谭运章	85553188	办理开办厂场业务
东莞市塘厦林村工业发展公司	李成发	87722262	外引内联企业的咨询及洽谈
广州志诚科技工程服务有限公司东莞凤岗分公司	陈浩铭		科技工程服务

1-5 营业收入超5000万元的外资企业（2009年）

Foreign-funded Enterprises with Business Revenue over RMB 50 Million (2009)

单位名称	负责人	联系电话	主要产品(或服务)
农副食品加工业			
东莞市飞亚达益富可华南油脂有限公司	阿姆利	88230055	棕榈油精炼
东莞兴业生物科技有限公司	王耀辉	22652130	预混合配合饲料
中粮新沙粮油工业(东莞)有限公司	王印基	88825601	豆油
东莞光华饲料有限公司	蔡初强	88817756	猪饲料
东莞卡尔吉蛋白饲料有限公司	安博泰	88236732	豆油
东莞欧陆食品有限公司	郭洪有	86246898	西式肉类食品
统一嘉吉(东莞)饲料蛋白科技有限公司	谢志鹏	88225888	豆油
食品制造业			
东莞锦泰食品有限公司	袁汉思	22400818	饼干
东莞荣华饼家有限公司	袁应驱	86633692	月饼
东莞徐记食品有限公司	徐 乘	22259888	糖果
华嘉食品有限公司	张尚羽	22464101	饼干
广东太阳神集团有限公司	骆 辉	83621288	猴头菇胃肠口服液
东莞福满多食品有限公司	赵慧敬	88230290	粮食制品
东莞万好食品有限公司	钟明发	81016222	点心食品
饮料制造业			
金威啤酒(东莞)有限公司	叶旭全	22898999	啤酒
东莞石龙津威饮料食品有限公司	龚志勇		葡锌乳酸菌饮料
华润雪花啤酒广东有限公司	王 群	88772999	啤酒
东莞雀巢有限公司	张俊峰	22404088	速溶咖啡
可口可乐装瓶商生产(东莞)有限公司	戴嘉舜	22401678	茶饮料及果汁饮料
广东加多宝饮料食品有限公司	张树容	85331688	王老吉
纺织业			
东莞达利盛时装有限公司	林富华	87756188	服装
东莞合迅服装设计有限公司	许莉娜	86244388	针织化纤胸围
东莞通盈纺织制衣有限公司	麦俊鹏	88188015	梳织布
东莞百宏实业有限公司	郑国烟	88869615	粘扣带
东莞东兴商标织绣有限公司	孙贺宜	85545888	商标
东莞富达染厂有限公司	刘进基	88844490	棉针织色布
东莞超盈纺织有限公司	卢煜光	88231808	双拉布
惠宜制衣(东莞)有限公司	李剑伟	83331110	棉裤
东莞忆凯制衣有限公司	赖炎山	83185898	全绵婴儿毛衫
东莞励发制衣厂	欧淦坤	85822228	全棉男庄针织长袖T恤
宏达纺织(东莞)有限公司	陈少婷	87982238	灯芯绒坯布、全棉坯布
东莞胜丰针织有限公司	黄志坚	88879742	纺织服装
东莞福珍针织制衣有限公司	卢华胜	88321475	针织服装
东莞弘裕纺织科技有限公司	叶芳樱	88563858	特多龙塑胶布
东莞永联弹力织物有限公司	颜华兴	88852801	橡根带
东莞明辉商标织造有限公司	史提芬·戴维森	87797688	布商标
东莞念辉家饰用品有限公司	萧雅玲	83392366	桌巾
东莞东美线业有限公司	弗烈积逊	88339333	缝纫线涤纶短纤维线

1-5　续表 1

(2009年)

单位名称	负责人	联系电话	主要产品(或服务)
东莞光晖针织有限公司	戴瑞恒	83112278	针织毛衫
东莞益富制衣有限公司	罗乐凤	83812288	针织成衣、梳织成衣
东莞新兴织造厂有限公司	王志元	85562795	毛染整精
东莞沙田丽海纺织印染有限公司	夏松芳	88866583	印染布
多宝针织服装(东莞)有限公司	白礼达	83820563	针织毛衣
东莞富山纺织漂染有限公司	邢仁寿	88841755	漂染针织布、梳织布
东莞明海整染厂有限公司	李逢乐	38831553	染色布
东莞福安纺织印染有限公司	夏松芳		棉针织用纱线
必富针织(东莞)有限公司	陈锡光	87293365	毛衫
东莞虎门科艺纺织印花有限公司	刁锦嫦	85561798	丝绸印花
东莞世丽纺织有限公司	邓业中	88843806	全棉针织色布
东莞立春纺织有限公司	许承男	88862325	粘扣带
东莞富阳针织有限公司	郑裕耀	88603688	毛衣
东莞泰广玻璃纤维有限公司	陈志强	88384898	方格布
东莞康俊胶布有限公司	陈锦标	83913222	胶尼龙布
建大纺织(东莞)有限公司	吕荣团	88855355	毛线
东莞联丰巨川纤维膊棉有限公司	骆大川	86914666	人造纤维制品
东莞同广纺织品有限公司	钟棣豪	85933301	各类针织胚布
东莞晶苑毛织制衣有限公司	罗乐凤	83982212	纺织品
东莞乐升植绒有限公司	冯治国	86668899	棉、化纤印染精
东莞联庆纺织有限公司	蔡文钦	86784606	棉、化纤纺织
广东联发毛纺织有限公司	周伟权	22262232	纺织
东莞厚宏制衣有限公司	苏伟年	83341382	针织服装
东莞德兴胸围内衣有限公司	刘兆明	85616668	胸围
东莞新锦江印花有限公司	李庆铭	88843112	全棉针织印花布
东莞茂志针织有限公司	李谋任	83209838	针织服装
东莞奥康德思宏针织品有限公司	萧玉妍	83828858	毛衣(针织)
东莞裕发纺织漂染有限公司	高明星	88850188	纺织漂染
东莞百和织造有限公司	郑国烟	88862371	粘扣带
东莞德永佳纺织制衣有限公司	黎兆强	88821738	棉针织染整布
联亚制衣(东莞)有限公司	李雍熙	82081818	梭织服装
东莞市小猪班纳服饰有限公司	张良义	87125086	童装
东莞宝达日用品制造有限公司	詹耀良	83311690	布手套
东莞嘉鹏纺织有限公司	李敏华	88826666	毛
东莞润达弹性织造有限公司	卢煜光	85593366	织带
东莞德福制衣有限公司	吴圣宗	83335273	毛衣针织
东莞市新马毛织时装有限公司	梁炘尧	83313441	羊毛衫
东莞市远梦家用纺织品有限公司	许镇智	85991010	床上用品
纺织服装、鞋、帽制造业			
东莞市帼制衣有限公司	程　隽	88516316	服装
东莞高业制衣有限公司	潘静玲	22784602	服装
东莞永达利纺织有限公司	钟湛豪	85588751	全棉针织坯布
东莞澳思制衣有限公司	周一俊	83332225	毛衣及针梭织服装
东莞福井制衣有限公司	朱镇波	85440871	服装

1-5 续表 2

(2009年)

单位名称	负责人	联系电话	主要产品(或服务)
东莞福泉制衣有限公司	水耀敏	88666698	棉针织服装
东莞盈富制衣有限公司	曹建华	88838386	男装衬衫
东莞益豪时装有限公司	连乙文	86618323	服装
东莞力凯鞋业制造有限公司	廖俊荣	85583101	运动鞋
东莞联泰制衣有限公司	陈亨利	86807613	衣服
东莞菲力制衣有限公司	邱允恭	88786698	服装
东莞众信制衣有限公司	叶锡乾	88318125	服装
东莞永信鞋业有限公司	刘枝煌	85918320	运动鞋
东莞成笑服装有限公司	黄其成	88709991	服装
东莞利来远东针织有限公司	李旭傍	22851333	服装
东莞璒录普制衣有限公司	吴文和	85551363	服装
东莞精致针织有限公司	方元德	86836260	各类服装
东莞宏宇制衣有限公司	郭玉美	88462208	针织服装
东莞绰豪制衣有限公司	方安宁	86244388	服装
东莞亿城服装有限公司	石培珍	85311107	各类纺织品服装
东莞昱胜鞋业有限公司	张志邦	88808168	皮鞋
东莞启松服装有限公司	林少文	87722174	服装
东莞新记制衣印花有限公司	林柏奇	86176508	服装
得福(东莞)制衣有限公司	欧阳家辉		服装
东莞诠立鞋业有限公司	柯瑞桐	85992586	女装便鞋
东莞富程鞋业有限公司	萧扬晔	22265418	休闲鞋
东莞冠昌制衣有限公司	赖仁剑	88703966	服装
东莞丰泰制衣有限公司	吕美玲	86179848	纺织服装
东莞美商制衣有限公司	达斯瓦尼·帕尔因	22902688	服装
东莞海星服装有限公司	夏松芳	85300702	各类服装
东莞宏大制衣有限公司	吕建东	88468668	各类针织衣服
东莞冠丽时装有限公司	钟伟明	86016001	服装
东莞励进制衣有限公司	黎兆强	85822228	全棉男装针织长袖T恤
东莞海琪运动服装有限公司	陈建忠	85701202	化纤成人运动装
东莞永嘉盛针织有限公司	李旭江	22407788	纺织毛衫
东莞三骏时装有限公司	张益麟	85326098	针梳织服装
长江西服东莞有限公司	黄柏林	83384250	西服及西服套装
东莞大明制衣有限公司	何婉芬	85192121	服装
东莞盈升制衣有限公司	黄柏坤	86655401	服装
东莞市东方叶杨实业有限公司	叶国雄	22634282	羊绒衣服
东莞台昌鞋业有限公司	张家铭	85980666	鞋类产品
东莞时利制衣有限公司	邓维安	85709662	服装
东莞迅捷环球制衣有限公司	黄志坚	85441918	服装
东莞美商新力鞋业有限公司	叶癸三	83261991	运动鞋
东莞宝基鞋业制造有限公司	林陈春英	85582985	鞋
东莞邦胜鞋业有限公司	吴振贤	85835990	各类鞋及鞋面
乐活制衣(东莞)有限公司	莫文漳	83729200	成衣
东莞绰荣制衣有限公司	陈爱菁	83936788	针梳织服装

1-5 续表 3

(2009年)

单位名称	负责人	联系电话	主要产品(或服务)
东莞奇兴服装有限公司	院秀琼	83382968	西装衫
东莞胜德织造有限公司	黄志坚	88738293	毛织品
东莞茶山永联织造厂	谢庆华	88655088	婴儿服装
真至美服装(东莞)有限公司	张尔平	83726111	服装
东莞种子制衣厂	陈川豪	88876660	内衣裤
东莞怡信针织有限公司	黎佩瑜	86836268	服装
东莞泰富服装有限公司	郑文彪	88830780	服装
联业制衣(东莞)有限公司	李雍熙	87738280	服装
东莞凯威针织制衣有限公司	陈英杰	86830510	布料服装
东莞上杰鞋业有限公司	周硕煜	81663185	鞋
纳美(东莞)服装有限公司	颜纯炯	83200999	帽子
东莞泉泰服饰有限公司	陈亨利	86808062	衣服
东莞大森鞋材有限公司	郭进福	85901546	鞋材
东莞高品服装有限公司	蔡兆安	83501111	服装
东莞宝升制衣有限公司	林安娜	85549971	衣服
皮革、毛皮、羽毛(绒)及其制品业			
东莞嘉应制鞋有限公司	刁辉荣	86631175	皮鞋
东莞联运鞋业有限公司	蔡子仲	83303350	鞋类
东莞永盛鞋业有限公司	刘枝煌	85918310	运动鞋
东莞大森手袋有限公司	戴郭珍芳	85554130	手袋银包
东莞加明时装有限公司	贾安坤	87724718	皮草服装
东莞泽荣箱包有限公司	杨明深	83228386	旅行袋
东莞裕村鞋业有限公司	林英男	81833678	人造皮革鞋
东莞台威运动用品有限公司	许云川	85534587	运动鞋、滑板
东莞汇博鞋业有限公司	陈朝乐	85826256	成品鞋
东莞绿扬鞋业有限公司	尤以力	85876969	鞋以及鞋材
东莞陆威运动用品有限公司	蔡茂俊	85080276	各类滑板护具
宏盛皮具(东莞)有限公司	邓宏达	22665668	皮箱
东莞亮智服装有限公司	张国良	83305288	皮革服装
东莞朗福皮鞋有限公司	梁日昌	87761380	皮鞋
东莞凯祥塑胶制品有限公司	王敏隆	85415571	手袋
东莞高埗裕元制造第一分厂	李　权	88874202	鞋
威华(东莞)鞋业有限公司	陈宝常	87732368	皮鞋
东莞强发制鞋有限公司	吴坤和	85753911	鞋底
东莞环艺实业有限公司	朱文俊	88755578	手袋
东莞超丰手袋有限公司	方瑞铭	22627688	手袋
东莞佳展手袋有限公司	李文恩	88871735	手袋
新百丽鞋业(深圳)有限公司东莞分公司	黄为民	85261438	皮鞋
东莞聚保手袋有限公司	徐保荣	22252261	旅行袋
东莞诚达鞋业有限公司	于日江	88806888	休闲鞋
东莞钜盛鞋业有限公司	穆新元	83214345	皮鞋
东莞安阳鞋业有限公司	卓锦和	83318919	牛皮鞋
东莞市汉皇鞋业有限公司	马锦汉	83790019	鞋类
东莞好利包袋制品有限公司	罗　同	87906032	钱包、手袋

1-5　续表 4

(2009年)

单位名称	负责人	联系电话	主要产品(或服务)
雄进塑料制品(东莞)有限公司	柯永聪	83320081	PVC造革
东莞绿洲鞋业有限公司	萧瑞芬	85880975	皮鞋女鞋以及运动鞋
东莞泰亿袋业有限公司	蔡文维	87862228	皮箱
安迈特提箱(东莞)有限公司	谢明振	83356051	旅行箱包
东莞金莹鞋业有限公司	许玲玉	85900471	皮鞋
东莞尚昇鞋业有限公司	李匡如	83050099	鞋制品
东莞东禾鞋业有限公司	陈正忠	22662588	鞋类产品
东莞华南皮革有限公司	陈毓仁	86642187	轻革
东莞万鑫鞋业有限公司	徐哲雄	86226699	皮鞋
东莞博励图鞋业有限公司	陈玉环	83266168	各类鞋业
东莞三元鞋业有限公司	林炽昌	22181972	皮鞋
东莞韦旭鞋业有限公司	庄金殿	85321666	皮鞋
东莞奥天奴皮草服装有限公司	吴锡龙	86786993	皮草服装
东莞昕晋手袋制造有限公司	黄文贤	85379861	手袋旅行袋
东莞伯爵鞋业有限公司	林炜翔	85588033	皮鞋
东莞台育鞋业有限公司	刘建宗	86323168	皮鞋
东莞卫仕皮具有限公司	苗大卫	88386228	皮具制品
东莞普威鞋业有限公司	宋家彰	85586102	运动鞋
东莞邦荣鞋业有限公司	黄景明	85835990	各类鞋
东莞聚美手袋有限公司	谭玉莲	85374168	手袋
东莞协和鞋业有限公司	吴荣芳	85595058	童鞋
东莞莱得利皮具有限公司	王振邦	85554590	皮具
东莞华宝鞋业有限公司	肖启恒	22908300	鞋
东莞宏国制鞋有限公司	刘文忠	85559400	皮鞋
东莞威腾皮革有限公司	伟大利	85080096	皮革
圣马可(东莞)制革皮草有限公司	周巨龙		皮革
东莞鼎力鞋业有限公司	黄素琴	85586102	运动鞋
东莞钜旺鞋业有限公司	穆春华	22251840	皮鞋
东莞伯产合成皮革有限公司	金相和	88820807	PU合成皮革
东莞高埗彰元鞋材厂	李尚智	88872837	鞋材
东莞朝代鞋业有限公司	陈正熙	85588915	皮鞋
东莞星浩手袋有限公司	英豪云	87939288	各类手袋
东莞爱莉莎皮具有限公司	计兴棠	88868969	皮箱、包袋
东莞建成鞋业有限公司	曾昭伟	87734968	运动鞋
东莞宏业制鞋有限公司	李志强	86859812	运动鞋皮鞋
东莞时代皮具制品厂有限公司	杨华强	85595771	手袋
东莞飞力达鞋业有限公司	王水镗		女式皮鞋
东莞源亨皮具制品有限公司	邱泰年	83312003	手袋
东莞颖龙皮件制品有限公司	王谦如	88730366	皮箱
东莞瑞辉鞋业有限公司	上原正辉	22656056	女装牛皮鞋
东莞茂德塑胶制品有限公司	王九全	85015628	塑胶制品(胶袋)
东莞福聚皮革有限公司	迈克尔·海吉亚格	88326331	皮革鞣制
东莞永义鞋业有限公司	刘枝煌	85918310	牛皮运动鞋
东莞黄江宝亮鞋材厂	曾锦昌	83367386	PU人造皮

1-5　续表 5

(2009年)

单位名称	负责人	联系电话	主要产品(或服务)
东莞大邦鞋业有限公司	张堂钱	23066010	成品鞋
东莞大田鞋业有限公司	尤曦紫	87732488	皮鞋
东莞威霖鞋业有限公司	林戊坤	83093999	运动鞋
东莞雄师皮具有限公司	刘尚敏	81663838	皮带
东莞捷希皮革制品有限公司	何淑愉	83731678	手袋鞋
东莞兆鑫鞋业有限公司	徐哲雄	88998989	PU童鞋
木材加工及木、竹、藤、棕、草制品业			
东莞承达木材制品有限公司	梁继明	87712640	木门
亿丰(东莞)制帘有限公司	许碧珠	83988300	木制百叶窗
东莞市嘉声音响器材制造有限公司	骆伟光	88810027	木制音箱
东莞中城木业有限公司	王梓洪	88331338	装饰板
京木木制品(东莞)有限公司	杨永聪	86516096	木制家具
东莞达艺家私有限公司	曾志雄	83351335	木制家私
合和胶板(东莞)有限公司	林英智	88381666	装饰防火胶板
家具制造业			
东莞事达家具有限公司	许建丰	83098832	家具及家居饰品
东莞美时家具有限公司	朱卓文	82031091	办公家具
东莞豪文塑胶五金制品有限公司	苏致诚	87316206	办公家具
东莞稳耐五金塑胶制品有限公司	张秀如	87778036	电脑桌
东莞宜庆家具有限公司	陈先助	22632705	家具
东莞宏展家具有限公司	庄清约	83433133	家私
东莞台升家具有限公司	郭山辉	83352715	木制家具
东莞朗顺五金塑胶制品有限公司	刘嘉纹	87331399	铁制餐桌椅
东莞辰森木制品有限公司	徐源森	83627078	木制家具
东莞超信金属有限公司	吴松柏	83320898	铁制家具
瑞丰木业(东莞)有限公司	梁厚镇	87310180	家具
东莞大众木业有限公司	林相顾	85619320	木制品
立富木器(东莞)有限公司	黄庆富	83356577	家具业
东莞柚隆木业有限公司	曾文山	83358666	木制品家具
东莞益新家私装饰有限公司	曾志雄	85658912	木制家私
东莞永鹏家具有限公司	赵宗礼	85617546	家具
东莞上丰家具有限公司	赖丰胜	83221455	五金家具
维斯福(东莞)家具有限公司	戴维汤生	87921007	家具零件
东莞大欣家具有限公司	安东尼察李	23160288	沙发
东莞富运家私有限公司	陈爱民	83055888	客厅家俱
东莞乡源木器业有限公司	欧秋中	83355145	家具木业
东莞冠良兴家具有限公司	李函倩	85613431	家具
东莞强盛五金制品有限公司	朱季夫	87338588	铁管
东莞新兴钢具厂有限公司	严志明	88872618	办公家具
东莞雄伟木业有限公司	林明顾	83352804	木制品家具
东莞冠威绿之宝实业有限公司	叶仲伦	83351030	塑胶制品
东莞天山金属家具有限公司	李瑞堃	83305743	金属家具
东莞米德兰五金塑胶制品有限公司	王清海	87312071	金属椅子
东莞震兴家私有限公司	赵宗礼	85551784	家具

1-5 续表 6

(2009年)

单位名称	负责人	联系电话	主要产品(或服务)
东莞志佳木业有限公司	林明源	83623301	木椅
东莞世昌五金制品厂有限公司	林文生	85537699	桌椅
东莞康桥家具有限公司	林进登	83054021	木制家具
东莞汉平家具有限公司	刘珍财	86814555	木制家具
东莞雅克沙发有限公司	汉森·约翰·温特	85087789	沙发
优先家具(东莞)有限公司	安东尼·雷曼	22691495	其他家具
富鼎木业(东莞)有限公司	颜明德	83357899	家具
东莞高丰木业制品有限公司	陈锦堂	83629708	木制家具
东莞巨千家具有限公司	蒋顺风	86306168	铁制家具
荣锋家具(东莞)有限公司	张游全	86249688	办公椅
东莞明辉家私有限公司	郭瑞添	83351928	木制家具
东莞金石家具有限公司	何起澐	83355678	家具
东莞中铤家具厂有限公司	张庆全	87727725	钢木家具
东莞威捷家具制品有限公司	姚家祥	87943088	家具配件
瑞丰木业(东莞)有限公司三中分公司	谭厚镇	87310180	家具
东莞马山五金塑胶制品有限公司	李素娥	87312780	五金塑胶家具
东莞铭晋家具有限公司	吕邱进	22653362	木质家具
东莞诺华家具有限公司	何远征	88313444	木质家具
东莞东和家具有限公司	黄健伟	87914361	组合床
东莞益新家俬装饰有限公司	曾志雄	83351335	家具
运时通(中国)家具有限公司	陈燕木	83358888	家具床垫家具复合材料
东莞泰冠时钟有限公司	林怀德	87730352	婴儿床
东莞勤筑五金塑胶制品有限公司	曾春富	87311390	铁制休闲椅
东莞明昌家俱有限公司	李添成	88687918	金属家具
东莞莱富家具有限公司	洪文德	83432299	咖啡茶几桌
造纸及纸制品业			
东莞华成纸业有限公司	洪重祺	87988111	其他纸制品
东莞理文造纸厂有限公司	朱国龙	88888168	纸及纸制品
东莞新森奇纸品有限公司	罗树显	83391366	纸箱
广东理文造纸有限公司	李运强	88432168	造纸
东莞龙成纸业有限公司	李逢春	81125111	瓦楞纸板
东莞华南印刷有限公司	何建中	82098700	纸盒
东莞骏佳纸业有限公司	纪家贤	87712467	纸类制品
安姆科国际容器(广东)有限公司	陈世彬	83303343	纸制品
东莞金源研磨有限公司	杨　璐	85618339	砂纸
东莞派克奇包装有限公司	吴　同	85585950	纸制品
东莞虎门恒辉彩印有限公司	郑敬辉	85521115	彩盒
东莞天兴纸业有限公司	刘桂棠	85700268	纸品
东莞江南纸业有限公司	邵振明	88184305	瓦楞纸
正隆(广东)纸业有限公司	游晴辉	82273288	纸板
东莞地龙纸业有限公司	张　茵	88234888	牛卡纸
东莞扬铭纸品有限公司	蔡宪仁	22773061	纸张裁切
东莞顺诚纸品有限公司	邵振明		纸板
东莞佳木纸品有限公司	香富安	83375868	纸板

1-5 续表 7

(2009年)

单位名称	负责人	联系电话	主要产品(或服务)
东莞顺盈纸业有限公司	邵振明	88112123	瓦楞原纸
东莞建晖纸业有限公司	黎祖球	88888363	涂布白板纸
东莞顺益纸品制造有限公司	杨广强	86641635	纸箱
东莞恒基纸品有限公司	香荣光	83391999	纸板
怡高纸品印刷(东莞)有限公司	梁沛辉	83122188	纸箱
东莞顺裕纸业有限公司	刘沛雄	88560003	瓦楞纸
东莞中世拓纸业有限公司	刘　磊	85033228	数码打印纸
东莞永和工艺盒有限公司	林　贵	87318720	工艺盒
广源兴纸品(东莞)有限公司	黄天水	85631665	纸板
东莞明彩纸品有限公司	吴燕子	87713003	纸制品
东莞大荣纸品有限公司	江国兴	87734999	纸箱
东莞高昇纸品有限公司	黄家业	87983362	瓦楞纸品
永丰余纸业(东莞)有限公司	张燕忠	87566668	高档纸
东莞骏成纸业有限公司	纪家慧	87505300	其他纸制品
东莞长安昌众造纸有限公司	王　雷	85534024	铜板纸
东莞台聚包装有限公司	何澄松	85353369	纸合制品
耐帆包装工程(东莞)有限公司	博安格尔斯特兰德	83784130	可折叠木包装箱
东莞力捷纸品有限公司	许家印	87313089	纸类印刷品
东莞福门纸品制造有限公司	王廷坤	22405762	鞋盒
东莞寮步中大纸品有限公司	商海泉	83211760	纸箱
东莞理文纸品有限公司	李文丽	88888168	纸板
东莞玖龙纸业有限公司	张　茵	88234888	牛卡纸
斯默菲石东包装(东莞)有限公司	左格逊	81331300	瓦楞芯纸
永固(东莞)纸业有限公司	黄宜弘	87932383	纸箱
东莞市中堂江南造纸厂	邵振明	88184305	包装用纸
东莞金洲纸业有限公司	黎景均		瓦楞纸
东莞正隆纸制品有限公司	胡明进	83630032	纸箱
东莞大新彩印纸品有限公司	曾城锜	87736060	纸制品
东莞高绮印刷有限公司	简明添	83355498	铭板
有余纸品(东莞)有限公司	邝志强	85630000	纸箱
东莞市振兴纸品有限公司	张玉珍	88871188	纸板
东莞海龙纸业有限公司	张　茵	88234888	灰底白板纸
东莞浩文纸品有限公司	杨文德	87198718	坑纸
坚碧包装制品东莞有限公司	梁永禧	85780088	包装制品
东莞合意印刷有限公司	吴玲玲	87138221	纸制品
东莞映佳纸业有限公司	李奇泓	22277747	纸品
东莞进益纸品有限公司	许森国	87758302	纸箱
东莞利通包装有限公司	黎永棠	22408186	纸箱纸板
印刷业和记录媒介的复制			
东莞市智源彩印有限公司	李卓然	88556888	包装装潢印刷印刷
永发印务(东莞)有限公司	左　敏	85650898	包装装潢印刷品
东莞新扬印刷有限公司	李达扬	22259209	印刷成品书
东莞万诚彩印包装有限公司	何　永	83355238	印刷纸张印刷包装
东莞冠文彩印有限公司	卢志诚	22278166	纸板印刷

1-5 续表 8

(2009年)

单位名称	负责人	联系电话	主要产品(或服务)
丰耀包装印刷(东莞)有限公司	黄鹭红	85995096	鞋盒
东莞恒业印刷制品有限公司	陈丽琴	85099366	包装装潢印刷品印刷
东莞忠柏彩印工艺制品有限公司	王金旭	22024071	纸浆
东莞建隆纸制品有限公司	张及时	83849909	包装装潢印刷品印刷
东莞勤和纸品有限公司	吕振邦	85544224	纸制品
东莞隽思印刷有限公司	郑稳伟	87712112	彩色纸箱
利丰雅高包装印刷东莞有限公司	卢建章	85630000	包装印刷
东莞大朗中编印刷厂	李礼河	83314723	书籍印刷
建泰印刷(东莞)有限公司	孙奕雄	85375818	彩盒说明书
东莞明泰彩色包装印刷有限公司	许进富	85316011	说明书印刷
东莞新洲印刷有限公司	苏周艳屏	85625222	包装印刷
东莞晨光印刷有限公司	杨荣实	86551928	纸张塑料工艺商标印刷品
东莞金杯印刷有限公司	杨金溪	83394888	印刷书刊
东莞运城制版有限公司	介骏鸿	83395297	凹印版辊
东莞新丰印刷有限公司	麦秉衡	87142581	书、报、刊印刷
东莞永洪印刷有限公司	谭少丽	87711961	彩色纸盒
东莞佳艺包装制品有限公司	卢佳莉	22285667	彩色包装印刷品
敬业(东莞)印刷包装厂有限公司	林源华	85551734	纸盒
东莞当纳利印刷有限公司	毛可·詹姆斯·汤普金	81126499	印刷服务
美锐电路(东莞)有限公司	萧铭铧	87724932	印刷电路板
东莞虎彩印刷有限公司	陈成稳	85252189	包装印刷品
东莞昌明印刷有限公司	雷　志	83356851	包装物
东莞广发印刷钉装有限公司	黄子健	88339316	书籍
东莞勤达印刷有限公司	郭志辉	85538880	纸类印刷品
文教体育用品制造业			
东莞清溪三中永威电子二厂	邱　杰	87731195	电狗感应器
东莞飞达鞋业有限公司	罗远茂	83344547	运动鞋皮鞋
联志玩具礼品(东莞)有限公司	邱庆华	83737875	塑胶玩具
东莞长安锦厦邦劲电子厂	李志强	85535441	塑胶发声玩具
东莞兴发玩具厂有限公司	杜志辉	22201697	塑胶玩具
东莞开达电子有限公司	丁午寿	88811559	玩具
东莞冠贺运动器材有限公司	欧聪明	85551210	球类产品及用具
东莞南栅利高文具制品厂有限公司	杜振安	85561878	五金文件夹
东莞兴华玩具有限公司	殷国华	81818839	玩具
东莞源泰运动器材有限公司	尤景三	87722669	网球拍壁球拍高尔夫球杆
东莞宝柏新威玩具有限公司	马国林	83384113	玩具业
东莞龙鑫运动用品有限公司	向华炉	86851318	运动器材
东莞桥头中星电器厂	陈沛南	83344504	电器配件
东莞大扬运动器材有限公司	杨文祥	85594466	棒球
东莞联弘玩具有限公司	邱庆华	83376123	玩具
达宇运动器材有限公司	王景聪	83882808	运动器材
东莞峰达电子有限公司	严夏良	88811559	玩具制售
东莞台塘旅游用品有限公司	陈永楙	87912521	制品旅游袋
东莞南辉塑胶电子有限公司	邓泽民	88861619	塑胶玩具

1-5 续表 9

(2009年)

单位名称	负责人	联系电话	主要产品(或服务)
东莞康达玩具礼品有限公司	温国雄	86178588	毛绒玩具
东莞虎门南栅国际文具制造厂	王永泰	85561686	文具夹
东莞巨佑体育用品有限公司	廖卿霖	85582170	运动鞋
东莞建力体育器材有限公司	黄陈服	87739858	高尔夫球具
东莞虎门南栅国际文具制造有限公司	杜振安	85561686	文具夹
长荣玩具(东莞)有限公司	张赛娥	87314418	玩具
锦美运动用品(东莞)有限公司	陈勇雄	87333971	高尔夫球具
东莞大迪音响器材有限公司	陈明智	83326201	音箱
东莞龙昌玩具有限公司	梁 麟	86836266	玩具
东莞稳健高尔夫球用品有限公司	郑玉珠	87739826	高尔夫球用品
东莞冠越玩具有限公司	理查德·艾勒特	89968888	塑胶玩具
宝钜(中国)儿童用品有限公司	郑丽玉	87893231	婴儿手推车
东莞利达运动用品有限公司	李秋林	88806900	运动用品
东莞祥兴玩具有限公司	吴毅群	85541020	塑胶玩具
东莞登富鞋业有限公司	黄玉绢	87736010	运动鞋
东莞力威高尔夫球用品有限公司	饶郑睦	87316101	高尔夫球用品
东莞广声五金塑胶制品有限公司	翟所容	86061888	木制玩具
东莞大德电子有限公司	王德财	85544242	各类玩具
东莞美联玩具有限公司	罗拨特西门氏	86648128	填充玩具
高仕文具(东莞)有限公司	佩里奥斯蒂芬·亚历山	85585588	文具
明安运动器材(东莞)有限公司	郑锡坤	85555321	高尔夫球类用品
富国运动器材(东莞)有限公司	傅庆材	85252033	高尔夫运动器材
山打根实业(东莞)有限公司	徐荫球	22272416	塑胶电子玩具
东莞康贝童车玩具有限公司	榎本照夫	87720591	童车
东莞广达塑胶制品有限公司	丁炜章	83318515	塑胶玩具
盛昌布艺品(东莞)有限公司	贾安良	88516028	塑胶电子玩具
东莞富美高文具制品有限公司	谢豊全	87898682	文具制品
东莞仁美玩具制品有限公司	柯鸿振	83051388	玩具
东莞联欣运动器材有限公司	谢 超	85259998	远动器材
东莞乐迪卡游戏机制造厂有限公司	格雷·史特费尼	85159455	游戏机、电子液晶体显示器
东莞永鑫运动用品有限公司	洪永裕	83236641	背包
东莞惠丰鞋业有限公司	柯铭奎	85589441	运动鞋
东莞润田服装工艺制品有限公司	洪启辉	86633899	儿童玩具
东莞盈利幼童用品有限公司	刘永新	87736157	儿童三轮车
东莞胜辉健身器材有限公司	希尔·道格拉斯	82098838	健身器材
东莞大发玩具厂有限公司	周启文	85315256	玩具
东莞英德玩具塑胶电子有限公司	傅慧任	22295251	塑胶制品
东莞易达文具有限公司	萧耀民	81032000	文件夹类文具
东莞达成金属制品有限公司	罗振章	85026632	电镀文具夹
东莞旭科电子制品有限公司	邓健伟	87932700	电子玩具
明珠高尔夫制品(东莞)有限公司	江伟清	86812699	高尔夫球
东莞广德运动用品有限公司	洪永裕	83283992	背包
东莞意志高纸品有限公司	冯广发	22259730	笔记本
东莞金冠运动器材有限公司	卢振芬	83526163	体育器材及配件

1-5 续表 10

(2009年)

单位名称	负责人	联系电话	主要产品(或服务)
东莞康博复材科技有限公司	林哲光	83028181	体育器材及配件
东莞鑫达玩具礼品有限公司	高约翰	83375750	合金塑胶玩具
东莞永湖复合材料有限公司	廖国廷		棒球棒
展恒玩具电子(东莞)有限公司	梅志明	86655372	塑胶玩具
东莞兴利五金塑胶有限公司	文丽霞	86551728	玩具
东莞龙昌数码科技有限公司	陈自健	86836266	玩具
东莞龙华玩具厂	梁钟羡	22263686	塑料玩具
东莞银辉玩具有限公司	蔡奇逢	85551910	玩具
东莞飞达玩具制造有限公司	蔡灿鸿		塑胶玩具
东莞御丰文具有限公司	何钦鍊	85154611	文具
东莞东发玩具厂有限公司	周启文	85315256	玩具
东莞司贸文教赠品有限公司	林为恭	85598898	文具
东莞宝熊渔具有限公司	廖清桓	87722967	渔具
东莞凤岗竹尾田玩具厂	赖静思	87753128	玩具
明门(中国)幼童用品有限公司	郑钦明	87733251	婴儿手推车
东莞佳畅玩具有限公司	胡斯诺	86856166	塑胶玩具
东莞镇扬玩具有限公司	朱其昆	87736471	玩具(电子塑胶)
石油加工、炼焦及核燃料加工业			
东莞泰和沥青产品有限公司	叶　军	88803013	普通沥青
化学原料及化学制品制造业			
东莞市润营有机硅科技有限公司	连丽娜	86533772	有机硅
东莞秉顺制漆有限公司	马修慈	86801888	油漆
东莞荣和化工有限公司	吴思毅	88337898	橡胶助剂
东莞三联热缩材料有限公司	鲁尔兵	81120158	热缩套管
东莞华宝树脂有限公司	陈主游	85587517	胶水
东莞康耀录像盒带制品有限公司	温锡钻	87711691	录像带空盒
东莞毅兴塑胶原料有限公司	许国光	85588755	精色粉
东莞大东树脂有限公司	施泽民	88806780	胶水
东莞鸥哈希化学涂料有限公司	邱奕诚	83317997	塑胶涂料
东莞瑞安高分子树脂有限公司	李元龙	85533620	非化学危险品的聚丙烯树脂
阿克苏诺贝尔涂料(东莞)有限公司	尹凯实	86520333	工业涂料
东莞杜邦华佳高性能涂料有限公司	侯永生	22288858	涂料
东莞宏德化学工业有限公司	郭秀明	85533620	胶浆树脂化工类
东莞宝丽美化工有限公司	贾雪雷	83392980	印染助剂
高宝化妆品(中国)有限公司	贾雪雷	83392980	护肤品
东莞东交沥青有限公司	周志辉	88807929	改进沥青
罗门哈斯电子材料(东莞)有限公司	杜　华	86225511	铜添加剂
东莞立茂化工有限公司	林长庚	88330956	化学用品
鲁道夫化工(东莞)有限公司	王铁群	88466888	纺织品助剂
东莞安舍日用品有限公司	徐尔恒	22253908	合成洗涤剂
日立化成工业(东莞)有限公司	石井隆夫	86413898	线路板专用光致抗蚀工膜
东莞威威日用品有限公司	陈伟珠	86632080	合成洗涤剂
东莞佳和化工厂	郭宏芬	88853308	纺织助剂
东莞大宝化工制品有限公司本部	陈贺生	83352051	油漆

1-5 续表 11

(2009年)

单位名称	负责人	联系电话	主要产品(或服务)
东莞誉展化工有限公司	郭国庆	87509919	涂料油漆
东莞普立万氯乙烯聚合体有限公司	庄荣忠	85878800	乙稀昱化合物
汉高胶粘剂技术(广东)有限公司	艾狭甫	85563700	粘合剂
宣伟涂料(东莞)有限公司	符起鹏	83220251	油漆
广东中成化工股份有限公司	汪志良	88822402	保险粉
东莞好利精细化工有限公司	傅妙君	83351634	环氧密封胶
东莞鼎丰聚胺酯有限公司	林峰雪	22781510	聚氨酯薄膜
东莞三星道达尔工程塑料有限公司	安寅淳	82781999	尼龙塑胶
东莞丽利涂料有限公司	潘德森	83353187	钢木家具涂料
大丰电研科技(东莞)有限公司	大野隆生	88487888	油墨
东莞新长桥塑料有限公司	廖有章	88663077	工程塑料
东莞永达彩印有限公司	陈永通	88830968	印刷彩盒
益海(东莞)油化工业有限公司	李福官	88238729	皂粒
东莞新东方化工有限公司	朱德洪	83639068	硅橡胶
医药制造业			
东莞万成制药有限公司	辜荣如	22176249	药品
东莞奥美医疗用品有限公司	崔金海	83630000	医用敷料
化学纤维制造业			
东莞东港化纤有限公司	辛　宇	89505888	丙纶制品
橡胶制品业			
诠立电子科技(东莞)有限公司	周耀威	87294721	橡胶制品
东莞国信鞋业有限公司	林景培	87721640	EVA拖(凉)鞋
东莞胜百吉鞋业有限公司	朱哲良	81608888	成品鞋
东莞英树电子科技有限公司	徐文麟	88642999	塑胶制品
东莞国汇实业有限公司	邵鑑棠	88387000	橡胶制品
东莞德州鞋业有限公司	张玄明	85531584	鞋
中星婴儿用品(东莞)有限公司	王凤萍	86652872	婴儿用品
东莞益宝鞋材有限公司	谢慧娇	85536565	化合成橡胶片
东莞群宏矽酮科技有限公司	简旭锐	85412126	橡胶制品
东莞东坑鸿图电业有限公司	冯就中	83382863	硅胶制品
东莞扬泰电子有限公司	廖吉甫		橡胶件
东莞兴宝密封件有限公司	练彦麟	22666410	橡胶密封件
东莞宏美鞋业有限公司	张志邦	88808618	皮鞋
东莞宝建鞋材有限公司	黄长泽	83631221	PU树脂
东莞兴鑫电子科技有限公司	许舒恭	85226956	塑料制品 电子电器零配件
东莞彰昱实业有限公司	陈松和	22260168	各类鞋材
东莞捷讯橡胶有限公司	李立新	86724551	硅橡胶制品
东莞铧冠橡塑制品有限公司	曾成戎	85876868	复合橡胶
东莞新桥鞋业有限公司	张世欣	22184688	橡胶鞋底
东莞南阳橡胶制品有限公司	萧登波	83236641	加硫鞋
东莞富华鞋业有限公司	张汉文	88788166	鞋类制品
东莞万泰橡胶有限公司	黄丽慧	88833021	橡胶靴鞋
东莞高大塑胶有限公司	方世莹	85596288	自粘塑胶皮
东莞金旺泡绵有限公司	白锡明	85591411	沙滩鞋
广东银禧科技股份有限公司	谭颂斌	88515828	改性塑料、PVL胶粒、阻燃ABS胶粒
东莞亚华胶粘带有限公司	顾青山	86316960	橡胶带
东莞太洋橡塑制品有限公司	黄佳莉	87197979	硅胶制品

1-5 续表 12

(2009年)

单位名称	负责人	联系电话	主要产品(或服务)
塑料制品业			
东莞百信塑胶制品有限公司	唐贯健	83456081	塑胶制品
东莞侑兴鞋业有限公司	邱镫仪	83083455	运动鞋
东莞华庆塑料有限公司	陈瑞坡	22295808	泡沫塑料
东莞金金碧电子有限公司	邱谦信	87574026	塑胶制品
东莞黄江福泰塑料厂	曾锦昌	83363017	塑料
亚化科技(东莞)胶粘制品有限公司	檀兆麟	85312270	胶粘带
东莞劲胜精密组件股份有限公司	王九全	82288188	塑胶制品
鸿特利塑胶制品(东莞)有限公司	萧宽仁	87738200	塑胶制品
东莞高成精密注塑科技有限公司	胡明进	83632679	工程塑料及塑料合金
东莞华唯塑胶制品有限公司	黄建铭	82055789	塑胶制品
东莞协宇塑胶制品有限公司	张岳明	85495868	塑胶制品
东莞普隆塑胶制品有限公司	罗凤珠	88181588	塑胶地砖(软体)
海格五金(东莞)有限公司	范德礼		五金制品
东莞百代塑胶制品有限公司	林照德	86767688	塑胶玩具
东莞木村塑胶制品有限公司	木村正治	88865581	打印机塑胶配件批发
港龙包装制品(东莞)有限公司	施毓群	87903336	塑料薄膜
东莞厚特双色塑胶有限公司	黄文锋	86954889	其他塑料制品
东莞正和塑胶有限公司	蔡俊宏	85311408	塑胶配件
东莞联全鞋材有限公司	李锦富	22250887	鞋材塑胶制品
东莞利士包装有限公司	蔡国镇	83910878	塑料罐
东莞华源玩具有限公司	钟耀华	88455176	塑胶五金玩具
东莞佑茂五金塑胶有限公司	郭明华	87686300	电脑五金塑胶配件
东莞宏华塑胶制品有限公司	袁满华	82201616	五金塑胶制品
东莞高惠电子有限公司	李建亮	85319188	连接器
东莞群福塑胶制品有限公司	刘显洲	85827756	塑胶制品
东莞坚利塑胶制品有限公司	甄东刚	87775341	塑胶制品
东莞井上高分子材料有限公司	赤松政雄	86176861	聚氨酯橡胶
东莞三和塑胶制品有限公司	郑聪敏	83392589	手握箱
东莞厚街三屯创机塑胶制品厂	曾建强	82728888	塑料制品
东莞冠晖塑胶制品有限公司	陈永铨	22404249	塑胶充气制品
东莞丽佳塑胶有限公司	周敏朝	83138028	有机玻璃
东莞坤胜五金制品有限公司	李淑贞	85564158	五金配件
东莞荒井橡胶制品有限公司	下山田好辉	87925725	传真机、复印机、打印机
东莞维鸿化工有限公司	许进成	83342979	聚素胶树脂成型粉
东莞竞业塑胶五金制品厂有限公司	黎颂荣	88812843	塑料餐具及厨具
东莞同成塑胶五金制品有限公司	余明宗	86640256	塑胶五金配件
东莞富增泡棉塑胶有限公司	程明宗	88462258	塑胶泡棉
东莞增立塑料制品有限公司	吴益仁	88680500	PVC人造革
银禧工程塑料(东莞)有限公司	谭颂斌	88387388	工程塑料
东莞伟嘉塑胶电子制品有限公司	郑镇炎	88232838	塑胶制品

1-5 续表 13

(2009年)

单位名称	负责人	联系电话	主要产品(或服务)
永塑(东莞)塑料有限公司	黄復楹	87331245	塑胶粒
昌煜塑胶(东莞)有限公司	刘朝明	87750453	塑胶产品
东莞富宏塑胶原料有限公司	孔伙永	87280018	PVC塑吸原料料
东莞田氏化工厂有限公司	田庆光	85118638	塑料人革
东莞合旺塑胶颜料有限公司	林旺生	87758710	颜料塑胶鞋、ABS胶鞋、HIPS胶鞋
东莞衍青塑胶五金制品有限公司	王清珍	87733701	水杯
兆丰(东莞)制帘有限公司	许碧珠	86716666	门框形百叶窗
东莞华美人造皮厂有限公司	陈　铭	88839163	PVC、PW人造革
东莞贯新幼童用品有限公司	胡荣财		婴幼儿车及制品
东莞恒发五金塑胶制品有限公司	陈庆顺	83345000	五金塑胶制品
东莞宝华利塑胶制品厂有限公司	杨东成	87773870	PVC塑胶
东莞兴昂鞋业有限公司	谢东壁	85631888	鞋材和鞋的开发
东莞高登鞋材有限公司	施教进	88830578	塑料鞋
东莞富采包装制品有限公司	源而细	85551972	吸塑
晋德塑料科技(东莞)有限公司	钟春重	87929956	工程塑料
东莞远展包装制品有限公司	陆耀忠	83354716	发泡胶
东莞万豪五金电子有限公司	黄美龄	83379213	数码机相机上盖
东莞高文内衣制品有限公司	洪彩霞	83792939	海棉、脯棉
东莞高富达塑料制品有限公司	麦带喜	22636148	塑胶材料
东莞保利文塑胶制品有限公司	郑钟伟	83989198	胶花
东莞市立新塑胶有限公司	高天平	86658588	塑胶制品五金制品
东莞沛恩旅行箱制品有限公司	李宇杰	22700530	箱袋类制品
东莞珂维斯日用品有限公司	迪根·罗伯特·迈克	22089885	化妆品
东莞大银塑胶制品有限公司	吴伊丽	85412001	塑料制品
东莞南星塑胶有限公司	蔡香海	87713408	聚乙烯胶袋(筒)
东莞敬记容器有限公司	李崇伟	85151012	塑料制品
东莞裕胜拉链五金配件有限公司	翁景进	85490660	尼龙拉链
东莞华心塑胶制品厂	陈华昌	87775513	PVC袋
东莞凡进工业模具有限公司	朴正吉	81895181	塑胶模具
东莞伸丰人造革有限公司	郑兴旺	88315005	人造革
东莞泛昌窗帘制品有限公司	许碧珠	88399789	塑胶百叶窗帘
东莞进升塑料制品有限公司	蔡玉兰	85357081	CD袋
东莞冠诚塑胶模具有限公司	刘诸彰	87739270	遥控器
东莞美哲塑胶制品有限公司	罗凤珠	88181588	塑胶地砖
东莞德源塑胶制品有限公司	关鸿基	85566181	塑胶制品
东莞玮锋电子包装材料有限公司	颜永裕	85381227	塑料型材
东莞天步鞋材有限公司	张志邦	88808168	橡胶鞋底
东莞誉铭电业科技有限公司	梁伯和	85373322	塑胶制品
东莞光群雷射科技有限公司	郭维文	85601301	塑料软包装新科技新产品
东莞穗联包装制品有限公司	李炳根	87559119	塑胶瓶
东莞华通发泡塑料制品有限公司	姚根沛	86789888	泡沫包装薄膜
东莞祥曜塑胶制品有限公司	叶金建	87758622	塑胶制品
东莞卓越光像薄膜有限公司	梁宝璋	83395440	光像薄膜
台翰模具制品(东莞)有限公司	杨剑平	87087888	精冲模模具标准件

1-5　续表 14

(2009年)

单位名称	负责人	联系电话	主要产品(或服务)
伟易达(东莞)塑胶制品有限公司	陈德荣	85581806	塑胶制品
东莞卓荣实业有限公司	谢卓华	83698138	塑胶衣架
东莞嘉多利塑胶制品有限公司	黄春美	87504968	PVC薄膜
加福塑胶制品(东莞)有限公司	王敏萍	85310681	塑胶原料
东莞骏威电子制品有限公司	罗运鹏	81119390	塑胶门钟
东莞中央化学有限公司	渡边信	86788666	塑料包装容器
东莞稻畑工程塑料有限公司	西村修	86188280	工程塑料
东莞胜乔鞋业有限公司	苏恒贵	87887018	各类鞋
东莞绿树塑胶制品有限公司	谢月美	22765001	塑胶配件
东莞奇妙包装有限公司	何德才	83034888	塑料软包装产品(塑料袋)
日本电产日新(东莞)工机有限公司	江森文雄	87085211	数码相机镜片
东莞金富包装材料有限公司	叶树华	85114144	塑料制品
乔福塑胶(东莞)有限公司	郭宏志	87787166	塑胶塑料
腾翔精密塑胶(东莞)有限公司	林品雅	83368096	塑胶制品
广东紫泉包装有限公司	周洁碧	22679188	瓶盖
东莞万善美耐皿制品有限公司	戴庆林		美耐皿制品
东莞普能塑料科技实业有限公司	林成香	88735183	塑料再生胶粒
东莞丽骏塑胶制品有限公司	刘镇国	87811708	衣架
舒尔曼塑料(东莞)有限公司	特利李·轩尼斯	83422777	工程塑料
东莞利富高塑料制品有限公司	小野寺优	86106921	汽车零部件
东莞欣仪五金塑胶制品有限公司	林振雄	83439116	五金塑胶制品
金旺塑胶制品(东莞)有限公司	郑立铭	87515170	窗帘配件
东莞广丰兴塑胶有限公司	叶贞兴	87727051	塑胶色母料
东莞市佑忠电子有限公司	徐志瑜		发泡胶
东莞信柏塑胶有限公司	吴文松	82016888	塑料原料
东莞丰佳塑胶有限公司	江茂煨	85999799	PCC胶粒
东莞富利达塑胶制品有限公司	叶志成	87750770	PVC薄膜
中侨路易塑胶制品(东莞)有限公司	谭礼坚	22655287	塑胶袋
东莞加能鞋材有限公司	陈桂英	22400092	鞋材
东莞贺捷塑胶有限公司	吴祯权	83392512	旅行箱塑胶配件
东莞三荣日化容器有限公司	陈进登	86415046	塑料容器瓶
东莞市永捷塑胶制品有限公司	黄玉玲	86920526	塑胶制品
东莞益卓电子科技有限公司	薛文富	86263266	塑胶外壳
东莞市乐福塑胶电子有限公司	蓝春秋	88968988	塑胶制品
东莞恒骏吸塑制品有限公司	罗松标	85350072	塑胶盖
东莞裕元制造厂	李　权	88874202	运动鞋
圣诺盟聚氨酯(东莞)有限公司	林汉立	87881068	海棉制品
东莞宇光塑胶制品有限公司	陈燕雄	87753066	吸塑罩
东莞盛泓五金塑胶制品有限公司	谢新居	87772450	复印机的塑胶五金配件
富裕注塑制模(东莞)有限公司	何尔吉	83378570	塑胶模具
泽冠塑胶电子(东莞)有限公司	刘家应	83086666	塑胶配件
东莞南新塑胶制品有限公司	谭容波	83996222	塑胶玩具制品
东莞欣意医疗保健制品厂	吴富源	83361381	医疗用品
东莞三阳塑胶有限公司	敖景宁	87515998	塑胶浴帘

1-5　续表 15

(2009年)

单位名称	负责人	联系电话	主要产品(或服务)
东莞兴腾鞋材有限公司	谢东壁	83058898	鞋材鞋底
赫比(东莞)电子科技有限公司	姚晓东	81886111	模具、塑胶制品
东莞家宝生活用品有限公司	邱锡鉠	86666668	塑料披覆
品翔电子塑胶制品(东莞)有限公司	蔡福气	86636668	电子塑胶制品
东莞威塑可塑胶原料有限公司	张俊璋	87719561	塑胶原料
东莞虎邦五金塑胶制品有限公司	蔡俊宏	85544660	运动器材塑胚配件
东莞荣泰塑化材料有限公司	李超伦	86869211	PVC塑胶粒
东莞市志朗包装制品有限公司	钟铁生	22204828	其他塑料制品
东莞泉声电子有限公司	温增丰	86325251	新型电子元器件
非金属矿物制品业			
东莞市森泰玻璃制品有限公司	高泉森	81082261	玻璃制品
益龙建材东莞有限公司	邱奕团	83885678	轻型建材及配套产品
东莞泰升玻璃有限公司	李锦亮	85557608	玻璃
东莞南玻太阳能玻璃有限公司	李卫南	88281785	光伏发电盖板玻璃
东莞南玻工程玻璃有限公司	吴国斌	88288656	中空玻璃
台玻华南玻璃有限公司	林伯实	88841000	浮法玻璃
环球石材(东莞)有限公司	朱荣驹	85544338	石材
信义超白光伏玻璃(东莞)有限公司	董清波	85266666	超白光伏玻璃
西斯尔(广东)岩棉制品有限公司	魏杰夫	86111401	岩棉制品
信义汽车玻璃(东莞)有限公司	李贤义	85266666	汽车玻璃
东莞华润混凝土有限公司	周龙山	88321319	水泥
东莞住秀电子有限公司	卯月准二	87552682	钕铁硼磁铁
信义汽车部件(东莞)有限公司	李圣根	85266666	汽车玻璃
力美有机玻璃东莞有限公司	毛炜堂	87885398	有机玻璃
东莞华润丰诚混凝土有限公司	周龙山	88326100	预拌商品混凝土
信义玻璃工程(东莞)有限公司	李贤义	85266666	建筑玻璃
东莞华润水泥厂有限公司	周龙山	88867530	水泥
广东可耐福新型建筑材料有限公司	戈大卫	88222708	环保石膏板
东莞可见优玻璃制品有限公司	舒耀星	87315335	玻璃转盘
信义超薄玻璃(东莞)有限公司	李贤义	85266666	玻璃
东莞万德镜片科技有限公司	陈正茂	22676816	镜片
黑色金属冶炼及压延加工业			
爱思开钢铁(东莞)有限公司	都重燮	81112111	金属材料剪切
东莞谦华五金厂有限公司	尹　虹	85537869	焊接钢管
宝威钢铁制品(东莞)有限公司	尹　虹	85539156	裁剪铁片
东莞万顺昌钢铁制品有限公司	莫非凡	85520198	金属管
东莞宇新钢材制品有限公司	郭诗珍	87313331	电镀锌铁(钢)板
东莞住金物产金属制品有限公司	霜鸟悦功	88439668	铝材
东莞伟腾五金塑胶有限公司	陈振福	85599181	不锈钢餐具厨具
东莞永冠铸造厂有限公司	张贤铭		铸坯制品
滨川金属(东莞)有限公司	萧钦铭	85322971	其他电脑零配件
东莞川电钢板制品有限公司	橘隆二	85543073	矽钢片
东莞大洲钢铁有限公司	尹吾烈	85557451	五金铁片

1-5 续表 16

(2009年)

单位名称	负责人	联系电话	主要产品(或服务)
有色金属冶炼及压延加工业			
东莞兆隆五金有限公司	丁　苏	87751742	铜线铝线
东莞瑞城压铸制品有限公司	周黄秋香	87511225	铝合金制品
东莞合立五金制品有限公司	胡维邦	85520161	五金制品
东莞铁和金属制品有限公司	矶部光男	22903361	镀钢板
东莞泛亚金属制造有限公司	潘正中	82888138	铝合金接头
阪和钢板加工(东莞)有限公司	藤塚正彦	81821038	电镀锌钢板
东莞翔腾金属制品有限公司	庄清标	83036688	金属制品
东莞新文钦金属有限公司	黄林美兰	88810666	铝合金条
东莞裕升薄板有限公司	尹定庭	88807688	镀锌薄板
日立金属(东莞)特殊钢有限公司	安达谦一	81869783	模具钢材
东莞东钜有色金属制品有限公司	吴祯权	86402606	铝合金
东莞华昌导体有限公司	曾秋平	85507296	红铜线
东莞升贸锡制品有限公司	李三莲	85508193	锡制品
东莞升洋焊锡材料有限公司	李三莲	82126112	锡线、锡棒、助焊剂
东莞日鑫铜材有限公司	陈巧云		裸铜杆
东莞宜安电器制品有限公司	李扬德	87737777	镁铝合金精密铸件
东莞联茂电子科技有限公司	蔡茂祯	88623268	覆铜板
东莞三星钢材加工有限公司	梁熙晳	81129215	电镀锌板
东莞市石碣华丰五金厂	吕　安	86313720	铝合金
金属制品业			
东莞今日兴五金表面处理有限公司	侯有庆	88860398	五金电镀
东莞恒旺五金有限公司	罗根旺	83737616	冷板
东莞高丽喷涂有限公司	李钟植	86407956	手机外壳喷涂
东莞力群金属厂有限公司	林耿煌	88826058	铁管
东莞精明五金科技有限公司	王明康	87862898	五金配件
东莞科达模具机器有限公司	陈洪顺	88857718	模坯
东莞爱可玛金属线有限公司	赖弘崇		铜线
东莞台端电子有限公司	刘美惠	85540507	各种端子
志联钢线钢缆(东莞)有限公司	刘春兴	85312723	钢材
东莞泉睿精密五金有限公司	宋贵修	85315643	五金轧制设备
东莞茂森金属冲压有限公司	陶伟洪		金属冲压件及组件
东莞惠昌电子有限公司	李建亮	85542566	电子
东莞万成模具五金制品有限公司	黄宣和	88731998	电脑配件
东莞冠德五金制品有限公司	赵杰丰	83723626	冷扎铁马口铁
东莞鼎翰铝制品有限公司	陈汉宗	87769786	铝制品
东莞智得电子制品有限公司	谢清泉	87883069	五金配件
东莞明耀金属制品有限公司	黄灿明	87942266	五金制品
东莞良佳五金塑胶制品有限公司	吴华德	87725096	五金塑胶制品
东莞豪达金属制品有限公司	萧柱祥	83391432	金属钮扣
富士精工(东莞)五金制品有限公司	斋藤胜雄	22782111	五金制品
丹麦马士基集装箱工业有限公司	柏安松	88826668	集装箱
东莞番尔康金属制品有限公司	黄广甜	86803388	铁五金制品
东莞韦腾五金塑胶制品有限公司	张珮蓉	85785101	烤肉炉
东莞雄罐印铁制罐有限公司	薛来雄	83226869	马口铁制品铁罐

1-4　续表 17

(2009年)

单位名称	负责人	联系电话	主要产品(或服务)
东莞雅康皮塑五金有限公司	郑可明	86957222	金属制品
东莞翡致伟五金制品有限公司	福门帝·吉昂卡罗	88837504	金属工具
锌辉扬热浸锌(东莞)有限公司	詹汉权	88661928	热浸锌钢铁件
东莞以利沙五金塑胶制品有限公司	柯志萍	87811756	五金塑胶制品
东莞欣晟五金制品有限公司	曾春荣		烤炉
东莞承光五金制品有限公司	董俊毅	85926110	塑胶制品
东莞雄昌五金塑胶制品有限公司	罗文达	22209873	矽钢片
东莞华懋五金有限公司	林清启	83399130	螺丝
东莞维信五金塑胶制品有限公司	谢百錬	85411861	金属家具
东莞马士基集装箱工业有限公司	BentErikCarlsen	88826668	集装箱
东莞华震电器有限公司	黄明祥	83218666	喇叭金属零件
东莞四方技研五金制品有限公司	田中晴通	87811636	精密冲模
东莞嘉丰机电设备有限公司	许永松	83226777	五金机箱机动性柜
东莞亿量五金制品有限公司	郭春田	81160085	线材
东莞顺牛金属制品有限公司	宋朝阳	85931595	金属制品
合胜五金制品(东莞)有限公司	赖芬妙	87383625	五金制品
东莞柏威金属制品有限公司	黎新宇	88835933	机械镑
东莞华尔泰装饰材料有限公司	邢　锦	22716312	铝塑复合板
东莞茂盈五金科技有限公司	朱季夫	82038300	五金制品及配件
东莞龙兴五金制品有限公司	邱瑞鸿	87916380	铁线
东莞原创金属结构有限公司	李启鸿	88688080	金属结构制品
东莞荣成塑胶五金制品有限公司	余峯德	81811503	塑胶五金配件
东莞群晔五金制品有限公司	王启人	85589170	五金制品
东莞璋泰五金制品有限公司	赵金和		铁制品
东莞特嘉塑胶五金电子有限公司	陈锦棠	87314676	电动罐头刀
东莞欣鼎五金塑胶制品有限公司	曾春荣	87338888	沙滩桌椅
东莞汉源精密五金制品有限公司	黄辰兴	86851000	五金制品
东莞宝金山五金制品有限公司	王德发	82068588	五金制品
东莞圣雅洁具有限公司	蒋素珍	88863568	有机玻璃按摩池
永金金属材料(东莞)有限公司	郑贵美	85330095	锡条
东莞怡敦实业有限公司	马可史蒂芬	22031000	水龙头
大量(东莞)五金制品有限公司	张民亭	83110970	金属丝
东莞正升五金制品有限公司	蔡明江		折合桌椅
东莞长谷川金属制品有限公司	长谷川泰正	83721269	铝梯
东莞立亚达电子有限公司	张　强	86511283	电子产品
东莞智信五金制品有限公司	王志华	87925656	五金制品
东莞翎乔五金塑胶制品有限公司	赖富康	88386188	五金制品
东莞陇亿自行车配件有限公司	郭碧伶	87723781	铁车架
同明金属制品(东莞)有限公司	粟饭原俊行	87903150	铜带片
东莞凤岗雁田财迎五金电子厂	邓祖派	87770958	摄录机机芯
自力钢构(东莞)有限公司	欧灿田	86310711	钢构房屋承建
东莞升业五金压铸制品有限公司	赖日升	83630412	锌配件
东莞创意真空镀膜有限公司	张国明	87881046	真空镀膜
新晟五金制品(东莞)有限公司	林茂南	87733601	五金制品

1-5 续表 18

(2009年)

单位名称	负责人	联系电话	主要产品(或服务)
东莞精锐电器五金有限公司	陆学中	88941998	金属制品
东莞住商益安金属制品有限公司	原　宽	88863093	剪切钢卷
惟可五金塑胶制品(东莞)有限公司	张香德	85615886	烤肉炉
东莞众富五金制品有限公司	石明发	87945998	电脑电器散热片
东莞铿利五金制品有限公司	许红超	87790560	五金配件
东莞华新五金家具有限公司	廖国璋	83385013	五金制品
东莞建兴塑胶五金制品有限公司	黄颂富	87753012	五金日用品
英联卫浴器材(东莞)有限公司	廖志铭	83387970	水槽
东莞世泉家电五金制品有限公司	苌钦杉	83885906	五金制品
东莞济安塑胶五金制品有限公司	洪秋美	88870555	五金饰品
东莞振华特种包装有限公司	钟存仁	88828115	特种包装铁桶
东莞清溪光华制锁厂有限公司	廖文良	87731333	锁具产品
灿荣五金(东莞)有限公司	陈　灿	88488118	电视架
东莞顺传五金制品有限公司	钟长庆	87732273	自行车五金零件
通用设备制造业			
东莞泰德电机有限公司	廖明杭	83020111	吊扇
东莞奄美弹簧有限公司	佐佐木富雄	85537655	弹簧
东莞蓝旋电子有限公司	刘威强	87079268	小型交流风扇
东莞斯穆碧根柏五金制品有限公司	郭锦明	85191603	模块经营活动
东莞市高亿电子五金配件有限公司	森津对	87923840	螺丝
东莞塘厦林村太阳茂森金属制造厂	李后昌	87929299	金属冲压
东莞长益五金制品有限公司	林瑞宝	83723671	铁管
东莞冠翔电机有限公司	洪英智		汽车空压机
协隆(东莞)塑胶电子有限公司	杨宗宪	87916200	其他金属机械
东莞富鼎兴精密电子科技有限公司	叶云安	87686518	电脑周边配件
东莞吉田塑料制品有限公司	伊藤义弘	83395533	机芯塑料件
东莞益新五金有限公司	王干文	83393762	五金制品
东莞皇冠螺丝有限公司	佐久间功	85418758	精密螺丝
东莞珉强五金塑胶制品有限公司	王世煌	87314470	铁管
东莞钜升塑胶电子制品有限公司	陈世昌	88611111	手机模型
东莞宝峰金属制品有限公司	陈云山	87136078	铁制品
日立粉末冶金(东莞)有限公司	坂本靖雄	86170115	气门导管
东莞百利达健康器材有限公司	谷田大辅	22298309	电子机械衡具
东莞建越精密轴承有限公司	梁伸夫	88431300	轴承
成行精密部件(东莞)有限公司	重本丰生	87282609	精密部件
大船科技(东莞)有限公司	洪启宗	22899666	精密轴承
东莞市瑞电电器有限公司	松本重幸	88703880	工业用空调
比安达五金(东莞)有限公司	吴锦旺		精密轴承
东莞三美空调配件有限公司	三尾一彦	83862444	空调配件接管
东莞强韧机械铸造有限公司	吴子建	83455397	铸件
东莞日技金属加工有限公司	原　宽	83394631	钢材
东莞信易电热机械有限公司	吴一夫	83313588	干燥机
东莞大集精密五金制品有限公司	黄清义	87913346	精密五金制品
东莞高德电动工具有限公司	吴丰哲	85924071	木材机床

1-5 续表 19

(2009年)

单位名称	负责人	联系电话	主要产品(或服务)
东莞富鸿齐电子有限公司	翁祖晋	87187028	各类主机轴承
春雨(东莞)五金制品有限公司	李明晃	83310921	钢材
东莞东运镁业有限公司	刘克礼	83500019	镁合金制品
东莞庆安制冷设备配件有限公司	李杰深	83346775	分离器
东莞群马电子有限公司	上野文雄	83860001	电子零配件
东莞耐力五金配件有限公司	翁英美	85338531	铁螺丝
东莞君雄精密五金制造有限公司	郭　军	86710181	钢铁铸件
东莞百乐仕汽车精密配件有限公司	加藤一彦	87987779	工业用的塑料
东莞双叶金属制品有限公司	寺田武久	85658197	汽车部件
东莞邑鸿金属有限公司	陈树兰	88959666	铁金属复合材料的分条裁切
东莞邦达五金有限公司	费业龙	83818660	光控开关
东莞保来得粉末冶金有限公司	菊池正史	83133077	轴承零配件
东莞千石家电有限公司	千石唯司	83732881	冷气机
东莞艾尔发自动化机械有限公司	施复兴	83180326	机械手(注塑机)
东莞群胜粉末冶金有限公司	杨潮钰	85303351	粉末冶金制品及电动工具传动器
东莞瑞智压缩机有限公司	陈修明	85528857	气体压缩机
瑞智制冷机器(东莞)有限公司	陈修明	85528857	制冷空调设备
东莞东成空调设备有限公司	袁世民	83632222	中央冷水机
希克斯电子(东莞)有限公司	松谷伸规	85601508	充电器
东莞鹏驰五金制品有限公司	周启胜	83668128	螺丝
专用设备制造业			
科广电子(东莞)有限公司	杨志龙	83302929	微型二极管
东莞伟易达电子产品有限公司	陈德荣	85581806	电子玩具
东莞宏威数码机械有限公司	刘惠森	22901516	旋涂机
一胜百模具(东莞)有限公司	尼古拉斯	22897888	精密型模具
东莞万德电子制品有限公司	白毅松	88775555	硅胶按键
东莞东坑富港电子制品厂	苏汉平	83882225	电子制品
东莞塘厦光裕灯泡厂	刘耀庭	87727255	灯泡
东莞丰裕电机有限公司	郑锡辉	87902888	喷涂环保工业自化设备
东华机械有限公司	邓　焘	22806233	注塑机
东莞大泉传感器有限公司	平绵孝之	88953366	传感器
东莞立诚电子有限公司	叶德波	86532010	电线
先锐模具配件(东莞)有限公司	李象烈	85376810	热流管
东莞佑能工具有限公司	庄景佳	88848901	钻头
忠信制模(东莞)有限公司	崔宗杰	83732298	非金属制品模具
东莞井上五金橡塑有限公司	村川尚则	88863344	印刷机部件
大宇(东莞)电器有限公司	李素华	83020257	榨汁机
东莞伊斯丹电子有限公司	藤森直和	87338301	变压器
东莞胜美达(太平)电机有限公司	何伟洪	85111118	电子原件
保德科技(东莞)有限公司	王乐得	81896936	电动化电渡机械设备
东莞泛邦电子有限公司	张瑞德	85310926	各类电子产品
东莞豪力机械有限公司	邝贯晴	88658999	直线封边机
大宝(东莞)模具切削工具有限公司	远藤徹	83182598	螺丝
东莞明利钢材模具制品有限公司	何英麟	83316878	精密型腔模

1-5 续表 20

(2009年)

单位名称	负责人	联系电话	主要产品(或服务)
东莞中兴模具有限公司	胡建华	87735508	模具标准件
东莞康佳模具塑胶有限公司	王友来	82071360	模具
永大精密模具(东莞)有限公司	陈显崇	85312541	精密模具
毅昌金型(东莞)五金制品有限公司	陈锦华	87761209	塑胶模具
台光五金制品(东莞)有限公司	巫典勋	87685123	精密五金模具
比美高精密模具(东莞)有限公司	颜乙清	87753128	其他橡胶模具制品
东莞顺兴电子有限公司	安承奎	83039160	电子塑胶零配件
东莞添威电子制品有限公司	曾侠奎	87779805	电源供应器
东莞富强鑫塑胶机械制造有限公司	王伯祥	83313753	全自动身拙或型机
长成电子(东莞)有限公司	任志刚	22035023	非金属制品模具
东莞安联电器元件有限公司	罗杰肖	85500410	电器开关
新崧塑胶(东莞) 有限公司	洪焕青	85079188	非金属制品模具
捷荣模具工业(东莞)有限公司	赵晓群	82387988	模具
东莞毅昌模具制造注塑有限公司	陈锦华	87761209	五金模具
东莞恒晖彩印机械厂有限公司	谢林翰	87751438	彩印机器设备
东莞亿东机器有限公司	陆柯雅	85785003	全自动注塑机及零配件
东莞鑫佑光电科技有限公司	吴志明	86534198	背光板
东莞胜方电子有限公司	詹胜琴	86216886	导电薄膜
东莞极盛电子有限公司	权石雄	88953118	激光头塑料配件
东莞佳鸿机械制造有限公司	李伟宏	88859861	吹瓶机
峰川模具东莞有限公司	陶伟洪	87513998	五金模具
东莞艾玛电子有限公司	王音樵	87725209	红外线感知灯光控制器
东莞骆恒塑胶制品有限公司	林朝熙	87312310	精密成型钢模
东莞今富五金机械有限公司	黄金男	87632358	针织机
东莞宝豪灯饰有限公司	吴文彰	88627888	灯饰及其配件
东莞东城天祥电子塑胶制品厂	许鸿仪	88990909	电视机外壳
东莞塘厦顺扬精密五金厂	刘秀朗	87989888	五金模具制作
东莞富强电子有限公司	田国英	83882225	耳机
交通运输设备制造业			
美尔顿车业(东莞)有限公司	林碧玉	81118000	电动助力车
广东中远船务工程有限公司	王兴如	88286988	金属船
东莞泰合复合材料有限公司	张国萃	86913288	自行车零配件
东莞信丰五金机械塑胶工业有限公司	刘松柏	85411186	汽车零件
爱地雅(东莞)自行车有限公司	李志文	88951888	自行车
小仓离合机(东莞)有限公司	市川洋光	86361603	离合器
东莞龙达科技有限公司	林胜源		自行车配件
格尔翰汽车配件(东莞)有限公司	格拉咸则田泰拿	81828988	汽车配件
东莞鸿图精密压铸有限公司	冯就图	86062888	铝合金压铸件
东莞方皓汽车配件有限公司	李孝中	87725576	捆绑器
东莞鸿益雨刷有限公司	古原钦	86646707	汽车雨刷
东莞联志五金制品有限公司	高志庆	83195767	汽车刹车盘零件
东莞京滨汽车电喷装置有限公司	大沼公纪	22658290	汽车零部件及配件
东莞杰腾造船有限公司	陈弘文	85921699	制售FRP游艇
东莞大和化成汽车零配件有限公司	池田雅史		汽车配件

1-5 续表 21

(2009年)

单位名称	负责人	联系电话	主要产品(或服务)
东莞山口实业有限公司	山口哲夫	87128480	汽车塑胶制品
东莞恩斯克转向器有限公司	出川光夫	22620960	汽车零部件及配件
古河汽车配件(东莞)有限公司	中田庄一郎	87295600	汽车用电线
东莞井上建上汽车部件有限公司	福原浩路朗	88682171	汽车零部件
电气机械及器材制造业			
东莞艾帝思电子科技有限公司	郑起龙	88637292	电子元件
东莞万迪电子有限公司	刘金利	82988519	其他输配电及控制设备
东莞创机电业制品有限公司	邓联泰	82728888	电动工具
世雅电子科技(东莞)有限公司	欧阳婉琳	85414388	高效率变频器
京都电工(东莞)有限公司	井手敏明	85428288	电子元器
东莞基业电气设备有限公司	苏洪新	22273666	高低成套开关柜
东莞东峰铝型材制品有限公司	陈汶良	87913344	铝型材
东莞永力电业有限公司	赖文达	83335989	电源线插头
东莞华兴电器有限公司	温异强	82995698	小型变压器
东莞德宏电线电子有限公司	游忠德	87724535	电线
东莞广宇精密电子有限公司	宋光斗	85509706	电线
东莞海韵电子有限公司	魏金花	22610501	电子设备
东莞福登机电有限公司	许永福	81035111	电机小型电器
东莞南玻光伏科技有限公司	柯汉奇	88288808	晶体硅太阳能电池
东莞三雄电业制造有限公司	顾文雄	83436611	电源线
东莞积信电器有限公司	陆程鹏	87799639	电烤炉
东莞亚大电子科技有限公司	林振兴		电线、电缆
东莞宏翔电器有限公司	张淑蓉	87772581	电风扇
东莞清溪合力电器制造厂	刘炳坤	87731111	搅拌机
东莞优电电线电缆有限公司	王世传	86632563	电线电缆
东莞塘厦伊南电器制品厂	钟庆辉	87880237	连接线
东莞港电电器制品有限公司	廖顺祺	86518228	直发器
东莞荣星电线有限公司	王东宪	87913003	漆包线绫线
东莞盛时五金塑胶制品有限公司	萧 诚		五金塑胶灯具及配件
东莞泰德灯饰有限公司	刘红涛	83620988	灯饰
东莞溢丰电器有限公司	林振让	83519616	家用房电器
东莞特伟电机有限公司	五协盛	83691717	马达
东莞六源电线电缆有限公司	徐陈吉子	83336789	电话线
东莞启益电器机械有限公司	柯志萍	87989065	变压器
东莞市雅科精密线材有限公司	熊泽均	83888869	电线电缆
东莞昌亿电器有限公司	叶民发	88847319	电器开关制
荣文灯饰(东莞)有限公司	林建南	81667888	灯饰及配件
东莞东马电子厂	钟任根		微型马达及附件
东莞林发电子有限公司	林世雄	83085888	音响插头线
港芝(东莞)电子制造厂有限公司	廖锦昌	87720639	健身器材
智宝电子(东莞)有限公司	郑建忠	87914676	电解电容器
东莞泽龙线缆有限公司	叶炽德		特种漆包线
东莞可比世电子有限公司	小岛雄幸	83623093	变压器
东莞华明灯具有限公司	王忠琦	87311200	灯具

1-5 续表 22

(2009年)

单位名称	负责人	联系电话	主要产品(或服务)
东莞川电电机有限公司	廖仁宽	83020001	定子
东莞宏大电器制品有限公司	劳天智	22269073	家用电器
东莞信浓马达有限公司	金子八郎	87772818	微电机
东莞永大电子有限公司	丁永详	83339366	插头连接线
东莞新光电线有限公司	和田启	88316705	电线电缆
东莞文邦电线有限公司	潘俊明	87731000	电线电缆
东莞威煌电器制品有限公司	梁小玲	87727984	电动剪发器
东莞华新电线电缆有限公司	焦佑慧	83195252	8.0铜杆
东莞苏泊尔电器有限公司	苏显泽	86365011	电磁炉
丽宾电子通讯(东莞)有限公司	罗善美	87188102	耳机线材
东莞大东电业有限公司	杨淑媖	83340838	电线电缆
东莞宏智电器配件有限公司	吴汉基	87136136	家用电器配件
东莞松藤电子有限公司	关　亨	83457291	吹风
东莞富钜电器有限公司	王建文	81508099	电源插座
东莞澳利电器制品有限公司	梁锦荣	83330419	变压器
东莞恒忻电子有限公司	谢明明	87915567	电感线圈
华展照明(东莞)有限公司	李思薇	83222228	落地灯
东莞光距电子有限公司	姜其求	87288988	网络线
四国电线(东莞)有限公司	佐佐木康裕	87735432	同轴电线
东莞莹辉灯饰有限公司	钟少鸿	85551445	灯饰
东莞宇隆电工材料有限公司	林福群	86642861	漆包线
金霸王(中国)有限公司	胡韬盟	22403615	电池
东莞东江电线电缆有限公司	林　俊	83391335	电话线
东莞建通电子五金有限公司	苏敦义	85565684	端子
东莞万利信新材料元件有限公司	高伯安	86069888	铝电解电容器
易达威锐电源设备科技(东莞)有限公司	龙　格	22651108	智能化电源设备系统
东莞美群电器制品有限公司	文肇伟	87981800	家用电力器具
东莞达晨电业制品有限公司	林麦升	86631818	电线
东莞巨汉灯饰有限公司	蔡纯昌	22096948	灯饰
丰岛电子制品(东莞)有限公司	江长霖	87312590	精密按键
东莞迅德电器有限公司	陈嘉雄	87739411	小型变压器
东莞维升电子制品有限公司	吴瑞雄	83622694	电源线连插头
勤诚电脑(东莞)有限公司	李连富	83420011	电子元件
东莞新立电线有限公司	蔡永秋菊	86520268	橡胶电线
飞宏(东莞)电子有限公司	林中民	87319026	电源供应器及半成品
东莞蒂雅克电子有限公司	桐章造	85548848	音响视听设备
东莞宏桦电器有限公司	张正育	87935001	电风扇
东莞金星电线有限公司	洪培琪	83195297	电线电缆
长青林电子(东莞)有限公司	林铅廷	83340851	电线
东莞厚街三屯创力电器制品厂	曾建强	82728888	吸尘器
东莞杰扬五金电器有限公司	李伟崇	83020011	吊灯
易事特电力系统技术有限公司	黎丽珍		不间断电源
东莞怡盛电业有限公司	叶浩然	83016688	电线电缆
东莞九州电器有限公司	张家瑜	83188854	筒灯

1-5 续表 23

(2009年)

单位名称	负责人	联系电话	主要产品(或服务)
东莞永成电器制品厂有限公司	沈广河	87738870	吸尘器
东莞冠宏电子有限公司	潘耀昇	88619858	组合音响、电子钢琴
福华电子设备(东莞)有限公司	蓝荣裕	83193767	开关
东莞龙杰电子有限公司	何涵箴	87734425	线材组合
东莞东进照明有限公司	贺维格·彼克勤(Herwig)	22024968	灯饰
永新电线电缆(东莞)有限公司	萧泉利	85411045	电线电缆电脑连接线
新宝电机(东莞)有限公司	陈盛沺	85504417	线路转换板
东莞桥梓周氏电业有限公司	周礼谦	83332731	电线电缆PVC胶粒
东莞光晋灯饰有限公司	林世铭	85586035	灯饰及灯饰配件
东莞三星电机有限公司	刘晓星	83305000	电源
东莞明电电气工程有限公司	胜沼正和	88750012	高压配电柜
东莞卡妮尔灯饰有限公司	周时彬	87723088	台灯
呈威电子(东莞)有限公司	邱明贤	83377756	微型变压器
东莞嘉盛照明科技有限公司	谢雅芬	85700057	灯具
东莞世福电器有限公司	郑荣辉	87923483	电源控制盒
金淞制冷设备(东莞)有限公司	廖文淦	83394468	移动式冷气机
东莞世昕电子有限公司	廖林展	87917888	新型电子元器件
东莞亚飞电器有限公司	陈文捷	86983888	灯头
东莞柏杰灯饰有限公司	陈锦樑	85551219	塑料五金灯饰
东莞润泰电线电缆有限公司	张程博	88620999	电线
东莞庆龙电线电缆有限公司	林建吾	83665661	电线
东莞毓华电子科技有限公司	马家豪	86668107	开关电源
东莞依安达电子有限公司	胡卫成	83344574	电解电容
东莞安硕电子有限公司	蔡文芳	87882595	电子式镇流器、微型变压器
东莞赫升机电有限公司	陈启文	82095588	各类机电设备
东莞卡斯特照明有限公司	曹淑琴	88655066	照明灯具及其配件
杰群电子科技(东莞)有限公司	方家俊	83635267	新型电子元器件
光宝电子(东莞)有限公司	宋恭源	86070888	电源供应器
东莞联立电器实业有限公司	区国辉	87721921	小家电
东莞正宏机械有限公司	廖国忠	85566078	电容器机械
东莞统元电源连接有限公司	陈忠明	83101598	电源线连插头
东莞耀台五金电子有限公司	黄中兴	83355496	电器五金件
东莞华巨特殊线材有限公司	郭来卿	88389008	镀锡线
东莞汇勋电器制品有限公司	麦立志		电风扇、暖风机、增湿机
东莞星地电子有限公司	林成玉	85545751	带插头电线
东莞永德电业制品有限公司	梁永进		电线
东莞汉华金属制品有限公司	林淑芬	83188845	铜线
东莞利通电器二厂	罗日全	86070888	电源供应器
东莞莞城协益电子厂	陈志文	22264550	微型电机及零部件
东莞虎门沙角豪特五金塑胶厂	张锡潮	85561965	插头
东莞金波罗电业科技有限公司	宋生泉	88886808	电线电缆
东莞大新科技有限公司	马钦佳	88865753	气量测试器
日立蓄电池(东莞)有限公司	铃木幹十	86400790	汽车铅酸蓄电池
海蓝星光学科技(东莞)有限公司	林丽华	87184998	镇流器

1-5 续表 24

(2009年)

单位名称	负责人	联系电话	主要产品(或服务)
万泰光电(东莞)有限公司	张铭烈	88620666	单模光纤
东莞进泰电子有限公司	邢家蓁	87725650	音响
东莞旭光五金氧化制品有限公司	吴焯光	83371090	电热壶
奇烨电子(东莞)有限公司	舒铁汉	86925028	变压器
东莞瀚宇电子有限公司	沈孝玉	83193666	KF线
东莞天扬电子有限公司	王镝程	82011299	电力电子元器件
正规电线电缆(东莞)有限公司	高士钦	83624357	电源线连插头
东莞库柏电子有限公司	刘金利	81605288	变压器
东莞庆泰电线电缆有限公司	叶泰隆	83330265	电线、电源
东莞美盛电器制品有限公司	周礼谦	83816178	小型变压器电感线圈镇流器
东莞长联电线电缆有限公司	张伟良	85703585	电线电缆
东莞钜权电器有限公司	吴蓓馨	22183056	厨房电器
东莞金山电池有限公司	许永新	87723007	锂离子电子
太阳电线东莞有限公司	谷口直毅	22401739	电线、电缆
日本电产三协电子(东莞)有限公司	松尾史朗	86111234	微型步进电机
东莞桥功电子有限公司	张永京	86937682	塑胶五金
东莞道滘建和五金制品厂	岑炎波	88836680	开关电线接插件
东莞市井南电子有限公司	韩吉九	88410266	新型电子材料
东莞泰欣照明有限公司	魏春水	87135999	灯饰
东莞乐域塑胶电子制品有限公司	劳应海	86550011	光管手提灯
东莞元太电业有限公司	林振兴	87881778	电线
亚士吉灯饰(东莞)有限公司	艾文德·沽文森	88492087	灯具、照明装置
东莞威德电子科技有限公司	武济群	23061648	背部按摩椅座垫
东莞新能源科技有限公司	陈棠华	88989162	高技术绿色电池
大盛照明(东莞)有限公司	陈正雄	87503918	各种灯具及配件
东莞实英电子有限公司	邱秋林	88630999	电脑接插件
东莞景盛电线材料有限公司	邓进成	85157538	PVC胶粒
亚弘(东莞)电器有限公司	黄晋益	86851766	家用电器
东莞伸金电子有限公司	郑裕丰	22266314	各种电子接插件
东莞镒台电子有限公司	张次男	83305834	电脑连接线
东莞创宝达电器制品有限公司	陈顺结	83335747	漏电保护器
东莞宏致电子有限公司	袁万丁	85393066	电子零配件
东莞铭励电器制品有限公司	叶民发	88437043	电器开关制
立信杰(东莞)精密模具制造有限公司	黄奇勇	86800088	汽车线材
万裕三信电子(东莞)有限公司	高伯安	86069888	电子电容器
东莞志丰电子有限公司	林纯正	83183457	蜂鸣器
东莞常禾电子有限公司	陈周万	85551202	音箱、喇叭、扬声器
东莞理士电源制品有限公司	彭　辉	87325187	高能阀控密封蓄电池
东莞新能源电子科技有限公司	曾毓群	88989052	电池
东莞首资宝电器制造有限公司	谢树安	87130808	电暖器
东莞伟能五金电子有限公司	林美慧	87510872	家用电器配件及电脑配件
东莞升隆电线塑胶有限公司	郑莲清	83608118	电线
东莞亿得电器制品有限公司	萧铭任	85554635	电热炉
东莞亿泰电线电缆有限公司	王银河	85500951	电线

1-5 续表 25

(2009年)

单位名称	负责人	联系电话	主要产品(或服务)
东莞强盛电线电缆有限公司	宋生泉	86633470	电线、电缆
东莞力达电机有限公司	麦立志		微电机及其它电机
东莞新亚电子科技有限公司	白建功	85702888	电线通讯电缆
东莞石龙粤龙电器厂	叶汉泉		微电机
东莞吉联电线电缆有限公司	王光添	85551155	PVC电线
谊邦电工材料(东莞)有限公司	林国标	22654837	漆色线
东莞珀韵电子有限公司	吴进枝	83720950	音圈
东莞超霸电池有限公司	许永新	87910215	电池
实盈电子(东莞)有限公司	黄凰洲	87318688	连接器
东莞艾天电池科技有限公司	李明九	88973706	锂离子电池
东莞明晖不锈钢厨具有限公司	王毅俊	87313210	高身雪柜
东莞新元电子有限公司	朴进铉	87815229	锂离子电池
东莞鸿呈电子有限公司	简忠正	88636000	电脑连接插头
东莞万宝至电机设备制造有限公司	羽渊展世	22267409	微电机其他电机
东莞苏扬灯饰有限公司	潘文芳	83342116	圣诞饰品
东莞安达电器制品有限公司	李伟明	87771128	不锈钢咖啡壶
东莞星志厨具厂有限公司	陈清富	86634017	厨具
东莞高力电池有限公司	蒙小兵	87739390	干电池
东莞苏扬电器有限公司	潘文芳	83391502	圣诞灯串
东莞启东电线电缆有限公司	于健平	88867234	电线电缆
东莞新隆漆包线有限公司	袁锦标	86415025	漆包线
东莞唯可灯饰有限公司	许火南	87713153	灯饰及灯饰零件配件
东莞丰盛电线电缆有限公司	颜念威	83343591	漆包线
东莞航升实业有限公司	梁简用	83668283	家用电器用品
富士林电子(东莞)有限公司	洪英顺	83882225	连接线
东莞固邦灯饰电线有限公司	陈林素珍	85553167	节日灯饰、红铜线
东莞基立线缆有限公司	潘俊业	82061078	电脑连接线
东莞威霸清洁器材有限公司	乔根·延森	83283988	清洁器材
东莞市银晖电制品有限公司	许永新	87723007	开发锂离子电池
通信设备、计算机及其他电子设备制造业			
东莞南阳电子有限公司	尹亮坤		电子元器件
东莞沛波电子有限公司	吴俊谊	86310316	小型变压器
东莞斯普电子有限公司	骆伯昭	83726800	MP3录放机
东莞中探探针有限公司	陈志峯	85151668	电子测试探针
东莞冠坤电子有限公司	苏辉雄	87318000	片式电容
东莞东远机械制造有限公司	介俊明	83501527	制版设备
大东俊通(东莞)电子有限公司	李泰夏	83394379	组合音响
东莞市王氏港建电子有限公司	何树灿	83903333	电子产品
东莞栢能电子科技有限公司	王锡豪	85822002	电脑主机
东莞国瑞电子有限公司	曾加兴	82063511	电感器
东莞首邦电子有限公司	侯清渊	86632772	变压器
东莞泰峰电子有限公司	金大中	83437030	汽车音响高频头
东莞英特科电子有限公司	吴知焕	87937821	打印机及其零部件
东莞新洋电子有限公司	梁熙成	86171021	手机外壳

1-5 续表 26

(2009年)

单位名称	负责人	联系电话	主要产品(或服务)
泓凯电子科技(东莞)有限公司	张灿能	83365942	电脑机箱
东莞石排联鑫电子厂	邓柱锦	86591818	彩色电视机
富加宜连接器(东莞)有限公司	陈 也	88682108	电子连接器
东莞国创电子有限公司	郑玉慧	87720275	片式电阻器
东莞华强三洋电子有限公司	周 力	87910998	彩电
东莞华龙电子有限公司	施宪雄	83376575	变压器
康舒电子(东莞)有限公司	高青山	87915950	电源供应器
东莞康创电子科技有限公司	张贵益	85889989	收音机
东莞亚锋电脑零配件有限公司	陈胜彬	87727888	电脑零配件
益伸电子(东莞)有限公司	官有文	83796198	五金电子
东莞顺晟电脑实业有限公司	李振南	86801188	电脑机箱
东莞爱铭数码电子有限公司	李世运	83038000	激光头
东莞市三协精工科技有限公司	吕礼志	88787202	电子产品
东莞时力科技电子厂	谭旭明	85415668	电子元件
奥托仑光电子(东莞)有限公司	林志允	86401060	玻璃光学镜片
东莞捷盛电子有限公司	陈卓平		零件印制电路板
东莞南城新科磁电制品厂	梁永乐	22810033	电脑磁头
东莞鹏龙光电有限公司	吕子鹏	88787202	平板显示器件
东莞长安厦岗成铭电子制品厂	麦永强	85419999	电脑机箱
东莞柏能电子厂	曾庆馀	85822002	计算机主板显卡
东莞柏狮赛格精密电子有限公司	刘谨铭	88233068	半导体
东莞铭异精密电子有限公司	克雷格·托马斯	86387383	电脑支架
业强科技(东莞)有限公司	王台光	85421928	新型电子元器件
东莞微迅电子科技有限公司	王 瑜	87735130	数字音、视频编解码设备
东莞皓讯电子有限公司	王秀瑾	87313056	电脑电子周边线
东莞康特尔电子有限公司	王成群	88462888	数字电视机
东莞全策电器有限公司	甄东刚	82069922	收音机
东莞嘉茂电子科技有限公司	林天元	88606888	喇叭
三轴电子(东莞)有限公司	沈再清	86639298	印制电路板
东莞高盛电子有限公司	林 威	83813136	电话机
东莞日线线缆有限公司	川添徹郎	83344845	铜材
兴科电子(东莞)有限公司	许舒恭	85106058	手机按键
泰科电子(东莞)有限公司	陈顺结	85817613	通讯终端设备
东莞长安镇时力电子厂	孙学斌	85533151	磁臂组合半成品
东莞东坑先益电子厂	卢集祥	83381857	发光二极管
东莞红板多层线路板有限公司	喻红棉	86060111	电子元器件
天弘(东莞)科技有限公司	叶克裕	22899333	网络游戏机
品佳电子(东莞)有限公司	董裕华	88800318	液晶显示器
东莞市捷伟讯电子有限公司	谢拥军	85993708	手机
东莞清溪三清半导体厂	黄泰稳	87734139	半导体晶体管
东莞宣得电子有限公司	江长霖	85546400	电子元器件
东莞秀特电子有限公司	陈育男	87773572	磁性材料
泰宏电子(东莞)有限公司	王凤平	87313956	数位答录机
东莞万年富电子有限公司	张国华	87724667	线路板

1-5 续表 27

(2009年)

单位名称	负责人	联系电话	主要产品(或服务)
东莞太华半导体有限公司	姜模勋	83263688	手机用液晶显示器部件
东莞光阵显示器制品有限公司	沈振权	87738870	摄像头
广东南方宏明电子科技股份有限公司	邓春华	22407479	电容器
东莞加玮华电子有限公司	蔡镇雄	22257469	耳机
东莞电创电子有限公司	麻生繁	88834807	电子接插件
唯耀电子(东莞)有限公司	何荣珍		电源板
东莞台庆精密电子有限公司	林鉴荣	83365488	电子零件
东莞首富电子有限公司	李泰祺	87710688	电子产品
东莞歌乐东方电子有限公司	村上浩一	83387001	汽车音响
东莞通华液晶有限公司	黄华达	88774388	液晶显示板
东莞泰富电子有限公司	郑玉清	88730138	电话
东莞日联精钢有限公司	冯永茂	22203677	不锈钢螺丝
东莞加炜电子有限公司	杨峰慧	86310071	电子连接器
东莞石龙粤龙光学制品厂	叶汉泉		收音机
东莞华春电子有限公司	徐金旗	88888850	路由器
东莞东英电子工业有限公司	藤原匡男	87328201	DVD机蕊
东莞东原电子有限公司	河棅朝	83228000	手机充电器
台达电子零组件(东莞)有限公司	柯子兴	86639008	散热风扇(电脑)
高效电子(东莞)有限公司	许昆泰	88901888	电脑零配件
东莞建永数码科技有限公司	李建福	87880818	CD镭射机
东莞领航电子有限公司	杨　森		变压器整流器
东莞立德电子有限公司	林碧珍		变压器
东莞爱美克电子有限公司	江玟慧	87775085	放大器
东莞三星视界有限公司	尹晋赫	85582000	液晶显示片
东莞凡振工业电子有限公司	朴正吉	87635181	电子音响
东莞长安涌头富贵电子厂	文德亮	85328418	电位器
东莞洲磊电子有限公司	李明顺	87631888	磷化镓
雅新电子线路板(东莞)有限公司	黄恒俊	86331999	印刷线路板
东莞宝桥电子科技有限公司	卢金柱	83632679	新型平板显示器件
东莞辉城电子有限公司	陈瑞星		电子组件
东莞宝山电子有限公司	莫建邻	87712264	电子产品
东莞动利电子有限公司	许文昉		电脑散热风扇
品基电子(东莞)有限公司	林茂生	87910231	电子元件
东莞爱维泰电子有限公司	约翰·密切尔	83377651	电脑散热器
东莞黄江威成科技电子厂	曾锦昌	83632679	液晶显示屏
升荣电子(东莞)有限公司	庄信裕	87311036	电脑周边产品
东莞同昌电子有限公司	庄跃灿	83318960	PCB
东莞东骏电器有限公司	毛　冬	22401688	电子变压器用铁心片
东莞谢岗钨珍电子厂	吴勇日	82126950	手机外壳
联德电子(东莞)有限公司	陈铭智	83072288	电子电源供应器
东莞益衡电子有限公司	叶陇西	87755689	电源供应器
东莞安美时电子有限公司	叶克裕	83394581	网络控制设备
诺基亚通信有限公司东莞分公司	蔡志强	22402844	移动电话
东莞微端电子科技有限公司	鲁景岱	83975888	新型平板显示器

1-5　续表 28

(2009年)

单位名称	负责人	联系电话	主要产品(或服务)
东莞友华电子有限公司	桥本悦男	83326171	端子连接器
东莞市旭进光电有限公司	藤森知雄	85413789	光学镜头
东莞三泰电器有限公司	周　哲	83331722	电子元件
东莞建玮电子制品有限公司	黄陈素美	87734800	电脑连接线
东莞怡科电子有限公司	陈政宽	87086668	汽车移动电话充电器
东莞保辉电子有限公司	李庭津	87727701	电子玩具
东莞成乐电子有限公司	邱庆华	83713213	电子产品
东莞耀升机电有限公司	蔡崇志	87338900	电子零件、压铸产品
中名(东莞)电子有限公司	源而细	85559636	耳机
东莞华科电子有限公司	朱有义	83115168	片式电容
东莞相川铁龙电子有限公司	相川猛	83395551	电子元件
恩智浦半导体广东有限公司	叶昱良	83668268	开发半导体
台达电子(东莞)有限公司	柯子兴	86639008	线圈
东莞达宏电子有限公司	林冠宏	87736405	电源供应器
东莞矽德半导体有限公司	邱贤德	87313240	集成电路
东莞山本电子科技有限公司	高桥俊雄	88227094	印刷线路板
东莞德利信电子有限公司	铃木直人	83395111	各种机芯产品
东莞技嘉电子有限公司	刘明雄	83367140	电脑主板
美信音响器材(东莞)有限公司	吴维忠	86856188	音箱、喇叭、扬声器
东莞广通事务机有限公司	郑文涛	85312190	电子元件及组件
东莞恒辉电阻制造厂有限公司	张志宏	83315373	电阻器
东莞瑞智电子有限公司	史达芬	83222959	传感器元件
东莞新进电子有限公司	陈其镰	85613846	电子计算机外部设备
东莞凯升电子有限公司	李礽辉	87883521	电脑机箱
华磁电子(东莞)有限公司	徐道训		电感器
达创科技(东莞)有限公司	梁克勇	86637008	集线器
东莞利保迅电子有限公司	方传仁	86408844	变压器
棠裕电子(东莞)有限公司	陈志湧	87332588	液晶显示器
东莞福满生电子有限公司	沈秀美	82207777	电脑显示器托架
东莞超悦电子有限公司	朴虎范	83305007	电脑键盘
东莞达电电子有限公司	孙文伟	86323500	耳机
东莞黄江瑞升科技电子厂	曾锦昌	83633303	电脑及周边产品
东莞创盟电子有限公司	林宪昌	85505799	半导件集成电路
茂瑞电子(东莞)有限公司	刘松平	87077888	键盘
东莞狮龙电子有限公司	毛巧茹	83283391	DVD
弘星通讯电子(东莞)有限公司	林海德	88492771	通讯零部件
东莞黄江精成科技电子一厂	曾锦昌	83632679	电脑主板
三井高科技(广东)有限公司	犬塚和人	86070008	新型电子元器件
东莞陆和电子有限公司	廖禄堙	88885117	键盘
东莞昆盈电脑制品有限公司	卓进兴	85825810	鼠标器
东莞欧珀移动通信有限公司	金乐亲	85545555	手机
东莞高埗昭和电子厂	冯灿荣	88873451	遥控器
东莞石碣源利电子厂	杨　伟	86638923	液晶显示器
永胜电脑五金(东莞)有限公司	廖志铭	83387140	电脑机箱

1-5 续表 29

(2009年)

单位名称	负责人	联系电话	主要产品(或服务)
东莞意华电子有限公司	李振松	85379731	插头
东莞展翊五金电器有限公司	余允平	87735052	电脑机箱
东莞健益五金制品有限公司	陈省炎	86487999	DVD机芯五金件
富相电子科技(东莞)有限公司	潘梅玉	88737888	液晶显示器件
东莞嘉盈电子有限公司	刘增炳	85812455	电脑塑胶配件
东莞永冠电子科技有限公司	洪志刚	22033699	DVD播放机
飞比达电子元器件(东莞)有限公司	张绍鹏	83725088	新型电子元器件
平易电子(东莞)有限公司	陈广兴	83820333	印刷电路板
东莞鑫联数码科技有限公司	黄其昌	86591818	数码DVD播放机
东莞创慈磁性元件有限公司	苏天寅	86327771	变压器
东莞力罗电子科技有限公司	李明九	83712772	新型电子元件
东莞诠盛电器有限公司	洪月逢	85825373	电源插座
东莞合宝电器制品有限公司	颜礼华	83715169	电器开关
东莞仲屏电子有限公司	张君碧	81868166	扬声器
东莞艾斯光电科技有限公司	尹焞鑛	22667703	新型电子元器件
锦旭电子(东莞)有限公司	孙国钦	87737118	电脑周边产品
东莞富鼎塑胶五金有限公司	翁祖晋	86279588	电脑托架
先锋信泰(东莞)光学有限公司	赖以仁	85535435	精密光电电器件
飞磁电子材料(东莞)有限公司	范德豪	87382420	磁芯、磁环
东莞凯鸿光电科技有限公司	徐华基	85524576	电器保护管
东莞旺宏科技有限公司	刘瑀洁		鼠标
东莞普思电子有限公司	曹规源	85538871	高频滤波器
东莞生益电子有限公司	唐翔千	22272074	多层印刷电路板
东莞太阳诱电有限公司	吉野泰司	86636888	电容器
东莞万士达液晶显示器有限公司	黄显雄	22668178	光电子器件及其他电子器件
东莞海湘电声有限公司	肖铁飞	83624245	扬声器
太阳诱电(广东)有限公司	吉野泰司	86636888	电容器
东莞近江电子有限公司	细川清司	81036276	线路主板
东莞翔国光电科技有限公司	赖麒瑜	81833588	印刷电路板
东莞益新实业有限公司	王干文	87811000	电子零配件
东莞汇和电子有限公司	余丽瑜	87768410	印刷线路板
东莞优威王电子塑胶五金有限公司	陈锦鼎	85701800	计算机用PC塑胶配件
东莞正阳电子有限公司	林淑敏	87916258	音箱
东莞世华电子有限公司	蔡清梅	87910021	电子设备
国巨电子(东莞)有限公司	颜荣昆	87720275	电阻器
圣华电子(东莞)有限公司	巩　卫	87882707	电脑连接线
东莞高美电子有限公司	李景载	83300880	电子配件
东莞裕光数码电子有限公司	姜文昌	88382101	手机LCD电路板
东莞康佳电子有限公司	姚健平	87755689	电子元件
东莞企达电器制品有限公司	颜礼华	83715169	电子元件
极讯电子(东莞)有限公司	廖正民	88953310	电子元件
东莞盛和电子有限公司	胡清河	86076988	电子
东莞音音电子绘本有限公司	陈世雄	83668068	电子式音乐卡
东莞高伟光学电子有限公司	李南午	83307111	电子组件

1-5 续表 30

(2009年)

单位名称	负责人	联系电话	主要产品(或服务)
东莞艾利博电子有限公司	丁海云	22899100	电子词典显示器
东莞旭福电脑有限公司	宋恭源	87318190	电脑主机板
东莞协盈电脑有限公司	徐文助	85880090	鼠标器
广东升威电子制品有限公司	洪金镳	87287777	电位器编码器
东莞致力电脑有限公司	宋恭源	87312821	电脑配件
派登电子科技(东莞)有限公司	王永辉	86091666	键盘
东莞盛世科技电子实业有限公司	郑　犁	86914800	电子元器件
东莞奇力新电子有限公司	詹炎生	87730251	线圈
东莞柏业五金制品有限公司	林忠祥	86259665	电脑机箱
盛恒达电子(东莞)有限公司	陈俊德	86633718	ADLS路由器
东莞宝顺力电子塑胶制品厂有限公司	何志强	83353827	电子产品音响
东莞全台电子有限公司	曾瑞铭	83697606	平板显示器
东莞宏松精密组件有限公司	李武宗	28129588	键盘
东莞美捷电业有限公司	梁锦樟	83903378	镭射收录机
东莞福哥电子有限公司	刘兴旺	86649438	电子产品电位器
东莞福摩斯托电子有限公司	张文贤	85541200	家用电子元件
东莞成谦音响科技有限公司	梁志强	85380808	喇叭
华容电子(广东)有限公司	徐道训		电容器
东莞富饶精密五金制品有限公司	源而细	85556266	五金制品
东莞冠诚塑胶模具有限公司清溪分厂	陈锐文	87315088	遥控器
东莞普悦电子有限公司	廖文瑛	81660860	线路板插件
东莞裕佳电子有限公司	吴树财	87739418	光盘驱动器
东莞婕讯电子科技有限公司	孙昌盛	83088028	宽带接入网通信系统设备
东莞稀世电子有限公司	金钟锡	88383096	空气净化器
东莞长江电脑制品有限公司	朱　昀	87736209	电脑机箱
富声(东莞)电器配件有限公司	周文仁	85701082	耳机多媒体喇叭
东莞宇宙电路板设备有限公司	陈德和	87569928	电路板水平机组
东莞联桥电子有限公司	蔡汉林	86485066	印刷电路板
东莞常平桥沥大东大明电子厂	马沛强	83914086	塑胶制品
东莞劲捷电子有限公司	王万喜	85895863	电池充电器
东莞贯达电子有限公司	江富春	88786000	电感
振曜电子(东莞)有限公司	廖文章	83188470	网络交换机
东莞宝星电子有限公司	朴镇秀	83288770	微型麦克风
东莞友讯电子有限公司	龚志富	85318000	网络卡
东莞磁威电子科技有限公司	廖世芳	86787388	宽带网洛活音分歧器
日本电产（东莞）有限公司	泽村贤智	88873011	大容量光磁盘驱动器
东莞联聿电子有限公司	沈茂松	85322996	电脑机箱
快捷达通信设备(东莞)有限公司	文汉耀	83936688	数据通
东莞美城电子电器有限公司	谢鸿强	22250946	收录音机
东莞爱电电子有限公司	塚本年治	83434525	线路板
群光电子(东莞)有限公司	许昆泰	87311688	电脑键盘
东莞英格尔电子有限公司	黄廷光	87934928	电子元件
东莞宇声电子有限公司	郑甲烈	83732276	麦克风
东莞中建塑胶有限公司	刘玉清	88788261	塑胶配件

1-5 续表 31

(2009年)

单位名称	负责人	联系电话	主要产品(或服务)
东莞创群石英晶体有限公司	张铭宗	83119395	石英晶体谐振器
先锋高科技(东莞)有限公司	内藤真	83287704	磁盘驱动器
艾利和电子科技(中国)有限公司	丁海云	22899100	MP3、MP4
东莞耀胜电子有限公司	许春风	83737691	电脑周边产品
东莞新劲电子有限公司	陈其镳	87810780	电脑周边产品
东莞东力电子有限公司	凌少文	87723276	DVD机
东莞友华通信配件有限公司	须贺泉	22982285	天线
金笔电子东莞有限公司	林阿森	22200489	电子零配件件
成翔电子(东莞)有限公司	李振南	87733511	电源供应器
东莞广濑拓展电子有限公司	井泽隆		复印线路
东莞淳安电子有限公司	周耀威	87317941	薄膜开关
东莞基杰五金制品有限公司	刘德华	87735140	电脑机箱
东莞致通电脑有限公司	宋恭源	87312821	数据机网络卡
东莞呈杰电子有限公司	吴仲修	23102088	液晶显示器配件
东莞得泰电子有限公司	吴晏辉	86316090	耳机
富港电子(东莞)有限公司	卜庆藩	83882225	变压器
东莞东聚电子电讯制品有限公司	潘武龙	86631652	鼠标
东莞金士宝电子元件有限公司	李灯辉	87730695	电子元器件
东莞台霖电子通讯有限公司	林祺生	85655858	电脑线连插头
瑞讯电子(东莞)有限公司	潘良荣	88753288	网络卡、路由器
东莞美隆电声器材有限公司	吴维忠	86856288	各类型喇叭
东莞标帆塑胶五金制品有限公司	刘少凡	83189617	电脑机箱
旗利得电子(东莞)有限公司	饭岛克夫	87766645	印刷线路板
东莞塘厦建永塑胶电子厂	赵耀南	87880818	CD镭射机
东莞华强三洋马达有限公司	鞠耀明	87720523	微型马达
立维腾电子(东莞)有限公司	谭斯哈其	81038888	电子元件及组件
永捷电路版(东莞)有限公司	黄志国	85812542	印制电路板
东莞怡富电路板厂	杨锦堂	22274021	电路板
东莞高埗微太电子科技有限公司	简俊雄		数码产品
东莞森泰电子有限公司	喻红棉	87751663	手机
特新电路板器材(东莞)有限公司	冯志威	86403328	线路板钻孔
东莞保力电子有限公司	骆子云	86511771	电子新产品
东莞双盈电子有限公司	王义隆	87310135	电脑接线手机连接线
东莞精恒电子有限公司	杨明龙	88977068	公共广播器材
祥发电子(东莞)有限公司	黄恒俊	86331999	电源供应器
东莞上端电子有限公司	蔡胜枝	85099191	电脑配件
东莞惠伦顿堡电子有限公司	赵积清	83362809	电子元器材
雅新电子(东莞)有限公司	黄恒俊	86331999	空白印刷电器板
东莞亿润电子制品有限公司	谢明宗	88730855	光电子元器件
东莞德英电子通讯设备有限公司	卢德林	22024422	婴儿监督器
东莞亚联科技电子有限公司	黄　震	87727680	电脑及其周边配件、充电器
广东佳彩数码科技有限公司	张福柱	86727181	机顶盒
东莞托普顿电子有限公司	廉大植	86902111	扬声器
东莞翔辉插头零件制造厂	杨日安	85561480	五金塑胶电器配件、端子产品

1-5 续表 32

(2009年)

单位名称	负责人	联系电话	主要产品(或服务)
东莞伟特电子有限公司	殷明康	83345241	调制及调谐器
东莞明鑫电子有限公司	黄献洲	86731868	电子元件及组件
东莞长安乌沙李屋上川电子制品厂	李雪华	85549235	电子制品
东莞清溪德丽电子厂	黄海涛	87311036	电脑键盘
东莞勤德五金制品有限公司	谢阿田		计算机五金制品
东莞易迅电子制品有限公司	郑玉清	88788261	开关电源器CAC、DC换能器
东莞石龙京瓷光学有限公司	久芳彻夫	86119611	液晶制品
东莞鸿爱斯通信科技有限公司	金圭泰	88783009	电子元件
东莞鸿万电子有限公司	罗秀英	86785330	游戏机配件
新豪(东莞)电子有限公司	周进文	83216200	电脑键盘
东莞力音电子有限公司	李庆杉	86637826	电子线圈
东莞捷讯电子有限公司	莫建邻	87712009	手提标签机
东莞科达五金制品有限公司	崔少安	86313419	精密驱动器部件
最上(东莞)电子有限公司	后藤善文	87883718	喇叭鼓纸
东莞科泰电子有限公司	黎德明		合路器
东莞骅国电子有限公司	陈正煌	85597201	连接器
东莞辉煌电子有限公司	黄　震	87727680	电脑连线
东莞彩嘉电子有限公司	郑敏聪	87762803	录放机
东莞亨域电子有限公司	张颖杰	88859838	恒温器
松普科技(东莞)有限公司	骆建针	87937608	宽带接入网通信系统设备
东莞长安科得电子有限公司	杨福来	85546130	主板机
东莞森玛仕格里菲电路有限公司	丹提·乔瓦尼	81822047	多层线路板
东莞东源光电有限公司	章启侨	22633913	光纤跳接线
东莞智富五金制品有限公司	徐如松	86853888	电器外壳、散热片、音响面板
东莞明崴电子科技有限公司	张立国	22265628	光电子器件其他电子器件
东莞翊凯电器制品有限公司	陈東学	86812999	电脑机箱外壳
东莞怡发塑胶制品有限公司	王国强	83392238	电话充电器胶件
东莞泰硕电子有限公司	薛永胜	85321851	连接器
东莞诚信电子塑胶有限公司	毕国豪	85507263	变压器胶架
品嘉电子(东莞)有限公司	赵亨泰	85903505	电脑显示卡
东莞长安华南电子厂	谭永璋	85307366	磁性产品
东莞东骅电子科技有限公司	张连生	86986160	电脑机箱
东莞雅士电子有限公司	陈秉阶	85545115	收放组合机
东莞东煦五金电镀厂有限公司	萧　杰	85564222	LED引线架
杰特电子(东莞)有限公司	吴金彩	87725351	电脑音箱
东莞百音电子有限公司	柏木正和	22984320	扬声器
东莞美京电子有限公司	卢满基	83222370	散热片
联一小原光学(东莞)有限公司	陈忠政	86240666	光学玻璃毛胚
东莞伟易达电脑有限公司	陈德荣	83231806	电源控制口
特新微电子(东莞)有限公司	宋本中	86403328	电路板钻孔
东莞利源电子有限公司	黄一城	83723988	灯光控制器
亚电电子(东莞)有限公司	黄晋益	87982616	黑胶唱机
东莞伟易达卫星设备有限公司	陈德荣	83231806	室内无线电话

1-5 续表 33

(2009年)

单位名称	负责人	联系电话	主要产品(或服务)
东莞彩显有机发光科技有限公司	刘惠森	87738875	新型平放显示器
东莞迈虹电子有限公司	伊滕春美	85378311	印刷线路板
东莞厚街鸿亮机电设备有限公司	邓联泰	83099888	剪草机
东莞凤岗三和盛科技电子厂	朴晶柱	87862222	计算机及周边设备、仪表仪器
奥泰斯电子(东莞)有限公司	福井真一	83365026	防盗热感应器
特新电路材料(东莞)有限公司	冯志威	86403328	多层线路板
东莞船井电机厂	陈志明	83665999	液晶电视机
东莞中钜资讯光电有限公司	方健文	85994660	电子原配件
东莞芝浦电子有限公司	关根厷行	85412371	热敏电阻
东莞常平土塘大根电子光学制品厂	黄伟文	83395446	扫描器镜头
东莞航大电子有限公司	小林兼男	83392291	电话单机
东莞奕华电子有限公司	邓 洪	88759333	电子产品
东莞令特电子有限公司	丹尼班纳安简	81515186	压敏电阻
东莞市兴奇宏电子有限公司	沈丽美	86731868	电脑主机
世擎光电(东莞)有限公司	李柾橐	81821666	手机摄像模组
东莞新动电子有限公司	陈其镰	88962920	汽车组合仪表
嘉益电子(东莞)有限公司	蔡奕炎	22207821	印制电路板
旭丽电子(东莞)有限公司	宋恭源	86638923	键盘
矽谷电子科技(东莞)有限公司	李昱锦	83366696	液晶显示器
东莞环亚高科电子有限公司	谭伟豪	85316946	个人数码助理
东莞巨丰铜线有限公司	曾顺龙	22266314	漆包线
东莞岳丰电子科技有限公司	叶春荣	86634236	电话线连插头
东莞康源电子有限公司	周庆泉	85562002	线路板
东莞广原电子有限公司	朴瑛信	86366010	扬声器
研华电子科技(东莞)有限公司	何春盛	87308088	电脑机箱
东莞莫仕连接器有限公司	麦敌漢	86310328	电脑连接线
东莞高信电子有限公司	全禹昶	83283743	印刷电路板
东莞友华汽车配件有限公司	桥本悦男	83326172	各种开线塑胶配件
东莞科乐波电子有限公司	宋汉准	83281822	变压器
东莞虎门大宁泰生电机制造厂	蔡金成	85552521	电器开关漏电保护器
东莞明泰电讯设备有限公司	陆柯雅	83356898	各类电话机
东莞七盟电子有限公司	刘炎棋	83621007	电子专用设备
东莞美维电路有限公司	唐庆年	86228000	印制线路板
东莞清溪晶达电子制品厂	王润光	87320077	液晶器件
东莞嘉德电子科技有限公司	陈松漂	83025777	塑胶配件
东莞日矿富士电子有限公司	辻正博	88431720	液晶背光源用电极
东莞塘厦裕华电路板厂	姚彩凤		空白线路板
东莞东佳电子塑胶制品有限公司	徐浩元	87723276	组合音响
台达电子电源(东莞)有限公司	柯子兴	86639008	电源供应器
乐依文半导体(东莞)有限公司	李永松	85647662	集成电路
雅邦电子(东莞)有限公司	黄恒俊	86331999	电子成品组装
东莞宏易电子有限公司	钟乾庚	87881584	音响分频器
东莞世技电子有限公司	张英一	83224133	防盗器
东莞友池精密机械有限公司	陈俊安	87369900	机械
东莞捷仕美电子有限公司	黄振文	83125678	电子连接器
东莞樟洋电子有限公司	佐藤义则	87197011	摄像头

1-5　续表 34

(2009年)

单位名称	负责人	联系电话	主要产品(或服务)
仪器仪表及文化、办公用机械制造业			
东莞侨运表业有限公司	陈汉生	83086066	手表
东莞奇信电子有限公司	林荣俊	83799600	液晶平板显示器
东英精密轴承(东莞)有限公司	寺本英树	88666101	打印机配件
东莞清溪优品电子厂	刘伟军	87311417	计数机
东京光学(东莞)科技有限公司	塚田正三		镜头组件
东莞均益精密五金制品有限公司	熊汉生	88937100	表带表壳
东莞富国橡塑工业有限公司	森川慎	85656968	防振垫
希比希真空电子(东莞)有限公司	林　薰	82389200	数码相机零配件
东莞虎门泰达电子有限公司	唐锡麟	85558622	电子计算器
柯尼卡美能达商用科技(东莞)有限公司	铃木诚一		复印机
东莞新溢眼镜制造有限公司	陈智燊	85540945	眼镜
陆逊梯卡华宏(东莞)眼镜有限公司	路易吉·弗兰卡维拉	88870241	金属塑胶眼镜
东莞精熙光机有限公司	郑文涛	85312190	照相机、复印机主要零部件
东莞宏光光学制品有限公司	陈懋常	88705659	手机镜头
京瓷美达办公设备(东莞)有限公司	驹口克己		打印机
宏达光电玻璃东莞有限公司	钟志明	81625988	TFT-LCD显示屏材料
盈利时表业(东莞)有限公司	姚汉明	83103333	表带
敦朴光电有限公司	詹仕国	85926660	照相机
东莞华仪仪表科技有限公司	叶继贤	87309005	仪器仪表
东莞日精电子有限公司	长束隆	86857999	遥控器、打印机、复印机控制面板
东莞福泰电子有限公司	王铁君	85318100	碎纸机
三和盛电子科技(东莞)有限公司	内山修	87862222	数码相机关键件
万金机械配件东莞有限公司	陶伟洪	82039188	复印机零配件
东莞奥美佳电子有限公司	陈竹均	87503835	数码相机
东莞晓视眼镜制造厂有限公司	吴基鸿	87754133	眼镜
东莞力维时钟有限公司	林怀德	87732284	时钟
东莞泰联光学有限公司	赖以仁	85535435	照相器材
东莞新旭光学有限公司	梁启泰	86240898	光学镜片
东莞信泰光学有限公司	赖以仁	85535435	数码相机
东莞石龙粤龙办公设备制造厂	叶柱安		影印机
恩倍福显示器(东莞)有限公司	菊泽靖	87737851	电脑显示器
高铁检测仪器(东莞)有限公司	陈景长	22400899	试验机
东莞大泰光电科技有限公司	朱清福	85503858	照相机配件
东莞贝盈激光仪器有限公司	容伟霖	86907088	激光仪器
金宝电子(中国)有限公司	许胜雄	85321555	电子计算机
优利德科技(东莞)有限公司	洪佳宁	85729892	电器仪表
镰仓光学(东莞)有限公司	镰仓一郎	85562870	望远镜及其配件
东莞雄福五金有限公司	王进福	83723390	数码相机零配件

1-5 续表 35

(2009年)

单位名称	负责人	联系电话	主要产品(或服务)
工艺品及其他制造业			
三铃制绒(东莞)有限公司	山元俊司	83395435	铜线
东莞又福伞业有限公司	刘振德	87731901	雨伞
东莞三大电子科技有限公司	韩继人	83997278	电脑零件
东莞隆富精密模具有限公司	马英枰	85311526	手机按键
东泰机械工具(东莞)有限公司	黄俊杰	83939183	冲床
东莞大信装饰礼品有限公司	赖文程	86293999	蜡烛灯
东莞优立化工有限公司	黄志辉	87727642	电泳涂料
永泰电子(东莞)有限公司	许庆红	83918040	电脑连接线
东莞恒耀日用制品有限公司	杨鹏耀	87310715	婴儿手推车
东莞广泽汽车饰件有限公司	余泽民	85903898	汽车饰件
东莞大洋硅胶制品有限公司	黄佳莉	87712088	硅胶制品
东莞台新纤维制品有限公司	谢亚男	87311541	汽车地毯
东莞长安港芝电子塑胶制造厂有限公司	廖锦昌	85543500	健身器材
东莞精美拉链配件有限公司	梁伸夫	88849521	各类型拉链
东莞宝树工艺制品有限公司	施建基	83355481	健身器材
东莞安泰玩具有限公司	罗文启	87790368	充气塑胶玩具
欣泰家具(东莞)有限公司	李丰裕	87313008	太阳伞、户外伞
东莞安居家饰有限公司	林宗福	87306597	窗帘
东莞大日化工厂有限公司	高木志朗	85556675	ABS粒
东莞盈大服饰有限公司	魏志良	85323312	五金纽扣
东莞赛诺家居用品有限公司	张水英	87881068	家具用品
东莞庆章光机有限公司	郭水木	87381610	分光镜
东莞富美康电器科技有限公司	胡永梅	87631613	直发器
东莞海金杜门五金制品有限公司	莫大钧	22401768	特殊五金冲压件
大毅科技电子(东莞)有限公司	江财宝	83394790	新型电子元器件
东莞星系手袋厂有限公司	英豪云	87939288	其他日用杂品
东莞永腾电子制品有限公司	邓淑贞	87755269	铝制散热片及散热器
东莞晟富电子科技有限公司	黄坤章	81120130	降频器
东莞杜邦电子材料有限公司	郑宪志	22852951	电子浆料
东莞华艺铜业有限公司	周礼谦	83918628	铜杆
东莞宇源精密金属实业有限公司	李台勇	86968798	金属工艺品
东莞素艺儿童用品有限公司	李贞礼	88382301	婴儿手推车
东莞西文商标织绣有限公司	程锦德	81767999	商标织绣
东莞华生精密制品有限公司	萧宝荣	87187900	组装音响
东莞富钢电子有限公司	罗基云	83399000	电路板组件
东莞婴宝幼童用品有限公司	李英桃	87738800	童车
东莞日太灯饰有限公司	林涂结	87724201	玻璃制品
广濑电机(东莞)有限公司	森元泉	83817840	连接器
东莞爱福赛保安制品有限公司	伊安·嘉利·琼斯	83631663	五金
电力、热力的生产和供应业			
东莞深能源樟洋电力有限公司	李英峰	87198888	天然气发电站
广东广合电力有限公司沙角发电厂C厂	朱志飞	85135124	火力发电
东莞市科伟环保电力有限公司	黎俊东	83715838	垃圾焚烧发电

1-5　续表 36

(2009年)

单位名称	负责人	联系电话	主要产品(或服务)
深南电(东莞)唯美电力有限公司	傅　博	88463006	天然气发电
东莞天明电力有限公司	尤　伟	22788336	火力发电
东莞虎门电厂	王建清	85042288	电力、火力发电
东莞通明电力有限公司	黄爱清	83525188	天然气发电站
东莞中科环保电力有限公司	梁　军	22667772	垃圾余热发电
燃气生产和供应业			
东莞长安新奥燃气有限公司	李志荣	85475722	管道燃气的建设
道路运输业			
东莞发展控股股份有限公司	尹锦容	22083225	高速收费
广东省虎门大桥有限公司	童德功	85509333	高速公路管理养护
顺丰速运(东莞)有限公司	曾治平		普通货物道路运输业务
水上运输业			
东莞虎门龙威客运有限公司	钟绍良	85511759	沿海旅客运输
仓储业			
东莞永得利仓储有限公司	小寺元	88236909	物流服务
东莞三江港口储罐有限公司	林海川	88862888	液体化工仓储服务
电信和其他信息传输服务业			
中国联通有限公司东莞分公司	袁　健	89826239	通信服务
中国移动通信集团广东有限公司东莞分公司	温乃粘		移动通信业务
批发业			
东莞太平洋博高润滑油有限公司	黄文俊	38876660	发动机油
金光纸业(广州)有限公司东莞分公司	朱兴华	22992511	纸品
东莞明瑞电子有限公司	赖金兰	86072000	调解器
东莞市创盛贸易有限公司	萧人杰	82289868	钢材制品
隆原(东莞)机电贸易有限公司	孙福奎	81607192	柴油发电机
东莞金丰物流设备有限公司	许伟基	88333981	叉车
嘉顿食品贸易(中国)有限公司	张尚羽	23024830	蛋糕
东莞柳道贸易有限公司	魏　巍	85394406	热流道条流及配件
大同机械(东莞)销售有限公司	李天来	22806163	机械设备
东莞市喜威液化石油气有限公司	霍世杰	22497388	液化气
东莞加德士石油产品有限公司	何俊康	22367236	石油产品
东莞市恒镒钢铁有限公司	陈晓君	88182648	钢材
东莞硕宇电子有限公司	赖新煜	85710300	电源插座
零售业			
东莞沃尔玛百货有限公司	陈耀昌	22323055	超级市场
东莞擎达汽车销售服务有限公司	王中和	85580180	汽车
华润万家生活超市(东莞)有限公司君豪店	陈　硕	22761852	百货
东莞市家乐福商业有限公司	贝多拉	22201897	百货
东莞百安居装饰建材有限公司	马立思	22719121	其他室内装修材料
东莞永佳中通汽车服务有限公司	叶志荣	81633000	汽车零配件
中油碧辟石油有限公司东莞分公司	刘国柱	88338556	机动车燃料
东莞美东汽车服务有限公司	叶　帆	82319819	汽车
东莞新奥燃气有限公司	李志荣	88992299	管道燃气输配

1-5　续表 37

(2009年)

单位名称	负责人	联系电话	主要产品(或服务)
青岛润泰事业有限公司东莞大朗分公司	王哲音	83034798	百货
东莞意美汽车服务有限公司	王阳乐	85050911	汽车
东莞市洛加斯润滑油有限公司	池甜熹	85617000	润滑油
东莞仁孚溢华汽车服务有限公司	唐玉华	22902080	汽车
住宿业			
东莞丽池海悦酒店有限公司	张文和	85885888	服务行业
东莞新都会酒店有限公司	钟汉强	87713333	住宿业
东莞御景湾酒店	李民立	22625029	旅业
东莞山庄	叶树红	22300000	餐饮服务
餐饮业			
东莞泛亚饮食有限公司	郭洪有	87708232	餐饮
东莞肯德基有限公司	朱宗毅	83588288	快餐
东莞海悦花园大酒店有限公司	蔡云生	85318888	餐饮服务
东莞麦华食品有限公司	施乐生	22115051	西式快餐
东莞豪门大饭店	徐振鉴	85117888	餐饮
银行业			
汇丰银行(中国)有限公司东莞分行	刘少莉	23093088	吸收公众存款
恒生银行(中国)有限公司东莞分行	唐泽维	23138838	金融企业
保险业			
美国友邦保险有限公司东莞支公司	周健森	22418628	人寿保险
信诚人寿保险有限公司东莞营销服务部	王绍斌	22763188	人寿保险
中德安联人寿保险有限公司广东分公司东莞营销服务部	关中流	22827268	人寿保险
房地产业			
东莞骏豪房地产开发有限公司	朱鼎健	28022593	房地产开发经营
东莞水濂山水库商品住宅建造有限公司	张田同		房地产开发经营
东莞市佳兆业房地产开发有限公司	罗汉郭	22801111	房地产开发
东莞市金地房地产投资有限公司	黄俊灿	88991111	房地产
东莞万科置业有限公司	周　彤	23013547	房地产开发及建设
东莞东泰花园建造有限公司		22482388	房地产
东莞新中银花园建造有限公司	徐国流	22900668	房地产开发
东莞市庆丰房地产有限公司	何瑞莲	22619005	房地产中介
东莞雁田工业区发展有限公司	邓耀辉	87771905	房地产开发经营
商务服务业			
东莞派诺蒙鞋业服务有限公司	费阿里	22491889	鞋类产品设计
东莞康美雅咨询有限公司	梁杰伦	87513260	提供家庭电器用品的咨询
斯凯奇鞋业(东莞)有限公司	保尔·克梯斯	85994908	鞋类产品技术咨询
(丹麦)森海塞尔通信有限公司东莞代表处	马宏业	22360850	业务联络
研究与试验发展			
东莞新科技术研究开发有限公司	田　宏	22810033	研究开发磁电制品
娱乐业			
东莞观澜湖高尔夫球会有限公司	朱鼎健	28020888	高尔夫球场及配套设施建设经营
东莞长安今宇高尔夫球场俱乐部有限公司	庄舜而	85539288	提供高尔夫球娱乐活动
东莞峰景高尔夫有限公司	马伟钊	22253459	高尔夫球

1-6 星级以上酒店名单（2009年）

List of Star-ranking Hotels (2009)

酒店名称	星级	电话	地址
银城酒店	五星	22828888	东莞市莞太大道48号
樟木头三正半山酒店	五星	87799333	樟木头镇石新大道
凤岗金凯悦大酒店	五星	87759888	凤岗镇凤深大道158号
龙泉国际大酒店	五星	85188688	虎门镇连升路金洲段
豪门大饭店	五星	85117888	虎门镇虎门大道
嘉华大酒店	五星	85928888	厚街镇家具大道1号
富盈酒店	五星	85888888	厚街镇赤岭路段
索菲特御景湾酒店	五星	22698888	东城区迎宾路8号
莲花山庄	五星	85538388	长安镇莲花山
长安海悦花园大酒店	五星	85318888	长安镇霄边管理区二环路
长安国际酒店	五星	85333333	长安镇锦绣路1号
石龙金凯悦大酒店	五星	86188888	石龙镇莞龙路西湖路段
喜来登大酒店	五星	85988888	厚街镇S256省道莞太路段
新都会怡景酒店	五星	87883888	塘厦镇环市东路6号
太子酒店	五星	83363333	黄江镇江北路32号
塘厦三正半山酒店	五星	87299333	塘厦镇迎宾大道
汇华国际饭店	五星	83938888	常平镇常平大道2号
帝豪花园酒店	五星	83122222	大朗镇美景中路769号
丰泰花园酒店	五星	85708888	虎门镇S358省道大板地路段
寮步金凯悦大酒店	四星	83326328	寮步镇教育路1号
文华大酒店	四星	85911111	厚街镇莞太路新塘路段
珊瑚大酒店	四星	85826888	厚街镇S256省道莞太路段
东莞宾馆	四星	22222222	莞城区东正路11号
江龙大酒店	四星	85838888	厚街镇S256省道莞太路段
新都会酒店	四星	87713333	樟木头镇维多利商业大道38号
君爵酒店	四星	22288888	万江区石美广深路段
宏远酒店	四星	22418888	南城区宏远路1号
汇美酒店	四星	83918888	常平镇中元路9号
花园酒店	四星	87799888	樟木头镇南城广场
长安酒店	四星	85532388	长安镇中心S358省道旁
桥头三正半山酒店	四星	83341868	桥头镇碧莲路
司马假日酒店	四星	83391888	常平镇司马管理区

1-6 续表 1

(2009年)

酒店名称	星级	电话	地址
新世纪酒店	四星	83338888	常平镇常平大道8号
梵尔赛酒店	四星	83816888	常平镇下墟工业区
厚街海悦花园大酒店	四星	85885888	厚街镇厚街大道东
华翔国际酒店	四星	83728888	横沥镇瑞康路
汇源华美达酒店	四星	85244888	虎门镇虎门大道
业丰大酒店	四星	83113888	大朗镇莞樟路金朗大道23号
万盈酒店	四星	88828888	麻涌镇麻涌大道
中汇文华酒店	四星	88788888	高埗镇振兴路
方中假日酒店	四星	86866666	茶山镇茶山大道西28号
半岛酒店	四星	83988888	常平镇北环路
华禧酒店	四星	85383888	长安镇S358省道上沙路段
嘉辉会酒店	四星	87563388	凤岗镇官井头嘉辉路
美怡登酒店	四星	83028888	常平镇中元路
石龙宾馆	三星	86613333	石龙镇绿化中路2号
广彩城酒店	三星	22402088	南城区莞太路
石碣豪华大酒店	三星	86633333	石碣镇新城区
金湖粤海酒店	三星	87869888	塘厦镇塘厦大道南99号
莲城酒店	三星	85536888	长安镇莲峰路接一环路口
乌沙大酒店	三星	85548888	长安镇乌沙环东路228号
黄江假日酒店	三星	83362888	黄江镇黄江大道3号
西湖大酒店	三星	22822888	南城区西平板岭
明苑大酒店	三星	85122918	虎门镇金龙大道南
盛御酒店	三星	86111888	石龙镇西湖大道1号
篁胜酒店	三星	22463888	南城区体育路11号
宝石大酒店	三星	86662188	企石镇振华路1号
恒丰酒店	三星	83343333	桥头镇恒丰新村2号
西湖酒店	三星	86112288	石龙镇西湖区
金岛山庄	三星	87729018	塘厦镇128工业区
绿洲酒店	三星	88832788	道滘镇振兴路156号
沙头酒店	三星	85418888	长安镇沙头管理区
华通城大酒店	三星	86732288	企石镇湖滨南路

1-6 续表 2

(2009年)

酒店名称	星级	电话	地址
丰田酒店	三星	87771199	凤岗镇雁田管理区怡安路
丽江酒店	三星	88872888	高埗镇捷达工业村13座
嘉福海港酒店	三星	88682888	沙田镇中心区港口大道17号
中明酒店	三星	88883368	中堂镇新兴路1号
乐怡酒店	三星	85823888	厚街镇康乐北路
御烽酒店	三星	22186888	万江区107国道拔蛟窝路段
莱莉雅酒店	三星	87507888	凤岗镇永盛商业大街中银大厦
东逸酒店	三星	85396388	长安镇莲峰路103号
鸿茂酒店	三星	83508888	常平镇常黄路
四季酒店	三星	88566666	望牛墩镇新电城A8座
宏信假日酒店	三星	87363888	清溪镇香芒西路
美景湾酒店	三星	83739888	横沥镇沿江路1号
天鹅湖酒店	三星	83338388	常平镇天鹅湖路8号
富豪酒店	三星	83998888	常平镇金美路256号
中青旅山水设计师酒店	三星	21988888	东城区东纵大道189号
亚都酒店	三星	85343888	长安镇长中路
金沙亚都酒店	三星	85413888	长安镇靖海中路36号
金澳花园酒店	二星	22496966	东城大道金澳花园A座
耀豪酒店	二星	88865333	沙田镇中心区
东海酒店	二星	83335484	常平镇东元路1号
银星酒店	二星	83987333	常平镇木棆大道9号
雄狮大酒店	二星	83911540	常平镇振兴路1号
盈丰酒店	二星	83333333	常平镇振兴路中段
新港大酒店	二星	83331000	常平镇新市一街6号
悦华大酒店	二星	83336888	常平镇东兴路275号
海霞酒店	二星	83815222	常平镇板石霞村路段
昇平酒店	二星	83812888	常平镇中元街
冠城酒店	二星	83337788	常平镇中元街常平广场
龙源大酒店	二星	85551028	虎门镇S358省道北栅路段
恒安酒店	二星	88868868	沙田镇横流中心区
海月酒店	二星	85926888	厚街镇涌口海月公园侧
悦凯酒店	一星	83398808	常平镇东元东路28号

1-7 高新技术企业名录（2009年）

List of High-tech Enterprises (2009)

企业名称	企业负责人	联系电话	行业类别
东莞市领航通通信科技有限公司	杜明德	22486699	应用软件服务
东莞市弘明空调服有限公司	郭 震	22766088	纺织服装
东莞市维信电脑科技有限公司	杨吉伟	22300106	应用软件服务
广东宏达工贸集团有限公司	袁 斌	22380008	建筑安装业
东莞市太平洋计算机科技有限公司	朱伦宏	22333699	其他计算机服务
东莞德英电子通讯设备有限公司	卢德林	22412008	其他通信设备
广东智通人才连锁股份有限公司	叶 菁	87078398	职业中介服务
东莞市TR轴承有限公司	张顺成	22469450	轴承
东莞市神州视觉科技有限公司	王锦峰	22620877	电子工业专用设备
东莞市依时利科技有限公司	朱伦宏	22320338	其他计算机服务
广东华南药业集团有限公司	张绍日	86100111	化学药品制剂
东莞市龙基电子有限公司	邓泰均	81862666	电子元件及组件
广东开普互联信息科技有限公司	汪 敏	13901376603	基础软件服务
广东众生药业股份有限公司	张绍日	86100111	中成药
东莞市石龙联兴实业有限公司	张锦明	88496069	纸和纸板容器
东莞市石龙万通实业有限公司	王苏仔	88492100	其他未列明的金属制品
东莞市石龙富华电子有限公司	黄子田	86022222	电子元件及组件
东莞市光华实业有限公司	陈锦麟	81862888	电子元件及组件
东莞市广安电气检测中心有限公司	林志力	86106683	工程管理服务
东莞泽龙线缆有限公司	叶炽德	81388623	电线电缆
泰阳电子(东莞)有限公司	张志光	81862666	电子元件及组件
广东巨龙信息科技有限公司	黄锦麦	86189809	应用软件服务
东莞市虎门金山电线电缆有限公司	洪曲波	85198111	电线电缆
东莞市众誉电子有限公司	陈伟贤	13929255003	电子计算机外部设备
东莞中探探针有限公司	陈志峯	85151668	电子元件及组件
东莞市中实焊锡有限公司	梁静珊	85231818	其他未列明的金属制品
东莞市广大制冷有限公司	方福兴	85519986	制冷、空调设备
东莞市科达计算机系统工程有限公司	吴惠霞	85109166	其他计算机服务
东莞虎彩印刷有限公司	陈成稳	85252189	包装装潢及其他印刷
东莞市联升电线电缆有限公司	张玉良	13602391175	电线电缆
信义汽车玻璃(东莞)有限公司	李贤义	85266666-8155	其他玻璃制品
中名(东莞)电子有限公司	谭美伦	85709915	家用音响设备
广东银禧科技股份有限公司	谭颂斌	85151828	其他合成材料
东莞市天盛特种纸制品有限公司	叶建忠	85169468	其他纸制品
优利德科技(东莞)有限公司	洪佳宁	85723888-893	电工仪器仪表
东莞市霸菱实业有限公司	陈光华	85553636	社会公共安全设备及器材
东莞科威医疗器械有限公司	王安勤	21985698-801	医疗诊断、监护及治疗设备
东莞康视达自动化科技有限公司	王 华	23395662	光电子器件及其他电子器件
东莞市百分百科技有限公司	安 波	88754392	照明灯具
东莞生益电子有限公司	唐庆年	22272074	印制电路板
广东宏远集团药业有限公司	杨 杰	22261081	化学药品制剂

1-7 续表 1

(2009年)

企业名称	企业负责人	联系电话	行业类别
东莞市邦臣光电有限公司	徐朝丰	22086466	工程和技术研究与试验发展
东莞市桦业土木基础工程有限公司	刘淑芬	22308398	其他土木工程建筑
东莞市大忠电子有限公司	李正中	22010620	电子元件及组件
东莞市宏磊达电子塑胶有限公司	姚　斌	87070008	光电子器件及其他电子器件
东莞市高能电气股份有限公司	罗素芳	22291876	其他输配电及控制设备
东华机械有限公司	何秉廉	22806033	塑料加工专用设备
东莞徐记食品有限公司	徐　乘	22268955	糖果、巧克力
东莞市建邦计算机软件有限公司	叶建辉	22499660	应用软件服务
东莞市凯格精密机械有限公司	邱国良	22767281	印刷专用设备
东莞市晖速天线技术有限公司	陈　晖	85388505	通信传输设备
东莞市德生通用电器制造有限公司	梁　伟	23160713	家用音响设备
东莞市一信通信科技有限公司	谢造辉	23171138	移动通信及终端设备
东莞市至诚涂料有限公司	李志民	22182252	涂料
东莞市康源节能科技有限公司	胡　杰	22710536	泵及真空设备
东莞万成制药有限公司	曾昭利	22282309	化学药品制剂
东莞基业电气设备有限公司	苏洪新	22273666	其他输配电及控制设备
东莞市科达机电设备有限公司	伍耀均	22188788	制冷、空调设备
东莞市银华生物科技有限公司	陈东明	22188099	饲料
东莞市金翔电器设备有限公司	周沛池	22038808	电子计算机外部设备
东莞市大族粤铭激光科技有限公司	张建群	89838888-308	电工机械专用设备
广东五星太阳能股份有限公司	胡广良	22176388	燃气、太阳能及类似能源的器具
东莞市百思维软件有限公司	张　蓓	22384201	基础软件服务
广东开心信息技术有限公司	陈建章	22023588	计算机系统服务
广东万维博通信息技术有限公司	江善东	22852898	应用软件服务
高铁检测仪器(东莞)有限公司	陈景长	22400899	实验分析仪器
广东南方宏明电子科技股份有限公司	秦经建	13316639972	电子元件及组件
广东省东莞电机有限公司	黄进安	22412480	电动机
东莞市杉杉电池材料有限公司	李智华	22035233	专项化学用品
东莞市福地电子材料有限公司	王约庚	22406001	电子元件及组件
广东科旺电源设备有限公司	方旺根	22900009-221	其他未列明的电气机械
东莞市凯诺德软件科技有限公司	冯燕全	13316688928	应用软件服务
东莞新能源电子科技有限公司	曾毓群	22405338	电子元件及组件
东莞市保得生物工程有限公司	张新雄	22886693	谷物的种植
中域电讯连锁集团股份有限公司	李建明	88777888	通信设备零售
东莞市中大科教网络科技有限公司	朱振寰	26982898	其他计算机服务
广东迪奥技术工程有限公司	张红斌	22771688-606	提供施工设备服务
东莞宏威数码机械有限公司	刘惠森	22909612	电工机械专用设备
东莞锦泰食品有限公司	袁汉思	22400818	饼干及其他焙烤食品
东莞市新雷神仿真控制有限公司	章晓明	22386051	应用软件服务
广东丹宝利酵母有限公司	李小周	88896528	其他调味品、发酵制品
东莞市广益食品添加剂实业有限公司	梁炳坤	88886882	食品及饲料添加剂

1-7 续表 2

(2009年)

企业名称	企业负责人	联系电话	行业类别
东莞市东兴铝材制造有限公司	何旭坤	88813671	其他未列明的金属制品
东莞理文造纸厂有限公司	李運強	88888168-6269	机制纸及纸板
东莞市凯迪克高分子材料有限公司	吴达文	81335656	涂料
东莞金波罗电业科技有限公司	宋生泉	88886808	电线电缆
广东一品鲜生物科技有限公司	黎锐深	13622648447	其他未列明的食品
东莞佳鸿机械制造有限公司	李伟宏	88850268	其他医疗设备及器械
东莞德永佳纺织制衣有限公司	陈知行	88821738	棉、化纤印染精加工
东莞玖龙纸业有限公司	张　茵	88234888	机制纸及纸板
东莞太平洋博高润滑油有限公司	黄文俊	88823886	原油加工及石油制品
广东中远船务工程有限公司	李　荣	13922960808	金属船舶
东莞海龙纸业有限公司	张　茵	88234888	机制纸及纸板
广东龙马化学有限公司	卢文书	88232288	涂料
广东信力特种橡胶制品有限公司	郑日土	88220800	车辆、飞机及工程机械轮胎
广东中成化工股份有限公司	钟存仁	88822402	无机盐
东莞市奥莱克电子有限公司	莫启旭	88229781	家用音响设备
东莞市贝特利新材料有限公司	王　全	88283198	油墨及类似产品
东莞市英芝堂生物工程有限公司	亢祝纯	88826118	生物、生化制品的
东莞市华兰海电子有限公司	刁翠香	88823105-823	电子元件及组件
东莞市前锋电子有限公司	袁灿荣	86633990	家用厨房电器具
东莞市盈聚电子有限公司	赵星宝	81837999	电子元件及组件
东莞创慈磁性元件有限公司	蘇天寅	86327771	电子元件及组件
台达电子电源(东莞)有限公司	柯子兴	86639008	电子元件及组件
台达电子(东莞)有限公司	柯子兴	86639008	电子元件及组件
品翔电子塑胶制品(东莞)有限公司	蔡福气	86323266	变压器、整流器和电感器
东莞岳丰电子科技有限公司	宋泰维	81837666	电线电缆
台达电子零组件(东莞)有限公司	柯子兴	86321008	电子元件及组件
旭丽电子(东莞)有限公司	胡雅兴	86638923	电子计算机外部设备
东莞市智高文具有限公司	梁佛南	86316728	文具
东莞市旭田电子有限公司	王肖鹏	86300096	电子计算机外部设备
东莞广发制药有限公司	牟永新	81839922	中成药
东莞莫仕连接器有限公司	麦启汉	86310328-8868	电子元件及组件
东莞泉声电子有限公司	温增丰	13509823070	电子元件及组件
达创科技(东莞)有限公司	梁克勇	86637008	计算机网络设备
广东福利龙复合肥有限公司	郝志辉	2259816921	复混肥料
广东正业科技股份有限公司	徐地华	86279555	其他科技服务
东莞市科磊得数码光电科技有限公司	欧　文	88782660	光电子器件及其他电子器件
东莞洲亮通讯科技有限公司	李月亮	88326318	通信传输设备
广东大众农业科技有限公司	赵小云	88430005	农业科学研究与试验发展
东莞市亚洲制药有限公司	梁　峰	22463054	中成药
东莞市邦泽电子有限公司	徐　宁	89191288	电子元件及组件
东莞市沙田顺发畜禽实业有限公司	许爱顺	88686610	牲畜的饲养

1-7 续表 3

(2009年)

企业名称	企业负责人	联系电话	行业类别
东莞市东方科技有限公司	方敬湖	85583500	电子计算机外部设备
东莞市金河田实业有限公司	方植宁	85585691	电子计算机外部设备
东莞昆盈电脑制品有限公司	卓进兴	13809634101	电子计算机外部设备
东莞市远梦家用纺织品有限公司	许镇智	83085188	其他纺织制成品
东莞广泽汽车饰件有限公司	余泽民	85903898	橡胶加工专用设备
东莞市力凯科技发展有限公司	黄建新	88910888	应用软件服务
东莞骅国电子有限公司	陳正煌	85597201	电子元件及组件
东莞市南兴木工机械有限公司	林旺南	13809625008	木材加工机械
东莞市龙记环保科技有限公司	李思梅	85588479	其他环境治理
东莞市金银丰机械实业有限公司	李　智	85911093	其他未列明的电气机械
东莞市东阳光电容器有限公司	吕文进	85315288	电子元件及组件
万裕三信电子(东莞)有限公司	高伯安	88619118-8118	电子元件及组件
环球石材(东莞)有限公司	朱荣驹	85544338	建筑用石加工
东莞市国菱机械有限公司	杨东佐	85544423	金属结构
东莞劲胜精密组件股份有限公司	王九全	85395280-620	通信终端设备
广东加多宝饮料食品有限公司	张树容	85331688	茶饮料及其他饮料
金宝电子(中国)有限公司	许胜雄	88521555	其他通信设备
东莞友讯电子有限公司	龚志富	85318000	通信传输设备
东莞市奥普特自动化科技有限公司	陈炎景	86068128	其他未列明的电气机械
东莞普思电子有限公司	曹规源	85538871-1122	电子元件及组件
广东万濠精密仪器股份有限公司	蒋小丽	85316127-181	绘图、计算及测量仪器
先锐模具配件(东莞)有限公司	李象烈	85376810	其他未列明的金属制品
东莞市铁志电子有限公司	王会泽	82311301	其他文化、办公用机械
东莞市达成机械设备制造有限公司	易应新	83217777	其他专用设备
东莞市佳景印刷材料有限公司	陈健强	82318231	油墨及类似产品
东莞市开关厂有限公司	陆少雄	83233911	配电开关控制设备
东莞市永强汽车制造有限公司	陈灶金	83307688	改装汽车
东莞市友美电源设备有限公司	颜晓英	83239405	其他专用设备
东莞市蓝冠环保节能科技有限公司	申卫红	83309018	燃气、太阳能及类似能源的器具
东莞市康达机电工程有限公司	沈剑山	88989999	发电机及发电机组
东莞宇球电子有限公司	钱济高	83529888	电子元件及组件
东莞市三联科技实业有限公司	叶满芳	83215622	其他专用化学产品
东莞市科隆威自动化设备有限公司	唐岳泉	83228201	电子工业专用设备
东莞光群雷射科技有限公司	陈祖洪	85601301-886	日用塑料杂品
东莞市瑞德丰生物科技有限公司	高焕森	83359225	化学农药
东莞市新时代新能源科技有限公司	谢　坤	85653393	家用空气调节器
东莞华科电子有限公司	朱有义	83115168	电子元件及组件
东莞富强鑫塑胶机械制造有限公司	王伯祥	83313753	塑料加工专用设备
环球工业机械(东莞)有限公司	阮文德	83118946	金属切削机床
东莞市飞尔液晶显示器有限公司	邓　宏	88953386	电子计算机外部设备
东莞信易电热机械有限公司	吴一夫	83313588-1018	塑料加工专用设备

1-7 续表 4

(2009年)

企业名称	企业负责人	联系电话	行业类别
东莞市台冠起重机械设备有限公司	周文来	83019666	其他交通运输设备
东莞市迈科新能源有限公司	李中延	83015363	电池
东莞市迈科科技有限公司	李中延	83197555	电池
东莞市中一合金科技有限公司	林羽锦	13825724576	其他建筑、安全用金属制品
泓凯电子科技(东莞)有限公司	张灿能	83365942	电子计算机外部设备
东莞市莱钢钢结构有限公司	刘衍敏	83666666	钢铁铸件
东莞市盛和化工有限公司	周祖俊	87132000	有机化学原料
东莞惠伦顿堡电子有限公司	赵积清	38879888	电子元件及组件
东莞维升电子制品有限公司	吴瑞雄	83622694	电线电缆
东莞新东方化工有限公司	何百祥	13790415799	有机化学原料
东莞星火机电设备工程有限公司	刘水庆	83666848	其他输配电及控制设备
东莞市柏百顺石油化工有限公司	蔡伟清	87189883-888	工程和技术研究与试验发展
东莞贰发毛绒有限公司	陈　熹	87718080	其他纺织制成品
东莞永洪印刷有限公司	刘绚强	87711991	包装装潢及其他印刷
东莞市兄奕塑胶制品有限公司	罗新勇	87792188-888	其他家具
东莞顺传五金制品有限公司	钟长庆	87732273	脚踏自行车及残疾人座车
东莞市瑞柯电机有限公司	杨　琪	87899858	气体压缩机械
东莞市粤林电脑科技股份有限公司	邓会英	87890888	电子计算机外部设备
东莞华明灯具有限公司	王忠琦	87311200	照明灯具
实盈电子(东莞)有限公司	黄凰洲	87318688	电子元件及组件
东莞致通电脑有限公司	宋恭源	87312821-282	电子计算机外部设备
东莞华仪仪表科技有限公司	田　军	87309018	电工仪器仪表
东莞宜安电器制品有限公司	李卫荣	87327777	金属结构
东莞光阵显示器制品有限公司	舒伟平	87738870	光电子器件及其他电子器件
东莞市快意电梯有限公司	罗爱文	87731075	其他交通运输设备
广东星河生物科技股份有限公司	叶运寿	87916623	蔬菜的种植
东莞丰裕电机有限公司	郑锡辉	87902888	其他专用设备
康舒电子(东莞)有限公司	高青山	87915950	电子元件及组件
广东升威电子制品有限公司	洪金镳	87287777	电子元件及组件
东莞正阳电子有限公司	林淑敏	82776360	电子元件及组件
广东志成冠军集团有限公司	周志文	87722374	电工机械专用设备
东莞市理士奥电源技术有限公司	刘飞平	87925180-1039	其他能源发电
广东坚朗五金制品有限公司	白宝鲲	86851116	建筑、家具用金属配件
东莞市力王电池有限公司	李维海	86201111	其他未列明的电气机械
东莞宇宙电路板设备有限公司	陈德和	87569928	电工机械专用设备
东莞奥美佳电子有限公司	陈竹均	87503835	光电子器件及其他电子器件
广东楚天龙智能卡有限公司	苏尔在	87508618	应用软件服务
东莞康佳模具塑胶有限公司	向天顺	87758888	家用影视设备
东莞李洲电子科技有限公司	李明顺	13509020769	光电子器件及其他电子器件
东莞市大兴化工有限公司	蔡双儿	87766346	涂料
东莞东海龙环保科技有限公司	骆国豪	83506181	照明灯具

1-7　续表 5

(2009年)

企业名称	企业负责人	联系电话	行业类别
东莞东运机械制造有限公司	秦学锋	13902697864	印刷专用设备
东莞市环宇激光工程有限公司	林　鹏	83364999	电子工业专用设备
东莞欧达电子有限公司	艾伯特·加勒	83977722-2233	光学仪器
东莞市麦蒂科技有限公司	陈向定	13669850668	应用软件服务
东莞市特尔佳电子有限公司	陈东明	89962233	电子元件及组件
东莞益新五金有限公司	王干文	87811000	移动通信及终端设备
东莞市宇洁新材料有限公司	王宝柱	83998003	涂料
东莞龙昌数码科技有限公司	梁钟铭	86836266	游艺用品及室内游艺器材
东莞市鼎聚光电有限公司	李雪勇	86769535	光学仪器
东莞市华立实业股份有限公司	谭洪汝	83333239	其他家具
东莞宝丽美化工有限公司	贾雪雷	83392980-728	其他日用化学产品
东莞市世通国际快件监管中心有限公司	周柱桃	83828727	装卸搬运
东莞运城制版有限公司	介骏鸿	83393446	包装装潢及其他印刷
东莞勤上光电股份有限公司	李旭亮	83395678	光电子器件及其他电子器件
东莞三泰电器有限公司	李　智	86836688	通信交换设备
智嘉通讯科技(东莞)有限公司	张锡帆	83335430	通信传输设备
东莞市日新传导科技股份有限公司	李明斌	82803333	光电子器件及其他电子器件
意拉德电子(东莞)有限公司	鲁道夫·法弟	82208920	电子元件及组件
忠信制模(东莞)有限公司	赵孝纯	83732298	模具
东莞盈拓科技实业有限公司	林小玉	83798101	金属切削机床
广东明家科技股份有限公司	周建林	87061828	社会公共安全设备及器材
东莞市源殿电子科技有限公司	龚芙英	85317295	灯用电器附件及其他照明器具
东莞市凯晟灯头实业有限公司	姚利民	86787878	电光源
东莞市创普光电技术有限公司	梁　昆	13602335578	金属切割及焊接设备
东莞市兆明光电科技有限公司	张铄冰	86720016	电子元件及组件
广东佳彩数码科技有限公司	张福柱	86732328	其他家用电力器具
东莞明鑫电子有限公司	黄献洲	86731868	电子计算机外部设备
东莞市智乐堡儿童玩具有限公司	王志光	86550188	日用塑料杂品
东莞市益达实业有限公司	谢松登	86409230	电线电缆
东莞市英科水墨有限公司	刘润林	86179118	油墨及类似产品
东莞市贻嘉光电科技有限公司	吴新伟	13829232567	光电子器件及其他电子器件
广东洛贝电子科技有限公司	张宏志	22895188	电子元件及组件
广东生益科技股份有限公司	刘述峰	22271828	电子元件及组件
东莞市万科建筑技术研究有限公司	肖　楠	22890188	房地产开发经营
领亚电子科技股份有限公司	白建功	85550688	家用影视设备
广东力优环境系统股份有限公司	方沛明	22899195	应用软件服务
广东康菱动力科技有限公司	田爱民	22895555	发电机及发电机组
广东东阳光药业有限公司	朱英伟	85315888-2695	化学药品制剂
东莞泛亚太生物科技有限公司	王耀辉	22892600	牲畜的饲养
广东易事特电源股份有限公司	何思模	87883369	电力电子元器件
东莞新能源科技有限公司	曾毓群	88989080	电子元件及组件

第四部分　政策法规

Part Four　Policies and Legislation

东莞市生态控制线管理规定

Regulations on Ecology Control Line in Dongguan

第一章　总　则

第一条　为加强生态环境保护，防止城市建设无序蔓延，促进社会经济可持续发展，根据有关法律、法规，结合本市实际，制定本规定。

第二条　本规定所称生态控制线是指根据本规定第六条、第七条划定的生态保护范围界线。

第三条　生态控制线的划定、调整以及生态控制线范围内各项土地利用、建设活动，适用本规定。

第四条　规划、国土、综合执法、建设、环保、发改、农业、林业、水利、工商、城市管理等行政主管部门按照有关法律、法规和规章规定，在各自职责范围内，共同做好生态控制线监督和管理工作：

（一）规划主管部门负责组织编制生态控制线的划定和调整方案；依法对线内新建、改建项目实施规划管理；利用遥感或航拍等技术，每半年一次对线内的建设情况进行监测，发现违法建筑应及时通报市城市管理综合执法部门和所属镇街，并配合做好查处工作。

（二）国土主管部门依法对线内土地进行监管；依法收回、收购土地并纳入政府土地储备；做好线内违法用地行为的查处工作。

（三）城市管理综合执法部门按照其职责对线内违法建设行为进行查处，加强巡查工作，每半年一次将违法建筑及其查处情况向市政府报告，并向社会公布。

（四）建设主管部门负责对线内建筑的质量和安全进行监控，做好对未取得施工许可证的违法建设行为的查处工作。

（五）环境保护主管部门负责线内环境监测，并依法对环境违法行为进行查处，逐步提高环保要求，削减线内污染负荷。

（六）农业、林业、水利等主管部门按各自的职责加强对线内农田、林地、水源保护区等监管，做好生态保护和生态恢复工作。

（七）发改、工商、城市管理等主管部门依法履行相应的生态控制线管理职责。

各有关部门在查处线内违法建设行为过程中应紧密配合，共享信息，及时将查处情况通报其他部门。

各镇街负责维护本辖区范围内生态控制线的完整，组织、协调对线内违法用地、违法建设行为的查处工作。

第五条　鼓励公民、法人或其他组织从事生态保护活动，对做出突出贡献的给予奖励；鼓励单位和个人对生态控制线内的违法建设行为进行举报，并给予适当奖励，具体奖励办法另行制定。

第二章　划定和调整

第六条　生态控制线的划定包括下列范围：

（一）自然保护区、基本农田保护区、一级水源保护区、森林公园、郊野公园及其它风景旅游度假区；

（二）坡度大于25%的山地、林地以及海拔超过50米的高地；

（三）主干河流、水库、湿地及具有生态保护价值的海滨陆域；

（四）维护生态系统完整性的生态廊道和隔离绿地；

（五）其他需要进行生态控制的区域。

第七条　生态控制线按以下程序划定和公布：

（一）市规划主管部门组织编制生态控制线划定方案；

（二）方案征求市相关职能部门和各镇街意见；

（三）方案根据有关意见论证修改后，由市规划主管部门报市城市规划委员会审议；

（四）方案审议通过后，修改完善形成规划成果，报市政府批准；

（五）生态控制线应自批准之日起30日内，在市主要新闻媒体和政府网站上公布。

公布的生态控制线范围应当清晰，并附有明确地理坐标及相应界址地形图。

第八条　因国家、省、市重大建设项目或城市发展战略的重大变化，需要对生态控制线进行局部调整的，应遵循总量不减、占一补一原则，按照下列程序进行：

（一）建设单位依据重大建设项目的相关批准文件，委托具有甲级规划资质的设计单位编制生态控制线调整方案报市规划主管部门（因城市发展战略的重大变化需要对生态控制线进行调整的，由市规划主管部门组织编制调整方案）；

（二）由市规划主管部门对调整方案初审后征求市相关职能部门和所涉及镇街的意见；

（三）市规划主管部门将调整方案进行公示，公示时间不少于15日，必要时可通过召开论证会、听证会等形式广泛征求意见；

（四）调整方案根据有关意见论证修改后，报市城市规划委员会审议；

（五）调整方案审议通过后，报市政府批准；

（六）调整方案自批准之日起15日内，在市主要新闻媒体和政府网站上公布。

第九条　市城市管理部门统一设立生态控制线保护标志。任何单位和个人不得破坏或擅自改变生态控制线保护标志。

第三章　管理与监督

第十条　禁止在生态控制线范围内进行建设，属下列情形之一的除外：

（一）国家、省、市的重大道路交通设施；

（二）国家、省、市的市政公用设施；

（三）旅游设施；

（四）公园；

（五）根据本规定第十二条第（一）项、第十四条确定的建设项目。

市政公用设施包括供电设施，供水、排水、排污、防洪排涝、水土保持、水利工程管理设施，供气、供热设施，通信设施，环卫环保设施，防灾、减灾和公共安全保障设施，直接为农、林、渔业生产服务的各类设施，以及经国家、省、市政府批准建设的特殊用途设施等。

旅游设施是指提供旅游服务所依托的游览娱乐设施、交通运输设施、食宿接待设施和旅游购物设施等。在生态控制线内，旅游设施的任意一公顷用地的容积率都不应大于 0.2、硬地率不应大于 10%，食宿接待设施建筑面积占旅游设施总建筑面积的比重不应大于 20%。

生态控制线内的公园不纳入所在镇街的总体规划以及控制性详细规划进行指标平衡。

法律、法规和规章对生态控制线内的建设项目有更严格限制的，按照有关法律、法规和规章的规定执行。

第十一条 符合第十条规定的建设项目，应按以下程序办理相关手续：

（一）进行项目可行性研究、环境影响评价及规划选址论证；

（二）建设项目选址方案经市规划主管部门初审后征求市相关职能部门和所在镇街的意见；

（三）市规划主管部门将建设项目选址方案公示，公示时间不少于 15 日，必要时可通过召开论证会、听证会等形式广泛征求意见，因国家安全和保密需要不宜公开的除外；

（四）建设项目选址方案由市规划主管部门报市城市规划委员会审议；

（五）市城市规划委员会审议通过后，报市政府批准；

（六）建设项目选址方案应自批准之日起 15 日内，在市主要新闻媒体和政府网站上公布；

（七）建设单位到市相关职能部门依法办理有关建设手续。

第十二条 从尊重历史、实事求是、分类处理的原则出发，慎重、妥善地处理好本规定实施前生态控制线内的建设用地和建设项目：

（一）已办理土地使用证、签订国有土地使用权出让合同或集体土地流转合同，但尚未开工的建设项目，原则上不得批准建设，应置换到生态控制线外根据规划进行建设，或由市国土主管部门依法补偿后收回土地，纳入政府土地储备。

确需建设的，应转为资源消耗低、环境影响小的用途，容积率不得超过 0.8，并按本规定第十一条规定的程序进行报批。

（二）已建合法建设项目，可按现状保留使用，但不得擅自改建、扩建或拆旧建新，使用期满后由市国土主管部门依法收回土地使用权。

已建合法建设项目在使用年期届满前转让土地使用权的，市国土主管部门可依法收购其土地使用权并纳入政府土地储备。

已建合法建设项目要优先考虑环境保护，加强各项环保及绿化工程建设，转为资源消耗低、环境影响小的用途；市环保主管部门应加强监管，对环保不达标的项目应责令其整改，拒不整改或整改不达标的应依法予以取缔。

（三）已建的违法建设项目，市规划、国土、建设、发改、房管等主管部门不再补办有关手续，市工商部门不再办理企业设立登记，市环保部门应加强环保监管，市国土主管部门依法收回占用土地。

第十三条 市国土主管部门在生态控制线内依法收购、收回纳入政府储备的土地，经过整合调配后主要用于生态建设。

第十四条 生态控制线内的原农村居民点，市政府和各镇街制定引导政策，鼓励其在线外进行异地统建。

不能搬迁确需原址改造的，应遵循用地规模、建设规模不增加的原则，制定详细规划，并按本规定第十一条的程序进行报批。

第十五条 市政府和各镇街制定财政转移支付政策，保障线内受控村组的社会事务管理支出和基本生活生产需要。

第四章 法律责任

第十六条 违反本规定在生态控制线内进行建设的，由相关行政主管部门按照《东莞市在建违法建筑处理办法》的有关规定进行处理，并依法对建设、施工单位或个人进行处罚；构成犯罪的，依法追究刑事责任。

第十七条 毁坏或擅自改变生态控制线保护标志的，由城市管理部门责令恢复原状，并依法进行处理。

第十八条 各镇街应采取有效措施保护生态控制线，对新的违法建设行为未能及时制止的，取消镇街当年评优资格，取消镇街及其城市管理综合执法部门直接责任人员的当年评先资格。

第十九条 违反本规定擅自调整生态控制线的，对主管领导和直接责任人员依法予以行政处分；构成犯罪的，依法追究刑事责任。

在生态控制线范围内擅自审批建设项目或批准建设的，对主管领导和直接责任人员依法予以行政处分；构成犯罪的，依法追究刑事责任。

第五章 附 则

第二十条 依本规定划定的生态控制线及其范围图为本规定组成部分，具有同等效力。

第二十一条 本规定由市城建规划局负责解释。

第二十二条 本规定自 2009 年 8 月 1 日起施行，有效期至 2014 年 7 月 31 日。

东莞市推进“三旧”改造工作方案

Program on Propelling the Transformation of “Old Town, Old Villege and Old Factory Building” in Dongguan

为深入贯彻落实国务院《珠江三角洲地区改革发展规划纲要（2008—2020）》、省委省政府《关于争当实践科学发展观排头兵的决定》及《关于加快建设现代产业体系的决定》，完成全省节约集约用地和“三旧”（旧城镇、旧村庄、旧厂房）改造试点市的“先行先试”工作任务，进一步加快推进全市产业结构调整和转型升级，现结合我市实际，制定本工作方案。

一、加快推进“三旧”改造的重要性和紧迫性

“三旧”是以往粗放用地方式的历史产物，也是在新增建设用地资源有限的条件下，拓展用地空间的重要资源。省委省政府高度重视，把“三旧”改造作为全省深入贯彻落实《珠江三角洲地区改革发展规划纲要（2008—2020）》、争当实践科学发展观排头兵和加快建设现代产业体系的重要工作来部署，明确各市人民政府是本行政区域内推进“三旧”改造工作的执行主体，各市人民政府主要负责人是第一责任人；从2009年起，各市人民政府须每年向省人民政府专题报告“三旧”改造工作情况；对推进“三旧”改造工作规范认真、成效显著的地级市，省人民政府将给予表扬，并在分配下一年度新增建设用地指标时予以倾斜。省即将出台的“三旧”改造政策，规定各类历史用地手续工作须在三年内完成。

国家和省赋予我市“三旧”改造“先行先试”的政策探索任务，为我市实事求是解决历史遗留用地问题提供了政策机遇。开展“三旧”改造是解决当前我市建设用地供需矛盾、实现保增长的重要途径，是推进产业结构调整和产品转型升级的重要保障，是优化产业布局、完善城市功能和提升城市形象的重要措施。通过“三旧”改造，我市可以拓展约30万亩存量建设用地空间；同时将有利于“三来一补”企业就地转型及企业以房地产权融资。因此，全市必须抢抓机遇，大胆探索创新，加快推进“三旧”改造工作。

二、工作目标

（一）促进产业结构调整升级。通过“三旧”改造打通建设用地的调整使用和产权登记的关口，促进“退二进三”、“优二强二”和“三来一补”企业就地转型，从土地资源配置上支持产业结构调整和转型升级。

（二）优化产业布局和城市布局。通过有计划、有秩序的拆迁改造，对历史原因造成的粗放用地按现行城镇建设规划、产业规划和土地规划进行重新开发，整合和完善城镇配套设施和绿化建设，落实“四整四聚”和空间转型，进一步优化产业布局、城市布局和城市配套功能。

（三）推进土地节约集约利用。通过“三旧”改造激励建设用地的二次利用和复合利用，提高土地容积率、投资强度、产出率和综合效益，减少新增建设用地占用，促进用地节约集约。

（四）保障经济持续快速增长。以“三旧”改造拓展用地空间，为新增项目和原有项目的转型升级与增资扩产提供用地保障；以“三旧”改造促进城镇拆迁改造，支持集体经济组织和企业改造现有物业，拉动固定资产投资，保障经济增长。

（五）解决历史遗留用地难题。利用“三旧”改造“先行先试”的政策机遇，妥善解决历史遗留的不规范用地问题，畅通房地产权抵押融资渠道，强化土地权能保护。

三、基本原则

（一）改革创新，先行先试。以科学发展观和《珠江三角洲地区改革发展规划纲要（2008—2020）》为指导，尊重历史事实，立足当前实际，着眼经济社会的可持续发展，按照省对节约集约用地和“三旧”改造试点市的“先行先试”要求，大胆改革创新、先行先试。

（二）节约集约，盘活资产。通过各类改造全面提高土地的综合效益，实现节约集约用地；利用“三旧”改造全面推动现代产权制度的建设和完善，明晰土地产权，盘活土地资产。

（三）规划先行，统筹推进。坚决落实用途管制和规划控制，严格遵循城市功能布局规划和产业政策；市对“三旧”改造项目实行统一规划和统筹管理，建立统一台账，按中长期规划和中短期规划稳步推进。

（四）政府引导，市场运作。坚持市政府在“三旧”改造中的主导地位，并充分发挥市场机制配置资源的作用；通过规划、财税、用地等政策手段和制度安排，充分调动各级政府、土地权益人和市场主体共同参与的积极性。

四、实施步骤和工作安排

（一）调研阶段（2008年8月—2009年4月）

深入各镇（街）、有关企业及基层村组进行调查研究，掌握“三旧”的类型，分析改造的必要性、可行性和政策障碍，制定《东莞市推动产业结构调整和转型升级实施“三旧”改造土地管理暂行办法》。

（二）准备阶段（2009年5月—2009年9月）

1. *成立领导机构。*市、镇两级成立“三旧”改造工作领导小组和办公室，加强组织领导、政策研究和统筹协调，明确工作责任，落实工作任务。

2. *制定工作方案。*明确实施“三旧”改造的总体目标、主要任务和分阶段工作安排，按照调研、准备、实施、总结四个阶段稳步推进“三旧”改造工作。

3. *建立台账，制定“三旧”改造专项规划。*加强台账管理、规划控制和规划协调，防止“越改越乱”。市国土、规划、拆迁部门共同开展“三旧”改造清查摸底，建立台账，逐宗填表造册；区分轻重缓急，并建立中短期规划（到2012年）和中长期规划（到2020年）。

4. *制定配套政策措施。*市国土、发改、财政、建设、规划等部门就税费、改造项目方案编制技术规程和改造规划审批等制定配套政策，全面规范“三旧”改造工作。

5. *召开动员大会。*9月底召开全市“三旧”改造工作动员大会，全面部署全市“三旧”改造工作。

（三）实施阶段（2009年9月—2012年10月）

1. *先行先试，探索经验。*分类型进行试点，建设样板点，探索经验，制定操作细则。

2. *召开示范现场会，总结试点经验。*通过试点示范，总结经验，完善操作办法，以点带面向全市铺开；通过加强政策和试点经验宣传，充分调动各级政府、土地权益人和市场主体共同参与的积极性。

3. *组织培训，规范操作。*以试点总结完善的操作办法为范本，统一设置办事流程、办事材料目录和审批要求，统一组织“三旧”改造业务培训，确保严格按政策规范运作，依法有序进行。

4. 全面铺开，快速推进。把示范点经验向全市推广，集中力量启动一批“三旧”改造项目，推动“三旧”改造工作的全面铺开。

（四）总结阶段（2012 年 11 月—2012 年 12 月）

总结运作情况，提高运作效率，进一步规范审批程序，研究“三旧”改造转入日常化运作等有关事宜。

五、主要措施和要求

（一）加强组织领导。各级政府是本行政区域内推进“三旧”改造工作的执行主体，政府主要负责人是第一责任人。市“三旧”改造领导小组由市长任组长，各镇（街）“三旧”改造领导小组由各镇镇长（街道办主任）任组长。市法院、检察院、监察、国土、财政、建设、农业、规划、发改、综合执法、文广新、经贸、外经贸、工商、地税、法制、房产、公安消防、拆迁等部门是“三旧”改造的相关成员单位。市“三旧”改造领导小组研究决定“三旧”改造的具体操作措施，解决“三旧”改造中的重大问题；研究审批“三旧”改造工作计划及方案；督促、检查各镇（街）和成员单位的工作，加强全程监管。市“三旧”改造领导小组下设工作办公室，由市国土资源局抽调人员负责日常工作，各部门派出业务骨干常驻办公室工作。各镇（街）要成立相应的领导小组和办公室，负责制定本辖区“三旧”改造的台账、规划和项目实施方案，并具体组织实施。

（二）落实工作责任。“三旧”改造工作实行属地负责制，各镇（街）负责本辖区内“三旧”改造工作的具体组织和相关材料的真实性审查。参照省与市签订责任书的做法，市政府与各镇政府（街道办事处）签订《东莞市推进“三旧”改造工作责任书》。各镇（街）要认真抓好“三旧”改造的基础工作，认真开展“三旧”用地的摸底排查，对每宗“三旧”用地要在土地利用总体规划图和土地利用现状图标注并列表造册；要认真制定本区域“三旧”改造规划和年度实施计划，分步实施，有序推进；要对纳入“三旧”改造范围需补办用地手续涉及材料的真实性、合法性负责，不得借“三旧”改造的名义，擅自扩大完善历史用地手续的范围，将不进行改造的用地或不符合改造条件的用地“搭车”完善手续。各镇（街）在 2009、2010、2011 年的每年底对本区域的“三旧”改造工作进行自查，并于第二年的 1 月底前向市政府专题报告。对“三旧”改造工作进展缓慢或弄虚作假的，市政府将给予通报批评，并依法追究主要负责人和相关责任人的责任。

各相关职能部门负责配套政策的制订和报批材料的审核把关。监察部门和市预防职务犯罪工作领导小组负责对制度建设、组织领导、联合会审的全程监督，对各镇（街）“三旧”改造政策执行情况进行检查监督，既确保有效预防职务犯罪，又确保“三旧”改造政策落到实处，为“三旧”改造保驾护航。各级各部门要各负其责，各司其职，同时要加强协调，部门联动，加强对“三旧”改造工作的指导、服务、协调和监督。

（三）明确改造范围。现状已建，建筑物和构筑物存在安全隐患、外观破旧、需要拆旧整治的区域；因城镇规划调整原因需要改变用途、重新改造的旧工业厂房、旧居民住宅、旧公共设施；国家产业目录规定的禁止类、淘汰类产业转为鼓励类产业、现代服务业、先进制造业的原厂房用地，“三来一补”、个体工商户转型升级调整使用的原厂房用地；布局分散、公共服务设施配套不完善的城镇、村庄；城乡建设用地增减挂钩项目的农村建设用地等均可列入“三旧”改造范围。

（四）建立台账和规划。纳入“三旧”改造范围的土地，要按照《东莞市推动产业结构调整和转型升级实施“三旧”改造土地管理暂行办法》规定的五种类型分别统计归类，登记造册，编制台账，形成工作底表。据初步估算，当前我市符合“三旧”改造条件的用地约占建设用地总规模的20%—25%，总量约30万亩。按照分步改造、逐步推进的原则，中短期规划（2009—2012年）改造10万亩，平均每年2.5万亩；中长期规划（2013—2020年）改造20万亩，平均每年2.5万亩。

（五）完善配套政策。一是市国土部门牵头制订《“三旧”改造土地管理实施细则》，参照市已建房屋补办房地产权手续相关流程，明确“三旧”改造审批流程，并制定相应文书格式、图表。二是市国土部门会同市规划、拆迁管理部门编制“三旧”改造台账，制订中短期和中长期规划，明确改造项目所需审批要素，形成格式化表格。三是市规划部门牵头制订《“三旧”改造成片拆迁专项规划编制规程》，指导各镇街编制成片拆迁专项规划。四是市规划部门根据城市总体规划、控制性详细规划等制定“三旧”改造具体项目规划审批办法。五是市财政部门牵头制订具体收费标准，包括改变土地用途补缴出让金差额固定标准、成片拆迁改造项目资金运作、税费优惠等政策。六是市建设部门会同消防等部门出台“三旧”改造项目房屋安全检测适用标准、项目实际建成时间确定依据。七是市发改部门会同经贸、外经贸、环保部门出台产业发展政策和行业规划，明确纳入“三旧”改造范围的项目准入门槛。八是监察部门和市预防职务犯罪工作领导小组制定《关于对“三旧”改造加强职务犯罪预防工作的通知》，预防和查处“三旧”改造中的职务犯罪。

（六）妥善处理历史遗留问题。对“三旧”改造拆迁范围的各类违章建筑，要甄别具体情况，分类处置。对已批建设用地（指已办理土地使用证或已取得建设用地批准文件）明晰产权、超占面积补办手续和改变土地用途等调整使用的申请，按《东莞市推动产业结构调整和转型升级实施“三旧”改造土地管理暂行办法》及其实施细则办理；未经批准的土地（指无任何用地手续或用地手续部分完善的土地，其中后者包括已办理批次报批手续或经省登记备案确认但未完善供地手续的情形）申请补办历史遗留用地手续的，按《东莞市已建房屋补办房地产权手续总体方案》及其实施细则办理。

（七）依法组织拆迁。认真做好建设项目的规划和改造方案，按期实施拆迁；对无法协商的应及时适用法定程序处理，保障项目建设。各职能部门要通力配合，共同处理拆迁中的矛盾纠纷。切实保障被拆迁人的利益，制定拆迁补偿方案时应充分考虑和保障被拆迁人的利益不因拆迁受到损失，不能以牺牲或减少拆迁户的利益来降低项目成本。拆迁安置房的建设应先于项目建设，减少拆迁的临时安置。认真做好拆迁户办证办税、搬迁回迁以及处理房屋相关设施等服务工作。拆迁安置补偿必须公开公平公正，拆迁补偿的资金要及时足额到位，安置房的过户手续要及时给予办理。

（八）加强舆论引导。抓好舆论宣传和引导，是“三旧”改造顺利开展的重要保障。“三旧”改造涉及土地利益的深层次调整，容易诱发社会矛盾和负面炒作。宣传部门必须牢牢把握正确的舆论导向，组织媒体积极宣传“三旧”改造的好典型、好做法和取得的成效，引导社会各界支持和积极参与“三旧”改造。市“三旧”改造工作领导小组要适时组织新闻发布会，主动做好政策解释和指引，各职能部门及镇（街）须在市“三旧”改造工作领导小组的统筹指导下接受新闻媒体的采访活动，切实防止负面炒作和不实报道，维护社会稳定和土地管理秩序的稳定。

东莞市总部企业认定暂行办法

Interim Measures on Recognizing Company Headquarters in Dongguan

第一章　总　则

第一条　为鼓励国内外企业在我市设立总部，推动我市总部经济的发展，根据《东莞市关于鼓励总部经济发展的工作方案》，制定本办法。

第二章　组织领导

第二条　建立由市有关领导为召集人的市鼓励总部经济发展工作联席会议制度，由联席会议统筹协调推动总部经济发展工作。

第三条　市经贸局负责总部企业认定的组织工作，主要包括：受理企业申请，协调相关职能部门初审，提出初审意见报市鼓励总部经济发展工作联席会议讨论，对符合认定条件的企业报请市政府批准认定，对需取消总部企业资格的企业提请市政府取消其资格等。

第三章　认定范围

第四条　本市认定的总部企业是指其核心营运机构或具备总部性质的职能机构设在我市，并对其所投资的全部或部分企业行使经营、管理和服务职能，且符合规定条件的企业（包括我市现有企业和新设立或迁入我市的企业）。

第五条　现有企业申请认定，应同时具备以下基本条件：

（一）在我市工商登记注册，具有独立法人资格；

（二）在我市税务登记，实行统一核算，并在我市（合并）汇总缴纳企业所得税；

（三）企业投资或授权管理和服务的企业不少于3个。

第六条　营业收入中来自下属企业的比例原则上不低于20%，作为参考条件。

第七条　综合型总部是指具有较强综合竞争力，具有决策管理、行政管理、资产管理、资金结算、研发管理、采购管理等总部综合职能的大型企业。现有企业申请综合型总部认定，应符合本办法第五条规定，注册资金或净资产1.5亿元及以上，上年度营业收入8亿元及以上，上年度在我市纳税（指企业所得税、增值税、营业税，下同）的地方分成部分2000万元（房地产企业3000万元）及以上。

第八条　职能型总部是指具有部分总部职能的企业。现有企业申请职能总部认定，应分别符合以下条件：

（一）制造业总部。符合我市制造业发展方向，以八大支柱产业、装备制造业的总部企业为主，符合本办法第五条规定，注册资金或净资产5000万元及以上，上年度营业收入3亿元及以上，上年度在我市纳税地方分成部分 1000 万元及以上。

（二）高端服务业总部。符合我市现代服务业发展方向，以设计研发、现代物流、品牌会展、信息服务、文化创意、服务外包、金融服务业为主，符合本办法第五条规定，注册资金或净资产 1000 万元及以上，上年度营业收入 5000 万元及以上，上年度在我市纳税地方分成部分 300 万元及以上。

（三）商贸服务业总部。符合我市服务业发展方向，以大型商贸总部企业为主，符合本办法第五条规定，注册资金或净资产 1000 万元及以上，上年度营业收入 10 亿元及以上，上年度在我市纳税地方分成部分 500 万元及以上。

（四）一般职能总部。符合我市产业发展方向，符合本办法第五条规定，注册资金或净资产 8000 万元及以上，上年度营业收入 3 亿元及以上，上年度在我市纳税地方分成部分 1500 万元及以上。

第九条 企业如未能达到相关指标要求，但其本身在国内外具有行业领军优势地位、对市财政或经济增长贡献大，经联席会议讨论通过，报请市政府批准，可适当放宽条件。

第十条 新设立或迁入我市的企业应同时具备以下条件：

（一）世界 500 强、中国 500 强、中国民营 500 强企业，或经联席会议讨论通过，并报请市政府批准的国内外大型企业；

（二）在我市工商登记注册，具有独立法人资格；

（三）在我市税务登记，实行统一核算，并将在我市汇总（合并）缴纳企业所得税；

（四）接受该企业管理和服务的企业不少于 3 个。

第十一条 申请认定的总部企业应承诺 5 年内不将注册地址迁离本市，不改变其在本市的纳税义务。

第四章　认定程序

第十二条 总部企业认定程序如下：

（一）企业申报。企业从东莞市经贸局网站下载申请表格，按要求进行申报，并提供各类有效证明文件。

（二）初步审核。市经贸局对企业申报的资料进行初步审核。企业报送资料中需要其他部门进行审核的，由市经贸局统一提交有关部门审核。市经贸局根据相关职能部门的审核意见，提出初审意见，上报市鼓励总部经济发展工作联席会议讨论。

（三）联席会议讨论。由市鼓励总部经济发展工作联席会议召集人主持召开由市经贸局、发改局、教育局、科技局、公安局、财政局、人事局、劳动局、社保局、国土资源局、城建规划局、外经贸局、统计局、外事局、国税局、地税局、工商局、质监局、金融办及市府法制局等职能部门参加的联席会议，对市经贸局提请认定的企业名单进行讨论，并确定公示企业名单。

（四）社会公示。将联席会议讨论通过的企业名单在《东莞日报》政务公布版进行 5 个工作日的社会公示。

（五）批准认定。公示无异议的，报请市政府批准认定，如企业发生经核查证实的重大问题，则取消该企业的认定资格。

第五章　申报材料

第十三条　申报认定的企业需提交如下材料：

（一）现有企业申请总部企业认定应提交以下材料：

1. 公司法人代表签署的认定申请表原件；

2. 公司法人代表签署的对第三章第十一条的承诺书原件；

3. 企业营业执照、组织机构代码证、税务登记证复印件（原件查验）；

4. 经审计的企业上年度的财务会计报表复印件（原件查验）；

5. 下属的控股公司或分支机构的证明文件复印件（包括工商营业执照、税务登记证明、批准证书等）；

6. 由税务部门出具的企业上年度纳税证明文件原件；

7. 其它相关证明文件。

（二）新设立或迁入我市的企业申请总部企业认定除提交第十三条第（一）款规定的前三项材料外，还需提交以下材料：

1. 公司投资计划书和市场报告书复印件；

2. 接受本市新设立企业管理和服务的控股公司或分支机构的证明文件复印件（包括工商营业执照、税务登记证明、批准证书等）；

3. 其它相关证明文件。

第十四条　提供证明资料、数据的相关职能部门对有关数据、资料的真实、准确性负责并承担相应的法律责任。

第十五条　申报认定的企业应根据要求如实提供材料并承担相应的法律责任。管理部门有权核查提供材料的真实性，如发现弄虚作假行为，经查证属实将取消其资格。

第六章　表彰扶持

第十六条　对经认定的总部企业由市政府授予证书，并对符合相关条件的总部企业从资金扶持、用地保障、投融资服务、人员培训等方面进行扶持，具体实施细则由市经贸局会同有关部门研究制定。

第七章　动态监督

第十七条　经认定的总部企业发生下列情况之一的，由市政府取消其总部企业资格。

（一）因各种原因，不再具备总部职能的；

（二）以虚假资料申报认定总部企业资格和享受政策扶持的；

（三）违反第三章第十一条规定的；

（四）有其它违反国家法律法规情节严重的。

第十八条　被取消资格的企业，其享受的有关优惠政策相应终止。注册地在 5 年内迁离我市的，由市政府责令其按一定比例退回所得奖励和补助。以虚假资料获得财政奖励和补助的，由市政府责令其全额退回所得奖励和补助，情节严重的，将依法追究相关负责人的责任。

第八章　附　则

第十九条　本办法由市经济贸易局负责解释。

第二十条　本办法自公布之日起执行。

关于鼓励总部经济发展的工作方案

Program of Encouraging Headquarters Economy Development

总部经济是指某区域由于特有资源优势吸引企业将总部在该区域集群布局，将生产基地布局在具有比较优势的其他地区，而使企业价值链与区域资源实现最优耦合，以及由此对该区域经济发展产生积极影响的一种经济形态。为鼓励国内外企业在我市设立总部，推动我市总部经济的发展，优化我市产业结构和城市功能，推进经济社会双转型，现结合我市发展实际，提出如下工作方案。

一、目的意义

经过近30年的粗放型发展，如何保持经济社会的持续发展和繁荣，实现新的跨跃式发展是我市迫切需要解决的问题。发展总部经济是优化产业结构，提升产业集群层次，应对产业转移、解决资源能源紧缺的有效途径，也是推动企业做大做强，扎根东莞的必要措施。发展总部经济将为我市实现新一轮的经济结构调整优化和城市功能转型升级提供新的发展模式和发展领域，对推动经济社会双转型具有重要意义。

总部经济是国际分工的高端环节。发展总部经济，承接制造业和服务业的高端环节，吸引国内外具有总部性质的企业在我市集聚发展，对改变我市在国际分工中的地位，进一步增强综合竞争力有着积极的促进作用。同时，发展总部经济可以为我市带来税收贡献效应、产业乘数效应、消费带动效应、劳动就业效应和社会资本效应等五种经济效应。

二、指导思想

以科学发展观为指导，以优化产业结构和城市功能为目标，充分发挥我市产业优势和区位优势，大力营造适合总部经济发展的政策环境、体制环境、服务环境，不断完善城市功能，加快承接国际制造业和服务业高端环节，引进和培育一批总部企业在我市聚集，推动我市在更高层次融入全球经济，增强参与国际竞争的能力，加快实现经济社会双转型。

三、基本原则

坚持总部经济与城市发展相结合的原则，把我市总部经济定位与城市发展定位有机结合起来；坚持总部经济与支柱产业相结合的原则，充分发挥我市的产业优势，以服务我市支柱产业的职能总部为重点，发展总部经济；坚持制造业与服务业相结合的原则，既要发展直接为制造业服务的总部，也要发展独立的服务型总部；坚持培育和引进相结合的原则，既要引进国内外大企业总部，也要鼓励和引导现有企业特别是民营企业在我市设立总部。

四、组织领导

建立由市有关领导为召集人的“市鼓励总部经济发展工作联席会议”制度，不定期召集市经贸局、发改局、教育局、科技局、公安局、财政局、人事局、劳动局、社保局、国土资源局、城建规划局、外经贸局、统计局、外事局、工商局、质监局、国税局、地税局、金融办及市府法制局等部门，统筹协调指导推动总部经济发展工作，包括：研究鼓励总部经济发展的政策，重点招商方向和目标，协调解决发展总部经济过程中的重大问题以及对发展总部经济的各项措施进行绩效评价等。

市经贸局负责研究制定支持总部经济发展的政策，组织协调有关部门开展对总部企业的认定，会同有关部门根据《工作方案》制定相关政策的实施细则，研究分析总部经济的发展状况，协调有关部门共同解决总部经济发展过程中的问题，对需报请市政府批准的重大问题，提出初步意见，会同有关部门共同为总部企业提供优质服务等工作。

五、科学规划

（一）以市中心区莞城、东城、南城、万江四个街道和石龙、塘厦、长安、樟木头、麻涌、大朗、虎门、常平等八个中心镇以及松山湖、虎门港、东莞生态园、长安滨海新区为主要空间载体，科学规划总部经济基地。积极发挥政策导向作用，引导总部集聚布局，形成高新技术产业总部与产业园区紧密结合，综合型总部与职能型总部相对集中的总部经济基地。

（二）加强对总部经济基地的规划建设，把项目建设和总部经济发展紧密结合起来，加快松山湖等园区的基础设施和商务配套设施建设，加快市中心区四个街道资源的统筹整合，带动全市资源向市中心区和三个龙头园区集聚，同时，进一步提升中心镇的集聚力和辐射力，为总部经济的发展提供高层次的物质承载空间。市中心区四个街道重点引进和培育商贸、会展、金融、信息、中介等企业总部；松山湖主要强化总部与支柱产业、高新技术产业的融合，重点引进和培育研发、测试、品牌孵化、产业创新、工业设计、创意产业等企业总部，打造支柱产业和高新技术产业总部基地；虎门港重点引进和培育物流配送、供应链管理、仓储、能源、化工、汽车、装备制造等企业总部，打造物流总部基地；东莞生态园以发挥先进制造优势为重点，引进和培育先进制造业核心机构，打造先进制造业总部基地；长安滨海新区重点发展创意设计、软件开发、服务外包、经济技术中介、网络信息、金融和投资服务等高端服务业总部。

（三）八个中心镇可根据实际发展需要，制定政策措施，加大力度引进和培育有利于优化提升本地特色产业水平的总部企业。

（四）除了从全市的层面做好总部经济总体规划外，市规划的总部经济基地要根据本地区的区域优势和产业发展实际，制定总部经济发展规划，提出发展方向、目标和措施。

六、发展方向

把城市发展定位、产业优势与总部经济的发展方向结合起来，充分发挥我市强大的产业优势，以发展各种职能总部为主，明确引进和培育的重点。一是吸引现有外资企业的专业职能总部，如研发中心、营销中心、检测中心、采购中心、培训中心、物流配送中心、电子商务中心、投资中心、结算中心等；二是加强与香港的合作，吸引香港高端服务业的大陆总部；三是培育特色产业总部，按照“内强总部，外拓基地”的思路，重点培植本土特色产业民营企业总部，鼓励有实力的民营企业走出去，外建新的生产基地，把研发、营销、人才、品牌等根植东莞，内强总部，做强做大；四是发挥毗邻香港，莞港关系密切的优势，吸引国内有意开拓国际市场的中国500强和中国民营500强企业总部落户东莞；五是吸引国外大型企业，争取引进国际上影响大的尤其是世界500强企业总部或地区总部。

七、配套服务

（一）建立专业化服务体系。大力发展物流、会展、商贸、金融、咨询、设计、法律、教育、培训、中介等与产业配套的生产性服务业，建立专业化、国际化、高端化的生产性服务体系。改造提升生活性服务业，优化服务业结构和空间布局，推进服务业与总部经济的良性互动发展，为总部企业提供良好的支援服务。

（二）完善城市规划管理。有效推进交通设施、市政配套设施、文化体育设施、医疗卫生保健设施等公共设施的规划和建设，优化城市配套功能，强化科学管理，有效解决城市交通、社会治安等热点难点问题。推进市容市貌综合整治，加强生态、环保建设，营造舒适优美的城市环境。

（三）建设“数字化东莞”。大力发展电子政务、电子商务和教育信息化，构建多层面信息体系；建设高质量的现代化通讯系统，为总部企业提供方便、快捷、全面的咨讯服务。

（四）加大城市营销力度。创新城市营销的理念、策略、手段和方式，形成完整的营销体系和制度，对城市定位、城市精神、城市文化以及优势产业、特色产业进行系统的、全面的整合推广，努力提高城市品位，打造城市品牌，增加城市知名度，扩大城市影响力。

（五）实施名牌带动战略。鼓励发展较成熟的产业集群打造区域品牌，形成具有较强竞争力的品牌孵化培育中心和品牌集聚辐射中心。鼓励行业中拥有自主品牌的企业集体参加国际展会，提升在国际市场上的整体形象和实力，增强对跨国公司的吸引力。

（六）建设培育人才载体。加快引进国内一流高等院校、著名研究机构来莞设置分院校和技术开发总部；积极推进我市高等院校、科研机构、行业组织和具备条件的企业与跨国公司人力资源部合作，建设各类引进和培育精英人才的联合培训平台；加快留学人员创业园、博士创业园以及多元投入、面向社会、资源共享的科技创新基地的建设，充分发挥现有高层次人才载体的引领作用。

（七）加大基础教育投入。进一步加大我市基础教育的投入，一方面要进一步提升我市现有中小学的教育水平，另一方面积极引进国际教育机构，通过举办国际学校及中外合作办学等形式，满足国际、国内高端人才子女教育的需要。

八、鼓励扶持

（一）制定发展总部经济的实施细则。由市经贸局负责牵头，会同相关职能部门，根据《工作方案》执行过程中的实际需要，分批制定有关配套实施细则，加强对总部企业的鼓励和扶持。

（二）加大对总部经济的资金扶持力度。2009 年 5 月 1 日后新设立或迁入经市政府认定的总部企业，达到相关指标要求的，给予一次性奖励，综合型总部最高不超过 1000 万元，职能型总部最高不超过 300 万元。对于其高管，在住房、探亲、子女教育等方面给予一次性财政补贴，补贴金额以该企业当年获一次性奖励金额的 10% 确定。2009 年 5 月 1 日前已在我市注册登记的现有企业，符合相关指标要求，经认定为总部企业的，予以 5 年补助奖励，奖励数额参照该企业上年度税收（指企业所得税、营业税、增值税，下同）地方分成并缴入我市地方库部分中相对前一年度增量的 30% 核定。新设立的总部企业从认定次年起，享受本政策。经市政府认定为总部企业后，新设立或迁入的总部企业购置、自建自用办公用房（不包括附属和配套用房）的，按每平方米 500 元人民币的标准给予一次性补助，最高不超过 500 万元；租赁自用办公用房的，按照其房屋租赁合同价格的 30% 给予一次性 12 个月的补助，最高不超过 100 万元。原有企业因扩大规模或迁入我市规划的总部基地需要新增自用办公用房的，也可享受该项补助政策。总部企业违反上述规定租售、转租办公用房或改变办公用房用途的，应当退还已经领取的补贴并按银行同期贷款利率补交利息。总部企业及其在东莞的附属企业，在申请企业研发投入资助、企业工程中心、企业技术中心、技改技创、人才发展专项资金等财政资金支持时，符合申报条件的给予优先安排。总部经济的奖励扶持资金在“科技东莞”工程专项资金中统筹安排，有关实施细则由市经贸局会同市财政局另行制定。

（三）加强总部企业用地保障。总部企业用地优先纳入年度土地供应计划，在推出市场公开交易时，对总部企业用地中属于工业用途的，可将招标、拍卖、挂牌的对象设定为总部企业。凡经市政府认定的总部企业，均可参与市场竞投。对总部企业竞得的土地，属客观因素影响导致无法及时开发的，可向市国土资源部门提出申请，适当延长开发期限。总部企业用地构成闲置的，经市财政、国土资源部门联合会审，符合不予征收或减免征收土地闲置费征收条件的，可不予或减免征收土地闲置费。有关实施细则由市经贸局会同市财政局、国土资源局另行制定。

（四）支持总部企业拓宽融资渠道。积极利用我市扶持企业上市的政策，支持总部企业利用资本市场进行融资，市金融办负责统筹协调有关部门解决企业在上市融资过程中的问题。鼓励总部企业积极利用外资和民间资本，争取引进国内外风险投资。

（五）加强政府与总部企业的沟通。及时了解并掌握总部企业的需求，帮助解决实际问题；定期举办各种互动活动，加强双方的交流。政府在制定有可能对企业生产经营产生重大影响或涉及企业重大利益的经济政策时，事先广泛征询总部企业的意见和建议。

（六）总部企业的高层管理人员培训纳入政府培训计划。结合总部企业的实际需求，市组织人事部门在制定培训计划时，将总部企业高层管理人员培训纳入政府培训计划，加强有关法律法规、外贸政策、国际惯例、国内外经济形势等知识的培训。

（七）支持和鼓励总部企业引进人才。对总部企业引进人才，按我市人才引进政策和人才迁户规定优先办理工作调动或户口迁移，其配偶和未成年子女户口可随迁。各级人才服务机构要为总部企业引进人才提供优质服务。

（八）为总部企业提供义务教育优质学位。在认定的总部企业中，其年纳税额的地方分成部分增长幅度达到规定标准的，市教育部门为其就近提供2个我市义务教育阶段等级学校优质学位。有关实施细则由市经贸局会同市教育局、财政局另行制定。

（九）为总部企业人才出入境提供便利。在莞的总部企业外籍管理人员，公安出入境管理部门可优先为其办理签证、居留许可等，工作时限由5个工作日缩短至3个工作日；在企业备案工作中，对于年纳税额未能达到规定数额的总部企业，酌情予以受理；对于企业商务备案续期而备案人员无变动的，在5个工作日内办结；对确需到港澳处理紧急商务的总部企业，予以优先受理，并将工作实现由10至15个工作日缩短至5至7个工作日。总部企业中层以上中方管理人员因公务出访可按规定通过因公渠道申办出国（境）手续。

（十）为总部企业提供通关便利。市外经贸局要积极协调海关等有关部门为企业做好政策辅导、通关业务咨询等相关服务。总部企业办理进出口业务，享受优先服务。对企业在通关过程中碰到的困难，市外经贸部门要加强和海关的联系，建立专人跟踪协调制度。

九、工作机制

（一）建立总部企业信息库。市工商、税务和统计部门要增加总部企业的识别标志，建立总部企业信息库，定期反馈总部企业的数量和主要经济指标，为动态掌握总部企业的变动情况提供基础性资料。

（二）加强总部经济分析和监测。建立总部企业定期统计分析监测制度，市统计局将总部企业全部纳入统计范围，市经贸局负责全面分析总部经济发展态势及存在问题，为市政府准确掌握总部经济的发展状况、制定扶持政策、明确鼓励发展方向提供依据。

（三）市经贸局在经贸网站上开辟总部经济专栏，全面推广我市发展总部经济的政策环境、政务环境、商务环境和生活环境，宣传我市的投资优势和总部经济的发展状况，形成有利于总部经济发展的良好氛围。

（四）市经贸局会同有关职能部门对经认定的总部企业进行动态跟踪，每年牵头组织有关部门对总部企业的运作情况进行评价。市财政每年安排专门经费用于开展总部企业的认定、统计以及其他后续管理工作。

（五）经认定的总部企业不再具备总部职能或违反国家法律法规情节严重的，市经贸局上报市鼓励总部经济发展工作联席会议审定确认后，报请市政府取消其总部企业资格，其享受的有关优惠政策同时终止。注册地在 5 年内迁离我市的，由市政府责令其按一定比例退回所得奖励和补助。以虚假资料获得财政奖励和补助的，由市政府责令其全额退回所得奖励和补助，情节严重的，将依法追究相关负责人的责任。

十、其他

（一）我市现有其他对总部企业的奖励、补贴和扶持政策与本方案相抵触的，以本方案为准。

（二）本方案由市经济贸易局负责解释。

（三）本方案自公布之日起实施。

中国统计出版社最新图书简目

（仅供参考，以最后出书为准）

统计资料

中国统计年鉴－2010
中国统计摘要－2010
国际统计年鉴－2010
2010 中国发展报告
中国第三产业统计年鉴－2010
中国区域经济统计年鉴－2010
中国劳动统计年鉴－2010
中国社会统计年鉴－2010
中国城市统计年鉴－2009
中国建筑业统计年鉴－2010
中国人口和就业统计年鉴－2010
中国工业经济统计年鉴－2010
中国商品交易市场统计年鉴－2010
中国房地产统计年鉴－2010
中国能源统计年鉴－2010
中国民政统计年鉴－2010
中国贸易外经统计年鉴－2010
2010 中国地区经济监测报告
中国科技统计年鉴－2010
中国农村统计年鉴－2010
中国农产品价格调查年鉴－2010
中国高技术产业统计年鉴－2010
中国教育经费统计年鉴－2009
中国农村贫困监测报告－2010
全国农产品成本收益资料汇编－2010
中国科学技术协会统计年鉴－2010
工业企业科技活动资料－2010
第二次全国残疾人抽样调查资料系列
中国棉花年鉴－2008/2009
中国城市（镇）生活与价格年鉴－2010
中国县（市）社会经济调查年鉴－2010
中国农村住户调查年鉴－2010（中、英文）
中国农村全面建设小康监测报告－2010
中国国内生产总值核算历史资料（1952－2004）
中国季度国内生产总值核算历史资料（1992－2005）
中国零售和餐饮业连锁企业统计年鉴－2010
大中型批发零售和住宿餐饮企业统计年鉴－2010
2005 年中国 1%人口抽样调查系列资料

2010 年省级综合统计年鉴系列

北京　天津　河北　山西　内蒙古　辽宁　吉林　黑龙江　上海　江苏　浙江　安徽　福建　江西　山东
河南　湖北　湖南　广东　广西　海南　重庆　四川　贵州　云南　西藏　陕西　甘肃　青海　宁夏
新疆　新疆生产建设兵团

2010 年市（县）级综合统计年鉴系列

天津滨海新区　石家庄　唐山　邯郸　太原　大同　长治　阳泉　晋城　朔州　晋中
运城　忻州　临汾　呼和浩特　包头　沈阳　大连　长春　吉林市　四平　延吉　哈尔滨　齐齐哈尔
黑龙江垦区　上海浦东新区　苏州　无锡　常州　徐州　南通　盐城　镇江　江阴　丹阳　杭州
宁波　绍兴　台州　舟山　温州　金华　嘉兴　衢州　安庆　福州　福州经济技术开发区
厦门经济特区　南昌　上饶　济南　青岛　潍坊　东营　郑州　洛阳　三门峡　南阳　武汉　宜昌
十堰　荆州　黄冈　长沙　广州　东莞　惠州　深圳　桂林　南宁　柳州　来宾　河池　海口　成都
贵阳　昆明　西安　庆阳　银川　乌鲁木齐　吐鲁番

"十一五"规划教材

非参数统计　医学统计学　概率论与数理统计　统计学　现代金融投资统计分析
多元统计分析　经济计量学教程　应用时间序列分析　统计指数理论及应用
统计数据处理概论　质量管理统计方法　社会统计学　多元统计分析实验
企业经营管理统计　市场调查与预测　统计学原理（非统计专业使用）
统计学：从数据到结论　国民经济核算教程（国民经济统计学）　概率论与数理统计（经济、管理类专业使用）

重点图书

新中国六十年　挑大学选专业 2010—高考志愿填报指南　挑大学选专业 2010—考研择校指南

欲购以上图书请与中国统计出版社发行部联系
电话：（010）63376907，63376908　同椇行书店电话：68783171，68783172
通讯地址：北京市西城区三里河月坛南街 57 号。邮政编码：100826